Pearson New International Edition

Research in Education
Evidence-Based Inquiry
James McMillan   Sally Schumacher
Seventh Edition

Pearson Education Limited
Edinburgh Gate
Harlow
Essex CM20 2JE
England and Associated Companies throughout the world

Visit us on the World Wide Web at: www.pearsoned.co.uk

© Pearson Education Limited 2014

ISBN 10: 1-292-02267-1
ISBN 13: 978-1-292-02267-3

British Library Cataloguing-in-Pu
A catalogue record for this book is av

Printed in the United States of Ameri

Table of Contents

Glossary

A-B design   A single-subject design that compares frequency of behavior during the baseline (A) with intervention (B) conditions

A-B-A design   A single-subject design that compares the baseline (A) with the intervention (B) and then with the baseline (A)

abbreviated time-series design   Adaptation of the time-series design in which there are only a few pre- and post-measures prior to the intervention

achievement tests   Tests that measure knowledge, skills, or behavior

action research   Studies undertaken by practitioners in schools that address an actual problem or issue in the school or classroom

agreement   A type of reliability based on the consistency of ratings or observations among two or more persons

alpha level   Predetermined level of probability to reject the null hypothesis

alternative assessment   Procedures used to measure performance through constructed-response answers, unlike traditional paper-and-pencil tests

alternative hypothesis   A statistical statement that is opposite the null hypothesis

analysis of covariance (ANCOVA)   An inferential statistical test used to adjust statistically the effect of a variable related to the dependent variable

analysis of variance (ANOVA)   An inferential statistical procedure for determining the level of probability of rejecting the null hypothesis with two or more means

analytical research   An analysis of documents to investigate historical concepts and events

anonymity   Ensures that none of the participants are identified

applied research   Research that is conducted in a field of common practice and is concerned with the application and development of research-based knowledge

aptitude test   A test used to predict performance

artifacts   Material objects of a current or past event, group, person, or organization that reveal social processes, meanings, and values

assent   A procedure whereby children aged 7–17 agree or do not agree to participate in a study

attenuation   The lowering of a measure of relationship between two variables because of the unreliability of the instruments used

attrition   A threat to internal validity in which loss of subjects affects the results

authenticity   The faithful reconstruction of participants' multiple perceptions

basic research   Research that tests or refines theory; not designed to be applied immediately to practice

behavioral objectives   Objectives of a practice that are stated in terms of observable terminal performances, which can be measured; also called *performance objectives* or *measured objectives*

beta weight   A standardized regression coefficient

bivariate   Refers to correlation between or testing of two variables or categories for differences

bivariate regression   A regression analysis in which the dependent variable is predicted by a single independent variable

boolean   Operators such as *and* and *or* that are used to limit a literature or Internet search

box-and-whisker plot   A graphic illustration of variability of a set of scores

case study   Qualitative research that examines a bounded system (i.e., a case) over time in detail, employing multiple sources of data found in the setting

categorical variable   A variable used to divide subjects, objects, or entities into two or more groups

categories   Abstract terms that represent the meaning of sets of related topics

central question   A general question that identifies the main phenomenon that is examined in a qualitative study

chi-square   A nonparametric statistical procedure that is used with nominal data to test relationships between the frequency of observations in categories of independent variables; also called *goodness of fit*

closed form   A type of questionnaire item in which the subject chooses between or among predetermined options

cluster sampling   A form of probability sampling in which subjects are first grouped according to naturally occurring traits

code   A descriptive name for the subject or topic of a data segment

coefficient of concordance   A type of interrater reliability based on the rank-order agreement among raters

coefficient of determination   A squared correlation coefficient that indicates the percentage of variance accounted for in a relationship

coefficient of multiple correlation   An indicator of the combined relationship of several independent variables with the dependent variable

Cohen's kappa   A type of interrater reliability for categorical data

collective case   A type of case study design in which more than a single example or setting is used

comparative   *See* comparative research

comparative research A type of nonexperimental quantitative research that examines differences between groups

complete observer An observer who remains completely detached from the group or process of interest

comprehensive sampling The type of sampling in qualitative research in which every participant, group, setting, event, or other information is examined

concept analysis A study that clarifies the meaning of a concept by describing its generic meaning, different meanings, and appropriate use

concurrent triangulation design A type of mixed method design in which quantitative and qualitative methods are used simultaneously

confidence interval A range that describes probable population values

confidentiality Only the researcher has access to the data and participants' names and subjects know beforehand who will see the data

construct A complex abstract concept that is not directly observable, such as anxiety, intelligence, and self-concept

construct irrelevant variance The extent to which an assessment measures facets that are not related to its purpose

construct underrepresentation The extent to which an assessment fails to incorporate important facets that are related to its purpose

construct validity A type of experimental validity that refers to the extent to which a study represents the underlying construct

context sensitivity In qualitative research, integrating aspects of the context in conducting the study and interpreting the results

continuous observation An observational data-gathering technique in which the observer records all important behaviors

continuous variable A variable in which the property or attribute of an object, subject, or entity is measured numerically and can assume an infinite number of values within a range; also called a *measured variable*

control group interrupted time-series design A quasi-experimental time-series study that compares the intervention group to a control group

control or comparison group Group of subjects in an experiment compared to the intervention group

convenience sampling A nonprobability method of selecting subjects who are accessible or available

correlation coefficient A calculation that represents the size and direction of the degree of relationship between two variables

correlational research Research in which information on at least two variables is collected for each subject in order to investigate the relationship between the variables

cost-effective analysis An evaluation that compares the outcomes of similar programs and practices in relation to their costs when the programs have the same objectives and measures

credibility The extent to which the results of a study approximate reality and are thus judged to be trustworthy and reasonable

criterion variable In a prediction study, the variable that is predicted

criterion-referenced Refers to instruments whose scores are interpreted by comparing them to set criteria or standards rather than to the performance of others

critical studies Qualitative research in which the researcher is committed to exposing social manipulation and changing oppressive social structures and in which he or she may have emancipatory goals

Cronbach's alpha A measure of internal consistency reliability for items with scaled responses

cross-sectional Refers to a research strategy in which several different groups of subjects are assessed at the same time

crystallization An analytical style in which the researcher combines segmenting, categorizing, and pattern seeking into an extensive period of intuition-rich immersion in the data

culture Shared norms and expectations for behavior among members of the same group

data The results obtained by research from which interpretations and conclusions are drawn

deception A procedure in which participants are not informed of the actual purpose of the study

decision-oriented evaluation An evaluation that supplies information for prespecified decisions, such as needs assessment, program planning, program implementation, and outcomes

degrees of freedom A mathematical concept that indicates the number of observations that are free to vary

demand characteristics A possible source of bias when any aspect of a study reveals its purpose and may influence subjects to respond differently because they know that purpose

dependent variable The measured variable that is the consequence of or depends on antecedent variables

descriptive Refers to research that describes an existing or past phenomenon in quantitative terms

descriptive statistics Statistical procedures used to describe something

diffusion of intervention A threat to internal validity in which the subjects are influenced by other conditions of the independent variable

discrepant data In qualitative studies, evidence that some data are not in agreement with other data

documents Records of past events, whether written or printed, such as letters, diaries, and journals, newspapers, and regulations

double-barreled questions Single questions that contain two or more ideas to which the subject must make one response

duration recording A type of observer recording procedure in which the duration of behavior is recorded

ecological external validity The extent to which the results of research can be generalized to other conditions and situations

effect size A statistical index of the practical or meaningful differences between groups

emergent design A research plan in which each step depends on the results of the field data obtained in the previous step

enquiring Action research in which new data are collected

empirical What is guided by evidence, data, and sources

equivalence A type of test reliability in which the scores from equivalent or parallel forms of the same instrument, obtained at about the same time, are correlated

ERIC (Educational Resources Information Center) A comprehensive database and index of education literature

ethnography A description and interpretation of a culture, social group, or system

evaluation A study that uses a formal design to collect and analyze data about a practice or anticipated practice and then determines the worth of that practice

evaluation approach   A strategy used to focus evaluation activities and produce a useful report

evidence based on contrasted groups   Validity evidence based on scores from groups expected to show differences

evidence based on internal structure   Validity evidence that shows appropriate correlations among items

evidence based on relations to other variables   Validity evidence that shows appropriate correlations with other measures

evidence based on test content   Validity evidence in which scores represent an underlying meaning, interpretation, trait, or theory

examining   Action research in which already collected data are analyzed

exempt   Category or review used by Institutional Review Boards (IRB) to designate that proposed studies are not subject to procedures to obtain informed consent or continuing IRB review.

expedited   Category of review used by Institutional Review Boards (IRB) to designate that proposed studies having no more than minimal risk to participants do not need full IRB review

experiencing   Action research with a focus on observation to better understand the participants and the setting

experimental design   Research in which the independent variable is manipulated to investigate a cause-and-effect relationship between it and the dependent variable

experimenter effects   A threat to internal validity in which the researcher's differential treatment of the subjects affects results, also called *experimenter contamination*

explanatory design   Mixed method design in which quantitative data gathered first, followed by qualitative data

exploratory design   Mixed method design in which qualitative data gathered first, followed by quantitative data

experimental group   *See* intervention group

ex post facto design   *See* ex post facto research

ex post facto research   Research that investigates events that have already occurred and implies a cause-and-effect relationship from the results

external criticism   Analytical procedures carried out to determine the authenticity of the source—that is, whether the source is the original document, a forged document, or a variant of the original document

external validity   The extent to which the results of a study can be generalized to other subjects, conditions, and situations

extraneous variable   Uncontrolled variable that influences research results

factorial ANOVA (analysis of variance)   An analysis of variance statistical procedure using two or more independent variables that permits testing each independent variable and the interaction among the variables

factorial designs   Research in which there are at least two independent variables that are analyzed together

facts   In analytical research, descriptions of who, what, when, and where an event occurred; obtained from decisive evidence

fidelity of intervention   The extent to which an experimental intervention was completed as planned

field log   Documents the nature, dates, and duration of work in the field

focus group interview   A small group interview of selected individuals to assess a problem, concern, new product, program, or idea

foreshadowed problems   Anticipated research problems that will be reformulated during data collection

formative evaluation   Evaluation that is used to improve an ongoing practice or program

frequency-count recording   A type of observer recording procedure in which the frequency of a behavior is recorded

frequency distribution   A display of a set of scores that is organized by the number of times each score was obtained

frequency polygon   A graphic representation of a frequency distribution formed by connecting in a line the highest frequency of each score

gatekeeper   The individual(s) who provide(s) access to the field in qualitative and mixed method studies

generalization   The extent to which the results of one study can be used as knowledge about other populations and situations; also, summaries of facts

grounded theory   Qualitative procedures that are used to develop detailed concepts or conditional propositions for substantive theory

high inference   A type of observation in which the observer records judgments about what has occurred

histogram   A graphic illustration of a frequency distribution in which a bar is used to represent the frequency of each score

historical analysis   The application of analytical methodology to the study of the past, as in biographies and studies of movements, institutions, and concepts

historiography   A study of the procedures that different historians use in their research; also a study of the changing revisions and interpretations of the past

history   A threat to internal validity in which incidents or events that occurred during the research affect results

inadequate preoperational explication of the constructs   A threat to the construct validity of a study in which insufficient explanation is provided of the nature of the construct being measured or manipulated

independent samples *t*-test   An inferential statistical procedure for determining the probability level of rejecting the null hypothesis using two samples of subjects that have no relation to each other

independent variable   A variable that is antecedent to or that precedes the dependent variable; in experimental design, also called the *experimental* or *manipulated variable*

in-depth interviews   Purposeful conversations that use a general interview guide with a few selected topics and probes (i.e., not a set of standardized questions); should last for at least an hour

inductive reasoning   An analysis in which categories and patterns emerge from the data rather than being imposed on them prior to data collection

inferential statistics   Procedures that are used to indicate the probability associated with saying something about a population based on data from a sample

informed consent   Obtaining permission from individuals to participate in research before the research begins

Institutional Review Board (IRB)   An organization that reviews research involving human subjects to ensure that ethical and legal practices are followed

instrumental case   A type of case study design in which the focus is on a specific theme or issue

instrumentation   A threat to internal validity in which changes in instruments and unreliability affect the results

interaction   The unique effect that different levels of independent variables have on the dependent variable

internal consistency   A type of test reliability in which the homogeneity of the items of an instrument is assessed after it has been administered once

internal criticism The use of analytical procedures to determine the credibility of the statements in a source; the accuracy and trustworthiness of the facts

internal validity The degree to which extraneous and confounding variables are controlled

interpretive/constructivist Use of systematic procedures with multiple socially constructed realities

interval A type of measurement scale in which numbers are rank ordered with equal intervals between ranks

interval recording A type of observer recording procedure in which behavior that occurs during a given time interval is recorded

intervention group The group of participants that receives the intervention

intervention, experimental, or treatment group Group of subjects in an experiment who receive the intervention the researcher hypothesizes will change thinking or behavior

intervention replications A threat to internal validity in experiments that occurs when the number of intervention replications does not equal the number of subjects

intrinsic case A type of case study design in which the emphasis is on the case itself

in vivo **codes** In qualitative data analysis, the coding of participants' voices from the data

Kuder-Richardson (KR) A type of internal consistency reliability for items that are scored right or wrong

kurtosis A distribution that is either more peaked or more flat than a normal distribution

leading question A question that suggests a particular answer

level of significance A value that is selected to indicate the chance that it is wrong for the purpose of rejecting the null hypothesis; also called *level of probability* or *level of confidence*

Likert scale A type of scale in which the subject expresses a degree of agreement or disagreement with a statement

loaded question A question for which there is an obvious or desirable answer

logical positivism A rationalistic view of the world holding that humans can be studied like nature, with objective methods, with a single reality

logistic regression A type of regression analysis in which the dependent variable is dichotomous

longitudinal A research strategy in which quantitative data are collected on subjects over a period of time

low inference A type of observation in which the observer records the occurrences of specific behaviors

magnitude of effect A measure of the extent to which findings have practical significance

mapping the field Identifying the social, spatial, and temporal relationships among participants and the setting

margin of error Range of likely population values from the sample mean

matrix sampling A type of sampling in which parts of the test items are randomly assigned to each subject

maturation A threat to internal validity in quantitative research in which maturational changes in the subjects (e.g., growing older or becoming tired or hungry) affect the results

maximum variation sampling Type of qualitative sampling in which participants are selected to represent differences on characteristics of interest

MAXMINCON An acronym for maximizing systematic variance, minimizing error variance, and controlling extraneous variance

mean A measure of central tendency; the arithmetical average of the scores

measurement scales Properties that describe the relationships between numbers

measures of central tendency Summary indices of a set of scores that represent the typical score in a distribution

measures of variability Numerical indices that describe the degree of dispersion of scores from the mean

median A measure of central tendency; the point or score in a distribution that is the midpoint

member checking Participant review of notes and recordings for accuracy

meta-analysis A research procedure that uses statistical techniques to synthesize the results of prior independently conducted studies

metasearch engines Research tools that allow multiple Internet searches to be conducted at one time

mixed method Refers to a study that combines qualitative and quantitative techniques and/or data analysis within different phases of the research process

mode A measure of central tendency; the most frequently occurring score

mono-method bias A threat to construct validity due to the use of a single exemplar or measure

mono-operation bias A threat to construct validity due to the use of a single method in implementing an intervention or measuring the dependent variable

multilevel mixed method sampling Selection in which individuals are nested in larger groups

multiple-baseline designs A type of single-subject design that uses several subjects, types of behavior, or situations simultaneously

multiple regression A statistical procedure for using several variables to predict an outcome

multisite evaluation A type of qualitative research designed to report the practices at each site and to make generalizations across sites

multistage cluster sampling The use of several stages of clustering in selecting a sample

multivariate Refers to a family of statistics that are used when there is more than one independent variable and/or more than one dependent variable

negative case In qualitative research, a case that is found to contradict other cases

negatively skewed A distribution of scores that has a disproportionately large number of high scores

nominal A type of measurement scale in which objects or people are named, classified, or numbered

nonequivalent groups posttest-only design A pre-experimental design in which one or more groups of subjects (who have not been randomly assigned) receives an intervention and a posttest and another group of subjects receives only a posttest

nonequivalent groups pretest–posttest control or comparison group designs Quasi-experimental designs in which groups that have not been randomly assigned to interventions are compared using both a pretest and a posttest

nonexperimental Research that contains no direct manipulation of variables, such as descriptive and correlational research

nonparametric Types of statistical procedures used when the assumptions necessary to use parametric procedures have been violated

nonprobability sampling A sampling procedure in which the probability of selecting elements from the population is not known

nonproportional sampling   Stratified sampling in which the number of subjects selected from each stratum is not based on the percentage of the population represented by that stratum

norm-referenced   Refers to an interpretation of test results in which a score or group of scores is compared with the typical performance of a given (i.e., norm) group

normal distribution   A symmetrical, bell-shaped distribution of scores that have the same mean, median, and mode

null hypothesis   A formal statistical statement of no relationship between two or more variables

objectives-oriented evaluation   An evaluation that determines the degree to which the objectives of a practice have been attained by a target group

objectivity   Refers to data collection and analysis procedures from which only one meaning or interpretation can be made

odds ratio   The nature of the results from a logistic regression that indicates the probability of some outcome

open form   A type of questionnaire item in which the subject writes in a response to a question

operational definition   A definition of a variable that is produced by specifying the activities or operations necessary to measure, categorize, or manipulate it

oral history   A form of historical research in which individuals' spoken words and testimonies about the past are recorded

oral testimonies   The records or interview transcripts of witnesses or participants to a past event that is being studied

ordinal   Refers to a type of measurement scale in which the objects or persons are rank ordered from lowest to highest

outlier   A data point that is extremely high or low and thus is very different from the other data collected

paired *t*-test   An inferential statistical procedure for determining the probability level of rejecting the null hypothesis with two samples of subjects that are matched or related; also called *correlated samples* or *dependent samples t-test*

parametric   Refers to types of statistical procedures that assume normality in population distributions, homogeneity of variance, and interval or ratio scale data

participant observer   One who uses interactive data collection strategies such as limited participation, field observation, interviewing, and artifact collection

participant-oriented evaluation   A holistic approach to evaluation that uses multiple methods to uncover the divergent values of a practice from the various participants' perspectives

participants' perspectives   The language of participant descriptions

path analysis   A statistical procedure that uses correlations among a set of variables that are logically ordered to reflect causal relationships

pattern   A relationship among categories in qualitative analyses

percentile rank   The point in a distribution at or below which a given percentage of scores is found

phenomenological   Research that describes the meanings or essence of a lived experience

plagiarism   Not giving credit to an original source of an idea or writing

planned comparisons   Predetermined statistical tests of selected pairs of means

plausible rival hypotheses   Possible explanations (i.e., other than the effect of the independent variable) for cause-and-effect relationships

policy analysis   Research to investigate and formulate policies and programs

population   A group of individuals or events from which a sample is drawn and to which results can be generalized

population external validity   The extent to which the results of a research study can be generalized to other people

portfolio   A form of alternative assessment in which the materials demonstrating student performance are purposefully collected, organized, and evaluated

positionality   A researcher's display of position or standpoint by describing his or her own social, cultural, historical, racial, and sexual location in the study

positively skewed   A distribution of scores that has a disproportionately large number of low scores

post hoc comparison   Statistical tests used with pairs of means that are usually conducted after statistical test of all means together; also called *multiple comparisons*

postpositivism   Allows for contextual limitations and determinants for logical positivism

pragmatic   A research paradigm that includes common sense and practical thinking along with quantitative and qualitative methods

prediction study   Research in which behaviors or skills are predicted by one or several variables

predictor variable   The antecedent variable in a prediction study

pre-experimental designs   Experimental designs that generally have very weak internal validity due to no pretest or no control group

pretesting   A threat to internal validity in which taking a pretest affects the results

primary source   In analytical research, a document or the testimony of an eyewitness to an event; in reviewing literature, studies with original data

probability   A statement of the degree of confidence about predicting some outcome

probability sampling   A type of sampling in which subjects are drawn from a population in known probabilities

probing   Questions designed to lead to more detail in interviews

propensity score matching   A statistical procedure in which participants are matched on a number of variables

proportional sampling   A type of stratified sampling in which the number of participants selected from each stratum is based on the percentage of participants in the population in that stratum

psycINFO   Database of psychological research and other literature sponsored by the American Psychological Association

purposeful sampling   A type of sampling that allows choosing small groups or individuals who are likely to be knowledgeable and informative about the phenomenon of interest; selecting cases without needing or desiring to generalize to all such cases

purposive random sampling   In mixed method studies, a small, targeted random sample

qualitative   A type of research that refers to an in-depth study using face-to-face or observation techniques to collect data from people in their natural settings

quantitative   A research paradigm in which objective data are gathered and analyzed numerically

quasi-experimental designs   Research designs in which there is no random assignment of subjects

questionnaire   A written set of questions or statements that is used to assess attitudes, opinions, beliefs, and biographical information

quota sampling   A nonprobability method of sampling in which subjects are selected in proportion to the characteristics they represent in the general population

random assignment   A procedure used to assign subjects to different groups so that every subject has an equal chance of being assigned to each group

random sampling   A procedure for selecting subjects from a population in such a way that every member of the population has an equal chance of being selected

randomized posttest-only control and comparison group design   A true experimental design in which one or more randomly assigned groups of subjects receives an intervention and a posttest and one randomly assigned group of subjects receives only a posttest

randomized groups pretest-posttest comparison group design   Experiment in which there is random assignment, a pretest, a posttest, and at least two interventions are compared

randomized groups pretest-posttest control group design   Experiment in which there is random assignment, a pretest, a posttest, and a control group

range   A measure of variability; the difference between the highest and lowest scores in a distribution

rank order   Listing of results from highest to lowest

ratio   A type of measurement scale in which the numbers are expressed meaningfully as ratios

realist ethnography   A detailed description of a cultural group

recursive   In qualitative studies, findings that occur repeatedly

reflexivity   Refers to the researcher's rigorous self-scrutiny throughout the entire qualitative research process

reflex journal   *See* reflex records

reflex records   Records the researcher makes immediately after leaving the field; contains summaries of observations, addresses quality of data, suggests next steps, and provides for self-monitoring

regression coefficient   A factor used in multiple regression to weight the contribution of each variable in the equation

relics   In historical research, objects that provide information about the past, such as textbooks, equipment, and examinations

replication   A study that duplicates the findings of a prior study using different participants, settings or techniques

research   A systematic process of collecting and logically analyzing data for a specific purpose

research design   The plan that describes the conditions and procedures for collecting and analyzing data

research methods   The procedures used to collect and analyze data

research problem   A formal statement of the question or hypothesis that will be investigated through empirical research

research role   The relationships acquired by and ascribed to the researcher during interactive data collection; should be appropriate for the purpose of the study

response set   Tendency to respond the same way to multiple questions

responsive evaluation   An evaluation designed to supply information about the issues and concerns of the audiences; uses an emerging design to provide an understanding of the program

restriction in range   Small variation among scores

reversal, removal, or withdrawn design   A type of single-subject design in which an intervention is changed or discontinued

sample   The group of subjects from whom data are collected; often representative of a specific population

sampling by case type   Sampling in qualitative research that depends on the type of participant that is selected, such as typical case or unique case

sampling distribution   The frequency distribution of possible samples from a given population

scale   Questionnaire items for which the responses consist of gradations, levels, or values that describe various degrees of something

scatterplot   A graphic representation of the intersections of subjects' scores on two variables

search engines   Services that allow for cataloging and retrieving information from the Internet

secondary data   Data that were collected previously and are available in a database for further use

secondary data analysis   Statistical analysis that uses secondary data

secondary sources   In historical research, documents and testimonies of individuals who did not actually observe or participate in the event being studied; in literature reviews a summary of primary sources

segment   A part of a dataset that is comprehensible by itself and contains one idea, episode, or piece of information relevant to the study

selection   A threat to internal validity in which differences between groups of subjects affect the results

semantic differential   A type of scale in which subjects respond by choosing between adjective pairs in relation to a concept or object

semistructured questions   Fairly specific interview questions that allow for individual, open-ended responses

sequential explanatory design   A mixed method design in which a quantitative phase is followed by a qualitative phase

sequential exploratory design   A mixed method design in which a qualitative phase is followed by a quantitative phase

sensitivity   The ability of interventions and measures to show relationships

simple random sampling   A sampling method in which every member of the population has the same chance of being selected

single-group interrupted time-series design   A quasi-experimental design in which multiple observations of the dependent variable are made before and after the intervention

single-group posttest-only design   A pre-experimental design in which a single group of subjects receives an intervention and a posttest

single-group pretest-posttest design   A pre-experimental design in which a single group of subjects receives a pretest, an intervention, and then a posttest

single-sample *t*-test   An inferential statistical test of the difference between the mean of a set of scores and a set value

single-subject designs   Research done with individual subjects in order to study the changes in behavior that are associated with the intervention or removal of the intervention

site selection   The specification of site criteria implied in the foreshadowed problems; used to obtain a suitable and feasible research site

skewed   *See* positively skewed *and* negatively skewed

snowball sampling (network sampling)   A qualitative strategy in which each successive participant or group is named by a preceding group or individual

social desirability   The tendency of subjects to respond to items in ways that will seem desirable to others

Social Science Citation Index (SSCI)   Provides access to the bibliographic and citation information to find research data, trends, journals, and researchers

sources of variability   Systematic, error, and extraneous influences related to research design

split-half reliability   A type of internal consistency reliability in which equal halves of a test are correlated

spurious correlation   A correlation that overrepresents or underrepresents the true relationship

stability   A type of test reliability that correlates scores from the same instrument given on two occasions

stakeholder   A person, organization, or group that is interested in or impacted by the evaluation

standard deviation   A measure of variability; a numerical index that indicates the average dispersion or spread of scores around the mean

standard error   The standard deviation of a sampling distribution

standard scores   Numbers that have been converted from raw distributions with constant means and standard deviations

standardized tests   Tests that are administered and scored according to highly structured, prescribed directions

standards-based   A type of test in which performance is compared to set standards of proficiency

statistical conclusion validity   The extent to which statistics provide accurate information about the relationship being studied

statistical hypothesis   A hypothesis that is stated in terms of statistical results

statistical power   The ability of a statistical analysis to detect relationships with a given variance and a given number of participants

statistical regression   The tendency for extreme scores to move closer to the mean score on a second testing

statistically significant   Refers to evaluating the results of inferential statistics and indicating that the differences noted are not likely due to chance

statistics   Procedures for organizing and analyzing quantitative data

stem-and-leaf display   A method of showing a frequency distribution

stratified purposeful sampling   In mixed method studies, targeted selection from each stratum

stratified random sampling   A form of random sampling in which a population is first divided into subgroups (i.e., strata) and then subjects are selected from each subgroup

structural equation modeling   Statistical method for using correlational relationships among latent variables to explain causal conclusions

structured questions   Types of interview questions that provide a predetermined set of responses from which the participant is to choose; also called *limited-response questions*

subject directories   Lists of cataloged Internet resources

subject effects   Changes in subject behavior that result from being in a study

summative evaluation   An evaluation designed to determine the merit, the worth, or both of a developed practice and to make recommendations regarding its adoption and widespread use

survey research   The use of a questionnaire or interview to assess the current opinions, beliefs, and attitudes of members of a known population

systematic sampling   A form of sampling in which subjects are selected from a continuous list by choosing every nth subject

t-test   An inferential statistical procedure for determining the probability level of rejecting the null hypothesis that two means are the same

target group   The group whose behavior is expected to change as a result of a given practice

teacher-researcher   Teacher engaged in action research

test reliability   The extent to which scores from an instrument are consistent

test validity   The extent to which inferences based on instrument scores are reasonable

theory   A prediction and explanation of natural phenomena

thesaurus   A publication that lists and cross-references the key terms used in an index for a reference service (database), such as ERIC or *Psychological Abstracts*

time sampling   A type of observer recording procedure in which behaviors are observed for specific time periods

time-series design   Quasi-experimental design in which one group of subjects is measured repeatedly before and after an intervention

transformative   A research paradigm in which social, political, cultural, racial, and ethnic factors contribute to the design and interpretation of results

treatment group   *See* intervention group

triangulation   Qualitative cross-validation among multiple data sources, data collection strategies, time periods, and theoretical schemes

triangulation design   A mixed method design in which quantitative and qualitative data are collected at the same time

true experimental   A type of experimental research design that uses random assignment of subjects to different groups

Type I error   The error that results from rejecting the null hypothesis when it is in fact true

Type II error   The error that results from failing to reject the null hypothesis when it is in fact false

typicality   The degree to which a phenomenon may be compared or contrasted with other phenomena along relevant dimensions

unit of analysis   Smallest element used as the number of replications employed in statistical analyses.

unit of study   Independent element that corresponds to the number of participants

univariate   Refers to a statistical analysis in which there is a single dependent variable

unobtrusive measures   Methods of collecting information in which the subject is unaware of being a participant in the research; also called *nonreactive measures*

unstructured questions   Interview questions that are broad and allow for open-ended responses

variability   *See* measures of variability

variable   An event, category, behavior, or attribute that expresses a construct and has different values, depending on how it is used in a study

variance   Generically, the degree of spread or dispersion of scores; mathematically, the square of the standard deviation

verification   Confirming or modifying the results of a research study in subsequent research

visual representation   An organized assembly of information (e.g., figures, matrices, integrative diagrams, and flow charts) that assists in qualitative data analysis

z-score   A type of standard score that has a mean of 0 and a standard deviation of 1

8

Introduction to Evidence-Based Inquiry

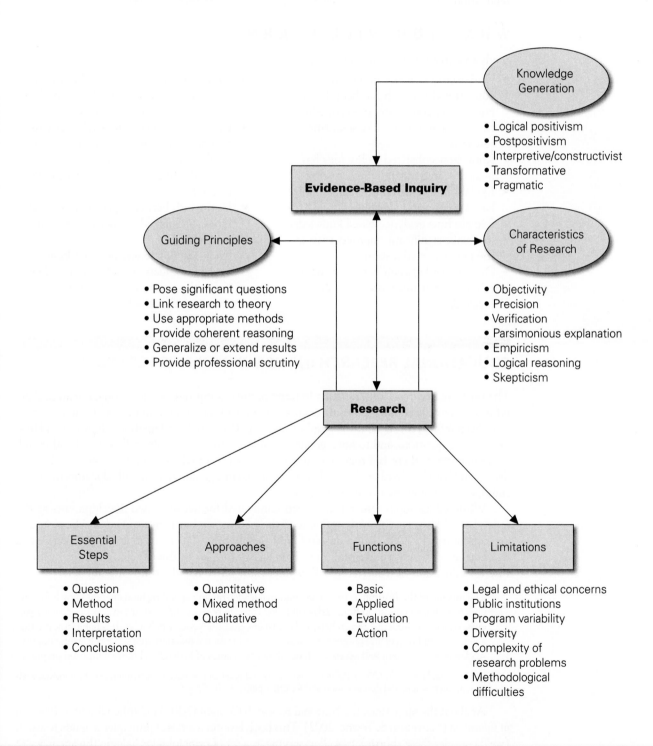

KEY TERMS

logical positivism	evidence-based inquiry	mixed method
postpositivism	generalization	basic research
interpretive/constructivist	research	theory
quantitative	research methods	applied research
qualitative	objectivity	evaluation research
transformative	verification	action research
pragmatic	empirical	
replication	data	

WHAT YOU WILL LEARN

Study this chapter and you will:

- Understand that the importance of educational research has been heightened by federal efforts to make educational research more like scientific research.
- Know how enhanced technology has made research much more accessible.
- Explain how research is fundamentally based on human judgments.
- Explain how evidence-based knowledge can make significant improvements in the practice of education.
- Distinguish between various epistemologies that influence research methods.

- Understand that educational research is systematic inquiry guided by established principles and characteristics.
- Distinguish between research methods that are quantitative, qualitative, or a combination of the two.
- Know the five steps required to conduct research.
- Distinguish between quantitative, qualitative, and mixed methods approaches to research.
- Know the differences between basic, applied, evaluation, and action studies.
- Know the constraints and limitations of educational research.

EDUCATIONAL RESEARCH IN THE TWENTY-FIRST CENTURY

The times we live in are truly amazing in terms of the possibilities for educational research! Powerful tools have been afforded us through the variety of technology and research methods that have been refined throughout the past half century. These tools and methods allow us to address challenging questions and to have greater confidence that our results will be valid and useful. More important, there is a renewed interest at all levels of education for decisions to be data driven and based on hard evidence. This has resulted in a greater need for all educators to understand, conduct, and use research findings.

While educational research has been conducted for decades, two developments at the federal level have significantly influenced the nature of what is researched and how studies are conducted. In 2002, based on No Child Left Behind, President George W. Bush signed the Education Scientific Reform Act. This legislation led to the development of the Institute for Education Sciences (IES). This important office has the following mission:

> The mission of the Institute is to provide national leadership in expanding fundamental knowledge and understanding of education from early childhood through post-secondary study, in order to provide parents, educators, students, researchers, policymakers, and the general public with reliable information about the condition of and progress of education . . . educational practices that support learning improve academic achievement and access . . . [and] the effectiveness of Federal and other education programs.
>
> Source: From H. R. 3801 (2002). An act to provide for improvement of federal education research, statistics, evaluation, information, and dissemination and for other purposes. (p. 5)

At about the same time, the National Research Council (NRC) published *Scientific Research in Education* (Shavelson & Towne, 2002). This book lays out a series of principles to guide research (we'll consider these shortly), as well as serving as a set of principles for judging the adequacy of empirical studies. Together, these two developments have had a strong, ubiquitous influence on educational research. They have had a direct impact on what is studied, how studies are conducted, and how results are reported and disseminated. Most importantly, there is a new attitude about the importance of scientific or evidence-based research as the basis for establishing knowledge about what educational practices have the greatest impact. Consistent with No Child Left Behind, there is an emphasis on outcomes—in this case, scientifically based results.

The other major development affecting educational research is technology. Technology has changed how research is conducted, such as the use of Web-based surveys and statistical software, making it very easy to analyze data. Online journals, websites, and search engines also provide amazingly fast access to studies and other literature.

Although these developments may suggest a more objective approach to educational research, we need to be clear about the role of human judgment. Many would argue that, in the end, all of our research and the knowledge generated from that research are fundamentally based on subjective premises. For example, isn't it the researcher who decides how to frame survey questions? Isn't the choice of statistical analysis up to the researcher? What about the interpretation of results? Is *cooperative learning* defined the same way for different studies? Our perspective is that human judgment is indeed critical to research, but we also believe that there are principles of evidence-based thinking that make such judgments more accurate. After all, at the end of the day, we want information that will enhance student motivation and achievement and improve attitudes. Research framed as evidence-based inquiry helps us generate more credible information. We'll expand on this last point in the next section.

Why Educational Research Is Important

Why has educational research become a valuable source of information? We suggest six reasons for the importance of evidence-based inquiry.

First, *educators are constantly trying to understand educational processes and must make professional decisions.* These professional decisions have immediate and long-range effects on others: students, teachers, parents, and, ultimately, our communities and nation. How do educators acquire an understanding to make decisions? Most of us tend to rely on several sources, including personal experience, expert opinion, tradition, intuition, common sense, and beliefs about what is right or wrong. Each of these sources is legitimate in some situations, yet in other situations, each source may be inadequate as the only basis for making decisions.

Second, *noneducational policy groups, such as state and federal legislatures and courts, have increasingly mandated changes in education.* How do policy groups acquire their views of education and obtain their information about schools and instruction? Most policy-makers prefer to have research-based information relevant to the specific policy issue. Many state legislatures require state education departments to conduct studies on state educational policies. Both federal and state departments of education also commission funded studies. Researchers are increasingly being asked to work on complex problems in highly politicized environments.

Third, *concerned public, professional, and private groups and foundations have increased their research activities.* Professional educational associations, teacher labor unions, Parent-Teacher Associations, and foundations such as the National Science Foundation have conducted or commissioned studies on topics of special concern to the organization.

Fourth, *reviews of prior research have interpreted accumulated empirical evidence.* For example, research reviews have addressed such topics as thinking aloud and reading comprehension; hypermedia and learner comprehension, control, and style; why parents become involved in their children's education; parameters of affirmative action in education; teacher efficacy; the effects of single-sex and co-educational schooling on social, emotional, and academic development; and teacher occupational stress, burnout, and health. Other research reviews identify areas of needed research.

Fifth, *educational research is readily available.* Research about educational practices is found in professional and research journals, funding agencies' published reports, books, library databases, newspapers, television, and the Internet. Although the quality of the research may vary with the specific source, educational research is very accessible.

Sixth, *many educators who are not full-time researchers conduct studies to guide their decisions and to enhance classroom, school, and system accountability.* Teachers can conduct action research that is relevant for their needs and for the issues about which they feel passionately, such as second-language students, students with disabilities, and approaches to teaching school subjects. Educators often collaborate to conduct research and to form partnerships in projects. Seemingly insignificant findings can add to the current body of evidence in the search for answers to important educational questions. Furthermore, all educators must be able to demonstrate effectiveness in an age of accountability. Educators also need to interpret results accurately and to be responsible in their use of research findings. Evidence-based inquiry provides valid information and knowledge about education that can be used to make informed decisions.

Because research systematically describes or measures phenomena, it is often a better source of knowledge than one's own experiences, beliefs, traditions, or intuition. Some studies provide general information about common educational practices and policies; this type of research influences the way one thinks about education. Other studies provide detailed information about specific practices at particular sites, such as a school, a classroom, or an office; this type of research can be used immediately to improve or justify a specific practice.

Using Evidence-Based Knowledge to Improve Educational Practices

The impact of educational research on schools and policy-makers seeking to improve educational practices may be seen as a process. Figure 1.1 shows the five phases of the process of developing evidence-based knowledge to improve educational practices: (1) identification of research problems, (2) empirical studies, (3) replications, (4) research synthesis and review, and (5) practitioner adoption and evaluation. The identification of research problems (Phase 1) begins with determining valued outcomes. Practical fields, like education, are concerned with valued outcomes such as learning. Research questions and problems come from the following sources: common observation, practical wisdom, policy controversies, prior research, and new methods applied in the study of education. Researchers conduct evidence-based studies (Phase 2), and then they attempt research replication (Phase 3) with different subjects and in a variety of settings and circumstances. In research synthesis and review (Phase 4), comparable studies are systematically evaluated and statistically or narratively summarized. Such an analysis helps to organize and make sense of the overall findings of prior research. Thus, the preponderance of evidence from many careful fully conducted studies, rather than a few exact replications of the original research, builds an evidence-based body of knowledge in education. Practitioners and policy-makers can reasonably accept the implications of research findings that are consistent without harmful side effects. Continuing local evaluation (Phase 5) is the final phase in the process.

To illustrate the potential impact of evidence-based research on educational outcomes, here are some examples of practices that were found to be effective (National Center for Educational Evaluation and Regional Assistance, 2004):

- **One-on-one tutoring by qualified tutors for at-risk readers in grades 1–3** The average tutored student read more proficiently than approximately 75% of the untutored students in the control group.
- **Life-skills training for junior high students** Implementing a low-cost, replicable program reduced smoking by 20% and a serious level of substance abuse by 30 percent by students' senior year compared to the control group.

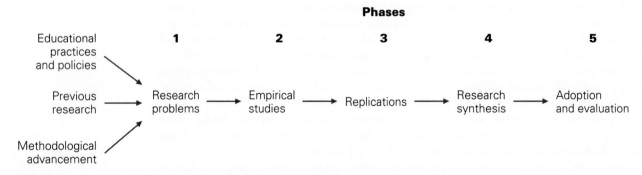

FIGURE 1.1 **Development of Evidence-Based Knowledge to Improve Educational Practice**

TABLE 1.1 Topics Researched by the NCEE	
School choice	Magnet school assistance programs
Technology	Preschool reading
School-based drug use and violence prevention	Reading instruction in the primary grades
Mentoring	Teacher quality and preparation
Career and technical education	Professional development
After-school programs	English language learning
Charter schools	Remedial reading
Comprehensive technical assistance centers	

- *Reducing class size in grades K–3* On average, students in small classes scored higher on the Stanford Achievement Test in reading/math than 60 percent of the students in regular-sized classes.
- *Instruction for early readers in phonemic awareness and phonics* The average student in these interventions read more proficiently than approximately 70 percent of the students in the control group.
- *Enhancing students' literacy and early reading skills* Early Reading First students' average score of 102.69 was slightly above the national average for the print and letter knowledge subtest.

Clearly, the federal emphasis is on supporting a new generation of rigorous research.

The National Center for Educational Evaluation and Regional Assistance (NCEE) was established as part of the IES's goal to focus on evidence-based program effectiveness and impact questions. As illustrated in Table 1.1, the NCEE has initiated program effectiveness studies in areas that are directly related to student achievement. All of these nationally funded evaluation studies take either two or three years to address the bottom-line question of causality: Was the program or specific intervention effective? The NCEE supports only those studies that can provide credible scientific evidence. The results of these studies are widely disseminated in scholarly and professional journals and are available on the NCEE website. As evidenced by the number of different areas studied, many topics, issues, and programs are now viewed through the evidence-based lens of educational research.

RESEARCH AS SCIENTIFIC, EVIDENCE-BASED INQUIRY

Conducting research is a relatively new activity in the history of education. In the centuries before reading and writing were common, individuals developed knowledge of the world around them primarily by three means. The first was through personal experiences and observation of others' experiences. Collective wisdom was conveyed as a series of detailed stories of people and events. Stories provided an understanding, a repertoire of wisdom from which one could extrapolate or apply known experience to an unknown area and thus form reasonable expectations.

A second method of knowledge generation could be identified as logical positivism. This approach emphasized that there is a single reality within known probability, objectivity, empiricism, and numbers. **Logical positivism** was the foundation for the scientific method. The idea was that the study of humans could be done the same way as the study of nature, with an accepted set of rules for conducting and reporting the results. This rationalistic view of knowledge is illustrated by the work of Francis Bacon, John Locke, and August Comte. Prior to World War II, logical positivism gave way to **postpositivism**, which allows for limitations, contextual factors, and use of multiple theories within which research findings are interpreted.

Logical positivism: a rationalistic view of knowledge with single realities

Postpositivism: allows for limitations to rationalism and contextual factors

Interpretive/constructivist: emphasis on multiple socially constructed realities

Quantitative: methods based on postpositivism epistemology and numerical data

Qualitative: methods based on interpretive/constructivist epistemology and numerical data

Transformative: research based on social, gender, and race factors

Pragmatic: emphasis on common sense and practice in addition to the scientific method

A third paradigm for generating knowledge is called **interpretive/constructivist**. Interpretive/constructivist researchers use systematic procedures but maintain that there are multiple socially constructed realities (unlike postpositivism, which postulates a singe reality). Rather than trying to be objective, researchers' professional judgments and perspective are considered in the interpretation of data. There is less emphasis on numbers and more emphasis on values and context.

These two major paradigms, postpositivism and interpretive/constructivism, provide the foundation for different types of educational research (**quantitative** and **qualitative**, respectively). More important, though, is the emphasis of any kind of research on gathering empirical evidence, using systematic procedures, and using accepted rules for determining quality and rigor.

It should also be noted that there are two additional paradigms that have had a more recent impact on research methods—transformative and pragmatic. The **transformative** paradigm emphasizes that social, political, cultural, gender, and ethnic factors are significant contributors to the design and interpretation of studies (Mertens, 2005). This is reflected by feminist and critical theorist perspectives. In the **pragmatic** paradigm there is a belief that the scientific method, by itself, is insufficient. Rather, common sense and practical thinking are used to determine the best approach (e.g., quantitative, qualitative), depending on the purpose of the study and contextual factors. This approach provides the theoretical basis for conducting mixed-method studies.

Although for a time there was great debate about which paradigm leads to the best knowledge about teaching and learning, we believe that guiding principles contained in the NRC's report are essential for all the paradigms. Until the late twentieth century, there was a clear emphasis on logical positivism and postpositivism in educational research—what could be thought of as a quantitative orientation, built on research methods used in science, agriculture, and psychology. Constructivist thinking was very influential since 1980, branding the term *qualitative*. In Washington, there has recently been more emphasis on postpositivism and quantitative methods, especially experiments—the so-called gold standard of different methodologies.

Evidence-based inquiry: guided by empirical findings from systematic data-gathering

Moreover, among the disciplines, there are variations in designs and methods in the process of conducting a study. What is common, though, is the principle of **evidence-based inquiry**. Evidence-based inquiry is the search for knowledge using systematically gathered empirical data. Unlike opinion or ideology, evidence-based inquiry is conducted and reported in such a way that the logical reasoning can be painstakingly examined. The term *evidence-based* does not refer to ritualization and using narrow forms of investigation, nor does it necessarily refer to following formal procedures. A study is evidence-based when investigators have anticipated the traditional questions that are pertinent and instituted techniques to avoid bias at each step of data collection and reasoning. If the errors or biases cannot be eliminated, investigators discuss the potential effects of these issues in their interpretations and conclusions. Consistent with the NRC report, it is appropriate to describe evidence-based inquiry as scientific, as long as we are not referring solely to logical positivism or postpositivism studies.

Guiding Principles of Scientific, Evidence-Based Inquiry

Scientific evidence-based inquiry, in educational research, is guided by six principles (National Research Council, 2002). Each is briefly explained with certain modifications reflected in scholarly reviews of the report (Erickson & Gutierrez, 2002; St. Pierre, 2002). (See Table 1.2 for a summary of the six principles.)

Guiding Principle 1: Pose Significant Questions That Can Be Investigated Empirically

The quality of a posed question often determines whether a study will eventually have an impact on the current state of knowledge. A question may be investigated to fill a gap in prior knowledge, to seek new knowledge, to identify the cause or causes of some phenomenon, or to formally test a hypothesis. A good question may reframe a prior research problem in light of newly available methodological tools or theory. The significance of a question can be established by citing prior research, relevant theory, and important claims regarding practice or policy. A new question may be articulated at the end of a study, when the researcher has a better understanding of the phenomenon.

Guiding Principle 2: Link Research to a Relevant Theory or Conceptual Framework

Much of scientific inquiry is linked, either explicitly or implicitly, to some overarching theory or conceptual framework that guides the entire research process. Sometimes the conceptual framework is not formally stated but is easily recognized by the community of scholars working in the particular discipline. For example, the concept of *culture* provides a framework for anthropologists, just as the notion of *group* or *community* often frames the work of sociologists. Theory enters the research process in two important ways. First, scientific research is usually guided by a conceptual framework or theory that suggests possible questions or answers to questions posed. In a second, more subtle way, a conceptual framework influences the research process in the selection of what and how to observe (i.e., methodological choice). Thus, the conceptual framework or theory drives the research question, the use of methods, and the interpretation of results.

Guiding Principle 3: Use Methods That Allow Direct Investigation of the Research Question

A method can only be judged in terms of its appropriateness and effectiveness in undertaking a particular research question. Scientific claims are strengthened when they are tested by multiple methods. Specific research designs and methods are best suited to specific types of questions and can rarely illuminate all the questions and issues in a given line of inquiry. Very different methodological approaches must often be used in different parts of a series of related studies.

Debates about the merits of various methods, especially quantitative versus qualitative, have raged for years. Simply stated, the method used to conduct scientific research must fit the question posed, and the link between question and method must be clearly explained and justified.

Guiding Principle 4: Provide a Coherent and Explicit Chain of Reasoning

A logical chain of reasoning, which proceeds from evidence to conclusions, is coherent, shareable, and persuasive to the skeptical reader. The validity of inferences made through this process is strengthened by identifying limitations and biases, estimating uncertainty and error, and systematically ruling out other plausible explanations in a rational, convincing way. Detailed descriptions of procedures and analyses are crucial.

Most rigorous research—quantitative and qualitative—embraces the same underlying logic of inference. Nonetheless, the nature of the chain of reasoning will vary depending on the design, which will, in turn, vary depending on the question being investigated.

Guiding Principle 5: Replicate/Generalize or Extend across Studies

Scientific inquiry emphasizes checking and validating individual findings. However, the role of contextual factors and the lack of control that exists in social settings make **replication** difficult. In both social sciences and education, many generalizations are limited to particular times and places. And because the social world changes more rapidly than the physical world, social generalizations usually have shorter life spans than generalizations in the physical world.

Some quantitative research aims at replication and generalization. **Generalization**, in research, is the extent to which the results of one study can be used as knowledge about other populations and situations. For instance, the findings of one quantitative study may also describe the current status of another group and its members' opinions, beliefs, and actions. The goal of most qualitative research, however, is to illuminate what is unique and to understand the particulars of a specific situation (i.e., case) in all its complexity. A body of scientific knowledge is built through the *logical extension* of findings rather than through the statistical generalization of such information. The term *extension of findings* (sometimes used synonymously with *analytical synthesis, extrapolation, transferability,* or *assertion*) means that others can use the information to understand similar situations and can apply the information in subsequent research. Knowledge is produced not by replication but by the preponderance of evidence found in separate case studies over time.

Replication: repeating previously conducted studies to verify results

Generalization: extending results to other people and situations

Guiding Principle 6: Disclose Research to Encourage Professional Scrutiny and Critique

Scientific research does not contribute to a larger body of knowledge until its findings have been widely disseminated and undergone professional scrutiny by peers. The intellectual debate at professional meetings, in collaborative projects, and in other situations provides a

TABLE 1.2	Guiding Principles of Scientific, Evidence-Based Inquiry

Principle	Description
1. Pose significant questions that can be investigated empirically	Questions should have an impact on the knowledge base and/or practice and lend themselves to empirically derived answers
2. Link research to a relevant theory or conceptual framework	Theories and conceptual frameworks help explain results by showing how phenomena are related
3. Use methods that allow direct investigation of the research question	Appropriate methods that provide empirical data are based on the research questions
4. Provide a coherent and explicit chain of reasoning	Shows how all aspects of the study are related
5. Replicate/generalize or extend across studies	Findings need to be checked by others and generalized appropriately to other settings
6. Disclose research to encourage professional scrutiny and critique	Findings need to be disseminated to professional peers for their evaluation

forum by which scientific knowledge is refined and accepted. A collaborative public critique is a sign of the health of scientific inquiry.

No single study or series of related studies can completely satisfy all six of the guiding principles. A single study may adhere to each principle in varying degrees, and the extent to which it does assists in gauging its scientific quality. The features of education and of educational research, in combination with the guiding principles of science, set the boundaries for the design of a study. The design per se does not make the study scientific. A wide variety of legitimate scientific designs are available for educational research, ranging from experiments to in-depth qualitative case studies (National Research Council, 2002). To be scientific, the design must allow empirical (i.e., evidence-based) investigation of an important question, suggest appropriate methods for exploring the question, account for the context in which the study occurred, utilize a conceptual framework, demonstrate a chain of logical reasoning, and disclose results to encourage professional examination.

Definition of Research

Research: systematic inquiry

Briefly defined, **research** is the systematic process of collecting and logically analyzing data (i.e., evidence-based) for some purpose. This definition is general because many methods are available to investigate a problem or question. Although educational research is not limited to the approaches used in the physical and natural sciences, the word *research* should not be used indiscriminately to describe what is actually casual observation and speculation or what one does in the library or online to "research" a topic. **Research methods** (sometimes called *methodology*) are the ways in which one collects and analyzes data. These methods have been developed for acquiring knowledge reliably and validly. Data collection may be done with measurement techniques, extensive interviews and observations, or a set of documents.

Research methods: approaches to designing studies and collecting information

Research methodology is systematic and purposeful. Procedures are not haphazard; they are planned to yield data on a particular research problem. In a broader context, the term *methodology* refers to a design whereby the researcher selects data collection and analysis procedures to investigate a specific research problem.

Characteristics of Educational Research

The following characteristics are common to many types of evidence-based research conducted in education: objective, precise, verifiable, explanatory, empirical, logical, and skeptical. Taken together, these characteristics describe the nature of research (see Table 1.3):

Objectivity: data support for a single interpretation

1. *Objectivity* Objectivity is both a procedure and a characteristic. To the lay person, objectivity means unbiased, open-minded, not subjective. As a procedure, **objectivity** refers to data

collection and analysis procedures from which a single reasonable interpretation can be made. Objectivity refers to the quality of the data produced by procedures that either control for bias or take into account subjectivity.

2. **Precision** Technical language is used in research to convey exact meanings. Expressions such as *validity* and *reliability* in measurement, *research design, random sample,* and *statistical significance* refer to technical procedures. Other phrases, such as *constant comparison* and *reflexivity,* refer to strategies in qualitative inquiry. Precise language describes the study accurately so that the study may be replicated or extended and the results may be used correctly.

3. **Verification** To develop knowledge, a researcher attempts to design and present a single study in a manner that allows **verification**—that is, the results can be confirmed or revised in subsequent research. Results are verified in different ways, depending on the purpose of the original study. If the research tests a theory, then further testing with other groups or in other settings could confirm or revise the theory. Most qualitative studies, however, provide descriptive interpretations about the selected situation or case. These interpretations are extended but not replicated in subsequent research of other similar situations for revision. Qualitative research is not verified in the same manner or to the same degree as quantitative research.

Verification: confirming or verifying the results of other studies

4. **Parsimonious explanation** Research attempts to explain relationships among phenomena and to reduce the explanation to simple general rules. The principle "Frustration leads to aggression" is a rule that predicts, and it can be tested for verification. The summary generalization "Teacher learning and curriculum change cannot be isolated from the social situations in which the curriculum is implemented" is a rule that can be investigated further. The ultimate aim of research, then, is to reduce complex realities to simple explanations.

5. **Empiricism** Research is characterized by a strong empirical attitude and approach. The word *empirical* has both lay and technical meanings. The lay meaning of *empirical* is that which is guided by practical experience, not by research. According to this pragmatic perspective, if it works, it is right; regardless of the reasons, it must be right because it works. To the researcher, **empirical** means guided by evidence obtained from systematic research methods rather than by opinions or authorities. Generally, an empirical attitude requires a temporary suspension of personal experience and beliefs. Critical elements in research are evidence and logical interpretations based on the evidence.

Empirical: what is guided by systematically obtained evidence and data

To a researcher, evidence is **data**, that is, information obtained from research from which interpretations or conclusions are drawn. In a general sense, the terms *data, sources,* and *evidence* are used synonymously, to mean information obtained by research methods. Test scores and computer printouts, field notes and interview records, artifacts and historical documents are all called *data*.

Data: research results used to generate interpretations and conclusions

6. **Logical reasoning** All research requires logical reasoning. Reasoning is a thinking process, using prescribed rules of logic, in which one proceeds from a general statement to the specific conclusion (deduction) or, the reverse, from specific statements to a summary generalization (induction). Both kinds of reasoning are employed in the research process, regardless of the type of design or method being used.

TABLE 1.3 Characteristics of Educational Research

Characteristics	Quantitative	Qualitative
Objectivity	Explicit description of data collection and analysis procedures	Explicit description of data collection and analysis procedures
Precision	Measurement and statistics	Detailed description of phenomenon
Verification	Results replicated by others	Extension of understandings by others
Parsimonious explanation	Least complicated explanation preferred	Summary statements
Empiricism	Numerical data	Narrative
Logical reasoning	Primarily deductive	Primarily inductive
Skepticism	Predicted results obtained	Verification by others

7. *Skepticism* A skeptical, critical perspective is needed to ensure that weaknesses or problems with the research design and analyses do not seriously affect the results, leading to different conclusions. This includes being wary of sampling procedures and measures used to gather information and challenging, if appropriate, specific interpretations (what the results mean).

The Research Process

Research is conducted using a sequence of steps. The researcher's goal is to obtain credible answers to research questions by designing and conducting the study and reporting data that others will view as trustworthy, that is, as reasonable answers that make sense.

In its most simple form, research involves five essential sequenced steps:

$$\textit{Question} \longrightarrow \textit{Method} \longrightarrow \textit{Results} \longrightarrow \textit{Interpretation} \longrightarrow \textit{Conclusions}$$

Based on a need for knowledge in a particular area and a review of literature, the researcher formulates specific, concise research questions or statements. This is followed by selecting and implementing appropriate methods to gather data. After the results are in, the critical next step is to interpret them. Finally, conclusions are drawn that provide answers to the research questions. For example, suppose you are interested in whether the type of teacher feedback given to students affects their achievement. The study could include the five steps in the following manner:

Question	*Method*	*Results*	*Interpretation*	*Conclusions*
What is the effect of feedback on student achievement?	Give different kinds of feedback and use tests for a sample of tenth-grade students.	Students given specific feedback achieve more than students given general feedback.	Results are consistent with the literature—no serious weaknesses in the design.	Student achievement can be increased by having teachers use specific feedback when grading students' work.

An expanded version of these five steps is illustrated in Figure 1.2. This shows in more detail how researchers actually go about planning and conducting research. Every step contributes to the credibility and usefulness of the study, and the steps should be thought of as a chain, which is as strong as its weakest link.

Research begins with the identification of a general issue or problem that warrants thought and a review of related literature. Often this is a topic that arises from an obstacle to effective decision making, a barrier of some kind, or the need to choose from among different programs. The second step, reviewing the literature, involves locating relevant research on the same topic. This research is analyzed and related to the initial problem or question.

Next, the researcher formulates a specific research hypothesis or question or a more general question. The research hypothesis (expected or anticipated result) and the specific question are used with research that follows a positivist/postpositivist approach. Research that follows an interpretive/constructivist orientation typically involves a more general question.

The design of the study is based on what will be an adequate test of the hypothesis or what will provide the best answer to the question. It should be noted, then, that the method follows from the question. Though you may be tempted, don't decide on a method (e.g., a survey, focus group interview, experiment) before coming up with the appropriate hypothesis or question. The methodology of the study includes four kinds of information related to the overall design: (1) the nature of the intervention if the study is an experiment, (2) the procedures for collecting data, (3) the measures used to gather data, and (4) a description of the subjects or participants in the study. A good study is designed so that the methods used will give the most credible answer to the question. These characteristics are also the ones that can be criticized as being flawed so that more than one conclusion may be correct. So, for example, we might say that a biased sample explains the strong attitudes reported or that the test scores obtained were invalid.

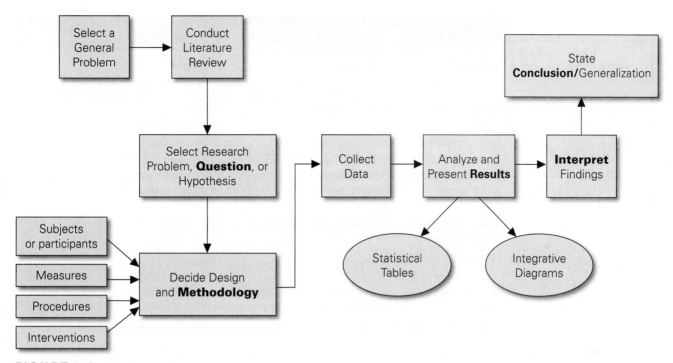

FIGURE 1.2 The Research Process

Once the data are gathered and analyzed, the results are reported. Here we get into statistics in quantitative studies and new terminology in qualitative studies. Interpretation and discussion follow from the results. The researcher integrates aspects of the study design and the previous literature to make an argument about what the results *mean*. Because different methods can lead to different interpretations of the data, researchers discuss whether other rival explanations may mitigate the credibility of the explanation that was intended (one of the goals of this book is to make you an expert at finding rival explanations!). The last step is to draw conclusions based on answers to initial research questions, the discussion, and the literature. This step also includes a discussion of the limitations of the study and of what generalizations are appropriate.

Throughout these steps, a reflective inquiry orientation is used to ensure that when taken together, the different parts of the research process are supported as being appropriate to lead to credible conclusions. Decisions are often explicit, with a rationale for a particular choice. High-quality research is conducted when all the parts come together to make a complete, interesting, and thorough study that makes a positive impact.

QUANTITATIVE, QUALITATIVE, AND MIXED METHOD RESEARCH APPROACHES

As noted earlier, the terms *quantitative* and *qualitative* are used frequently to identify different modes of inquiry or approaches to research. The terms can be defined on two levels of discourse. At one level, they refer to distinctions about the nature of knowledge: how one understands the world and the ultimate purpose of the research. On another level, the terms refer to research methods—how data are collected and analyzed—and the types of generalizations and representations derived from the data.

Recently, many researchers have used mixed method designs. A **mixed method** study combines characteristics of both quantitative and qualitative approaches to research. This mix could emphasize one set of characteristics or the other. Because mixed method studies are based on

Mixed method: combination of qualitative and quantitative designs

TABLE 1.4 Quantitative and Qualitative Research Approaches

Orientation	Quantitative	Qualitative
Assumptions about the world	A single reality, i.e., measured by an instrument	Multiple realities, e.g., interviews of principal, teachers, and students about a social situation
Research purpose	Establish relationships between measured variables	Understanding a social situation from participants' perspectives
Research methods and process	Procedures (sequential steps) are established before study begins	Flexible, changing strategies; design emerges as data are collected
Prototypical study (clearest example)	Experimental design to reduce error and bias	Ethnography using "disciplined subjectivity"
Research role	Detached with use of instruments	Prepared person becomes immersed in social situation
Importance of context	Goal of universal context-free generalizations	Goal of detailed context-bound summary statements

the more established quantitative and qualitative designs, we will focus here on how these two approaches are different.

Purists suggest that quantitative and qualitative research methods are based on different assumptions about the world, the research purpose, research methods, prototypical studies, the researcher's role, and the importance of context in the study (Denzin & Lincoln, 2000; see Table 1.4):

1. *Assumptions about the world* As mentioned earlier, quantitative research is based on some form of *positivism*, which assumes that there are stable, social facts with a *single reality*, separated from the feelings and beliefs of individuals. Qualitative research is based more on *constructionism*, which assumes that *multiple realities* are socially constructed through individual and collective perceptions or views of the same situation.

2. *Research purpose* Quantitative research seeks to establish relationships and explain *causes* of changes in measured outcomes. Qualitative research is more concerned with *understanding* the social phenomenon from the participants' perspectives. This often occurs through the researcher's participation to some degree in the lives of those persons.

3. *Research methods and process* In quantitative studies, there is an established set of procedures and steps that guide the researcher. In qualitative studies, there is greater flexibility in both the strategies and the research process. Typically, qualitative researchers use an *emergent design* and revise decisions about the data collection strategies during the study. In contrast, quantitative researchers choose methods as part of a *pre-established design*, determined before data collection.

4. *Prototypical studies* The quantitative researcher usually employs *experimental* or *correlational* designs to reduce error, bias, and the influence of extraneous variables. The prototypical qualitative study of ongoing events is an *ethnography*, which helps readers understand the multiple perspectives of the social scene or system by the persons studied. Whereas quantitative research seeks to control for bias through design, qualitative research seeks to take into account subjectivity in data analysis and interpretation.

5. *Researcher role* The ideal quantitative researcher is *detached* from the study to avoid bias. The qualitative researcher becomes *immersed* in the situation and the phenomenon being studied. For example, qualitative researchers may assume interactive social roles in which they record observations and interviews with participants in a range of contexts. Qualitative scholars emphasize the importance of data collected by a skilled, prepared *person* in contrast to an *instrument*. Qualitative research is noted for "disciplined subjectivity" (Erickson, 1973) and "reflexivity" (Mason, 1996), that is, critical self-examination of the researcher's role throughout the entire research process.

6. *Importance of the context in the study* Most quantitative research attempts to establish *universal, context-free generalizations*. The qualitative researcher believes that human actions are strongly influenced by the settings in which they occur. The researcher cannot understand human behavior without understanding the framework within which subjects interpret their thoughts, feelings, and actions. This framework or context is noted by the qualitative researcher during data collection and analysis. Qualitative research develops *context-bound* summaries.

Many of these distinctions between quantitative and qualitative research are not absolute when one conducts research or reads a completed study. As indicated, researchers can and do combine quantitative and qualitative research methods in a single study, although this can be more difficult than it may appear. The distinctions between quantitative and qualitative approaches are essential for describing and understanding research methods.

THE FUNCTIONS OF RESEARCH: BASIC, APPLIED, EVALUATION, AND ACTION

Another way to think about differences in research is to examine the function or purpose of the study with respect to how the new knowledge can be used. There are four major functions: basic, applied, evaluation, and action. Although the differences between these functions are becoming blurred to a certain extent, knowing the intent of the researcher is helpful in your evaluation of the design, analyses, and conclusions of studies.

Basic Research

The purpose of **basic research** (sometimes called *pure* or *fundamental research*) is to know and explain by testing specific theories that provide broad generalizations. A **theory** predicts and explains a natural phenomenon. Instead of explaining each specific behavior of adults, for example, the scientist seeks general explanations that link different behaviors. By explaining which variables relate to which other variables and how, the researcher can make predictions.

> **Basic research:** generates knowledge and tests or refines theories
>
> **Theory:** predicts and explains generalizable findings

A theory may or may not have empirical support. When a theory has considerable empirical support, it is called a *scientific law*. A scientific law, such as the law of gravity, is generalizable—that is, it explains many individual cases.

Basic research is not designed to solve social problems. The researcher is preoccupied with developing knowledge but is not required to spell out the practical implications of his or her work. Both goals usually cannot be achieved by a single study. Basic research, after considerable time, can indirectly influence the ways people think about and perceive phenomena. Much valuable social science research, however, is not specifically theory oriented. Although having modest, limited, and specific aims is good, formulating and verifying theories is better because theories are more general and explanatory.

Applied Research

Applied research is conducted in a field of common practice and is concerned with the application and development of research-based knowledge about that practice. Medicine, engineering, social work, and education are all applied fields. Applied research (as opposed to basic research) produces knowledge relevant to providing solutions to general problems. In other words, applied studies focus on research problems common to a given field.

> **Applied research:** field- and application-oriented

In the field of education, applied research usually focuses on problems that need to be solved to improve practice. To the extent that general theories are tested, the results may be generalized to many different educational settings. For example, basic theories of human memory, developed through basic research, could be tested in a new curriculum to discern improved retention of science concepts. Other examples of applied research in education are studies that compare different teaching styles, identify characteristics of effective schools, and examine the effects of lengthening the schoolday on student achievement. Educational research thus focuses on knowledge about *educational* theories and practices rather than on *universal* knowledge.

Because applied research usually investigates problems that are integral to making decisions, its impact may be immediate. Depending on the topic of study, applied research also may have an indirect effect over time by influencing how practitioners think about and perceive common problems. With the federal government's emphasis on conducting and evaluating field studies of "what works" to enhance student achievement, applied research is now dominant in educational studies, with much less emphasis on basic research.

Evaluation Research

Evaluation research: determines the merit and worth of a practice

Evaluation research focuses on a particular practice at a given site. The practice may be a program, a product, or a process. Evaluation research assesses the *merit* and *worth* of a particular practice. Evaluation determines whether the practice works—that is, whether it does what is intended at the site. Evaluation also determines whether the practice is worth the associated costs of development, implementation, and widespread adoption. Those costs may involve materials, space, staff development, teacher morale, and/or community support.

Along with applied research, the federal government has instituted evaluation requirements in virtually all projects that are funded. The quality of the *evaluation design* is a key factor that has a significant impact on what is approved for funding. Furthermore, the emphasis is clearly on conducting assessments of how students and/or professional personnel have changed as a result of the program or project. This suggests that the evaluations need to use some kind of experimental design so that causal conclusions can be drawn. This is a very different emphasis from the previous one, namely, gathering data to improve the program and documenting successful implementation.

Action Research

Action research: used by practitioners to address a specific problem or issue

Action research involves the use of research methods by practitioners to study current problems or issues. Action research may focus on three levels: individual teacher research, research by teams in a single school or department, and schoolwide research. Because the focus is on a solution to common problems or everyday concerns in classrooms or a school, the results of action research tend to be localized. Rigorous research control is not essential, and both quantitative and qualitative research approaches may be used.

A more recent variation is *collaborative action research* (Oja & Smulyan, 1989; Stinger, 1996; Stringer, 2004), in which practitioners conduct the study with the help of a consultant. For example, teachers may work with university-based researchers in their classrooms doing participatory research. Collaborative action research usually focuses on both the processes and the outcomes of a change strategy, such as a staff development program.

Keep in mind that the *purpose* of research and the *quality* of research are two separate dimensions of inquiry. Researchers use the same kinds of designs and methods for these different functions. The criteria for determining the quality of a study are related to the design and procedures chosen for the question being investigated. As such, there can be poorly designed basic research and excellent applied studies. Similarly, small-scale action research can be well designed, and large-scale evaluation studies can be poorly designed.

LIMITATIONS OF EDUCATIONAL RESEARCH

Education, as an interdisciplinary field of inquiry, has borrowed concepts and theories from psychology, sociology, anthropology, political science, economics, and other disciplines. Theories based on concepts such as *role, status, authority, self-concept,* and the like have been tested in education, and new educational concepts have emerged. Evidence-based educational research uses methodologies developed originally in the social sciences. Psychology has been a dominant influence on educational research. Other methodologies employed in education are the sociological survey, anthropological participant observation, historical research, and political analysis.

The presence of many disciplinary perspectives in education research has at least two implications for evidence-based inquiry. First, because different disciplinary perspectives focus on different parts of the education system, many legitimate research frameworks and methods are available (National Research Council, 2002). But, because most disciplines focus on different parts of the educational system, this also means that contradictory conclusions are possible. Second, advances in educational research often depend on advances in related disciplines and fields.

The development of a scientific basis for educational knowledge is limited by features specific to education. Most practitioners are well aware of these features, but these aspects also affect research activities. Education is multilayered, constantly shifting, and involves interaction among institutions (e.g., schools, universities, families, communities, and government). It is value laden and embraces a diverse array of people and political forces. Because the U.S. educational system is so heterogeneous and the nature of teaching and learning is so complex, research generalizations are limited in scope.

Furthermore, educational research relies on having relationships with professional practitioners. Few studies can be conducted without the participation or cooperation of these professionals. Educational research depends on its links with practice, which exist along a continuum: Some types of research involve only a short, distant, one-time interaction, whereas others require long-term, full partnerships or collaborations with schools or other agencies.

Educational research is limited by the following six constraints, which ultimately influence the knowledge gained (see Figure 1.3):

1. *Legal and ethical considerations* Educational research focuses primarily on human beings. The researcher is ethically responsible for protecting the rights and welfare of the subjects who participate in a study. Most studies require that informed consent be obtained from students, their parents, or a relevant institution, and laws are in place to protect the confidentiality of the data and the privacy of the subjects. These principles often impose limitations on the kinds of studies that can be conducted. For example, the physical and mental discomfort of subjects may affect the length of testing periods, the replication of studies, the types of treatments, and ultimately the conclusions that are supported.

2. *Public institutions* Education, for the most part, is a public enterprise that is influenced by the external environment. Since the report of a presidential commission, A *Nation at Risk*, was issued in 1983, the United States seems to be in a constant process of reforming its schools. Legislative mandates and judicial orders have changed the structure of schools and added, deleted, and modified programs. As waves of reform have swept the schools, instability has

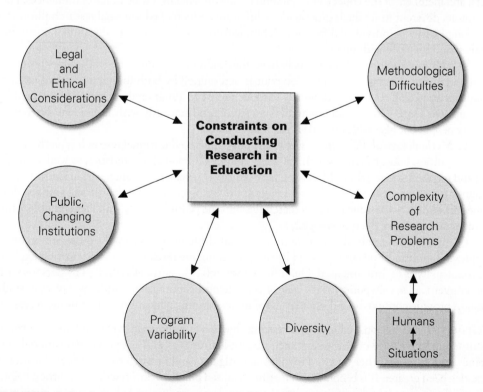

FIGURE 1.3 **Constraints on Educational Research**

occurred in curriculum, standards, and accountability. Longitudinal and replication studies that evaluate changing clientele, programs, and institutions are difficult to conduct. In addition, the ultimate effects of these changes on schooling may not be known because such effects often occur years later, outside the educational setting.

The public nature of education also influences the kinds of research questions investigated. In most studies, the subjects and other groups are made aware of the research topic. Some topics may be too controversial for a conservative community or too divisive for a given institution's staff. Some studies are not conducted because the subsequent reactions may be detrimental to maintaining an educational organization.

3. *Program variability* A third constraint on research in education is the wide variety of programs that exist. Even within reform movements, state and local control of education markedly shapes how instructional programs and other changes are implemented. Evaluations of curriculum changes may be influenced by high-stakes accountability systems and national college entrance exams. Researchers must specify the local and state conditions under which their findings were produced.

4. *Diversity* The U.S. population is becoming increasingly diverse, and this is mirrored in schools. The linguistic diversity that characterizes many schools is the most obvious manifestation of this trend. But beyond the common characteristic of lacking English fluency, there are notable differences between students from newly arrived immigrant families and those whose families have lived in this country for generations. Along with linguistic diversity come differences in culture, religion, academic preparation, and ties to the homeland. The parents' education and current socioeconomic circumstances may affect a child's academic success more than his or her not speaking English.

Examining linguistic and sociocultural contexts is critical to understanding the ways in which cultural differences affect learning in diverse classrooms. Attention to different contexts implies close coordination between the researcher and practitioners. Greater emphasis should be placed on the impact of schooling on diverse populations of students. Contextual factors necessitate a careful delineation of the limits of scientific generalization.

5. *Complexity of research problems* Another constraint on educational research is the complexity of research problems. The people involved—students, teachers, administrators, parents, and members of the collective community—are affected by a wide range of influences. Furthermore, different individuals process ideas differently. Much of educational research illustrates the complexities of individual differences. Thus, within a single study, the educational researcher deals simultaneously with many variables.

In addition, most social scientists believe that individuals cannot be studied meaningfully by ignoring the context of real life. Behavior is determined by both individual and situational characteristics, and to study individuals without regard to situational characteristics would be incomplete. Thus, educational researchers must contend not only with individual differences among people but also with myriad situational elements.

6. *Methodological difficulties* The final constraint on educational research is methodological difficulties. Educational research measures complex human characteristics, as well as thinking and problem-solving skills. Moreover, to measure achievement, intelligence, leadership style, group interaction, or readiness skills involves formulating conceptual definitions and deciding issues of validity. Some educational research has become possible only as valid and reliable forms of measurement have been developed.

Qualitative research also has methodological difficulties, especially those inherent in employing multimethod strategies, addressing the reflexive research role, and making explicit the data analysis techniques used. Qualitative research is sometimes criticized by persons with the conventional viewpoint for its lack of reliable and generalizable findings, but case study designs provide context-bound summaries for understanding education and for future research.

Despite these limitations, educational research has made important evidence-based contributions to our knowledge of how to enhance student learning, as well as to other educational outcomes. In fact, at no other time has the idea of using data and research to influence educational practice been greater. It is becoming an institutionalized practice. So, on with our journey, beginning with a summary of different research designs and an introduction to how research is reported and critiqued.

CHAPTER SUMMARY

This chapter has introduced the field of educational research, including the six guiding principles of scientific, evidence-based inquiry; the development of educational knowledge; the characteristics of educational research; distinctions between quantitative and qualitative research; the functions of research; and the limitations of educational research. The major ideas in this chapter can be summarized as follows:

1. Evidence-based inquiry uses systematically gathered empirical data that are reported in such a way that the logical reasoning that underlies them can be painstakingly examined.
2. Two major paradigms, positivism and interpretive/constructivist, provide the foundation for different methods and approaches to conducting educational research.
3. There are five essential steps in conducting educational research: question, method, results, interpretation, and conclusions.
4. Federal government involvement in research has had an important influence in making educational research and evaluation more visible and influential.
5. The process of developing educational knowledge involves identification of research problems, empirical studies, replications, research synthesis, and practitioner adoption and evaluation.
6. The guiding principles of scientific inquiry are to pose significant empirical questions, to link research to theory, to use appropriate methods for investigating the research question, to demonstrate a specific chain of reasoning, to generalize or extend across studies, and to disclose results for professional scrutiny.

7. *Research* is the systematic process of collecting and logically analyzing data for some purpose.
8. Characteristics of research in education are objectivity, precision, verification, parsimonious explanation, empiricism, logical reasoning, and conditional conclusions.
9. Quantitative and qualitative research differ in terms of their assumptions about the world, research purposes, research methods and processes, prototypical studies, research roles, and the importance of considering context in the physical, behavioral, and social sciences.
10. Applied research tests the usefulness of scientific theories in an applied field and investigates relationships and analytical generalizations common to that given profession.
11. Evaluation research assesses the merit and worth of a specific practice at a given site or several sites against one or more scales of value.
12. Action research involves teachers, counselors, and administrators using research methods to study classroom problems
13. The scientific quality of a study depends on the design and methods used, not the type of research (e.g., basic, applied, evaluation, or action research).
14. Education is an interdisciplinary field of inquiry. That is, educational researchers borrow concepts and methodologies from other academic disciplines and apply them in educational research.
15. Educational knowledge is limited by ethical and legal concerns, the public nature of education, program variability, diversity, the complexity of research problems, and methodological difficulties.

APPLICATION PROBLEMS

Research results can be used in a number of ways:

A. to influence the way the reader thinks about or perceives a problem
B. to generate decision making that leads to action
C. to generate a new research question or problem

The following are examples of research results. In which of the ways just listed might each be used? Provide examples. There is no single correct answer. For feedback, compare your answers with the sample answers in at the end of this chapter.

1. A teacher reads a research study reporting that children from broken homes are more likely to exhibit deviant behavior in school than are children from intact homes.
2. A study reports that a test measuring reading comprehension in grades 1 through 4 has been validated on students in grades 1 and 2 but not those in grades 3 and 4.

3. An educational historian notes that a well-known study of the organization of public schools from 1900 to 1950 stops short of the 1954 Supreme Court ruling on "separate but equal" education.
4. Upon reading the results of a survey of the parents of his pupils, a principal realizes that the parents do not understand the new report card and the grading system.
5. A curriculum developer field tests a pilot module to help adult basic education teachers teach a reading strategy. The results of a study of a representative sample of the teachers in the state suggest that the module should be revised to include a rationale for the strategy, a clear specification of the type of student who would benefit from the strategy, and alternative techniques to respond to student difficulties.

6. Previous research indicates that school systems have been tightly structured organizations with hierarchical authority. A professor of school administration recalls that several superintendents and principals have seen many elements of autonomous behavior by principals and teachers at the school level, even though no empirical studies have reported this finding.

ANSWER TO THE APPLICATION PROBLEMS

1. A. The teacher is more aware that classroom misbehavior might be related to the home environment.
2. C. A new research question might concern whether the reading comprehension test is also valid for grades 3 and 4.
3. C. A new research problem would be to study the organization of schools since the 1954 Supreme Court rulings.
4. B. The principal decides to send an information letter to parents that explains the new report card and grading system.
5. B. The curriculum developer decides to revise the module to reflect the suggestion from the field testing of the pilot module.
6. C. The professor proposes a new study to investigate the degree and type of autonomous behavior of superintendents, principals, and teachers.

Research Designs and
Reading Research Articles

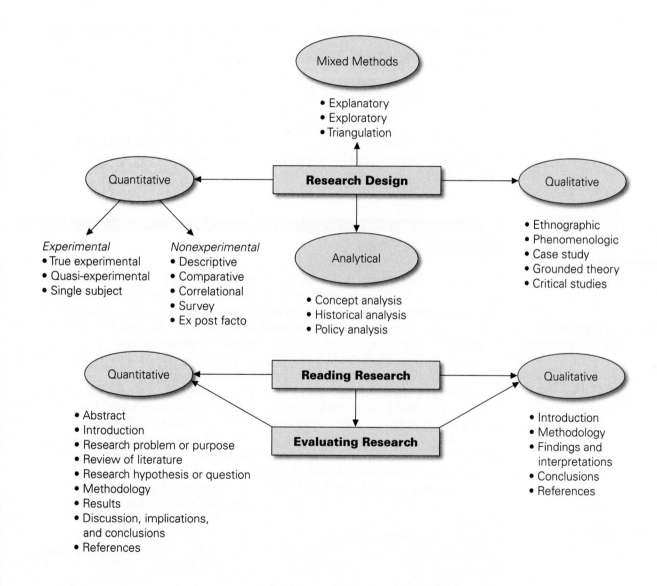

KEY TERMS

research design
experimental
true experimental
random assignment
quasi-experimental
single-subject
nonexperimental
descriptive
comparative

correlational
survey
ex post facto
secondary data analysis
ethnography
phenomenological study
case study
grounded theory
critical studies

analytical research
concept analysis
historical analysis
policy analysis
mixed method
explanatory design
exploratory design
triangulation design
transparency

WHAT YOU WILL LEARN

Study this chapter and you will:

- Identify different types of research designs.
- Understand the fundamental characteristics of quantitative, qualitative, mixed method, and analytical research designs.
- Identify the fundamental characteristics of experimental and nonexperimental quantitative designs.
- Know about different types of basic qualitative designs.

- Know about different types of mixed method designs.
- Know about different types of basic analytical designs.
- Know what is included in different sections of quantitative and qualitative research reports.
- Know how to read and evaluate quantitative and qualitative studies.

RESEARCH DESIGNS

Research design: plan for interventions and collecting data

Consider that research can be viewed as scientific inquiry and evidence-based inquiry, that approaches to research can be primarily quantitative or qualitative, and that research can be categorized as basic, applied, evaluation, or action. Another way to think about research is based on the research design of the study. A **research design** describes the procedures for conducting the study, including when, from whom, and under what conditions the data will be obtained. In other words, the research design indicates the general plan: how the research is set up, what happens to the subjects, and what methods of data collection are used.

The purpose of a research design is to specify a plan for generating empirical evidence that will be used to answer the research questions. The intent is to use a design that will result in drawing the most valid, credible conclusions from the answers to the research questions. Because there are many types of research questions and many types of research designs, it is important to match the question to an appropriate design. Research design is very important because certain limitations and cautions in interpreting the results are related to each design and because the research design determines how the data should be analyzed.

To help you identify and classify different research designs, we have classified them as four major categories: quantitative, qualitative, mixed method, and analytic. The first two are the most common. Within each major category, there are different types. These types of designs, listed in Table 2.1, are often used to describe the research (e.g., "This is an experimental study," "This is a case study," "Correlational research was used"). The designs will be reviewed briefly in this chapter. Once you become familiar with the primary orientation of each design, it will help you identify that design when reading studies or when thinking about a study of your own.

These categories are independent of the classification of research as basic, applied, action, or evaluation. That is, for example, basic research can be experimental or nonexperimental, and applied research can be single-subject or correlational.

TABLE 2.1 Research Designs

Quantitative		Qualitative	Mixed Method	Analytical
Experimental	**Nonexperimental**	**Qualitative**	**Mixed Method**	**Analytical**
True experimental	Descriptive	Ethnographic	Explanatory	Policy analysis
Quasi-experimental	Comparative	Phenomenological	Exploratory	Concept analysis
Single-subject	Correlational	Case study	Triangulation	Historical analysis
	Survey*	Grounded theory		
	Ex post facto	Critical studies		
	Secondary data analysis			

*Surveys are classified here as a type of research design. Surveys can also be classified as a type of data collection technique.

QUANTITATIVE RESEARCH DESIGNS

Quantitative research designs emphasize objectivity in measuring and describing phenomena. As a result, the research designs maximize objectivity by using numbers, statistics, structure, and control.

A very important subclassification of quantitative design is experimental/nonexperimental. Once you have determined that the study being reviewed is quantitative, you should think about whether it is experimental or nonexperimental. This difference has major implications for both the nature of the design and the types of conclusions that can be drawn.

Experimental Designs

In an **experimental** design, the researcher intervenes with a procedure that determines what the subjects will experience. In other words, the investigator has some control over what will happen to the subjects by systematically imposing or withholding specified interventions. The researcher then makes comparisons either (1) between subjects who have had and others who have not had the interventions or (2) between subjects who have experienced different interventions. An experimental design also has a particular purpose in mind: to investigate cause-and-effect relationships between interventions and measured outcomes.

Here we will describe the three most common experimental designs.

Experimental: includes an intervention for participants

True Experimental   The unique characteristic of a **true experimental** design is that there is random assignment of subjects to different groups. With **random assignment**, every subject used in the study has an equal chance of being in each group. This procedure, when carried out with a large enough sample, helps ensure that there are no major differences between subjects in each group before intervention begins. This enables the researcher to conclude that the results are not due to differences in characteristics of the subjects or to most extraneous events.

True experimental: includes random assignment of participants

Random assignment: the same chance of being in different groups

The physical and biological sciences frequently use true experimental designs because they provide the most powerful approach for determining the effect of one factor on another. In these disciplines, it is also relatively easy to meet the conditions of random assignment and manipulation. For example, if a group of farmers wants to determine which of two fertilizers causes the best growth, they can divide large plots of land into smaller sections and randomly give some sections fertilizer A and the others fertilizer B. As long as the same amount of rain and sun and the same insect problems and other factors affect each section—which would probably be the case—the farmers can determine which fertilizer is best. In the social sciences, however, and especially in education, it is often difficult to meet these conditions. True experiments are especially difficult to employ in applied research, in which researchers minimize changes to naturally occurring conditions. Yet, these designs are the ones identified by federal guidelines as the gold standard for evidence-based research.

Quasi-experimental: no random assignment

Quasi-Experimental

A **quasi-experimental** design approximates the true experimental type. The purpose of the method is the same—to determine cause and effect—and there is an intervention controlled by the experimenters. However, there is no random assignment of subjects. A common situation for implementing quasi-experimental research involves several classes or schools that can be used to determine the effect of curricular materials or teaching methods. The classes are intact, or already organized for an instructional purpose. The classes are not assigned randomly and have different teachers. It is possible, however, to give an intervention to some of the classes and treat other classes as the "control group."

Single-subject: one or a few participants

Single-Subject

Research in education has been influenced heavily by a tradition in which groups of subjects, rather than individuals, are studied. In many situations, however, it is impossible or inconvenient to study entire groups of subjects. Furthermore, the researcher may be interested in one or two subjects, not large groups of subjects. **Single-subject** designs offer an alternative by specifying methods that can be used with a single individual or just a few subjects and still allow reasonable cause-and-effect conclusions. Similar to quasi-experimental research, there is an intervention but no random assignment.

Nonexperimental Designs

Nonexperimental: no active or direct intervention

Nonexperimental research designs describe phenomena and examine relationships between different phenomena without any direct manipulation of conditions that are experienced. There are six types of nonexperimental designs: descriptive, comparative, correlational, survey, ex post facto, and secondary data analysis.

Descriptive: simple quantitative summary

Descriptive

Research using a **descriptive** design simply provides a summary of an existing phenomenon by using numbers to characterize individuals or groups. It assesses the nature of existing conditions. The purpose of most descriptive research is limited to characterizing something as it is.

Comparative: differences between groups

Comparative

In a **comparative** design, the researcher investigates whether there are differences between two or more groups on the phenomena being studied. As with descriptive designs, there is no intervention; even so, the comparative approach takes descriptive studies a step further. For example, rather than simply describe pupils' attitudes toward discipline, a comparative study could investigate whether attitudes differ by grade level or gender. Another example would be to compare the grades of athletes and nonathletes. Often, comparative modes of inquiry are used to study relationships between different phenomena, for example, the relationship between participation in athletics (yes or no) and grade-point average.

Correlational: a relationship between phenomena

Correlational

Correlational research is concerned with assessing relationships between two or more phenomena. This type of study usually involves a statistical measure of the degree of relationship, called *correlation*. The relationship measured is a statement about the degree of association between the variables of interest. A *positive correlation* means that high values of one variable are associated with high values of a second variable. The relationship between height and weight, between IQ scores and achievement test scores, and between self-concept and grades are examples of positive correlation. A *negative correlation* or relationship means that high values of one variable are associated with low values of a second variable. Examples of negative correlations include those between exercise and heart failure, between successful test performance and a feeling of incompetence, and between absence from school and school achievement.

Survey: information collected from groups

Survey

In a **survey** research design, the investigator selects a sample of subjects and administers a questionnaire or conducts interviews to collect data. Surveys are used frequently in educational research to describe attitudes, beliefs, opinions, and other types of information. Usually, the research is designed so that information about a large number of people (the population) can be inferred from the responses obtained from a smaller group of subjects (the sample).

Ex Post Facto   An **ex post facto** design is used to explore possible causal relationships among variables that cannot be controlled by the researcher. The investigator designs the study to compare two or more samples that are comparable except for a specified factor that occurred in the past. The possible causes are studied after they have occurred. Rather than control what *will* happen to subjects, as in experimental designs, the research focuses on what has happened differently for comparable groups of subjects, then explores whether the subjects in each group are different in some way. For example, an important question concerning day care for children is the relative effect the type of day-care program may have on school readiness. Some day-care programs are more academic than others. Because it would be very difficult to determine experimentally the type of day care a child attends, an ex post facto mode of inquiry would be appropriate. The investigator would identify two groups of children who have similar backgrounds but who have attended different types of day-care facility. The subjects would be given a school readiness test to see whether those who attended a highly academically oriented day-care facility differ from children who attended a less academically oriented day-care facility.

> **Ex post facto:** intervention from the past

Secondary Data Analysis   Often, researchers have access to data that others have gathered and conduct analyses using these data. This type of research design is called **secondary data analysis**. Secondary analysis is becoming more popular as large federal and state data sets are released to the public. Good examples include test score data and data relevant to the No Child Left Behind (NCLB) Act. According to the NCLB, for example, student test score data must be reported for different types of students (e.g., students with disabilities, English-language learners, African American students). Researchers can take these data and conduct studies that compare achievement among the groups or that examine trends.

> **Secondary data analysis:** using existing databases

QUALITATIVE RESEARCH DESIGNS

Qualitative research designs use methods that are distinct from those used in quantitative designs. To be sure, qualitative designs are just as systematic as quantitative designs, but they emphasize gathering data on naturally occurring phenomena. Most of these data are in the form of words rather than numbers, and in general, the researcher must search and explore with a variety of methods until a deep understanding is achieved.

We will cover five interactive qualitative designs, as listed in Table 2.1. These designs can be organized by (1) a focus on *individual lived experience*, as seen in phenomenology, case study, grounded theory, and some critical studies, and (2) a focus on *society and culture*, as defined by ethnography and some critical studies.

Ethnography

An **ethnography** is a description and interpretation of a cultural or social group or system. Although there is some disagreement about the precise meaning of the term *culture,* the focus is on learned patterns of actions, language, beliefs, rituals, and ways of life. As a process, ethnography involves prolonged fieldwork, typically employing observation and casual interviews with participants of a shared group activity and collecting group artifacts. A documentary style is employed, focusing on the mundane details of everyday life and revealing the observation skills of the inquirer. The collective informants' point of view is painstakingly produced through extensive, closely edited quotations to convey that what is presented is not the fieldworker's view but authentic and representative remarks of the participants. The final product is a comprehensive, holistic narrative description and interpretation that integrates all aspects of group life and illustrates its complexity.

> **Ethnography:** study of a culture or social system

Phenomenology

Phenomenological: meanings of lived experiences

A **phenomenological** study describes the meanings of a lived experience. The researcher "brackets," or puts aside, all prejudgments and collects data on how individuals make sense out of a particular experience or situation. The aim of phenomenology is to transform lived experience into a description of its "essence," allowing for reflection and analysis. The typical technique is for the researcher to conduct long interviews with the informants directed toward understanding their perspectives on their everyday lived experience with the phenomenon.

Case Study

Case study: examines a single entity

A **case study** examines a *bounded system*, or a case, over time in depth, employing multiple sources of data found in the setting. The case may be a program, an event, an activity, or a set of individuals bounded in time and place. The researcher defines the case and its boundary. A case can be selected because of its uniqueness or used to illustrate an issue (Stake, 1995). The focus may be one entity (within-site study) or several entities (multisite study).

Grounded Theory

Grounded theory: examines a phenomenon as related to theory

Although the hallmark of qualitative research is detailed description and analysis of phenomena, **grounded theory** goes beyond the description to develop *dense* (detailed) concepts or conditional propositional statements that relate to a particular phenomenon. The term *grounded theory* is often used in a nonspecific way to refer to any approach to forming theoretical ideas that somehow begins with data. But grounded theory methodology is a rigorous set of procedures for producing substantive theory. Using a constant comparative method, the data analysis simultaneously employs techniques of induction, deduction, and verification. The researcher collects primarily interview data, making multiple visits to the field. The initial data collection is done to gain a variety of perspectives on the phenomena; then the inquirer uses constant comparison to analyze across categories of information. Data are collected until the categories of information are *saturated*. At this point, the researcher selects the central phenomenon, develops a *story line*, and suggests a conditional matrix that specifies the social and historical conditions and consequences influencing the phenomenon.

Critical Studies

Critical studies: nontraditional perspectives, theories, and approaches

Researchers who conduct **critical studies** draw from critical theory, feminist theory, race theory, and postmodern perspectives, which assume that knowledge is subjective. These researchers also view society as essentially structured by class and status, as well as by race, ethnicity, gender, and sexual orientation. Thus, a patriarchal society maintains the oppression of marginalized groups (Lather, 1991). Critical researchers are suspicious of most research designs for ignoring the power relations implicit in the data collection techniques and for excluding other ways of knowing. Whereas feminist and ethnic research focus on gender and race as the problems of a study, postmodernism and critical theory tend to focus more on society and social institutions.

ANALYTICAL RESEARCH DESIGNS

Analytical study: analysis of documents

In an **analytical study**, the researchers investigate concepts and events through an analysis of documents. The researcher identifies, studies, and then synthesizes the data to provide an understanding of the concept or a past event that may or may not have been directly observable. Authenticated documents are the major source of data. The researcher interprets facts to provide explanations of the past and clarifies the collective educational meanings that may be underlying current practices and issues.

Concept analysis: describes meaning

Examples of analytical research include concept analysis, historical analysis, and policy analysis. **Concept analysis** is the study of educational concepts such as *cooperative learning, ability grouping,* and *leadership* to describe the different meanings and appropriate use of the concept. **Historical analysis** involves a systematic collection and criticism of documents that describe past events. Educational historians study past educational programs, practices, institutions, persons, policies, and movements. These are usually interpreted in the context of historical economic, social, military, technological, and political trends. The analysis examines causes and the subsequent events, often relating the past to current events.

> **Historical analysis:** describes past events, policies, and/or persons

In **policy analysis** the researcher examines policy and policy-makers to make determinations about policy formulation, implementation of programs, revisions of policy, and evaluations of policy effectiveness and efficiency.

> **Policy analysis:** studies of policies and policy-makers

MIXED METHOD RESEARCH DESIGNS

The use of **mixed method** research designs, which combine quantitative and qualitative methods, is becoming increasingly popular because the use of both approaches together can provide a more complete investigation. With mixed method designs, researchers are not limited to using techniques associated with traditional designs, either quantitative or qualitative. For example, a study of how teachers apply the results of high-stakes tests to their instruction might use a written questionnaire to survey a large number of teachers, as well as qualitative interviews to probe the reasons for the use documented in the survey. An important advantage of mixed-method studies is that they can show the result (quantitative) and explain why it was obtained (qualitative).

> **Mixed method:** incorporates both quantitative and qualitative approaches

Explanatory Designs

How mixed method designs are used can vary considerably, depending on the weight given to each approach and when each is used. It is common, for instance, to use methods sequentially. In an **explanatory design**, quantitative data are collected first and, depending on the results, qualitative data are gathered second to elucidate, elaborate on, or explain the quantitative findings. Typically, the main thrust of the study is quantitative, and the qualitative results are secondary. For example, this kind of design could be used to study classroom assessment and grading. A large sample of teachers could be surveyed to determine the extent to which they use different factors in classroom assessment and grading; this would provide a general overview of the teachers' practices. In a second phase, teachers could be selected who represent extremely high or low scores on the factors in the survey. These teachers could then be interviewed using a qualitative method to determine why they used certain practices. Thus, the qualitative phase would be used to augment the statistical data and thus explain the practices.

> **Explanatory design:** quantitative, then qualitative

Exploratory Designs

In a second type of mixed method design, the qualitative data are gathered first and a quantitative phase follows. The purpose of this kind of study, which is called an **exploratory design**, is typically to use the initial qualitative phase with a few individuals to identify themes, ideas, perspectives, and beliefs that can then be used to design the larger-scale quantitative part of the study. Often, this kind of design is used to develop a survey. By using a qualitative component in the beginning, researchers are able to use the language and emphasis on different topics of the subjects in the wording of items for the survey. Doing so increases the validity of the scores that result because they will be well matched with the way the subjects, rather than the researchers, think about, conceptualize, and respond to the phenomenon being studied.

> **Exploratory design:** qualitative, then quantitative

Triangulation Designs

The third kind of mixed method study is called a **triangulation design**. In this design, both qualitative and quantitative data are collected at about the same time. Triangulation is used

> **Triangulation design:** Quantitative and qualitative together

Sometimes you can use a qualitative or quantitative approach. Go to MyEducationLab for Research at www.myeducationlab.com and practice planning qualitative and quantitative approaches. Click on the topic "Introduction to Educational Research," then select the Activities and Applications titled "Planning Qualitative and Quantitative Studies."

when the strengths of one method offset the weaknesses of the other, so that together, they provide a more comprehensive set of data. To the extent that the results from each method converge and indicate the same result, there is triangulation and thus greater credibility in the findings. Theoretically, the triangulation design is used because the strengths of each approach can be applied to provide not only a more complete result but also one that is more valid. An example of a triangulation design would be a study on school culture. A quantitative survey of school culture could be used in conjunction with focus groups of students, teachers, and administrators. The more the survey results match the focus group results, the greater the validity of the conclusion that a certain type of culture exists in the school. The advantage of using the survey is that a large number of students, teachers, and administrators can be represented, and the advantage of using the focus groups is that descriptions are provided in voices specific to each group.

READING, UNDERSTANDING, AND EVALUATING RESEARCH REPORTS AND ARTICLES

Research is reported in a variety of ways, most commonly as a published article or as a paper delivered at a conference. The purpose of the report is to indicate clearly what the researcher has done, why it was done, and what it means. To do this effectively, researchers use a more or less standard format. This format is similar to the process of conceptualizing and conducting the research. Because the process of doing research is different for quantitative compared with qualitative methods, there are differences in the reporting formats used for each approach. Mixed method studies, as might be expected, combine elements of both quantitative and qualitative report formats. Although there is typically one review of the literature, there are often separate Methodology sections for the quantitative and qualitative parts of the study. Explanatory studies present quantitative methods first, exploratory studies present qualitative methods first, and triangulation studies present both at the same time.

At this point, it will be helpful simply to jump in, so to speak, and to begin reading research reports. Two articles have been provided in this chapter to get you started: one quantitative study and one qualitative study. Each contains notes to help you understand what you read, but you are not expected to comprehend everything. That will come with further experience and study. Each type of research is introduced with a description of the major parts, and each article is followed by questions that will help you understand what is being reported.

In reading research, it is important to judge the overall credibility of the study. This judgment is based on an evaluation of each of the major sections of the report. *Each part of the report contributes to the overall credibility of the study.*

According to guidelines published by the American Educational Research Association (AERA), there is a standard set of components that should be used to organize the report or article (American Educational Research Association, 2006). The reporting standards are divided into six areas aligned with the steps that are taken to conduct the study. There is an emphasis on providing adequate evidence to justify results and conclusions and on what is called *transparency*. **Transparency** refers to how well the study communicated the logic of inquiry and activities, collection and analysis of evidence, and conclusions. That is, there should be sufficient detail so that readers can see what occurred and why.

Transparency: clear, complete communication about the study

The AERA standards for reporting are shown in Figure 2.1, with traditional language used in the research literature for decades. The standards are explained in much more detail than is reported in this figure, which helps readers to understand why particular elements are needed. It will be interesting to see how quickly the AERA standards will be adopted. In the meantime, the research that has already been conducted will follow reporting conventions primarily for either quantitative or qualitative studies (mixed method studies will use a combination). Until there is greater adoption of the AERA language, the research you read will use more traditional words to describe each part of the report or article, and it would certainly be appropriate to use the new guidelines now and in the future.

2006 AERA standards	Traditional report/article format
Problem Formulation	
• Clear statement of the purpose and scope of the study	Introduction
• Contribution to knowledge	Problem
• Review of relevant scholarship	Questions
• Rationale for the conceptual, methodological, or theoretical orientation	Review of literature
Design and Logic	
• Methods used	Methods
• Logic of inquiry	Methodology
• Methodology describing data collection and analysis	Design
Sources of Evidence	
• Units of study	Subjects
• Selection of units of study	Participants
• Relevance of evidence to the research problem	
• Data collection	
• Description of interventions	
Measurement and Classification	
• Development of measurements and classifications rationale for use	Instruments
• Inclusion of relevant descriptive statistics	Measurement
• Reliability and validity	Procedures
• Description of transcriptions	
Analysis and Interpretation	
• Procedures used for analysis	Findings
• Analytic techniques and interpretation	Results
• Intended or unintended circumstances	Discussion
• Conclusions	
• With quantitative methods	
– Descriptive and inferential statistics	
– Data collection and processing	
– Data analysis	
– Statistical results	
• With qualitative methods	
– Process of developing descriptions, claims, and interpretations	
– Evidence for each claim	
– Search for disconfirming evidence and alternative interpretations	
– Interpretive commentary	
Generalization	Conclusions
• Specific descriptions of participants, contexts, activities, data collection, and intervention	
• Intended scope of generalization	
• Logic used for generalization	

FIGURE 2.1   **Recent and Traditional Guidelines for Reporting Research**

With the recent popularity of qualitative designs, it is helpful to see how these studies differ in format and language from what is used in quantitative articles. We use two methods to illustrate these differences. In Figure 2.2 there is a list of common elements used in reporting any kind of research, followed by a column for both quantitative and qualitative articles to show where there are differences. We also describe each stage or phase of each kind of research in

Report Element	Quantitative	Qualitative
Title and Authors	✓	✓
Abstract	✓	✓
Introduction and Statement of the Problem	✓	✓
Review of Literature	Extensive, detailed	Brief
Research Question	Specific, narrow questions and/or research hypotheses	General with foreshadowed question
Method and Design	Participants or subjects, instruments, procedures, intervention	Participants, settings, sites, and context
Results	Statistical	Narrative, descriptive
Discussion	✓	✓
Conclusions	✓	✓
References	✓	✓

FIGURE 2.2 **A Comparison of Quantitative and Qualitative Research Report Formats**

more detail, followed by examples of published studies—one quantitative and one qualitative. Our experience is that it is best to learn how quantitative and qualitative studies are done and reported separately using the quantitative/ qualitative distinction, then move on to mixed method research. With that in mind, we'll begin with the quantitative study, the type of study that is most often conducted and reported.

How to Read Quantitative Research: Anatomy of an Experimental Example

Although there is no universally accepted format for reporting quantitative research, most studies adhere to the sequence of scientific inquiry. There may be variation in the terms used, but the components indicated in Figure 2.2 are included in most studies.

Abstract The *Abstract* is a short paragraph that summarizes the entire journal article. It follows the authors' names and is usually italicized or printed in type that is smaller than the type in the article itself. Most abstracts contain a statement of the purpose of the study, a brief description of the subjects and what they did during the study, and a summary of important results. The abstract is useful because it provides a quick overview of the research.

Introduction The *Introduction* is typically limited to the first paragraph or two of the article. The purpose of the introduction is to put the study in context. This is often accomplished by quoting previous research in the general topic, citing leading researchers in the area, or developing the historical context and/or theoretical rationale of the study. The introduction acts as a lead-in to a statement of the more specific purpose of the study. In Figure 2.3, the introduction includes the first nine paragraphs.

At the beginning of the article, researchers state a general research problem drawn from issues, topics, or questions. It is a general statement of the purpose and scope of the study that addresses what is being researched and why it is significant. Significance is established by indicating how the findings from the study will make a contribution to or challenge knowledge and/or theory in an area of inquiry, practice, or, in the case of researching something that is new, why that would be important. The problem statement or question is usually located at the end of the introduction, as illustrated in Figure 2.3.

Review of Literature The *Review of Literature* summarizes and analyzes previously reported scholarship that bears directly on the proposed study. This should include an indication of the scope of the search for relevant studies, that is, what criteria were used to identify and select the articles and reports. Often, the theoretical rationale for the study is included. The length of the review can vary, but it should be selective and focus on other empirical studies (primary sources). It should be long enough to demonstrate to the reader that the researcher has a sound understanding of the relationship between what has been done and what will be done. There is usually no separate heading to identify the review of literature (Figure 2.3 does have one, however), but it is always located before the methods section.

Research Hypothesis or Question   Following the literature review, researchers state the more specific hypothesis or question. Based on information from the review, researchers write a hypothesis that indicates what they predict will happen in the study. A hypothesis can be tested empirically, and it provides focus for the research. For some research, it is inappropriate to make a prediction of results, and in some studies, a research question rather than a hypothesis is used. Whether it is a question or a hypothesis, the sentence(s) should contain objectively defined terms and state relationships in a clear, concise manner. (See the hypotheses in Figure 2.3.)

Methodology   In the methods or *Methodology* section, the researcher indicates the research design, subjects, instruments, interventions, and procedures used in the study. This section may contain information to enable other researchers to replicate the study. It should be presented so that there is a clear logic of inquiry that begins with the research problem and continues through the review of literature and finally the design. There is usually a subheading for each part of the methods section.

In the *Participants* subsection (sometimes referred to as the *Subjects* or *Data Source* or *Source of Evidence*), the researcher describes the characteristics of the individuals or groups from whom information was gathered. There is an indication of the number of subjects and the way they were selected for the study.

The *Instruments* or *Measures* subsection describes the techniques used to gather information. This includes tests, surveys, observation, and interviews. There should be an indication of the validity and reliability of the results for each measuring device to show that the techniques are appropriate for the study. Sometimes examples of items are included to help the reader understand the nature of the instrument.

The *Procedure* or data collection subsection is used to explain how the study was conducted. The authors describe when the information was collected, where, and by whom. They describe what was done to the subjects (i.e., the intervention) and the manner in which the data were collected. It is important to provide a full description of the procedures. There needs to be sufficient information so that the reader would know how to proceed in replicating the study. The procedures may also affect the ways subjects respond.

Results   A summary of the analyses of the data collected is reported in the *Results* or *Findings* section. This section may appear confusing to the beginning researcher because statistical language, symbols, and conventions are used in reporting the results. The results are usually presented within the text of the article. The results should be presented objectively, without interpretation or discussion, summarizing what was found. There should be a clear indication of the statistics used, with a rationale for why these procedures are appropriate. Fairly detailed, specific descriptive statistics are needed. Inferential statistics, which give an index of uncertainty, should not be used without accompanying statistical tests of the magnitude of the relationships and differences.

Discussion, Implications, and Conclusions   In this section, the researchers indicate how the results are related to the research problem or hypothesis as well as to previous research. It is a nontechnical interpretation of whether the results support a hypothesis or answer a research question. If the study is exploratory or contains unexpected findings, the researchers explain why they believe they obtained these results. The explanation should include an analysis of any deficiencies in the methodology utilized and an indication of other research that may explain why certain results were obtained. This section is also used to indicate implications of the study for future research and practical applications and to give overall conclusions. It is important to include an indication of the generalizability of the results to other persons and contexts. Often researchers delineate the persons and contexts to which the findings do *not* apply. This section is identified by several different labels. The most common are *Discussion, Conclusion,* and *Summary.*

References   A list of references and reference notes that are cited in the article follows the discussion. The style of the notation will vary. The journal in which Figure 2.3 was published uses the most recent APA (American Psychological Association, 2001) format.

Guidelines for Evaluating Quantitative Research

There is no agreed-upon method for or approach to reading research articles. Some readers begin with the conclusion, and others follow the written sequence of the article. Our experience suggests that you should begin with the abstract and then scan the introduction, research problem, and conclusion sections. If, after reading these sections, you are still interested in the article, then start at the beginning and read the entire article more carefully. Whenever reading research, keep in mind the practical or meaningful significance of the study. Research is significant if there are no serious weaknesses in the design and the differences obtained between groups or individuals or relationships reported are large enough to suggest changes in theory or practice.

Other questions also should be kept in mind in reading research. Although you need to become acquainted with these considerations now, a full understanding and application of the questions is expected after further study of each topic. The following questions, organized according to each major section of a quantitative research article, constitute a guideline for evaluating quantitative investigations.

Research Problem or Purpose

1. How clearly and succinctly is the problem or purpose stated?
2. Is it sufficiently delimited to be amenable to investigation? At the same time, does it have sufficient practical or theoretical value to warrant study?
3. Does it have a rationale? Has the problem been studied before? If so, should this problem be studied again? Is the study likely to provide additional knowledge?

Review of Literature

1. How adequately has the literature been surveyed?
2. Does the review critically evaluate previous findings from other studies, or is it only a summary of what is known?
3. Does the review support the need for studying the problem?
4. Does the review establish a theoretical framework for the problem?
5. Does the review relate previous studies to the research problem?

Hypotheses or Questions

1. Is the question or hypothesis succinct and clear?
2. Are hypotheses consistent with theory and known facts?
3. Are they testable?
4. Do hypotheses suggest an expected result?

Methodology

1. Are the procedures, design, and instruments employed to gather the data described with sufficient clarity to permit another researcher to replicate the study?
2. Is the population described fully? Did the researcher use the total population, or was a sample used? If a sample was used, is it representative of the population from which it was selected?
3. Is evidence presented about the validity and reliability of the scores?
4. Was a pretest used? Was there a pilot study? If so, why? What were the results? Was the problem or question or procedure changed as a result of the pretest or pilot study, and if so, was this modification justifiable or desirable?
5. Are there any obvious weaknesses in the overall design of the study?

(text continues)

To practice reading and understanding articles, go to: MyEducationlab for Research at www.myeducationLab.com and complete the Building Research Skills exercise. Click on the topic "Introduction to Educational Research" and select the exercise titled "Identifying Steps in the Research Process, Part 1."

The Effects of Computer-Assisted Instruction on First Grade Students' Vocabulary Development

Charlotte Boling, *The University of West Florida*
Sarah H. Martin, *Eastern Kentucky University*
Michael A. Martin, *Eastern Kentucky University*

The purpose of the present study was to determine the effect of computer-assisted instruction on first grade students' vocabulary development. Students participating in this study were randomly divided into experimental and control groups. The students in both groups were involved in DEAR (Drop Everything And Read) as part of their instruction in a balanced literacy program. During their normal DEAR time, the control group used a book and tape to explore stories. The experimental group explored stories using computerized storyboards. The results of the study show a significant difference for both groups on pre and posttests. However, the mean difference demonstrates a much larger gain for students in the experimental group.

Abstract

What can teachers do to insure that the children they teach will develop into successful readers? This is a question that has puzzled the educational community for years. Most educators have their individual opinion as to how the reading process occurs. Morrow and Tracey (1997) state that some educators believe in a behavioristic approach where reading is taught in a skills-based environment through a prescribed curriculum. Others believe in a more constructivist approach where a relationship between the context and child must be developed where students build knowledge and gain skills through immersion in a literature-rich environment (Czubaj, 1997; Daniels & Zemelman, 1999). Whatever one believes, these approaches to reading instruction—behaviorist or constructivist—continue to be the subject of debates in our classrooms and communities.

Introduction—Significance of topic

The core beliefs that teachers possess have a great impact on students learning to read. Teacher's personal beliefs concerning the processes involved in learning to read greatly influence their instructional choices. A teacher's beliefs are based on his or her personal knowledge, experiences with instructional techniques, and the way students respond to the instructional strategies in classroom situations (Dillon, 2000; Howard, McGee, Purcell, & Schwartz, 2000; Kinzer & Leu, 1999). Therefore, while teachers maintain their core beliefs about how children best learn to read, they are continuously striving to find the technique(s) that will have the greatest impact on their students.

Since the early 1920s, educators have used a multi-sensory approach to teaching reading by combining reading, writing, and speaking in a natural context and not through deliberate teaching (Chall, 1992). This has been particularly useful in the teaching of vocabulary. It stands to reason then that the most active vocabulary growth occurs in the early years of life. A child learns to connect an object with the sight, sound, smell, taste, and feel associated with the object. This experience is followed by certain sounds made to represent the object. Thus, communication begins and the concept associated with the object develops into vocabulary. For example, a child understands the physical properties of an apple. He knows how the object looks, tastes, feels, smells, and sounds. A loving parent then builds vocabulary in a natural context by adding the word associated to this object—apple. Then, this label is connected to the experience. "You are eating an apple."

Introduction—Background on importance of vocabulary

As the vocabulary increases, children realize words are used in many contexts. Children must then reach beyond the actual word and activate their schema of the context in which the word is used to understand the meaning. For example, the word "mouse" can have different meanings, such as, a small rodent or a computer device. A child needs to experience words being used in different contexts to understand the complexity of our language. The more children experience vocabulary in context, the sooner they will begin to realize that it is the concept of the word in question in the given context that provides meaning.

(continued)

As a child progresses through the various aspects of literacy development (listening, speaking, reading, and writing), their communication skills become more interdependent upon vocabulary development. Vocabulary development involves understanding the 'labeling' that goes with the 'concept' that makes the word meaningful. It is acquired through direct experience, multiple exposure, context, association, and comprehension. As students become comfortable with new vocabulary words, they are more likely to use the words when communicating.

Introduction—Background on importance of vocabulary (continued)

Elements of our 'Technological Age' often influence the instructional decisions that teachers make in the classroom. One such decision is the role that computers will play in the reading development of the children one teaches. Computer-based teaching and learning has produced positive effects in the classroom. Students seem to be motivated by learning through this medium (Forcier, 1999). Therefore, it is essential that today's teachers change as our society changes (Hoffman & Pearson, 2000). Children who enter today's primary classrooms have been processing multi-sensory concepts for most of their young lives. Home computers, interactive games, television, the Internet, and software companies capitalize on this multi-sensory concept.

Software companies have developed many programs for beginning reading that appeal to the senses and interests of the young child who is learning to read. This multimedia concept stimulates the learner with sight, sound, and action while integrating skills necessary for language development. Instructional technology offers virtual multi-sensory perception that should provide meaningful instruction.

Introduction—Background on importance of technology

Teacher-centered instruction is one approach to the use of instructional technology in the classroom (Forcier, 1999). The teacher-centered approach is similar to the direct-instruction approach in that the teacher is directing the children through the learning in order to achieve the goals of the lesson. One category of the teacher-centered approach is computer-assisted instruction. When using computer-assisted instruction the teacher organizes the learning situation. He/she selects the targeted learning goal, situates the learning environment, and then allows exploratory time as students engage in learning. The teacher then monitors the learning activities and modifies the instructional level as needed to meet the various needs of the children involved.

Introduction—Importance of teacher-centered instruction

Classroom teachers have the unique opportunity to infuse a variety of technological components with multi-sensory learning while situating the learning situation. One area where this is especially true is in the teaching of reading to young children. The research study being reported employed a teacher-centered, computer-assisted instructional technique that situated progressive reading material in an attempt to answer the following question:

Will a computerized multi-sensory approach to the teaching of reading increase first-graders' vocabulary development?

Research question

Review of Literature

Major heading

Many software programs offer 'read alongs' and 'edutainment' that assist students as they learn letter sounds, vocabulary concepts, comprehension, and to enjoy literature. Interactive multimedia allows the printed word to take on sight, sound, and action which visually and mentally stimulates the individual.

One such program is DaisyQuest I and II (Mitchell, Chad, & Stacy, 1984–2000). An in-depth study investigated the phonological awareness in pre-school children utilizing this software (Brinkman & Torgesen, 1994). Each child in the treatment group interacted with a computerized story concerning "Daisy the friendly dragon". A computer, monitor, mouse, and standard headphone were provided to allow the child, as he/she listened to the story, to discover clues revealing where the dragon was hiding. The clues were revealed by correctly answering at least four correct answers in a row. The skills assessed were rhyming words, beginning sounds, ending sounds, middle sounds, and whether a word contained a given number of sounds. This study revealed that children in the treatment group responded at a higher and faster rate of reading readiness than children in the control group. Not only did the children in the treatment group gain knowledge to aid in their ability to read; these pre-schoolers had fun!

Summary of findings from previous study

In another study, two literacy teachers (one a Reading Recovery teacher, the other a Title 1 Reading Teacher) wrote simple, predictable texts using a multimedia software, HyperStudio (Wagner, 1978–2000). These teachers created 'talking books' for their students with a focus on high-frequency words with graphics and animation to offer sight, sound, and movement. Students enjoyed experiencing the stories as the computer 'read' the story to them as the cursor (pointing finger) touched each word. This process came full circle by the end of the school year, as these students were writing and reading their own stories. Students were then encouraged to use invented spelling, graphics, and sounds, while they created their own stories using the Kid Pix Software program (Hickman, 1984–2000). "The computer serves as a motivational tool in their journey to literacy" (Eisenwine & Hunt, 2000, p. 456).

Summary of findings from previous study

There are many reasons why computer-assisted reading instruction has been effective. The computer provides immediate responses and practice for the child learning a skill. Struggling readers interface with the computer and practice a skill without embarrassing situations in the classroom. Interaction with a multi-sensory format provides motivation and a positive attitude toward reading and learning (Case & Truscott, 1999; Forcier, 1999).

Shows significance of technology

A word of caution accompanies much of the literature warning educators to focus on the targeted instructional goals and not be 'enchanted' by the entertainment that makes software packages so appealing (Case and Truscott, 1999; Sherry, 1996). While this multi-sensory approach is highly motivating for young readers, the instructional purpose is to enable them to become better readers. Educators should choose the types of software and technological resources carefully in order to maximize learning without being entangled in the 'bells and whistles'.

Indicates criteria for selecting software

The benefits of using instructional technology include "an intrinsic need to learn technology . . . motivation increases engagement time . . . students move beyond knowledge and comprehension and into application and analysis . . . and students develop computer literacy by applying various computer skills as part of the learning process" (Dockstader, 1999, p. 73). As Ray and Wepner (2000) suggest, the question as to whether or not technology is the valuable educational resource we think it is may be a moot point since it is such an integral part of our lives. However, the question concerning the most productive methods of using technology in the classroom still needs to be addressed. Therefore, the purpose of this study was to investigate the effects of computer-assisted instruction on first grade students' vocabulary development. Specifically, this study investigated the impact of the WiggleWorks program (CAST & Scholastic, 1994–1996) on first grade students' vocabulary development.

Shows need for study

Purpose

Research problem

Method

Sample

Identifies subjects

A first grade classroom at a mid-Atlantic elementary school was selected for this research project. The subjects were 21 first-grade students. There were 10 boys and 11 girls involved in this study. The ethnic background of this class was as follows: 13 Caucasian students, six African American students, one Hispanic student, and one Pakistani student. Students were from a lower socioeconomic status and had limited exposure to educational experiences outside the school. The subjects were assigned to either the control or experimental group by using a table of random numbers and applying those numbers to the students. Ten students were assigned to the control group and 11 to the experimental group.

Convenience sample

Description of subjects

Random assignment (low number of students in each group)

Computer Assisted Program

The WiggleWorks (1994–1996) software program was used in this study. Co-developed by CAST and Scholastic, Inc., this program offers a literacy curriculum based on a combination of speech, sounds, graphics, text, and customizable access features. The software program features 72 trade books, audiocassettes, and a variety of computer-based activities. Students use the trade books and audiocassettes to read independently with or without the support of the audiocassette. Using the software program, students may listen to a story, read along with a story, or read a story silently. As they read, students are encouraged

Detailed description of intervention

(continued)

to review the suggested vocabulary words by selecting My Words. Students may listen to a pronunciation of the word by clicking on it or hear the word contextually in the story. Students may add new words to their vocabulary list by clicking on the selected word and the plus sign or remove words by clicking on the subtraction sign. Students may read and reread the story as they wish. Students may also create word families or practice spelling using a magnetic alphabet.

After listening to or reading a story, students have the option of composing their own stories. WiggleWorks provides a story starter, cloze-structured text, or free writing to help young students write their story. After composing a story, students may illustrate personal stories using basic drawing tools, stamps of the story characters, and/or story event backgrounds. Students may share their stories with others by recording their stories or printing the story and creating a book. These functions are available in a Read Aloud, Read, Write, My Book, and Magnet Board menu available to the individual user.

WiggleWorks is a managed instructional system. The management functions allow the teacher the opportunity to customize the computer-assisted instruction for each child. For instance, in Read Aloud, the settings can be adjusted so that the story is read to the student using a word-by-word, line-by-line, or whole-page approach. The management system also keeps a running log of individual and class activities. The Portfolio Management feature provides a reading record for each child (tracks the stories read, date and time individual stories were read, etc.), including reading and writing samples. The WiggleWorks software program provides a multimedia approach to literacy while supporting traditional methods with the accompanying trade books and audiocassettes.

| Detailed description of intervention (continued) |

Variables

The research project tested the independent variable of computer-assisted instruction on reading vocabulary development. Eleven students received the treatment monitored by one of the researchers. The dependent variable was a pre and post vocabulary test. The test was an independent word list administered by the researcher to the experimental and control group at the beginning and end of each session.

| Intervention (independent) and outcomes (dependent) |

Measurement

| How data are collected |

The instrument used to determine the effect of computer-assisted instruction on vocabulary was a pre and posttest designed by one of the researchers. Six high-frequency vocabulary words from each of the seven stories were selected by the researcher and placed on an independent list. The independent list of words served as the pre and post vocabulary test for each. All results were compared to determine the effect the treatment had on these subjects.

| Locally developed instrument |

Procedure

| How intervention was implemented |

As a part of the regular curriculum, all students received reading vocabulary instruction. The teacher utilized the reading instructional curriculum adopted by the county which consist of reading text books, related materials, and charts provided by the publishing company. Students participated in daily reading instruction. Each student in the class was randomly assigned into two groups: a control group and an experimental group. In an attempt to limit extraneous learning, both groups continued to receive regular reading instruction by the researcher/teacher. The regular reading curriculum had a twenty minute time block where students participated in a DEAR (Drop Everything And Read) program. The researchers used this block of time to implement this research project.

Seven pre-determined stories were used for this research project. The stories were available on book and tape as well as interactive, computerized storyboards. The control group experienced the story in a variety of ways. First, they listened to the assigned story as the teacher/researcher read the story to them. Next, students listened to the story on tape and read along with an accompanying book. Lastly, students were provided with an assortment of literature: library books, classroom literature, or the student's personal books to read at their leisure after the pre-determined book and tape assignment had been completed. During that twenty-minute time span, the 10 students in the experimental group visited the Media computer lab and explored the same story using the computerized

| More detail about intervention and procedure |

storyboard. A computer, monitor, mouse, and headphone were provided for each subject. During the first session, the teacher/researcher explained the working mechanics of the computer laboratory and answered any questions from the students. Then, the lessons began as students listened to enjoy the story. Next, the students revisited and identified words unknown to them by clicking on the word. The computerized storyboards serve as a remediator. These subjects saw the printed word highlighted and heard as the word was produced in sound. Students were required to listen to the story once while reading along. After completing those requirements, students could listen and/or read any story previously read or any story at a lower level. Students were introduced to a new WiggleWorks story every other day. During this project, students experimented with seven different stories that became progressively more challenging. The ability levels of the stories ranged from Kindergarten to second grade. The project continued for six weeks.

> More detail about intervention and procedure (continued)

Results

The results were analyzed using a Paired-Samples *t*-test. An alpha level of .05 was set incorporating a two-tailed significance level. The analyses showed significant positive changes for both groups. The mean scores confirm that students using computerized storyboards demonstrate significant gains in their ability to recall a greater amount of new vocabulary words (See Table 1). The pre and posttest were analyzed using a Paired-Samples *t*-test. The results demonstrate a statistically significant difference ($p > .002$) in the experimental (computer) group. A significant difference ($p > .01$) was also found (See Table 2) in the control group (Book/Tape).

> Pretest-posttest analysis

> Description of results

The mean scores of the pre and post vocabulary tests indicate a significant gain in the experimental (computer story board) group (Mean Pre = 3.7; Mean Post = 16.9). A further analysis involving the reading ability of the individual students demonstrated that students with higher reading ability scored higher in the experimental and control groups than average ability or low ability students. Those students who were performing successfully in their reading scored significantly higher than those students who were performing at a lower level.

> Introduction of second independent variable

TABLE 1   Means and Standard Deviations

Group	Pretest		Posttest	
	M	SD	(M)	(SD)
Computer	3.7	4.37	16.9	13.17
Book/Tape	1.8	2.68	5.45	6.07

> Mean scores
> Standard deviation

TABLE 2   Paired-Samples *t*-test

Group	df	t	p
Computer	9	4.18	0.002
Book/Tape	10	3.17	0.010

> Inferential statistical test

Discussion

The stories selected for this project were progressively more challenging so as to meet the needs of as many young readers as possible. Students with greater reading ability scored higher on the pretests and showed greater improvement on the posttests. These students seemed to possess a greater command of reading and technological skills required in maneuvering the storyboards.

> Summary of results

(continued)

Students with less reading ability did not gain as much from the experience. While they seemed to enjoy the stories, they were greatly challenged by the pre and posttest. These students would have been more successful with stories developmentally appropriate for their reading ability. Overall, the ability level of the students in the classroom seemed to mirror their performance in the computer-based reading instruction. Strong readers worked somewhat independently, average-ability students were at an instructional level with reading and technology skills, while students with less reading ability needed assistance with reading and technology. Students in the experimental group (computer storyboards) were greatly motivated by the use of computers. They enjoyed the interactive, multi-sensory aspect of learning. This was evidenced by the students' request to spend more time listening to stories on the computers. Multi-sensory teaching seemed to make their learning fun.

Additional results and explanation of results

Implications and Significance

This research project was designed to investigate the effects of computer-assisted instruction on first grade students' vocabulary development. With the integration of sights, colors, sounds, actions, plus the printed word, vocabulary lessons took on a new meaning. Students recognized the word on sight, remembered the word through association and phonemes, and quite a few could use the word as a part of their spoken and written vocabulary. Students were able to recognize the words in isolation and in text.

Conclusions

Overall, implications of this research project are that a 20-minute DEAR time using computerized storyboards directly results in improved vocabulary development among first grade students. Learning new vocabulary words took place at a faster pace with greater accuracy than with the direct teaching format. "Technology brings to your classroom the capability of connecting dynamic, interactive vocabulary learning with reading, writing, spelling, and content learning" (Fox and Mitchell, 2000, p. 66).

Findings related to previous research

Computerized classroom instruction does not infer inflated test scores or a magic potion for teaching. It is a motivating medium that enhances good teaching. The infusion of technology and literacy is a lifelong learning gift we create for our students.

Significance

Recommendations

Computer-assisted instruction has a positive influence on student's motivation, interest, and learning. This research project validates the effect that computer-assisted instruction has on first graders' vocabulary development during a crucial time when they are learning to read. To improve upon this study, a concentrated effort should be made to determine the developmental reading level of each student. Students could then receive more individualized instruction at their appropriate reading level. Additionally, teachers/researchers need to move students from dependent direct instruction to more independent learning. A natural follow-up to this study could be to see if this move to more independent learning is facilitated by differing uses of technology in the classroom.

Restatement of conclusion

Suggestions for future research

References

Brinkman, D. & Torgeson, J. (1994). Computer administered instruction in phonological awareness: evaluation of the DaisyQuest program. *The Journal of Research and Development in Education, 27*(2), 126–137.

Case, C. & Truscott, D. M. (1999). The lure of bells and whistles: choosing the best software to support reading instruction. *Reading and Writing Quarterly, 15*(4), 361.

Chall, J. (1992). The new reading debates: evidence from science, art, and ideology. *Teachers College Record, 94*(2), 315.

Czubaj, C. (1997). Whole language literature reading instruction. *Education, 117*(4), 538.

Daniels, H. and Zemelman, S. (1999). Whole language works: sixty years of research. *Educational Research, 57*(2), 32.

Dillon, D. R. (2000). Identifying beliefs and knowledge, uncovering tensions, and solving problems. *Kids' insight: reconsidering how to meet the literacy needs of all students* (pp. 72–79). Newark, DE: International Reading Association, Inc.

Dockstader, J. (1999). Teachers of the 21st century know the what, why, and how of technology integration. *T.H.E. Journal, 26*(6), 73–74.

Eisenwine, M. J. & Hunt, D. A. (2000). Using a computer in literacy groups with emergent readers. *The Reading Teacher, 53*(6), 456.

Forcier, R. C. (1999). Computer applications in education. *The computer as an educational tool* (pp. 60–93). Upper Saddle River, NJ: Prentice-Hall. Inc.

Title of journal article: initial cap only

Title of journal: cap each word

Year published

Pages

Volume

Title of book: initial cap only

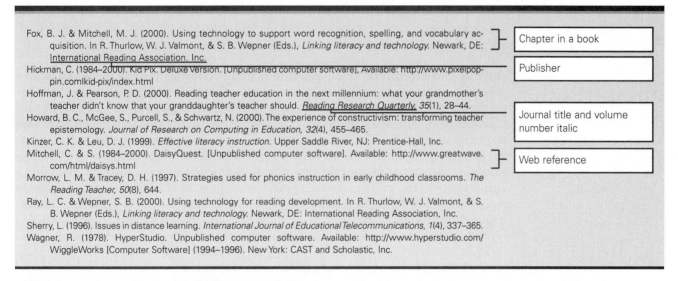

Fox, B. J. & Mitchell, M. J. (2000). Using technology to support word recognition, spelling, and vocabulary acquisition. In R. Thurlow, W. J. Valmont, & S. B. Wepner (Eds.), *Linking literacy and technology*. Newark, DE: International Reading Association, Inc.

Hickman, C. (1984–2000). Kid Pix. Deluxe Version. [Unpublished computer software], Available: http://www.pixelpoppin.com/kid-pix/index.html

Hoffman, J. & Pearson, P. D. (2000). Reading teacher education in the next millennium: what your grandmother's teacher didn't know that your granddaughter's teacher should. *Reading Research Quarterly, 35*(1), 28–44.

Howard, B. C., McGee, S., Purcell, S., & Schwartz, N. (2000). The experience of constructivism: transforming teacher epistemology. *Journal of Research on Computing in Education, 32*(4), 455–465.

Kinzer, C. K. & Leu, D. J. (1999). *Effective literacy instruction*. Upper Saddle River, NJ: Prentice-Hall, Inc.

Mitchell, C. & S. (1984–2000). DaisyQuest. [Unpublished computer software]. Available: http://www.greatwave.com/html/daisys.html

Morrow, L. M. & Tracey, D. H. (1997). Strategies used for phonics instruction in early childhood classrooms. *The Reading Teacher, 50*(8), 644.

Ray, L. C. & Wepner, S. B. (2000). Using technology for reading development. In R. Thurlow, W. J. Valmont, & S. B. Wepner (Eds.), *Linking literacy and technology*. Newark, DE: International Reading Association, Inc.

Sherry, L. (1996). Issues in distance learning. *International Journal of Educational Telecommunications, 1*(4), 337–365.

Wagner, R. (1978). HyperStudio. Unpublished computer software. Available: http://www.hyperstudio.com/ WiggleWorks [Computer Software] (1994–1996). New York: CAST and Scholastic, Inc.

Chapter in a book

Publisher

Journal title and volume number italic

Web reference

FIGURE 2.3 **Anatomy of a Quantitative Research Article**

Source: From Boling, C., Martin, S. H., & Martin, M. A. (2002). The effects of computer-assisted instruction on first grade students' vocabulary development. *Reading Improvement, 39*(2), 79–88. Provided by Reading Improvement, Phillip Feldman, Ed. Reprinted by permission.

Results

1. Were the most appropriate and meaningful statistical techniques employed?
2. Have the results been adequately and clearly presented?
3. Is there reference to *practical* as well as *statistical* significance?

Discussion, Implications, Conclusions

1. Are the conclusions and generalizations consistent with the findings? What are the implications of the findings? Has the researcher overgeneralized the findings?
2. Does the researcher discuss the limitations of the study?
3. Are there any extraneous factors that might have affected the findings? Have they been considered by the researcher?
4. Are the conclusions presented consistent with theory or known facts?
5. Have the conclusions (both those relevant to the original hypothesis and any serendipitous findings) been presented adequately and discussed?

How to Read Qualitative Research: Anatomy of a Qualitative Example

There is greater diversity in the formats used to report qualitative research than in the formats typical of quantitative studies. Published reports typically use four major sections: Introduction, Methodology, Findings, and Conclusions. In contrast to those found in quantitative studies, however, these sections may not be identified clearly or may be identified by descriptive terms related to the topic. Figure 2.4 provides an example of a qualitative research article.

Introduction   The *Introduction* provides a general background of the study, indicating the potential importance of the research. It summarizes the general intentions of the investigator, along with a general statement of the research problem or purpose. For a journal article, usually only one of many research foci are reported. The introduction includes a preliminary literature review to present possible conceptual frameworks that will be useful in understanding the data and results. The review justifies the need for the study. The introduction may also indicate the structure of the rest of the report.

Methodology   The *Methodology* section describes the design of the study, including the selection and description of the site, the role of the researcher, initial entry for interviews and observation, the time and length of the study, the number of participants and how they were selected, and data collection and analysis strategies. The amount of detail contained in this section will vary, depending on the type of research report. In relatively short published articles, the Methodology section may be part of the introduction.

Findings and Interpretations   In this section, the researcher presents the data that were gathered, usually in the form of a lengthy narrative, and analyzes the data. This should be done in sufficient detail to allow the reader to judge the accuracy of the analysis. The data are used to illustrate and substantiate the researcher's interpretations. Analysis is often intermixed with the presentation of data. The data are often in the form of quotes by participants. It is important to indicate the purpose of data analysis and to describe what has been learned by synthesizing the information. Because the presentation is in narrative form, there are frequently a number of descriptive subtitles connoting different findings. Most qualitative studies follow an iterative pattern of developing claims, seeking confirming and disconfirming evidence, exploring alternative claims, and making new claims. This process should be carefully described so that the reader can follow the process. Descriptive statistics are used sometimes to summarize data.

Conclusions   The *Conclusion* usually includes a restatement of the initial focus of the study and how the data results and analyses impinge on that focus. Implications of the results can be elaborated, as well as implications for further research, and the extent of transferability should be discussed.

References   The References section provides full bibliographic information for all previously completed work that is cited in the article. Although APA format is common, some journals have a unique style.

Guidelines for Evaluating Qualitative Research

To understand qualitative research, it is necessary to carefully read the entire report or article. This is how readers are able to identify with the investigators and understand how they have come to their conclusions. The process by which this occurs is important, and to understand this process, it is necessary to read from beginning to end. As with quantitative studies, certain questions should be asked about the report to judge its quality.

Introduction

1. Is the focus, purpose, or topic of the study stated clearly?
2. Are there situations or problems that lead to the focus of the study? Is there a rationale for the study? Is it clear that the study is important?
3. Is there background research and theory to help refine the research questions?
4. Does the Introduction contain an overview of the design?
5. Is the literature review pertinent to the focus of the research? Is the literature analyzed as well as described?

Methodology

1. Are the research sites described to identify their uniqueness or typicality?
2. Is entry into the field established?
3. Was the role of the researcher explained?
4. Are limitations of the design acknowledged?
5. Is the iterative process, used in data collection, clearly described?
6. Is the context clearly described?

Findings and Interpretations

1. Are the perspectives of the different participants clearly presented? Are participants' words or comments quoted?
2. Is sufficient detail and depth provided?
3. Are multiple perspectives presented?
4. Are the results well documented? Are assertions and interpretations illustrated by results?
5. Are researchers' personal beliefs accounted for?
6. Are the interpretations reasonable? Were researchers' preconceptions and biases acknowledged?

Conclusions

1. Are the conclusions logically consistent with the findings?
2. Are limitations of the research design and focus indicated?
3. Are implications of the findings indicated?

The Developmental Progression of Children's Oral Story Inventions

Eugene Geist   Jerry Aldridge

This study investigated stories that children created after being told the Grimm version of selected tales. These stories were told as an instruction to the children on story structure and to familiarize children with ideas of plot, character, and conflict in stories. This cross-sectional study considered what differences are evident in the oral fairy tales that children tell at different ages. Stories from children in kindergarten, first grade, second grade, and third grade were collected and analyzed. For the purpose of this study, the following research questions were asked. These questions guided the research and eventually became the major coding categories.

1) Is there a developmental difference in the type of story (i.e., personal narrative, fantasy, realistic fiction) children tell when they are asked to invent a fairy tale?
2) Are there developmental differences in the content of children's stories among age groups?
3) Are there developmental differences in how children organize the content of their invented fairy tales?

A qualitative research methodology was used for this study. Children's orally invented stories were tape recorded and transcribed. The data were analyzed using content analysis of the transcripts.

This study indicates that children's orally told invented fairy tales can be used (a) to promote cognitive development, (b) to assess cognitive development, and (c) to identify emotional conflicts that children are experiencing. This study also indicates that second grade is a good time to promote creativity and imaginations as this was the age in which children were most confident in their imaginative abilities.

Abstract (rather long)

Few studies have been conducted on children's oral story inventions (Aldridge, Eddowes, Ewing, & Kuby, 1994). Studies on children's interest in folk and fairy tales have not touched on children's invented "fairy tales" and how they can reflect developmental issues. There have been many examinations of written retellings of fairy tales (Boydston, 1994; Gambrell, Pfeiffer, & Wilson, 1985; Morrow, 1986). However, few works have examined oral stories invented by children. Invented oral stories can give a valuable insight into a child's cognitive, affective, and creative development (Allan & Bertoia, 1992; Markham, 1983; Sutton-Smith, 1985).

Suggests need for study

This study investigated stories that children created after being told the Grimm version of selected tales. These stories were told as an instruction to the children on story structure and to familiarize children with ideas of plot, character, and conflict in stories. The Grimm (1993) versions were chosen because the literature suggests that they are the closest to the oral tradition (Zipes, 1988). This cross-sectional study considered what differences are evident in the oral fairy tales that children tell at different ages. Stories from children in kindergarten, first grade, second grade, and third grade were collected and analyzed (Geist & Aldridge, 1999).

General research problem

For the purpose of this study, the following research questions were asked. These questions guided the research and eventually became the major coding categories.

1) Is there a developmental difference in the type of story (i.e., personal narrative, fantasy, realistic fiction) children tell when they are asked to invent a fairy tale?
2) Are there developmental differences in the content of children's stories among age groups?
3) Are there developmental differences in how children organize the content of their invented fairy tales?

Research questions

(continued)

Method

A qualitative research methodology was used for this study. Children's orally invented stories were tape recorded and transcribed. The data were analyzed using content analysis of the transcripts. According to Carney (1972), "content analysis is any technique for making inferences by objectively and systematically identifying specified characteristics of messages" (p. 25).

A semistructured interview format was used to collect data. The children were asked to make up a fairy tale and tell it to the researcher. The researcher prompted the subject if there was a long pause. The researcher also had the child start over if the child was engaging in a retelling of a story that the researcher recognized. The data were then analyzed using a content analysis.

> Overall research design

> Researcher conducted all interviews

Participants

> Not "subjects"

Convenience sampling was the method used to select study participants. The classrooms chosen were believed to facilitate the expansion of a developing theory because the sample was homogeneous. All subjects were African American and from low socioeconomic families. The subjects for this study were students in four classrooms at an elementary school in a low socioeconomic area of an urban city in the Southeastern United States. The racial make up of the sample was 100% African American.

> Indicates characteristics of participants

Data Collection

Each classroom participated in a 45-minute lesson on fairy tales and story structure each day for 4 days. The lesson consisted of reading and discussing the plots and characters of fairy tales. After the 4 days, the children were asked, individually, to make up a fairy tale and tell it orally. The stories were tape recorded and transcribed. A content analysis of the transcripts was performed as described by Carney (1992).

> Data gathered as tape-recorded interviews

> Data analysis

One kindergarten, one first-grade, one second-grade, and one third-grade classroom, each with approximately 15 students, participated in this study. Each classroom was given an identical session on fairy tales and story structure. This session consisted of reading fairy tales to the students and discussing the aspects of the story. The specific description of the 5 days of storytelling and discussion are found in Geist and Aldridge (1999). These procedures were modified from Allan and Bertoia (1992) by Boydston (1994). Allan and Bertoia developed a procedure to initiate the discussion of fairy tales. This outline was used for seventh graders; however, because this study was interested in students in kindergarten, first, second, and third grades, a procedure modified by Boydston (1994), was used for this study. Boydston's outline was developed for second graders but is appropriate for the ages targeted in this study.

> Shows modification of previously used methods

Data Analysis

Analysis of the data was generated from the transcripts of the audiotapes. The research questions served as a guide for conducting the analysis. Each question became a major coding category broken down by age. The results of each age were then compared to each other to build a model of children's invented fairy tales. Bogdan and Biklen (1992) stated that preassigned coding systems are developed when researchers explore particular topics or aspects of the study.

> Coding emerges from the data for many qualitative studies

Inter-rater reliability was conducted on this study by having an educational professional with extensive knowledge of fairy tales and their form, function, and uses independently categorize the data. Another rater was trained in content analysis and was experienced in the content analysis method. This researcher had performed qualitative studies on fairy tales and children's storytelling in the past. The two raters participated in two practice sessions of reading and analyzing children's oral invented stories.

> Use of trained, independent rater improves credibility

The recordings were transcribed and copied. The independent rater and the researcher received identical copies of the transcripts. Because the three foreshadowed questions were used as a framework for the categories, the independent rater was given a copy of the foreshadowed questions. Each rater read the transcripts as many times as needed and noted themes related to genre, content, and organization. Each rater then independently compared the common themes from each grade and constructed a model for genre, content, and organization.

Both raters discussed the method for analysis before beginning. When a theme or thread was identified, it was highlighted by a colored marker that identified it with other items that belonged with that thread. The rater wrote notes in the margin next to this highlighted text. Then all of the text passages with the same color highlight were collected by grade. The rater then reread the passages and came up with a phrase or word that best described the common characteristics of those passages. The descriptive phrases were then compared to the phrases for the other grades to determine if a model could be constructed. Often, there was more than one model that was evident in each of the categories.

These themes and models were then compared. The themes and models that were consistent between the two raters were retained and clarified. The themes and models that were not consistent between the two raters were not included. Each story was then categorized independently by each rater into the rough model that had been developed.

> Use of trained, independent rater improves credibility (continued)

Results

Findings from this study suggest a developmental shift in the genre, content, and organization of children's oral invented stories. The genre of the children's stories moved from the fantastical to stories based on personal experiences. Kindergarten children told mostly fantasy stories, first and second graders told mostly realistic fiction, and third graders told mostly personal narratives.

> Results directly related to research question

The content of the children's stories showed development in two areas. First, there was development in the basis of their stories. Kindergarten children based their stories on previously heard material, first graders based theirs on familiar surroundings, second graders based their inventions on their imagination, and third graders tended to base their stories on personal experiences.

Second, there was development in how parents were depicted in the stories. Kindergartners, first, and second graders depicted parents as heroes and comforters. Third graders depicted parents as authority figures.

The content of the stories of all the grades contained reflections of the children's fears and concerns from everyday life. Fears about being kidnapped or other stresses, such as performance anxiety and social pressures, were reflected in their stories.

> Examples from participants

The organization of the stories moved from disjointed sentences to a coherent whole story. States that could be delineated were (a) disjointed, (b) phrase disjointed, (c) short-utilitarian, (d) sidetracked, and (e) coherent whole.

> Inquiry paradigm

Genre

The development of genre moved from the fantastical notions of kindergartners to the realistic personal narratives of third graders. Kindergartners told fantastical stories of talking umbrellas, flying to Mars, magic, and evil witches that turned children into food. First and second graders told realistic fiction stories about hunters, kings, queens, and an occasional witch; however, almost all of the actions of the characters were in the realm of possibility. Third graders tended to tell personal narratives that related directly to their life experiences; they were simply retelling events that happened to them or to someone they knew.

> Detail provided to show depth of understanding

The study suggests the genre was influenced by 3 things. First it was influenced by the classroom context. In the kindergarten classroom, the researcher observed a lot of fantasy literature. Children heard stories daily about talking animals and fantastical actions in the books the teachers read to them. However, as the grades progressed, the researcher observed that the teachers provided more realistic literature and less fantasy. This, in turn, affected the genre of the stories that the children told. Second was the children's developing understanding of the difference between fantasy and reality. As children begin to

> Explanation of overall findings concerning genre

(continued)

understand the concept of causality and move into concrete operations, the concept of what is possible and logical versus what is illogical, magical and impossible becomes more delineated. The second and third grade stories reflect this move toward reality based stories. Third, was the base material that children chose. As we have already mentioned, children tended to choose more personal material as they got older until at third grade, they tell personal, true to life personal narratives. Obviously, this shift is going to affect the genre of the story that they tell. This will be discussed further in the examination of the content of the children's stories.

> Explanation of overall findings concerning genre (continued)

Content

There were two developmental themes that could be delineated in the content of the children's stories. The first was the basis that the children used to construct their stories. The second was the role of parents in the children's stories. Third, the content of all the grades contained reflections of children's fears and concerns.

Children in kindergarten based their stories on previously heard material. They did not appear confident in their ability to be successful in making up a story on their own, so they used stories that they had heard or read recently to build their story around. First graders were a little more sure of themselves so they did not need specific stories on which to base their inventions. However, they still needed to base the settings and characteristics on things that were familiar to them. This gave them the framework for their stories. By second grade, the children did not need outside structure on which to build their stories. They could rely on their imagination completely as the basis for their stories. In third grade, the surge of imagination noted in second grade appeared to be gone. Either by discouragement or development, children had given up on imagination as the basis of their stories. These children told personal narratives that used personal experiences as the basis for their inventions. These types of stories required little or no imagination.

> Researcher opinion

> Researcher synthesis of findings from each grade level

A second developmental theme evident in the content of the children's orally invented stories was that at around third grade children began to consider peers, rather than parents, as their primary social contacts. This transition was reflected in their stories. In kindergarten and first grade, children were still primarily dependent on their parents for social and emotional interaction. However, around second grade they began to bond with peers, and the peer group became their primary social group with many third graders.

Before third grade, parents in children's stories were heroes and comforters. It was they who rescued the child from the grasp of the monster. A major shift had occurred in the third graders' stories, when parents were depicted as strict authority figures who were present to judge and punish. Third grade children's stories showed a common theme of fear of parental reprisals in this sample.

The stories also show a reflection of children's fears and anxieties. Children are surrounded with stress that is often not released. Stories offer children this release. The stories of all the grades contained personal reflections of fears and stresses. Especially prevalent were fears of kidnap and murder. The children in this particular school had experience with a classmate being kidnapped and murdered so it is not surprising that this fear appeared in their stories.

> Researcher reflection on characteristics of participants

Organization

Three developmental aspects of children's organization of invented stories were determined in this study. These included:

1) There was a clear developmental sequence to the way children organized their stories.
2) Egocentrism decreased through interactions in the social environment.
3) The distinction of the difference between fantasy and reality developed with age.

Even after the children were involved in the 4-day workshop on fairy tales, a developmental pattern still emerged. This suggests that there are aspects to children's understanding of story structure that is developmental and cannot be totally directly taught. The workshop focused on the characters, settings, plot, and organization of fairy tales. The children were instructed that fairy tales have a clear beginning, middle, and end; the beginning contains an introduction of the characters, setting, and problems; the middle of the story discusses how the characters go about solving the problems; and the end of the story contains the resolution. Thus, the children were familiar with the parts of the stories, and still a majority of the children were unable to use the information in the workshops to construct a coherent whole story. This suggests that the progression through stages of organization is developmental and not based on training.

Review of salient characteristics of context

Conclusion

Implication of conclusion

There was a cognitive developmental sequence in the organization of children's oral invented stories. So distinct were the differences, a developmental model can be proposed based on the data. The first stage can be characterized by the children's being unable to form a coherent ordered whole story. They told disjointed stories in which individual thoughts were juxtaposed. This is consistent with the findings of Piaget (1958) that children could not order a story into a coherent whole until about the age of 8.

Synthesis of data to suggest model

In the second stage, the children could string a series of thoughts together into coherent phrases, however, the phrases of about two or three sentences were juxtaposed against other phrases to which they had little relationship. In the third stage, children told short, utilitarian stories that just included the basics of a story with no elaboration. The children were attempting to keep their stories ordered and coherent and, if there was too much information, they got confused.

The fourth stage showed the result of this confusion. Children got sidetracked because they included more elaboration and lost track of the original story line. Eventually, they got back on track, and ended the story on the same theme with which they started. The final stage was characterized by children telling a coherent, elaborate story from beginning to end without getting sidetracked.

Conclusions and Implications

This study showed that literacy is not totally in the domain of social knowledge. The learning of words, letters, and rules of language must be passed down through the culture; these aspects of literacy cannot be invented by children without help. However, there are aspects of literacy that involve what Piaget deemed logico-mathematical knowledge. This study suggests that story structure is, at least partially, logico-mathematical knowledge. The part-whole relationship (Piaget, 1970) plays a part in the structure of children's stories. The children in this study all received direct instruction on story structure, but still a developmental sequence was evident. Children's understanding of story structure is dependent on more than direct instruction.

Findings related to previous research

Story structure is learned through interaction with text and words rather than through direct instruction. Children will invent story structure by telling and writing stories. The reactions from the audience and from their rereading or listening to other students' stories cause disequilibrium, which according to Piaget (1970), leads to development.

This study indicates that children's orally told invented fairy tales can be used (a) to promote cognitive development, (b) to assess cognitive development, and (c) to identify emotional conflicts that children are experiencing. This study also indicates that second grade is a good time to promote creativity and imaginations as this was the age in which children were most confident in their imaginative abilities.

Overall conclusions

Orally invented stories can be used to promote cognitive development. Each time children tell a story, they must attempt first to order it mentally. This mental activity promotes the construction of knowledge. A developmental sequence to the organization of orally told stories appears evident from the stories children told in this study. To promote the movement through these developmental stages, children must be provided with the opportunity to tell stories to an audience and receive social interaction. Each time the child tells a story, the reaction from the audience causes disequilibrium. If the audience does not understand the story, the child must examine why the audience did not understand it. This type of construction through social interaction was also described by Kamii (2000) in math development. This works just as well for storytelling. The feedback from peers helps the child to overcome the limitations of egocentrism and egocentric thought.

Implications

Points related to previous research

(continued)

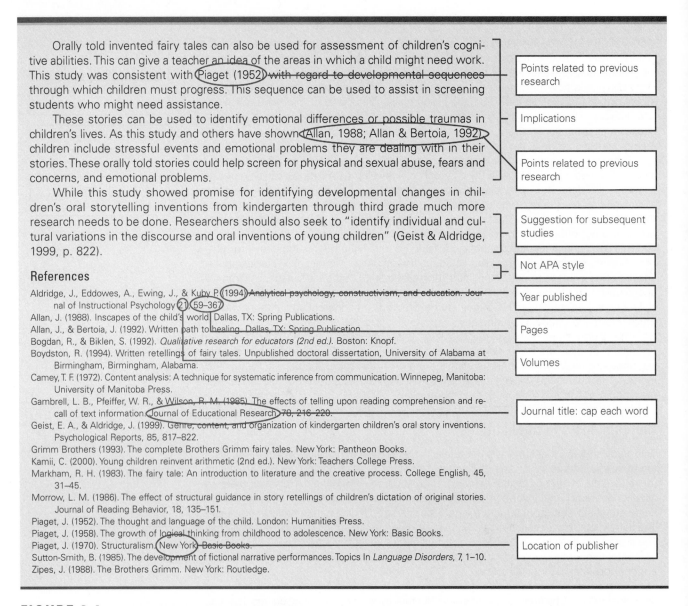

FIGURE 2.4 **Anatomy of a Qualitative Research Article**
Source: From Geist, E., & Aldridge, J. (2002). The developmental progression of children's oral story inventions. *Journal of Instructional Psychology, 29,* 33–39. Reprinted with permission of the Journal of Instructional Psychology.

CHAPTER SUMMARY

This chapter has provided an overview of common terminology of types of research designs and the standard formats of published articles. The major points in this chapter are as follows:

1. Research design is the general plan of the study, including when, from whom, and how data are collected.

2. An important difference in quantitative research is whether it is experimental or nonexperimental.

3. In experimental designs, the investigator studies cause-and-effect relationships by introducing an intervention and seeing how that intervention relates to the outcome of the study.

4. True experimental research is characterized by random assignment of subjects to groups.

5. Quasi-experimental research investigates causation without random assignment.

6. Single-subject research investigates the causal relationship between a factor and the behavior of a single individual.

7. *Nonexperimental* is a generic term that refers to research in which there is no direct control over causation. Nonexperimental designs can be classified as descriptive, comparative, correlational, survey, ex post facto, and secondary data analysis.

8. Qualitative modes of inquiry use face-to-face data collection to construct in-depth understandings of informants' perspectives.
9. An ethnography is a detailed description and interpretation of a culture or system.
10. A phenomenological study describes the meanings of a lived experience from the perspective of the informants.
11. A case study investigates a single bounded system over time using multiple sources of data.
12. Grounded theory is used to develop detailed concepts or propositions about a particular phenomenon.
13. Critical studies emphasize the subjectivity of knowledge and contemporary perspectives of critical, feminist, and postmodern theory.

14. Analytical research investigates historical, policy, and legal events through document analysis.
15. Mixed method studies include explanatory, exploratory, and triangulation designs, using elements of both quantitative and qualitative designs.
16. Quantitative studies follow a well-established report format. In qualitative studies, the format will vary but will usually include an introduction and literature review, methodology, findings and interpretation, and conclusions.

APPLICATION PROBLEMS

1. Classify each study described below as a type of research design: experimental, nonexperimental, quantitative, qualitative, or mixed method.
   a. A pilot investigation of the validity of the Back Stroke Test to identify problem swimmers
   b. A comparison of the effect of two reading programs on fourth-grade classes in Kalamazoo
   c. An investigation of the structure of attitudes of college students
   d. The effect of extrinsic rewards on the motivation of randomly assigned children to play groups
   e. A survey of principals' general attitudes toward collective bargaining as well as interviews with a small number of principals
   f. A study of the relative effectiveness of different counseling techniques used by counselors over the past five years
   g. An investigation of the difference in attendance between students in two high schools with different leadership styles

   h. A posttest-only study of the effect of humorously written review sentences on comprehension for two groups of children
   i. A study of the meaning of merit pay to teachers

2. Locate one quantitative and one qualitative journal article. For each article, identify the major sections and answer the questions provided in the guidelines for evaluating each type of article. Rate the overall credibility of each article.

3. Write a brief statement that indicates which type of research design—quantitative or qualitative—is used most commonly in your field of study.

4. Ask a professor in your field of study how he or she reads a research article. Ask what he or she reads first, second, and so forth. Also ask what the professor does about statistical procedures included that he or she does not understand and what features he or she focuses on to judge the overall credibility of the study.

ANSWERS TO APPLICATION PROBLEMS

1. a. nonexperimental
   b. experimental or nonexperimental
   c. nonexperimental or qualitative
   d. experimental
   e. nonexperimental
   f. nonexperimental
   g. nonexperimental
   h. experimental
   i. qualitative
2. (individual student response)
3. (individual student response)
4. (individual student response)

Research Problems, Questions, and Hypotheses

Research Problems, Questions, and Hypotheses

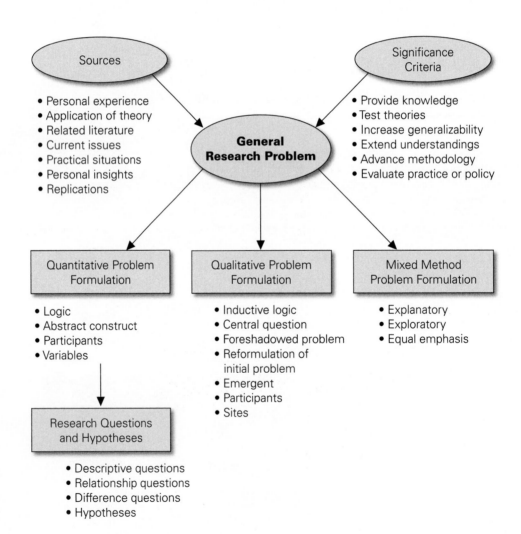

KEY TERMS

research problem

construct

variable

categorical variable

continuous variable

dependent variable

independent variable

predictor variable

criterion variable

extraneous variable

operational definition

research hypothesis

central question

foreshadowed problem

WHAT YOU WILL LEARN

Study this chapter and you will:

- Recognize three components of research problems: context, purpose, significance.
- Know about sources for constructing research problems, including those based on contradictory findings and application of theory.
- Understand the nature and importance of doing replications.
- Understand different variables in quantitative research, especially independent, dependent, and extraneous variables.

- Learn how to write specific research questions and hypotheses.
- Learn about problem and research question formulation in qualitative research.
- Distinguish between quantitative and qualitative research questions.
- Understand problem and research question formulation in mixed method research.
- Be able to apply criteria for establishing the significance of research.

THE NATURE OF RESEARCH PROBLEMS

Empirical studies begin with research questions. But where do these questions come from? What is the context in which they are embedded that suggests that the questions are appropriate and important? How does the reader get an understanding of *what* is proposed and *why* is it important? To address these questions, investigators formulate a research problem. The **research problem** is the issue, controversy, or concern that initiates the study. The research problem is included in the introduction section of a research report or article. It consists of several sentences or a few paragraphs that show how the problem is formulated, and provides the foundation for the meaningfulness of the study. This results in an understanding of how the research will contribute to a body of knowledge or to practice.

Research problem: issue, controversy, or concern

Sometimes the research problem begins with a *topic*. A topic is a general indication of the subject that is being researched. It indicates the starting point of initial interest. Each of the following would be considered a topic:

- Reading difficulties of elementary students
- Doing research on the Internet
- Formative classroom assessment
- Student motivation
- Social development of adolescents
- Adult literacy

Topics are communicated in the titles of studies and in the first few sentences of the introduction. As such, they provide a simple and easily understood general idea of what is being investigated.

The research problem follows from the topic. You will find that many styles are used in presenting the research problem, and usually there is no separate section of the report named "Research Problem." In short articles the research problem may consist of only a few sentences. In doctoral dissertations there may be several pages devoted to the research problem. One rule is that the purpose and context of the study are presented before the review of literature. Statements related to the justification and significance of the study may be placed before or after the review of literature.

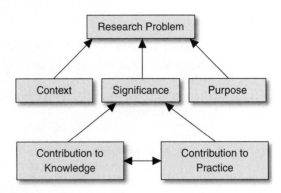

FIGURE 3.1 **Components of Research Problems**

As illustrated in Figure 3.1, research problems typically have three components: context, purpose, and significance. Context, or background, places the research problem within a larger subject or area. For example, a researcher might say, "There has been growing interest in the process of student self-assessment" or "For many years researchers have documented the importance of student self-efficacy to motivation" or "This researcher was interested in investigating the effect of a new approach to teaching basketball." Sometimes researchers use the first person effectively for example, "For several years, I have been concerned about my expectations of autistic students in my class" or "As principal, I need to know which kind of classroom observation format provides the best feedback to teachers." Excerpt 3.1, a sample statement from a published article, further illustrates context as a part of the research problem.

The purpose is a statement that indicates in a more specific manner what is being investigated. This is indicated by the ubiquitous phrase "The purpose of this study is to. . . ." This kind of phrase is a formal problem statement. It can be rather broad, such as:

- The purpose of this study is to investigate effective approaches to mainstreaming exceptional students.
- The purpose of this study is to determine the dropout rate.
- The purpose of this study is to identify factors predicting teacher satisfaction.
- The purpose of this study is to provide empirical evidence of students' views of performance assessment.

Purpose statements can also be much more specific, very similar to the research question:

- The purpose of this study is to investigate the relationship between teachers' experience and student disruptions in the classroom.
- The purpose of this investigation was to relate student knowledge of test-taking strategies to student performance on high-stakes tests.
- Our goal was to examine which of three learning styles were best suited to differentiated instruction for elementary students.

Significance is addressed by showing how the study will make a contribution to current knowledge and/or practice. For basic and applied studies, it is crucial for the study to be clearly related to the existing body of knowledge and theory. For practice, the problem needs to be

EXCERPT 3.1 Context in Research Problems

In recent years there has been a growing concern regarding the current state of the educational system in the United States. For example, in comparison to other countries, high school students in the United States are falling behind students in other countries on various measures of academic achievement . . . given these concerns, one goal of this research was to examine the relative contributions of cognitive abilities to students' science achievement. (p. 161)

Source: From O'Reilly, T., & McNamara, D. S. (2007). The impact of science knowledge, reading skill, and reading strategy knowledge on more traditional "high-stakes" measures of high school students' science achievement. *American Educational Research Journal, 44*(1), 161–196.

EXCERPT 3.2   Research Problem Significance

This work attempts to move this larger body of research on school accountability policies forward by examining the influence of accountability policies on teacher motivation . . . this empirical investigation of motivational theories in the CPS accountability context provides important insights into the motivation response of teachers to school accountability policies . . . understanding the factors that imp[rove] teacher motivation in low-performing schools . . . Contributes to a broader knowledge base around improving teacher performance and, as a result, student performance. (p. 595)

Source: From Finnigan, K. S., & Gross, B. (2007). Do accountability policy sanctions influence teacher motivation? Lessons from Chicago's low-performing schools. *American Educational Research Journal, 44*(3), 594–629.

concerned with what occurs in actual educational situations. Action research emphasizes practical significance. Whether based on contributions to knowledge and/or practice, significance is essentially the justification for the study—why does it need to be done and reported? That is, it consists of reasons that indicate why the research problem is important.

Excerpt 3.2 shows how researchers indicate the significance of a study of school accountability and teacher motivation. In this case, contributions to both knowledge and practice are presented.

Sources for Research Problems

How do researchers begin to develop and identify good research problems? Although there are several excellent strategies for this purpose, the process can be rather arduous and time-consuming. Ideas that seem promising initially typically need revision as literature and practical constraints are clarified and analyzed. For some studies, especially doctoral dissertations, this process can take weeks or months. I like to characterize this process that the researcher experiences as a "psychological cycle" that builds over time to eventually result in a good problem. As illustrated in Figure 3.2, initially promising ideas generate optimism and hope, only to be lessened with further reading and thinking. Then another idea seems good, but it too isn't the best. One implication of this process is that researchers should be patient and allow the process to unfold. It took me a year to get from the initial topic to a focused research problem for my dissertation.

There are two excellent sources for identifying a topic that can be molded into a research problem. The first is to read recently published books and journal articles. An example of a good resource is *Education Week*. Each week this publication presents contemporary topics and results of research

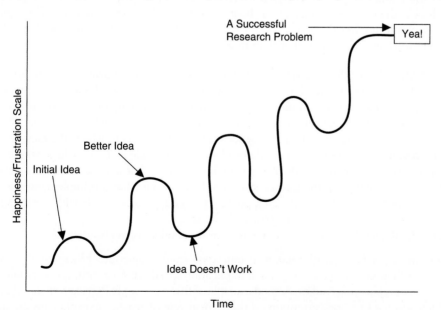

FIGURE 3.2   Psychological Profile for a Doctoral Student Developing a Good Research Problem

that may trigger identification of a topic and eventually a research problem. Another good strategy is to talk with knowledgeable professionals about the current issues, policies, and directions of a field of study. For researchers in university environments, discussions with faculty can (and should!) be helpful in developing a research problem. This is especially true in cases where the faculty member has an ongoing line of research. Students doing theses and dissertations are sometimes given a research problem that fits well within a line of research or an externally funded project.

Although no single strategy is best, following are some further sources that are used to establish good research problems.

Investigator's Observations, Interests, and Experience   Everyday observations and experiences can be a good source of research problems, especially for action research projects. Teachers encounter many problems and issues during their work day in and day out, e.g., concerns about how students are grouped for instruction, the effectiveness of teaching methods, grading, and differentiated instruction. School administrators may encounter issues about communicating with teachers and parents, dealing with parent advocacy groups, and identifying leadership styles that are effective with department chairs. Faculty in higher education may want to investigate the effect of different grading schemes on student motivation, how student teachers handle classroom management challenges, and how cooperating teachers' relationships are developed. Counselors may want to know whether group or individual sessions with students are most effective. For virtually any position, there will be problems or difficulties that hinder practice, things that can be improved to enhance student motivation and achievement. Your own experience in professional positions provides this virtual wealth of possible topics and research problems. In addition to these experiences, each of us is interested in various topics that can be used for research problems. The topic may be something we have heard about or read about, or it may be a long-standing interest of some kind.

Applying Theory   A common source of problems for basic and applied research is theories that have implications for practice. One approach is to take a theory in a related field, such as sociology and psychology, and develop problems that test or extend the theory to educational contexts. A good example of this is the substantial amount of work done on motivation theory in psychology. Here the broader topics of intrinsic and extrinsic motivation, and of self-efficacy and values, have been the basis for many studies in education. For example, an educational study could identify what kinds of feedback and grading would be considered intrinsic and extrinsic for middle school students and whether the effects of such feedback would vary by socioeconomic status, race, or gender. Other examples include the use of knowledge of how the brain works for designing instruction, the use of behavioral theories for reinforcement and behavior modification, and the use of theories of leadership for studying the effectiveness of principals. In each case, the theories provide ideas about what the implications would be when applied to educational settings. Existing educational theories can also be tested, revised, or clarified, with the intent to change theories rather than to apply theories in other disciplines.

Replication   One of the hallmarks of good scientific inquiry is replication. There is no question that the process of replicating already completed studies gives us the information we need to build a body of knowledge. Some replications that are essentially the same as earlier studies are needed, though most replications include minor changes to methodology or analyses. We think of this as "tweaking" previous studies. The idea is to identify ways in which the measures, subjects, procedures, and interventions could be changed to provide better conclusions. For example, suppose you read about a study of a specific intervention that was used to improve reading. In examining the nature of the intervention, you believe that what was implemented wasn't a good model of the theory. Your research could replicate the earlier study with changes in the intervention so that it is more consistent with the theory.

Gall, Gall, and Borg (2007) give five reasons for conducting replications:

1. *To confirm the findings of a major or milestone study.* Sometimes blockbuster studies are reported that seem to have exceptional implications. In these situations, it is very important to conduct replication studies. A good example of this is the study *Pygmalion in the Classroom*, which was used to draw attention to the critical role of teacher expectancies on student achievement. Hundreds of replications have been done since that initial study that have had significant influence on how such expectations actually affect students.

2. ***To extend the validity of research findings to different participants.*** An important aspect of research is to determine the extent to which the conclusions will hold for subjects who are not like the ones used in the original study. Thus, many replications use the same procedures with new subjects. For example, in Kohlberg's initial research on moral development, the studies used mainly men. It would be appropriate, then, to see if the results would be the same for women. When new subjects are very similar to ones used in previous studies there is no need to replicate just because of these minor differences.

3. ***To extend the validity of the research using different methods of measurement.*** Usually, research findings are limited to a single method of measurement. This may mean that the findings are true only when that same measure is used. That is, different measures may result in different conclusions. In this circumstance, the results are unduly influenced by the instrument or methods used to collect data, including the protocols used to administer the measures. For example, there are many instruments that purport to measure self-concept, each with an emphasis on different aspects of self-concept. The same is true for many other variables, including critical thinking, problem solving, creativity, and intelligence. When replication studies confirm findings using different measures, the conclusions are verified and strengthened. A related reason to replicate is to check findings by using different methods to analyze the data.

4. ***To determine trends or changes over time.*** Replications are needed to see if initial findings are consistent over time. This kind of information is more important than ever with high-stakes accountability testing. With this kind of testing, schools are able to identify trends over time for targeted groups of students. This is helpful in determining the effectiveness of curricula and practices that are targeted to students at risk of failure. On the national level, the National Assessment of Educational Progress (NAEP) has measured student performance since 1969, providing a trend that allows us to see if, overall, the country is improving student achievement.

5. ***To develop more effective or efficient interventions.*** With the increased emphasis on experimental research, there is a need to improve interventions so that they maximize student achievement. Thus, replications are needed that tweak or fine-tune the intervention. For instance, an after-school tutoring intervention could be researched to see if it helps students pass accountability tests. There are many aspects of this kind of intervention, and it would be good to determine if the results are the same if the procedures are changed (e.g., lengthening the intervention by 30 minutes, going three days a week rather than two, hiring special tutors to work with the students). Also, small-scale and controlled interventions can be replicated on a larger scale in more complex settings.

Clarification of Contradictory Findings It is not difficult to find contradictory findings across many studies that investigate the same problem. Perhaps you have come across a situation like this—one study comes up with one conclusion and other studies, of the same thing, reach a different conclusion. This is a great situation for doing further research! New studies can be designed to resolve the discrepancies in order to explain the reasons for these contradictions. For example, suppose some studies on retaining children in kindergarten for another year show that such students do better, whereas other studies show that some students don't do better. These studies can be examined to see if changes in methods or situations make a difference. Likewise, some research indicates that dropout prevention programs work well and other studies show no or few positive outcomes. Why?

Significance of the Problem

The significance of the problem is the rationale for a study. It justifies why an evidence-based inquiry is important and indicates the reasons for the researcher's choice of a particular problem. Because research requires knowledge, skills, planning, time, and fiscal resources, the problem to be investigated should be important. In other words, the study should have a potential payoff.

A research problem is significant when it aids in developing theory, knowledge, or practice. That significance increases when several reasons can be provided to justify the inquiry. Justifications may be based on one or more of the following criteria: whether the study provides knowledge about an enduring practice, tests a theory, is generalizable, extends understanding of a broader phenomenon, advances methodology, is related to a current issue, evaluates a specific practice at a given site, or is an exploratory study.

EXCERPT 3.3 Significance: Add to Knowledge of an Enduring Practice

The study adds to parent involvement research by examining parents' beliefs about involvement in different domains. (p. 201)

Source: From Drummon, K. V., & Stipek, D. (2004). Low-income parents' beliefs about their role in children's academic learning. *The Elementary School Journal, 104*(3), 197–214.

Knowledge of an Enduring Practice   The study may provide knowledge about an enduring educational practice. Perhaps previous research on the practice has been done, but this particular research problem has not been investigated. The practice being studied may be common to many schools but not necessarily found in every school. The study will add knowledge about an enduring common practice (see Excerpt 3.3).

Theory Testing   The study may be significant because it tests an existing theory with a verification design. The focus may be on social science theories of child or adult development, organizational development, conflict, and so on. Educational theories may focus on curricula, instructional models, staff development, learning styles, teaching strategies, and the like. By testing a theory in different situations or on different populations, the researcher may modify or verify it.

Generalizability   The study may be designed so that the results will be generalizable to different populations or practices. A study may replicate or include other variables not investigated in previous research, or it may call for using a different population than the original research to enhance generalizability (see Excerpt 3.4).

Extensions of Understanding   Many qualitative studies conducted in the phenomenological tradition extend understanding rather than generalizability. By describing a selected case of a social situation in detail, such a study provides an understanding of the phenomena observed. That understanding provides an image or configuration of reasonable expectations that might be useful in similar situations.

Methodological Advancement   The study may be significant because it increases the validity and reliability of an instrument or uses a methodology different from the methodologies used in previous studies. Much of the research on educational measurement investigates questions related to assessment, such as testing procedures, the order of the items on an instrument, the item format or response set, and the information processes of the respondent. Another study may develop a statistical or methodological technique and elaborate on its usefulness for research.

Current Issues   The study may focus on a social issue of immediate concern. Organized political movements such as those for women's rights and civil rights have generated educational research. Public recognition of social problems has frequently led to assessment of their educational effects. The increasing prevalence of single-parent families, for example, has raised questions about the impact of single parenting on student self-concept and achievement. Similarly, studies on the instructional effects of students having laptops and Internet access have originated from social concerns about living in a highly technological society (see Excerpt 3.5).

EXCERPT 3.4 Justification: Replication and Generalization

Thus, the objective of the present inquiry was to replicate and extend the work of Witcher et al. (2001). Specifically our purpose was to investigate what preservice teachers view as important characteristics of effective teachers. (p. 118)

Source: From Minor, L. C., Onwuegbuzie, A., Witcher, A. E., & James, T. L. (2002). Preservice teachers' educational beliefs and their perceptions of characteristics of effective teachers. *Journal of Educational Research, 96*(2), 116–127.

EXCERPT 3.5 Justification: Current Issue

[Being aware of] the No Child Left Behind Act . . . can enable educators to get a head start not only on hearing the concerns of African American parents but also on improving their relations with these parents and seeking effective ways to improve the quality of education that they offer to African American students. (pp. 277, 279)

Source: From Thompson, G. L. (2003). Predicting African American parents' and guardians' satisfaction with teachers and public schools. *Journal of Educational Research, 96*(5), 277–285.

EXCERPT 3.6 Justification: Evaluation of a New Program at a Site

[For] our research project, "The Effects of Standards-Based Assessments on School and Classrooms," [we] selected Washington because of the newness of its reform effort. We decided to study implementation at the local level, persuaded by the generally accepted belief that large-scale reforms succeed or fail based on issues of local implementation. (pp. 171–172)

Source: From Borko, H., Wolf, S. A., Simone, G., & Uchiyama, K. P. (2003). Schools in transition: Reform efforts and school capacity in Washington state. *Educational Evaluation and Policy Analysis, 25*(2), 171–201.

Evaluation of a Specific Practice or Policy at a Given Site   The study may evaluate a specific practice or policy for decision makers at a given site or for external groups. Evaluation research determines worth: Does the practice need improvement? Is it effective? Should its usage be expanded? Similar questions are addressed in policy studies. Such research supplies information for immediate use in site decision making, which may be at the local, state, or national level. Although the study is not concerned initially with generalizability or theory development, it may have implications for developing such knowledge (see Excerpt 3.6).

Exploratory Research   Exploratory research is usually conducted in new areas of inquiry, and such studies may be quantitative or qualitative. For example, a study might field test a particular assessment format to determine whether it can be used by sixth-grade students and if it discriminates against any particular student groups. Qualitative exploratory studies often examine phenomena that have not been studied previously. Some exploratory studies develop theory or components of a concept (see Excerpts 3.7 and 3.8).

EXCERPT 3.7 Significance: To Develop Components of a Concept

The purpose [is] . . . to begin the process of fleshing out the construct of leadership content knowledge, [that is] . . . how and why subject matter knowledge matters in educational leadership; . . . [to] analyze three cases of instructional leadership [principal, associate superintendent, and central office team], . . . and [to] examine each for evidence of leadership content knowledge in use. (p. 424)

Source: From Stein, M. K., & Nelson, B. S. (2003). Leadership content knowledge. *Educational Evaluation and Policy Analysis, 25*(4), 423–448.

EXCERPT 3.8 Justification: Explore to Develop Theory

Several objectives guided this study. Specifically . . . to (1) identify and explore (and ultimately develop a conceptual framework for) the various domains of discomfort that teachers face; (2) explore dimensions within these various discomfort domains that define whether moments of discomfort for students and teachers become debilitating or educative; (3) explore the impact of discomfort on teacher's beliefs and pedagogical practices; and (4) explore the notion of teaching *toward* discomfort. (p. 130)

Source: From Frykholm, J. (2004). Teachers' tolerance for discomfort: Implications for curricular reform in mathematics. *Journal of Curriculum and Supervision, 19*(2), 125–149.

PROBLEM AND RESEARCH QUESTION FORMULATION IN QUANTITATIVE RESEARCH

For quantitative studies, there is need for concise research questions that clearly communicate the nature of the study. The questions are based on the research problem but are more specific in showing the logic of the design and variables. Logic begins with a clearly defined abstract construct that links with variables. Each variable is then defined operationally:

$$abstract\ construct \longrightarrow variables \longrightarrow operational\ definitions$$

Constructs

Construct: abstract concept

In research, an abstract concept is called a **construct**. Often derived from theory, a construct expresses the idea behind a set of particulars. Examples of constructs are motivation, intelligence, thinking, anxiety, self-concept, achievement, and aptitude. Another way to define a construct is to say that it is created by combining variables in a meaningful pattern. For example such variables as visual perception, sight/sound discrimination, audio acuity, and left-to-right orientation are meaningfully combined to suggest the construct of reading readiness.

Variables

Variable: antecedent factor that varies

Variable is perhaps the most frequently used word in quantitative research. A variable is a name or label that represents a concept or characteristic. A concept is a noun that describes a class of objects, such as desk, teacher, school, or curriculum, whereas a characteristic describes a trait, such as achievement, attitude, creativity, height, gender, or socioeconomic status. Quantitative studies use *variable* rather than *noun* or *characteristic* because what is studied varies, or has different values. Thus, a **variable** is a noun or characteristic that represents numerical or categorical variation. For example, characteristics such as speed, height, intelligence, and artistic ability can be represented by a numerical range of values.

For quantitative studies, many variables have different *levels* or *attributes*. The attributes or levels show the different categories of the variable. Thus, for example, gender as a variable has two levels, male and female. Race is a variable that could have four levels, Caucasian, African American, Hispanic, and other. Such variables could also be called **categorical**, in which subjects or objects are divided into mutually exclusive groups. The most simple categorical variable has two levels and could be called *dichotomous* (e.g., gender, high group/low group, dropout/graduate, marital status). Categorical variables with more than two levels are common, such as grade level, nationality, type of graduation diploma, and athletic teams.

Categorical: a set of discrete levels

Continuous: an infinite number of levels

A **continuous** variable is one that theoretically has an infinite number of values within a specified continuum of possible values. Thus, each subject trait can be located within a range of numbers. The possible range of scores is determined by rank-ordering the scores from low to high or from small to large. Continuous variables are very common in quantitative studies and include such traits as achievement, aptitude, age, and motivation.

It is possible that the same variable can be either continuous or categorical. This occurs when categories are defined from continuous values. For example, years of experience is a continuous variable if the range is 0–35. This could be a categorical variable by forming three groups—low, medium, and high years of experience (e.g., 0–10 = low, 11–20 = medium, and 20+ = high).

Dependent variable: consequence or outcome

Independent variable: antecedent factor

Independent and Dependent Variables The idea of variables arose as a way of describing and explaining experimental studies. In an experiment the outcome "depends on" what is caused by the intervention, hence the name *dependent variable*. The **dependent variable** is affected by the intervention. The **independent variable** in experimental studies is a name for the intervention and control groups (see Excerpt 3.9). It describes what was done by the experimenter to influence the dependent variable. In addition to the intervention variable, other variables, that are not controlled, can also be used in the design. For example, if a study uses two methods to teach reading as the intervention, or independent variable, as well as gender to

EXCERPT 3.9 Experimental Research: Independent and Dependent Variables

Research questions to examine the effects of teaching a lesson of emotionally charged issues on achievement, attitude, . . . [using Multisensory Instructional Packages {MIP}]:

1. Will there be significantly higher student achievement test gains when the Holocaust is taught using the MIP as opposed to when it is taught traditionally?

2. Will there be significantly higher student attitude test scores toward instruction methods when the Holocaust is taught with the MIP as opposed to when it is taught traditionally? (p. 43)

Source: From Farkas, R. D. (2003). Effects of traditional versus learning-styles instructional methods on middle school students. *Journal of Educational Research, 97*(1), 42–51.

examine differences between boys and girls, gender is also an independent variable. Another way to think about independent and dependent variables in experimental studies is that the independent variable is the *antecedent* and the dependent variable is the *consequence*.

The following is a more abstract way of thinking about independent and dependent variables in experiments:

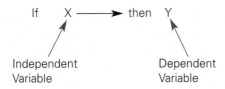

Figure 3.3 shows a variety of common independent and dependent variables in educational research. Note that these examples are restricted to experimental designs. We now turn to the identification of variables in nonexperimental studies. As you will see, this is not as straightforward as it is in experimental research.

In nonexperimental research, the independent variable *cannot* be manipulated. For example, a study of the effect of school size (independent variable) on achievement (dependent variable) may use large, medium, and small schools (levels of the independent variable). Obviously, the researcher will not manipulate the sizes of the selected schools but will choose the schools from enrollment records. In some correlational research, the antecedent variable is called the **predictor variable** and the predicted variable is called the **criterion variable**. In a study that examines the relationship of scores on the SAT to success in college, the predictor variable is the SAT scores and the criterion variable is college success. In other correlational studies, there is no obvious antecedent variable—for example, in considering the relationship between self-concept and achievement. In this case, the researcher is not interested in prediction but in

Predictor variable: factor used to predict the outcome

Criterion variable: outcome or result

Independent	Dependent
Method of instruction	Student achievement
Type of feedback	Student motivation
Type of curriculum	Student achievement
Induction programs	Teacher satisfaction
Test preparation programs	Student confidence

FIGURE 3.3 Examples of Independent and Dependent Variables in Experimental Designs

EXCERPT 3.10   Correlational Research: Predictor and Criterion Variables

The present study has two main purposes: (1) to develop a comprehensive set of kindergarten prereading tasks that would predict reading achievement at the end of first and second grade, and (2) to determine at what point in the kindergarten year—beginning, middle, or end—the various tasks would exert maximum predictive power. (p. 95)

Source: From Morris, D., Bloodgood, J., & Perney, J. (2003). Kindergarten predictors of first- and second-grade reading achievement. *The Elementary School Journal, 104*(2), 93–110.

determining the strength and direction of the relationship between the variables (see Excerpt 3.10). Some researchers use the terms *independent* and *dependent* with correlational and other non-experimental research when it is clear that one variable precedes the other variable or that categories have been created to allow comparisons. For example, in a study that examines the relationship between the amount of time students are engaged to achievement, time on task logically precedes achievement. Hence, time engaged is the independent variable and achievement is the dependent variable. In comparative studies the variable that is categorical is typically independent. If a researcher looks at whether there is a relationship between socioeconomic status and GED scores, and socioeconomic status has three levels, SES is the independent variable and GED scores is the dependent variable. If race is also included, with four levels, then it is a second independent variable.

You need to be aware that the same variable can be independent in one study and dependent in another. Think about the relationship between college student achievement and motivation. You could make a case that achievement leads to more motivation or that more motivation leads to higher achievement. As another example, a variable like graduation could be used as a dependent variable to study factors that are related to whether or not students graduate from high school. Variables such as test performance, hobbies, socioeconomic status, level of co-curricular activities, and attendance could be used as independent variables to predict graduation. Graduation could also be used in a predictive manner to examine the relationship between obtaining a high school diploma and income.

Extraneous and Confounding Variables   In every study, consideration must be given to the likelihood that outside or unanticipated events and factors have influenced the results. Two types of variables are used to identify these events and factors. **Extraneous variables** are conditions, events, or occurrences that affect the subjects in a particular group, changing the outcome. In other words, these variables compromise the interpretation of what the results mean. That is, they provide an alternative explanation and "mess up" the study.

Extraneous variable: external factors affecting the outcome

Usually we think about an extraneous variable as something that is external to the protocol or context of the study. For example, unplanned and unwelcome events could occur during an intervention that influence the results. Suppose the intervention consists of after-school tutoring. If, during the tutoring, there are many distractions caused by extraneous variables, such as announcements or students visiting the room, the effectiveness of the tutoring could be compromised. In this kind of study we might find that the intervention did not help, but the explanation would need to include these extraneous variables.

A confounding variable is one that varies systematically with levels of the independent variable and affects the dependent variable. These variables may be responsible for differences observed between treatment groups. For example, consider a study that investigates the effect of using an individualized, technology approach to learning on small-group instruction. Two classes of students are selected. One class is assigned the technology treatment, the other small-group instruction. If students in the technology intervention group, as a whole, are more capable, then it is not possible to separate the effect of the treatment from differences in student ability. Thus, student ability is confounded, intertwined if you will, with one level of the independent variable. If students in the technology group do better, you would not know if it is because of the intervention or the students' ability.

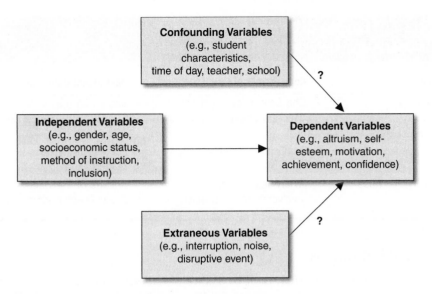

FIGURE 3.4 **Relationship of Different Types of Variables**

Identifying extraneous and confounding variables is key to an appropriate evaluation of the worth of conclusions from quantitative studies. They are very important for both designing and interpreting research. Figure 3.4 shows how the variables relate to each other.

See Table 3.1 for a list of variables used in quantitative studies, along with definitions and examples.

TABLE 3.1 Variables Used in Quantitative Research

Type of Variable	Definition	Examples
Independent	Cause or antecedent, factor that precedes another one, used to establish comparison groups	Method of instruction Gender Attendance Age
Dependent	Outcome or consequence, what is affected by the independent variable	Achievement Attitudes Values Occupational choices
Extraneous	Uncontrolled factor that has an undesirable effect on the dependent variables	Noise Interruption Acting out
Confounding	Factor that exists more in one group than in another and affects the dependent variable	Time of day Student characteristics Teacher
Continuous	Variable with an infinite scale of possible values	Achievement Attitudes Self-Concept Intelligence
Categorical	Variable that divides subjects into separate groups	Tenured vs. untenured teachers Dropouts vs. completers Small school vs. large school

TABLE 3.2 Examples of Variables and Conceptual versus Operational Definitions

Variable	Conceptual Definition	Operational Definition
Self-concept	Characteristics used to describe oneself	Scores on the Coopersmith *Self-Esteem Inventory*
Intelligence	Ability to think abstractly	Scores on the Stanford-Binet
Teacher with-it-ness	Awareness of student involvement and behavior	Results of the *Robinson Scale Teacher With-It-Ness*

Operational Definitions

Each variable in a quantitative study must be defined operationally and subsequently categorized, measured, or manipulated. A conceptual (i.e., dictionary) definition defines a word by using other terms, such as defining *anxiety* as "apprehension or vague fear." In contrast, the researcher uses an **operational definition**, which assigns meaning to a variable by specifying the activities or operations necessary to measure, categorize, or manipulate that variable. An operational definition tells the researcher and the reader what is necessary to answer the question or test the hypothesis. Variables frequently can be defined operationally in several ways, and some operations may be more valid for certain research problems than others. For example, one study might operationalize achievement as scores on the Stanford Achievement Tests, whereas in another study achievement is defined by scores on a state-specific accountability test.

Table 3.2 provides some examples of variables, each described with a conceptual definition and an operational definition.

Operational definition: how a variable is measured, categorized, or implemented

Specific Research Questions, Statements, and Hypotheses

Once the problem is identified in quantitative studies, researchers state a more specific research question, statement, and/or hypothesis that sets the stage for the study. It is in these questions and statements that researchers specify the nature of the variables, the logic of the design, and, sometimes, an indication of the population. Suppose a supervisor is interested in determining whether organizing programs for gifted elementary students in different ways will affect student creativity. The gifted programs are organized as (1) special programs, in which students remain together for a comprehensive program; (2) pull-out programs, in which students attend regular classes except for two hours' daily instruction by selected teachers; and (3) enrichment programs, in which students complete enrichment activities as an extension of their regular instruction. The research question is, Is there a difference in creativity (the dependent variable) among gifted elementary students (the population) who participate in a special program, a pull-out program, or an enrichment program (three levels of one independent variable)? This question is narrowed to the degree that it identifies the population and the two variables. The logic behind the question is clear because the relationship between the independent and dependent variable can be identified.

A question phrased as Does mainstreaming do any good? is too broad and has neither a population nor variables. The researcher must narrow the problem to be more specific: Is there a difference between high school students' (the population) attitudes toward students with disabilities (the dependent variable) who participated in a six-week mainstreamed class and the attitudes of those students who did not participate in the class (two levels of the independent variable)? Now the question is focused. In addition, it explicitly implies the logic of the experimental design.

You will find that researchers use questions or statements to communicate the variables and logic of the study. Note how the following examples of statements convey the same information as questions:

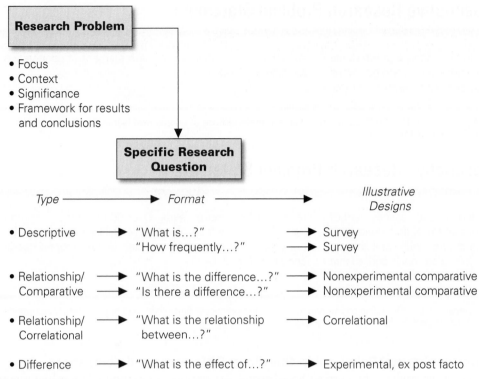

FIGURE 3.5 Components of Specific Research Questions

Questions

What is the relationship between college professors' knowledge of the subject and pedagogical skills to student ratings of instructor effectiveness?

What is the effect of three group strategies on the anxiety of middle school students?

Statements

This study examined the relationship between college professors' knowledge of the subject and pedagogical skills to student ratings of instructor effectiveness.

The purpose of this study is to determine which of three group strategies best reduces middle school students' anxiety.

The question format is preferred because it is simple and direct. Psychologically, it orients the researcher to the immediate task: to develop a design to answer the question. Research questions may be descriptive questions, relationship questions, or difference questions. Each type of question implies a different design (see Figure 3.5).

Descriptive Questions   Descriptive research questions and specific research problem statements do just that—describe. Studies using descriptions typically use frequencies, percentages, averages, total scores, graphs, and other indicators of how much or how frequently something has occurred. There are no comparisons or correlations, and often there are no independent variables. Note the following examples of descriptive research questions:

- What is the achievement level of fourth-grade students on the state accountability test?
- What are parents' beliefs about the best way to redraw school boundaries?
- What do teachers perceive to be the area in which they would like training for professional development?

Excerpts 3.11 and 3.12 illustrate specific descriptive research problem statements. Excerpt 3.11 is a descriptive study in which the extent of the use of cooperative learning is reported. In Excerpt 3.12 the authors report the difference between beliefs and practices for two groups (Head Start and Pre-K professionals). This means that descriptive results are provided for each group, not that a comparison or relationship is examined. This excerpt also illustrates a typical way in which descriptive results are reported in the narrative of the article.

EXCERPT 3.11 Descriptive Research Problem Statement

In the present study, we examine the degree to which exemplar teachers reported using cooperative learning versus the degree to which they would prefer to use this method, as well as the relative use of each element of cooperative learning. (p. 234)

Source: From Lopata, C., Miller, K. A., & Miller, R. H. (2003). Survey of actual and preferred use of cooperative learning among exemplar teachers. *The Journal of Educational Research, 96*(4), 232–239.

EXCERPT 3.12 Descriptive Research Problem Statement

This article provides the results of a needs assessment of beliefs, skills, and training needs of Pre-K and Head Start teachers about including young children with disabilities in EDCE settings. . . . Both groups of professionals agreed that they had the ability to arrange the classroom environment to meet all children's needs. Over 80 percent . . . agreed that they could effectively observe children with and without disabilities to learn about their developmental needs and skills. (pp. 230–231)

Source: From Bruns, D. A., & Mogharreban, C. C. (2007). The gap between beliefs and practices: Early childhood practitioners' perceptions about inclusion. *Journal of Research in Childhood Education, 21*(3), 229–242.

Nonexperimental Relationship Questions: Differences and Correlations   In most quantitative studies, the purpose goes beyond description to examine relationships among variables. The term *relationship* is used extensively. It refers to how one variable relates to another, that is, can results of one variable predict results of the other variable? Nonexperimental relationship questions include two types. One type analyzes differences or comparisons between groups of subjects. Examples include: Do sixth-grade students have stronger motivation than fifth-grade students? What differences exist in the motivation of students across grade level? In both of these questions there is an implied relationship between grade level and motivation. That is, can stronger student motivation be predicted by knowing the grade level? In Excerpt 3.13 the authors indicate that grade level is the independent variable in a relationship study that examines differences in student attitudes.

A second, more common type of nonexperimental relationship question uses a correlational procedure rather than differences between groups. This typically is done with two continuous variables—for example, socioeconomic status, achievement, self-concept, attitudes. The intent is to measure the relationship with a correlation coefficient. Often the stated purpose is to predict one variable from another. Examples of that include:

- To what extent do preservice ratings during student teaching predict teaching effectiveness?
- Do preschool aptitude test scores predict achievement in kindergarten and first grade?
- What is the predictive relationship between first-semester grades of college students and retention?
- Do SAT scores predict success in college?
- The purpose of this study is to examine the relationship between socioeconomic status and achievement of students attending rural high schools.

EXCERPT 3.13 Nonexperimental Difference Research Statement

The purpose of the study reported in this article was to provide empirical evidence of students' views about a state performance assessment and its effects in science and social studies classrooms in Maryland. . . . These grades were selected to allow comparison of responses from students in tested grades (5 and 8) to those in nontested grades (4 and 7). (p. 305)

Source: From Parke, C. S., & Lane, S. (2007). Students' perceptions of a Maryland state performance assessment. *The Elementary School Journal, 107*(3), 305–324.

EXCERPT 3.14 Specific Problem Statement for Correlational Research

In this study, I examined variables that predict how African American parents and guardians of school-aged children rate their children's elementary and secondary school teachers, and the public school system as a whole. (p. 279)

Source: From Thompson, G. L. (2003). Predicting African American parents' and guardians' satisfaction with teachers and public schools. *The Journal of Educational Research, 96*(5), 277–285.

EXCERPT 3.15 Nonexperimental Difference and Correlational Research Questions

The present study was designed to address four primary questions: (a) What is the relationship between intrinsic and extrinsic motivation, (b) are there significant age differences in intrinsic and extrinsic motivation when these two constructs are measured independent of one another, (c) how are these two motivational orientations related to academic outcomes, and (d) with respect to the previous three questions, are there significant differences between European American and Asian American children? (p. 186)

Source: From Leper, M. R., Corpus, J. H., & Iyengar, S. S. (2005). Intrinsic and extrinsic motivational orientations in the classroom: Age differences and academic correlates. *Journal of Educational Psychology, 97*(2), 184–196.

In these examples the predicted variable is the dependent variable, and the one that logically precedes is the independent variable. Excerpt 3.14 illustrates a specific research problem statement for correlational research. In Excerpt 3.15 the authors present four nonexperimental questions, some of which are analyzed as differences and others with correlations.

Experimental Difference Questions   In most experiments, groups of subjects are compared to determine the effect of the intervention. The differences between the groups are analyzed to investigate whether one group scores higher on the dependent variable than another group or groups. For example, asking, "Are there significant differences in achievement between traditional and computer-assisted learning groups?" implies that the achievement scores of one group will be compared to the scores of the other group to detect differences. Some experimental research uses a single group, giving it a pretest, then the intervention, and then a posttest. With this design, the difference between the pretest and posttest is examined.

Suppose you have three different methods of working with autistic children, and you design an experiment to see which is most effective. A specific research question could be something like this: What is the effect of three different interventions on the academic achievement of first-grade autistic children? This question clearly implies a causal intent, consistent with doing an experiment. It indicates three levels of the independent variable, a single dependent variable, and something about the nature of the sample. It would also be appropriate to include names for each of the interventions, resulting in this statement: The purpose of this study is to compare the effectiveness of three learning strategies (behavioral, small group, and student self-monitoring) on the academic achievement of first-grade autistic children.

Excerpt 3.16 shows specific research questions for a study investigating the effect of a science course on teachers' efficacy beliefs, personal teaching, and outcome expectancies.

EXCERPT 3.16 Experimental Difference Questions

What effect did the science and mathematics content-based earth systems science course have on elementary preservice teacher[s'] personal science [and mathematics] teaching efficacy and science [mathematics] teaching outcome expectancy? (p. 1)

Source: From Moseley, C., & Utley, J. (2006). The effect of an integrated science and mathematics content-based course on science and mathematics teaching efficacy of preservice elementary teachers. *Journal of Elementary Science Education, 18*(2), 1–12.

Research Hypotheses

A research hypothesis is a tentative statement of the expected relationship between two or more variables. Problem statements and research hypotheses are similar in substance, except that research hypotheses are declarative statements, more specific than problem statements, clearly testable, and indicative of the expected results. That is, a research hypothesis is the investigator's expectation or prediction of what the results will show. It is a conjectural statement that is a prediction made prior to data collection.

Research hypotheses are used because they represent a synthesis of the researcher's expectation based on previous literature and experience. The research hypothesis, then, follows from the related literature. It is a way to connect the literature to the current study, providing a framework for developing explanations. It also helps the researcher keep focused on the purpose of the study. Finally, research hypotheses provide a framework for reporting results and making interpretations of the data. This helps the reader understand the meaning and significance of the findings.

It should be noted that there is another commonly used type of hypothesis, the *null* hypothesis. The null hypothesis is a statement that there are no statistically significant differences or relationships. It is used for making a decision about whether to reject or fail to reject the statement that there are no differences or relationships. The rejection or failure to reject provides support or no support, respectively, for the research hypothesis. The null hypothesis is technically needed for statistical reasoning, but it will not be covered in detail here. At this point, it is sufficient to understand that research and null hypotheses serve different purposes in quantitative studies. Table 3.3 illustrates how research problems could be stated as both research and null hypotheses.

When developing and writing research hypotheses, four standards should be met:

1. *The hypothesis should state the direction of the difference or relationship.* Although you may see some *non*directional research hypotheses, it is better to clearly indicate the direction of the anticipated results. That is, it is better to say, "Students of teachers who use specific comments as feedback score higher than students who receive brief praise" than "The scores of students receiving specific comments are different from the scores of students receiving brief praise."

2. *The hypothesis should be testable.* A testable hypothesis is verifiable through data analyses. Conclusions are drawn from empirical data to indicate statistically whether an expected relationship or difference occurred. This means that the researcher has decided, before data are gathered, what specific statistical test will be used and what rules will be used for making statistical decisions. In this sense, the more specific the research hypothesis, the better. Too many researchers proceed without being sufficiently focused and then wonder what to do with the results. Notice in the three following examples the difference in the level of specificity of the hypotheses.

TABLE 3.3 Examples of Research Problems, Research Hypotheses, and Null Hypotheses

Research Problem/Question	Research Hypothesis	Null Hypothesis
What is the effect of an ELL workshop on the confidence of teachers?	Teachers attending an ELL workshop will show greater confidence in working with ELL students than teachers not attending the workshop.	There is no difference in confidence in working with ELL students between teachers who do or do not attend an ELL workshop.
This study examined the relationship between teacher use of technology and student achievement.	There is a positive relationship between the amount of technology used by teachers and student achievement.	There is no relationship between the amount of technology used by teachers and student achievement.
What is the relationship between class size and teacher satisfaction?	There is a negative relationship between class size and teacher satisfaction.	There is no relationship between class size and teacher satisfaction.

Too General	Acceptable	Better
Disruptive student behavior improves with small-group instruction	Students working in small groups will show less disruptive behavior than students working individually	Students working in small groups will show 50% less disruptive behavior than students working individually

3. *The hypothesis should have a clear rationale.* It is important for the hypothesis to be grounded in theory and/or previous research so that the explanation for the findings is reasonable. In other words, you need to be able to connect results with the theory and literature. This helps avoid investigating trivial topics and forces the researcher to focus on relevant topics and ideas. This relevance does not need to be based on a single theory or idea. Often, in fact, fruitful research is conducted that tests different predictions based on different theories.

4. *The hypothesis should be clearly stated.* Writing research hypotheses that are clear and easily understood can take some time but, when achieved, becomes essential in helping both researchers and readers of research understand why there are specific variables and what is being tested. An ambiguous or incomplete hypothesis indicates a weakness in the researcher's ability to understand previous literature and use it to know the specific purpose of the research. There needs to be a clear chain of reasoning from research problem to hypothesis to methods to data analyses to results. An unclear hypothesis will break the chain.

To practice developing a hypothesis, go to: MyEducationLab for Research at www .myeducationlab.com. Click on the topic "Selecting and Defining a Research Topic" and then select the Building Research Skills activity titled "Developing a Hypothesis."

A study may have one or several research hypotheses. It is best to frame one or just a few hypotheses to keep things relatively simple and focused. When there are multiple variables, just stating them may make the study tedious and overly complex. This is consistent with what we think is a good general rule about variables for conducting quantitative research— fewer is better than many.

Excerpts 3.17 and 3.18 illustrate research hypotheses in published studies.

PROBLEM FORMULATION AND RESEARCH QUESTIONS FOR QUALITATIVE DESIGNS

In qualitative research, the logic and specifics of research problems and questions differ from those used in quantitative studies. These differences are summarized in Table 3.4. To understand qualitative research problems, it is helpful to consider the logic that is used. In qualitative

EXCERPT 3.17 Research Hypothesis

The foregoing literature review suggests that parents who attend school meetings or conferences and interact with school personnel are likely to have children who demonstrate higher levels of achievement at school than children of parents who fail to participate in their child's school program. (p. 92)

Source: From Shaver, A. V., & Walls, R. T. (1998). Effect of Title I parent involvement on student reading and mathematics achievement. *Journal of Research and Development in Education, 31,* 90–97.

EXCERPT 3.18 Research Hypothesis

In this field study, . . . we investigated the relationships among . . . instructional practices, motivation, and writing performance. We expected that instructional practices would be motivating when teachers provided challenging tasks, highlighted real-life relevance, stimulated curiosity, allowed a high level of autonomy, recognized students' effort, and provided useful feedback. We also expected that students would have better writing performance when they were motivated in the writing task. (p. 147).

Source: From Shui-Fong, L., & Law, Y. K. (2007). The roles of instructional practices and motivation in writing performance. *The Journal of Experimental Education, 75*(2), 145–165.

TABLE 3.4 Differences Between Quantitative and Qualitative Research Problems

Quantitative	Qualitative
Specific	General
Deductive	Inductive
Narrow	Broad
Closed-ended	Open-ended
Static	Emergent
Outcome-oriented	Process-oriented
Confirms	Describes
Contains variables	Contains concepts and ideas

studies the logic is a *continual process* of *inductive* reasoning. In contrast, quantitative studies use inductive reasoning to formulate the problem and then use deductive reasoning to answer the research questions with a fixed design. With qualitative studies, research questions are continually being revised as data are collected and analyzed. That is, the research questions "emerge" from findings. This fluid process allows for an interactive relationship between the questions and what the researcher has learned. The research problem is typically reformulated during data collection so that the data closely represent the reality of the individual and/or shared social experiences. The focus changes, depending on what is needed to have a deep understanding of the phenomena.

Qualitative research questions tend to be flexible and open-ended, less specific than those found in quantitative studies. They are evolving rather than static. There is an orientation toward process, probing the phenomena for deeper understanding. This results in a tendency to use specific kinds of words, such as *generate*, *understand*, *describe*, *discover*, and *explore*, rather than *relate*, *differ*, or *compare*. Generally, qualitative problems are neutral with respect to what will be learned. There are no predictions, expected results, or research hypotheses.

Initial Purpose or Research Problem

Like quantitative studies, qualitative studies begin with a general research problem. The qualitative problem will include the primary issue or topic that is studied, sometimes referred to as the *central question*. The **central question** is an open-ended idea or purpose that identifies, in a broad way, the *central phenomenon* that will be investigated. The central phenomenon is the overarching concept, process, issue, or idea (Creswell, 2008). It provides a starting point from which more specific subquestions are framed as data are gathered. Examples of a central phenomenon include teenage alienation, teacher retention, principal burnout, teacher induction, and accountability testing. In some studies the researchers may refer to the *foreshadowed* problem. The **foreshadowed problem** is like a central question. It is a general problem that will frame the initial data collection process.

The central question or foreshadowed problem should not be so broad that almost anything can be included; it needs to provide a general direction for the researcher to gather information to learn more about the phenomenon. It is stated as a single concept or process, and it is sufficiently general so that any pertinent information gathered during the study can be used to understand the phenomenon. Discovery and understanding lead to an emerging design that changes along the way with further, more specific and targeted questions. Note in Excerpt 3.19 that the researchers indicate that research questions emerged from discussions and experiences with participants.

Consider the following central questions. In each case, a general topic is introduced. Note how some questions include a description of the participants and/or the research site. The central phenomenon is given in italics.

What factors are used by teachers in *grading students*?
What are the characteristics of *resilient at-risk students*?

Central question: captures the overarching issue

Foreshadowed problem: frames initial data collection

EXCERPT 3.19 Initial Problem and Reformulation from the Sites

[Initially] show how teachers and their administrators were attempting to come to terms with top-down . . . [state], and district mandates to make more and better use of computer technologies in teaching and learning...

How are existing power relations in schools reinforced and/or reorganized by the introduction of computer technologies? How do these new technologies change the work of

teaching and how do these changes undermine or encourage the teacher's . . . sense of control and ownership?. . . These questions emerged from a series of conversations and experiences we had with individual teachers . . . [who] consistently raised issues of gender inequities both in the context of schooling and in relation to the technology itself. . . . [We] did not set out to study gender. (pp. 170–171)

Source: From Jenson, J., & Rose, C. B. (2003). Women at work: Listening to gendered relations of power in teachers' talk about new technologies. *Gender and Education, 15*(2), 169–181.

How is *school culture* identified and maintained?
How do schools change with the *inclusion of ESL students*?
The purpose of this study is to understand the reasons elementary students give for their *motivation to do well in school.*

In Figure 3.6, the steps involved in developing qualitative research problems are illustrated. You will see that the initial topic is the starting point and that once the central question is formulated, data are gathered to identify subquestions that guide further data collection. The central phenomenon in this example is choice implementation.

Excerpts 3.20 and 3.21 illustrate research problems and questions in published qualitative studies. In Excerpt 3.20 the central phenomenon is student learning strategies; in Excerpt 3.21 the central phenomenon is cultural and identity formation among Vietnamese immigrants. Excerpt 3.22 shows somewhat more specific central questions for studying kindergarten teachers' expectations (central phenomenon).

When developing and writing qualitative research problems and questions, keep the following criteria in mind:

1. *The central question should not be too specific or too general.* A central question that is too general or broad will not give sufficient direction to know what methods will be used. If the central question is too narrow, the researcher may be limiting and focusing so much that important information will not be gathered. This essentially is inconsistent with the goal and strength of qualitative research.

2. *The central question should not be biased by the researcher's assumptions or desired results.* The researcher's bias and assumptions need to be made clear so that possible effects due to these factors will not lead to central questions that direct data gathering that results in findings consistent with these factors. Here is an example of a biased central question: The purpose of this study is to explore reasons college faculty give to explain a lack of multicultural awareness in their teaching. A better statement would be: The purpose of this study is to explore college faculty's multicultural awareness while teaching.

Topic	→	Central Question	→	Data Gathered	→	Subquestions	→	Further Data Gathered
Instructional choice		The purpose of this study was to better understand the role of teachers in the choice-implementation process		Initial teacher interviews		Why do teachers give students choices? What is their rationale for doing so?		Further teacher interviews

FIGURE 3.6 Steps in Forming Qualitative Research Questions

EXCERPT 3.20   Qualitative Research Central Question

This research study used grounded theory in an attempt to explain how 10th-grade public school students in average and advanced classes used strategies to learn material in their high school social studies classes. This study sought to understand the strategies that students used to learn information, the frequency of the strategy used, and student student's method of acquiring these strategies. (p. 63)

Source: From Martin, L. A. (2005). Use of cognitive strategies by high school social studies students. *Action in Teacher Education, 26*(4), 63–73.

EXCERPT 3.21   Qualitative Research Central Question

By exploring the tensions that students perceive and struggle with as they bring their own values and practices into the school site, we seek to better understand the ways in which the categories of gender and cultural identity are connected to the academic and social experience of recent immigrant students . . . we ask the following questions: In what way does transition to U.S. schooling influence how Vietnamese immigrant students negotiate aspects of cultural norms and values related to gender? How do the ways in which they understand and define gender roles and expectations influence their academic experiences? (p. 855)

Source: From Stritikus, T., & Nguyen, D. (2007). Strategic transformation: Cultural and gender identity negotiation in first-generation Vietnamese youth. *American Educational Research Journal, 44*(4), 853–895.

EXCERPT 3.22   Qualitative Research Questions

In order to understand this complex situation more deeply, I designed a qualitative study to investigate kindergarten teachers' experiences [in] responding to the challenges presented by the changing expectations for kindergarten teaching. The study's research questions were: 1) How do kindergarten teachers satisfy both their commitment to de- velopmentally appropriate teaching practices and their responsibility to teach the predetermined knowledge and skills mandated by their state?; and 2) What challenges do kindergarten teachers feel they are facing, and how do they respond to those challenges? (p. 383)

Source: From Goldstein, L. S. (2007). Embracing pedagogical multiplicity: Examining two teachers' instructional responses to the changing expectations for kindergarten in U.S. public schools. *Journal of Research in Childhood Education, 21*(4), 378–400.

3. *The central question should be amenable to change as data are collected.* It is important for the central question to be somewhat open-ended and general. This allows for changes that can and probably will be made to the question as data are collected and analyzed. The continuing refinement of the central question reflects the emergent design characteristic of qualitative research. Suppose an initial central question is: What do students say about whether graduation tests are fair? This question is less amenable to change than the central question: What are students' perceptions of tests for graduation?

4. *The central question should be written with "how" and "what" to keep the focus on understanding the phenomenon.* The most important goal of qualitative research is to be able to provide an in-depth description and understanding of the central phenomenon. This goal is best achieved if the researcher focuses on *what* occurs and *how* it occurs. An initial focus on *why* it occurs tends to limit the scope of what is collected and focus on causal conclusions.

5. *The central question should indicate the participants and site.* Good qualitative central questions contain three elements—the central phenomenon, an indication of participation, and an indication of the site or location of the study. Creswell (2008) suggests using the following script to guide central question formation: The purpose of this study is to _____(describe/understand/explore/discover) the _____ (central phenomenon) for _____ (participants) at _____(research site). An example would be "The purpose of the study is to understand the reluctance of social studies teachers to engage in discussions about religion at James River High School."

To practice reviewing and identifying quantitative and qualitative research, go to: MyEducationLab for Research at www.myeducationlab.com. Click on the topic "Selecting and Defining a Research Topic" and then select the Activities and Application activities "Reviewing Research Proposals A & B."

PROBLEM FORMULATION AND RESEARCH QUESTIONS FOR MIXED METHOD RESEARCH

Like a study that is either completely quantitative or qualitative, a mixed method investigation begins with identification of a general problem, which provides context and background. Identifying the general problem is followed by indicating a more specific purpose for the study. At this point, the researcher could indicate that a mixed method design will be used and write specific quantitative research questions and central qualitative problems. In addition, some researchers present more specific questions and problems after their review of the literature.

Because a good research problem implies design, the questions and central problems should be presented in a way that is consistent with the way the methods will be used. The *relative importance* of how each method functions in the study should be communicated (e.g., whether a quantitative or qualitative approach is emphasized or both are given equal weight) along with the overall purpose of the research. Knowing the relative importance of each method used in the study helps determine the type of mixed method design.

Typically, researchers doing mixed method studies will provide a justification for why both approaches are needed. This is nicely illustrated in Excerpt 3.23 with a longitudinal study of accountability and school reform issues.

Equal Priority to All Questions

When a variety of questions are asked and all are equally important, both quantitative and qualitative data are collected at about the same time. In this case, research questions for both quantitative and qualitative questions are usually presented together. Doing so communicates that both kinds of data have equal priority. Suppose a researcher is interested in studying beginning teachers and has formulated this general problem: What kinds of help are most important in ensuring the success of beginning elementary teachers? The following questions are more specific:

1. To what extent have several kinds of help been received by beginning elementary teachers? (quantitative)
2. How do beginning elementary school teachers rate the helpfulness of the assistance received? (quantitative)
3. How does the elementary school principal rate the helpfulness of assistance provided to beginning teachers? (quantitative)
4. Why have certain kinds of assistance proven most helpful? (qualitative)
5. How does the context of the teaching situation influence the need for different kinds of assistance? (qualitative)

The first three quantitative questions could be addressed with an instrument that lists the types of assistance received (e.g., from a mentor, principal, other teacher) and provides a rating scale for evaluating the extent of helpfulness. The qualitative questions (items 4 and 5) could be answered by conducting interviews with teachers and principals at about the same time that the surveys are being completed. Findings from both kinds of data would be analyzed and interpreted to determine if similar results are obtained. The questions imply a *triangulation design* because using both methods provides a more complete result.

EXCERPT 3.23   Justification for Using a Mixed Method Design

The present investigation was based on a longitudinal mixed methodology case study of a large, high poverty district's experiences during a decade of accountability-focused reform efforts. A mixed method design was chosen in a pragmatic effort to capture the widest range of effects of accountability efforts (the so what of reform efforts together with a range of participants' perspectives of how and why various reforms were attempted).

Source: From Stringfield, S. C., & Yakimowski-Srebnick, M. E. (2005). Promise, progress, problems, and paradoxes of three phases of accountability: A longitudinal case study of the Baltimore City Public Schools. *American Educational Research Journal, 42*(1), 43–75.

Measured Results Explained by Qualitative Data

Suppose these research questions were being considered: Are there differences in the amounts of helpful assistance that beginning teachers receive? If so, how do beginning teachers explain why some types of assistance are helpful and others are not? Researchers must see the results of the first question to decide if they need further data to explain the findings. A survey could be used to identify individual teachers who have received the greatest amount of effective assistance and those teachers who have received the least amount of assistance. Once those individuals have been identified, qualitative interviews could be conducted with a small sample from each group. The interviews could explore reasons that particular kinds of assistance were helpful or not helpful. The research design could be represented this way:

Quantitative	Qualitative
Which elementary teachers have received the greatest amount of assistance? Which elementary teachers have received the least amount of assistance?	What explanations do teachers have about why some kinds of assistance are helpful and other kinds are not?

When data are collected sequentially—quantitative first, qualitative second—the quantitative phase provides general results that are then explained with qualitative data. When data are collected sequentially, an *explanatory design* is implied.

Qualitative, Then Quantitative Questions

When there is little prior research on a topic or a practice is new, qualitative methods may be used first to investigate the scope of the phenomenon, followed by quantitative methods. The data identified in the qualitative phase will then be investigated in a more structured way using quantitative approaches. For example, in a study of beginning teacher assistance, it may be necessary to explore the types of assistance received before measuring the relationship among the types. The quantitative results extend what is found in the qualitative phase. The following research design could be used:

Qualitative	Quantitative
What types of assistance are beginning teachers receiving? How do beginning teachers feel about the helpfulness of the different types of assistance?	Is there a relationship between the types of assistance that beginning teachers receive and the grade levels they teach? Is there a difference in terms of helpfulness between assistance received from mentors and assistance received from principals?

When qualitative methods initiate the inquiry and are followed by quantitative techniques, the problem implies an *exploratory design*. Exploratory designs are often used to develop instruments. A topic will be studied in depth to clarify all important dimensions, and then these dimensions will be used as a framework for developing a questionnaire. For instance, a researcher could spend considerable time in a school observing the nature of school climate and then use that information to develop an objectively scored instrument that captures all aspects of school climate.

STANDARDS OF ADEQUACY FOR PROBLEM STATEMENTS AND RESEARCH QUESTIONS

Research problems are critically evaluated on the three elements discussed in this chapter: the statement of the general research problem, the significance of the problem, and the specific research purpose, question, or hypothesis. In addition, other criteria may be applied.

General Research Problem The following questions appraise the general statement of the problem:

1. Does the statement of the general research problem imply the possibility of empirical investigation?
2. Does the problem statement restrict the scope of the study?
3. Does the problem statement give the educational context in which the problem lies?

Significance of the Problem Readers assess the significance of the problem in terms of one or more of the following criteria:

- Develops knowledge of an enduring practice
- Develops theory
- Generalizable—that is, expands knowledge or theory
- Provides extension of understandings
- Advances methodology
- Is related to a current social or political issue
- Evaluates a specific practice or policy at a given site
- Is exploratory research

Specific Research Question or Hypothesis Different criteria are applied in the evaluation of quantitative, qualitative, and mixed methods research questions.

Quantitative

1. Does the specific research purpose, question, or hypothesis state concisely what is to be determined?
2. Does the level of specificity indicate that the question or hypothesis is researchable, or do the variables seem amenable to operational definitions?
3. Is the logic of the research question or hypothesis clear? Are the independent and dependent variables identified?
4. Does the research question or hypothesis indicate the framework for reporting the results?

Qualitative

1. Do the research questions, foreshadowed problems, and condensed problem statement indicate the particular case of some phenomena to be examined?
2. Is the qualitative methodology appropriate for the description of present or past events?
3. Is the logic of the research reasonably explicit?
4. Does the research purpose indicate the framework for reporting the findings?

Mixed Method

1. Is the relative emphasis of each method made explicit?
2. Is the order in which quantitative and qualitative data are collected clear (e.g., how each type of data will be used in the study)?

Other Criteria for Standards of Adequacy Before conducting a study, the researcher, a possible funding agency, review committees, and other groups also evaluate the problem according to additional criteria. These criteria concern the ability of the researcher to conduct the study and the feasibility and ethics of the research design. Typical questions asked include the following:

1. Is the problem one in which the researcher has a vital interest and a topic in which the researcher has both knowledge and experience?

2. Are the problem and the design feasible in terms of measurement, access to the case, sample, or population, permission to use documents, time frame for completion, financial resources, and the like?

3. Does the researcher have the skills to conduct the proposed research and to analyze and interpret the results?

4. Does the proposed research ensure the protection of human subjects from physical or mental discomfort or harm? Is the right of informed consent of subjects provided? Will ethical research practices be followed?

CHAPTER SUMMARY

This chapter has examined the major aspects of research problem statements, problem formulation in quantitative, qualitative and mixed method research, the significance of the problem, and standards of adequacy for a problem statement. The primary concepts can be summarized as follows:

1. A research problem implies the possibility of empirical investigation.

2. Sources for research problems are casual observations, theory, literature, current issues, practical situations, and personal insights.

3. A research problem statement specifies the focus, educational context, importance, and framework for reporting the findings.

4. In quantitative research, deductive logic is employed in selecting the construct, variables, and operational definitions.

5. A construct is a complex abstraction and as such is not directly observable. A variable is an event, category, behavior, or attribute that expresses a construct and has different values, depending on how it is used in a study.

6. Variables may be categorical or continuous. Variables may be dependent, independent, manipulated, experimental, predictor, or criterion variables in different designs.

7. An operational definition assigns meaning to a variable by specifying the activities or operations necessary to measure, categorize, or manipulate the variable.

8. To formulate a quantitative problem, the researcher decides the variables, the population, and the logic of the design.

9. A research problem is significant if it provides knowledge about an enduring practice, tests a theory, increases generalizability, extends empirical understanding, advances methodology, focuses on a current issue, evaluates a specific practice, or is an exploratory study.

10. Problem statements are judged by the criteria for statement of a research problem, the problem significance, the specific research questions or hypotheses, and the appropriate logic and feasibility.

11. Specific quantitative research problems may ask descriptive, relationship, or difference questions or state a hypothesis.

12. Qualitative research problems and questions change as a result of continuing inductive reasoning.

13. The central question for a qualitative study is an open-ended question that summarizes the main focus of the study.

14. The central question should not be biased, too general or specific, amenable to change, indicate the site and participants, and keep the focus on understanding in depth.

15. In qualitative research, the general topic, the case, and the methodology are interrelated and selected interactively, rather than in separate research steps.

16. Qualitative research problems are reformulated several times during data collection; quantitative research problems are stated before data collection begins.

17. Mixed method problem statements indicate the relative importance of quantitative and qualitative data (i.e., how the method will function in the design).

APPLICATION PROBLEMS

1. The following are examples of research topics. Indicate the decisions necessary in order to conduct the study, and restate each as a useful research question.
   a. Effects of different ways of learning social studies
   b. Effects of cooperative versus competitive instruction on attitudes toward learning
   c. Opinions of parents toward education
   d. Family characteristics and school attendance
   e. Validity of the Wechsler Intelligence Scale for Children (WISC) for school performance

2. Write a directional hypothesis for the following problem statement, and identify the type of variables in the

hypothesis: Low-achieving students frequently respond positively to behavior modification programs. Is there any relationship between the type of reward (tangible or intangible) and the amount of learning?

3. State a hypothesis based on each of the following research questions:
   a. What is the effect of individualized and structured social studies on high school students?
   b. Are there any differences in students' engagement in tasks when a teacher uses a positive introduction and when a teacher uses a neutral introduction to tasks?
   c. Does nonpromotion of elementary pupils improve their social adjustment?
   d. Do teachers' perceptions of job stress differ among teachers of mildly retarded, moderately retarded, and nonretarded children?

4. In the following qualitative problem statements, identify a central question to be studied:
   a. This study describes and analyzes how women faculty members at an urban university perceive their professional and personal lives and how they integrate their lives.
   b. School board records of a suburban school system were analyzed for the ideologies articulated by various school board members to legitimize systemwide curriculum policies from 1950 to 1980.
   c. The research problem is to describe how Sue Olson, a first-year elementary school teacher, develops a professional role with students, faculty, administrators, and parents and how she develops an understanding of teacher professionalism.
   d. The research problem is to describe and analyze a faculty social system in the implementation of an innovative middle school program for grounded theory.

ANSWER TO THE APPLICATION PROBLEMS

1. a. Need to specify the population, "different ways of learning," and "effects." Example: Is there a difference between the SRA social studies achievement scores of eighth-graders who had an inquiry approach and those who had a lecture approach?
   b. Need to specify the population and measures of two variables. Example: Do the attitudes toward learning of middle school students differ between those in cooperative instruction and those in competitive instruction?
   c. Need to specify which educational opinions of which parents (population) are the focus. Example: What are the opinions of the parents of Fox School pupils toward the proposed athletic eligibility regulations?
   d. Need to specify which family characteristics are to be measured or categorized and measurement for school attendance. Example: Is there a relationship between educational level of parents and number of siblings and their average daily school attendance?
   e. Need to specify type of validity sought, population, and criterion for validity. Example: Is there a relationship between the scores on the WISC and the CAT among primary-grade minority children?

2. Directional hypothesis: Low-achieving students reinforced with tangible rewards will demonstrate greater achievement in basic skills than low-achieving students reinforced with intangible rewards. The independent variable is type of reward (categorical), and the dependent variable is achievement (continuous or measured).

3. a. High school students in an individualized curriculum will score higher on a social studies test than students in a structured curriculum.
   b. Teachers' use of positive task introduction compared to neutral task introduction will produce sustained student engagement in those tasks.
   c. Students who are retained have higher scores on a measure of personal adjustment than comparable students who are promoted.
   d. There are significant differences in the scores of a teacher burnout inventory among teachers of mildly retarded, moderately retarded, and nonretarded children, or the degree of teacher burnout increases as the students' level of intellectual ability decreases.

4. a. Female faculty members of an urban university
   b. The school board records of a suburban school system, 1950 to 1980
   c. Sue Olson's first year as a teacher in an elementary school
   d. A faculty implementing an innovative middle school program

Review of Literature

with Amanda Connor and Jess ca Hearn

From Chapter 4 of *Research in Education: Evidence-Based Inquiry*, 7/e. James H. McMillan. Sally Schumacher.

Review of Literature
with Amanda Connor and Jessica Hearn

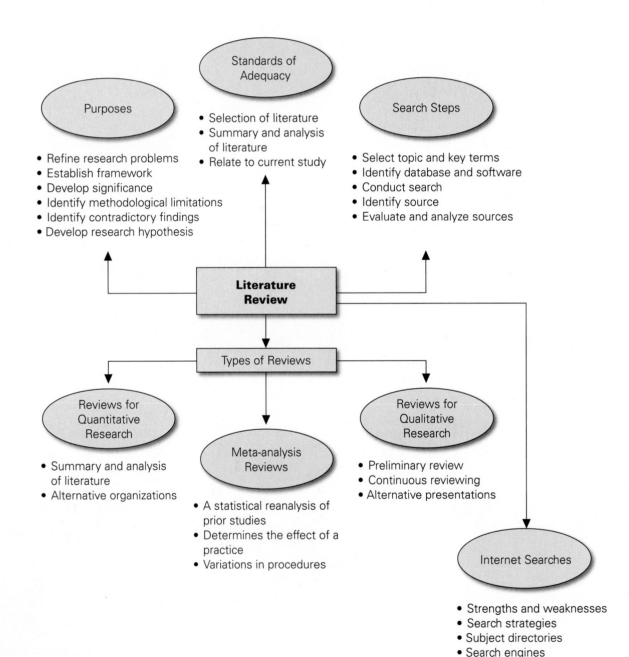

Standards of Adequacy
- Selection of literature
- Summary and analysis of literature
- Relate to current study

Purposes
- Refine research problems
- Establish framework
- Develop significance
- Identify methodological limitations
- Identify contradictory findings
- Develop research hypothesis

Search Steps
- Select topic and key terms
- Identify database and software
- Conduct search
- Identify source
- Evaluate and analyze sources

Literature Review

Types of Reviews

Reviews for Quantitative Research
- Summary and analysis of literature
- Alternative organizations

Meta-analysis Reviews
- A statistical reanalysis of prior studies
- Determines the effect of a practice
- Variations in procedures

Reviews for Qualitative Research
- Preliminary review
- Continuous reviewing
- Alternative presentations

Internet Searches
- Strengths and weaknesses
- Search strategies
- Subject directories
- Search engines
- Scholarly communication
- Educational websites

KEY TERMS

primary source	PsycINFO	subject directories
secondary source	Social Science Citation	search engines
thesaurus	Index (SSCI)	metasearch engines
ERIC	boolean	meta-analysis

WHAT YOU WILL LEARN

After studying this chapter you will:

- Understand why the review of literature is an essential component of credible research.
- Be able to identify various purposes for the review of literature.
- Be able to write a review of literature.
- Know how to evaluate the review of literature section of reasearch reports and articles.

- Become skilled at using the Internet for reviewing literature.
- Understand the differences between primary and secondary sources.
- Identify sources as either primary or secondary.

WHY REVIEW RELATED LITERATURE?

When we teach our graduate students about reading and doing research, the one topic that comes up as essential *throughout the process* is the review and use of literature. There are two major reasons: (1) the review establishes important links between existing knowledge and the research problem being investigated, which enhances significance, and (2) the review provides very helpful information about methodology that can be incorporated into a new study. Use of these ideas, materials, and experiences enhances the overall credibility of new studies. Consider the following for would-be researchers:

- What questionnaire should be used? What has been used in other studies?
- What sample size is appropriate? How many subjects were used in previous investigations?
- What data analysis procedures are appropriate? What analyses have been used in previous studies?
- How should the intervention be monitored? How was it monitored in other studies, and how successful were these methods?
- How should the intervention be implemented? What were other researchers' experience with similar interventions?

Almost every question about doing new research can be answered by knowing what others have done and reported. This is why the review is so important. Researchers need to know why the review is essential, how to locate previous studies, how to analyze and interpret the study, and how to use what others have done in writing their own review of literature.

Broadly stated, the purpose of the review is to relate previous research and theory to the problem under investigation. McMillan (2008) lists six more specific purposes:

- *Refining the research problem.* Researchers typically begin with a general problem in mind or some idea of what they want to investigate. This is a good starting point, but eventually more specific research questions are needed (particularly in the case of quantitative research). The previous literature helps to narrow down the topic to these specific questions. As other similar empirical studies are found, ideas and examples of how to narrow down the topic to researchable questions are provided. Variables are clarified on the basis of how others have operationalized them. In one sense, the literature provides the "data" for developing specific research questions.

For qualitative studies, the review helps establish the appropriate foreshadowed or central questions that guide the investigation. Previous research is used as a justification for how these questions will achieve the purpose of the study. The literature also helps frame the more specific subquestions that guide data gathering.

EXCERPT 4.1 Developing Significance Based on Previous Research

In general, researchers who have explored the relationship of part-time employment to educational outcomes have found mixed results—from no effects to small, negative, and sometimes positive effects. . . . Some researchers have argued also that differences between working and non-working students may be attributable to pre-work, differences in attitudes, values, and behaviors. . . . Bachman and Schulenberg (1993) suggested that work intensity might be the result, rather than the cause, of low academic achievement. In the present research we explore the relationship of work and school performance, controlling for different sets of variables at successive steps. . . . By controlling for those important predictors of academic achievement, we can determine the true effect of part-time work on school engagement and grades. Thus, we build on prior research and extend the empirical knowledge on the effect of part-time work on educational outcomes of youth. (p. 15)

Source: From Singh, K., Chang, M., & Dika, S. (2007). Effects of part-time work on school achievement during high school. *The Journal of Educational Research, 101*(1), 12–23.

• *Establishing a conceptual or theoretical framework.* By placing the research into a more general conceptual framework or theoretical orientation, a rationale is provided for the research questions. Essentially, the intellectual or scholarly perspective in which the problem is embedded is described. The framework is also used to justify the selection of the subjects, variables, and design. Results are interpreted and explained in light of theory. Establishing this framework is essential in applied quantitative studies, especially when researching a problem that has been extensively studied. Qualitative studies differ in the emphasis of theory. Some qualitative studies rely heavily on existing theories, whereas others take the perspective that it's not best to incorporate theory initially because this may focus the study in a way that limits the inductive process from the data gathered. Finally, theory can show a logical link between questions and methodology.

• *Developing significance.* Research needs to make a meaningful contribution to existing knowledge or practice. By basing the study on what has been reported, a stronger case for significance can be made. It is best to indicate specifically how the results will be significant, how they will add to, expand, and build on what has already been done. The review will also help identify new directions that are worth investigating and will avoid unnecessary duplication. Furthermore, the findings from previous research can be used to interpret results, making conclusions and recommendations more meaningful. Note in Excerpt 4.1 how the authors developed an argument for significance based on previous research.

• *Identifying methodological limitations.* One of the best ways to justify the significance and contribution of the study is to focus on methodological limitations of previous research. This involves an *analysis* of the literature, not simply a reporting of what others have found. In addition, this kind of analysis helps researchers identify methods related to sampling, measurement, procedures, and interventions that are useful in designing their studies. New approaches can be explored and considered, and past mistakes can be avoided. Often methodological limitations are used as a rationale for conducting replications. Two excerpts (4.2 and 4.3) are provided to illustrate how authors point out these limitations.

• *Identifying contradictory findings.* The review of literature may uncover studies in which the findings contradict one another (e.g., in Excerpts 4.1 and 4.3). This is common and healthy to the research enterprise and is an excellent justification for designing new research that would change the methodology to resolve the contradictory results. This may involve the variables used,

EXCERPT 4.2 Identifying Methodological Weaknesses

Unfortunately, the vast majority of research on this important issue has fallen short of scientific standards for drawing causal inference. . . . Virtually all published evaluations of state pre-K programs, as well as the national studies, have failed to correct for selection bias; many have relied on tests that have not been normed or validated, and it has not been uncommon for studies to rely on pre-K teachers' reports in pretest-posttest designs, thus introducing strong evaluator bias. None of the studies examined used random assignment. (p. 873)

Source: From Gormley, W. T., Jr., Gayer, T., Phillips, D., & Dawson, B. (2005). The effects of universal pre-k on cognitive development. *Developmental Psychology, 41*(6), 872–884.

EXCERPT 4.3 Identifying Methodological Weaknesses

Why is there so little agreement on the short-term effects of retention? There are three methodological reasons why studies differ in their conclusions about the short-term achievement effects of retention: (a) the point at which researchers estimate achievement effects; (b) the compara-bility of test scores across grades; and (c) the ability of researchers to construct adequate comparison groups of retained and promoted children and account for their prior characteristics. (p. 311)

Source: From Roderick, M., & Nagaoka, J. (2005). Retention under Chicago's high-stakes testing program: Helpful, harmful or harmless? *Educational Evaluation and Policy Analysis , 27*(4), 309–340.

EXCERPT 4.4 Identifying Contradictory Findings

Results of research on the effects of immediate feedback on anxiety during testing have not been consistent. Some researchers have found immediate feedback to be associ-ated with decreases in anxiety. . . . On the other hand, researchers have also frequently observed increases in anxiety . . . as well as reductions in test performance. (p. 313)

Source: From DiBattista, D., & Gosse, L. (2006). Test anxiety and the immediate feedback assessment technique. *Journal of Experimental Education, 74*(4), 311–327.

EXCERPT 4.5 Developing Research Hypotheses

We based our predictions about the number and nature of the dimensions underlying students' attributions on the work of Wimer and Kelley (1982) and Weiner (1979, 1985). First, as Wimer and Kelley note, "researchers do not agree on a single set of attributional categories" (p. 1143). However, with few exceptions exploratory analyses of the structure of attribution have identified a locus of causality, or internal versus external, dimension (Meyer, 1980). . . . Although less consistently, several investiga-tions have also revealed a "good-bad" dimension. . . . Wimer and Kelley (1982), for example, argue that attribu-tors draw a major distinction between positive causes and negative causes, and term this the Good-Bad fac-tor. . . . this view suggests that causes tend to be va-lenced: "good" causes increase the likelihood of success, whereas "bad" causes increase the likelihood of failure. We therefore expected to find evidence of both a locus of cause and a good-bad dimension in our analyses. . . . Second, we also predicted that the causes obtained would be hierarchically structured.

Source: From Forsyth, D. R., Story, P., Kelley, K. N., & McMillan, J. H. (2008). What causes failure and success? Students' perceptions of their academic outcomes. *Social Psychology of Education.*

selection of subjects, and measures. Excerpt 4.4 provides another example of how researchers compare contradictory findings.

• *Developing research hypotheses.* Good research hypotheses that are used in quantitative research are based on what is suggested from previous studies. Similar research may suggest that a specific result is likely, and the hypotheses would be consistent with those findings. When there are few previous empirical studies on the topic, existing theories should be used to justify the hypotheses. Thus, a thorough review of the literature is needed to find other empirical studies and/or theories that can be used to formulate the hypotheses. Sometimes researchers need to search for studies in other fields, such as psychology or sociology, which are also rich in the use of theo-ries. Excerpt 4.5 illustrates the development of research hypotheses based on the literature.

TYPES OF LITERATURE SOURCES

When you review the literature, you will come across many different types of articles and reports. This can be somewhat confusing because there are hundreds of journals, agencies, associations, and organizations that publish studies or what is called *research*, especially because the Internet has access to so much information. Although it is important to know about the quality of any source, there is one fundamental difference that it is essential to understand—the difference between what are called *primary* and *secondary* sources.

Primary Sources

Primary source: contains original or firsthand information

A **primary source** is one in which original data and firsthand information are used. This is "raw" or initial material or data. Primary sources in quantitative research consist of what the subjects did or reported. This is presented in an article, report, monograph, book, website, or other format with an analysis of the initial data that were gathered. This is typically reflected in a detailed report that is addressed to others who are interested in primary data. When there is reference to "empirical research," this means that the source is primary.

In qualitative studies, primary sources are the artifacts and individuals with whom the researcher has direct interaction. The participants in a qualitative study are primary sources, and the researcher would interview or observe them directly. Firsthand documents, such as memos, reports, films, minutes, photographs, relics (such as equipment), diaries, or correspondence, would be read by the researcher. Observations are conducted in naturally occurring settings and provide original data that are subsequently analyzed.

Primary sources are identified by looking for certain characteristics of the report or article. These include:

1. *The title:* Does the title suggest that data have been gathered? The words *study* and *investigation* usually denote a primary source, as do phrases such as *an investigation of*, *the effect of*, *the relationship between*, or *an analysis of*. Here are some examples of titles that suggest that the work is primary:
   A Study of Teacher Use of Benchmark Assessment
   The Relationship between Age of Coaches and Style of Interaction with Athletes
   The Effect of Mentors on Beginning Teacher Satisfaction and Retention
   An Analysis of College Students' Perceptions of Influential Faculty
2. *Have new data been collected?* In a primary source there will be a description of data or information that is unique to the study, that is, new in the sense that the collection of data is part of the study. This is reflected in sections of the article or report that use terms such as *instruments*, *source of data*, *measures*, *procedure*, or *data collection*.
3. *Is there a design, methods, or methodology section?* Primary sources will contain an explanation of how the data were gathered, as well as from whom they were collected. This includes a description of the sampling, procedures, and an intervention.
4. *Is there a section on findings or results?* This section is always part of an article or report that is a primary source. There are typically tables and figures in quantitative studies and often quotations from participants in a qualitative study.

As you become familiar with the journals in your field, you will see that particular journals publish mostly empirical studies. This is the case, for instance, with *The Journal of Educational Research*, *American Educational Research Journal*, *Journal of Research in Science Teaching*, *Reading Research Quarterly*, and many other journals. Dissertations are primary sources, as are most technical reports.

Secondary Sources

Secondary source: summary or other use of original work

Secondary sources summarize, review, analyze, or discuss primary source information as well as what is contained in other secondary sources. There is no firsthand gathering of data. Typically, a secondary source is something written *about* the primary source information. The secondary source may be a review of research or a conceptual paper about a topic. It could be a digest, a book, or an article in a journal that rarely publishes primary studies (e.g., *Educational Leadership*, *Phi Delta Kappan*, *Educational Horizons*).

There are four major types of secondary sources:

1. *Quarterly and Annual Reviews and Yearbooks.* These reviews give detailed syntheses of narrow topics with extensive lists of primary sources. For example, the *Review of Research in Education* is published annually as a book. Each year different topics are targeted. The National Society for

the Study of Education (NSSE) *Yearbook* also contains articles that summarize studies on a number of different topics. *Review of Educational Research* is published quarterly by the American Educational Research Association and contains excellent reviews, also on different topics.

2. **Professional Books.** Books written by scholars for other professionals give detailed analyses of the literature in a field from particular perspectives. Textbooks are also secondary sources, and although they are written for students, they also contain useful summaries of a topic and references. Some publishers are known for their professional books, such as Teachers College Press, Corwin Press, and Jossey-Bass.

3. **Encyclopedias.** These books contain brief summaries of other literature and can provide a good overview in an area. The *Encyclopedia of Educational Research*, for example, with numerous articles and extensive bibliographies, represents a comprehensive analysis of 15 or more educational topics. There are also more specialized encyclopedias that contain articles about specific fields, such as early childhood education, school administration, and teacher education.

4. **Handbooks.** Recently, many handbooks in different areas have been published. They are excellent secondary sources. The chapters in these books are more comprehensive than those found in other secondary sources and are more scholarly because the audience is other professionals as well as students. The chapters are usually authored by noted scholars in the field. They are often published by professional associations. Here is a *partial* list:

   - *Handbook of Educational Psychology*
   - *Handbook of Reading Research*
   - *Handbook of Research on Curriculum*
   - *Handbook of Research on Educational Administration*
   - *Handbook of Research on Mathematics Teaching and Learning*
   - *Handbook of Research on the Teaching of English*
   - *Handbook of Research on Science Education*
   - *Handbook of Research on Science Teaching and Learning*
   - *Handbook of Research on Teaching*
   - *Handbook of Research on School Supervision*
   - *Handbook of Sport Psychology*
   - *Handbook of Research on Multicultural Education*

For a number of years, ERIC produced what were called *ERIC Digests*. The Digests are short reports that synthesize research ideas about contemporary educational issues. There are over 2,000 Digests, and all are available online. To search the ERIC database for the digests, go to the Advanced Search screen, as illustrated in Figure 4.4, and select "ERIC Digests in Full Text" as the publication type.

STEPS IN CONDUCTING A REVIEW OF LITERATURE

Your goal in reviewing the literature is not simply to find some sources, it is to find the best sources that can help you establish significance and help you design your study. With the Internet, searching literature is easy if you are only looking for something; identifying the right literature, especially relevant primary sources, requires a more sophisticated approach. By following the steps summarized in Figure 4.1, you will increase the quality of your search and locate the most appropriate studies more quickly. We will consider each of these steps in more detail.

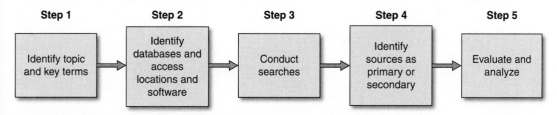

FIGURE 4.1 **Steps in Conducting a Review of Literature**

However, we want to emphasize that any search of literature should be preceded by complete familiarization with the library you will use (*if* you use one—it isn't nearly as essential now as it once was). A librarian will help you understand the nature of the databases that are accessible and what journal articles can be obtained electronically. Soon there will be few sources that are not electronic. Working with a librarian who understands educational and psychological literature is especially helpful. Searching the literature can take quite a long time, though not nearly as long as it would take when doing a manual search. Computer resources are ubiquitous but also change frequently, so you need to keep up-to-date with what is available and how it can be accessed.

The most effective sequence of steps in searching the literature has changed recently because of the electronic availability of reports and articles. In previous editions of this book we recommended identifying and using secondary sources first, then moving on to primary sources, and that still is a logical sequence of steps. Now, however, as you will see, we think it is best to simply choose key terms, identify a database, and then search, distinguishing between primary and secondary sources as you conduct the search.

Step One: Select a Topic and Key Terms

The first step in reviewing literature is to have some idea of the topic or subject about which you are interested. This could be rather general, like "what teaching methods are best for students with learning disabilities," or more specific. Identify the most important terms in the problem and then think about other terms that are closely related. These terms are then used in computerized databases to find literature. For example, you may be interested in *student motivation*. It would be wise to use related terms, such as *engagement, effort, persistence, intrinsic motivation,* and *self-efficacy.* All of these terms could be used, and different sources will be identified by each one.

Thesaurus: source of key terms for searching

Once terms are identified, you may want to jump right into a computerized database and see what literature comes up, or you may want to begin by refining the terms used in the search. For most searches of educational literature, it is best to use a special **thesaurus** that is available to help select the most appropriate key terms. You will want to use either the ERIC *Thesaurus* or the *Thesaurus of Psychological Index Terms* (accessed in the PsycINFO database, with definitions and uses that are somewhat different from those in the ERIC *Thesaurus*). ERIC, the Education Resources Information Center, is your best friend when it comes to educational literature. **ERIC** is a digital library of education-related resources (more on ERIC soon). Although a hard copy of the *Thesaurus of ERIC Descriptors* could be used, the most recent and continually updated version is online (http://www.eric.ed.gov; other database vendors, such as EBSCO, use their own online format).

ERIC: Educational Resources Information Center

ERIC has a "controlled vocabulary" of terms called *descriptors*. Descriptors are used to organize and index database materials by subject. Each record is assigned several descriptors. The *Thesaurus* also uses *keywords*. Keywords match words found in the indexed record, whereas descriptors locate records that may not contain the specific keyword. This means that if you use keywords for a search, you will locate many more records. For example, in September 2007, we used the term *guidance centers* as both a keyword and a descriptor. The keyword search identified 1,811 records (PsycINFO has only 59 records); the descriptor search located 610.

You can search the ERIC *Thesaurus* by entering a specific term or phrase, or by browsing alphabetically or by category, to determine a match between how the *Thesaurus* defines a term and your use of the term. A critical aspect of using terms is to understand that a given topic probably has both general and narrow terms, as illustrated in Figure 4.2. When beginning a

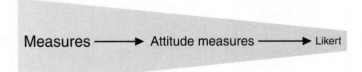

FIGURE 4.2 **Specificity of ERIC Descriptors**

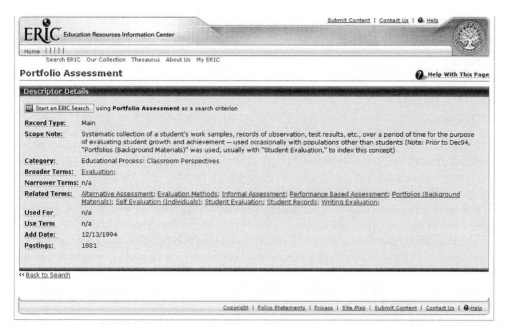

FIGURE 4.3 Example of ERIC's *Thesaurus* Descriptor Details
Source: Used with permission of the U.S. Department of Education.

search, it is best to use general rather than specific terms (e.g., categories rather than keywords). You can get an idea of the specificity of a term by pulling up the *Thesaurus* record on it, as illustrated in Figure 4.3. The record shows other, broader and narrower terms, as well as related terms. Suppose your topic is "the effect of using portfolio assessment on student achievement." You put *portfolio assessment* in the *Thesaurus*, and it shows up as Figure 4.3. The results give you the definition ERIC has used. It is in the educational process: classroom perspectives category, with *evaluation* as a broad term and no narrow terms. Interestingly, *authentic assessment* is not a related term. For many this would be a characteristic of portfolio assessment. However, when *authentic assessment* is used as a keyword for an ERIC search overall, 1,000 records are identified. This illustrates an important point in using key terms for your search: You must spend considerable time trying different searches with different terms, and you cannot assume that the way you think about and define terms is the same as that of the ERIC personnel who maintain the database.

As an alternative to searching ERIC or PsycINFO with key terms, you may want to search a more traditional library card catalog, a database of a wide range of books, or the Internet, which could be helpful in focusing your research problem and key terms.

Step Two: Identify the Database and Access Software

There are many different databases that can be accessed. We will consider in some detail two that are used most frequently for educational research—ERIC and PsycINFO. Equipped with a fairly focused set of key terms, you can use ERIC to identify articles and reports that can be reviewed in more detail to determine how helpful they will be for the review of literature. ERIC is a database of resources sponsored by the federal government. It contains journal and non-journal articles and reports obtained since 1966. ERIC is essentially a Web-based library for accessing historical and current resources. With the Education Sciences Reform Act of 2002 ERIC underwent significant changes, and it continues to adopt new procedures to further modernize the database, including the criteria for selecting resources and journals to be included.

There are several different ways to access ERIC, each involving different software. The most direct route is to go to the ERIC website (http://www.eric.ed.gov). In addition, you may reach the ERIC database by using another server such as EBSCOhost, FirstSearch, or CSA Illumina (Cambridge Scientific Abstracts). Interestingly, even though there is only one ERIC database, different servers will give you somewhat different search results. For example, we conducted a search using the term *school culture* as a descriptor for the year 2008, and this is the number of documents identified in each server:

ERIC	70
FirstSearch	59
CSA ILLUMINA	42
EBSCOhost	59

It has been our experience that using http://www.eric.ed.gov will usually give you more hits. It is not clear why there are differences. Simply keep this in mind, and try more than one server. The convenient aspect of university library access points, such as EBSCO, is that more than one database can be searched, and it is easy to determine if the article or report is available online. You will be able to access library resources and databases from home as well as going directly to http://www.eric.ed.gov.

PsycINFO: psychology and related fields database

The **PsycINFO** database contains documents, articles, dissertations, and books on psychology and related disciplines, including education. This database is accessible online. It contains over 2 million records covering 2,000 journals (98% are peer reviewed). All university libraries provide access to PsycINFO. Individuals can use PsycINFO at a cost determined by time or the number of records used. There are also databases on sociology, business, medicine, and other fields related to education that will search sources that are not included in ERIC. For many topics PsycINFO needs to be used along with ERIC. PsycINFO contains different journals and a different process for categorizing the articles. Like ERIC, PsycINFO is available on the Web; your university library will also have it, without access costs.

One additional database used by many libraries is InfoTrac Onefile. This database has access to over 50 million articles, about half of which are online and available to print from your computer. This file combines scholarly and popular journals and magazines in all fields.

There are also a number of more specialized indexes that have narrower coverage, focusing on single subjects related to education. These include:

- Sociological Abstracts
- Physical Education Index
- State Education Journal Index
- Educational Administration Abstracts
- Dissertation Abstracts International
- Higher Education Abstracts
- Exceptional Child Education Resources
- Sociology of Education Abstracts
- American Statistics Index
- Exceptional Child Education Resources

Check with your librarian for a list of all databases on education. Our library at Virginia Commonwealth University lists 27. Some of these databases related to education may provide good sources.

Social Science Citation Index (SSCI): connects studies and authors

A unique type of database is the **Social Science Citation Index (SSCI)**. This index enables a researcher to determine the impact of a key study or theory on the works of other scholars and researchers. This is particularly important if the first report or article was controversial or if it initiated a new subfield or series of studies. Once you find a key author, you can trace subsequent articles that referenced that particular person and study. This is an excellent way to find additional sources. There is also a Science Citation Index (SCI).

The final very important database that you can search is the Internet. This vast repository of websites contains something on almost every topic. More about the Internet later.

Step Three: Conduct a Search

Searches are conducted in different databases. We will focus on the two most popular kinds of searches for education—ERIC and the Internet. In this section we will describe the steps using ERIC and then cover the Internet in a separate section of the chapter.

The specific nature of the procedures to use to search ERIC depends on the server. Using the http://www.eric.gov.ed website as an example, you begin by simply typing in words that describe your topic in the Search box. We strongly recommend that you click on "Advanced Search" and use that screen for your search. As illustrated in Figure 4.4, there are a number of options to make choices that can improve your search. The first decision in using the Advanced Search screen is whether you want to limit your search to the author, title, ERIC number, descriptor, journal name, or keywords (all fields), which is the default. These options appear when you click on the box to the right with an arrow, along with some infrequently used options. The author, title, or other information is typed in the box to the right. With Publication Date you can select documents appearing in specific years. It is often best to begin with the most recent five years. If you find too many documents during that period, do another search limited to one year. If too few documents are identified, lengthen the number of years to 10 or even more. The quality of the studies accessed has not changed appreciably for at least 20 years. Some topics researched heavily many years ago with strong studies provide excellent information. So, although it is important to use recent studies, don't ignore the old ones. The latter studies may be more directly related to what you are researching.

The next decision has to do with Publication Type(s). You have a large number of choices here, though typically only a few are relevant. Obviously, Any Publication Type encompasses all records (even those not formally published in an article). You can select specific types of documents by checking as many as apply on the rather long list. Book/Product Reviews is excellent for identifying secondary sources. If you check Journal Articles, the search is limited to records appearing in published journals. Often the best search of primary sources uses Journal Articles and Reports/Research. The Tests/Questionnaires choice is good to find sources that use a particular measure.

Most students find that they need to tailor the search until they can identify a reasonable number of sources that appear to be closely related to their research problem. The most common way of refining a search is to use the **boolean** operators *and*, *or*, and *not*. These operators will alter the search, either by including more records (*or*) or fewer records (*and*, *not*). The most frequently used operator is *and*. It will reduce the search because the computer will look for entries that are categorized by all the descriptors or keywords indicated. Put parentheses around sets of terms, quotations around phrases, and commas between terms. For example, a search of *teaching styles and elementary education* would have fewer hits than a search using only one of these terms

Boolean: connectors for specifying searches

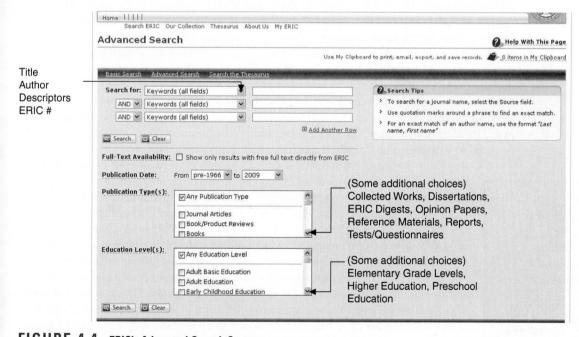

FIGURE 4.4 **ERIC's Advanced Search Screen**
Source: Used with permission of the U.S. Department of Education.

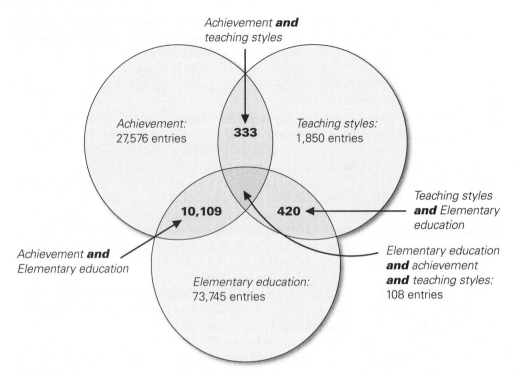

FIGURE 4.5   Narrowing an ERIC Search with *and*

(*teaching styles* by itself would include elementary, middle, and high schools, as well as colleges and universities). If a third descriptor, *achievement*, is added, the search is further refined. This process of narrowing the search is illustrated in Figure 4.5, using Any Publication Type and Publication Date years 1998–2008.

When a topic is searched with http://www.eric.ed.gov, the user is presented with a list of articles and documents, with summary information and an abstract. By clicking on the title of the document or on "more details," further specifics about the record will be provided, as illustrated by the Records Detail screen in Figure 4.6. This entry resulted from a search using *student motivation*. Figure 4.6 shows that there is an ERIC # assigned to the entry. This number is permanent and will be the same for all servers. Most journal articles have some kind of peer review, which tends to result in better quality than what you will find with nonjournal documents. But there are exceptions! Many journal articles, even with peer review, are not very credible, and many nonjournal documents are excellent. One advantage of searching nonjournal documents is that conference presentations are often included. Some of these presentations eventually become articles, but there may be a significant time lag between submission of a manuscript to a journal for publication and the time when the article appears in print. With this format (Figure 4.6) there is sufficient information to determine if it would be useful to locate the full article or report.

Once you have limited your search to a reasonable number of documents (e.g., between 5 and 20), you need to obtain the article or report to examine each one in greater detail in order to determine if it could be used in the review. Obtaining the actual article will depend on whether it is available online (increasingly, journal articles are available on the Internet, either from home or through your library) or as hard copy in your library. You may need to use other libraries or interlibrary loan. ERIC has a *Find in a Library* feature that lists the nearest library that contains the record.

The typical process, then, involves taking a large number of possible documents and reducing it to the relatively few to be used for the review. For example, you might begin a study on science and mathematics teaching strategies with some 12,000 hits, reduce that number by restricting your search to a few years, reduce it again by accessing only journal articles, locating those, and then, finally, pick 8 articles from among the 22 you obtained.

To practice conducting a database search, go to MyEducationLab for Research at www.myeducationlab.com. Click on the topic "Reviewing the Literature" and then select the Activities and Applications activity titled "Conduct a Database Search."

FIGURE 4.6 Sample ERIC Records Detail

Source: Used with permission of the U.S. Department of Education.

Step Four: Identify Sources as Primary or Secondary

Separating the sources by whether they are primary or secondary is helpful in organizing the information. Use the secondary sources to provide an overview of work in the area, the historical context, and as a summary of what other researchers have found. A good review of research is a great starting point for considering in greater detail the primary studies. You will want to focus most of the review on a discussion of primary sources, and a review of literature is excellent for placing priority on the primary studies.

Step Five: Evaluate and Analyze Sources

The last step is the toughest. This is the point at which you need to make decisions about the extent to which the source will be used and whether, initially, it will be used in the introductory section or the review of literature. Use these criteria to help guide your decision:

1. *Credibility.* Does the study appear objective, with little or no researcher bias? Are the conclusions reasonable, and was the methodology appropriate for the investigation? Was the study supported by external funds? Is it part of a line of research the investigator has developed over years of work?

2. *Source reputation.* Is the journal refereed (this is indicated in the ERIC Records Detail screen for an article [Figure 4.6])? What is the circulation? What is the acceptance rate? Generally, journals sponsored by national associations have excellent reputations and use a blind review procedure. An excellent source for detailed information about journals, including circulation figures, is available on *Ulrich's Periodicals Directory* (http://www. Ulrichweb.com). Acceptance rates vary considerably. The rate for *Harvard Educational Review* is 1–5 percent; other journals may accept 60 or 70 percent of the manuscripts submitted. For some pay journals, almost all manuscripts are accepted! For journals published by the American Psychological Association, acceptance rates, along with other details, are located at http://www.apa.org/journals/statistics. Educational journal acceptance rates can be found at *Cabell's Educational Set* (8th ed., 2007–2008); go to http://www.cabells.com. Individual journals may indicate acceptance rates at their website.

3. *Relevance.* Each study included in the manuscript should be clearly related to the research problem. Typically, a search will turn up far more articles than can be used. In this case, include those that are credible, directly related, recent, and representative. Sometimes there are classic sources and seminal work that should be included.

As you read each study, it is useful to record your notes electronically or on paper or index cards. The advantage of using note cards is that they are easy to organize and reorganize to achieve the proper sequence that will be used as the basis for the review. Begin by reading the abstract of the article, if there is one, and the purpose or research problem. Next, read the results and decide if it is worthwhile to read the entire article more carefully and take notes on it. Begin your notes by writing out or copying and pasting the complete bibliographic citation. There are software products that can assist you to do this electronically, including Son of Citation Machine (http://citationmachine.net), Endnotes (http://endnote.com), and RefWorks (http://www.refworks.com). The Citation Machine will convert reference information to APA, Modern Language Association (MLA), or *Chicago Manual of Style* formats. It is very easy to learn and work with, and it is ideal for short-term projects. Endnotes can be used to search databases, organize references, and format bibliography information in APA or other formats. RefWorks is an online research management, writing, and collaboration tool designed to help researchers gather, manage, and store information, as well as generate citations and bibliographies. RefWorks requires up to an hour or so to learn, but it has excellent capabilities and is especially valuable for long-term projects like dissertations.

Whether you take notes electronically or on paper, it is helpful to include essential information in "shorthand" to allow you to capture much about the study in a small space. That would include the purpose, variables, design (e.g., E for experimental, NE for nonexperimental), results, and conclusions. You should also record interesting and insightful quotations, weaknesses or limitations in the methodology, analysis of the data and conclusions, and how the study is related to your research problem. Make reference to quotations (but don't use many in the written report). Also, devise and use a system for judging the overall credibility and relevance of the study. If you find it to be closely related and highly credible, you could rate the source as an A, somewhat related and credible as a B, and so forth. Codes can also be developed to indicate the major focus of the study by topic. For example, in reviewing studies on student engagement, you may find that some studies examine the effect of engagement on student achievement, others focus on strategies to improve student engagement, and still others emphasize different approaches to student engagement, depending on the types of students.

Using the skills you have learned about evaluating and analyzing sources, test your understanding by Abstracting in a real article. Go to MyEducationLab for Research at www.myeducationlab.com and click the topic "Reviewing the Literature." Then, select and complete the Building Research Skills exercise titled "Abstracting a Quantitative Article."

INTERNET SEARCHES

Strengths and Weaknesses of the Internet for Educational Research

Because the Internet is a worldwide network of interconnected computers, the amount of information at your fingertips is unprecedented. The challenge is to sift through a plethora of websites to find high-quality information. A careful consideration of the Internet's strengths and weaknesses will help you determine when and how to search it for a specific topic. The Internet is particularly good at delivering current and niche information. On the other hand, it is not an exhaustive source for searching educational literature. It is not organized with the educational researcher in mind and has not been reviewed for accuracy or quality.

With the ERIC database, you can search through the contents of more than 800 education journals dating back to 1966, all at the same time. In comparison, when searching the Internet for education journals, you must find each journal's website and then browse through its archives. Although most education journals now have their current issues available online, only some have an archive that extends farther than the previous five years.

Every item in the ERIC database has been assigned a series of subject headings. The consistency and quality of these subject headings allow you to retrieve specific information from the database. The Internet does not have such a system of controlled vocabulary. There is no thesaurus to consult to find out what the best search terms are. For example, if you were looking for educational research about teenagers, the search would be conducted using a number of different terms, such as *teens, adolescents,* or *high school* and *middle school students.*

Everything that you find in ERIC has been through some type of review process. Many journals in ERIC have an editorial staff of experts who judge the quality of the submissions. This does not mean that everything in ERIC is of high quality, but the overall quality will be better than what is available from the Internet. Anyone can publish a webpage. Although there is an appealing democratic beauty to the Internet, it is crucial to evaluate the quality of Internet sources.

Even though ERIC offers a more comprehensive, better-organized, and mostly peer-reviewed set of information about educational research, the Internet does have advantages. If a journal has an online version, you will be able to browse the most recent issues. Also, online journals will often contain the full text of each article, whereas ERIC entries are often limited to abstracts. ERIC covers educational research and issues in the United States very well; the Internet offers access to educational research from other countries. You will also find useful information on the Internet beyond journal articles and research reports, such as statistics, email links to experts, governmental information, datasets, and discussion forums.

Fortunately, you are not limited in your research to either the Internet or journal indexes like ERIC. In framing your research question, think about the type of information that each source might offer. This will help with your searches in each source. For example, you would certainly want to know what the research on your topic has been for the past 10 years as well as the past months. This will help you capture a well-rounded and diverse portrait for your topic.

Internet Search Strategies

The research strategies that have been discussed for ERIC are also relevant for Internet searches. Before you start typing words into the first search engine that comes along, it is important to have a focused search strategy with a number of key terms and subject headings. Based on that search strategy, choose from an assortment of secondary finding tools including subject directories and search engines. Once you have identified appropriate Internet search tools, pay attention to the various search options that each one offers and construct your computer search accordingly. Finally, evaluate the sources that you find for their quality and relevance to your research question.

Each Internet search company (like Yahoo! or Google) compiles its own database of Internet sites. When you "search the Internet," you are really searching these databases. That is, your search does not go to the Web and look at every page in existence. In choosing an Internet search tool, you want to peer beyond the search screen and get some idea of the quality, content, organization, and scope of the data behind the scenes. The three primary types of Internet search utilities are *subject directories*, *search engines*, and *metasearch engines*. Understanding the differences between them will improve your Internet search considerably.

Subject directories: browse by topic

Subject Directories   Internet **subject directories** are the Yellow Pages of the Internet where you are able to browse through lists of Internet resources by topic. Typically, each topic is located within a hierarchy of subjects. For example, in a subject directory there may be a choice for *education*, then numerous choices under that subject like *universities*, *K–12*, *government*, *history*, and so on. Examples of subject directories include Yahoo!, WWW Virtual Library, and the Librarians' Index to the Internet. The advantage of subject directories is that the content has been reviewed and organized by a human. Subject directories rely on teams of editors who have knowledge of specific disciplines. Thus, under each category, you will find a high degree of relevance and quality. Subject directories are often the quickest way to assemble a manageable list of Internet resources for a topic. Here are some research questions that would be especially good for a subject directory:

> Where can I find a list of educational associations?
> Where can I find the department of education from each state?
> Where can I find a list of online education journals?

Although subject directories are well organized, they are much smaller than the average search engine. Some subject directories have partnered with search engines in order to increase their coverage. For example, if you use the search box in Yahoo!, there will be options to run the same search in any number of search engines. The search function of a subject directory is most useful when you are not sure what category to choose for a particular subject. For example, in Yahoo! it is somewhat difficult to find Montessori education, especially if you choose the education category *K–12*. If you search Yahoo! for *Montessori education*, you will find that it is listed in the education category of *Theory and Methods*.

Search engines: search a database

Search Engines   **Search engines** are large searchable databases of webpages. Whereas subject directories are assembled and organized by human editors, search engines are compiled in an automated fashion. Each search engine uses a *spider* or *robot* that trolls through the Web from hyperlink to hyperlink, capturing information from each page that it visits. Therefore, the content of each search engine is dependent on the characteristics of its spider:

- How many pages has it visited?
- How often does it visit each page?
- When it visits, how much of the webpage does it record?

In terms of "freshness," the addition of new pages or modifications to existing pages can take several months to appear in various search engines. Especially interesting is that there is no consistent amount of overlap between search engines. This means that the Internet researcher is wise to try several search engines.

Despite their limitations, search engines index hundreds of millions of webpages. They offer a quick way to search for specific words that may appear in webpages. Here are some research questions that would be especially appropriate for a search engine:

> Are there any webpages that cover standardized testing in the state of California?
> Are there any webpages that deal with John Dewey's *Democracy in Education*?
> Are there any webpages with a biography of Paulo Freire?

In searching through a large set of data like a search engine, there are a number of strategies to keep in mind. One is the use of boolean connectors. Note that in all of the examples above, you would want to combine two or more concepts for an effective search. Your Internet search can be more effective if you pay attention to search language, special search features, and the most relevant search results.

There is no standard search language that is consistent across all search engines. Some search engines understand logical connectors like *and*, whereas others insist that you use a + before each word if you wish to limit your results to combined terms. Despite the lack of standards, there are several features that are common to most search engines. For example, even though some engines use *and*, whereas others look for +, the feature of combining more than one idea into a single search is available across all search engines. One of the best places to find information about each engine's search language is its online help page. Even seasoned Internet searchers need to revisit the help pages of their favorite search engine periodically.

Search engines continue to make advances in the area of special search features. You will find these on the "advanced search" options within most search engines. Special search features help you construct very complex searches by selecting various options from a menu that give you the ability to limit your search by language, date, location, and medium (such as audio or images). For example, in Yahoo!, from the search page click on Options and then Advanced Search. In Google you will want to use Google Advanced Search and Google Scholar.

Google's searching tips are available at http://www.googleguide.com/. This site offers many tips to search more effectively and a guide that can be printed out from a PDF file (http://www.googleguide.com/print_gg.html). There is also a "cheat sheet," at http://www.googleguide.com/cheatsheet.html, that offers examples for quick searching.

Relevancy   In addition to search options, it is helpful to be familiar with the retrieval algorithms of various search engines. Retrieval algorithms determine both how many pages each search retrieves and how the results of each search are ordered. For example, if you were searching for *cooperative learning*, the webpages that appear at the top of your search results should be the most relevant. Perhaps these pages have both words as part of their title, whereas the webpages that appear at the very end of your search results might simply have the word *cooperative* somewhere in their text. If your results start to look less and less relevant, don't keep looking through the same list. Move on to a new search or a new search engine.

Metasearch Engines   Metasearch engines submit your search to multiple search engines at the same time. Examples of metasearch engines include Dogpile and Metacrawler. Metasearch engines can be especially useful because studies have shown that each search engine includes pages that others do not. On the other hand, no single metasearch engine includes all of the major search engines. Also, you cannot take advantage of the specific search language or features that are native to each search engine. For this reason, it is best to use search engines for your complex Internet searching and rely on metasearch engines for searches that are very simple, involving one or two words. With metasearch engines it is especially important to pay attention to relevancy, because you have less control over how each search engine interprets your metasearch query.

Metasearch engines: search several databases

The line between search engine and search directory is often difficult to discern. Advanced search technology that makes it easier to find the information you need can mask the type of tool that you are using. In search engines, there will often be an associated directory listing. For example, when you use Google, your search will also be matched against the Open Directory project for categories that may be relevant to your search. Likewise in Yahoo!: If there are no matches in their directory, your search will get kicked over to a subset of Google's database.

Table 4.1 lists several subject directories and search engines that you will find useful in using the Internet to find educational research and other information on contemporary educational issues. Search Engine Showdown (http://www.searchengineshowdown.com) and Engine Watch (http://www.searchenginewatch.com) for the latest information about search directories, search engines, and metasearch engines. The University of California at Berkeley maintains an excellent website comparing features of different search engines and directories (http://www.Lib.berkeley.edu/TeachingLib/Guides/Internet/).

Scholarly Communication Strategies for Reviewing the Literature

Perhaps the most revolutionary aspect of the Internet is its ability to connect people with shared interests. This is especially powerful in highly technical and specific areas of study where geographical boundaries might otherwise hinder communication between

In this chapter you have been exposed to many tools for conducting a literature search, as well as examples and activities using existing literature. Now practice conducting a literature review on something of particular interest to you. Go to MyEducationLab for Research at www.myeducationlab.com. Click on the topic "Reviewing the Literature" and then select the Activities and Applications activity titled "Conduct a Literature Search on a Topic of Your Choice."

TABLE 4.1 Internet Search Tools

Subject Directories

About	http://about.com
Complete Planet	http://aip.completeplanet.com
Google Directory	http://google.dir.com
Infomine	http://www.infomine.ucr.edu
Internet Public Library	http://www.ipl.org
KidsClick!	http://kidsclick.org
Librarians' Internet Index	http://lii.org
Link Library	http://www.eduplace.com/linklibrary/
WWW Virtual Library	http://vlib.org

Education Subject Directories

Education Index	http://www.educationindex.net
Educator's Reference Desk	http://www.eduref.org

Search Engines

AlltheWeb	http://www.alltheweb.com
AltaVista	http://www.altavista.com
Ask	http://www.ask.com
Google	http://www.google.com
Lycos	http://www.lycos.com
MSN Search	http://search.msn.com
Yahoo!	http://www.yahoo.com

Metasearch Engines

Clusty	http://clusty.com
Dogpile	http://www.dogpile.com
Metacrawler	http://www.metacrawler.com
Search.com	http://www.search.com
SurfWax	http://www.surfwax.com
Vivisimo	http://vivisimo.com

a limited number of experts. For example, it might be hard to find a group of scholars in any one location who were all interested in the sociology of education. Through the Internet, however, such groups are able to form and discuss various issues specific to their field of study. GENIUS (Global Expertise Network for Industry, Universities, and Scholars) is a database that allows users to identify individuals working on a similar topic. Through the use of email, mailing lists, newsgroups, blogging, social networking, and conferencing, educational researchers have ready access to their peers and do not need to be isolated by location.

Email Email can be an especially valuable tool in conducting research. The speed and ease of email communication allow you to find resources and experts. Through email, it is possible to easily contact researchers, librarians, or institutions for guidance on a specific research question and relevant literature. Email is also an excellent way to collaborate with colleagues on works in progress by sharing ideas, drafts, and files. You can locate experts on your topic by using Ask an Expert or the Directory of Educational Researchers, and by searching university departments and schools of education that list faculty members and their research interests. Simply type in the name of the college or university in a search engine, go to the appropriate school or department, and peruse the list of faculty, which will include email addresses.

Newsgroups, Email Discussion Groups, and Listservs The Internet has thousands of newsgroups, mailing lists, and listservs that cover every conceivable area of interest. For example, there is a mailing list called arlist-l that is solely dedicated to the discussion of action research. Most Internet browsers, such as Netscape and Microsoft Internet Explorer, include a *news reader*, which allows you to read and post messages about various subjects to a newsgroup. A discussion group is similar to a newsgroup, except that the messages are transmitted as email and are therefore available only to individuals who have subscribed to the mailing list. A listserv (registered trademark of Lsoft.com) is a specific type of software for managing email lists.

There are many newsgroups and discussion groups that are very active in providing scholarly content and commentary. Through them, researchers can identify new viewpoints and new strategies for research identified by others with similar interests. They are an excellent way to stay current in your area of interest. The ERIC Educational Listserv Archive at http://ericir.syr.edu/Virtual/Listserv_Archives provides an excellent menu of high-quality educational mailing lists as well as a searchable archive of previous discussions.

Education Websites

There are a number of education websites that contain excellent information for educational researchers. Many of these are worth visiting.

Associations and University Webpages All large professional associations and universities have a substantial Web presence. At each of these sites you can find useful information, such as lists of faculty, publications, resolutions, and links to other websites. By visiting these pages, you not only gain knowledge of educational research but also get a feel for the culture and activity of each organization.

Two national associations, the American Educational Studies Association at http://www3.uakron.edu/aesa/ and the American Education Research Association (AERA) at http://www.aera.net, provide valuable information for the educational researcher. AERA (http://www.aera.net) is the leading national association for educational research. It is a large, diverse group of professors, school professionals, and students. There are 12 divisions within AERA. Each division focuses on broad substantive or professional interests, ranging from administration and curriculum to teacher education and education policy and politics. There are also nearly 200 small Special Interest Groups (SIGs) in more specific areas. Membership in either a division or a SIG facilitates communication among researchers with similar interests.

Table 4.2 describes several education associations and organizations. One that matches your interests can be very helpful. Students are typically given steep discounts for membership.

Institute of Education Sciences (IES) The IES is a particularly noteworthy part of the U.S. Department of Education for researchers. IES maintains a leadership role in the field of educational research by conducting, collecting, and distributing research studies and statistics. The IES home page website includes current news on educational research, grant opportunities, statistics, and publications. It publishes the *Research e-News*, an electronic newsletter that summarizes ongoing IES programs. IES hosts four centers:

- National Centers for Education Research (NCER)
- National Center for Education Statistics (NCES)
- National Center for Education Evaluation and Regional Assistance (NCEE)
- National Center for Special Education Research (NCSER).

The Regional Educational Laboratory Program (REL), which is sponsored by IES, consists of a network of 12 *laboratories* that serve the educational needs of a designated region by providing access to high-quality, scientifically valid education research through applied research and development projects, studies, and other related technical assistance activities. The network of Regional Laboratories (see Table 4.3) works to ensure that those involved in educational

TABLE 4.2 Examples of Education Associations and Organizations

Association/Organization	Description
American Association for Health, Physical Education, Recreation, and Dance Research Consortium (http://www.aahperd.org/research)	Purpose is to further and promote research in health education, physical education, dance, athletics, exercise, and recreation.
American Association of School Administrators (http://www.aasa.org)	Focuses on improving the condition of children and youth, preparing schools and school systems for the twenty-first century, connecting schools and communities, and enhancing the quality and effectiveness of school leaders.
American Educational Research Association (http://www.aera.net)	Concerned with improving the educational process by encouraging scholarly inquiry related to education and by promoting the dissemination and practical application of research results.
American Federation of Teachers, Research Department (http://www.aft.org/research)	Features research-oriented publications such as salary surveys, legislative updates, newsletters, histories, research reports, position papers, and example forms.
Association for Supervision and Curriculum Development (http://www.ascd.org)	Includes everything from full-text articles published in *Educational Leadership* to descriptions of every ASCD professional institute. Also features new initiatives and programs, new distance learning opportunities at PD Online, and interactive forums.
Center for Data-Driven Reform (http://www.bestevidence.org)	Distills evidence from several different research groups on promising practices and interventions in education.
International Reading Association (http://www.reading.org)	Seeks to promote high levels of literacy for all by improving the quality of reading instruction through studying reading processes and teaching techniques; serving as a clearinghouse for the dissemination of reading research through conferences, journals, and other publications; and actively encouraging the lifetime reading habit.
National Association for the Education of Young Children (http://www.naeyc.org)	Primary goals are improving professional practice and working conditions in early childhood education and building public understanding and support for high-quality early childhood programs.
National Association of Elementary School Principals (http://www.naesp.org)	Dedicated to ensuring that all children get the best education possible by serving the professional interests of elementary and middle school principals and promoting the highest professional standards.
National Association of Secondary School Principals (http://www.nassp.org)	Seeks to be at the forefront in establishing standards for exemplary schools and leaders by fostering a greater understanding of the global marketplace, the influence of technology, and the effects of the Information Age on teaching and learning.
National Council of Teachers of English (http://www.ncte.org)	Provides a forum for the profession, an array of opportunities for teachers to continue their professional growth throughout their careers, and a framework for cooperation to deal with issues that affect the teaching of English.
National Education Association (http://www.nea.org)	America's oldest and largest organization committed to advancing the cause of public education. Works on the local, state, and national levels to influence and set education policy.
National Middle School Association (http://www.nmsa.org)	The only educational association exclusively devoted to improving the educational experiences of young adolescents.
National Science Teachers Association (http://www.nsta.org)	Committed to promoting excellence and innovation in science teaching and learning for all.
Phi Delta Kappa International, Inc. (http://www.pdkintl.org)	Promotes quality education, with particular emphasis on publicly supported education, as essential to the development and maintenance of a democratic way of life.

TABLE 4.3 Regional Educational Laboratories

Laboratory	States	Mission
Appalachia (http://www.RELAppalachia.org)	Kentucky, Tennessee, Virginia, West Virginia	REL Appalachia's mission is to provide high-quality research, analysis, and technical assistance that help state and local education systems in the region achieve higher educational standards and close the achievement gap.
Central (http://mcrel.org/)	Colorado, Kansas, Missouri, Nebraska, North Dakota, South Dakota, Wyoming	Making a difference in the quality of education and learning for all through excellence in applied research, product development, and service.
Mid-Atlantic (http://info@relmid-atlantic.org)	Delaware, Maryland, New Jersey, Pennsylvania, Washington DC	REL Mid-Atlantic is a collaboration of five partners working together to meet the research needs of educational leaders and policy makers in the region.
Midwest (http://www.learningpt.org)	Illinois, Indiana, Iowa, Michigan, Minnesota, Ohio, Wisconsin	Learning Point Associates believes that all learners deserve the opportunity to reach their full potential. For this reason, they focus on making the education system work for everyone. They tackle the most problematic issues in education by combining research, evaluation, and hands-on support to make a lasting impact. Clients turn to them for high-quality information and tested strategies so that they can replicate what works and change what doesn't.
Northwest (http://www.nwrel.org)	Alaska, Idaho, Montana, Oregon, Washington	The mission of the Northwest Regional Educational Laboratory (NWREL) is to improve learning by building capacity in schools, families, and communities through applied research and development.
Pacific (http://www.prel.org)	American Samoa, Federated States of Micronesia, Guam, Hawaii, North Mariana Islands, Republic of the Marshall Islands, Republic of Palau	PREL serves the educational community with quality programs, services, and products developed to promote educational excellence. It works throughout school systems, from classroom to administration, and collaborates routinely with governments, communities, and businesses. Above all, it specializes in multicultural and multilingual environments.
Southeast (http://www.serve.org)	Alabama, Florida, Georgia, Mississippi, North Carolina, South Carolina	SERVE is a university-based research, development, dissemination, evaluation, and technical assistance center. Its mission is to support and promote teaching and learning excellence in the pre-kindergarten to grade 12 education community.
Northeast and Islands (http://www.edc.org)	Connecticut, Maine, Massachusetts, New Hampshire, New York, Puerto Rico, Rhode Island, Vermont, Virgin Islands	Education Development Center, Inc., is an international nonprofit organization with more than 325 projects dedicated to enhancing learning, promoting health, and fostering a deeper understanding of the world.
Southwest (http://www.edvanceresearch.com)	Arkansas, Louisiana, New Mexico, Oklahoma, Texas	Southwest's mission is to be a leader in the advancement of rigorous education research. The laboratory is dedicated to improving student achievement by supporting educational organizations in learning about evidence-based practices and using that information to improve their work and results.
West (http://www.wested.org)	Arizona, California, Nevada, Utah	Success for every learner is the goal at WestEd. A nonprofit research, development, and service agency, WestEd enhances and increases education and human development within schools, families, and communities.

improvement at the local, state, and regional levels have access to the best available educational research and information.

IES also sponsors the What Works Clearinghouse (WWC). The WWC (http://ies.ed.gov/ncee/wwc) is a program that is charged with producing user-friendly practice guides for educators with research-based recommendations. It assesses the rigor of research evidence on the effectiveness of interventions that are designed to improve student learning and keeps a registry of evaluation researchers to assist schools in designing and carrying out rigorous studies. The WWC reports are excellent for researchers because of the review process of studies on particular interventions, such as a reading or mathematics curriculum. It is sobering, though, that only a small percentage of the studies reviewed are graded sufficiently positive to be evaluated as credible evidence.

State Government Sites   All state governments and state departments of education have websites. These are ideal for learning about current programs and initiatives, as well as publications and reports. They include contact information for individuals in different areas of expertise. A comprehensive listing of state education agencies can be found at http://www.ed.gov/Programs/bastmp/SEA.htm.

Online Journals, Reviews, and Abstracts   The following three websites maintain extensive listings of electronic journals in education. Many are categorized as scholarly, peer-reviewed, and full-text. Most university libraries also maintain institution-specific subscriptions to electronic journals. In addition to journal listings, Education Line hosts an archive of reports, conference papers, working papers, and preprints in the fields of education and training.

- Electronic Journals in the Field of Education: http://aera-cr.ed.asu.edu/links.html
- Education Journals and Newsletters: http://www.scre.ac.uk/is/webjournals.html
- Education-Line: http://www.leeds.ac.uk/educol/

Table 4.4 shows examples of research-oriented online education journals.

Two websites that index conference proceedings and other research reports are the Education Policy Analysis Archives at http://olam.ed.asu.edu/epaa and The Qualitative Report at http://www.nova.edu/ssss/QR.

Information obtained from the Internet can be an excellent complement to print research, but it can also be low in quality, even deceptive and misleading. Researchers using the Internet need to critically evaluate resources found there, just as they would evaluate information found in a library, government office, center report, or journal. Remember that in most cases there is no peer review of information. As a result, the quality of the information varies considerably. Some of it may be of high quality and credible; other information may be biased, presenting a particular point of view, or simply of low quality. Your evaluation of Internet material will be strengthened by asking the following questions:

- Who is the author or publisher of the information?
- What is the author's reputation and qualifications in the subject covered?
- Is the information objective or is there a noticeable bias?
- Are the facts or statistics verifiable?
- Is there a bibliography?
- Is the information current?

It is common when searching for contemporary topics to find websites of centers and nonprofit organizations. Many of these organizations have a clear agenda to promote, so it is advisable to understand these points of view in order to detect bias and opinion rather than a more balanced, scholarly perspective. The key to evaluating any type of research is to carefully read and analyze the content. It is also helpful to find a variety of sources so that you can compare and contrast them in order to get a fully informed view of any subject. If you are interested in learning more about evaluating sources on the Internet, see *Evaluating Web Sites for Educational Uses: Bibliography and Checklist* at http://www.unc.edu/cit/guides/irg-49.html.

As with all other research, it is important to document your Internet sources so that other researchers can visit the sites you have found. In addition to the author, title, publication date, and address, most citation formats encourage you to list the date that you accessed the site. Most

TABLE 4.4 Examples of Research-Oriented Online Education Journals

Title	Subject	Address
Alan Review	Young adult literature	http://scholar.lib.vt.edu/ejournals/ALAN/
American School and University	Educational administration	http://www.asumag.com
Community Updates	Newsletter on school reform	http://bcol01.ed.gov/CFAPPS/OIIA/communityupdate/page1.cfm
Education Next	School reform	http://www.educationnext.org/
Education Policy Analysis Archives	Research and policy	http://epaa.asu.edu/
Education Week	Current education news	http://www.edweek.com
Educational Theory	Educational theory	http://www.ed.uiuc.edu/EPS/Educational-Theory/
Educause Quarterly	Educational technology	http://www.educause.edu/pub/eq/eq.html
Effective Teaching	Higher education	http://cte.uncwil.edu/et/
Exploring Adult Literacy	Adult education	http://literacy.kent.edu/cra/
From Now On	Educational technology	http://www.fromnowon.org
IT Journal	Instructional technology	http://etext.virginia.edu/journals/itjournal/
Journal for Research in Mathematics Education	Educational research	http://www.nctm.org/jrme
Journal of Technology Education	Instructional technology	http://scholar.lib.vt.edu/ejournals/JTE/
Journal on Excellence in College Teaching	Higher education	http://ject.lib.muohio.edu/
OERI Bulletin	Educational research	http://www.ed.gov/bulletin/
Rethinking Schools	Urban education	http://www.rethinkingschools.org/
The Online Chronicle of Distance Education and Communication	Distance education	http://www.fcae.nova.edu/disted/
T.H.E. Journal	Instructional technology	http://www.thejournal.com/
TESL-EJ	Teaching English as a second language	http://www-writing.berkeley.edu/TESL-EJ/

educational research is documented in APA format (see Excerpt 4.6). You can find the APA's official guidelines for citing electronic sources in the *APA Style Guide to Electronic References* (2007) and on the APA Web page at http://www.apastyle.org/elecref.html.

WRITING A REVIEW OF LITERATURE

The nature of the written review of literature will depend on whether the study is quantitative, qualitative, or mixed method. Quantitative reviews are often detailed and found in the beginning sections of articles. Qualitative reviews tend to be brief in the beginning but more integrated

EXCERPT 4.6 APA Citation of an Online Journal Article

VandenBos, G., Knapp, S., & Doe, J. (2001). Role of reference elements in the selection of resources by psychology undergraduates. *Journal of Bibliographic Research, 5,* 117–123. Retrieved October 13, 2001, from http://jbr.org/articles.html

EXCERPT 4.7 Relating Prior Research to Current Study

It would seem, however, that studies on the relationship between families and Black college students are more limited. The present study was designed to examine this gap in the literature on Blacks in higher education. The purpose of this study was to explore the role of family in the life of African American college students. (p. 494)

Source: From Herndon, M. K., & Hirt, J. B. (2004). Black students and their families: What leads to success in college. *Journal of Black Studies, 34*(4), 489–513.

throughout the complete article. Mixed method study reviews of literature tend to be consistent with the dominant approach (quantitative or qualitative).

Quantitative Reviews of Literature

The review of the literature can be organized in several ways, but the most common approach is to group studies that investigate similar topics or subtopics. This can be done more easily if you coded the studies as you read them. Index cards about articles with one code can be put in one pile, those with another code in a second pile, and so forth. The cards or articles then can be put in order, usually with articles related to the problem in a more general way first and those more specifically related to the problem last. Within each article topic, it may be possible to organize the studies by date, with the most recent studies last. This arrangement provides a sense of the development of the research over time. Studies that are only generally related to the research problem should be summarized briefly. If several studies have similar results, they should be grouped and their findings summarized as such—for example, "Several studies found that teachers' expectations are related to student achievement (Jones, 1978; Smith, 1984; Watson, 1982)."

For a few studies, specifically those that are closely related to the problem, the review should include three elements: a *summary* of the study, an *analysis* of the study, and a statement of how the study *relates* to the research problem (see Excerpt 4.7). The review should not contain long quotations or use the same wording in discussing different studies. Quotations, in general, should be used sparingly and only when a special or critical meaning cannot be indicated using your own words. You should use short sentences, as well as transitional sentences, to provide a logical progression of ideas and sections.

Some reviews are organized in alternative ways, depending on the type of study and the topic researched. For instance, reviews may be organized by (a) variables, (b) treatments, (c) research designs and methods, (d) different results from investigations of the same problem, or (e) any combination of these (see Excerpt 4.8). A study that is better designed than the previous research emphasizes methodological criticism (see Excerpt 4.9).

The length of the review depends on the type of study, its purpose (e.g., class paper, thesis or dissertation, manuscript for publication), and the topic. The literature review for an exploratory study may not be very long, whereas that in a thesis or dissertation may be 30 or 40 typed pages. A lengthy review requires structuring with major and minor headings and periodic summaries. Excerpt 4.10 is an example of a quantitative research literature review.

EXCERPT 4.8 Organizing Previous Studies by Similar Conclusions

Despite more than 30 years of extant scholarship, . . . the myth remains that the ideal leader for most schools conforms to a White, masculine stereotype, especially at the secondary level (Brunner & Peyton-Caire, 2000; Murtadha & Larson, 1999; Shakeshaft, 1989). The educational literature offers limited knowledge construction based on data gathered from African American women principals (Alston, 2000; K. W. Collins & Lightsey, 2001; Henry, 2001; Lo-motey, 1989). (p. 346)

Source: From Bloom, C. M., & Erlandson, D. A. (2003). African American women principals in urban schools: Realities, (re)constructions, and resolutions. *Educational Administration Quarterly, 39*(3), 339–369.

EXCERPT 4.9 Methodological Criticism

Although results supported the effectiveness of cooperative learning, school favorableness toward cooperative learning might have created a selection bias that threatened the validity of the results. Specifically, schools whose faculty agreed to implement the structured model of cooperative leaning were included in the treatment group. Despite this weakness, Stevens and Slavin (1995) contended that cooperative learning positively affected academic achievement. (p. 233)

Source: From Lopata, C., Miller, K. A., & Miller, R. H. (2003). Survey of actual and preferred use of cooperative learning among exemplar teachers. *Journal of Educational Research, 96*(4), 232–239.

EXCERPT 4.10 Quantitative Research Literature Review

Often, African American and Hispanic parents do not attend school functions. Consequently, there is a widely held belief among educators in poor and urban schools that those parents do not care about their children's education (Delpit, 1995; Flores, Tefft-Cousin, & Diaz, 1991; Poplin & Weeres, 1992; Thompson, 2002). Moreover, in its Schools and Staffing Surveys for 1990–1991 and 1993–1994, *The Digest of Education Statistics* (U.S. Department of Education, 1999) reported that lack of parent involvement was a great concern for many public school teachers.

Summary

Some researchers have found that there is a mismatch between teachers' perceptions of parent and guardian involvement and reality (Flores et al., 1991; Poplin & Weeres, 1992). For example, Thompson (2002) conducted a study of the K–12 schooling experiences of nearly 300 African American students in a southern California region that had many underperforming schools. Although there was a widespread assumption among educators in the region that the parents and guardians of most children of color were apathetic about their children's formal education, Thompson found that when the African American students in her study were asked to rate the level of their parents' involvement, the majority of students rated it as excellent or good. The students' ratings were compared later with data from African American parents in the same region. The overwhelming majority of the parents also rated their involvement in their children's education as excellent or good (Thompson, 2003). Furthermore, in their examination of the National Education Longitudinal Study data, Cook and Ludwig (1998) found that African American parents were as involved in their children's education as were White parents from similar socioeconomic backgrounds. These findings are similar to those of other researchers who found that educators are not always the most reliable judges of parent involvement (Flores et al., 1991; Poplin & Weeres, 1992).

Analysis

Furthermore, some researchers have specifically described the positive correlation between parent involvement and the schooling experiences of African American students. . . . Floyd (1995) examined variables that contributed to the academic success of a group of lower socioeconomic status (SES) African American high school students. She found that good parental relationships or positive relationships with other adults played an important role in the students' academic success. Wilson and Allen (1987) studied African American adults to identify links between educational attainment and family practices. They concluded that parents play a significant role in their children's education. Clark (1983) studied the home environments of high- and low-achieving poor African American high school seniors and found that parents of high achievers used regular routines to assist their children academically. Conversely, the parents of low achievers were so overwhelmed by adversity that they made few positive contributions to their children's formal schooling. . . .

A logical first step is for educators to begin to listen to the voices of parents in order to hear their concerns. In an effort to begin this discussion, I sought to provide educators with feedback from African American parents about their children's schooling experiences. In this study, I examined variables that predict how African American parents and guardians of school-aged children rate their children's elementary and secondary school teachers, and the public school system as a whole. (pp. 278–279)

Related to current study

Source: From Thompson, G. L. (2003). Predicting African American parents' and guardians' satisfaction with teachers and public schools. *Journal of Educational Research, 96*(5), 277–285, (2003) Reprinted with permission of the Helen Dwight Reid Educational Foundation. Published by Heldref Publication, 1319 Eighteenth St., NW, Washington, DC 20036-1802.

EXCERPT 4.11 Providing a Conceptual Framework and Relating to Current Research

Building on the work of Weedon (1987), Peirce (1995) developed a concept of *social identity* . . . as 'the conscious and unconscious thoughts and emotions of the individual, her sense of herself and her ways of understanding her relation to the world' (p. 32, quoted in Peirce, 1995). In opposition to the Western notion of identity as centered, singular, and unitary, [social identity] takes on three characteristics. . . . This article uses Peirce's (1995) conception of social identity as a means to identify the unique qualities that the foreign-born ESL teacher brings to instruction and curriculum. (pp. 126–128)

Source: From Case, R. E. (2004). Forging ahead into new social networks and looking back to past social identities: A case study of a foreign-born English as a second language teacher in the United States. *Urban Education, 39*(2), 125–148.

Qualitative Reviews of Literature

Similar to a review of quantitative research literature, a review of literature in qualitative research is used to document the importance of the topic. Otherwise, the literature is used differently in qualitative research. Rather than provide a detailed analysis of the literature prior to the methods section, the review is a preliminary one. A qualitative review simply introduces the purpose of the study and the initial broad questions that will be reformulated during data collection. Qualitative researchers usually provide the conceptual framework that they began with, as well (see Excerpt 4.11).

Unlike a quantitative researcher, a qualitative researcher conducts a continuing literature search during data collection and analysis. This approach to reviewing the literature merely reflects the discovery orientation typical of qualitative research. A continuing literature review is done because the exact research focus and questions evolve as the research progresses. Using this approach, the researcher can better understand what he or she is actually observing and hearing. The literature may provide meaningful analogies, a scholarly language to synthesize descriptions, or additional conceptual frameworks to better organize the findings. As with quantitative research, the literature review in qualitative research is integrated with the discussion and conclusion sections of the article or report. At this point, additional new literature may be introduced to better explain and interpret the findings. Thus, by the completion of a study, the researchers have done an extensive literature review (see Excerpt 4.12).

The literature review in a qualitative study is (a) presented as separate discussion and/or (b) integrated within the text. Seldom is an entire section of a journal article or an entire chapter in a report called a "Literature Review." The literature is found in the introduction and the more detailed discussion is located in the concluding interpretations of the study. Given the format required by some journals, a "Literature Review" header may be provided for readers.

Mixed Method Reviews of Literature

In mixed method studies the review of literature is typically presented in a single section, rather than having separate sections for qualitative and quantitative reviews. For this reason, these reviews tend to resemble more closely what is found in quantitative research. However, there is less standardization with mixed method studies, so a variety of approaches can be found. It is best, in our view, if the literature review is consistent with the logic of the design. For example, in an explanatory design, the review would initially look like what is typical for quantitative literature. An explanatory study would probably have a review that resembles what is written for qualitative research. It is very helpful if you are able to find other mixed method studies on your topic.

META-ANALYSIS LITERATURE REVIEWS

Meta-analysis: statistical summary of many studies

Our discussion of reviewing literature would not be complete without some mention of meta-analysis. Unlike a narrative analysis and summary of studies, a **meta-analysis** uses statistical techniques to provide an overall average result, based on the results of prior studies that have been

EXCERPT 4.12   Qualitative Research Literature Review

Background

The interrelationships among gender, higher education, and inequality in the workplace have been examined from diverse theoretical perspectives and through a number of different disciplines. Probably the most influential idea to account for women college students' lower career aspirations and their resignation to accepting lower-paying, less prestigious careers has been that institutions of higher education discourage or discriminate against women (Astin 1978; Dweck et al. 1978; Hall and Sandler 1982; Holmstrom and Holmstrom 1974; Sadker and Sadker 1994; Stacey et al. 1974; Sternglanz, and Lyber-Beck 1977). . . . . — **Summary**

Holland and Eisenhart's [1990] long-term study of women students on two southern campuses moves away from social reproduction theory to a theory of "cultural production." Their approach allows us to see students as active agents who construct "systems of meaning" through which they relate to and act within their world. The most important construction that Holland and Eisenhart uncover in their study is a "culture of romance" that privileges males and is generated within student peer groups. Some women students fall into the "culture of romance" as they become discouraged in their studies. . . . — **Summary of major study**

The Holland and Eisenhart study provides rich material on women students' ideas about romance and marriage, but, curiously, it does not touch on students' ideas about motherhood or how these ideas might be related to students' decisions about their careers. By contrast, Anne Machung's (1989) study of Berkeley students, conducted at about the same time, indicates that senior women students planned to interrupt their careers for child rearing. Likewise our study reveals that a "culture of motherhood" rather than a "culture of romance" may lie behind women students' lower career aspirations. — **Analysis of second major study**

Granted, this difference between our findings and those of Holland and Eisenhart may be partly because of the different foci and methods of these two studies. The Holland and Eisenhart research focused only on women students, whereas our study compared women and men. This allows us to highlight those views of women students that stood out in strong contrast to those of men, in particular their contrasting views about the compatibility between their careers and their roles as parents. Another difference is that our study looked at students only over one academic year, whereas Holland and Eisenhart followed a group of women students over several years during and after college. This allowed them to document the women's lowering aspirations and their increasing involvement in romantic relationships over time, whereas our methods could not detect major shifts in students' interests and involvements. Yet we were able to uncover something that may have been missed in the Holland and Eisenhart study. Our study shows that a perceived incompatibility between motherhood and full-time careers is a central theme in students', especially women students', discussions of their futures. (pp. 68–70) — **Analysis and relationship to current research**

Source: From Stone, L., & McKee, N. P. (2000). Gendered futures: Student visions of career and family on a college campus. *Anthropology and Education Quarterly, 37*(1), 67–89.

independently conducted. It is a statistical synthesis of many studies of the same topic or problem, giving an overall pooled result. Meta-analysis is used widely in biomedical sciences, where it is possible to locate and summarize many experimental trials. In educational research meta-analysis is becoming more important, although in education it isn't possible to meet the same levels of specificity found in medical studies. Note in Excerpt 4.13 how the researchers differentiated their narrative review from a meta-analytic one.

It makes great sense from a scientific perspective to use meta-analysis as a way of showing whether many individual studies, when taken in the aggregate, suggest an overall pattern of effects by systematically combining the results of many studies. Typically, an overall *effect size* is calculated and reported. There is a result, then, that is statistical in nature. Indeed, this kind of study is often considered a primary source.

To conduct a good meta-analysis, it is necessary to develop and carefully apply criteria to guide the selection of studies. If there are excluded studies, a rationale for this action needs to be included. Sometimes a researcher will judge the credibility of the located studies and include

EXCERPT 4.13 Narrative Best-Evidence Synthesis Compared to Meta-Analysis Review of Literature

In this research synthesis, we sought to identify all high-quality research studies that analyzed implementation or reported outcomes of one-to-one initiatives from English-language journals and Web sites. We adopted a narrative, rather than meta-analytic approach to synthesizing findings, both because there were so few outcome studies and because the vast majority of studies reported on implementation processes that could better be summarized and synthesized using a narrative approach. In this section, we describe in detail our approach to identifying, selecting, and analyzing studies for the synthesis. (p. 331)

Source: From Penuel, W. R. (2006). Implementation and effects of one-to-one computing initiatives: A research synthesis. *Journal of Research on Technology in Education, 38*(3), 329–348.

EXCERPT 4.14 Meta-Analysis

Articles for this meta-analysis were identified using two methods. First, a computer literature search of PsycInfo and ERIC databases was conducted from 1980 to 2003. The descriptors included WM matched with dyslexia/reading disability/learning disability/LD. . . . The initial search yielded 75 studies . . . only 31 articles met the criteria for inclusion. . . . In the present meta-analysis 28 articles compared WM [Working Memory] performance of RD [Reading Disability] with that of skilled readers. . . . The 28 studies produced 208 effect sizes, for an average of 7 comparisons per study. The overall mean effect size across all studies was -0.81 (SD = 0.92). Based on Cohen's criteria, that is a large effect size that indicated that the overall mean performance of the RD group was almost one standard deviation below that of the normally achieving group. (pp. 37–38)

Source: From Swanson, H. L. (2005). Memory and learning disabilities: Historical perspective, current status, and future trends. *Thalamus, 23*(2), 30–44.

only those that meet strict requirements of quality. Other meta-analytic studies may include all the studies that were found. A key question is whether it makes sense to include *any* study that is poorly conducted. Would the addition of many poorly constructed studies have validity if the result was more positive than the studies by themselves? Because there are many different ways of identifying the studies that comprise a meta-analysis, as well as different approaches to combine them statistically, it is necessary to examine the methodology to ensure credibility. When well conducted, a meta-analysis can be very helpful and influential in summarizing many studies on the same problem to reach an overall conclusion.

A summary of a meta-analysis study is shown in Excerpt 4.14. We should also point out that there are methods for synthesizing qualitative studies as well. These are referred to as *qualitative metasynthesis* or *qualitative meta-analysis.*

STANDARDS OF ADEQUACY

The adequacy of a narrative literature review is judged by three criteria: the selection of the sources, summary and analysis of the literature, and the relevance of the literature to the current study.

Selection of Literature

1. Is the purpose of the review (preliminary or exhaustive) indicated?
2. Are the parameters of the review reasonable? Why were certain bodies of literature included in the search and others excluded?
3. Is primary literature emphasized in the review and secondary literature, if cited, used selectively?
4. Are most of the sources from reputable, refereed journals?
5. Are recent developments in the literature emphasized in the review?
6. Is the literature relevant to the problem?
7. Are complete bibliographic data provided for each source cited?

Summary and Analysis of Literature

1. Is the review organized by topics or ideas, not by author?
2. Is the review organized logically?
3. Are major studies discussed in detail and the actual findings cited?
4. Are minor studies with similar results or limitations summarized as a group?
5. Is there adequate analysis or critique of the methodologies of important studies so that the reader can determine the quality of previous research?
6. Are studies compared and contrasted and conflicting or inclusive results noted?
7. For some basic and applied studies and qualitative research, is the conceptual framework or theory that guides the study explained?

Relationship to Current Study

1. Does the summary provide an overall interpretation and understanding of prior research?
2. Does the review of major studies relate explicitly to the research problem and methods?
3. Do the methodological analyses provide a rationale for the design to follow?
4. Does the review of the literature help establish the significance of the research?

A literature review is not judged by its length or by the number of references it includes. Rather, it is judged in the context of the proposal or the completed study. The problem, the significance of the study, and the research problem all influence the type of literature review.

CHAPTER SUMMARY

This chapter summarized the reasons for conducting a literature review, the nature of the search process, literature reviews in quantitative and qualitative studies, Internet and Web resources, and meta-analysis. In summary:

1. Literature for review is taken from journals, reports, monographs, government documents, dissertations, and electronic resources.
2. Reviewing the literature enables the researcher to focus the problem, to select key terms, to establish a framework, to develop significance, to identify methodological limitations, and to suggest research hypotheses.
3. Steps in conducting a review of literature include selection of the topic and key terms, databases, and software, gathering documents, and identifying and evaluating each source.
4. Primary sources of original work are essential.
5. Secondary sources are found in reviews of research, yearbooks, handbooks, and professional books. They are useful in providing context, providing significance for the study, and identifying primary sources.
6. Reviews are organized by topic, based on an analysis and categorization of primary sources.
7. Sources are evaluated by three criteria—credibility, source reputation (e.g., refereed or nonrefereed journal), and relevance to the study.
8. In quantitative research, the review of literature includes a summary of minor studies as a group and analysis of major studies individually, proceeding from the most general topic to the most closely related topic.

9. In qualitative research, a preliminary literature review suggests the need for the study and the conceptual framework employed, but the literature search continues during data collection and analysis. Literature is presented in the introductory discussion and integrated within the text.
10. The strengths of using the Internet for educational research include access to full-text documents, the most current research, discussion forums, and information from around the world.
11. The Internet does not contain controlled vocabulary, consistent quality, or a significant archive for educational research.
12. The three primary types of Internet search tools are subject directories, search engines, and metasearch engines. Subject directories contain lists of websites organized by topic. Search engines are large searchable databases of websites. Metasearch engines simultaneously query multiple search engines.
13. Scholars and researchers are able to share information over the Internet through the use of email, mailing lists, newsgroups, and teleconferencing.
14. Accessing known locations on the Internet such as associations, newspapers, online journals, government pages, and statistical sites can lead the researcher to high-quality information.
15. National research centers and regional educational laboratories sponsored by the U.S. Department of Education are excellent resources for combining educational reasearch with practice.

APPLICATION PROBLEMS

1. Suppose that a supervisor wants to locate mathematics curriculum guidelines and evaluation studies of mathematics programs formulated under Title I of the Elementary and Secondary Education Act and those most recently done through Chapter 1. Which database and type of search would be most efficient?

2. Below is a problem statement and descriptors for each concept. The descriptors are listed in order of importance to a literature search.

   How do teacher-questioning techniques affect fourth-grade students' learning in social studies?

   A. questioning techniques
   B. questioning
   C. questioning behavior
   D. questions
   E. achievement
   F. skills
   G. recall
   H. social studies
   I. history
   J. upper elementary
   K. elementary education

   a. Direct a narrow search to obtain pertinent literature, using *and* to join the descriptors from A through K that most closely match the research question.

   b. Direct a more thorough search using *or* to join the different key terms for the same concept and using *and* to connect the descriptors A through K.

3. A reviewer has classified his or her relevant sources in the following manner:
   A. evaluations of behavior modification programs: effects on instructional approach, teacher questioning style
   B. descriptions of behavior modification programs and management implications
   C. evaluations of behavior modification programs and management implications
   D. theories of stimulus-response learning
   E. studies of operant conditioning on animals
      Organize these in order for a literature review on the problem of "evaluation of instruction, student behavior, and learning in a behavior modification program."

4. A researcher is interested in studying the resilience of high school students who are at risk of failure. Conduct an electronic search of possible sources on the Internet, using two different search engines. Compare the results from each search for relevance and credibility.

5. Identify four known locations on the Internet that correspond to your professional area of expertise (e.g., primary teacher, counselor, principal). List each one and summarize the nature of the information contained. What new information did you learn about at each of the sites?

6. Search the WWC for studies that investigate the effectiveness of different programs and curricula for improving reading skills. Determine the number of reviewed studies that were not included in the WWC summary, and identify the reasons for each study. Which reasons are most prevalent? Why?

ANSWERS TO APPLICATION PROBLEMS

1. Search *RIE* by type of document: curriculum guidelines and evaluation studies for Title I ESEA Act mathematics programs and by years desired. By using connecting identifiers with key terms, Chapter 1 (new terminology) can be located.

2. a. For a narrow search:
      A and E and H and J
   b. For a more thorough search:
      Search 1: (A or B) and (E or F) and (H or I) and J
      Search 2: (A or B) and (E or F) and (H or I) and (J or K)
      Search 3: (A or B or C or D) and (E or F or G) and (H or I) and J
      Search 4: (A or B or C or D) and (E or F or G) and (H or I) and (J or K)

3. The order of priority for presenting sources in a literature review is from the least related or most general to the most related literature. The sources would thus be organized as (d) theories, (e) studies on animal behavior, (b) program descriptions, (a) evaluations of instruction, and (c) evaluations of students.

4. (individual student response)

5. (individual student response)

6. (individual student response)

Designing Quantitative Research: Purpose, Validity, and Ethical Considerations

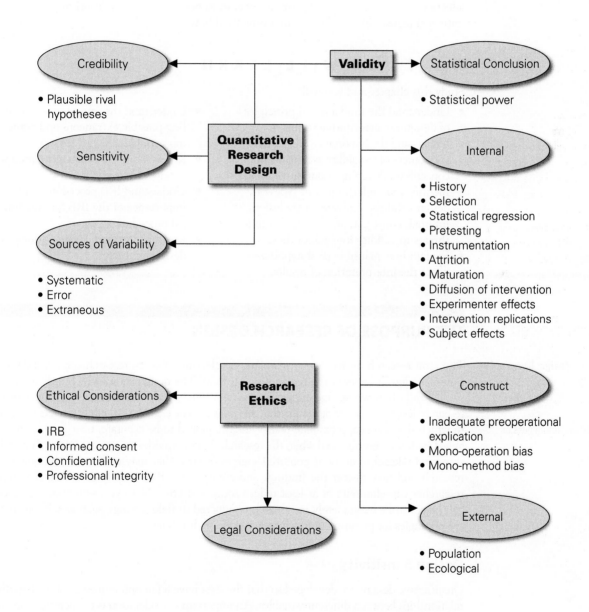

KEY TERMS

research design
credibility
sensitivity
variability
sources of variability
MAXMINCON
plausible rival hypotheses
statistical power
statistical conclusion
   validity
internal validity
history
selection
statistical regression

pretesting
instrumentation
attrition
maturation
diffusion of intervention
experimenter effects
intervention replications
subject effects
demand characteristics
construct validity
inadequate preoperational
   explication of constructs
mono-operation bias
mono-method bias

external validity
population external
   validity
ecological external validity
informed consent
assent
deception
anonymity
Institutional Review Board
   (IRB)
exempt
expedited
plagiarism

WHAT YOU WILL LEARN

Study this chapter and you will:

- Understand the fundamental principles of designing quantitative studies.
- Understand the importance of sensitivity and sources of variability as fundamental concepts for designing quantitative studies.
- Identify and understand four types of design validity—statistical conclusion, internal, construct, and external—and threats to validity for each of these.
- Explain how plausible rival hypotheses affect the interpretation of results.

- Understand the importance of controlling possible extraneous and confounding variables.
- Know about the ethics associated with conducting research.
- Understand IRB procedures and the importance of the IRB for ensuring ethical procedures.
- Know about legal considerations when designing studies.

THE PURPOSE OF RESEARCH DESIGN

Research design: blueprint for the study

The term **research design** refers to a plan for selecting subjects, research sites, and data collection procedures to answer the research question(s). The design shows which individuals will be studied and when, where, and under which circumstances they will be studied. The goal of a sound research design is to provide results that are judged to be *credible*. **Credibility** refers to the extent to which the results approximate reality and are judged to be accurate, trustworthy, and reasonable. Credibility is enhanced when the research design provides an opportunity to show relationships and takes into account potential sources of error that may undermine the quality of the research and may distort the findings and conclusions. By carefully designing the study, the researcher can eliminate or at least reduce sources of error. Not every potential source of error can be controlled completely in research conducted in field settings, such as schools, but there are principles for planning research to minimize such influences.

Credibility: truthfulness of results

Design Sensitivity

Quantitative designs are developed so that the data have a fair opportunity to show hypothesized relationships between different variables. An important consideration is to operationalize and use variables that can show these relationships. One way to think about this important feature is to examine the *sensitivity* of the variables as measured to show relationships. **Sensitivity** refers to the ability to detect differences or correlations between the variables. Some variables are insensitive, others very sensitive. Suppose a researcher is studying the relationship between teaching effectiveness and achievement. This is a reasonable research problem. From a sensitivity perspective, the

Sensitivity: ability to detect differences

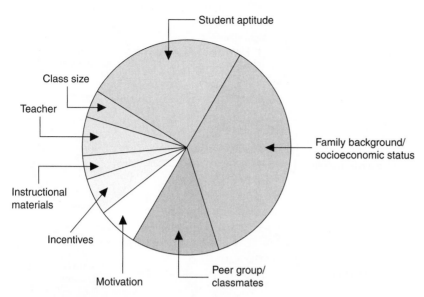

FIGURE 5.1 **Determinants of Achievement Variation**

goal is to operationalize these variables so that there is a good opportunity to show a relationship. On the face of it, these variables can and should be related. If the design calls for observations of teaching effectiveness and recording test scores at the end of the school year, sensitivity depends in part on the ability of these variables to be related. What potential exists to show a relationship?

One approach to determining this potential is to think about all the factors that contribute to scores obtained on each variable. This is illustrated in Figure 5.1, which shows how different factors influence the variability of a general measure of achievement. Clearly, the most important factor is student socioeconomic status—aptitude, background, and family. There are also many other factors that affect achievement, including teacher effectiveness. But as illustrated in Figure 5.1, when you parcel out these factors, only a small amount of the possible variation can be directly related to teaching effectiveness. Thus, the potential for showing a relationship is small to begin with, and the correlation of these factors is likely to be small or moderate at best. In other words, there is low sensitivity.

Figure 5.2 illustrates different degrees of sensitivity of two variables that could be correlated—this time motivation and achievement. Note how, as the variables become more specific and targeted, the sensitivity improves (circles become smaller and arrows become larger). From a design standpoint, then, it is very important to use variables that will have a high degree of sensitivity.

Sources of Variability

In quantitative research, researchers consider different *sources of variability*. **Variability** refers to how much observations of something take on different values. For example, we know that our mood varies from day to day, just as we know that a student's academic performance will not be the same each time he or she takes a test.

From the standpoint of design, it is important to recognize and control three **sources of variability**: systematic, error, and extraneous. *Systematic variance* is related to the variables that are being investigated. What you want is a design that will *maximize* this kind of variation. For instance, when studying the relationship between engaged time and achievement, you want to design the research so that the two variables of interest, engagement and achievement, both have high variability. On the other hand, if the study was designed so that all the students received the same or very similar achievement scores, then you would not be able to demonstrate the relationship.

Similarly, in an experiment, you want to maximize the variance of the dependent variable when comparing the groups. This is often accomplished by making sure that the intervention in the study will potentially produce quite different results. For example, systematic variance is likely to be greater in a study comparing individualized instruction with small-group discussion than in a study comparing two kinds of small-group discussion formats.

Variability: different values

Sources of variability: what causes different values

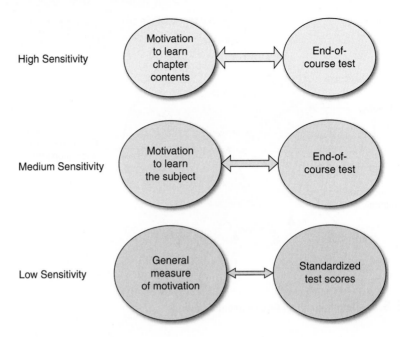

FIGURE 5.2 **Variables with High, Medium, and Low Sensitivity**

Systematic variance is assured by selecting the sample and measurement techniques that can be related to the dependent variable. Thus, it is difficult to show achievement differences among a group of advanced placement class students simply because this group is homogeneous with respect to ability. Using a class that contains students with different levels of aptitude will provide a much better opportunity to show variation in the results. Similarly, the measure used needs to allow for differences. A ceiling or floor effect will make it hard to show relationships or differences.

Error *variance* is something to be minimized. It includes sampling and measurement error and other kinds of random events that make it difficult to show relationships. *Extraneous variance* needs to be controlled. This kind of variability affects relationships directly, rather than in a random fashion. For instance, in examining the relationship between test scores and class size, the socioeconomic status of the students is a variable that would need to be controlled. That is, you would get a better estimate of the relationship if the effect of socioeconomic status, which is related to achievement, were removed statistically.

In the end, good quantitative research puts a priority on making sure that the selection of participants, measures, procedures, and interventions is such that there is adequate systematic variation and little error variance. How will you know if that is likely for a study? The answer is something we literally drill into graduate students: Read the literature and pilot test. By examining the results of similar previous studies, you will get an idea of the variability that can be expected, and a pilot test, with participants similar to what you use, will give you a trial run to be confident about the expected variability.

MAXMINCON: acronym for sources of variability

It is helpful to use the following acronym to remember the three sources of variability in designing and evaluating research: **MAXMINCON**. Quantitative research needs to MAXimize systematic variance, MINimize error variance, and CONtrol extraneous variance. Methods to achieve these goals are summarized in Table 5.1.

DESIGN VALIDITY

In the context of research design, the term *validity* (sometimes referred to as *experimental validity*) means the degree to which scientific explanations of phenomena match reality. It refers to the truthfulness of findings and conclusions. Explanations about observed phenomena *approximate* what is reality or truth, and the degree to which explanations are accurate comprises the validity of design.

TABLE 5.1 Principle of MAXMINCON		
MAXimize Systematic Variance	**MINimize Error Variance**	**CONtrol Extraneous Variance**
1. Use design measures that provide sufficient variability.	1. Standardize measurement procedures.	1. Make potential confounding variables constant.
2. Use a sample to provide sufficient variability.	2. Use measures with high reliability.	2. Use random assignment; use matching if random assignment is not possible.
3. Use design interventions that are very different.	3. Aggregate individual scores into group scores.	3. Build a possible confounding variable into the design as another independent variable.
	4. Use large samples.	
	5. Assure standardization in implementing the intervention in an experiment.	4. Use statistical adjustment procedures to help control the effects of confounding variables.

There are four types of design validity in quantitative research:

- *Statistical conclusion validity* refers to the appropriate use of statistical tests to determine whether purported relationships are a reflection of actual relationships.
- *Internal validity* focuses on the viability of causal links between the independent and dependent variables.
- *Construct validity* is a judgment about the extent to which interventions and measured variables actually represent targeted, theoretical, underlying psychological constructs and elements.
- *External validity* refers to the generalizability of the results and conclusions to other people and locations.

These four types of design validity can also be expressed as questions to be addressed in considering the overall quality of the findings and conclusions:

- Is there a relationship among the variables? (Statistical conclusion validity)
- Is there a causal relationship between the intervention and the dependent variable? (Internal validity)
- What is the nature of the constructs? (Construct validity)
- What is the generalizability of the results? (External validity)

As illustrated in Figure 5.3, these four types of validity derive from two categories, internal and external, that were set out in what is now a classic research design paper by Campbell and Stanley (1963). Cook and Campbell (1979) and Shadish, Cook, and Campbell (2002) showed how these two categories became four.

In designing or reading quantitative research with these four types of design validity in mind, it is necessary to consider who will be assessed (subjects), what they will be assessed by (instruments), how they will be assessed (procedures for data collection), and, for experimental designs, how experimental interventions will be administered. Once statistical conclusion validity has been assured, it is important to ask whether anything that occurred or was done could provide an explanation of the results by means of a rival hypothesis. *Rival* is used in the sense that it is in addition to the stated hypothesis of the research. (A rival hypothesis to the study of whether smoking causes lung cancer, for example, is that diet may contribute to the development of lung cancer.) This question represents the search for confounding and extraneous variables.

Campbell and Stanley (1963) refer to such explanations as **plausible rival hypotheses**. The search for plausible rival hypotheses is essential to ensure the quality of the research. Consider, for example, the questions below. Each addresses a possible source of error that could lead to a plausible rival hypothesis that could explain the results:

Plausible rival hypothesis: alternate explanation for results

1. Does the researcher have an existing bias about the subjects or about the topic researched?
2. Are the subjects aware that they are being studied?
3. Are the subjects responding honestly?

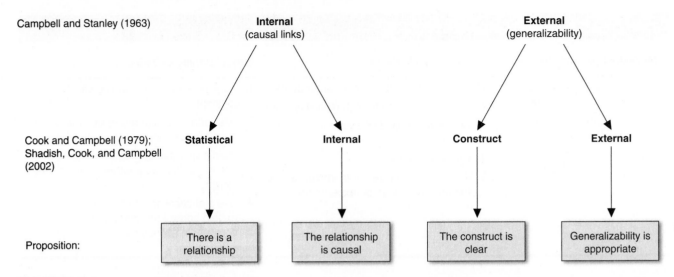

FIGURE 5.3 **Types of Design Validity**

4. Did both groups receive the intervention as described?
5. Does the sex of the interviewer make a difference?
6. Did very many subjects drop out before the end of the study?
7. Did the time of day the research was done affect the results?

If the researcher believes that the conditions of data collection might affect the results, the study can be designed to ensure that all conditions are as similar as possible. For example, in an observational study of the relationship between teacher behavior and student attention to material, the time of day the observer records data and the subject matter of the lesson (e.g., mornings versus afternoons, math versus history) could make a difference in student attention. One way to control this potential source of error is to make sure that all the observations are done at the same time of day during lessons on the same topic. In this example, the researcher could also control these potential influences by making them independent variables. This could be achieved by assigning observers to each subject of interest and having each topic observed in both the morning and the afternoon. Then the researcher could assess the effect of time of day and subject rather than simply control for it.

In quantitative studies, to the extent possible, control of confounding and extraneous variables is essential. Because educational research rarely exhibits the degree of control evident in studies of physical phenomena or even psychology, identifying alternative explanations is critical. This highlights the importance of internal validity. In our opinion, the principles of internal validity lie at the heart of designing good quantitative studies, as well as in the evaluation of research reported in journals, at conferences, and in the media.

The concern is with the way the procedures, sampling of subjects, and instruments affect the extent to which extraneous variables are present to complicate the interpretation of the findings. A study high or strong in internal validity successfully controls all or most confounding and extraneous variables so that the researcher can be confident that the intended explanation is correct. Studies low or weak in internal validity are hard to interpret, because it is difficult to tell whether the results were due to the independent variable or to some extraneous variable that was uncontrolled or unaccounted for. It is important for researchers to be aware of common factors that may be extraneous and to conceptualize and read research with these factors in mind. Because complete control of extraneous variables in educational research is difficult, if not impossible, all relevant threats to internal validity that cannot be prevented should be accounted for in interpreting the results.

We want to make one last point about design validity before considering each of the four types in greater detail. Although there are important design considerations and procedures that help control factors so that the explanations and conclusions are accurate, the extent to which design validity is strong *is always a matter of professional judgment*, guided by known "threats" according to the research design and specifics of where and how the research was conducted. Professional judgment is needed by both producers and consumers of research. It is your responsibility, in either role, to analyze the design, understand its strengths and weaknesses, and determine the truthfulness of the findings and conclusions. In the words of noted scholar Lee Shulman (2005):

> Truth is, research is all about exercising judgment under conditions of uncertainty, and even experimental designs don't relieve us of the judgment burdens. The acts of designing experiments themselves involve value judgments, and interpreting the results always demands careful judgment. (p. 48)

This judgment plays out with quantitative designs by distinguishing among factors that might affect the results so that they fall into four categories: (1) controlled, (2) possible/potential rival hypothesis, (3) plausible/probable rival hypothesis, and (4) fatal flaw. The term *threat* is often used to refer to factors that would compromise the conclusions or lead to the wrong conclusion. Thus, for each of the four categories of design validity, there is a list of potential threats. Some designs provide control of many or even most threats. Random assignment is the best-known feature of experimental designs to control threats.

As illustrated in Figure 5.4, you can use a series of decisions to establish the seriousness of a given threat. Some designs essentially control threats so that they are not a concern for internal validity, and some designs don't lend themselves to some threats. Possible/potential threats are those that are not controlled by the design. They need to be considered, although not controlling them does not mean that the research is flawed. Many threats that are not controlled still will not be a factor in overall design validity. Plausible/probable threats are ones that could constitute a definite rival hypothesis. Evidence is needed to argue that these are not an issue, as are any threats that rise to the level of a fatal flaw. If there is a fatal flaw, the results are judged to be uninterpretable in the sense that no conclusion can be reached concerning the impact of the independent variable.

Statistical Conclusion Validity

In quantitative research, statistics are used to determine whether a relationship exists between two or more variables. The issue is the extent to which the calculated statistics accurately portray the actual relationship. Doing the statistics is the first step in determining results, interpretations, and conclusions. In other words, statistics guide the findings. Although we have not yet discussed typical statistical procedures, it is important to realize that certain factors may invalidate the statistical results. That is, there are reasons that researchers may draw incorrect inferences about the relationship between variables. Although a complete consideration of these threats is beyond the scope of this chapter, being familiar with these ideas is important.

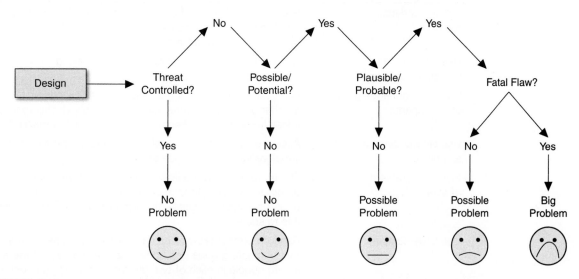

FIGURE 5.4 Internal Validity Decision Tree

Statistical conclusion validity: correctness of statistical analyses

Shadish, Cook, and Campbell (2002) list nine threats to **statistical conclusion validity**. The first seven are pertinent to our discussion:

1. *Low statistical power* An incorrect conclusion of no relationship due to lack of power, or the ability to detect relationships.
2. *Violated assumptions of statistical tests* Violated assumptions may under- or overestimate the size of a relationship.
3. *"Fishing" and error rate problem* Repeated tests for statistical significance can inflate statistical significance.
4. *Unreliability of measures* Measurement error weakens relationships.
5. *Restriction of range* Reduced, small differences among a set of scores weakens relationships.
6. *Unreliability of treatment implementation* Unstandardized treatments underestimate the effects of an intervention (also referred to as *treatment fidelity*).
7. *Extraneous variance in the experimental setting* Features of an intervention setting may inflate error, making it more difficult to show a relationship.

Statistical power: capability of finding a relationship

Statistical analyses convert raw data into results. An important concept in interpreting the results is to know that the design will make it possible to detect relationships and differences. The likelihood of finding these relationships and differences is estimated by what is called *statistical power*. **Statistical power** denotes the ability to detect relationships and differences as statistically significant. Adequate power makes it possible for a finding of no relationship or difference to be judged actual. Power increases the likelihood that the researcher is correct in concluding that there is no difference or relationship. Power makes the study more sensitive to what might be small differences, allowing findings to be statistically significant. In effect, power is a way of estimating whether true or actual relationships or differences exist. If there is inadequate power, there is a greater risk that if the researcher finds no relationship or differences, the conclusion is wrong. Although there are statistical estimates of power, which go beyond what we are able to present here, the elements of design in Table 5.2 show what researchers can do to increase power (Mitchell & Jolley, 2007). Essentially, random error needs to be lessened and the effect of an intervention needs to be strengthened (see Figure 5.5).

TABLE 5.2 Design Elements That Increase Statistical Power

Design Element	Description
Use a standardized protocol	Standardizing a study reduces random error by assuring that the same conditions exist each time interventions and measures are administered.
Use instruments that provide reliable scores	Reliable scores reduce random error by making measurement more consistent.
Use homogeneous groups of participants	Participants in each group should be just like those in another group (e.g., same age, gender, ability). This makes it less likely that the effect of the intervention is masked.
Use careful data coding and entry	Accurate coding and entry of data is a relatively easy and inexpensive way to reduce errors.
Increase intervention effects	The more different the intervention is from the control group or another intervention, the greater the opportunity to find significant results—the bigger the effect, the easier it is to see it.
Use large samples	Random error is likely to be canceled out in experiments that compare groups (e.g., power is much greater if there are 40 people in each of two groups rather than 8 people).

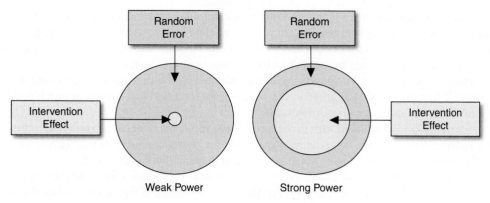

FIGURE 5.5 **Illustration of Strong and Weak Statistical Power**

Internal Validity

Because causal conclusions are the focus of experimental research, **internal validity** is the *sine qua non* of these studies. The possible threats to internal validity are described and illustrated below. These categories are taken from Campbell and Stanley (1963), Cook and Campbell (1979), Shadish, Cook, and Campbell (2002), and McMillan (2008). It is best to keep in mind that the names of these various threats to internal validity should not be interpreted literally. Often, each has a broader meaning than the name may suggest at first. Although some of the names are unique to this book, most were originally conceived for experimental research. Some of the threats relate to both experimental and nonexperimental designs; some make sense only in the context of an experiment.

Two conditions must be present to establish that a threat is plausible/probable: (1) the threat must influence the dependent variables, and (2) the threat must represent a factor or variable that differs in amount or intensity across levels of the independent variable. Thus, a factor could influence the dependent variables but would not be a threat if it affects the dependent variables of each group equally. For example, suppose a researcher is interested in investigating the effectiveness of a new training program for school counselors on counselor self-confidence. School counselors from two different schools participate in the study, with one school receiving the new program and the other school acting as a control. Both groups are given a pretest and a posttest two months later. One factor that is a clear threat is that teachers in one of the schools may be more motivated to learn, which then affects self-confidence. Taking a pretest on self-confidence could also affect the posttest, but because this test is the same for both groups, it would not be a threat to internal validity.

Keep in mind that the names of these threats to internal validity should not be interpreted literally. Many of the names have a broad meaning. Most of the names used here were established many years ago by Campbell and Stanley (1963). Some of the names are unique to this chapter, and other researchers have recently suggested labels that may better describe the category of threats. What is most important is not categorizing threats correctly; what is most important is to recognize when a factor may offer a plausible rival explanation. Knowing the names of the threats, however, will help you to be aware of possible problems in the studies you design or read about.

History History is a category of threats to internal validity that refers to uncontrolled events or incidents that affect the dependent variable (not the effect of events occurring in the past). These events can affect both experimental and nonexperimental research. In an experiment, some amount of time elapses between the onset of the intervention and measurement of the dependent variable. This time is necessary to enable the intervention to work. Events or incidents could occur during the study *in addition* to the intervention that plausibly affect the dependent variable. If this happens, you don't know whether results are due to the intervention, to the unplanned, uncontrollable event(s), or to a combination of the intervention and the event. Thus, the event is confounded with the independent variable—the two cannot be separated.

In an experiment, history threats can occur "within" the intervention in the sense that something occurs in the context of the setting in which the experiment is taking place. This is called

Internal validity: causal truthfulness

History: threats of concurrent events

local history because the unforeseen events are contained within the local setting or context. For example, consider a simple experiment in which a reading intervention is administered to one class, with a control class for comparison. A series of unexpected announcements that distracts the control group class may adversely affect their posttest scores. The researcher would not know the extent to which the control group scores are affected by the distraction. This would make it difficult to conclude that a difference between the intervention and control groups is due to the intervention and not to the distractions.

A related kind of problem with experiments is the influence of variables related to levels of the independent variable. Suppose an experiment has been designed so that two teaching method interventions are tested. One intervention is in Ms. Orlando's class in the morning; one is done by Mr. Abrams in the afternoon. We have at least two confounding variables, teacher and time of day, that would severely weaken the internal validity of the design. In fact this is a situation in which a "fatal flaw" exists in the design.

Other threats can occur "externally" in the sense that they are completely outside the context of the intervention but still affect the dependent variable. For example, suppose a class is studying the Far East and researchers are trying to determine what effect this unit has on students' multicultural attitudes. During the unit, a major crisis occurs in China (e.g., protesting the Olympics). If the students are affected by the crisis, which in turn influences the way they respond to a multicultural attitude questionnaire, this event will constitute a history threat to the internal validity of the study (see Figure 5.6).

Unexpected events can also influence results in longitudinal nonexperimental research. Suppose you are investigating the effect of a new department chair on faculty productivity. Data on faculty productivity can be summarized for several years before the new chair was hired and for several years afterward. However, at about the same time that the new chair was hired, the promotion and tenure guidelines for faculty were revised. Now there's a problem: You don't know if the change in productivity, if there is one, is caused by the new chair or the revised promotion and tenure guidelines.

Selection: threats related to participant characteristics

Selection   There are two types of **selection** threats to consider: (1) those that occur in experiments and ex post facto designs and (2) those that are related to the manner in which participants are selected for the sample. Selection threats are especially important because most measures of study outcomes are variables that are strongly affected by the characteristics of the participants. First, let's consider experimental and ex post facto designs.

In most experiments, two or more groups are compared. Selection is a factor if the groups differ in ways that affect the dependent variable. This threat could also be referred to as *group composition differences*. That is, for example, if one group is brighter, is more motivated, or has more positive attitudes, these differences could differentially influence the dependent variable, to one extent for one group, with a different degree of influence for the other group.

To avoid selection threats, experiments are typically designed so that each group has participants who, when put together as a group, have statistical equivalence with characteristics of a comparison or control group. Random assignment, when carried out correctly and in sufficient numbers, is used whenever possible to control threats associated with selection. However, in many situations, it is not possible to randomly assign participants or to randomize a sufficient

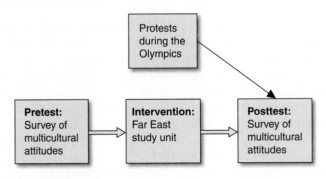

FIGURE 5.6   **History Threat to Internal Validity**

number of units (e.g., students, classes, schools). In both cases, selection is a threat that must be considered (McMillan, 2007).

Suppose a teacher wants to investigate whether the mastery or discovery approach is best for teaching adjectives and adverbs. The teacher secures the cooperation of another class in order to conduct a study. The two teachers flip a coin to decide who will use the discovery approach and who will use the mastery approach. The teachers assess achievement by giving each group a pretest and a posttest to determine growth in knowledge. It happens, however, that the average ability score of the mastery group is 115, whereas that of the discovery group is 95. Here selection is a major problem, since we would expect the higher-ability group to achieve more than the lower-ability group under almost any condition. If uncontrolled and unaccounted for in some way, then such a threat to internal validity could be a fatal flaw. The teacher would falsely conclude that the mastery learning method is more effective, when its apparent success is really due to initial differences in ability.

This design is also an example of the misuse of random assignment, which, if true, would be important for credibility. In fact, this method of assigning one intervention to one group and another to a different group is not random assignment after all, despite the flipping of a coin to assign different interventions. Sufficient units must be randomly assigned to reach the goal of similar group composition. In this case, students would need to be randomly assigned to both classes. Although there are methods that can be used when random assignment is not possible, such as matching and something called *covariance analysis* that adjusts the posttest scores on the basis of the pretest, whenever selection is possible, it is imperative to examine this threat.

As discussed previously, selection is also related to the manner in which the researcher chooses a sample. As pointed out, a common problem in research is using volunteers for the sample. The volunteer group may be more motivated or motivated for special reasons; hence, they will respond differently to the treatment or questions than a nonvolunteer group will respond.

Statistical Regression   **Statistical regression** (also called *regression artifacts* or *regression to the mean*) refers to the tendency of subjects who score very high or low on a pretest to score closer to the mean (i.e, *regress* to the mean) on the posttest, regardless of the effects of the treatment. Regression to the mean is entirely a statistical phenomenon. All measures have some degree of error, and statistical regression occurs because of changes in error from the pretest to the posttest. Because of this error, scores on a posttest will be different from those on the pretest for students on the basis of mathematical probability alone. For groups of students who score either very high or very low on a pretest, this error works to change the scores on the posttest so that they are closer to the mean of the posttest than they were to the mean of the pretest.

> **Statistical regression:** scores of extreme groups move closer to the mean

To illustrate this concept, think of Figure 5.7 as representing the same test taken twice by two groups of students in a class in which the average score is 100. The average score for the Superstars on the first test was 150, whereas the score for the Challengers was 40. On the second test, we would expect the average score for the Superstars to be lower and the Challengers' score to be higher, even if their true ability or knowledge remains the same.

Regression is a problem whenever the researcher purposely chooses groups on the basis of extremely high or low scores. For example, a school district may want to implement a special program to improve the self-concept of children who score low on a self-concept inventory. An assessment of the impact of the program could examine self-concept scores after the program (in a posttest), but the researcher would have to keep in mind that even if there is no program effect whatsoever, the initially low scores (on a pretest) would improve to some degree because of statistical regression. Similarly, it is usually difficult to find positive changes in programs for gifted children. (Because of regression, posttest scores will tend to be slightly lower on average.)

Here are six conditions or factors to keep in mind when considering statistical regression:

- Regression affects only groups of participants, not individuals.
- Regression is relative, so that even though the entire group scores higher on a posttest, regression still occurs.
- Regression is directly related to the reliability of the scores. The less reliable they are, the greater the regression; if there is no random measurement error, there is no regression.
- Regression is related to the distance of the group scores from the mean. The more extreme the scores, the greater the regression.

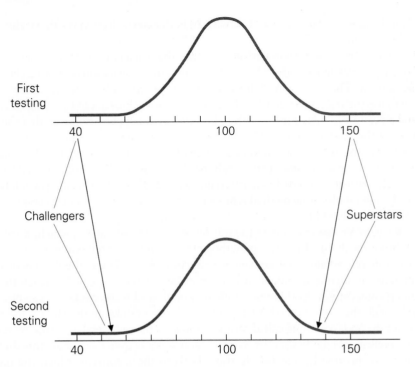

First
testing

40   100   150

Challengers   Superstars

Second
testing

40   100   150

FIGURE 5.7 **Illustration of Statistical Regression**

- Regression influences both high- and low-scoring groups.
- Statistical procedures can be used to correct, or adjust for, the effect of regression.

Pretesting: effect of the pretest on intervention results

Pretesting   Whenever research utilizes a pretest (i.e., some form of measurement that precedes a treatment or experience), it is possible that the test itself will have an impact on the subjects. Just taking a pretest could provide the subjects with motivation or practice on the types of questions asked or familiarize the subjects with the material tested. This kind of **pretesting** (or *testing*) effect is found in experiments measuring achievement over a short time and in research on attitudes or values when a single group is given a pretest and a posttest. If an attitude questionnaire is used as a pretest, simply reading the questions might stimulate the subjects to think about the topic and even change their attitudes. A researcher might, for instance, be interested in evaluating the effect of a series of films on changes in students' attitudes toward children with physical disabilities. The researcher would give a pretest, show the films, and then give a posttest to find out whether changes occurred. Any observed changes, however, might be caused by the pretest. The items in the questionnaire could have been enough to change the attitudes. Pretesting is not a threat for nonexperimental designs.

Instrumentation: effect of variations in measurement

Instrumentation   A threat to internal validity that is related to testing is called **instrumentation**. It refers to the way changes in the instruments or persons used to collect data might affect the results. This threat is particularly serious in observational research, when the observers may become fatigued or bored or change in some other way so as to affect the recording of data. A good example of how instrumentation could affect results occurs when scores from the same standardized test are used to track achievement across several years. If there has been a renorming of the test and a new form, it is problematic to compare results from the old test with those from the new one. The 1995 renorming and other planned changes in the SAT is a good illustration of how this can lead to errors in interpretation, because the meaning of the same score—for example, 500—is different in the new form. *Testing* is a change in the subject resulting from taking the test, whereas *instrumentation* is a recorded change in the results due to inadequacies of the testing.

Another kind of instrumentation threat occurs if the observer or rater knows which group is the intervention group and which one is the control group. In this situation, scoring is likely to be influenced by this knowledge through expectations of what should occur. Ideally, the observers and raters are "blind" to which group they are assessing. For example, an experimenter is carrying out a study on the behavior of students taught by master teachers compared to the behavior of students taught by novice teachers. If observers are used to record the behavior of students with both types of teachers, they should not know which teachers are the masters and which are the novices. This knowledge could easily affect what is observed. Similarly, if possible, raters should not know which measure is the pretest and which is the posttest.

Attrition Attrition (also called *mortality* or *differential attrition*) occurs in a study when subjects systematically drop out or are lost during the investigation. This is a threat to many longitudinal studies that last for several weeks or months. For example, a study of the effect of a program to assist low-achieving ninth graders conducted between the ninth and twelfth grades would have apparent success if the lowest-achieving students dropped out of school before twelfth grade and were not even included in the posttest analyses. For most nonexperimental and short-duration research, attrition is not a threat unless the intervention is especially demanding and systematically causes low-performing subjects to drop out. In studies that have differential loss of participants from different groups because of selection bias or the nature of the treatments, mortality is a serious threat to internal validity. Mortality is essentially the same problem as selection, but it happens after the study is already set up and underway.

Attrition: loss of participants

Maturation Maturation refers to normal growth or changes in the participants of a study over time that affect the dependent variable. It consists of natural and biological developmental changes. Subjects develop and change as part of growing older, and in interpreting research that occurs over an extended period of time, such changes should be considered. Some changes, such as getting hungry, tired, bored, or discouraged, can occur in a relatively short time and are also considered maturational threats to internal validity. Suppose a researcher is investigating the attitudes of fourth graders toward reading, mathematics, and science. The researcher has developed an instrument and gives it to all subjects in the same way. It takes the subjects a half hour to finish the reading instrument and another half hour to complete the mathematics questions. How will they respond to the science instrument? They will probably be tired, bored, and inattentive, and maturation would thus be a major problem in using their responses to the science items as an indication of their attitude toward science. Other examples are students who become more knowledgeable because of experience and first-graders who learn to dribble a basketball not because of an effective teacher but because they are maturing physically.

Maturation: natural and biological changes

Diffusion of Intervention In an ideal experimental design, an intervention is given to one group, and the control or alternative condition group never comes in contact with the experimental intervention. For instance, if a psychologist is studying cheating behavior and manipulates the incentive to cheat as the independent variable, one group might receive a high incentive for cheating and the other group a low incentive, but neither group would be aware of the treatment the other group was receiving. If, however, a teacher decided to test this notion with a class of students and told half of the students that they would receive a high incentive and the other half that they would, at the same time, receive a low incentive, then each group would know the condition of the other. In such circumstances, the treatments would be "diffused" throughout all subjects. It is possible that both treatments could affect either group, resulting in **diffusion of intervention**. Diffusion also occurs if the effects of the treatment spread to subjects in a control or comparison group.

Diffusion of intervention: spread of the effect of the intervention

Experimenter Effects Experimenter effects (bias) refer to both deliberate and unintentional influences that the researcher has on the subjects. This may be reflected in differential treatment of subjects, such as using a different voice tone, being more reassuring to one group than to others, reinforcing different behaviors, displaying different attitudes, selectively observing different subject responses, and any other behavior that influences either the subjects' behavior or the evaluation of the behavior by the researcher. Experimenter effects also occur if the characteristics of the investigator or person collecting data, such as clothing, age, sex, educational level, and race, affect subjects' responses. Of particular note is a study in which the researcher wants to "show that something is true" or "prove a point," rather than taking the perspective of an

Experimenter effects: influence of the researcher on the results

objective investigator. This occurs when the researcher wants to prove something, find a result that is consistent with a bias about what is best, or is pressured to find a particular result. For instance, it is easy for a professor who thinks that cooperative teaching is the best thing since sliced bread to conduct research on this topic in a biased manner because of a strong desire to validate the research hypothesis. This effect also occurs when researchers are funded to test the effect of an intervention by the company or group that is promoting the program, curriculum, or product. For example, a company could hire a professor to evaluate their new computerized remedial education program. This would be a conflict of interest for the professor, however, and could lead to bias.

Intervention Replications   In an experiment, the intervention is supposed to be repeated so that each member of one group receives the same intervention separately and independently of the other members of the group. Thus, if the researcher is testing a new method of instruction with a whole class, there is really only one replication of the intervention: The intervention is conducted once. Each class is like one subject, and hence several classes are needed to do the research properly. **Intervention replications** are a threat to internal validity to the extent that the reported number of subjects in the study is not the same as the number of independent replications of the intervention.

This threat is a particularly troublesome limitation for educational research because it is so difficult to use multiple groups of students. Often a study will compare two interventions: one given to one class, the other to a different class. Although this type of design usually results in a technical sample size of two, rather than the number of students in the classes, the threat of intervention replications does not mean that the results are completely invalid. Rather, what needs to be recognized is that whatever the results, interpretations and conclusions should be made with great caution. Some experimental interventions are given to students as a group assignment, but the actual intervention condition, such as a particular type of homework assignment, is individualized. In this circumstance, intervention replication is not a threat to internal validity.

Subject Effects   In ideal research, the subjects behave and respond naturally and honestly. However, when people become involved in a study, they often change their behavior simply because they understand that they are subjects, and sometimes these changes affect the results. **Subject effects** refer to subject changes in behavior initiated by the subjects themselves in response to the research situation. If subjects have some idea of the purpose of the study or the motivation for doing well, they may alter their behavior to respond more favorably. Subjects will pick up cues from the setting and instructions, which will motivate them in specific ways. These cues are called **demand characteristics**.

Subjects in most studies will also want to present themselves in the most positive manner. Thus, there may be positive self-presentation, social desirability, or a belief that certain responses are expected, which may affect the results. For instance, most people want to appear intelligent, competent, and emotionally stable, and they may resist interventions that they perceive as manipulating them in negative ways or they may fake responses to appear more positive.

Some subjects may increase positive or desirable behavior simply because they know they are receiving special treatment. (This is termed the *Hawthorne effect,* considered by some researchers as a threat to external validity; see the section on ecological external validity.) Control group subjects may try harder because they see themselves in competition with an intervention group or may be motivated because they did *not* get the intervention. (This may be termed the *John Henry effect* or *compensatory rivalry.*) Other subjects, when they realize that they were not selected for what they believe is a preferred intervention, may become demotivated (i.e., *resentful demoralization*). A good case of compensatory rivalry that actually occurred in a school district concerned the Talent Development High School program, developed by Johns Hopkins University. Five high schools were randomly selected to participate in one of three levels of implementation. One school received a reading strategy only, a second school received a reading strategy training with class sets of novels and work guides with materials of high interest to students, and three schools were the control group, receiving no materials. One of the control schools was upset about not receiving the training, so school officials purchased multiple class sets of high-interest novels and student books (not from Johns Hopkins), and also hired a part-time reading specialist to work with teachers.

Intervention replications: number of separate interventions

Subject effects: influence of participants on the results

Demand characteristics: subject effect related to participant knowledge of the study

TABLE 5.3 Design Components of Strong and Weak Internal Validity

Strong Internal Validity	Weak Internal Validity
Composition of groups being compared is the same	Different group compositions
No differences in either local or external history events	Differences in local or external history events
Maturation effects accounted for	Maturation effects not accounted for
Statistical regression accounted for	Statistical regression not accounted for
No subject attrition	Substantial subject attrition
No experimenter effects	Experimenter bias
No subject effects	Subject effects
Correct unit of analysis	Incorrect unit of analysis
Use of reliable and valid scores	Use of unreliable and/or invalid scores
Effect of taking the pretest unaccounted for	Effect of the pretest accounted for
Effect of the intervention contained	Effect of the intervention spread to others
Intervention fidelity	Differences in interventions

Some participants will react positively, with increased motivation, because they are doing something new and different (this is termed the *novelty effect*). Finally, some subjects may be anxious about participating or being "measured." This could have a detrimental effect on the outcome, leading to a false negative about the impact of the intervention. This effect is termed *evaluation apprehension*. As you can see, there are many potential subject effects that can occur.

Table 5.3 summarizes design features for strong and weak internal validity.

Construct Validity

Research involves making inferences about unobservable mental states and about what interventions represent. Mental states include traits, abilities, and intentions of the participants, as described and measured by the researcher. Similarly, in experiments, researchers use interventions that they believe represent what is intended to cause changes in participants. **Construct validity** refers to inferences that are made from the nature of the measurement and interventions used to the constructs they purportedly represent. Suppose a researcher is studying the effect of curriculum alignment with high-stakes testing on student achievement. The test of student achievement is given to make inferences about what students know and can do, and the specifics of the intervention are used to make inferences about curriculum alignment. Construct validity concerns the efficacy of using the test as a measure of what students know and can do, as well as the representativeness of the intervention as an illustration of curriculum alignment. There are many ways of measuring student achievement and doing curriculum alignment, so if only one test is used and only one model of curriculum alignment is proposed, construct validity will be weak.

Shadish, Cook, and Campbell (2002) list 14 threats to construct validity, some of which were considered earlier as subject effect threats to internal validity. The three threats to construct validity with the greatest relevance for education research include the following:

1. *Inadequate preoperational explication of constructs* Inadequate preoperational explication of constructs refers to the failure to adequately define and explain the nature of the construct that is being investigated prior to data collection. This is a threat because what is named as a specific construct, such as group discussion, motivation, or computer-based instruction, may not be consistent with the way others and/or the literature define the construct. Expert review of the construct prior to initiating the study is helpful in reducing the likelihood of this threat.

2. *Mono-operation bias* Mono-operation bias is focused on the nature of the intervention. Typically, only a single method or version of an intervention is used in a study, and this may limit

Construct validity: labeling of inferences

Inadequate preoperational explication of constructs: starting with an incomplete definition

Mono-operation bias: limited inferences due to a single intervention

the way the results are interpreted. For example, there may be several ways to study the impact of teacher humor as an intervention (e.g., in lectures, scripted jokes, or spontaneous). If the study uses one method, such as scripted jokes, it would not be appropriate to infer that any kind of humor is effective. To avoid this threat, each version would need to be included in the study. This is often difficult to implement, so replications with other versions would be valuable.

Mono-method bias: limited inferences based on a single measurement

3. *Mono-method bias* **Mono-method bias** refers to limitations based on a single way of measuring variables. There are many ways, for example, to measure self-concept (e.g., observation, peer ratings, teacher ratings, self-report), and when only one method is used, inferences are limited to this method. In other words, the meaning of the result is tied to the operationalized variable. Using several methods to measure variables reduces this threat.

Construct validity is closely related to generalizability, because using a weak conceptualization or a single method of measurement will limit inferences about the details of the conceptualization and method. Suppose student achievement is limited to how students score on a multiple-choice test. Other ways of measuring achievement might give different results. Thus, what is meant by student achievement is limited to the method of measurement.

External Validity

External validity: generalizability of results

External validity refers to the generalizability of the results. For quantitative designs, there are two general categories of **external validity** that need to be considered when designing studies or evaluating research findings: *population* external validity and *ecological* external validity.

Population External Validity   The subjects used in an investigation have certain characteristics and can be described with respect to such variables as age, race, sex, and ability. Strictly speaking, the results of a study can be generalized only to other people who have the same, or at least similar, characteristics as those used in the experiment. The extent to which the results can be generalized to other people is referred to as **population external validity**.

Population external validity: generalizability limited to subject characteristics

Consider the prevailing situation in much psychological research. Because of time, money, and other constraints, psychologists often use college students as subjects in research. The results of such research, strictly speaking, are limited in generalizability to other similar college students. In other words, what might be true for certain college students might not be true for sixth-grade students. Similarly, research conducted with elementary students should not be generalized to secondary students, nor research with males generalized to females, nor research with Hispanic Americans generalized to African Americans, and so forth. A treatment might be effective with one type of student and ineffective with another. If subjects are volunteers for research, the findings may be limited to characteristics of the volunteers.

Ecological external validity: generalizability limited by the context

Ecological External Validity   **Ecological external validity** refers to the conditions of the research and the extent to which generalizing the results is limited to similar conditions. The conditions of the research include such factors as the nature of the independent and dependent variables, physical surroundings, time of day or year, pretest or posttest sensitization, and effects caused by the presence of an experimenter or treatment. Included in these factors is the well-known *Hawthorne effect*: the tendency for people to act differently simply because they realize they are subjects in research. (It is called the Hawthorne effect because the original study was conducted at the Western Electric Hawthorne Plant in Chicago. Although some research has questioned the validity of the original study, the label *Hawthorne effect* endures.) Much as with threats of subject effects, subjects may become anxious, fake responses in order to look good, or react in many other ways because of their knowledge of aspects of the research.

A variation of external validity is to be careful not to conclude that what may be true for an entire group of subjects is also true for subgroups of subjects. For example, if research with a large high school shows a positive relationship between amount of time spent on homework and achievement for all students, it does not necessarily follow that this same relationship holds for high-ability students or low-ability students or that it is just as true for sophomores as for seniors. This is called generalizing *across* a population and can lead to erroneous interpretations.

It is possible to be so strict with respect to external validity that practically all research is useful only in specific cases. Although it is necessary to consider the external validity of studies, we need to be reasonable, not strict, in interpreting the results. It is common, for example, for researchers to cite in the discussion or conclusion section of the article the limitations of generalizing their results.

ETHICAL AND LEGAL CONSIDERATIONS

Because most educational research deals with human beings, it is necessary to understand the ethical and legal responsibilities of conducting research. Often, researchers face situations in which the potential costs of using questionable methods must be balanced by the benefits of conducting the study. Questionable methods come about because of the nature of the research questions and the methodology designed to provide valid results. The costs may include injury and psychological difficulties, such as anxiety, shame, loss of self-esteem, and affronts to human dignity, or they may involve legal infringement on human rights. Such costs, if a potential result of the research, must be weighed against the benefits for the research participants, such as increased self-understanding, satisfaction in helping, and knowledge of research methods, as well as more obvious benefits to theory and knowledge of human behavior.

It is ultimately the responsibility of each researcher to weigh these considerations and to make the best professional judgment possible. To do this, it is necessary for the researcher to be fully aware of the ethical and legal principles that should be addressed. Although most studies must be approved by an Institutional Review Board (IRB) prior to implementation, the researcher must be able to apply these principals to each study.

Research Ethics

Ethics generally are concerned with beliefs about what is right or wrong from a moral perspective. Research ethics are focused on what is morally proper and improper when engaged with participants or when accessing archival data. Naturally, there is some disagreement about how to define what is ethically correct in research. But it is a very important issue, one of increasing concern for private citizens, researchers, and legislators. Many professional and governmental groups have studied ethical issues in depth and published guidelines for planning and conducting research in such a way as to protect the rights and welfare of the participants. Most relevant for educational research are the ethical principles published by the American Educational Research Association and the American Psychological Association.

In the next few sections, we will summarize and discuss the principles and guidelines that are most relevant for educational research. While these principles and guidelines cover what should be adhered to so that a study is done ethically, *the primary investigator is responsible for the ethical standards used in the conduct of the research*.

Full Disclosure or Deception   Researchers should generally be open and honest with participants about all aspects of the study. This usually involves a full disclosure of the purpose of the research, but there are circumstances in which either withholding information about the research or deceiving the subjects may be justified. Withholding information means that the participants are informed about only part of the purpose of the research. This may be done in studies where full disclosure would seriously affect the validity of the results. For example, in research on students' racial attitudes, it may be sufficient to inform students that the research is investigating attitudes toward others.

A more volatile issue involves research in which, to put it bluntly, the researcher deliberately misleads the subjects. A good example is the classic study on teacher expectations by Rosenthal and Jacobson (1968). The researchers informed the teachers that certain students had been identified as "bloomers" on a test designed to predict intellectual gain. In fact, the test was a measure of intelligence, and the students were identified at random. In this design, it was necessary to tell the teachers an untruth. Is such deception justified? After all, in this case the students would only benefit from the misinformation, and the results did have very important implications.

From one perspective, the deception may be justified on the basis of the contribution of the findings. On the other hand, it is an affront to human dignity and self-respect and may encourage mistrust and cynicism toward researchers. We believe that deception should be used only in cases where (1) the significance of the potential results is greater than the detrimental effects of lying; (2) deception is the only valid way to carry out the study; and (3) appropriate debriefing is used, in which the researcher informs the participants of the nature of and reason for the deception following the completion of the study. These conditions are often present in laboratory research, typically in psychology, but rarely occur in field studies in education. Deception does not mean that the subjects should not have a choice whether to participate at all in the study.

Voluntary Participation

Voluntary participation means that participants cannot be compelled, coerced, or required to participate. No one should be forced to participate in research. This is true whether the participants are a "captured" group, such as students and teachers in a public K–12 school, or university professors. This includes the use of information contained in a database if there is any chance that individual identities can be associated with specific data or results, as well as relatively passive data collection. For example, if a researcher wanted to observe a class of high school students, these students need to volunteer to be observed. This voluntary aspect of research can be a difficult barrier to conducting research, especially if large percentages of potential subjects decide not to participate, or if the very act of obtaining volunteers somehow contaminates the study by enhancing participants' sensitivity to the method of data collection.

Although people should never be coerced into participating, sometimes coercion is subtle. This occurs when researchers emphasize the benefits of participating. The researcher may tell the participants that they can choose to participate or not participate, but the implicit message that "You're letting us down if you don't participate" may also be clear and compelling. It is also problematic for researchers to bribe potential participants. The researcher has the responsibility of knowing about these subtle forms of coercion that diminish voluntary participation.

A key concept in determining that participants have in fact volunteered is informed consent. This aspect of ethical research is central to making sure that participants have the information they need to decide whether or not to participate.

Informed Consent

Informed consent: subjects agree to participate with knowledge of the study

Informed consent is achieved by providing subjects with an explanation of the research, an opportunity to terminate their participation at any time with no penalty, and full disclosure of any risks associated with the study. Consent is usually obtained by asking subjects (or the parents of minor subjects) to sign a form that indicates understanding of the research and consent to participate. Almost all data gathering in public schools that requires student participation beyond normal testing requires parental as well as school district and principal permission.

Informed consent implies that the subjects have a choice about whether to participate. Yet there are many circumstances when it seems acceptable that the subjects never know that they have been participants. Sometimes, it is impractical or impossible to locate subjects; sometimes, knowledge of participation may invalidate the results. Some educational research is quite unobtrusive and has no risks for the subjects (e.g., the use of test data of students over the past 10 years in order to chart achievement trends). Still, the researcher infringes on what many believe is the ethical right of participants to make their own decisions about participation. Typically, some kind of informed consent form is used with potential participants. Participants read and then sign the consent form, which is stored separately from the results of the study. This type of consent is considered *active*, and it is commonly used. This means that the participant has specifically agreed to be included in the study.

Occasionally, *passive* consent is obtained, in which participants or parents of minors are asked to return a signed form if they do *not* want to volunteer. However, if this procedure is used with parents of students, it is rarely possible to know that all parents received the form. If they are in a class or group, participants may be pressured to not indicate that they are not agreeing to being in the study.

Johnson and Christensen (2008) list 10 informational points that should be included in a consent form:

1. purpose of the study
2. description of the procedures and the length of time needed
3. description of any risks or discomforts that may be encountered
4. description of the benefits from the research
5. description of an alternate procedure or intervention that would be advantageous
6. statement of the extent of confidentiality
7. names of people who may be contacted about the study
8. statement that participation is voluntary and participants can refuse to participate at any time without penalty
9. statement of the amount and schedule of payment for participation
10. statements written at no more than an eighth-grade level

A sample consent form is presented in Figure 5.8.

Informed consent with minors requires parental or legal guardian approval. In this situation, students may be asked to **assent** to the study. This means that students agree to participate after knowing about the study and any potential for risk or harm. Assent is typically obtained from minors who are old enough to understand that they are volunteering to participate and may choose not to do so without penalty. In general, the age considered "old enough" is nine years, though in some institutions assent will be required for younger children. An example of a student assent form is shown in Figure 5.9.

Assent: minor agrees to participate

One of the challenges of informed consent forms is that the right information needs to be included in a format and style that are easily comprehended. If too much information is included, potential participants and their parents may not take the time needed to understand all aspects of informed consent.

No Harm or Risk to Participants

Research should never result in physical or mental discomfort, harm, or injury to the participants. This includes revealing information that may result in embarrassment or danger to home life, school performance, friendships, and the like, as well as direct negative consequences. The researcher needs to carefully anticipate such risks and do whatever is needed to minimize them. Asking participants to answer personal questions or questions about deviant behavior can make them feel uncomfortable, or may be a stimulus to further considerations and thinking. This could occur if students are asked about whether they had cheated on assignments and papers.

Although preventing harm or risk is essential and severe negative consequences are rare in educational studies, it is likely that most studies have some degree of risk or harm. Thus, when obtaining consent, participants are told that there is minimal risk to being involved in the study. What constitutes "minimal"? Determination of the extent to which risk is minimal is the responsibility of the primary investigator, but such a determination also needs to be reviewed by others. This is often an Institutional Review Board (IRB; see below) if the researcher has a position in a college or university or if the research is externally funded. Federally supported research grants and contracts require such a review.

Sometimes there is risk in analyzing and reporting the results. This is definitely a concern for most qualitative studies, in which there is a small sample size and keeping participants anonymous when reporting results is difficult. If participants have been observed or interviewed and that information is analyzed, there may be negative consequences when the participants read about the study.

In some studies, it is necessary to use **deception** about the nature and purpose of the research because, if participants knew the purpose, it would invalidate the results. For example, if an

Deception: participants do not know what is being studied

Teacher Consent

STUDY TITLE: The Relationship between Classroom Grading and Assessment Practices and Student Motivation

Dear Teacher,

If this consent form contains language that is unclear, please ask the study staff to answer any questions or address any concerns you may have about the consent process and/or the study in general. If you consent to participate in the study, please sign and return this form in the envelope provided.

The Richmond area superintendents of schools are sponsoring a study with VCU School of Education faculty to gather information about teachers' grading and assessment practices and students' perceptions of motivation and engagement. We hope that the study will identify assessment practices that enhance student motivation and engagement and ultimately contribute to improved academic success.

Your participation involves completing a short survey about your grading and assessment practices. You may not benefit personally from this study; however, your participation may provide a long-term benefit by identifying the grading and assessment practices associated with greater levels of student motivation and engagement. There are no costs for participating in this study other than the time you will spend completing the survey.

Your answers to the survey items will be strictly confidential. We will not tell anyone the answers you give us; however, information from the study and the consent form signed by you may be reviewed or copied for research or legal purposes by Virginia Commonwealth University. The findings from this study may be presented at meetings or published in papers, but your name will never be used in these presentations or papers. Further, only summary results of the study will be reported; results *will not be* reported at the school or classroom levels.

You do not have to participate in this study. If you choose to participate, you may stop at any time without any penalty. You may also choose not to answer particular questions that are asked in the survey. You may withdraw from the study at any time, for any reason, without any consequence from VCU or the school division.

In the future, if you have questions about your participation in this study, contact:

Dr. Jim McMillan
Professor of Education
804-827-2620
jhmcmill@vcu.edu

CONSENT

I have been given the chance to read this consent form. I understand the information about this study. Questions that I wanted to ask about the study have been answered. My signature says that I am willing to participate in this study.

| Participant name printed | Participant signature | Date |

Name of Person Conducting Informed Consent
Discussion / Witness
(Printed)

Signature of Person Conducting Informed Consent   Date
Discussion / Witness

Investigator signature (if different from above)   Date

FIGURE 5.8   Example of Consent Form

observational study is investigating whether teachers' use of specific feedback affects student motivation, if students know the intent of the study they might fake, to a certain extent, their on-task behavior. If deception is used, participants are often *debriefed* about the actual nature of the study. Debriefing is important in studies in which the welfare of the participants would be improved and in situations where, if there is no debriefing, there may be risk.

Youth Assent Form

TITLE OF STUDY: Evaluation of Partners in the Arts Professional Development

This form may have some words that you do not know. Please ask someone to explain any words that you do not know. You may take home a copy of this form to think about and talk to your parents about before you decide if you want to be in this study.

I am here to ask you questions because I am doing a study on some training that your teacher has been doing. Your teacher has learned some new things and new ways to teach. For example, your teacher has been using art to teach you other subjects, such as science or math. I want to find out whether or not you have enjoyed these new things.

I am going to ask you 8 questions. These questions will be about what happens during the times when your teacher uses art with your other subjects, such as math and science. I will be writing down and taping the things you say, but I will not tell your teacher or your parent what you have said. I will be writing a report about what all of the children are saying about this program, but I will not use anyone's name.

You may decide not to answer a question, and you may stop this interview at any time. This interview should last about 30 minutes. If you decide to be in this research study, you will be asked to sign this form. Do not sign the form until you have all your questions answered and understand what will happen to you.

We will not tell anyone the answers you give us. We will not share your answers with your teachers or parents or friends. If we talk about this study in speeches or in writing, we will never use your name.

You do not have to be in this study. If you choose to be in the study, you may stop at any time. No one will blame you or criticize you if you drop out of the study. If you have questions about being in this study, you can talk to the following persons or you can have your parent or another adult call:

Dr. James McMillan
1015 W. Main Street, Richmond, VA 23834-2020
(804) 827-2620

Do not sign this form if you have any questions. Be sure someone answers your questions.

CONSENT
I have read this form. I understand the information about this study. I am willing to be in this study.

_____   _____   _____
Youth name printed   Youth signature   Date

_____   _____   _____
Witness Signature **(Required)**   Date
The witness must be an adult aged 18 or older, present when signed

FIGURE 5.9   Example of Student Assent Form

Finally, a determination needs to be made about whether withholding a program from a control group has the potential to cause risk in the sense that, if the control group received the intervention, it could have improved behavior or performance.

Privacy

The privacy of research participants must be protected. This means that access to participants' characteristics, responses, behavior, and other information is restricted to the researcher. The researcher ensures privacy by using three practices: (1) anonymity, (2) confidentiality, and (3) appropriate storing of data.

Anonymity means that the researcher cannot identify the participants from information that has been gathered. When we say that the data are anonymous, there is no way for the

Anonymity: no link between data and participants

researchers to know who said or did what, even when inspecting data that are collected. This results in excellent privacy. Anonymity is easily achieved in much survey research in which little or no identifiable information is gathered and the participants' responses are objective, with no open-ended questions. This would be the case if a survey designed to assess the impact of technology consisted solely of 20 questions using a five-point response scale. In some kinds of research, such as face-to-face interviews and observational studies, strict anonymity is not possible. In other situations, such as using Internet surveys, anonymity may be "assured," but participants may not be confident that their responses will not be matched to them.

Confidentiality: only researcher has access to data and participants' names

Confidentiality means that no one has access to individual data or the names of the participants except the researcher(s) and that the subjects know before they participate who will see the data. Confidentiality is ensured by making certain that the data cannot be linked to individual subjects by name. This can be accomplished in several ways, including (1) collecting the data anonymously; (2) using a system to link names to data that can be destroyed; (3) using a third party to link names to data and then giving the results to the researcher without the names; (4) asking subjects to use aliases or numbers; and (5) reporting only group, not individual, results. Boruch and Cecil (1979) provide details of many different procedures for ensuring confidentiality.

The third strategy for protecting privacy is to store the data, including both paper copies of responses and electronic forms of data, in a way that provides maximum protection of the participants' identities. This is accomplished by securing information with locks, and destroying any linking information. For example, in a study that examined the relationship between grades and test scores, schools could match student names with grades and test scores and create a dataset that did not include any student names or identifying information.

Some research (e.g., studies of the effects of drugs) obviously has potential danger that must be considered carefully by the investigator. Although much educational research may not seem to involve any ethical problems, the investigator's view may be biased. It is best to seek the advice and approval of others. Consulting with others provides an impartial perspective and can help the researcher identify procedures for protecting participants from harm.

Understanding research ethics is an important responsibility of the researcher. Check your understanding of ethical considerations presented in this section by going to MyEducationLab for Research at www.myeducationlab.com. Click on the topic "Introduction to Educational Research" and then select the Building Research Skills exercise titled "Understanding Research Ethics."

There is also an interesting, if not frustrating, interaction between being ethical, on the one hand, and designing the research to provide the best, most objective data, on the other. It is relatively easy, for example, to observe behavior unobtrusively, such that the subjects might never know they were in an experiment. As previously noted, the Hawthorne effect can reduce the validity of the study. To maximize both internal and external validity, therefore, it seems best for subjects to be unaware that they are being studied. Suppose, for instance, that a researcher planted a confederate in a class in order to record unobtrusively the attending behavior of college students. Does the researcher have an obligation to tell the students that their behavior is being recorded? If the students are aware of being observed, will this awareness change their behavior and invalidate the results? Such situations present ethical dilemmas, and the researcher must weigh the criteria listed above in order to determine the best course of action.

See Table 5.4 for a summary of key points for conducting ethical research.

TABLE 5.4 Keys to Conducting Ethical Research

- Be knowledgeable about ethical principles, professional guidelines, and legal requirements.
- Maximize potential benefits.
- Minimize potential risks.
- Obtain needed permission.
- Minimize potential misinterpretations and misuses of results.
- Obtain informed consent.
- Protect the privacy and confidentiality of the subjects.

Institutional Review Board

Because it is not always clear whether studies are conducted in an ethical way, and because no set of guidelines can be used effectively by all researchers in all circumstances to assure that a study is meeting ethical standards, most organizations, including all universities, have put in place a panel of professionals that will review proposed studies. That panel is called the **Institutional Review Board (IRB)**. The IRB is responsible for reviewing and approving proposed *human subjects research*. This process is used to assure compliance with federal regulations and helps to assure that the researcher has considered all ethical issues. Each institution's IRB operation is unique, though the general guidelines are the same.

Institutional Review Board (IRB): panel that approves studies

The first very important function of the IRB is to determine whether a proposed study meets the criteria for human subjects research. The term *research* refers to a systematic investigation designed to develop or contribute to generalizable knowledge. *Generalizable* means that the purpose of the study is to add to the professional knowledge in a field that would be of interest to others around the country and throughout the world. It is based on the intent of the researcher. If the intent is to contribute to the knowledge base in a profession or discipline, then it meets the test of generalizability. This means that a local study, in which the results would only be used in a restricted context, may not need IRB approval. Class projects for research courses and evaluation studies also may not need IRB approval. However, if *ever* the results will be disseminated to the field, IRB approval may be needed.

A *human subject* is a living individual about whom an investigator obtains data through an intervention or interaction with the individual or uses identifiable private information. That is, any individual who participates as a recipient of an intervention or control, or from whom data are collected, is considered a human subject for IRB purposes. Hence, studies that employ existing databases, in which there is no identifiable information, would typically not need IRB approval, nor would instrument development research. In some organizations qualitative case studies, in which there is no *systematic* collection of data, would not need IRB approval.

What is important in dealing with an IRB is that each investigator needs to check carefully the requirements and protocols that have been established in his or her organization or, in the case of federally funded research, with IRB requirements of the federal funding agency. Although it may seem clear that a proposed study does not meet the definition of human subjects research, it is best to at least check in an informal way with the IRB office to be sure that IRB approval is not needed.

IRB reviews fall into three categories—full, exempt, and expedited. The full IRB review includes a formal inspection of all aspects of the research by everyone on the institutional board. It is used for studies that clearly meet the definition of human subjects research and where there is a need for careful review of the protocol, the nature of the intervention, if there is one, and the procedures for obtaining informed consent. An **exempt** review is one that does not need to meet all federal IRB guidelines but still requires some level of review. It usually involves studies in one or more of the following categories: research in a commonly accepted educational setting without changes in normal activities, regular testing, surveys, interviews, observations, and existing databases with identifiable information. An **expedited** review is a process in which a small number of IRB panel members approve studies that are judged to involve no more than minimal risk to the participants. *Minimal risk* means that the probability and magnitude of harm or discomfort anticipated are not greater than what would be experienced in routine, day-to-day activities (e.g., taking exams at the end of an instructional unit). Expedited reviews are appropriate for studies in which there is an examination of data, documents, or records that are collected regularly for established nonresearch purposes and for involvement with participants for whom there is minimal risk, such as the use of focus groups, program evaluations, and surveys. Both exempt and expedited reviews are processed more quickly than full reviews.

Exempt: moderate review

Expedited: minimal review

Professional Integrity

Both the AERA and the APA have ethical guidelines that researchers need to be aware of (see http://www.aera.net and http://www.apa.org/ethics/ for the latest information). These guidelines are used as the basis for conducting and publishing research. Strike (2006) emphasizes the need for researchers to be sensitive to issues such as beneficence (benefits more than risks), justice, respect for persons, protecting vulnerable populations (e.g., children), and social betterment. Strike concludes by stressing the need to "advanc[e] the aims of the community . . . [and] to promote individual and social welfare" (pp. 71–72). Most important, researchers must respect the rights and welfare of individuals and groups, as well as the institutions created to enhance this welfare.

Another category of ethical issues is concerned with the authorship and scientific integrity of researchers. The American Psychological Association (2001) lists two goals of their ethical principles (p. 48):

1. To ensure the accuracy of scientific and scholarly knowledge
2. To protect intellectual property rights

Accuracy is ensured when the methods of an investigation can be replicated so that others can verify the knowledge claims. Hence, researchers have an ethical obligation to report the methods in detail, not to make up, modify, or omit data, with immediate correction of errors. **Plagiarism** is avoided by giving appropriate credit to the contributions of others. This may involve the use of quotation marks for verbatim use of others' writing or oral communication, tables and figures (e.g., Conway, 2006, p. 34), or references to a source so that authors do not represent the work of others as their own (e.g., Conway, 2006). Authorship is appropriate for individuals who have made a substantial professional contribution to the work. With multiple authors, the order listed typically ranks the individuals on the basis of how much each has contributed. Obviously, the one who makes the most substantial contribution is listed first. This is rather obvious when the order of authorship is not alphabetical. When it is alphabetical the authors, unless otherwise noted, are indicating equal contributions.

Plagiarism: failure to acknowledge others' work

When one is seeking to publish, the same manuscript should not be sent to two different journals at the same time, nor should a new submission look substantially like a previous publication. If a book chapter is based on a previously published article, what is repeated should be identified. Data should be available on request by journal editors (raw data as well as instruments, instructions, intervention delivery manuals, and software are expected to be kept for five years after publication).

Legal Constraints

Most of the legal constraints placed on researchers since 1974 have focused on protecting the rights and welfare of human subjects. These requirements are generally consistent with the ethical principles summarized earlier, and are in a constant state of reinterpretation and change by the courts.

The Family Educational Rights and Privacy Act (FERPA) of 1974, known as the Buckley Amendment, allows individuals to gain access to information pertaining to them, such as test scores, teacher comments, and recommendations. The act also states that written permission of consent is legally necessary with data that identify students by name. The consent must indicate the information that will be disclosed, the purpose of the disclosure, and to whom it will be disclosed. Exceptions to this requirement are granted for research using school records in which the results are of "legitimate educational interest" and when only group data are reported. It should be noted that data gathered in a study can usually be subpoenaed by the courts, even if confidentiality has been promised to the participants by the researcher.

The National Research Act of 1974 requires review of proposed research by an appropriate group in an institution (school division or university) to protect the rights and welfare of the subjects. Although most research involving human subjects must be reviewed by such a group, there are some exceptions, such as research using test data that result from normal testing programs and analyzing existing public data, records, or documents without identifying individuals. These regulations were expanded and modified in 1991 with publication of the *Code of Federal Regulations for the Protection of Human Subjects*. The code was further updated in 2003.

FERPA was enacted to protect the privacy of student education records. The law applies to all schools that receive funds under an applicable program of the U.S. Department of Education. FERPA gives parents certain rights with respect to their children's education records. These rights transfer to the student when he or she reaches the age of 18 or attends a school beyond the high school level.

The major provisions of FERPA that have implications for researchers are as follows:

- Parents or eligible students have the right to inspect and review the student's education records maintained by the school.
- Generally, schools must have written permission from the parent or eligible student in order to release any information from a student's education record. However, FERPA allows schools to disclose those records, without consent, in certain circumstances, such as to school officials with legitimate educational interest, for audit or evaluation purposes; and to organizations conducting certain studies for or on behalf of the school
- Parents have the right to tell schools not to disclose information such as a student's name, address, telephone number, date and place of birth, honors and awards, and dates of attendance.

FERPA definitely constrains what student data may be shared with researchers, and any requests to the school division to access records must address FERPA guidelines. The prepared researcher will do this as part of a request for data.

In 2008, the U.S. Department of Education suggested revisions to FERPA to provide continued access to student data. These comprise the most sweeping changes to the law in decades. Because these changes were still being reviewed at the time this book went to press, readers should check the U.S. Department of Education's website to obtain details of the changes.

CHAPTER SUMMARY

This chapter introduced the fundamental characteristics of designing quantitative research. It focused particular attention on variables that should be considered in designing and interpreting the research. Key points include the following:

1. Research design refers to the way a study is planned and conducted.
2. The purpose of a good research design is to enhance the credibility of the results by taking into account three sources of variability: systematic, error, and extraneous.
3. Choice of variables should include consideration of the sensitivity to detect differences and relationships.
4. Valid research designs provide results that have few plausible rival hypotheses and that approximate what is reality or truth.
5. Strong design validity is always a function of professional judgment; there are no designs in field settings that do not have possible extraneous and confounding variables.
6. Threats to validity include those that are possible, not controlled by the design but rarely serious, and probable or plausible, having a likelihood of affecting the results.
7. Statistical conclusion validity is concerned with whether there is an actual relationship.
8. Threats to the internal validity of quantitative studies include selection, history, statistical regression, pretesting, instrumentation, subject attrition, maturation, diffusion of intervention, experimenter effects, intervention replications, subject effects, and statistical conclusion.

9. Construct validity considers the match between theoretical constructs and actual interventions and measures.
10. Threats to external validity that limit generalizability are classified as population characteristics or ecological conditions.
11. Researchers should be aware of ethical responsibilities and legal constraints that accompany the gathering and reporting of information.
12. Generally accepted guidelines for the ethical conduct of research with human subjects includes full disclosure, voluntary participation, informed consent, absence of coercion, confidentiality, and no risk or harm to participants.
13. Active informed consent includes participant knowledge and acceptance of procedures, any risks or discomforts, benefits, voluntary participation, nature of confidentiality, and assurance that nonparticipation will not result in any harm or detriment.
14. The Institutional Review Board (IRB) is responsible for approving human subjects research. The IRB determines if the study meets requirements for research with human subjects and ensures that appropriate ethical and legal guidelines are followed.
15. Every researcher has an obligation to conduct his or her study in a manner that is consistent with professional guidelines.
16. Legal guidelines for conducting research have been set by the federal government, including, most recently, revisions of the Family Educational Rights and Privacy Act (FERPA).

APPLICATION PROBLEMS

1. For each case described here, list potential threats to internal and external validity.

   a. Two researchers designed a study to investigate whether physical education performance is affected by being in a class with students of the same sex only or in a class with students of both sexes. A college instructor is found to cooperate with the researchers. Three sections of the same tennis class are offered: an all-male section, an all-female section, and a mixed section. The researchers control the instructor variable by using the same person as the instructor for each section, informing the instructor about the study and emphasizing to the instructor the need to keep instructional activities the same for each section. One section is offered in the morning, one at noon, and one in the afternoon. Students sign up for the course by using the same procedure as for all courses, although there is a footnote about the gender composition in the schedule of courses. A pretest is given to control for existing differences in the groups.

   b. In this study, the effect of day care on children's prosocial behavior is examined. A group of volunteer parents agree to participate in the study. (The investigators pay part of the day-care fees.) Children are assigned randomly from the pool of volunteers either to attend a day-care facility of their choice or not to attend. Observers measure the degree of prosocial behavior before and after attending day care for nine months by observing the children on a playground.

   c. A superintendent wishes to get some idea of whether or not a bond issue will pass in a forthcoming election. Records listing real estate taxpayers are obtained from the county office. From this list, a random sample of 10 percent of 3,000 persons is called by phone two weeks before election day and asked whether they intend to vote yes or no.

   d. The Green County School Board decided that it wanted a status assessment of the ninth-graders' attitudes toward science. A questionnaire was designed and distributed in January to all ninth-grade science teachers. Each teacher was told to give the questionnaire within six weeks, to calculate mean scores for each question, and to return the questionnaires and results to the district office. The instructors were told to take only one class period for the questionnaires in order to minimize interference with the course. Sixty percent of the questionnaires were returned.

ANSWERS TO APPLICATION PROBLEMS

1. a. Evidently, the instructor knew about the study, and his or her bias could affect the results. Subjects choose the sections they will be in; hence, selection is a major threat. The time of day that the sections meet may affect selection and is itself a threat to internal validity. There is no assurance that the instructor will treat each section the same way. Diffusion of treatment may be a problem if students from different sections interact. Some students may purposely score low on the pretest in order to show significant improvement in the course (instrumentation—the results may be inaccurate). History may also be a threat, depending on the nature of the class groups. Generalizability is limited to the students taking the course in this particular college, the course itself (tennis), the instructor, and the methods used in the class.

   b. Instrumentation is a potential threat, because details about the nature of the observations are lacking. Test validity could also be considered, because measuring prosocial behavior in a playground may not reflect the benefits of day-care attendance. Compensatory rivalry or resentment might be a factor, because mothers who were chosen as a control group might arrange other experiences for their children that would enhance prosocial behavior. External validity is limited because of the volunteer nature of the sample and the specific programs of the day-care institutions utilized. If many different day-care organizations are represented, it will be difficult to generalize about the cause of the difference. Each case will have to be examined individually.

   c. The question here is whether the population that votes is the same as the population from which the sample is drawn; after all, those who rent can also vote, so, depending on the percentage of renters in the district, sampling property owners alone may be misleading. In addition, not all property owners have children who go to school, and only a portion of the population ever votes. The generalizability of the results thus would be suspect. Depending on the nature of the issue at hand, some respondents may provide less than honest information. They may also change their minds within the two weeks before voting.

d. The major threat is selection, because only 60 percent of the population returned questionnaires, and teachers could withhold information if they want to. Instrumentation may be a threat, depending on the way the questionnaire was designed (validity and reliability, and the standardization of the way it is administered—that is, its directions). There is a chance for scoring error, because each instructor does his or her own scoring. Subject attrition might be a problem. Because the questionnaire was given only once, students who were absent would be excluded. The generalizability of the results would be limited by the nature of the sample that returned questionnaires and the time of year the study was done.

Participants, Subjects, and Sampling for Quantitative Designs

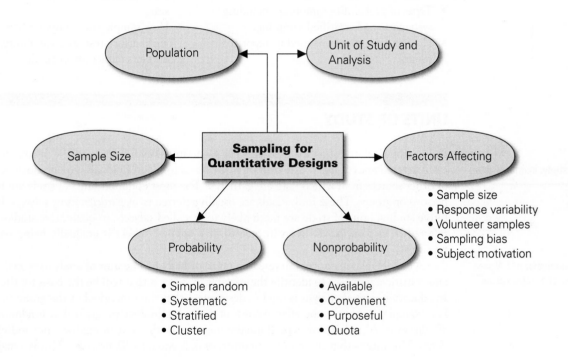

KEY TERMS

unit of study	stratified random sampling
unit of analysis	proportional sampling
sample	nonproportional sampling
population	cluster sampling
probability sampling	multistage cluster sampling
random sampling	nonprobability sampling
margin of error	convenience sampling
simple random sampling	purposeful sampling
systematic sampling	quota sampling

WHAT YOU WILL LEARN

Study this chapter and you will learn:

- The difference between populations and samples.
- The importance of determining the unit of study and unit of analysis.
- Types of probability sampling, including systematic and stratified sampling.
- How margin of error is used in reporting results.

- Types of nonprobability sampling, including available and purposeful sampling.
- How to estimate an appropriate sample size.
- How sample size, sampling bias, subject motivation, response variability, and volunteer samples affect results.

UNITS OF STUDY

Unit of study: individual data sources

Doing empirical investigations requires the gathering of data from someone or something, generally termed *units of study*. The **unit of study** refers to the individuals, groups, documents, sites, or other sources from which data are gathered. The most common units of study are individual persons or groups. These individuals are usually referred to as *participants* or *subjects*. In quantitative studies, units of study are more likely to be called *subjects*; in qualitative studies, they are referred to as *participants*. Even in quantitative studies, *subject* is gradually being replaced by *participant*.

Unit of analysis: *n* or *N* used for design and statistical purposes

A closely related concept in research is *unit of analysis*. The **unit of analysis** is used for design and statistical purposes to identify the variable of interest that will be the basis for the analyses. In education, *unit of analysis* is used to designate either the individual or the group as one unit. For example, a study of the effectiveness of a new technology program that is administered in 30 classes of 20 individuals would usually use class as the unit of analysis, not individual students. This means that the number of units, or *n*, is equal to 30, not 600. This is a major difference.

The manner in which units of study are selected is critical, and the descriptions of those individuals and/or groups are important in interpreting the results and in making generalizations of findings to other individuals and/or groups. Suppose you conduct a study of the relationship of adolescent loneliness to parenting styles. Notices are sent to parents so that permission can be obtained to survey high school students. You obtain a 30% response rate, limiting your sample significantly, which would affect the interpretation of the findings. For example, how likely are parents who believe that their child is lonely, or who are not confident about their parenting style, to give permission for their children to participate? This has an impact on the findings, especially if there is a small relationship, since a greater range of students might allow the researcher to detect a relationship.

Generalization is often part of the reason for doing quantitative studies, so it is imperative for the descriptions to be detailed. In qualitative studies there are far fewer participants. In these studies, researchers are very careful in selecting individuals who will provide needed information to result in a complete and thorough understanding of what is being studied. A good

EXCERPT 6.1   Descriptions of Units of Study

Students were enrolled in one of three kindergarten classes: 283 students (57.9%) attended half-day classes (157 half-day morning and 126 half-day afternoon) and 206 students (42.1%) attended full-day classes. Student ages ranged from 5 years 0 months to 6 years 6 months upon entering kindergarten; overall average age was 5 years 7 months. The total study included 208 girls (44.0%) and 256 boys (56.0%). The majority of students received no mone-tary assistance for lunch, which was based on parent income (89.0%, $n = 424$); 49 students (10.0%) received some assistance. Twenty-six students (5.3%) spoke a language at home other than English. The majority of students (90.5%), $n = 424$) were Caucasian; 31 students (6.3%) were Hispanic; and 14 students (2.8%) were African American, Native American, or Asian American. Those data reflect the community demographics within the school district. (p. 264)

Source: From Wolgemuth, J R., Cobb, R. B., Winokur, M. A., Leech, N., & Ellerby, D. (2006). Comparing longitudinal academic achievement of full-day and half-day kindergarten students. *The Journal of Educational Research 99*(5), 260–269.

description of the subjects contained in the narrative of a study is presented in Excerpt 6.1. Often researchers will use tables to present demographic information about the participants or subjects in their study (Excerpt 6.2).

SAMPLING

In quantitative studies, the group of subjects or participants from whom the data are collected is referred to as the **sample**. The sample can be selected from a larger group of persons, identified as the population, or can simply refer to the group of subjects from whom data are collected (even though the subjects are not selected from the population). The nature of the sampling procedure used in a particular study is usually described by one or more adjectives, such as *random convenience* or *stratified*. This describes the technique used to form the sample.

Sample: group of individuals from whom data are collected

We will consider two major categories of different sampling techniques: probability and nonprobability. First, though, some further discussion of *population* is needed.

What Is a Population?

A **population** is a group of elements or cases, whether individuals, objects, or events, that conform to specific criteria and to which we intend to generalize the results of the research. This group is also referred to as the *target population* or *universe*. The target population is often different from the list of elements from which the sample is actually selected, which is termed the *survey population* or *sampling frame*. For example, in a study of beginning teachers, the target population may be first-year teachers across the United States in all types of schools. The survey population may be a list of first-year teachers from 24 states. Thus, although the intent of the research is to generalize to all beginning teachers, the sampling frame places some limitations on such generalizations.

Population: total group to which results can be generalized

It is important for researchers to carefully and completely define both the target population and the sampling frame. This begins with the research problem and review of literature, through which a population is described conceptually or in broad terms. A more specific definition is then needed based on demographic characteristics such as age, gender, location, grade level, position, and time of year. These characteristics are sometimes referred to as *delimiting variables*. For example, in a study of rural first-grade minority students, there are four delimiting variables: rural, students, first-grade, and minority. A complete description is then included in the subjects section of the report or article.

Probability Sampling

In **probability sampling** subjects are drawn from a larger population in such a way that the probability of selecting each member of the population is known. This type of sampling is conducted to efficiently provide estimates of what is true for a population from a smaller group of subjects

Probability sampling: known probability of selection of units

EXCERPT 6.2   Table Summarizing Demographic Characteristics of Subjects

Table 1   Demographics of Respondents (n-120) by Number and Percentage

	Head Start (N = 83)		Pre-K (N = 37)	
	N	%	N	%
Gender				
Female	73	88%	35	95%
Male	3	4%	2	5%
Age				
20–29 years	20	24%	3	8%
30–39 years	17	21%	11	30%
40–49 years	11	13%	4	11%
50 years or older	12	15%	6	16%
Years working with young children				
0–2 years	5	6%	1	3%
3–5 years	20	24%	3	8%
6–10 years	25	30%	12	32%
Over 10 years	28	34%	20	54%
Years working with young children with disabilities				
Less than 1 year	15	18%	4	11%
1–3 years	17	21%	11	30%
More than 3 years	27	33%	13	35%
Types of disabilities				
Speech and language disorder	59	71%	28	76%
Physical impairments	28	34%	18	49%
Sensory impairments	19	23%	11	30%
Autism	30	36%	14	38%
Developmental delay	47	57%	25	68%
Social/emotional delay	38	46%	19	52%
Highest degree				
Associate	38	46%	n/a	n/a
Bachelor's	31	37%	28	76%
Master's	3	4%	7	18%
Ethnicity				
Anglo American	46	55%	27	73%
Hispanic American	1	1%	0	0%
African American	18	22%	4	11%
Asian American	0	0%	0	0%
Native American	4	5%	1	3%
Biracial/Bicultural	3	4%	1	3%

Note: Totals not equal to 100% are due to rounding or missing data.

Source: From Bruns, D. A., & Mogharreban, C. C. (2007). The gap between belief and practices: Early childhood practitioners' perceptions about inclusion. *Journal of Research in Childhood Education, 21*(3), 229–241. Reprinted by permission of D. A. Bruns and the *Association for Childhood Education International,* 17904 Georgia Avenue, Suite 215, Olney MD 20832. Copyright © 2007 by the Association.

(sample) (see Figure 6.1). That is, what is described in a sample will also be true, with some degree of error, of the population. When probability sampling is done correctly, a very small percentage of the population can be selected. This saves time and money without sacrificing accuracy. In fact, in most social science and educational research, it is both impractical and unnecessary to measure all elements of the population of interest.

Several methods of probability sampling can be used to draw representative, or *unbiased,* samples from a population. Each method involves some type of **random sampling**, in which each

Random sampling: each member of the population, or of subgroups, has an equal probability of being selected

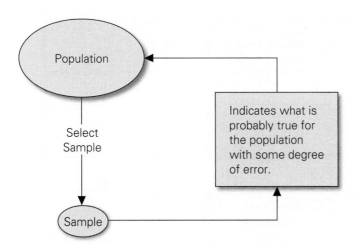

FIGURE 6.1   **Relationship of the Sample to the Population**

member of the population as a whole, or of subgroups of the population, has the same chance of being selected as other members in the same group. Bias is avoided with random sampling because there is a high probability that all the population characteristics will be represented in the sample. If the correct procedures are not followed, though, what may seem to be random sampling will actually produce a biased sample (biased in the sense that certain population characteristics are over- or underrepresented). For example, you may think that you can obtain a random sample of college students by standing at a busy corner and selecting every third or fourth student. However, you may not be able to keep an accurate count, and you may inadvertently select more males or females or more older or younger students. Such a procedure would result in a biased sample.

Random Sampling

The steps taken to draw a random sample are illustrated in Figure 6.2. These steps show how the sample is used to make statements about the population of interest. A key concept in sampling is that there is always some degree of error in random sampling, and that error must be considered in interpreting the results. The calculation of error is fairly complex, but the idea makes logical sense (see Figure 6.3). For example, consider a population of 1,000 high school seniors, from which a 10% sample (100) is drawn randomly to estimate the attitudes of the seniors toward technology. Suppose the average score for these students was 80, indicating a positive attitude. This number, 80, can be used to estimate the attitudes of all 1,000 seniors. But if you draw another 10% random sample, it is very likely that the average for these 100 seniors will not be exactly 80. Because we draw only one sample, therefore, we have to use statistics to determine the extent of the error we need to consider in evaluating the results. This is essentially what political pollsters do when they report that a certain percentage of the population will vote for one candidate or the other. For example, if the percentage calculated from the sample was 45 percent for Mr. Doright, the results

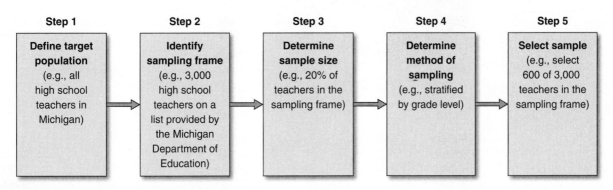

FIGURE 6.2   **Steps in Probability Sampling**

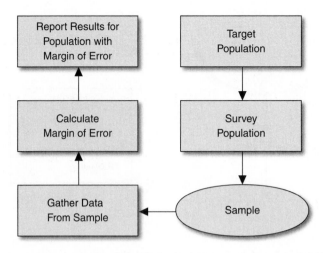

FIGURE 6.3 **Sampling and Margin of Error**

Margin of error: likely error in reporting population results

would be reported to be something like 45 percent +/− 3 percent. The plus or minus 3 percent is the *margin of error*. The **margin of error** indicates an interval within which the true or actual population result lies. In political polling there is typically a 95 percent probability that the *population* mean for Mr. Doright is somewhere between 42 and 48, but we can't be sure where.

In the next section, we consider four types of random sampling: simple random sampling, systematic sampling, stratified random sampling, and cluster sampling. The type used depends on the purpose of the study as well as on the investigator's resources and the size of the population.

Simple random sampling: every member of the population has the same chance of being selected

Simple Random Sampling In **simple random sampling**, subjects are selected from the population so that all members have the same probability of being chosen. This method is often used when the population is small. For example, a common type of simple random sampling is drawing names out of a hat.

With a large population, it is necessary to use a more precise procedure. One such procedure is to use a table of random numbers, which is a set of randomly assorted digits. Suppose, for example, that a researcher has a population of 100 third-graders and wants to select 20 by simple random sampling. First, each third-grader in the population is assigned a number from 001 to 100. (It could be 00 to 99.) Second, the researcher randomly selects a starting point in a table of random numbers. Then he or she reads all three-digit numbers, moving either across rows or down columns. The researcher follows the three-digit rows or columns while selecting 20 three-digit numbers between 000 and 100. Table 6.1 contains an example of simple random sampling.

TABLE 6.1 Randomly Assorted Digits		
46614	20002	17918
16249	05217	54102
91530	62481	05374
62800	62660	20186
10089	96488	59058
47361	73443	11859
45690	71058	53634
50423	53342	71710
89292	32114	83942
23410	41943	33278
59844	81871	18710
98795	87894	00510
86085	03164	26333
37390	60137	93842
28420	10704	89412

EXCERPT 6.3 Simple Random Sampling

The sample (*n* = 600) was randomly drawn from the enrolled population of University of Florida (UF) undergraduates (30,866) who were 18 years of age or older and holding a free computing account. . . . Because other population characteristics were not considered relevant to the research questions for this preliminary investigation, we chose not to draw a stratified sample. (p. 549)

Source: From Pealer, L. N., Weiler, R. M., Piggs, R. M., Jr., Miller, D., & Dorman, S. M. (2001). The feasibility of a web-based surveillance system to collect health risk behavior data from college students. *Health Education and Behavior, 28,* 547–559.

Five of the 20 subjects chosen to be included in the sample are circled, beginning with the top left and moving down each column.

A more efficient and increasingly popular way to draw a simple random sample is by using an appropriate computer software program, such as SPSS. This is especially easy and effective if the sampling frame is in an electronic format. Simple random sampling is easy to explain, but it requires each member of the population to be assigned a number or be available electronically. Often this is not possible or would take considerable time, energy, or resources. As we will now see, systematic sampling avoids some of these disadvantages. Excerpt 6.3 provides an example of simple random sampling.

Systematic Sampling   In **systematic sampling**, every *n*th element is selected from a list of all elements in the survey population, beginning with a randomly selected element. Suppose there is a need to draw a 10 percent sample from a population of 100. A number from 1 to 10 is randomly selected as the starting point. If 5 is selected, every 10th name on the list will then be selected: 5, 15, 25, 35, and so on. This approach can be used only when the researcher has a sequential list of all the subjects in the population, but it is easier than simple random sampling because not every member of the population needs to be numbered.

Systematic sampling is illustrated in Figure 6.4. From among 60 students, we need to select 6 to be in our sample (10 percent). We would randomly select a number from 1 to 10 (say, 2) and then select every 10th student for our sample.

Systematic sampling: taking every *n*th subject

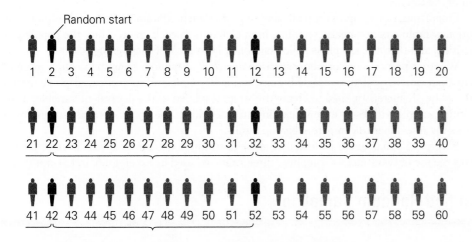

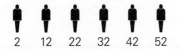

FIGURE 6.4 **Systematic Sampling**
Source: Adapted from Babbie (2007).

EXCERPT 6.4   Systematic Sampling

Using a list of kindergarten teachers supplied by the Department of Education in the State of Florida, 1,000 kindergarten teachers from different schools were selected by systematic sampling. The researcher selected every sixth name from the list. This was to ensure that the classroom would be represented from the sixty-seven counties in Florida. (p. 3)

Source: From Gayle-Evans, G. (2004). It is never too soon: A study of kindergarten teachers' implementation of multicultural education in Florida's classrooms. *The Professional Educator, 26*(2), 1–15.

There is a possible weakness in systematic sampling if the list of cases in the population is arranged in a systematic pattern that is related to what is being investigated. For example, suppose we are sampling teachers from many schools and the list obtained from each school is rank ordered in terms of length of service. If this cyclical pattern (referred to as *periodicity*) is related to every nth subject, the sample would systematically exclude teachers with certain ages and would not represent the population. Alphabetical lists do not usually create periodicity and are suitable for choosing subjects systematically.

An advantage of systematic sampling is that if the population is rank ordered on a variable that is related to the dependent variable, this ordering has the effect of making sure that the sample is represented by each level of that variable. For instance, if the population list is ordered by aptitude test scores (highest scores first, followed by lower scores), when we then select every nth subject, we will be assured that all levels of aptitude will be represented in the sample. Systematic sampling is illustrated in Excerpt 6.4. Notice that using systematic sampling resulted in geographic representation.

Stratified random sampling: selecting subjects from population strata or groups

Proportional sampling: reflects the proportion of different strata in the population

Nonproportional sampling: does not reflect the proportion of different strata in the population

Stratified Random Sampling   A common variation of simple random sampling is called **stratified random sampling**. In this procedure, the population is divided into subgroups, or strata, on the basis of a variable chosen by the researcher, such as gender, age, location, or level of education. Once the population has been divided, samples are drawn randomly from each subgroup. The number of subjects drawn is either *proportional* or *nonproportional*. **Proportional** (or *proportionate*) **sampling** is based on the percentage of subjects in the population that is present in each stratum. Thus, if 40 percent of the subjects in the population are represented in the first stratum, then 40 percent of the final sample should be from that stratum. In **nonproportional** (or *disproportionate*) **sampling**, the researcher selects the same number of subjects to be in each stratum of the sample.

Proportional or nonproportional sampling from each stratum is done with either simple random sampling or systematic sampling from elements in each group. Thus, the population is stratified, and then the sample is pulled randomly from each of these groups.

Whether proportional or nonproportional, stratified random sampling is often more efficient than simple random sampling because a smaller number of subjects needs to be used. As long as the characteristic used to create the strata is related to the dependent variable, using a stratified sample will result in less sampling error. Dividing the population into subgroups also allows the researcher to compare subgroup results.

Excerpts 6.5, 6.6, and 6.7 illustrate the use of stratified random sampling. Excerpt 6.5 illustrates the use of two strata for sampling; three strata are used in Excerpt 6.6. In Excerpt 6.7, the

EXCERPT 6.5   Stratified Random Sampling

A total of 126 elementary and 63 middle schools representing 22 of the 24 counties in Maryland were selected to participate in the research project. We used a stratified random sampling procedure to select schools, with the strata defined by three levels of percentage of free or reduced-price lunch and three levels of MSPAP performance (lower, middle, or upper third) . . . the percentage of schools with the cells varied, from approximately 8% to 14%. Next, we randomly sampled elementary and middle schools reflecting each of the combinations. (p. 310)

Source: From Parke, C. S., & Lane, S. (2007). Students' perceptions of a Maryland state performance assessment. *The Elementary School Journal, 107*(3), 305–324.

EXCERPT 6.6   Stratified Random Sampling

A stratified random sample of schools was selected across population density (i.e., urban, suburban, and rural), enrollment (i.e., 0–599, 600–999, 1000 and greater), and school levels (i.e., middle school and high school). Percentages of schools across population density and enrollment [and level] were established to maintain a sample consistent with the overall make-up of schools in Maryland. (p. 329)

Source: From Maccini, P., & Gagnon, J. C. (2002). Perceptions and application of NCTM standards by special and general education teachers. *Exceptional Children, 68*(3), 325–344.

EXCERPT 6.7   Stratified Random Sampling Participants

Thirty-six female elementary school teachers were randomly selected from a volunteer pool in a southern school district. The sample consisted of 18 second-grade teachers and 18 fifth-grade teachers and was restricted to female teachers, since there were few male teachers in the school district at the primary level. Based on the EFT* scores, 9 teachers at each grade level were randomly selected from those who were field independent, and 9 others were selected from those who were field dependent. There were 12 students (6 males and 6 females) who were selected randomly from each teacher's classroom for purposes of testing. The second-grade children ranged in age from 7 years to 7 years 11 months, whereas the fifth-grade children ranged in age from 10 years to 10 years 11 months. (p. 546)

*EFT refers to the Embedded Figures Test.

Source: From Saracho, O. N., & Dayton, C. M. (1980). Relationship of teachers' cognitive styles to pupils' academic achievement gains. *Journal of Educational Psychology, 72,* 544–549.

researchers have stratified the teacher population on the basis of grade level and scores on the EFT (Embedded Figures Test) and the student population by classroom. The sampling is diagrammed in Figure 6.5. To ensure that the final sample has a sufficient number of subjects in each group, nonproportional sampling is used.

Cluster Sampling   Cluster sampling is similar to stratified random sampling in that groups of individuals are identified from the population and subjects are drawn from these groups. In **cluster sampling**, however, the researcher identifies convenient, naturally occurring groups, such as neighborhoods, schools, districts, and regions, not individual subjects, and then randomly selects some of these units for the study. Once the units have been selected, individuals are selected from each one.

> **Cluster sampling:** selection of naturally occurring groups

Cluster sampling is needed in studies in which the researcher cannot obtain a complete list of all members of the population but can identify groups, or clusters, of subjects. For example, it would be very unusual to have a single list of all of the individuals participating in adult literacy programs in a state. However, all of the literacy centers in the state (which are known) could be sampled and then individuals could be sampled from the lists provided by the selected centers.

Thus, cluster sampling consists of at least two stages. Using more than two stages (e.g., school districts, schools within districts, classrooms within schools, students within classrooms) would be called **multistage cluster sampling**. We could begin by sampling 40 of 150 school districts, then 6 classrooms in each of the 40 districts, and then 10 students in each classroom (or all students in each classroom), using simple random or systematic sampling. Multistage cluster sampling is often used in states using geographic designations or districts as units that are initially selected, with schools selected from the geographic areas or districts. Cluster sampling usually results in a less representative sample of the population than either simple or stratified random sampling. See Figure 6.6, which shows different probability sampling procedures.

> **Multistage cluster sampling:** selection of two or more levels of clusters

Nonprobability Sampling

In many quantitative studies, particularly experimental and quasi-experimental investigations, probability samples are not required or appropriate, or it may be impossible or unfeasible to select

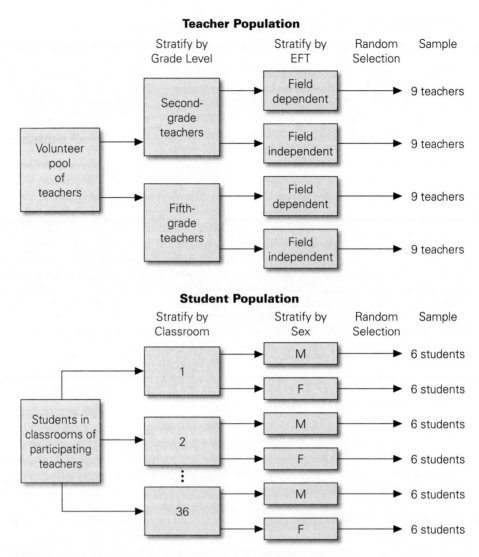

FIGURE 6.5 Stratified Random Selection of Subjects for Saracho and Dayton Study

Nonprobability sampling: no random selection

subjects from a larger group. Rather, **nonprobability sampling** is used. In fact, this form of sampling is the most common type in educational research. Nonprobability sampling does not include any type of random selection from a population. Rather, the researcher uses subjects who happen to be accessible or who may represent certain types of characteristics. For example, this could be a class of students or a group gathered for a meeting. Many circumstances bring people together in situations that are efficiently and inexpensively tapped for research.

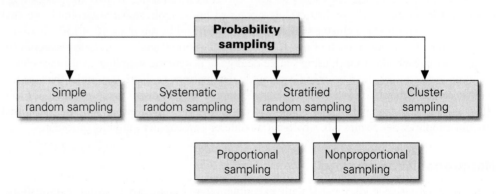

FIGURE 6.6 Types of Probability Sampling Procedures

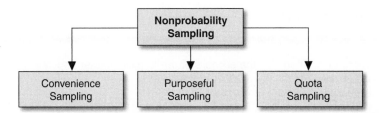

FIGURE 6.7 **Types of Nonprobability Sampling Procedures**

We will consider three types of nonprobability sampling approaches commonly used in quantitative studies: convenience sampling, purposeful sampling, and quota sampling (see Figure 6.7).

Convenience Sampling In **convenience sampling** (also called *available sampling*) a group of subjects is selected on the basis of being accessible or expedient. This could be a university class of a professor who is doing research on college student learning styles, classrooms of teachers enrolled in a graduate class, school principals who participate in a workshop or conference, people who decide to go to the mall on Saturday, or people who respond to an advertisement for subjects. Although this type of sample makes it easier to conduct the research, there is no precise way of generalizing from the sample to any type of population. This does not mean that the findings are not useful; it simply means that caution is needed in generalizing. Often, researchers will describe convenient samples carefully to show that although they were not able to employ random selection, the characteristics of the subjects matched those of the population or a substantial portion of the population.

Convenience sampling: using available subjects

Convenience samples are widely used in both quantitative and qualitative studies because this may be the best the researcher can accomplish due to practical constraints, efficiency, and accessibility. Also, the primary purpose of the research may not be to generalize but to better understand relationships that may exist. In such a case, it may not be necessary to use probability sampling. Suppose a researcher is studying the relationship between creativity and intelligence, and the only possible sample consists of children in an elementary school in his town. The study is completed, and the results indicate a moderate relationship: Children who are more intelligent tend to be more creative. Because there is no probability sampling, should we ignore the findings or suggest that the results are not credible or useful? That decision seems overly harsh. It is more reasonable to interpret the results as valid for children similar to those studied. If the school serves a low socioeconomic area, the results will not be as useful as they would be if the school represented all socioeconomic areas. The decision is not to dismiss the findings but to limit them to the type of subjects in the sample. As more and more research accumulates with different convenient samples, the overall credibility of the results will be enhanced.

Excerpts 6.8–6.10 illustrate different approaches to convenience sampling. In Excerpt 6.8 geography limits the sample, whereas in Excerpt 6.9 the sample is drawn from a school in which the researcher had worked. The approach in Excerpt 6.9 could be called *network sampling* because the researcher's network led to an opportunity to obtain a sample. This way of coming up with a sample is very common. In Excerpt 6.10 the often studied college student sample is

EXCERPT 6.8 Convenience Sampling

During the fall of 2002, the researcher surveyed the population of interest (specifically inservice teachers) with respect to their assessment literacy. The group of inservice teachers consisted of 197 teachers, representing nearly every district in a three-county area surrounding the researchers' institution. The schools were selected based on convenience due to their geographic location.

Source: From Mertler, C. A. (2003). Patterns of response and nonresponse from teachers to traditional and web surveys. *Practical Assessment, Research, & Evaluation, 8*(22). Retrieved May 10, 2004, from http://PAREonline.net/getvn.asp?v=8&n=22.

EXCERPT 6.9 Convenience Sampling

Data were collected from a rural high school in northern California at which the researcher had previously worked as a resource teacher . . . the sample ($N = 355$) consisted of the school's entire English learner population in the spring of 2002. (pp. 212–213)

Source: From Callahan, R. M. (2005). Tracking and high school English learners: Limiting opportunity to learn. *American Educational Research Journal, 44*(2), 305–328.

EXCERPT 6.10 Convenience Sampling

Participants in this investigation were 482 undergraduate students. Student volunteers were solicited primarily from educational psychology and human development courses at a large urban land-grant university in the mid-Atlantic states. (p. 704)

Source: From Buehl, M. M., & Alexander, P. A. (2005). Motivation and performance differences in students' domain-specific epistemological beliefs profiles. *American Educational Research Journal, 42*(4), 697–726.

used because they are captives with easy access. Notice too that participating is voluntary. As we will see later in this chapter, volunteering is a feature of studies that is ubiquitous in empirical studies, and it can have deleterious effects on the results.

Purposeful sampling:
selecting subjects with certain characteristics

Purposeful Sampling In **purposeful sampling** (sometimes called *purposive sampling*), the researcher selects particular elements from the population that will be representative or informative about the topic of interest. On the basis of the researcher's knowledge of the population, a judgment is made about which subjects should be selected to provide the best information to address the purpose of the research. For example, in research on effective teaching, it may be most informative to observe expert or master teachers rather than a sample of all teachers. To study school effectiveness, it may be most informative to interview key personnel rather than a random sample of the staff.

There are several types of purposeful sampling procedures for qualitative investigations. In quantitative studies, the emphasis is more on relying on the judgment of the researcher to select a sample that is representative of the population or that includes subjects with needed characteristics. That is, the emphasis tends to be on representativeness, whereas qualitative researchers are more interested in selecting cases that are information rich. Excerpts 6.11 and 6.12 are examples of using a purposeful sampling procedure in a quantitative study. In Excerpt 6.12 there is both convenience and purposeful sampling. The researcher had done other work for the school district, and all the schools in the sample met criteria related to diversity and socioeconomic status. Also, the final two schools volunteered, so that factor should be taken into consideration in interpreting the results.

Quota sampling: selecting based on characteristics of the population until an appropriate total is reached

Quota Sampling Quota sampling is used when the researcher is unable to take a probability sample but is still able to select subjects on the basis of characteristics of the population. Cer-

EXCERPT 6.11 Purposeful Sampling

Participants were chosen from three pullout resource room programs for students with mild disabilities. Participants met the following criteria:

1. They were identified as having LD under the 1986 Oregon administrative rules;

2. They were participants in special education programs;
3. They had an active Individualized Education Program (IEP) in reading; and
4. They had parent permission and gave their own permission to participate in the study. (p. 309)

Source: From DiCecco, V. M., & Gleason, M. M. (2002). Using graphic organizers to attain relational knowledge from expository text. *Journal of Learning Disabilities, 35*(4), 306–320.

EXCERPT 6.12 Purposeful and Convenience Sampling

Recruitment of schools for the study was completed the year before the implementation of the treatment. Ten principals from an urban school district in a professional development partnership with the researchers' university attended a meeting describing the study. . . . All schools had diverse student populations and a majority of students identified as both economically disadvantaged and culturally and linguistically diverse. . . . Two principals agreed to participate. (p. 7)

Source: From Reis, S. M., McCoach, D. B., Coyne, M., Schreiber, F. J., Eckert, R. D., & Gubbins, E. J. (2007). Using planned enrichment strategies with direct instruction to improve reading fluency, comprehension, and attitude toward reading: An evidence-based study. *The Elementary School Journal, 108*(1), 3–23.

tain quotas are established so that the sample represents the population according to these characteristics. Different composite profiles of major groups in the population are identified, and then subjects are selected, nonrandomly, to represent each group. For example, it is typical to establish quotas for such characteristics as gender, race/ethnicity, age, grade level, position, and geographic location. The advantage of this type of sampling is that it is more representative of the population than is a purposeful or convenience sample, but the reliance on the judgment of the researcher to select the subjects may be a limitation.

In deciding on a sampling procedure for quantitative studies, it is helpful to keep in mind the strengths and weaknesses of the different types, as summarized in Table 6.2. The final choice of procedure depends on the researcher's purpose, availability of subjects, and financial resources.

TABLE 6.2 Strengths and Weaknesses of Sampling Methods

Sampling Method	Strengths	Weaknesses
Probability		
Simple random	Easy to understand Little knowledge of population needed Free of subject classification error Easy to analyze and interpret results	Requires numbering each element in a non-electronic list of members of the population Larger sampling error than in stratified sampling for same sample size
Systematic	Simplicity of drawing sample Easy to understand Free of subject classification error Easy to analyze and interpret results Subjects do not need to be numbered	Larger sampling error than in stratified sampling for same sample size Periodicity in list of population elements
Proportional stratified	Allows easy subgroup comparisons Usually more representative than simple random or systematic Fewer subjects needed if strata are related to the dependent variable Results represent population without weighting	Requires subgroup identification of each population element Requires knowledge of the proportion of each subgroup in the population May be costly and difficult to prepare lists of population elements in each subgroup
Nonproportional stratified	Allows easy subgroup comparisons Usually more representative than simple random or systematic Fewer subjects needed if strata are related to the dependent variable Assures adequate numbers of elements in each subgroup	Requires subgroup identification of each population element May be costly and difficult to prepare lists of population elements in each subgroup Requires weighting of subgroups to represent population

(continued)

TABLE 6.2 Strengths and Weaknesses of Sampling Methods(*continued*)

Sampling Method	Strengths	Weaknesses
Cluster	Low cost Efficient with large populations Permits analysis of individual clusters	Less accurate than simple random, systematic, or stratified methods May be difficult to collect data from elements in a cluster Requires that each population element be assigned to only one cluster
Nonprobability		
Convenience	Less costly and time-consuming Ease of administration Usually assures high participation rate Generalization possible to similar subjects	Difficult to generalize to other subjects Less representative of an identified population Results dependent on unique characteristics of the sample Greater likelihood of error due to experimenter or subject bias
Purposeful	Less costly and time-consuming Ease of administration Usually assures high participation rate Generalization possible to similar subjects Assures receipt of needed information	Difficult to generalize to other subjects Less representative of an identified population Results dependent on unique characteristics of the sample Greater likelihood of error due to experimenter or subject bias
Quota	Less costly and time-consuming Ease of administration Usually assures high participation rate Generalization possible to similar subjects Tends to provide more representative samples than convenience or purposeful	Requires identification information on each subject Difficult to generalize to other subjects Less representative of an identified population Results dependent on unique characteristics of the sample Greater likelihood of error due to experimenter or subject bias More time-consuming than convenient or purposeful methods

Source: From Bruns, D. A., & Mogharreban, C. C. (2007). The gap between belief and practices: Early childhood practitioners' perceptions about inclusion. *Journal of Research in Childhood Education, 21*(3), 229–241. Reprinted by permission of D. A. Bruns and the *Association for Childhood Education International,* 17904 Georgia Avenue, Suite 215, Olney, MD 20832. Copyright © 2007 by the Association.

HOW SAMPLING AFFECTS RESEARCH

In both planning and evaluating research, you will need to know which type of sampling will provide the best answers to the research questions. At issue is how sampling procedures may have had an impact on the results. The nature of the sample is critical in determining statistical significance, in interpreting the meaning of the results, and in generalizing the conclusions. In this section, five important considerations about how sampling affects research are summarized: sample size, subject motivation, sampling bias, response variability, and use of volunteer samples.

Sample Size

A very important consideration in conducting and evaluating research is the size of the sample or the number of participants. The general rule in quantitative research is to obtain as many

			Sample Size			
Income Class	Number of Families	Population Data	1 in 10	1 in 20	1 in 30	1 in 50
A	1748	26.5	26.6	25.9	28.3	27.1
B	2477	22.7	22.9	23.5	22.3	22.6
C	2514	19.8	18.1	17.2	17.2	18.0
D	1676	15.8	16.0	14.4	17.1	16.9
E	3740	11.3	11.0	10.1	11.2	11.5

TABLE 6.3 Percentage of Income Spent on Rent

Source: From *Poverty and Progress: A Second Social Survey of York,* by B. S. Rowntree, 1941, London: Longman, Green. Reprinted by permission of The Joseph Rowntree Charitable Trust.

subjects as needed or possible to obtain a credible result, but there often are constraints to the number of participants: financial, logistical, or because of lack of availability.

In quantitative studies, the number of independent, individual units of study becomes the sample size, represented by the letter n (the size of the population is N). When selecting a sample from a population, a sample size that is only a small percentage of the population can approximate the characteristics of the population satisfactorily. Rowntree (1941) illustrated this point many years ago in a study of the percentage of income that was spent on rent by five categories of working-class families in England. Data were collected for the entire population and compared with the data that would have been reported by different sizes of random samples. As indicated in Table 6.3, there was little difference between a sample size of 2 percent (1 in 50) and 10 percent (1 in 10).

There are two approaches to determining adequate sample size. One uses published tables or sample size calculators (easily found on the Internet), based on established formulas. The tables and calculators use information provided by the researcher to determine what size of sample is needed for a given level of precision. This works well for some studies, but often the information needed is not readily available. A second approach uses various rules of thumb or general guidelines. It turns out that these more informal procedures are used most often in educational research. For example, when a population is very large—say, greater than 10,000—the size of the sample needed will usually range from 800 to 1,200. A 5 percent sample from a population of 2,000 (i.e., 100) would be insufficient. A 5 percent sample for a population of 40,000 is twice as many as needed.

A major consideration regarding sample size in quantitative studies is how the number of subjects is used in determining statistical significance. Statistical significance is directly related to sample size—the larger the sample, the smaller the difference or relationship needed to be statistically significant. This means that studies that have thousands of subjects will be very likely to show statistically significant results, even if the relationships or differences are very small.

Of particular concern is the impact of having a small sample in studies that show no statistically significant differences or relationships, especially because so many educational studies employ relatively small samples. For example, suppose you investigate the relationship between creativity and intelligence with 20 high school students and find that there is no stastically significant relationship. Is it reasonable to conclude that, *in reality*, there is no relationship? Probably not, because a plausible reason for not finding a significant relationship is that a small sample was used, in this case so small that the correlation would need to be rather high to reach the level of statistical significance. With more subjects, the relationship might very well be significant. Hence, a conclusion that there is no relationship has a pretty good chance of being wrong. This issue, interpreting results of studies with small samples in which there were no relationships or differences, is subtle, and is a contributor to determining practical significance.

On the other hand, in quantitative studies with a small sample that do show statistical significance, the relationship or difference is probably substantial. However, whenever there is a

TABLE 6.4 Rules of Thumb for Estimating Sufficient Sample Size for Quantitative Studies

Factor	Rules of Thumb
Type of design	Correlational studies should have a minimum of 30 subjects. Comparison and experimental studies should have at least 15 subjects in each group (some highly controlled experiments only need 8–10). In large-sample surveys, such as attitude surveys of all teachers in a state, a minimum of about 800 subjects is needed. About 100 subjects are needed for major subgroups and 20 for minor subgroups.
Research hypothesis	If small differences or relationships are expected (e.g., based on results of previous studies), a relatively large sample is needed. For instance, the effect of coaching on student performance on accountability tests may produce small but important results that might not be significant with a small number of coached students.
Financial constraints	Obviously, the cost of conducting a study will limit the number of subjects in the sample. These costs should be estimated before pulling the sample to be sure that there is an adequate total number of subjects. If the researcher is using an existing database, there may be no difference between a sample and the population. In that circumstance, the entire population should be used.
Importance	As the importance of the study increases, so should the sample size. These studies have serious consequences. For exploratory studies, a smaller sample is acceptable because the researcher is willing to tolerate a larger margin of error.
Number of variables	Generally, as the number of variables in a study increases, so should the sample size.
Reliability of scores	Because statistical significance is directly tied to error in measurement, low reliability needs to be offset by a larger sample.
Population size	As the population increases, a smaller percentage of subjects is needed to maintain the same level of estimation; the maximum number needed for any size population is 1,200.
Accuracy needed	The margin of error in sampling from a population is directly related to sample size; the larger the sample, the smaller the margin of error.
Subject attrition	If there is reason to believe that subjects may be lost during an intervention or in a longitudinal study, a sufficient number should be included in the initial sample to account for this attrition.

To check your understanding of some of the key terms introduced in this chapter, go to MyEducationLab for Research at www.myeducationlab.com and complete the Activities and Application activity "Defining Key Terms." Click on the topic "Selecting a Sample" and select the Activities and Application activity titled "Defining Key Terms."

small sample, other factors have a greater likelihood of influencing the results, such as bias in the sample (see below) or the presence of confounding variables.

In Table 6.4 further characteristics of quantitative studies are summarized to indicate how they help to determine adequate sample size.

Subject Motivation

The extent to which subjects are motivated to respond in certain ways can have substantial effects. Whether or not subjects are motivated for reasons that will skew the results is determined by the nature of the procedures used, especially in what subjects are told or how data are collected. For example, knowing that a teacher's future employment will be based to some extent on student achievement could motivate students to try harder than they otherwise would. In some studies, the sample is given an intervention with the expressed purpose of having positive outcomes. This purpose may motivate students to fake responses on the end-of-intervention questionnaire.

Clues that suggest an inappropriate influence of motivation will often be found in the way the subjects were selected. For example, if a researcher is interested in studying the effectiveness of computer simulations in teaching science, one approach would be to interview teachers who used these simulations. The researcher might even select only those science teachers who had used the simulations for more than two years. Understandably, because the teachers had been using the simulations, they would probably be motivated to respond favorably toward them. This could result in a finding like "Research shows that teachers support the use of computer simulations," whereas if all teachers had been included, the result could have been different.

Or suppose students in a college class want to get back at a professor who is an unfair grader by giving low student evaluations. In another class, students want to give excellent ratings because they want the teacher to be tenured, even if the teaching was not very good. In either case, students are motivated to respond in a certain way, and as a result the results are inaccurate.

Sampling Bias

Sampling bias occurs when the researcher consciously or unconsciously selects subjects that result in an inaccurate finding. This is deliberately accomplished by including subjects who have the point of view that is desired by the researcher. Suppose a researcher wants to survey college students to determine the extent to which they are engaged in altruistic behaviors. The researcher selects students who major in education and social work while ignoring those with majors that might have less of this orientation. The result may be front-page news—"College Students Strive to Help Others"—even though the small print would qualify this conclusion. Or suppose you obtained a sample of college students by standing at the entrance to the campus cafeteria. Even if you select every fifth student, only certain kinds of students actually eat at the cafeteria. This sample, then, would not be representative of all students. Especially egregious kinds of bias are to disregard subjects who do not respond as desired or to gather data continuously until the desired result is obtained.

Biased samples also occur nondeliberately, often because of inadequate knowledge of what is needed to obtain an unbiased sample. This occurs in studies in which the researcher wants, from the beginning, to "prove" that something is true. It is as though the researcher is wearing blinders because of the desire to obtain a specific result. For example, a proponent of cooperative learning could conduct studies on its effectiveness but bias the selection of subjects to provide evidence of the superiority of cooperative learning over other methods. Or suppose a large educational company conducts research on the effectiveness of its products. Is it likely to use biased sampling so that the company can prove its point? As we will see, attempting to prove something also affects other aspects of the research, especially in measurement and interpretation of the results.

Response Variability

In quantitative studies and maximum variation designs, there is a need to sample a sufficient number of participants so that adequate variability of responses is obtained. In quantitative studies, variation is needed to show differences and relationships. For example, if you want to study the relationship of principal leadership style to school climate, you need to sample enough schools so that there is variation in both leadership style and climate. In other words, if your sample does not contain enough subjects with different scores on the variables, you will not find relationships.

Volunteer Samples

A continual and nagging issue in educational and social science research is the use of volunteer samples and participants. It is well documented that volunteers differ from nonvolunteers in important ways, and these differences can obviously affect the nature of obtained responses. Volunteers, compared to nonvolunteers, tend to be

- better educated
- higher socioeconomically
- higher in aptitude and ability in quantitative studies
- higher in need for social approval
- more sociable
- somewhat less conventional
- less authoritarian
- less conforming
- female (except for studies of physical exertion)

These are only general trends. What is experienced in a specific study depends on the design and procedures for contacting individuals to participate. A design that is especially challenged with this issue is survey research, in which individuals are contacted "cold" and asked to complete a questionnaire and return it. Often the response rate is 40 to 50 percent or even much lower, and these respondents comprise a volunteer sample. At issue is whether these respondents are representative of the entire group that was asked to participate.

To practice describing and identifying aspects of sampling techniques in studies, go to MyEducationLab for Research at www.myeducationlab.com and complete the Activities and Applications activity titled "Describe the Sampling Technique." Click on the topic "Selecting a Sample" and select "Describe the Sampling Technique."

When only a small percentage of subjects who are asked to participate actually do so, the resulting sample should be considered volunteer. Suppose you identify 300 college faculty who are sent a survey to return. Only 60 respond. This low 20% response rate may result in a sample that may not be representative of the larger population. Or consider a study in which a researcher is interested in surveying elementary teachers' knowledge and understanding of mathematics. Of those surveyed, the teachers with a stronger background in mathematics may be more likely to respond.

Most research involving children requires parental permission. In this case, then, it is the parents who volunteer, not the children, so there is a need to consider if there are systematic differences between those parents who do choose to allow their children to participate compared to those who do not. As you might surmise, children of parents who volunteer tend to be more competent, popular, attractive, and involved in extracurricular activities. They tend to be less withdrawn, less aggressive, and less likely to smoke or use drugs (Gall, Gall, & Borg, 2007). These factors may be important in determining results, but their impact is a function of the nature of the research and the request for participation.

Whenever there is a volunteer sample, it is critical to carefully consider whether or not volunteering has an impact on the findings. This is usually determined by comparing the characteristics of the volunteer group to those of a larger group of possible participants on important demographic variables, such as gender, age, location, and socioeconomic status if possible, as illustrated in Excerpt 6.13. A low response rate of volunteers does not necessarily mean that the research is not helpful and/or useful. The importance of the results in these studies relies most on determining if the volunteers are likely to give particular responses.

EXCERPT 6.13   Matching Volunteer Sampling Results with Population Characteristics

A random sample of 350 was drawn from a list of 8,506 active elementary public school principals enrolled as members of the National Association of Elementary School Principals. An initial mailing, a follow-up, and two reminders yielded a 61% response rate. Surveys were returned from principals representing various regions of the United States: Midwest (32%), Northeast (27%), South (26%), and West (15%). These proportions closely reflected the membership of the population from which the sample was drawn. (p. 8)

Source: From *Journal of Research in Music Education*, Spring 2006, *54*(1), 6–20. Copyright © 2006 by MENC: The National Association for Music Education. Reprinted with permission.

CHAPTER SUMMARY

> Test your understanding of the fundamental principles of sampling in quantitative studies by going to MyEducationLab for Research at www.myeducationlab.com. Click on the topic "Selecting a Sample" and then select the Building Research Skills exercise titled "Sampling in a Quantitative Study."

This chapter has introduced fundamental principles of sampling used in quantitative studies. This discussion has included types of sampling procedures and a discussion of how sampling can affect the credibility and generalizability of the results. Key points include the following:

1. The unit of study is typically the number of subjects in the study and affects the nature of statistical analyses.

2. In probability sampling, a small percentage of the population is obtained randomly to be analyzed in order to make inferences about characteristics of the population.

3. Probability sampling procedures include simple random sampling, systematic sampling, stratified sampling, and cluster sampling.

4. Systematic sampling involves choosing individuals from a list and is as random as simple random sampling.

5. Stratified sampling, where subjects are selected from subgroups within the population, is used to decrease the margin of error in estimating population values and save resources. It is applied to represent the population proportionately or disproportionately.

6. Margin of error is used to report likely values for the population.

7. In nonprobability sampling there is no random sampling from the population. Rather, subjects are determined on the basis of availability, the purpose of the study, and the number of subjects needed (quota). This limits generalizability of the findings to similar individuals.

8. Sample size is critical for both accuracy and statistical purposes. Studies with a small number of subjects and lack of statistical significance are problematic.

9. The characteristics of the sample are important in determining subject motivation, sampling bias, and response variability. Subjects should be selected so that there is variation of responses to key variables.

10. Volunteer samples may provide biased results. Volunteers, compared to nonvolunteers, tend to be less conforming, have higher aptitude, and come from a higher socioeconomic group.

APPLICATION PROBLEMS

1. A researcher wants to make sure that a sufficient number of subjects is selected from a specific age category. Which type of sampling would be best?

2. Which sampling procedures (select from among all probability or nonprobability types) are illustrated in the following situations?

   a. Mr. Brown decides to assess his teachers' attitudes toward teaching autistic children. He identifies the teachers who have such students and interviews them to determine their attitudes.

   b. In this study Dr. Mathews wants to report to the board of education about the achievement of ESL students. He first identifies all the ESL students and then chooses 10 percent of them.

   c. Vicki Paris decides to do a study comparing children with high self-efficacy to those with low self-efficacy in order to see if there are differences in motivation and engagement. She identifies four classes to participate and surveys all the students in these classes.

   d. Paul Gerber is investigating the relationship between type of community (urban, rural, or suburban) and size of school. He obtains a list of all schools in the state, identifies each as urban, rural, or suburban, and then randomly selects 30 schools from each of the three categories.

   e. Lisa Abrams is conducting a study on the attitudes of faculty. She wants to know if there is a relationship between tenure status and job satisfaction and finds 54 faculty in her institution who are willing to complete the survey.

   f. In a study of high-stakes testing and student motivation, Dr. Hall identifies a group of schools with high student motivation ($n = 34$) and a group with low student motivation ($n = 55$). Dr. Hall then compares the achievement scores of the two groups of schools.

3. Give an example of a sampling procedure that has the following characteristics: a population of 400 and systematic sampling of every 20th student.

4. With a random number generator on statistical software, such as SPSS, and a database, select one simple random sample and one systematic sample. Compare the results.

5. Describe a study that has the following characteristics: fifth-grade students in seven schools, nonprobability,

purposeful, with two independent and two dependent variables.

6. Describe a study that has these characteristics: a stratified random sample based on two stratifying independent variables and one dependent variable.

7. What would be the four most significant points about sampling that you would present to a group of teachers who want to conduct a study in their own schools? Why?

8. What would be the best sampling strategy for a researcher who wants to conduct studies that would have the following strengths?

   a. Least amount of money and time used to conduct the study with probability sampling.

   b. Subjects from each subgroup are included.

   c. Simple for others to understand.

   d. Provides the most representative nonprobability sample.

ANSWER TO THE APPLICATION PROBLEMS

1. The best strategy would be to use a stratified random sample based on age categories and then take a nonproportional sample from each category to ensure an adequate number of subjects from each category.

2. a. nonprobability, purposeful

   b. probability, simple random sample, proportional

   c. nonprobability, convenience

   d. probability, stratified random sample, nonproportional (because of the same *n* from each group)

   e. nonprobability, convenience

   f. nonprobability, purposeful

3. (individual student response)

4. (individual student response)

5. (individual student response)

6. (individual student response)

7. (individual student response)

8. a. stratified random sample

   b. disproportional stratified random sample

   c. nonprobability—convenience or availability sampling; probability—simple random sampling

   d. quota sampling

Descriptive Statistics

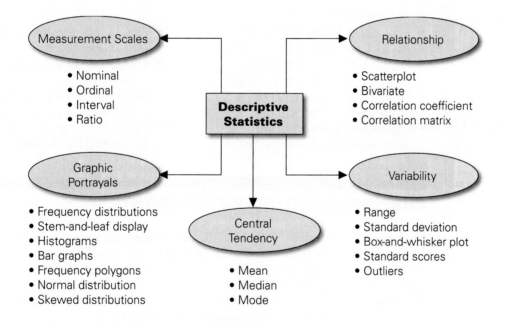

KEY TERMS

statistics	mode
descriptive statistics	normal distribution
inferential statistics	skewed
measurement scales	positively skewed
nominal	negatively skewed
ordinal	kurtosis
interval	measures of variability
ratio	range
univariate	standard deviation
bivariate	percentile rank
frequency distribution	variance
stem-and-leaf display	box-and-whisker plot
histogram	standard scores
bar graph	z-score
frequency polygon	outlier
measures of central tendency	scatterplot
mean	correlation coefficient
median	

WHAT YOU WILL LEARN

Study this chapter and you will:

- Differentiate between different types of statistics and levels of measurement.
- Understand the relationship between descriptive and inferential statistics.
- Be able to use frequency distributions and other graphic presentations of data.
- Explain how measures of central tendency are used to describe a dataset.

- Explain how measures of variability are used to describe a dataset.
- Understand the importance of outlier analysis.
- Know how bivariate correlations are used to measure relationships.
- Explain why scatterplots are essential for interpreting correlations.

INTRODUCTION TO DESCRIPTIVE STATISTICS

Quantitative research relies heavily on numbers in reporting results, sampling, and providing estimates of score reliability and validity. The numbers are often accompanied by unrecognized strange words and even stranger symbols, and are manipulated by something called *statistics*. Like magic, statistics lead to conclusions. Many readers of research simply prefer to skip over anything related to statistics. In the words of a prominent specialist in educational measurement: "For most educators, mere contemplation of the term 'statistics' conjures up images akin to bubonic plague and the abolition of tenure" (Popham, 1981, p. 66).

Even though some statisticians may like the image just described, in truth the fundamental concepts and principles of statistics are readily comprehensible. Advanced skills in mathematics are not a prerequisite to understanding statistics, and there is no need to memorize complex formulas. In fact, learning about statistics can actually be fun! (Consider the great new words learned that will be perfect for impressing friends and family.)

More seriously, there are important reasons for all educators to gain a functional command of statistical principles:

1. To understand and critique professional articles (for example, were appropriate statistical tools used?)
2. To improve evaluation of student learning
3. To conduct, even in modest and informal ways, research studies (for example, how should the results be analyzed?)

4. To understand evaluations of programs, personnel, and policies
5. To become better equipped as a citizen and consumer, making decisions based on quantitative data or arguments
6. To upgrade the education profession by providing standard skills to communicate, debate, and discuss research that has implications for educational practice

Types of Statistics

Statistics are methods of organizing and analyzing quantitative data. These methods are tools designed to help the researcher organize and interpret numbers derived from measuring a trait or variable. The mere presence of statistical procedures does not ensure high quality in the research. Although the contribution of some results does depend on applying the correct statistical procedure, the quality of the research depends most on proper conceptualization, design, subject selection, instruments, and procedures. Statistics is an international language that only manipulates numbers. Statistics and numbers do not interpret themselves, and the meaning of the statistics is derived from the research design. Of course, the improper use of statistics invalidates the research, but the interpretation of statistical results depends on carefully designing and conducting the study—that is, it depends heavily on producing high-quality quantitative data.

Statistics: tools for understanding data

There are two broad categories of statistical techniques: descriptive and inferential. **Descriptive statistics** transform a set of numbers or observations into indices that describe or characterize the data. Descriptive statistics (sometimes referred to as *summary statistics*) are thus used to summarize, organize, and reduce large numbers of observations. Usually, the reduction results in a few numbers derived from mathematical formulas to represent all observations in each group of interest. Descriptive statistics portray and focus on *what is* with respect to the sample data—for example, What is the average reading grade level of the fifth-graders in the school? How many teachers found the in-service valuable? What percentage of students want to go to college? and What is the relationship between the socio-economic status of children and the effectiveness of token reinforcers? The use of descriptive statistics is the most fundamental way to summarize data, and it is indispensable in interpreting the results of quantitative research.

Descriptive statistics: summarizes data

Inferential statistics, on the other hand, are used to make inferences or predictions about the similarity of a sample to the population from which the sample is drawn. Because many research questions require the estimation of population characteristics from an available sample of subjects or behavior, inferential statistics are commonly used in reporting results. Inferential statistics depend on descriptive statistics. Without a complete understanding of descriptive statistics, therefore, inferential statistics make very little sense. Figure 7.1 illustrates the relationship between descriptive and inferential statistics. It shows how a researcher would first take a sample from a population, use descriptive statistics to describe the sample, and then use inferential statistics to estimate the true value of the test score for the population.

Inferential statistics: describes the probability of results for populations

Researchers may choose from many types of descriptive statistics in characterizing a set of data. The choice usually depends on three factors: the type of measurement scale employed, assumptions about the data, and the purpose of the research. The purpose of the research, or *research problem*, actually depends on a knowledge of different statistical techniques, because each technique offers information for answering particular kinds of questions. Hence, each of the common descriptive techniques is presented here, with examples of the research problems it addresses.

 To practice using descriptive statistics related to a research plan, go to MyEducationLab for Research at www.myeducationlab.com. Click on the topic "Descriptive Statistics" and then select "Computing Descriptive Statistics."

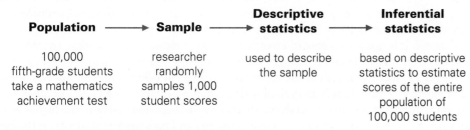

FIGURE 7.1 **Relationship of Descriptive to Inferential Statistics**

Scales of Measurement

Measurement in education usually involves assigning numbers to things in order to differentiate one thing from another. Unlike the measurement of physical phenomena, however, such as weight, density, and length, researchers can use numbers in different ways for investigating problems. These different ways are based on four properties of numbers: (1) numbers can be distinct from one another (e.g., 10 is different from 13; 0 is different from −5); (2) numbers are relative to one another (e.g., 13 is larger than 10; −3 is less than 0); (3) numbers can be related to each other in identified units (e.g., 10 is five units greater than 5); and (4) numbers can be related proportionately (e.g., 10 is twice as large as 5; 25 is to 5 as 30 is to 6).

These properties, in turn, determine what psychometricians refer to as **measurement scales**, or levels of measurement. There are four measurement scales: nominal, ordinal, interval, and ratio. These terms are often used to describe the nature of the measure, indicating, for example, that a nominal measure or nominal measurement was used.

Nominal The first and most rudimentary level of measurement is called **nominal**, *categorical*, or *classificatory*. The word *nominal* implies *name*, which describes what this scale accomplishes—a naming of mutually exclusive categories of people, events, or other phenomena. Common examples of nominal levels include classifying on the basis of eye color, gender, political party affiliation, and type of reading group. The groups are simply names to differentiate them; no order is implied (i.e., one group does not come before or after another), and there is no indication of the way the groups differ from each other. Often researchers assign numbers to the different groups (for example, yes = 1, no = 2, maybe = 3), but this is only for convenient coding of the groups in analyzing the data. Nominal data result in categorical variables, and results are reported as frequencies in each category.

Ordinal The second type of measurement scale is called **ordinal**, and as the name implies, measurement of this type assumes that categories of the variable can theoretically be rank ordered from highest to lowest. Each value can thus be related to others as being equal to, greater than, or less than. In other words, there is an inherent order to the categories. Examples of ordinal measurement include ranking class members by means of grade-point average, ranking ideas from most important to least important, and using percentile ranks in achievement tests.

Interval Interval measures share characteristics of ordinal scales and indicate equal intervals between each category. Interval scales give meaning to the difference between numbers by providing a constant unit of measurement. The difference or interval between 5 and 6, for example, is the same as the difference between 18 and 19. Percentile scores associated with the normal curve, for example, are not interval because the distance between percentile points varies, depending on the percentiles compared. There is a greater difference between extreme percentiles (e.g., 2nd and 3rd or 95th and 96th) than between percentiles near the middle of the distribution. Examples of interval scales include Fahrenheit and Centigrade temperature scales and most standardized achievement test scores.

Ratio Ratio scales represent the most refined type of measurement. Ratio scales are ordinal and interval and include a zero value, and the numbers can be compared by ratios: that is, a number can be compared meaningfully by saying that it is twice or three times another number or one-half or one-fourth of a number. Such observations as distance attained, strength expressed as weight lifted, or times in the mile run are ratio scale measurements. Most measurements in education, however, are not expressed as ratios. Educators think in terms of less than or greater than, not multiples (e.g., a student is more cooperative or less cooperative, not twice as cooperative or half as cooperative).

Although it is not always easy to identify the scale of measurement of some variables, it is important to distinguish between nominal and higher levels. The use of many of the more common statistical procedures, such as the mean and variance, usually requires an interval or ratio scale of measurement, although an ordinal scale is often acceptable. The choice of other, more advanced statistical procedures depends on whether the data are nominal or in the higher levels. If, for example, a researcher wants to compare minority and nonminority students on the basis of their choices of careers, the data are nominal and certain statistical procedures would be appropriate for analyzing them. If, on the other hand, these same students were being compared

Measurement scales: properties that describe the nature of data

Nominal: scales that name, classify, or number

Ordinal: ranking from lowest to highest

Interval: equal intervals between ranks

Ratio: relative size

TABLE 7.1 Characteristics and Examples of Measurement Scales

Scale	Description	Examples
Nominal	Numbers used to distinguish categories or types Assignment of numbers is arbitrary	Ethnicity, gender, country, marital status
Ordinal	Simple rank ordering of the measured variable	Percentile rank, socioeconomic status, school size, attitudes
Interval	Intervals between points represent equal differences on the trait being measured	Aptitude and achievement test scores, height
Ratio	Interval scales that include a zero amount of the trait measured	Growth, improvement, age, time, speed

on achievement or attitudes toward school, a different set of statistical procedures would be appropriate because the scale of the achievement and attitude data are ordinal or interval.

Table 7.1 summarizes the characteristics and provides further examples of the four scales of measurement. With many educational variables there are subtle but important differences between ordinal- and interval-level data. This difference is illustrated in Figure 7.2. Note that with ordinal data, the best we can conclude is that some scores are greater than or less than other scores. With interval data the degree of difference between data points is the same.

Types of Descriptive Analysis

There are several different ways to describe data, many of which will be familiar to you. One way to classify the methods is to determine whether they are univariate or bivariate. **Univariate** analysis is done to summarize data on a single characteristic or variable, usually the dependent variable. You probably already have an understanding of the univariate techniques, including the mean, median, and frequency distributions. Univariate analysis is especially important for descriptive studies.

Univariate: single dependent variable

Bivariate analysis is used when there is a correlation among variables or when different groups are compared. Thus, two variables are used for correlation (e.g., age and strength), and two or more categories are used for comparisons (e.g., males compared to females on self-concept; differences in achievement among African American, European American, and Hispanic American students; or trends in graduation rates for several school districts). The most common univariate and bivariate procedures are listed in Table 7.2.

Bivariate: two variables

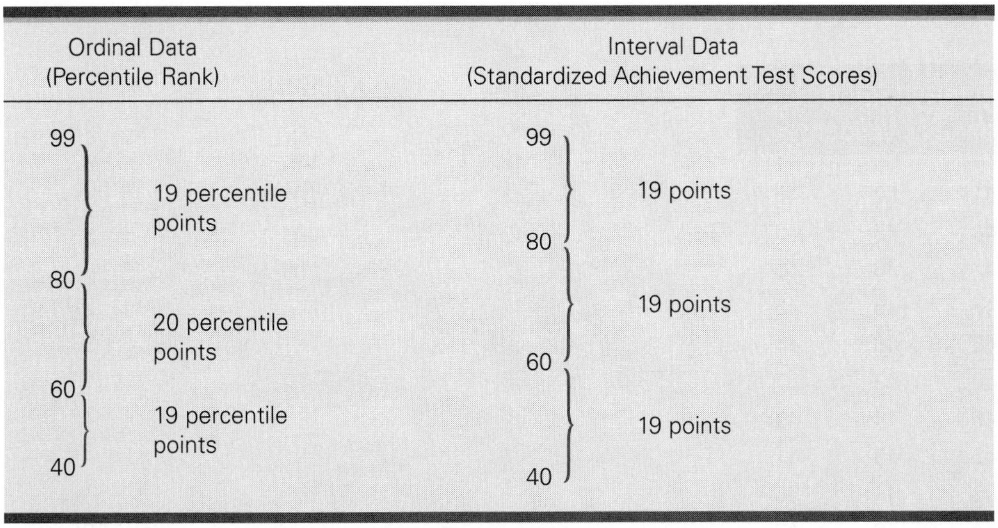

FIGURE 7.2 Illustration of Ordinal and Interval Scales of Measurement

TABLE 7.2 Univariate and Bivariate Statistical Procedures

Univariate	Bivariate
Frequency distribution	Correlation
Histogram	Comparing frequencies
Frequency polygon	Comparing percentages
Stem-and-leaf display	Comparing means
Percentage	Comparing medians
Mean	
Median	
Mode	
Range	
Standard deviation	
Box-and-whisker plot	

GRAPHIC PORTRAYALS OF DATA

When data are collected, the observations must be organized so that the researcher can easily and correctly interpret the results. This section presents five common methods of representing group data: frequency distributions, stem-and-leaf displays, histograms, bar charts, and frequency polygons.

Frequency Distribution or Count: A Picture of a Group

Frequency distribution: shows how often each score occurred

In most studies, there are many different scores, and if these scores are arrayed (arranged) without regard to their values, as in Table 7.3, it is difficult to make sense out of the data. The simplest organization of the scores is to list them from highest to lowest and create what is called a *rank-order distribution*. The rank-order distribution is transformed to a **frequency distribution** by indicating the number of times each score was attained, as indicated in Tables 7.3 and 7.4.

TABLE 7.3 Unorganized Examination Scores of 50 Students

47	37	41	50	46
39	49	44	43	40
42	43	42	46	40
44	45	47	45	45
36	45	46	48	44
42	48	40	43	37
46	45	45	44	42
43	43	42	43	41
44	45	42	44	36
44	38	44	46	42

TABLE 7.4 Frequency Distribution of Scores in Table 7.3

Scores in Rank Order	Tallies	Frequency (f)
50	1	1
49	1	1
48	11	2
47	11	2
46	1111	4
45	1111 111	8
44	1111 111	8
43	1111 1	6
42	1111 11	7
41	11	2
40	111	3
39	1	1
38	1	1
37	11	2
36	11	2
		n = 50

EXCERPT 7.1 Frequency Distribution

During an academic year, new clients at a university counseling center were recruited to participate in this study. All new clients requesting individual counseling services were eligible to participate. Ninety-four new clients (the majority of new clients at the center) agreed to participate. . . . The ages of participants ranged from 18 years to 47 years ($Mdn = 21.00$, $M = 22.4 . . .$).

Table 2 presents a frequency distribution of counseling duration. Participants completed from 1 to 28 sessions ($Mdn = 3.0$, $M = 4.6 . . .$). As [is] evident in the table, most participants completed a relatively small number of sessions. (pp. 171–180)

TABLE 2 Frequency Distribution of Counseling Duration

No. of Sessions Completed	f	%	Σ%
1–3	54	57.4	57.4
4–6	22	23.4	80.8
7–9	8	8.5	89.3
10–12	4	4.3	93.6
14–17	3	3.2	96.8
18–28	3	3.2	100.0

Note. $Mdn = 3$, Mode = 1, $M = 4.6$

Source: From Hatchett, G. T. (2003). Does psychopathology predict counseling duration? *Psychological Reports, 93,* 175–185. Copyright ©2003 by Psychological Reports. Reprinted with permission.

It is also common to combine scores into **class intervals** and tally the number of scores in each interval, as indicated in Excerpt 7.1. Intervals are especially useful for data in which few of the numbers are the same (e.g., ranking of states on median income).

Frequency distributions indicate quickly the most and least frequently occurring scores, the general shape of the distribution (e.g., clusters of scores at certain places or

EXCERPT 7.2 Use of Percentages to Report Results

TABLE 2 Percentages of Elementary Teachers' Responses to Selected Items for Mathematics Assessment Practices and Grading

Question	Not at all	Very little	Some	Quite a bit	Extensively	Completely
Factors Contributing to Grades						
Improvement of performance since the beginning of the year	13	17	38	21	7	2
Student effort—how much students tried to learn	6	14	44	27	7	2
Ability levels of students	10	13	31	24	19	4
Academic performance compared with other factors	2	3	12	29	44	10
Types of Assessments Used						
Objective assessments	2	8	28	36	21	5
Performance assessments	14	23	38	17	7	1
Cognitive Level of Assessments						
Assessments that measure student reasoning	0	2	25	44	25	4

Source: From McMillan, J. H., Myran, S., & Workman, D. (2002). Elementary teachers' classroom assessment and grading practices. *Journal of Educational Research, 95*(4), 203–213, (2002). Reprinted with permission of the Helen Dwight Reid Educational Foundation. Published by Heldref Publications, 1319 Eighteenth St., NW, Washington, DC 20036-1802. Copyright © 2002.

scores spread out evenly), and whether any scores are isolated from the others (i.e., outliers).

Along with the frequency of scores, researchers often summarize results by the percentage of responses for each score or interval (see Excerpt 7.1) and for subjects that provide different answers. The latter use is illustrated in Excerpt 7.2, which shows the percentages of responses to different points on a scale.

Stem-and-Leaf Displays

Stem-and-leaf: shows the number of cases of each value

Another technique for showing the distribution of scores is called a **stem-and-leaf display**. The "stem" is shown on a vertical column and represents the first number of each score. The "leaf" contains the last digit(s) of each score in the stem. Excerpt 7.3 presents an example of a stem-and-leaf display. It shows that there is one score in the distribution with a value of 0.78 (i.e., 0.7 stem and 8), one score that is 0.53, one that is 0.54, and two scores with values of 0.34.

Histograms and Bar Graphs

Histogram: graph that shows the frequency of scores in order

Frequency data are often effectively displayed pictorially. One type of illustration uses columns in a two-dimensional graph to represent the frequency of occurrence of each score or interval. This way of presenting a frequency distribution is called a **histogram**. The data from Tables 7.3 and 7.4 are presented as a histogram in Figure 7.3. In this example, the vertical dimension on the graph lists the frequencies of the scores, and the horizontal dimension rank orders the scores from

EXCERPT 7.3 Stem-and-Leaf Display

TABLE 3   Stem-and-Leaf Display of Unweighted Achievement Effect Sizes

Stem	Leaf
+.7	8
+.5	34
+.4	3
+.3	2448
+.2	22359
+.1	002223
+.0	3479
−.0	033446779
−.1	00
−.2	014
−.3	7
−.4	
−.5	6

Note. Effect sizes (*d* indexes) are based on each district as an independent sample (*n* = 39). The dotted line represents the value zero; the wavy line indicates a break in the distribution (there is no +.6 value in the stem column).

Source: From Cooper, H., Valentine, J. C., Charlton, K., & Melson, A. (2003). The effects of modified school calendars on student achievement and on school and community attitudes. *Review of Educational Research, 73*(1), 1–52. Copyright © 2003 by the American Educational Research Association. Reproduced with permission of the publisher.

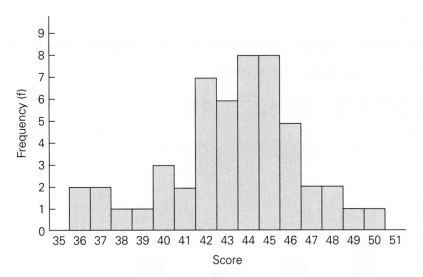

FIGURE 7.3 Histogram of Scores from Table 7.3

lowest to highest. The columns are drawn in the graph to correspond with the results. In similar fashion, Excerpt 7.4 shows how histograms can depict results in an article.

A **bar graph** looks very much like a histogram, with columns that present an image of the findings. In a bar graph, however, the ordering of the columns is arbitrary, whereas in a histogram, there is an order from least to most. Bar graphs are used, then, with nominal variables such as gender, state, political party affiliation, and similar categorical variables that have no implied order. A bar graph is illustrated in Excerpt 7.5.

Histograms are effective because they provide an easily comprehended image of results. However, the image may be distorted by manipulating the spacing of numbers along the vertical dimension of the graph. The intervals between score frequencies can vary, and the size of the units that are used can be changed to give different images. For example, a crafty researcher can make a very small difference appear great by increasing the space between measurement units. Consider the two graphs in Figure 7.4. Each graph has summarized the same data, but the visual results are clearly different.

Bar graph: graph that shows frequencies of categories

EXCERPT 7.4 Histogram

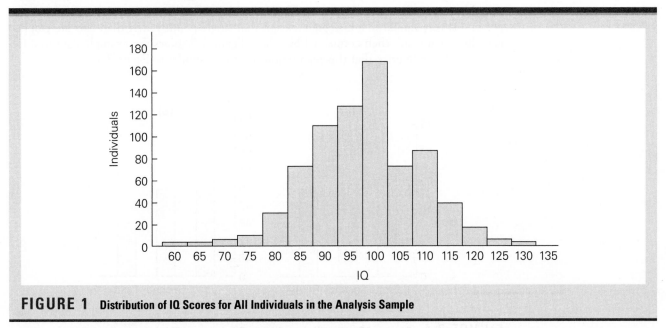

FIGURE 1 Distribution of IQ Scores for All Individuals in the Analysis Sample

Source: From Wadsworth, S. J., Olson, R. K., Pennington, B. F., and DeFries. J. C. (2000). Differential genetic etiology of reading disability as a function of IQ. *Journal of Learning Disabilities, 33*(2), p. 195. Copyright © 2000 by PRO-ED, Inc. Adapted with permission.

EXCERPT 7.5 Bar Graph

High School Grades of College Freshmen

The high school grade point averages of students entering four-year colleges and universities of all types continue to increase, according to an annual survey of freshmen by the University of California, Los Angeles.

Overall, a record high of 45.7 percent of freshmen reported earning A averages in high school in the fall 2002 survey. Students entering private universities reported the highest grades. (p. 4)

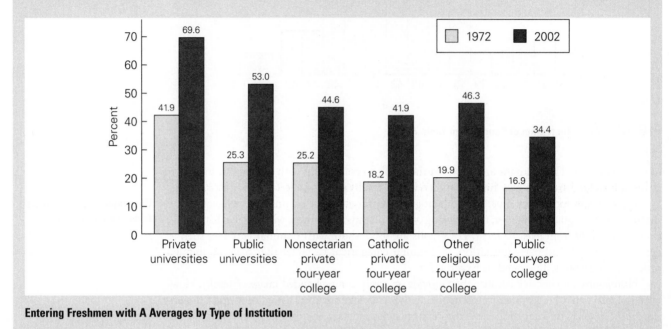

Entering Freshmen with A Averages by Type of Institution

Source: From "The American Freshman: National Norms for Fall 2002," Higher Education Research Institute, UCLA Graduate School of Education and Information Studies, 3005 Moore Hall, Box 951521, Los Angeles, CA 90095-1521. Reprinted by permission.

Frequency Polygons

Frequency polygon: curve of a histogram

Another way to illustrate a frequency distribution is to use a **frequency polygon**. A frequency polygon is very similar to a histogram except that single points rather than bars are graphed and these points are then connected by a line. Figure 7.5 shows the example data in a frequency polygon. Notice that this representation is very similar to Figure 7.3.

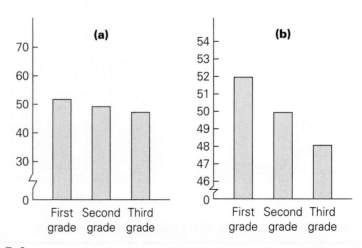

FIGURE 7.4 Graphs of Reading Scores of First-, Second-, and Third-Graders

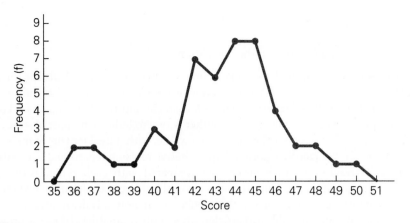

FIGURE 7.5 **Frequency Polygon of Scores from Table 7.3**

Finally, it is also useful to represent the distribution graphically by curving the straight lines of a frequency polygon. The well-known normal curve, discussed later in this chapter, is an example of using this technique.

MEASURES OF CENTRAL TENDENCY

For most sets of data, it is useful to get some idea of the typical or average score or observation in addition to knowing the frequency distribution. Although the word *average* has many connotations, in research only the *mean* refers to the average score. Two other indices, the *median* and the *mode*, also provide information about typical scores of a group. Together, these three indices are referred to as **measures of central tendency**. Each provides a numerical index of the typical score of a distribution.

Measures of central tendency: typical or average score

Mean

The **mean** is simply the arithmetic average of all the scores. It is calculated by summing all the scores and then dividing the sum by the number of scores. If, for example, we have a distribution of 5, 8, 9, and 2, the mean is 6 (5 + 8 + 9 + 2 = 24; 24 ÷ 4 = 6). The mean is the most frequently used measure of central tendency because every score is used in computing it. The weakness of the mean is that when a distribution contains extremely high or low scores (i.e., outliers), those very untypical of the rest of the distribution, the mean is pulled toward the extreme score. If, for example, a distribution contained scores of 4, 5, 7, and 40, the mean would be 14. Because in this case most of the scores are considerably lower than 14, the mean is somewhat misleading with respect to central tendency. You can think of the mean as the point that equally balances the sides, much like a seesaw that is level.

The calculation of the mean is simple. Using Σ to represent "the sum of," either or both of the following formulas can be used:

Mean: arithmetical average of scores

$$\overline{X} = \frac{\Sigma X}{n}$$

where $\overline{X}$ = sample mean
X = sample score
n = number of scores in the sample

or

$$\mu = \frac{\Sigma X}{N}$$

where μ = population mean
X = population score
N = number of scores in the population

Note that some of the symbols vary, depending on whether you are calculating the mean for the sample or for the population. Typically, lowercase Greek letters are used to indicate population statistics (parameters) and uppercase letters for sample statistics. Letters used for both population and sample statistics are italicized, as is either N or n to indicate number of scores. In some studies the uppercase N is used for the sample as a whole, with n used for part of the sample.

The mean is very frequently reported in quantitative research reports and is essential to the interpretation of results in which groups are compared with each other. Although some researchers and statisticians maintain that the mean should only be calculated when the data are at interval or ratio level and scores in the population are normally distributed, these assumptions routinely are not met in published articles, where only ordinal-level data are provided and the size of the sample is large. Excerpt 7.6 illustrates the use of means in an article. In this use of bivariate statistics, Russian and American students' attitudes, perceptions, and tendencies toward cheating are compared. Note the use of the lowercase n for samples.

Median

Median: midpoint of a distribution of scores

The **median** is the point that divides a rank-ordered distribution into halves that contain an equal number of scores. Fifty percent of the scores thus lie below the median and 50 percent of the scores lie above it. The median is unaffected by the actual values of the scores. This is an advantage when a distribution contains atypically large or small scores. For example, the median of the set of scores 10, 15, 16, 19, and 105 is 16, because half the scores are above 16 and half are below. Thus, 16 would be a better indicator of central tendency than the mean, which is 33. If a distribution contains an even number of scores, the median is the midpoint between the two middle scores (e.g., for the scores 2, 2, 4, 7, 8, and 12, the median is 5.5).

Because the value of the median is based only on the percentages of scores higher than and lower than the midpoint, the median is the preferred measure of central tendency when describing

EXCERPT 7.6   Use of Means to Report Results

TABLE 2   American and Russian Business Students' Beliefs about Cheating

	Overall Mean	American Students $n = 443$	Russian Students $n = 174$
Percentage of students believed to cheat on exams	36.53	24.18	69.59*
Most students cheat on exams	3.45	2.80	5.12*
Most students cheat on out-of-class assignments	4.09	3.88	4.64*
Cheating on one exam is not so bad	2.90	2.34	4.36*
OK to tell someone in later section about an exam	4.71	4.07	6.36*
Giving someone your past exams is cheating	2.26	2.02	2.87*
Using an exam from a prior semester is cheating	2.65	2.23	3.02*
Instructor must make sure students do not cheat	3.68	3.88	3.18*
Instructor discussing issues tied to cheating reduces amount of cheating	3.92	4.27	3.01*

Note: The first item in the table is a percentage (e.g., 36.53%). All other items are mean ratings using a seven-point scale, where 1 = Strongly disagree and 7 = Strongly agree.
*t = test of mean differences between nationalities significant at $\rho < 0.000$.

Source: From Lupton, R. A., & Chapman, K. J. (2002). Russian and American college students' attitudes, perceptions, and tendencies towards cheating. *Educational Research, 44,* 17–27. Reprinted by permission.

highly skewed data. The median is used to describe data that may have extreme scores, such as income level in the United States. Medians are also employed to divide one group of respondents into two groups of equal numbers. A researcher may, for example, get an indication of perceived degree of success from each respondent on a 7-point scale (extreme success = 7, extreme failure = 1). If the researcher wanted to divide the group of subjects into those with high and low self-perceptions of success, the median could be used. This procedure is called a *median-split technique*.

Mode

The **mode** is simply the score that occurs most frequently in a distribution. As such, it is a crude index of central tendency and is rarely used in educational research. It is useful only when there is an interest in knowing the most common score or observation or when the data are in nominal form. The word *mode* is used more frequently, to describe a distribution by indicating that the distribution is *bimodal* (two modes), *trimodal* (three modes), or *multimodal*. These terms are used even when, technically, there is only one mode but at least two scores that have definitely higher frequencies than the rest.

Mode: most frequent score

Relationships among Measures of Central Tendency

As long as a distribution of scores is relatively symmetrical, the mean, median, and mode will be about the same. In what is referred to as a **normal distribution**, these indices are exactly the same. The normal distribution (see Figure 7.11 on page 165) forms a bell-shaped symmetrical curve. The normal curve is the theoretical distribution that is used to transform data and calculate many statistics. Although many educational variables—for example, large numbers of achievement scores—are normally distributed, the data from a single research study may be distributed unevenly; that is, the distributions are unsymmetrical, and the scores tend to bunch up at one end of the distribution or the other.

Normal distribution: bell-shaped, symmetrical distribution of scores

Such distributions are called **skewed**, and with skewed distributions, the choice of the measure of central tendency becomes more important. Distributions are **positively skewed** if most of the scores are at the low end of the distribution, with a few high scores, and **negatively skewed** if most scores are located at the high end. To remember the difference between positive and negative skew, think of the curved shape of the distribution forming an arrow or a pointer. If it forms an arrow that points in a positive or higher direction, the distribution is positively skewed, and if it points in a negative or lower direction, the distribution is negatively skewed. That is, using the median or mode as a reference point, the mean is higher in a positively skewed distribution and lower in a negatively skewed distribution. Actually, you can think of the mean as being either positively or negatively skewed in relation to the median. In Figure 7.6, positively and negatively skewed distributions are illustrated with corresponding means, medians, and modes. Notice that the mean in each distribution is closer to the tail of the distribution than the median or mode, and the mode is farthest from the tail.

Skewed distribution: nonnormal

Positively skewed: disproportionately large number of low scores

Negatively skewed: disproportionately large number of high scores

To further illustrate this relationship, consider the following example. Suppose a teacher wants to report an "average" reading score for his class. He has a reading score for each of 20 students, ranging from 5 to 80. The distribution of scores is represented in Table 7.5.

If the teacher reports the arithmetic average as the mean, it would be 22.7. The median is 10, and the mode is 5. Which is correct? Because of a few students who scored very well (80), the distribution is positively skewed and hence the median is probably the most accurate single

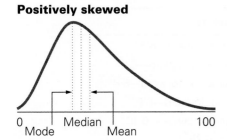

FIGURE 7.6 **Skewed Distributions**

TABLE 7.5 Frequency Distribution of Reading Scores

Scores	(f)
5	8
10	4
12	2
15	2
80	4
	$n = 20$

indicator. In such cases, however, it is probably best to report the mean for the students who scored between 5 and 15 (8.4) and to report the four high scores separately or to report both the mean and the median. Because many distributions in education are at least somewhat skewed, it is often best to report both the mean and the median.

Another way distributions can be characterized is related to what is called *kurtosis* (no, it's not a disease!). **Kurtosis** is a description used when a distribution is flat or peaked in comparison with the normal distribution. If a distribution is peaked, it is called *leptokurtic*; flat distributions are described as *platykurtic*. Distribution B in Figure 7.10 is clearly leptokurtic; distribution A is slightly platykurtic.

Kurtosis: flatter than or more peaked than the normal distribution

MEASURES OF VARIABILITY

Central tendency is only one index that can be used to represent a group of scores. In order to provide a full description, a second statistical measure is also needed. This statistic is referred to as a *measure of variability*. **Measures of variability** show how spread out the distribution of scores is from the mean of the distribution, how much, on the average, scores differ from the mean, or how different scores are from each other. Variability measures are also referred to in general terms as measures of *dispersion, scatter,* and *spread.*

Measures of variability: show the dispersion of scores

The need for a measure of dispersion is illustrated in Figure 7.7. This figure shows how two classrooms with the same mean score can actually be very different. In Class B, the students are rather homogeneous, or similar to each other, with few high- or low-achieving students. In Class A, however, the teacher has a great range of achievement, or a heterogeneous group of students whose scores spread from 55 to 100.

As another example, suppose Ernie is going to bet on Saturday's basketball game between the Bombers and the Dunkers. The sports section of the newspaper lacks the statistics on individual players, but the sports writer reports that the members of both teams have approximately equal height: the average height is 6′ 6½″ and 6′ 7½″, respectively, for the Bombers and Dunkers. With only the mean to help decide, Ernie places a bet on the Dunkers. When Ernie sees the program with the heights of the players, he discovers a shortcoming of the mean.

Bombers	Dunkers
Gerber, guard—6′0″	Regen, guard—6′5″
Bosher, guard—6′3″	Lambiotte, guard—6′6″
Davis, forward—6′5″	Hambrick, forward—6′8″
Gallagher, forward—6′7″	Lang, forward—6′9″
Robinson, center—7′3″	Wergin, center—6′10″
$\bar{X} = 6′6½″$	$\bar{X} = 6′7½″$

As the Bombers' offense proceeds to take advantage of Robinson's height over Wergin's to score, Ernie realizes that the mean fails to describe the characteristics of the distribution. The Dunkers have little variability, whereas the Bombers have high variability, and so Ernie loses the bet!

Variability, then, tells us about the difference between the scores of the distribution. Although we can use such words as *high, low, great, little,* and *much* to describe the degree of variability, it is necessary to have more precise indices. Two common measures of variability are *range* and *standard deviation.*

Range

The **range** is the most obvious measure of dispersion. It is simply the difference between the highest and lowest scores in the distribution. If, for example, the lowest of 30 scores on a test was 65 and the highest score was 90, the range would be 25 (90 − 65 = 25). Because there are only two scores involved in calculating the range, it is very simple to obtain. However, it is also a very crude measure of dispersion and can be misleading if there is an atypically high or low score. The range also fails to indicate anything about the variability of scores around the mean of the distribution. Sometimes researchers will use the *interquartile range*, which indicates the dispersion among the middle half of the scores.

Range: difference between the highest and lowest scores

Standard Deviation

The **standard deviation** is a numerical index that indicates the average variability of the scores. It tells us, in other words, about the distance, on the average, of the scores from the mean. A distribution that has a relatively heterogeneous set of scores that spread out widely from the mean (e.g., Class A of Figure 7.7) will have a larger standard deviation than a homogeneous set of scores that cluster around the mean (Class B of Figure 7.7). The first step in calculating the standard deviation (abbreviated *SD* or *s* for the sample and σ [sigma] for the population) is to find the distance between each score and the mean (see Figure 7.8), thus determining the amount that each score deviates, or differs, from the mean. In one sense, the standard deviation is simply the average of all the deviation scores, the average distance of the scores from the mean.

For any set of scores, then, a standard deviation can be computed that will be unique to the distribution and indicates the amount, on the average, that the set of scores deviates from the mean. The most common convention in reporting the standard deviation is to indicate that one standard deviation is equal to some number (e.g., $SD = 15.0$; $\sigma = 3.40$). One standard deviation added to and subtracted from the mean has a special meaning; it tells us the distance that most but not all of the scores are from the mean. For example, 68 percent of the scores will fall within the first standard deviation with a normal distribution. This property of standard deviation is illustrated in Figure 7.9, where 1 SD = 5. Notice that on both sides of the mean (15),

Standard deviation: average dispersion of scores around the mean

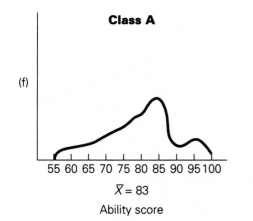
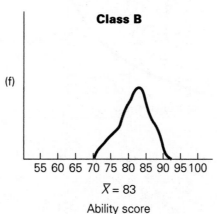

FIGURE 7.7 **Score Dispersion**

175

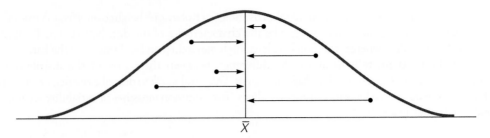

FIGURE 7.8 **Distance of Each Score from the Mean**

there is a line that designates −1 *SD* and +1 *SD*. The negative and positive directions from the mean are equivalent in score units (i.e., both − 1 and +1 *SD* = 5 units), and between −1 and +1 *SD*, there are about 68 percent of the total number of scores in the distribution. If we assume that the distribution is normal, then 50 percent of the scores are above the mean and 50 percent are below the mean. Now, because we know that there is an equal number of scores on either side of the mean, we know that 34 percent of the scores must be between the mean and − or + 1 *SD*, and if 50 percent of the scores are below the mean and we add 34 percent by going up +1 *SD*, then we know that about 84 percent of the scores of the distribution are below +1 *SD*. Similarly, if we subtract 34 from 50, we know that 16 percent of the scores are below −1 *SD*.

Percentile rank: percentage of scores at and below a certain score

When we indicate that a certain percentage of the scores is at or below a particular score, we are referring to the **percentile rank** of the score. If, for example, a score of 38 is at the 87th percentile, it means that 87 percent of the scores are the same as or lower than 38. In other words, only 12 percent of the scores are higher than 38. With normal distributions, +1 *SD* is always at the 84th percentile and −1 *SD* is at the 16th percentile.

The interpretation of 1 *SD* is always the same with regard to the percentages of scores within certain points of a normal distribution. Because the numerical units used to represent scores change, however, the standard deviation can equal 15 in one distribution and 0.32 in another distribution. Or in a circumstance with the same numerical units but two different distributions, the standard deviations will be unique to each distribution. That is, 1 *SD* has a meaning that is

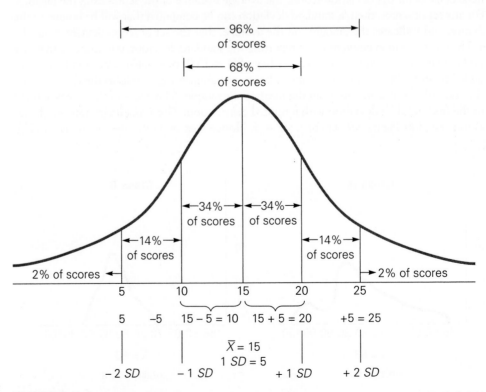

FIGURE 7.9 **Standard Deviation in a Normal Distribution**

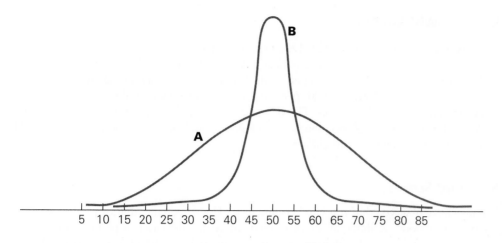

$\overline{X} = 50$, 1 *SD* for A = 15

$\overline{X} = 50$, 1 *SD* for B = 5

FIGURE 7.10   **Comparison of Distributions with Different Standard Deviations**

constant for any distribution regardless of the actual value of 1 *SD* for each distribution. For example, in Figure 7.10, two distributions are illustrated. Distribution A has a large standard deviation and distribution, B a small one; a score of 65 in distribution A has the same percentile rank as 55 in distribution B.

Along with the mean, the standard deviation is an excellent way to indicate the nature of the distribution of a set of scores. Standard deviation is typically reported in research with the mean. A measure of dispersion related to the standard deviation is termed the **variance** of a distribution (noted by σ^2 or s^2; thus, the standard deviation is equal to the square root of the variance). The term *variance*, however, is usually used as a general term in regard to dispersion (e.g., in stating that the variance is large or small) and is rarely reported as a specific number to indicate variability.

Excerpt 7.7 is an example of the way standard deviations can be reported. Standard deviations are almost always reported along with means.

Develop your descriptive statistics skills by reading the article on MyEducationLab for Research at www.myeducationlab.com and completing the questions provided. Click on the topic "Descriptive Statistics" and then select the Building Research Skill titled "Understanding Descriptive Statistics."

Variance: measure of dispersion of scores

EXCERPT 7.7   Reporting Means and Standard Deviations

TABLE 1   Mean, Standard Deviation, and Rank for Music Learning Outcomes in Current and Ideal Conditions

	Listen	Perform	Relate Culture/History	Read & Write Music	Relate to Other Subjects	Analyze	Create & Compose
Current							
M	**4.29**	**3.82**	**3.68**	**3.62**	3.54	3.31	**2.87**
SD	(0.66)	(0.98)	(0.93)	(1.01)	(0.94)	(1.02)	(1.14)
Rank	1	2	3	4	5	6	7
Ideal							
M	**4.57**	4.41	4.46	4.20	4.52	4.26	**4.00**
SD	(0.51)	(0.66)	(0.60)	(0.75)	(0.60)	(0.75)	(0.84)
Rank	1	4	3	6	2	5	7

Note: Bold numbers indicate the highest and lowest means for each condition.

Source: From *Journal of Research in Music Education*, Spring 2006, *54*(1), 6–20. Copyright © 2006 by MENC: The National Association for Music Education. Reprinted with permission.

Box-and-Whisker Plot

Box-and-whisker plot:
graphic display of dispersion of a set of scores

The **box-and-whisker** plot is used to give a picture or image of the variability. A "box" is formed for each variable. The size of this rectangular box is determined by the first and third quartiles of the distribution (i.e., 25th to 75th percentiles). The "whiskers" are lines drawn from the ends of the rectangle to the 10th and 90th percentiles. Sometimes additional points are included to show extremely high or low scores. The box-and-whisker plot in Excerpt 7.8 shows how U.S. student achievement in algebra compares with Japanese student achievement. Notice the wider variation in the achievement of U.S. students.

Standard Scores

Standard scores: converted scores based on the standard deviation

You may have observed that it is cumbersome to analyze several distributions if the means and standard deviations are different for each distribution. To alleviate this problem and expedite interpretation, raw score distributions are often converted to *standard scores*. **Standard scores** have constant normative or relative meaning. They are obtained from the mean and standard deviation of the raw score distribution.

Because a normal distribution has certain properties that are useful for comparing one person's score with the score of others, by converting to normalized standard scores, the normal curve properties can be assumed. Thus, raw score distributions with different means and standard

EXCERPT 7.8 Box-and-Whisker Plot

Given the differences in the patterns of coverage of algebra between these U.S. course types, what happens when U.S. achievement in algebra is disaggregated by course type?

Figure 3 presents such a disaggregation for class-level posttest scores—extended to include the parallel posttest achievement for Japan—and shows a striking pattern. (p. 21)

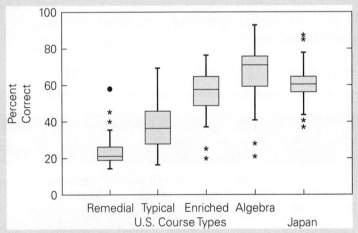

Note: In boxplots like those found in [this figure] . . . , the length of the box, the rectangle bounded by the "hinges," represents the proportion of the distribution that falls between the 25th and 75th percentiles. The line across the box represents the median. The length of the "whiskers" represents the min and the max or the adjacent outermost value,

$$1.5 = (pctile_{75} - pctile_{25}),$$

if this is less than the min and the max. The * and the • represent extreme values.

FIGURE 3 **United States and Japan: Posttest achievement in Population A Algebra**

Source: From Westbury, I. (1992). Comparing American and Japanese achievement: Is the United States really a low achiever? *Educational Researcher, 21*(5), 18–24. Copyright © 1992 by the American Educational Research Association. Reproduced with permission of the publisher.x

deviations that are difficult to compare can be transformed to the same standard scores and compared easily. Because standard scores are linear transformations, it is conceivable that a small raw score difference is exaggerated when converted to standard scores. For example, the SAT has a standard score mean of about 500 and a standard deviation of about 100, whereas the raw scores are much lower. Thus, a raw score difference of two or three questions may result in a standard score difference of 10 to 20 points.

The **z-score** is the most basic standard score, with a mean of 0 and a standard deviation of 1. Thus, a z-score of 11 is at the 84th percentile for a normal distribution, 21 is at the 16th percentile, and 22 is at the 2nd percentile. Other standard scores are linear transformations from the z-score, with arbitrarily selected means and standard deviations. That is, it is possible to choose any mean and any standard deviation. Most IQ tests, for example, use 100 as the mean and 15 to 16 as the standard deviation. The resultant IQ score is a standard score. (The ratio IQ, mental age divided by chronological age × 100, is rarely used today.) Figure 7.11 shows a normal distribution, standard deviations, percentiles, and some common standard scores.

z-score: mean of 0, standard deviation of 1

Outliers

An **outlier** (or *fringelier*) refers to a data point that falls far outside the main distribution of scores. Depending on how extreme it is and the total number of scores in the distribution (i.e., the fewer the scores, the bigger the impact), an outlier can distort statistical analyses that include actual values of all the scores, such as the mean and standard deviation. Although some researchers rely on a visual display to identify extreme scores, outliers are typically identified as data points that are three standard deviations from the mean. Osborne and Overbay (2004) point out three deleterious effects of outliers: (1) they increase the standard deviation, which exaggerates

Outlier: atypically high or low data point

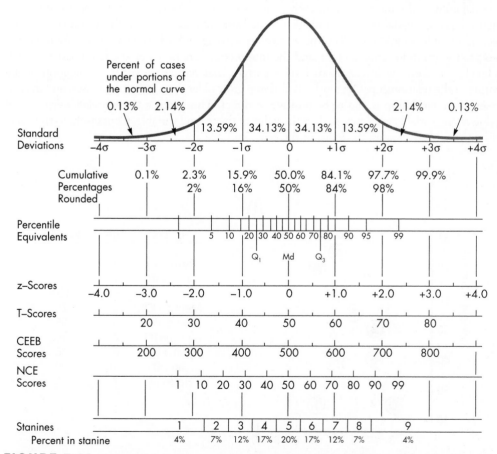

FIGURE 7.11 **Normal Curve, Standard Deviations, Percentiles, and Selected Standard Scores**
Source: Test Service Bulletin No. 148. Copyright 1955, updated 1980 by NCS Pearson, Inc. Reproduced with permission. All rights reserved.

variance; (2) they decrease the normality of the distribution (which is an assumption for using many statistics); and (3) they can bias results, leading to erroneous conclusions.

Outliers are like bad apples: One in a basket of good apples can spoil the whole bunch. What do we do with them? If it's clear on further investigation that the scores are invalid (e.g., a mistake in scoring or recording), then they should be corrected or dropped. When an outlier is valid, however, there is no consensus on what to do. Some researchers maintain that valid outliers should be dropped, whereas others believe that they should be included. A reasonable compromise to these choices is to conduct the statistical analyses twice—once with the outlier and once without it.

MEASURES OF RELATIONSHIP

Up to this point, we have been discussing descriptive statistics that are used to summarize or give a picture of groups on one variable at a time. There are, however, many questions of interest that depend on the way two or more variables are related to each other—for instance, are brighter students more motivated? If we increase the frequency of reinforcement, will the reinforced or target behavior also increase? Is there a relationship between self-concept and achievement? If students exert more effort in studying, will they feel better about their achievement? In each instance, two variables are measured for each subject in the group.

Scatterplot

Scatterplot: graphic display of a relationship of two variables

The most fundamental measure of relationship is called a *scatterplot, scatter diagram,* or *scattergram.* The **scatterplot** is a graphic representation of the relationship, achieved by forming a visual array of the intersection of each subject's scores on the two variables. As illustrated in Figure 7.12, one variable is rank ordered on the horizontal axis (age, in this example) and the second variable is rank ordered on the vertical axis (weight). Each subject's scores are indicated next to the graph in random order, and the intersections are noted by the letter assigned each subject. Together, the intersections form a pattern that provides a general indication of the nature of the relationship. Obviously, as children grow older their weight increases, and in such cases, the relationship is said to be positive or direct. Thus, with a *positive relationship,* as the value of one variable increases, so does the value of the second variable. Conversely, as the value of one variable decreases, the value of the other variable also decreases.

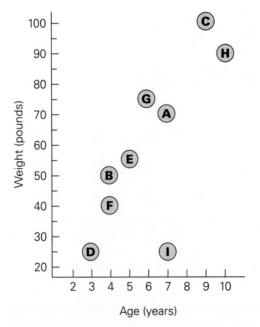

Subject	Age	Weight
Ryann (A)	7	70
Jessica (B)	4	50
Amanda (C)	9	100
Meghan (D)	3	25
Katie (E)	5	55
Cristina (F)	4	40
Emma (G)	6	75
Jan (H)	10	90
Helen (I)	7	25

FIGURE 7.12 Scatterplot

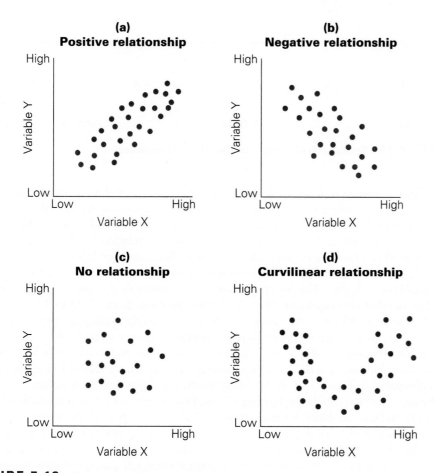

FIGURE 7.13 Scatterplots of Relationships

Scatterplots are useful in identifying outliers. For instance, in Figure 7.12, Helen was 7 years old and reported a weight of 25 pounds, which is very different from what is represented in points A through H. Scatter diagrams also provide a first hint about whether the relationship is linear or curvilinear (see Figure 7.13). (The usual approach in graphing relationships is to use dots, not circles, within the graph at the intersections.)

Several different types of patterns can emerge in scatterplots. When one variable decreases as the other increases (e.g., the number of miles on a tire and the depth of remaining tread), there is a *negative* (or *inverse*) relationship. If there is no pattern at all in the graph, there is no relationship. Figure 7.13 illustrates different scatter diagrams. Notice the curvilinear relationship in Figure 7.13(d). Curvilinear relationships are not uncommon but are usually detected only by plotting the scores. An example of a curvilinear relationship might be anxiety level and test performance. Performance could often be low during either high- or low-level anxiety and high during medium-level anxiety.

The direction of the pattern in the scatterplot, then, indicates whether there is a relationship and whether the relationship is positive, negative, or curvilinear. If a line is drawn through the plotted dots to minimize the distance of each dot to the line, then the degree of clustering around the line indicates the strength of the relationship. Plots that have mostly scattered dots have weak or low relationships, whereas dots clustered near the line indicate a strong or high relationship. The strength of the relationship is independent of its direction. Dots clustered so tightly as to form a straight line represent a perfect relationship (maximum strength). Correlations thus indicate three things: whether there is any relationship at all, the direction of the relationship, and the strength of the relationship.

Bivariate Correlation

Even though scatterplots are indispensable tools for evaluating the relationship between two variables, researchers rarely provide such graphs in published articles. The typical convention

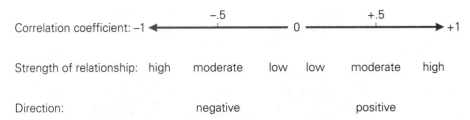

FIGURE 7.14 **Relationship of Strength and Direction of Correlations**

Correlation coefficient: number that shows the direction and strength of the relationship

is to calculate a number to represent the relationship, called a **correlation coefficient**.[1] There are many types of correlation coefficients, and the choice of the one to use is determined by the scale used in data collection, the research question, and the number of variables. When there are two variables and the purpose is to examine the relationship between them, the procedure used is a *bivariate* or *zero-order correlation*. Bivariate correlations are also used to investigate the many relationships that exist when there are many variables and a coefficient is calculated for each pair. The interpretation of the number used, however, is basically the same. The number that represents the correlation can range from −1.00 to +1.00. A high positive value (e.g., .85, .90, .96) represents a high positive relationship; a low positive value (.15, .20, .08) a low positive relationship; a moderate negative value (−.40, −.37, −.52) a moderate negative relationship; a value of 0 no relationship; and so on. Thus, the strength of the relationship becomes higher as the correlation approaches either +1 or −1 from zero. This is illustrated in Figure 7.14. Note that strength is independent of direction.

The most common correlation technique is the Pearson product-moment coefficient (represented by r), and the correlation is indicated by $r = 0.65$, $r = -0.78$, $r = 0.03$, and so on. (Notice that there is no plus sign before positive values, but there is a negative sign for negative values.)

Take a few moments to practice interpreting measures of relationships. Go to MyEducation-Lab for Research at www. myeducationlab.com and practice interpreting data from a study of fraternity members. Click on the topic "Descriptive Statistics" and then select "Interpreting Measures of Relationship."

The product-moment correlation is used when both variables use continuous scales, such as scores from achievement tests, grade-point average, self-concept inventories, and age. Because scores can also be reported as dichotomies, in several categories, or ranks, other correlation techniques, depending on the scale for the variables, are used to measure the relationship. Some of these techniques are summarized in Table 7.6.

Excerpts 7.9 and 7.10 show how to report correlational data. In Excerpt 7.9, there are lists of all correlations of interest in the study. In Excerpt 7.10 there is an *intercorrelation matrix*, in which many variables are correlated with each other. The numbers in the row on top of the table correspond to the variables listed vertically on the left. The correlation of teachers' disapproval and criticism with teachers' encouragement is −0.54; the correlation of engagement with teachers' long-term expectations is 0.44.

TABLE 7.6 Types of Correlation Coefficients

Type of Coefficient	Symbol	Types of Variables
Pearson product-moment	r	Both continuous
Spearman	r_s	Both rank ordered
Biserial	r_b	One continuous, one an artificial dichotomy
Point-biserial	r_{pb}	One continuous, one a true dichotomy
Tetrachoric	r^t	Both artificial dichotomies
Phi coefficient	ϕ	Both true dichotomies
Contingency coefficients	C	Both two or more categories
Correlation ratio, eta	η	Both continuous (used with curvilinear relationships)

EXCERPT 7.9 Pearson Product-Moment Correlation

Pearson product-moment correlations were computed between all demographic variables (i.e., percentage White; low income; attendance rate; percentage mobility; high school dropout rate; high school graduation rate; average class size; average teacher experience in years; pupil-teacher ratio; average teacher salary; average per-pupil expenditure) and the achievement scores (i.e., scores in reading and mathematics). The 1994 correlations (see Table 2) were similar across grade levels and subject matter within the 1994 data.

To summarize, we detected statistically significant relationships (or associations) between the school demographic variables and the achievement scores. The strongest relationships occurred for the following variables: low income, percentage White, high school graduation, and dropout rate. Moderate relationships existed for attendance, mobility, and high school pupil-teacher ratio. The weakest relationships occurred for average class size, elementary pupil-teacher ratio, teacher salary, teacher experience, and expenditure per pupil. (p. 332)

TABLE 2 Correlations of Attitude Measures with Achievement Scores

Variable	Grade 3		Grade 10	
	Reading	Mathematics	Reading	Mathematics
Percentage White	.78	.66	.75	.67
Low income	−.79	−.72	−.79	−.75
Attendance	.59	.53	.82	.72
Mobility	−.52	−.46	−.54	−.49
Dropout	—	—	−.69	−.61
High school graduation	—	—	.76	.69
Average class size, Grade 3	−.09**	−.06**	—	—
Average class size, high school	—	—	−.18	−.11**
Teacher experience	−.14	−.13	−.05	.00
Elementary pupil-teacher ratio	−.26	−.22	−.32	−.24
High school pupil-teacher ratio	—	—	−.32	−.24
Teacher salary	−.20	−.08	−.05	.07
Expenditure per pupil	−.31	−.19	.10*	−.01

Note: Grade 3, $n = 2{,}307$; Grade 10, $n = 644$. Correlations are statistically significant at the .001 level unless otherwise noted.
*$p < .05$. ** $p < .01$.

Source: From Sutton, A., & Soderstrom, I. (1999). Predicting elementary and secondary school achievement with school-related and demographic factors. *Journal of Educational Research, 92* (6), 330–338. (1999). Reprinted with permission of the Helen Dwight Reid Educational Foundation. Published by Heldref Publications, 1319 Eighteenth St., NW, Washington, DC 20036–1802. Copyright © 1999.

CHAPTER SUMMARY

This chapter introduced the fundamental principles of descriptive statistics. The statistical procedures are used in one way or another in quantitative research studies. The major points covered are as follows:

1. Descriptive statistics are indices that summarize or characterize a large number of observations.
2. Measurement scales (i.e., nominal, ordinal, interval, and ratio) and the purpose of the research suggest the descriptive statistics that are appropriate.

3. Descriptive statistical procedures can be classified as univariate (i.e., one variable) or bivariate (i.e., two variables).
4. Frequency distributions in the form of class intervals, histograms, bar graphs, frequency polygons, and stem-and-leaf displays provide an overview picture of all the data.
5. Measures of central tendency include the mean, median, and mode. Each measure provides a numerical index of the typical score in the distribution.

EXCERPT 7.10   Correlation Matrix

Zero-order correlations among the motivational context variables and behavioral signs of alienation are depicted in Table 2. All correlations were in the expected direction. Students' disciplinary problems were most strongly related to their reports of teachers' disinterest and criticism and teacher expectations. The strongest relation to emerge was between students' perceptions of teachers' expectations and student engagement. Peers' academic aspirations and their perceptions of the economic limitations of education were related to both disciplinary problems and engagement. (p. 67)

TABLE 2   Zero-Order Correlations between Perceived Motivational Context Variables and Indexes of Alienation

Motivation Context Variables	1	2	3	4	5	6	7	8	9	10
1. Teachers' disapproval and criticism	—									
2. Teachers' encouragement	$-.54^{***}$	—								
3. Teachers' long-term expectations	$-.39^{***}$	$.34^{***}$	—							
4. Peers' academic aspirations	$-.21^{***}$	$.13^{**}$	$.36^{***}$	—						
5. Peers' resistance to school norms	$.27^{***}$	$-.09$	$-.22^{***}$	$-.47^{***}$	—					
6. Peers' academic support	$-.32^{***}$	$.31^{***}$	$.29^{***}$	$.47^{***}$	$-.44^{***}$	—				
7. Economic limitations of education	$.38^{***}$	$-.24^{***}$	$-.35^{***}$	$-.38^{***}$	$.27^{***}$	$-.25^{***}$	—			
8. Economic benefits of education	$-.12^{*}$	$.21^{***}$	$.32^{***}$	$.32^{***}$	$-.12^{*}$	$.21^{***}$	$-.36^{***}$	—		
Indexes of Alienation										
9. Discipline problems	$-.35^{***}$	$.15^{**}$	$-.36^{***}$	$-.26^{***}$	$.17^{**}$	$-.21^{***}$	$.29^{***}$	$-.11^{**}$	—	
10. Engagement	$-.16^{**}$	$.04$	$.44^{***}$	$.27^{***}$	$-.14^{**}$	$.19^{***}$	$-.22^{***}$	$.11^{**}$	$-.47^{***}$	—

$^{*}p < .05.$ $^{**}p < .01.$ $^{***}p < .001.$

Source: From Murdock, T. B. (1999). The social context of risk: Status and motivational predictors of alienation in middle school. *Journal of Educational Psychology, 91*(1), 62–75. Copyright © 1999 by the American Psychological Association. Reprinted with permission.

6. The mean is the best measure of central tendency for distributions that have no extremely high or low scores; the median is the best for highly skewed data. Often, both the mean and the median should be reported.

7. Measures of variability indicate the spread of scores from the mean of the distribution.

8. Measures of variation include the range, standard deviation, and box-and-whisker plots.

9. Outliers are extreme scores that can distort findings.

10. Standard deviation is a measure of variability unique to each distribution that indicates, on the average, how much a score deviates from the mean.

11. Standard scores are converted raw score distributions with common units to indicate the mean and the standard deviation.

12. A scatterplot is used to indicate the general direction and strength of a relationship between two variables in one group or sample.

13. A correlation coefficient is a number that represents the direction and strength of the relationship between two or more variables.

APPLICATION PROBLEMS

1. For each case below, choose the most appropriate statistical procedure:
   a. A teacher of a low-level reading group wants to know the average score for the group of 25 students.
   b. An administrator wants to find out if there is a relationship between teacher absences and student achievement.
   c. A math teacher wants to know how many ability groups should be formed within a class of 30 students.
   d. A student teacher is interested in finding out the number of students who rate his performance as good, excellent, average, or poor.

2. Identify the scale of measurement in each of the following:
   a. attitudes toward school
   b. grouping students on the basis of hair color
   c. asking judges to rank order students from most cooperative to least cooperative

3. For the following set of scores, prepare a frequency distribution, a histogram, and a stem-and-leaf display for each variable. Also calculate the mean, the median, and the standard deviation of each score. Are there any outliers in the distribution? If so, what is the result if these scores are removed from the dataset? Draw a scatterplot that illustrates the relationship between the two variables.

Subject	Variable A: Attitude toward descriptive statistics (1 = low and 20 = high)	Variable B: Achievement on test of knowledge of descriptive statistics
Sam	12	80
Sally	10	60
Frank	19	85
Bob	8	65
Colleen	2	55
Isaiah	15	75
Felix	1	95
Dan	20	82
Robert	6	70
Jim	11	88
Michelle	3	59
Jan	7	60

4. If you have access to SPSS (Statistical Package for the Social Sciences), create a dataset that can be used for calculating descriptive statistics and making graphs. When you open SPSS, the title of the page will be *Untitled SPSS Data Editor*. The tab at the bottom (*Data View*) tells you that you are in the right screen to enter your data. The variables are named across the top, and each number on the left corresponds to a different subject. Once you have entered the scores, it is best to open the tab named *Variable View* and specify characteristics of each variable. Click on *Analyze* to see a number of different procedures. Select *Descriptive Statistics* and then *Descriptives* and *Explore*. To do the correlation, click on *Correlate* and then *Bivariate*. Click on *Graphs*, then Legacy Dialogs, to find *Histogram* and *Scatterplot*. Use these procedures to do the calculations in problem 3 and confirm your work.

NOTE

1. This discussion is limited to simple correlation. More advanced correlational procedures—such as multiple correlation, partial correlation, discriminant function analysis, and canonical correlation—are based on these principles to examine the combined relationships of several variables.

ANSWER TO THE APPLICATION PROBLEMS

1. a. mean
   b. Pearson product-moment correlation
   c. standard deviation (the wider the dispersion, the greater the number of groups)
   d. frequencies and percentages
2. a. interval or ordinal
   b. nominal
   c. ordinal

3.

	Variable A	Variable B
Mean	10.09	74.09
Median	10.00	75.00
Standard deviation	6.20	13.07

The correlation is .31. Felix is an outlier; when his scores are removed, the correlation is .76.

4. (Use SPSS to confirm answers to question 3.)

Quantitative Data Collection: Technical Adequacy

From Chapter 8 of *Research in Education: Evidence-Based Inquiry*, 7/e. James H. McMillan. Sally Schumacher.

Quantitative Data Collection: Technical Adequacy

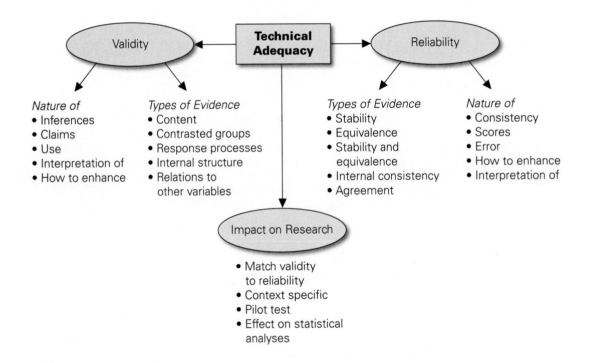

Validity

Technical Adequacy

Reliability

Nature of
- Inferences
- Claims
- Use
- Interpretation of
- How to enhance

Types of Evidence
- Content
- Contrasted groups
- Response processes
- Internal structure
- Relations to other variables

Types of Evidence
- Stability
- Equivalence
- Stability and equivalence
- Internal consistency
- Agreement

Nature of
- Consistency
- Scores
- Error
- How to enhance
- Interpretation of

Impact on Research

- Match validity to reliability
- Context specific
- Pilot test
- Effect on statistical analyses

KEY TERMS

test validity
construct underrepresentation
construct irrelevant variance
evidence based on test content
evidence based on contrasted groups
evidence based on response processes
evidence based on internal structure
evidence based on relations to other variables
test reliability

stability
equivalence
internal consistency
split-half reliability
Kuder-Richardson (KR)
Cronbach's alpha
agreement
coefficient of concordance
Cohen's kappa

WHAT YOU WILL LEARN

Study this chapter and you will:

- Know what test validity and reliability mean and how these technical characteristics affect research.
- Explain different types of evidence for validity and reliability.
- Understand how types of evidence for validity and reliability match different research designs.

- Identify validity and reliability of evidence in articles.
- Apply an understanding of validity to know what constitutes credible data collection.

FUNDAMENTALS OF QUANTITATIVE MEASUREMENT: TECHNICAL ADEQUACY

Quantitative measurement uses some type of instrument or device to obtain numerical indices that correspond to characteristics of the subjects. The numerical values are then summarized and reported as the results of the study. Consequently, the results depend heavily on the quality of the measurement. If the measure is weak or biased, then so are the results. Conversely, strong measures increase confidence that the findings are accurate. It is imperative, then, to understand what makes measurement strong or weak. Whether you need to choose instruments to conduct a study or to evaluate results, it is necessary to understand what affects the quality of the measure. In this section, two technical concepts of measurement, validity and reliability, are discussed as important criteria for determining quality for both cognitive and noncognitive assessment.

TEST VALIDITY

Test validity (or, more accurately, *measurement validity* to include noncognitive instruments) is the extent to which inferences made on the basis of numerical scores are appropriate, meaningful, and useful. Validity is a judgment of the appropriateness of a measure for specific inferences or decisions that result from the scores generated. In other words, validity is a situation-specific concept: It is assessed depending on the purpose, population, and environmental characteristics in which measurement takes place. A test result can therefore be valid in one situation and invalid in another. Consequently, in order to assure others that the procedures have validity in relation to the research problems, subjects, and setting of the study, it is incumbent on the investigator to describe validity in relation to the context in which data are collected.

This conceptualization of test validity implies much more than simply determining whether a test "measures what it is supposed to measure." The most recent *Standards for Educational and Psychological Testing* (American Educational Research Association, 1999) make it clear that it

Test validity: appropriateness of inferences

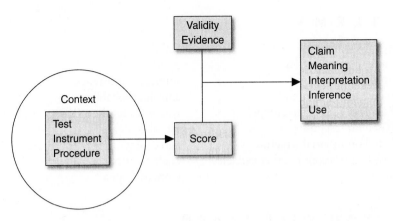

FIGURE 8.1 **Determining Measurement Validity**

is an *inference, use,* or *consequence* that is valid or invalid, not a test. That is, "Validity refers to the degree to which evidence and theory support the interpretations of test scores entailed by specific uses of tests" (*Standards,* 2000, p. 9). This means that the validation process is about professional judgments, which are "relative and ever evolving . . . evaluated in light of new evidence and desired interpretations" (Gorin, 2007, p. 461). Although technically validity is about interpretations made from scores, it is common to find the term *test validity* used when describing this characteristic. Indeed, some of the most recent professional standards use *test validity,* not *inference validity.* Keep this in mind concerning both what we present here and what is reported in research. Also, *test* means any kind of measurement, from content examinations to attitude scales and observations.

To assure validity, then, the researcher needs to identify assumptions or make arguments to justify an inference or use for a specific purpose (e.g., concluding that students in one group have more knowledge or have a stronger self-concept than students in another group) and then collect evidence to support these assumptions (Shepard, 1993; see Figure 8.1). This emphasis is consistent with the idea that validity is a single, unitary concept that requires evidence for the specific use that is cited. It follows, then, that a test by itself is not valid or invalid because the same test can be used for different purposes. For example, a college entrance test may lead to valid inferences about a student's future performance as an undergraduate but to invalid inferences about the quality of his or her high school program.

Two kinds of inferences are typically used in educational research. The first is related to assessing achievement, which depends primarily on how well the content of a test or other assessment represents a larger domain of content or tasks. For this kind of inference, evidence based on the content of the assessment is needed to support inferences that are made. A second kind of inference, one that is even more common in educational research, is about traits or characteristics that are more abstract than clearly defined content. These traits or characteristics are often called *constructs* and include, for example, intelligence, creativity, reading ability, attitudes, reasoning, and self-concept.

When inferences involve these constructs, it is important to have a clear theoretical conceptualization about what is being measured as well as evidence that there are no viable rival hypotheses to challenge the intended interpretation. Two types of rival hypotheses can be considered: *construct underrepresentation* and *construct irrelevant variance.* **Construct underrepresentation** occurs if the assessment fails to capture important aspects of the construct. For example, if a self-concept measure did not include items on social as well as academic areas, it would measure less than the proposed construct of self-concept. **Construct irrelevant variance** refers to the extent to which a measure includes materials or factors that are extraneous to the intended construct. An example of this kind of factor would be measuring mathematical reasoning ability with story problems. Because reading comprehension is needed to understand the problems, this ability is important to success as well as mathematical reasoning. Thus, the measure is influenced to some extent by factors that are not part of the construct. Figure 8.2 illustrates these threats to validity.

Construct underrepresentation: measuring less than what is claimed

Construct irrelevant variance: measuring facets unrelated to the purpose

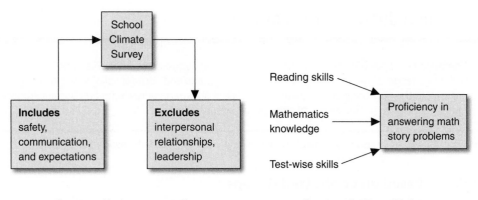

FIGURE 8.2 **Illustration of Construct Underrepresentation and Construct Irrelevant Variance**

Whether the inference involved in research is primarily content or construct, six major types of evidence can be used to both support intended interpretations and eliminate any rival hypotheses about what is being measured: evidence based on content, on contrasted groups, on response processes, on internal structure, on relations to other variables, and on consequences. We will consider the first five, which have the greatest relevance for research. The strongest cases are made when multiple sources of evidence are used.

Evidence Based on Test Content

In general, **evidence based on test content** demonstrates the extent to which the sample of items or questions in the instrument is representative of some appropriate universe or domain of content or tasks. This type of evidence is usually accumulated by having experts examine the content of the instrument and indicate the degree to which it measures predetermined criteria or objectives. Experts are also used to judge the relative criticality, or importance, of various parts of the instrument. For example, to gather evidence for a test of knowledge for prospective teachers, it is necessary to have experts examine the items and judge their representativeness (e.g., Is a question about Piaget representative of what needs to be known about child development?) and whether the percentage of the test devoted to different topics is appropriate (e.g., 20 percent of the test is on classroom management, but maybe it should be 40 percent). Evidence based on test content is essential for achievement tests. Also, the domain or universe that is represented should be appropriate to the intended use of the results.

Evidence based on test content: content matches specifications

Excerpts 8.1 and 8.2 show how "experts" are used to establish evidence based on content. Unfortunately, evidence based on test content for validity is often not reported in research articles, usually because there is no systematic effort to obtain such evidence for locally devised instruments. When standardized instruments are used, it is important to refer to previous research, reviews of the instrument, and technical manuals.

Evidence based on content is similar to *face validity*, but face validity is a less systematic appraisal between the measure and the larger domain. Face validity is a judgment that the items appear to be relevant, whereas validity evidence establishes the relationship systematically.

EXCERPT 8.1 Use of Expert Judges for Validity

The instrument titled "School Survey on Stalking" was modified from a previous stalking instrument. . . . The questions of this survey were developed in consultation with school counseling personnel who had experience working with law enforcement and school issues. A panel of four school counselors then reviewed and critiqued the instrument. (p. 26)

Source: Romans, J. S. C., Hays, J. R., Pearson, C., DuRoy, L. C., & Carlozzi, B. (2006). Stalking and related harassment of secondary school counselors. *Journal of School Violence, 5,* 21–33.

EXCERPT 8.2   Use of Expert Judges for Validity

A panel of five experts, two mathematics faculty and three mathematics education faculty, with knowledge of geometry and its teaching were asked to evaluate the appropriateness and relevance of each item on the instrument. Based upon comments and suggestions from this panel a few minor changes were made and content validity was again evaluated by the panel of experts prior to the first administration of the instrument. (p. 92)

Source: From Utley, J. (2007). Construction and validity of geometry attitude scales. *School Science and Mathematics, 107*(3), 89–94.

Evidence Based on Contrasted Groups

Evidence based on contrasted groups: validity evidence based on scores from groups expected to show differences

A straightforward approach to establishing validity is to see if groups that should be different respond as predicted. Usually, this is done with groups that clearly contrast with one another with respect to what is being measured. For example, a measure of teaching effectiveness should give very high results for individuals who have been recognized for their teaching (e.g., teachers of the year), whereas teachers who are judged by principals to be marginally effective should receive low scores. Excerpt 8.3 provides an example of how **evidence based on contrasted groups** is used.

Evidence Based on Response Processes

Evidence based on response processes: validity evidence that shows consistency between intended and actual response processes

Evidence based on response processes is focused on an analysis of performance strategies or responses to specific tasks and whether these strategies and responses are consistent with what is intended to be measured. For example, if students are to be involved in mathematical reasoning, it would be possible to ask them about their thinking in relation to solving problems to assure that reasoning, not rote application of an alogrithm, is used. Similarly, observers or judges can be asked to indicate criteria used for their judgments to be sure appropriate criteria are being applied.

Evidence Based on Internal Structure

Evidence based on internal structure: validity evidence that shows appropriate corelations among items

The *internal structure* of an instrument refers to how items are related to each other and how different parts of an instrument are related. **Evidence based on internal structure** is provided when the relationships between items and parts of the instrument are empirically consistent with the theory or intended use of the scores. Thus, if a measure of self-concept posits several types of self-concept (e.g., academic, social, athletic), then the items measuring the academic component should be strongly related to each other and not as highly related to the other components. A procedure called *factor analysis* is often used to provide internal structure evidence, as illustrated in Excerpt 8.4.

Evidence Based on Relations to Other Variables

The most common way that validity of interpretations is established is by showing how scores from a given measure relate to similar as well as different traits. There are several ways this can be done.

EXCERPT 8.3   Evidence Based on Contrasted Groups

The validation approach used both contrasted groups and correlational analysis. Contrasted groups are groups for whom there is prior expectation of different values and where we would therefore expect a valid instrument to produce significant inter-group differences. Thus, Israeli Druz students are expected to differ from Israeli Jewish students owing to cultural differences; Special Education students and school counselors are expected to hold more democratic beliefs than student-teachers in a regular programme, owing to differences in educational background and perhaps also to different vocational interests. Finally, effective teachers are expected to hold more democratic beliefs compared with non-effective teachers, given the evidence on the links between democratic beliefs and classroom effectiveness. (p. 367)

Source: From Schechtman, Z. (2002). Validation of the democratic teacher belief scale (DTBS). *Assessment in Education, 9*(3), 363–377.

EXCERPT 8.4 Evidence Based on Internal Structure

Using factor analysis (principal components with varimax rotation), we assessed the degree to which 19 teacher-level questions asked in the NAEP teacher survey . . . tap these four different dimensions of instruction. . . . The 19 items loaded on four factors with eigenvalues greater than 1. . . . These four factors mapped well to the dimensions. (p. 179)

Source: From Smith, T. M., Desimone, L. M., Zeidner, T. L., Dunn, A. C., Bhatt, M., & Rumyantseva (2007). Inquiry-oriented instruction in science: Who teaches that way? *Educational Evaluation and Policy Analysis, 29*(3), 169–199.

When scores from one instrument correlate highly with scores from another measure of the same trait, we have what is called *convergent* evidence. *Discriminant* evidence exists when the scores do not correlate highly with scores from an instrument that measures something different. Thus, we would expect that scores from a measure of self-concept would correlate highly with other measures of self-concept and show less correlation to related but different traits, such as anxiety and self-efficacy. In many research articles, this type of evidence will be referred to as *construct validity*.

An especially interesting kind of convergent and discriminant evidence is the multitrait, multimethod matrix (MTMM). With this technique, specific correlations among similar and different traits will be used as evidence to support validity. This is illustrated in Figure 8.3 with an intercorrelation matrix that shows both convergent and discriminant correlations. What is most important is the pattern of results—convergent correlations should be high compared to divergent ones. This is supported by the correlations in the table. Correlations that are bold are convergent. Others are either reliability, discriminant correlations among different subscales within each measure, or discriminant correlations among different subscales of different measures.

Another approach to gathering **evidence based on relations to other variables** pertains to the extent to which the test scores or measures predict performance on a criterion measure (i.e., test-criterion relationships). Two approaches are used to obtain test-criterion evidence: predictive and concurrent. With *predictive evidence,* the criterion is measured at a time in the future, after the instrument has been administered. The evidence pertains to how well the earlier measure can predict the criterion behavior or performance. For instance, in gathering evidence on a new measure to select applicants for leadership positions, the scores on the instrument would be correlated with future leadership behavior. If persons who scored low on the test turned out to be poor leaders and those who scored high were good leaders, predictive test-criterion evidence would be obtained.

Evidence based on relations to other variables: verification of what is measured

	Superior Measure of Self-Concept			Self-Concept Survey		
	Personal	Social	Academic	Personal	Social	Academic
Superior Measure of Self-Concept						
Personal	(.85)					
Social	.62	.92				
Academic	.50	.60	(.76)			
Self-Concept Survey						
Personal	**.79**	.48	.69	(.79)		
Social	.48	**.81**	.72		(.83)	
Academic	.52	.50	**.86**			(.90)

Reliability diagonal

FIGURE 8.3 **MTMM of Validity Evidence Using Correlations Among Subscale Scores**

EXCERPT 8.5 Predictive Test-Criterion Evidence for Validity

The predictive validity of this instrument is reflected in the findings that three of the four beliefs have predicted different aspects of learning. Belief in quick learning predicted comprehension monitoring, quality of summarizing, and test performance for social science and physical science passages. . . . Belief in certain knowledge predicted interpretation of tentative information. . . . Belief in simple knowledge predicted comprehension and monitoring of comprehension in mathematical passages. . . . Belief in fixed ability predicted students' appreciation of the value of education. (p. 11)

Source: From Schommer-Aikins, M., & Hutter, R. (2002). Epistemological beliefs and thinking about everyday controversial issues. *Journal of Psychology, 736*(1), 5–20.

EXCERPT 8.6 Concurrent Test-Criterion Evidence for Validity

The criterion-related or more specifically the concurrent validity of the UGAS and its three subscales was assessed by correlating them with the FSMAS and three of its subscales. A strong positive correlation ($r = .702$, $p < .001$) was found between the UGAS and the FSMAS. In addition, strong positive correlations were found on the corresponding confidence subscales ($r = .651$, $p < .001$), on the corresponding usefulness subscales ($r = .670$, $p < .001$), and between the enjoyment scale of the UGAS and the effectance motivation scale of the FSMAS ($r = .658$, $p < .001$). (p. 93)

Source: From Utley, J. (2007). Construction and validity of geometry attitude scales. *School Science and Mathematics, 107*(3), 89–94.

Excerpt 8.5 shows how predictive evidence is used to establish validity. With *concurrent evidence*, the instrument and the criterion are given at about the same time. Criterion-related evidence is often reported in research by indicating that a measure correlates with criteria that assess the same thing. An example of concurrent evidence is presented in Excerpt 8.6.

Validity is clearly the single most important aspect of an instrument and the findings that result from the data. The quality of the evidence judged by the users of the findings varies greatly in educational research. If standardized tests are used, there will be sophisticated evidence, whereas locally developed questionnaires may have little systematic evidence. In either case, good researchers always ask Are the inferences appropriate? What evidence supports my conclusion? The components of test validity are summarized in Table 8.1.

TABLE 8.1 Components of Test Validity

Component	Description	Procedure
Evidence based on content	Extent to which the items or factors represent a larger domain	Examine the relationship between content in the items and content in the domain.
Evidence based on contrasted groups	Whether groups that should be different are different in the predicted direction	Examine the differences between the groups.
Evidence based on response processes	Whether thinking and response processes are consistent with the intended interpretation	Examine the respondents' explanations and patterns of responses.
Evidence based on internal structure	Extent to which items measuring the same trait are related	Correlate items measuring the same trait.
Evidence based on relations to other variables	Whether the measure is related to similar or predicted variables and unrelated to different variables	Correlate the measure to other measures of the same trait and to measures of different traits.

Effect of Validity on Research

Because validity implies proper interpretation and use of the information gathered through measurement, it is necessary to judge the degree of validity that is present based on available evidence. In this sense, validity is a matter of degree, not an all-or-nothing proposition. Investigators should show that for the specific inferences and conclusions made in their study, there is evidence that validity exists. Consumers need to make the same decision based on their use of the results. Does this suggest that validity must be established for each research situation and possible use? Such a requirement would add a considerable amount of data collection and analysis to each study and is therefore impractical. In practice, it is necessary to generalize from other studies and research that interpretation and use are valid. That is one reason that already established instruments, for which some evidence on validity has probably accumulated, usually provide more credible measurement. On the other hand, it would be a mistake to assume that just because an instrument is established, its results are valid.

Locally devised instruments, which have no history of use or reviews by others, need to be evaluated with more care. When researchers develop new instruments, it is more important to gather appropriate evidence for validity and then report this evidence in the study.

Whether a locally prepared or established instrument is used, it is best to gather evidence for validity before the data for a study are collected. This is a major reason for a pilot test of the instrument and procedures for administering it.

Validity is important to consider when choosing an instrument. Read the research proposal and study notes provided on MyEducationLab for Research at www.myeducation-lab.com. Click on the topic "Selecting Measuring Instruments" and then select the Activities and Applications activity titled "Selecting an Instrument Given Three Choices." Review the notes and determine how this researcher made the choice, and see if the instrument has been changed since this proposal was made.

TEST RELIABILITY

Test reliability (or, more accurately, *reliability of scores*) refers to the consistency of measurement—the extent to which the results are similar over different forms of the same instrument or occasions of data collection. Another way to conceptualize reliability is that it is the extent to which measures are free from error. If an instrument has little error, then it is reliable, and if it has a great deal of error, then it is unreliable. We can measure error by estimating how consistently a trait is assessed.

Test reliability: consistency of scores

Think for a minute about tests you have taken. Were the scores you received accurate, or was there some degree of error in the results? Were some results more accurate than others? In measuring human traits, whether achievement, attitude, personality, physical skill, or some other trait, you will almost never obtain a result that does not have some degree of error. Many factors contribute to the less than perfect nature of our measures. There may be ambiguous questions, the lighting may be poor, some subjects may be sick, guessing on an achievement test may be lucky or unlucky, observers may get tired, and so on. What this means is that even if a trait remained the same when two tests were given a week apart, the scores would not be exactly the same because of unavoidable error.

According to classical test theory, the *obtained score* may be thought of as having two components: a *true* or *universe score*, which represents the actual knowledge or skill level of the individual, and *error*, sources of variability unrelated to the intent of the instrument:

$$obtained\ score = true\ or\ universe\ score + error$$

Common sources of error are listed in Table 8.2. The objective in selecting or evaluating instruments, then, is to look for evidence that error has been controlled as much as possible.

The actual amount of error variance in test scores, or the reliability, is determined empirically through several types of procedures.[1] Each type of reliability is related to the control of a particular kind of error and is usually reported in the form of a reliability coefficient. The reliability coefficient is a correlation statistic comparing two sets of scores from the same individuals. The scale for a reliability coefficient is from .00 to .99. If the coefficient is high, for example .90, the scores have little error and are highly reliable. The opposite is true for the correlation near .20 or .35. An acceptable range of reliability for coefficients for most instruments is .70 to .90.

TABLE 8.2 Sources of Measurement Error

Conditions of Test Construction and Administration	Conditions Associated with the Person Taking the Test
Changes in time limits	Reactions to specific items
Changes in directions	Health
Different scoring procedures	Motivation
Interrupted testing session	Mood
Race/ethnicity of test administrator	Fatigue
Time the test is taken	Luck
Sampling of items	Fluctuation in memory or attention
Ambiguity in wording	Attitudes
Misunderstood directions	Test-taking skills (test wiseness)
Effects of heat, light, ventilation on the testing situation	Ability to comprehend instructions
Differences in observers	Anxiety

The five general types of reliability estimates are stability, equivalence, equivalence and stability, internal consistency, and agreement. Each is addressed in a following section, and all five are summarized in Table 8.3.[2]

Stability

Stability: consistency of scores over time

A coefficient of **stability** is obtained by correlating scores from the same test on two different occasions of a group of individuals. If the responses of the individuals are consistent (i.e., if those scoring high the first time also score high the second time, and so on), then the correlation coefficient and the reliability are high. This *test-retest* procedure assumes that the characteristic measured remains constant. Unstable traits, such as mood, should not be expected to yield high stability coefficients. Furthermore, stability usually means that there is a long enough time

TABLE 8.3 Types of Evidence for Reliability

Type	Description	Procedure	Common Examples*
Stability (test-retest)	Consistency of stable characteristics over time	Administer the same test to the same individuals over time.	Aptitude tests IQ tests
Equivalence	Comparability of two measures of the same trait given at about the same time	Administer different forms to the same individuals at about the same time.	Achievement tests
Equivalence and stability	Comparability of two measures of the same trait given over time	Administer different forms to the same individuals over time.	Assessments of changes over time Personality assessment
Internal consistency (split-half; KR; Cronbach's alpha)	Comparability of halves of a measure to assess a single trait or dimension	Administer one test and correlate the items to each other.	Most measures except for speeded tests Attitude questionnaires
Agreement	Consistency of ratings or observations	Two or more persons rate or observe.	Observations and interviews

*These examples are not meant to suggest that forms of reliability other than those indicated are inappropriate (e.g., achievement tests also use test-retest reliability).

EXCERPT 8.7 Stability Evidence for Reliability

To evaluate the reliability of the survey, a separate test-retest study involving 113 introductory college chemistry students was conducted. These students completed the survey on two occasions, two weeks apart. The study produced reliability coefficients ranging from 0.46 to 0.69. (p. 49)

Source: From Wyss, V. L., Tai, R. H., & Sadler, P. M. (2007). High school class-size and college performance in science. *High School Journal,* 90(3), 45–54.

between measures (often several months) so that the consistency in scores is not influenced by a memory or practice effect. In general, as the time gap between measures increases, the correlation between the scores becomes lower. Excerpt 8.7 shows how stability estimates are reported.

Equivalence

When two equivalent or parallel forms of the same instrument are administered to a group at about the same time and the scores are related, the reliability that results is a coefficient of **equivalence.** Even though each form is made up of different items, the score attained by an individual would be about the same on each form. Equivalence is one type of reliability that can be established when the researcher has a relatively large number of items from which to construct equivalent forms. Alternative forms of a test are needed in order to test initially absent subjects who may learn about specific items from the first form or when an instructor has two or more sections of the same class meeting at different times.

Equivalence: consistency between two measures

Equivalence and Stability

When a researcher needs to give a pretest and posttest to assess a change in behavior, a reliability coefficient of equivalence and stability should be established. In this procedure, reliability data are obtained by administering to the same group of individuals one form of an instrument at one time and a second form at a later date. If an instrument has this type of reliability, the researcher can be confident that a change of scores across time reflects an actual difference in the trait being measured. This is the most stringent type of reliability, and it is especially useful for studies involving gain-scores or improvement.

Internal Consistency

Internal consistency is the most common type of reliability, because it can be estimated from giving one form of a test once. There are three common types of internal consistency: split-half, Kuder-Richardson, and the Cronbach alpha method. In **split-half reliability**, the items of a test that have been administered to a group are divided into comparable halves and a correlation coefficient is calculated between the halves. If each student has about the same position in relation to the group on each half, then the correlation is high and the instrument has high reliability. Each test half should be of similar difficulty. This method provides lower reliability than other methods, because the total number in the correlation equation contains only half of the items (and we know that other things being equal, longer tests are more reliable than short tests). (The Spearman-Brown formula is used to increase split-half reliabilities to estimate what the correlation would be for a whole test.) Internal consistency techniques should not be used with speeded tests. This is because not all items are answered by all students, a factor that tends to increase spuriously the intercorrelation of the items.

Internal consistency: consistency of items within an instrument

Split-half reliability: half of the items are consistent with the other half

A second method for investigating the extent of internal consistency is to use a **Kuder-Richardson (KR)** formula in order to correlate all items on a single test with each other when each item is scored right or wrong. KR reliability is thus determined from a single administration of an instrument but without having to split the instrument into equivalent halves. This procedure assumes that all items in an instrument are equivalent, and it is appropriate when the purpose of the test is to measure a single trait. If a test has items of varying difficulty or measures more than one trait, the KR estimate would usually be lower than the split-half reliabilities.

Kuder-Richardson (KR) reliability: consistency among right/wrong items

EXCERPT 8.8 Internal Consistency Evidence for Reliability (Cronbach's Alpha)

A three-part pre-tested instrument with 43 items was used to collect the research data. Section A with seven (7) items collected demographic data. This part of the instrument was designed by the researchers. Section B with 16 items consisted of a 6-point Likert-type attitude toward inclusive education scale (1 SD, 2 D, 3 Somewhat disagree, 4 Somewhat Agree, 5 A, 6 SA). This instrument was adopted from Wilczenski (1992). The alpha reliability for this scale was .86. . . . Section C contained the 21-item 4-point Likert-type concerns about inclusive education scale (1 Not at all concerned, 2 A little concerned, 3 Very concerned, 4 Extremely concerned). The scale's alpha reliability was 0.88. (p. 37)

Source: From Bradshaw, L., & Mundia, L. (2006). Attitudes to and concerns about inclusive education: Bruneian inservice and preservice teachers, *International Journal of Special Education, 21*(1), 35–41.

Cronbach's alpha: consistency among items measuring a single construct

Cronbach's alpha (or *coefficient alpha* or just *alpha*) determines agreement of answers on questions targeted to a specific trait. It is used when answers are made on a scale of some kind rather than as right or wrong. The scale could be levels of agreement; height; high, medium, and low socioeconomic status; extensive to little experience; and so on. Because many surveys and questionnaires use these types of items, alpha is the most common type of reliability reported in educational research. Alpha coefficients should be reported for every total and for each subscale score that is used as a variable.

The drawback to using a measure of alpha for internal consistency is that it requires at least three questions (preferably five or more) that measure the trait. These items are then used to calculate the reliability coefficient. For some traits, this means asking essentially the same question repeatedly. This not only lengthens the measure, it also affects subjects' attitudes because they wonder why they have to answer another question that was just like one they answered earlier! If there are many traits involved in the measure, which is what typically occurs when measuring something like self-concept, vocational interests, or school climate, this may result in a measure that is too long. For example, it would not be unusual to have five or six subscales for self-concept (academic, social, physical, etc.). If each of these dimensions has six items to obtain high reliability coefficients, the total length could be 30–36 items, which may be too many to maintain participants' focus.

Excerpts 8.8 and 8.9 illustrate examples of how Cronbach's alpha was used for reliability. Note that each scale and subscale warranted a separate alpha.

Agreement

Agreement: consistency of ratings or observations

The fifth type of reliability is expressed as a coefficient of **agreement**. It is established by determining the extent to which two or more persons agree about what they have seen, heard, or rated. That is, when two or more observers or raters independently observe or rate something, will they agree about what was observed or rated? If they do, then there is some consistency in measurement. This type of reliability is commonly used for observational research and studies involving performance-based assessments in which professional judgments are made about student performance. It will be reported as *inter-rater* reliability, *intercoder agreement*, or *scorer agreement* and will be expressed either as a correlation coefficient or as percentage of agreement.

Coefficient of concordance: reliability based on ranked data

Cohen's kappa: reliability based on categorization

There are two common procedures that result in a reliability coefficient: Kendall's coefficient of concordance and Cohen's kappa. The **coefficient of concordance** ranges from 0 to 1 and is used with ranked data. When raters agree completely on how to rank, the coefficient is 1. **Cohen's kappa**

EXCERPT 8.9 Internal Consistency Evidence for Reliability (Cronbach's Alpha)

Internal consistency coefficient for the scales in the instrument were as follows (Cronbach's alpha): Technology Integration Scale = .95; Exploration subscale = .84; Experimentation subscale = .93; Adoption subscale = .95; Integration subscale = .92; Barriers scale = .85; and Effectiveness scale = .91. (p. 209)

Source: From Kotrlik, J. W., & Redmann, D. H. (2005). Extent of technology integration in instruction by adult basic education teachers. *Adult Education Quarterly, 55*(3), 200–219.

EXCERPT 8.10 Agreement Evidence for Reliability

Videotaped observations were coded by two raters using the CBRS and MBRS. Each had a master's degree in developmental psychology and had completed approximately 30 hours of training until they had attained interrater agreement of 90% on each of the two scales. Reliability was computed based on interrater agreement for 70% of the observations used for the final study. . . . For the CBRS, overall exact agreement was 81%. . . . For the MBRS, overall exact agreement was 81%. (p. 34)

Source: From Kim, J., & Mahoney, G. (2004). The effects of mother's style of interaction on children's engagement: Implications for using responsive interventions with parents. *Topics in Early Childhood Special Education, 24*(1), 31–38.

EXCERPT 8.11 Agreement and Kappa Evidence for Reliability

Interrater agreement for the coding of the transcripts . . . was calculated by dividing the total number of agreements by the total number of agreements plus disagreements and multiplying by 100, as well as by using Cohen's (1960) kappa value. The interrater agreement across the 19 categories was 88% (median = 86%, range = 67%–96%), Cohen's kappa was .86 (median = .84, range = .66–.95). . . . According to Fleiss's (1981) general benchmark, a kappa value between .40 and .75 can be interpreted as intermediate to good, and a value above .75 can be considered excellent. (pp. 128–129)

Source: From Veenman, S., Denessen, E., van den Akker, A., & vander Rijt, J. (2005). Effects of a cooperative learning program on the elaborations of students during help seeking and help giving. *American Educational Research Journal, 42*(1), 115–151.

is used with raters when the data are nominal or categorical. This is used when raters classify items or performance into two or more discrete categories, such as grading an essay or performance assessment.

An important limitation of coefficients of agreement is that they do not indicate anything about consistency of the performance, behavior, or rating across time. (Ironically, internal consistency estimates don't either.) This means that it is one thing to obtain high inter-rater agreement, which is relatively easy to do, and quite another to obtain data that show that the behavior or trait is consistent over time. In Excerpt 8.10, observer agreement is used to provide reliability evidence. In Excerpt 8.11, the researchers used both percentage agreement and kappa for reliability.

The five types of reliability estimates are summarized in Table 8.4 according to when different forms of an instrument are given.

Interpretation of Reliability Coefficients

Several factors should be considered in interpreting reliability coefficients:

1. The more heterogeneous a group is on the trait that is measured, the higher the reliability.
2. The more items there are in an instrument, the higher the reliability.

TABLE 8.4 Procedures for Estimating Reliability[*]

	Time 1		Time 2
Stability	A		A
Equivalence	A	B	
Stability and Equivalence	A		B
Internal Consistency	A		
Agreement	R1	R2	

[*]A and B refer to different forms of the same test; R1 and R2 refer to rater 1 and rater 2, though more than two raters or observers can be used with agreement.

Source: Adapted from James McMillan, *Educational Research: Fundamentals for the Consumer*, 5th ed. Published by Allyn and Bacon, Boston, MA. Copyright © 2008 by Pearson Education.

3. The greater the range of scores, the higher the reliability.
4. Achievement tests with a medium difficulty level will have higher reliability than either very hard or very easy tests.
5. Reliability, like validity, when based on a norming group, is demonstrated only for subjects whose characteristics are similar to those of the norming group.
6. The more that items discriminate between high and low achievers, the greater the reliability.
7. Other things being equal, reliability is positively related to the number of participants.

Practice evaluating measures used in quantitative studies. Go to MyEducationLab for Research at www.myeducation-lab.com and complete the Building Research Skills exercise "Evaluating the Measuring Instruments Used in a Quantitative Study." Click on the topic "Selecting Measuring Instruments" and select the Building Research Skills exercise titled "Evaluating the Measuring Instruments Used in a Quantitative Study."

Researchers often ask how high a correlation should be for it to indicate satisfactory reliability. This question is not answered easily. It depends on the type of instrument (personality questionnaires generally have lower reliability than achievement tests), the purpose of the study (whether it is exploratory research or research that leads to important decisions), and whether groups or individuals are affected by the results (because action affecting individuals requires a higher correlation than action affecting groups). However, a good rule of thumb is to be wary of reliabilities below .70.

Effect of Reliability on Research

Like validity, the reliability of scores should be established before the research is undertaken and the type of reliability should be consistent with the use of the results. If you will use the results for prediction or selection into special programs, stability estimates of reliability are necessary. If you are interested in programs to change attitudes or values, equivalency estimates are needed. Reliability should also be established with individuals who are similar to the subjects in the research. For example, previous studies report good reliability with middle school students and you intend to use the results with elementary school students, the previously gathered reliability data may not be adequate. More commonly and appropriately, reliability is reported with the subjects used in the study. Failure to report reliability would be cause to interpret the results with caution, although there are some simple measures for which reliability coefficients are not needed (see below).

The most direct effect of low reliability is that it contributes to error when calculating inferential statistics to answer the research questions. Suppose you were studying different types of training college residence hall resident assistants (RAs). One group gets a four-day intensive workshop and one group a half-day seminar. Observations are conducted by the head resident of the residence hall to see if the RAs receiving more training have better interpersonal relationships with their students. The quality of interpersonal relationships is measured by observation. It would be difficult to establish strong observation reliability for this study, resulting in greater error, which would need to be overcome by very large differences between the RAs' interpersonal relationships with students.

You will read some research in which reliability is not addressed, yet the results of the research show statistical significance. This is an interesting situation in research because it is more difficult to find differences between groups with instruments that have resulted in scores that have low reliability. It is as if the differences were observed despite what may have been low reliability. Of course, it is possible that the measurement was reliable, even though no reliability estimates were reported. This situation is likely to occur in research in which the subjects are responding to questions so straightforward and simple that reliability is assumed. For example, in studies of students' perceptions of success or failure following performance on a test, the subjects may be asked to indicate on a scale from 1 to 10 (1 being a high degree of failure and 10 being a high degree of success) their feelings of success or failure. In much research, the subjects report information such as age, sex, income, time spent studying, occupation, and other questions that are relatively simple. For these types of data, statistical estimates of reliability are generally not needed.

Reliability is a function of the nature of the trait being measured. Some variables, such as most measures of achievement, provide highly reliable scores, whereas scores from personality measures have lower reliabilities. Consequently, a reliability of .80 or above is generally expected for achievement variables, whereas estimates of .70 may be acceptable for measuring personality traits. By comparison, then, a personality instrument reporting a reliability coefficient of .90 would be judged to have excellent reliability, and an achievement test with a reliability of .65 may be seen as weak. We need a much stronger reliability if the results will be used to make decisions about individuals. Studies of groups can tolerate a lower reliability. Measures of young children are usually less reliable than those of older subjects.

Keep in mind the following six points to enhance reliability. (1) It is best to establish standard conditions of data collection. All subjects should be given the same directions, have the same time frame in which to answer questions at the same time during the day, and so on. (2) Error is often increased if different persons administer the instruments. (3) It is important to know whether there were any unusual circumstances during data collection, because they may affect reliability. (4) The instrument needs to be appropriate in reading level and language to be reliable, and subjects must be properly motivated to answer the questions. (5) In some research, it is difficult to get subjects to be serious—for instance, when students are asked to take achievement tests that have no implications for them. (6) Reliability can also suffer when subjects are asked to complete several instruments over a long time. Usually, an hour is about all any of us can tolerate, and for younger children, less than a half hour is the maximum. If several instruments are given at the same time, the order of their administration should not be the same for all subjects. Some subjects should answer one instrument first, and other subjects should answer the same instrument last. This is called *counterbalancing* the instruments.

Finally, reliability is a necessary condition for validity. That is, scores cannot be valid unless they are reliable. However, a reliable measure is not necessarily valid. For example, we can obtain a very reliable measure of the length of your big toe, but that would not be valid as an estimate of your intelligence!

CHAPTER SUMMARY

This chapter has introduced essential principles to ensure that quantitative data collected as part of an empirical investigation are sound. These principles are based on technical aspects related to validity and reliability. Providing evidence for both validity and reliability is the responsibility of the researcher. Previously collected data can be helpful but may also be inadequate. Important points in this chapter include the following:

1. Validity is a characteristic based on the reasonableness of inferences drawn from a set of scores. Evidence is gathered to support an argument that the inferences are reasonable. Inferences are valid or invalid; tests or other instruments are not.
2. Instruments should not under- or over-represent what is claimed to be measured.
3. Several types of evidence are used in determining validity. The nature of the evidence should match the inferences.
4. Content-related evidence for validity is obtained by expert review.
5. Groups differing on the trait should attain different scores.
6. The response processes used by participants and internal structure analyses can be used to establish evidence for validity.

7. Correlations between the trait measured and other traits, both similar and different, can be used as evidence for validity, including the use of the MTMM.
8. Reliability is a way to indicate the extent to which error must be considered in interpreting scores. Scores are reliable; instruments are not.
9. There are many sources of error, including what is internal to individual subjects and what occurs in the context in which a measure is administered.
10. Consistency is the essential element of reliability. It can be determined by using several sources of evidence.
11. Stability and internal consistency are the most common types of reliability emphasis, though internal consistency can result in too many items. Different internal consistency coefficients may be used (primarily Kuder-Richardson[KR], and Cronbach's alpha).
12. The coefficient of concordance and Cohen's kappa are used along with percentage agreement to establish reliability for raters and observers.
13. The absence of reliability data may compromise the interpretation of a lack of significance.
14. Reliability is needed for validity; scores can be reliable but not valid.

APPLICATION PROBLEMS

1. For each of the following descriptions, identify the type of evidence presented for validity:
   a. Mr. Jones contends that his measure of athletic prowess is consistent with student self-reports.
   b. In this study, the investigator took deliberate steps to make sure that the test contained the right concepts. She asked several colleagues to review the items to see if, in their opinion, the right concepts were included.
   c. In a study of college student values, a researcher decided to correlate the measure of values with observations of values by residence hall assistants. The self-report results matched the observations.
   d. Dr. Lewis, a professor of education, is working on an instrument that can be used to predict which of his students will be effective teachers. He has several scores from classwork and observations in the classroom, and he considers how these correlate with principal evaluations that are done the year after students graduate.
2. For each of these descriptions, identify the type of evidence for reliability.
   a. Mr. Fox is the principal of Herring Middle School. He is working on a measure of teacher job satisfaction and has developed a number of items for different traits. He hopes that about six items per trait will be sufficient.
   b. A college counselor is interested in knowing whether small-group counseling with students having difficul-

   ties have made a difference. She has developed a measure of self-confidence and anxiety for her study and has given this measure to a control group of students four times during the semester.
   c. Kevin Sutherland is a professor of special education. He does single-subject research and needs to use several different graduate students to collect data. He gathers pilot data to see if the students agree on what they observe.
3. Search the literature in your field and identify a study that has a section on the reliability and validity of an instrument. Identify the types of evidence that are presented and evaluate whether the evidence is sufficient for the types of inferences that are made based on the results. What additional evidence could have been gathered?
4. Construct a short self-report instrument to measure attitudes of your classmates toward statistics. Summarize what kind of evidence for reliability and validity is needed for the inferences you propose and suggest a plan for collecting this evidence.
5. Suppose you were working with new teachers who want to do some action research in their classrooms. What would you tell them about the technical aspects of the measures they intend to use? How would you communicate principles of reliability and validity without being too technical?

NOTES

1. Most of the procedures are based on the assumption that there will be a sufficient dispersion or spread in the scores to calculate correlation coefficients. Some types of tests (e.g., criterion-referenced) do not provide much score variability, and traditional correlational indicators of reliability may be inappropriate. For such tests, researchers examine percentages of test takers who are classified in the same way after taking the test twice or after taking different forms of the same test, or the percentage of answers that are the same at different times, rather than the correlation coefficient. The presentation of reliability in this chapter will focus on traditional correlational procedures, since these are the ones most frequently used in the literature.

2. According to the *Standards for Educational and Psychological Testing* (2000) these traditional indices of reliability are special cases of a more general classification called *generalizability theory*. Generalizability theory has the ability to combine several sources of error into a single measure of variability. Although it is not reported frequently in the literature, it does provide a more accurate indication of the degree of error.

ANSWERS TO APPLICATION PROBLEMS

1. a. evidence based on relations with other variables (concurrent)
   b. evidence based on test content
   c. evidence based on relations with other variables (concurrent)
   d. evidence based on relations with other variables (predictive)

2. a. internal consistency
   b. stability
   c. interobserver agreement
3. (individual student response)
4. (individual student response)
5. (individual student response)

Collecting Quantitative Data

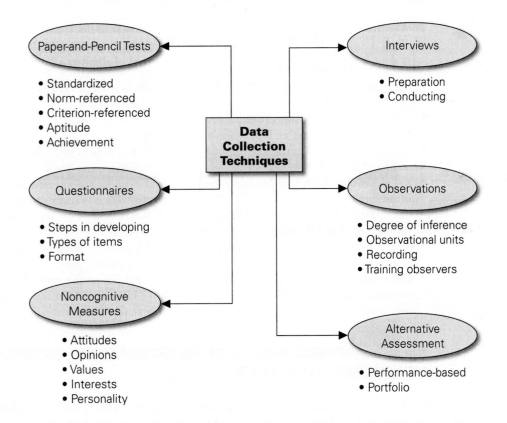

KEY TERMS

standardized tests
norm-referenced
criterion-referenced
standards-based
aptitude test
achievement test
alternative assessments
performance-based assessment
portfolio
response set
social desirability
questionnaire
double-barreled questions
loaded questions
leading questions
closed form
open form
scale

Likert scale
semantic differential
rank-order
contingency questions
structured questions
semistructured questions
unstructured questions
probing
complete observer
high inference
low inference
duration recording
frequency-count recording
interval recording
continuous observation
time sampling
nonreactive
unobtrusive measures

WHAT YOU WILL LEARN

Study this chapter and you will:

- Know how the nature of standardized tests affects research.
- Know different approaches to the interpretation of test scores.
- Explain differences between achievement and aptitude tests.
- Know how standards-based tests are used in research.
- Understand the advantages and disadvantages of using alternative assessments such as portfolio and performance-based assessments.
- Understand the differences between cognitive and noncognitive measurement.

- Be able to identify steps in designing a questionnaire.
- Know how to construct questionnaire items.
- Know how to write different kinds of questionnaire items.
- Know how to format a questionnaire.
- Know how to conduct an interview.
- Know how to use an observational schedule.
- Understand the impact of observer bias on gathered data.
- Understand the strengths and weaknesses of different types of noncognitive measurement.

MEASURING STUDENT PROFICIENCY

Much educational research is concerned with measuring student proficiency, whether achievement or aptitude. This assessment is usually done with tests, although other approaches, such as portfolios and performance assessments, can also be used. With the standards-based movement, there is now a heavy emphasis on traditional types of testing, especially multiple-choice formats, for accountability. The data from these assessments are rich resources for doing research. In this section of the chapter we'll consider different types of tests and alternative assessments that are used to assess student learning. Then we'll turn to assessments used for noncognitive traits.

The term *paper-and-pencil test* means that a standard set of questions is presented to each subject in writing (on paper or computer) that requires completion of cognitive tasks. The responses or answers are summarized to obtain a numerical value that represents a characteristic of the subject. The cognitive task can focus on what the person knows (achievement), is able to learn (ability or aptitude), chooses or selects (interests, attitudes, or values), or is able to do (skills). Different types of tests and their uses in research are summarized briefly in this chapter, but it is important to stress that all tests measure current performance. Tests differ more in their use than in their development or actual test items, particularly when comparing achievement and aptitude tests. In fact, it would be more accurate to say that there are different types of inferences and uses. It is what we do with the test results that creates distinctions such as achievement and aptitude.

Standardized Tests

Standardized tests provide uniform procedures for administration and scoring. The same or parallel questions are asked each time the test is used, with a set of directions that specifies how the test should be administered. This would include information about the qualifications of the person administering the test and the conditions of administration, such as time allowed, materials that can be used by subjects, and whether questions about the test can be answered during testing. The scoring of responses is usually objective, and most but not all standardized tests have been given to a norming group. The *norm group*, as it is called, allows comparison of a score with the scores of a defined group of individuals.

Most standardized tests are prepared commercially by measurement experts. This generally means that careful attention has been paid to the nature of the norms, reliability, and validity. This results in instruments that are "objective" and relatively uninfluenced or distorted by the person who administers them. Because most standardized tests are prepared commercially, they are intended to be used in a wide variety of settings. Consequently, whatever is tested is typically defined in broad and general terms. This may mean that for some research purposes, a standardized test may not be specific enough to provide a sensitive measure of the variable. For instance, if you were conducting a study to investigate the effect of general education at a university on students' knowledge in social science or humanities, a standardized test that you might use would be intended as a measure of social science and humanities knowledge at nearly *all* universities. This means that what is taught at one particular university may not be well represented on the test. This illustrates a trade-off in using standardized tests in research. On the one hand, you have a carefully constructed instrument, with established validity, reliability, directions, and scoring procedures. On the other hand, the test may not focus directly on the variable of interest in the study, may have inappropriate norms, or may cost too much. The alternative is to develop your own instrument; it will measure the variables more directly, but it may have questionable technical qualities.

An advantage to using a large-scale, standardized test or another instrument is that the researcher can say that "the reliability of the test is adequate," as demonstrated in previous studies. There is also something attractive about being able to say that the instrument was developed by a prestigious company, university, organization, or individual. But there are important trade-offs with using standardized tests in comparison with what the researcher can develop locally (e.g., an adaptation of an existing instrument or something developed by a researcher for a specific study). In the former case, the instrument is off the shelf; in the latter case, it is specific to the researcher's context and may be much more sensitive. Table 9.1 shows several characteristics that need to be considered when thinking about using a standardized or locally developed test or, for that matter, other kinds of instruments.

Norm- and Criterion (Standards)-Referenced Interpretation

A major distinction between tests is whether they are norm—or criterion—referenced. The purpose of a **norm-referenced** interpretation is to show how individual scores compare with scores of a well-defined reference or norm group of individuals. The interpretation of results, then, depends entirely on how the subjects compare with others, with less emphasis on the absolute amount of knowledge or skill. That is, what matters most is the comparison group and the ability of the test or instrument to distinguish between individuals. The goal is to determine, for example, whether the subjects know more or less than the norm group. Norm-referenced test scores are often reported to indicate specifically where the subject stands in relation to others (e.g., the 67th percentile or upper quartile).

Standardized tests: structured administration and scoring

Norm-referenced: interpretation based on the reference group

TABLE 9.1 Characteristics of Standardized and Locally Developed Tests That Researchers Should Consider[1]

	Large-Scale Standardized Tests	Locally Developed Tests
Relevance and sensitivity	Low	High
Technical quality (e.g., reliability, lack of test bias)	High	Low
Quality of test items	High	Low
Procedures to administer and score	Specific, set instructions	Flexible instructions
Score interpretation	May depend on national norms; complex scores	Limited to local context; simple scores
Content tested	General	Specific to local context
Ability to provide variability	High	Low

[1]This table shows general trends and considerations. It is quite possible for large-scale tests to be sensitive and for locally developed tests to have high technical quality.

Source: From McMillan, James H., *Educational Research: Fundamentals for the Consumer, 5e.* Published by Allyn and Bacon/Merrill Education, Boston, MA. Copyright © 2008 by Pearson Education. Reprinted by permission of the publisher.

Researchers need to keep two characteristics of norm-referenced interpretations in mind. First, because the purpose of the test is to differentiate between individuals, the best distribution of scores is one that shows high variance. To achieve high variability of scores, the items must discriminate between individuals. To accomplish this, the test items, particularly in standardized norm-referenced tests, are fairly difficult. It is not uncommon for students at the 50th or 60th percentile to answer slightly more than half of the items correctly. Easy items, ones that almost everyone answers correctly, are used sparingly. (Obviously, if all the items are easy, everyone gets a high score, and there is no differentiation between individuals.) Thus, important content or skills may not be measured, which will affect the meaning you give to the results. On the positive side, the large variability helps in establishing relationships.

Second, researchers should attend carefully to the characteristics of the norm or reference group. Perhaps you have had the same experience as we have, being enrolled in a class of bright, hardworking students with an instructor who graded by the curve. You could learn a lot but still get low marks! The interpretation of norm-referenced scores makes sense only when we understand what we are being compared against. Many standardized norm-referenced tests indicate that national norms are used. Despite the fact that the term *national* is subject to different interpretations, if you are studying gifted students and compare their scores with the national norm, the chances are good that your students will all score very high and show little variability. This gives you what is called a *ceiling effect* and a restricted range, which in turn may lead to nonsignificant results.

Criterion-referenced:
interpretation based on set criteria

Standards-based:
interpretation based on set standards

In a **criterion-referenced** or **standards-based** interpretation an individual's score is interpreted by comparing it with a professionally judged standard of performance. The comparison is between the score and a criterion or standard rather than the scores of others. The result is usually expressed as the percentage of items answered correctly or, for example, as pass-fail in the case of minimum competency testing. There is a focus on what the subjects are able to do, with a comparison of that performance with standards of proficiency.

Some criterion-referenced tests result in a highly skewed distribution, which lessens variability. If reliability is estimated with traditional indices, such as internal consistency, high coefficients are achieved with what approximates a normal distribution. Many state standards-based tests use these traditional indices, which are high with a normal distribution of scores, much like norm-referenced tests. It is actually better, with standards-based tests, to estimate the amount of error in making decisions about the category determined for each student (e.g., fail, proficient, advanced). The amount of error, then, is expressed as the percentage of students who are misclassified. When setting and using standards, there are always false positives (students rated proficient when in fact they failed) and false negatives (students who failed who were actually proficient). You want a test that minimizes these errors, though with a normal distribution the cut score is usually set so that misclassifications are higher than what would occur with a bimodal distribution. The percentage of students misclassified depends on where the cut score is placed in the overall distribution and the difference between the contrasted groups. As the difference between the means of the proficient and nonproficient groups increases, the percentage of misclassifications decreases. Despite this limitation, criterion-referenced tests are good to use for diagnosis and for categorizing subjects into groups as basic, proficient, and advanced. A related type of test, *domain-referenced*, is used to show how much of a specifically defined larger domain of knowledge is represented by the test. For example, if the domain is knowledge of addition with three-digit numbers, the test will sample this domain, and the researcher will make a professional judgment using the percentage of correctly answered items to judge the mastery of the domain.

The recent emphasis on high-stakes testing with state accountability systems and passage of the 2001 No Child Left Behind (NCLB) Act have resulted in the extensive use of standards-based tests for educational research. It should be noted that these tests are rarely diagnostic. They typically cover a lot of material and provide a single total score and some subscale scores. Moreover, the tests are usually specific to each state, so state-to-state comparisons are not possible. This is true even for NCLB data, because each state sets a beginning level of achievement as well as the difficulty of the test. So, although each state indicates what percentage of students is proficient, the meaning of *proficient* is not standardized across the states.

Often, high-stakes tests are used to document trends over time. This requires the tests used from year to year to be *equated* or *linked* so that comparisons across years are meaningful. When new standards are adopted, new test results should not be compared to previous results.

Aptitude Tests

The purpose of an **aptitude test** is to predict future performance. The results are used to make a prediction about performance on some criterion (e.g., grades, teaching effectiveness, certification, or test scores) prior to instruction, placement, or training. The term *aptitude* refers to the predictive use of the scores from a test rather than the nature of the test items. Some terms, such as *intelligence* and *ability*, are used interchangeably with *aptitude*, but aptitude tests tend to focus on specific characteristics.

Aptitude test: predicts future performance

Intelligence tests are used to provide a very general measure, usually reporting a global test score. Because they are general, intelligence tests are useful in predicting a wide variety of tasks. Intelligence is measured by an individual or group test. For most research, group tests of intelligence are adequate and cost much less than individual tests. Most group tests are designed so that researchers need training to administer and score them. Usually, these tests produce three scores: a verbal language score, a nonverbal or performance score, and a combined score. The scores are often used to adjust for ability differences in intact groups of subjects. Some of the common individual and group aptitude tests are listed in Table 9.2.

Many measures assess multiple aptitudes or specific kinds of aptitudes. Multifactor aptitude tests are used to provide separate scores for each skill or area assessed. Some would argue that this makes more sense than using a single score because relative strengths and weaknesses can be identified. Multifactor aptitude tests have become increasingly popular in vocational and educational counseling. However, the usefulness of factor scores in research is more problematic. Because just a few items may measure one factor, the reliability of the scores may be questionable. Total single scores, although more general, are often more stable and reliable. Special aptitude tests are good for research, because the focus is on an accurate indication of ability in one area. Table 9.2 contains examples of both multiple-aptitude and special-aptitude tests.

Achievement Tests

It is not always evident how achievement tests differ from aptitude tests. Often very similar items are used for both types of tests. In general, however, **achievement tests** have a more restricted

Achievement test: measures what has been learned

TABLE 9.2 Examples of Standardized Tests

Aptitude	Achievement
Group Intelligence or Ability	**Diagnostic**
Cognitive Abilities Test	Stanford Diagnostic Mathematics Test
Otis-Lennon School Ability Test	Woodcock Reading Mastery Test
SAT Reasoning Test	KeyMath Diagnostic Arithmetic Tests
Individual Intelligence	California Diagnostic Reading Test
Stanford-Binet 5	
Wechsler Scales	**Criterion-referenced**
Kaufman Assessment Battery for Children	Objectives-Referenced Bank of Items and Tests
McCarthy Scales of Children's Abilities	Skills Monitoring System
Multifactor	Integrated Writing Skills Test
Differential Aptitude Test	
General Aptitude Test Battery	**Specific Subjects**
Armed Services Vocational Aptitude Battery	Metropolitan Readiness Tests
	Gates-MacGinitie Reading Tests
Special	
Minnesota Clerical Test	**Batteries**
Law School Admissions Test	*Terra Nova* Achievement Test
Medical College Admission Test	California Basic Educational Skills Test
Bennett Mechanical Comprehension Test	Metropolitan Achievement Tests
Torrance Tests of Creative Thinking	Iowa Test of Basic Skills
Watson-Glaser Critical Thinking Appraisal	Stanford Achievement Test Series

coverage, are more closely tied to school subjects, and measure more recent learning than aptitude tests. Also, of course, the purpose of achievement tests is to measure what has been learned rather than to predict future performance.

There are many standardized achievement tests. Some are diagnostic, isolating specific areas of strength and weakness; some are concerned with measuring achievement in a single content area, whereas others (survey batteries) test different content areas; some are norm-referenced and others are criterion-referenced; some emphasize principles and skills rather than knowledge of specific facts. The choice of achievement test depends on the purpose of the research. If the research is concerned with achievement in a specific school subject, then it would be best to use a test that measures only that subject rather than using a survey battery. If comparisons between several schools will be made, it is best to use norm-referenced tests.

It is very important to assess evidence based on test content validity with a standardized achievement test before using it in research. This is because the curriculum in some schools may be different from the content of standardized tests that are designed for use in most schools. The best way to assess evidence for content validity is to examine the items of the test and make professional judgments of the match between what the item tests and the curriculum. Finally, those choosing a test should consider the difficulty level of the test and the abilities of the students. The desired goal is to have a fairly normal distribution of test scores. If results are skewed by a test that is too easy for bright students or too difficult for less able students, it will be difficult to relate the scores to other variables (e.g., measuring gain in achievement over a year or more with gifted students). Table 9.2 lists some popular standardized achievement tests.

Objective standards-based achievement tests are used extensively for accountability and screening of students for the purpose of remediation, advancement in grade, and graduation.

Many schools use *benchmark* tests every nine weeks or so to gauge student progress. For research, this means that these scores will often be used as dependent variables. It is important to remember that these tests *sample* student knowledge, understanding, and skills; that there is error that needs to be considered; and that a 40- or 50-item test designed to test nine weeks of content will provide general scores. It is best to use group rather than individual scores if possible. Examine the nature of the distribution of results. If it is more or less normal, error in classification needs to be considered.

It is also possible to measure student knowledge and understanding by using constructed-response tests, in which students supply an answer rather than select one, as in multiple-choice or matching items. Constructed-response items include essay and short-answer items and those in which students are assessed on their writing. Although the scoring of some of these responses is fairly objective, other items require subjective ratings. In using constructed-response items for research, it is important to know how the raters were selected and trained and whether procedures were in place to verify continued accuracy in scoring.

Alternative Assessments

In contrast to traditional paper-and-pencil testing formats, **alternative assessments** are designed to provide different ways of demonstrating student performance and achievement, often in more authentic contexts and relying on having students construct responses. Although there are many kinds of alternative assessments, including demonstrations and exhibitions, we will consider the two most often encountered in research: performance-based and portfolio.

Alternative assessment: nontraditional testing

Performance-Based Assessments

With **performance-based assessment**, the emphasis is on measuring student proficiency on cognitive skills by directly observing how a student performs the skill, often in an authentic context. Contexts are *authentic* to the extent that they reflect what students will actually do with what they are learning. For example, asking students to complete an oral history project based on a synthesis of interviews and written sources, write letters of inquiry about a job, complete a music recital, or prepare a portfolio of artwork could be considered performance-based assessments.

Performance-based assessment: observation of skill, behavior, or competency

Performance-based assessments have the advantage of providing a direct, holistic measure of thinking skills that are indirectly assessed in written tests. These assessments also provide a better measure of skill performance in contexts more like those students will encounter outside of school. Performance-based assessments are typically criterion referenced, without the sometimes unrealistic, arbitrary time constraints of written tests. Also, performance-based assessments are closely tied to instruction. This means that research on the relationships of instructional practices to dependent variables measured by performance-based assessments will be very sensitive, unlike more general standardized tests. However, the major drawback of performance-based assessments is the dependence on subjective ratings or observations of teachers, which often results in low reliability. This is most likely a problem when there is reliance on a single rating or observation. In addition, performance-based assessments are time-consuming to develop, administer to students, and score. Typically, teachers evaluate students singly or in small groups. Thus, from a research perspective, although these assessments can be very helpful in providing a direct measure of skills, careful planning is necessary to be certain that sufficient resources are allocated to provide reliable results.

Portfolio Assessment

A **portfolio** is a purposeful, systematic collection and evaluation of student work that documents progress toward meeting learning objectives. Portfolios have been used for years in fields such as architecture, art, and journalism as the primary method of evaluating learning and accomplishment. In education, portfolios are being used with increasing frequency, especially with the assessment of reading and writing skills.

Portfolio: systematic collection of work

Although portfolios have the advantage of providing many examples of student work over time, which can be used to evaluate growth or change, from a psychometric perspective, their reliability is often weak. The scoring of portfolios is done subjectively according to scoring guidelines or rubrics, and it is difficult to obtain high inter-rater reliability. This may result from scoring criteria that are too general and inadequate training of raters, even in national and statewide programs. If classroom teachers are scoring locally developed portfolios, even more scoring error can be expected.

Finally, evidence for validity needs to be carefully considered, because there is usually a desire to generalize from the examples to broader learning traits and objectives. For example, if judgments are being made about the ability of the student to communicate by writing and the only types of writing in the portfolio are creative and expository, then the validity of the inference to writing more generally is weak (i.e., construct underrepresentation).

PERSONALITY, ATTITUDE, VALUE, AND INTEREST INVENTORIES

Aptitude and achievement tests, projects, or presentations are called *cognitive* when what is assessed is focused primarily on what subjects know, understand, and can do. These assessments are often contrasted to noncognitive ones. Affective or *noncognitive* measures focus on emotions and feelings (even though all human responses have some degree of thinking or perceiving). Noncognitive traits include attitudes, values, interests, opinions, and other dispositions that relate to the extent to which individuals are attracted to, like, or prefer a task, idea, person (including themselves), product, or activity.

Although educators and psychologists have studied noncognitive factors for decades, the measurement of these traits is often more difficult than that of cognitive traits or skills. There are a number of reasons for this difficulty.

Response set: tendency to answer most questions the same way

First, noncognitive test results may be adversely affected by **response set**, which is the tendency of a subject's answer to be influenced by a general set when responding to items. There are several types of response sets, including responding with all positive or negative answers regardless of the content of the items, guessing, and sacrificing speed for accuracy. Response set is particularly prevalent with ambiguous items or items that use a continuum such as agree-disagree or favorable-unfavorable. Second, noncognitive items are susceptible to faking. Although there are some techniques that help reduce faking, such as using forced-choice questions, disguising the purpose of the test, and establishing good rapport with subjects, faking is always conceivable. One of the most serious types of faking is **social desirability**, in which subjects answer items in order to appear most normal or most socially desirable rather than responding honestly. Third, the reliability of noncognitive tests is generally lower than that of cognitive tests. Fourth, in most noncognitive tests, we are interested in evidence of construct validity, which is difficult to establish. Finally, noncognitive tests do not have "right" answers like cognitive tests. The results are usually interpreted by comparison with those of other individuals, so the nature of the comparison group is particularly important. Despite these limitations, noncognitive tests are used in research because they are an integral part of the learning process.

Social desirability: responding in order to look normal or good

Personality tests include a wide range of checklists, projective tests, and general adjustment inventories. Most are self-report instruments containing a structured question-response format, and they require specialized training for interpretation. Because of the psychometric weaknesses in many personality tests, the results should be used for groups of subjects rather than for individuals.

Attitude and interest inventories are used extensively in educational research. Most are self-report instruments and are subject to faking and response set. Interest inventories measure feelings and beliefs about activities in which an individual can engage. Attitude inventories measure feelings and beliefs about something other than an activity, such as an object, group, or place. Both are concerned with likes and dislikes, preferences, and predispositions.

A complete discussion of these types of inventories is beyond the scope of this chapter, although we will discuss questionnaires as one way to assess attitudes. Table 9.3 lists examples of personality, attitude, interest, and value inventories.

TABLE 9.3 Examples of Standardized Noncognitive Instruments

Personality	Attitudes	Values	Interests
Weinberger Adjustment Inventory	Survey of Study Habits and Attitudes	Study of Values	Strong-Campbell Interest Inventory
Minnesota Multiphasic Personality Inventory	Survey of School Attitudes	Rokeach Value Survey	Minnesota Vocational Interest Inventory
California Psychological Inventory	Minnesota School Affect Assessment	Gordon's Survey of Interpersonal Values	Kuder Career Search Inventory
Personality Inventory for Children	Children's Scale of Social Attitudes	Work Values Inventory	Vocational Preference Inventory
Omnibus Personality Inventory	Learning Environment Inventory		
Rorschach Inkblot Test	Student Attitude Inventory		
Thematic Apperception Test	Revised Math Attitude Scale		
Tennessee Self-Concept Scale			
Piers-Harris Children's Self-Concept Scale			
Coopersmith Self-Esteem Inventory			

QUESTIONNAIRES

For many good reasons, the questionnaire is the most widely used technique for obtaining information from subjects. A **questionnaire** is relatively economical, has the same questions for all subjects, and can ensure anonymity. Questionnaires can use statements or questions, but in all cases, the subject is responding to something written for specific purposes. In this section of the chapter, information about questionnaires is presented by following the sequence of steps researchers use in developing them. The steps are summarized in Figure 9.1.

Questionnaire: written set of questions

Justification

Before deciding to use a questionnaire, it is best to ask if there are other, more reliable and valid techniques that could be used. Answering this question requires knowing the strengths and weaknesses of each technique (which is addressed later in the chapter). Researchers should carefully consider whether they should develop new questionnaires. In many cases, existing instruments can be used or adapted for use instead of preparing a new one. If the researcher can locate an existing questionnaire, time and money will be saved and an instrument with established reliability and validity can be used.

Justification is strengthened to the extent that theory and previous research support use of the instrument. This requires a review of the literature in which the instrument or something similar to it has been used. The review is critical. It not only provides a conceptual framework, it shows limitations in using the instrument or approach. The review may result in the inclusion of specific items and examples of how questions should be asked.

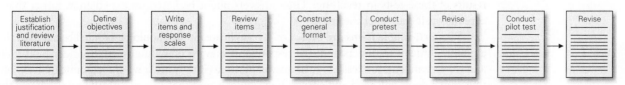

FIGURE 9.1 Steps in Developing a Questionnaire

Defining Objectives

The second step in using a questionnaire is to define and list the specific objectives that the information will achieve. The objectives are based on the research problems or questions, and they show how each piece of information will be used. They need not be strict behavioral objectives, but they must be specific enough to indicate how the responses from each item will meet the objectives. By defining objectives, the researcher is specifying the information that is needed. Unfortunately, many researchers include questions that have not been thought through properly, and the results are never used. Time and energy are wasted, and interested audiences are disenchanted.

Writing Questions, Statements, and Response Scales

It is best to write the items by objective and to be aware of the way the results will be analyzed once the data have been collected. There are two general considerations in writing the items: comply with rules for writing most types of items and decide which item format is best.

Babbie (2007), Colton and Covert (2007), and Johnson and Christensen (2008) suggest the following guidelines for writing effective questions or statements:

1. *Make items clear.* An item achieves clarity when all respondents interpret it in the same way. Never assume that the respondent will read something into the item. Often, the perspectives, words, or phrases that make perfect sense to the researcher are unclear to the respondents. The item may also be too general, allowing different interpretations. The question "What do you think about the new curriculum?" for example, would probably evoke counterquestions, for example, "Which curriculum? What is meant by 'think about'?" Finally, vague and ambiguous words like *a few, sometimes,* and *usually* should be avoided, as should jargon and complex phrases.

2. *Avoid double-barreled questions.* A question should be limited to a single idea or concept. **Double-barreled questions** contain two or more ideas, and frequently the word *and* is used in the item. Double-barreled questions and statements are undesirable because the respondent may, if given an opportunity, answer each part differently. If, for instance, a respondent is asked to agree or disagree with the statement "School counselors spend too much time with recordkeeping and not enough time with counseling of personal problems," it would be possible to agree with the first part (too much recordkeeping) and disagree with the second part (not enough time with counseling).

3. *Respondents must be competent to answer.* It is important that the respondents provide reliable information. Some questions that ask teachers to recall specific incidents or to reconstruct what they did several weeks earlier, for example, are subject to inaccuracy simply because the teachers cannot reliably remember the incidents. Similarly, it would be of little value to ask college professors who teach the historical foundations of education to judge the adequacy of a minimum competency test of reading readiness skills that prospective teachers should demonstrate knowledge of for certification. In many instances, the subjects are unable to make a response they can be confident of; in such circumstances, it is best to provide response options such as *unsure* or *do not know* in order to give the subjects an opportunity to state their true feelings or beliefs.

Consider too whether respondents have the literacy skills to understand the questions and how responses are made. The readability level needs to match literacy skills of the participants, and difficult or unfamiliar words should be avoided.

4. *Questions should be relevant.* If subjects are asked to respond to questions that are unimportant to them or deal with things they have not thought about or care little about, they will likely respond carelessly and the results will be misleading. This may occur, for instance, when teachers are asked their preferences in standardized tests when they rarely if ever use the results of these tests in teaching. Their answers might be based on expediency, rather than a careful consideration of the tests.

5. *Short, simple items are best.* Long, complicated items should be avoided because (a) they are more difficult to understand; (b) respondents may be unwilling to try to understand them; and (c) respondents are less likely to answer all items if they are long and complicated. Assume that respondents will read and answer items quickly and that it is necessary to write items that are simple, easy to understand, and easy to respond to.

Double-barreled questions: questions containing two ideas

6. *Avoid negative items.* Negatively stated items should be avoided because they are easy to misinterpret. Subjects will unconsciously skip or overlook the negative word, so their answers will be the opposite of the intended. If researchers use negative items, they should boldface, underline, or capitalize the key words (e.g., <u>not</u> or NO).

7. *Avoid biased items or terms.* The way in which items are worded, as well as the inclusion of certain terms, may encourage particular responses more than others. Such items are termed *biased* and, of course, should be avoided. There are many ways to bias an item. The identification of a well-known person or agency in the item can create bias. "Do you agree or disagree with the superintendent's recent proposal to . . . ?" is likely to elicit a response based on an attitude toward the superintendent, not the proposal. Some items provide biased responses because of the social desirability of the answer. For example, if you ask teachers whether they ever ridicule their students, you can be fairly sure, even if the responses are anonymous, that the answer will be *no* because good teachers do not ridicule students. Student responses to the same question or observations of other teachers might provide different information.

8. *Avoid loaded or leading questions.* Questions that include emotionally laden words that will quickly elicit a positive or negative reaction are called *loaded*. **Loaded questions** need to be avoided because they predispose respondents to view questions in ways that are consistent with the emotion that has been cued. **Leading questions** suggest or promote the idea that there is only one acceptable answer (e.g., "Have you taken the time needed to check students' learning?").

Loaded question: one that evokes emotion

Leading question: suggests a specific response

Researchers may also give a hint of what response they are hoping for. This occurs if the respondents want to please the researcher and provide responses they think the researcher wants, or it may occur if the subjects know the consequences of the responses. It has been shown, for example, that student evaluations of college professors are more favorable if the professor tells the students before they fill out the forms that the results will have a direct bearing on their (the teachers') tenure and salary raises. The students presumably feel less negative because of the important consequences of the results. Finally, items are ambiguous if the respondent thinks, "Well, sometimes I feel this way, sometimes I feel that way" or "It depends on the situation." Many items fail to specify adequately the situational constraints that should be considered, leading to inaccurate responses. If asked, for instance, to agree or disagree with the statement "The discovery method of teaching is better than the lecture method," a teacher would likely respond, "It depends on the student."

Given these general guidelines, how do you know if the items are well written? One approach is to ask friends, colleagues, and experts to review the items and look for any problems. Beyond this subjective method, a good way to demonstrate empirically that items are unbiased, unambiguous, and clear is to construct two equivalent forms of each item and give them to random groups. If the two groups' responses are nearly the same on each pair of items, then the items are probably good.

Types of Items

There are many ways in which a question or statement can be worded and several ways in which the response can be made. The type of item should be based on the advantages, uses, and limitations of these options.

Open and Closed Forms   The first consideration is to decide whether the item will have a **closed form**, in which subjects choose between predetermined responses, or an **open form**, in which the subjects write in any response they want. The choice of form to use depends on the objective of the item and the advantages and disadvantages of each type. Closed-form items (also called *structured, selected-response,* or *closed ended*) are best for obtaining demographic information and data that can be categorized easily. Rather than ask "How many hours did you study for the test?" for example, a closed-form question would provide categories of hours and ask the respondent to check the appropriate box, as indicated below:

Closed form: response selections provided

Open form: answers written by respondents

Check the box that indicates the number of hours you spent studying for the test.

☐ 0–2
☐ 3–5
☐ 6–8
☐ 9–11
☐ 12+

Obviously, it is much easier to score a closed-form item, and the subject can answer the items more quickly. It is therefore best to use closed-form items with a large number of subjects or a large number of items.

There are certain disadvantages to using structured items, however. With the question "How many hours did you study for the test?" for example, if every subject checks the response labeled 3 to 5 *hours*, the researcher has lost accuracy and variability (i.e., no spread of responses across all response categories) with this factor. In other words, if categories are created that fail to allow the subjects to indicate their feelings or beliefs accurately, the item is not very useful. This occurs with some forced-choice items. Another disadvantage is that a structured item cues the respondent with respect to possible answers. If asked, for example, "Why did you do so poorly on the test?" students might, if an open-ended format was used, list two or three factors that were relevant—things that they thought were important. A structured format could, however, list 25 factors and have the student check each one that was important (such as I *didn't study hard enough; I was sick; I was unlucky*); the student may check factors that would have been omitted in the open-ended mode. One approach to the situation in which both the open and closed forms have advantages is to use open-ended questions first with a small group of subjects in order to generate salient factors and then to use closed-ended items, based on the open-ended responses, with a larger group. Open-ended items exert the least amount of control over the respondent and can capture idiosyncratic differences. If the purpose of the research is to generate specific individual responses, the open-ended format is better: if the purpose is to provide more general group responses, the closed form is preferred.

Scale: choices that show different values

Scaled Items A **scale** is a series of gradations, levels, or values that describes various degrees of something. Scales are used extensively in questionnaires because they allow fairly accurate assessments of beliefs or opinions. This is because many of our beliefs and opinions are thought of in terms of gradations. We believe something very strongly or intently, or perhaps we have a positive or negative opinion of something.

The usual format of scaled items is a question or statement followed by a scale of potential responses. The subjects check the place on the scale that best reflects their beliefs or opinions about the statement. The most widely used example is the **Likert scale** (pronounced "Lick-ert"). A true Likert scale is one in which the stem includes a value or direction and the respondent indicates agreement or disagreement with the statement. Likert-type items use different response scales; the stem can be either neutral or directional. The following are examples of true Likert scales:

Likert scale: uses an agree-disagree scale

Science is very important:

| _____ | _____ | _____ | _____ | _____ |
| Strongly agree | Agree | Neither agree nor disagree (undecided or neutral) | Disagree | Strongly disagree |

| _____ | _____ | _____ | _____ |
| Disagree | Tend to disagree | Tend to agree | Agree |

| _____ | _____ | _____ | _____ | _____ | _____ |
| Strongly Agree | Agree | Slightly Agree | Slightly Disagree | Disagree | Strongly Disagree |

It should be pointed out that although the agree-disagree format is used widely, it can also be misleading. We might, for example, disagree with the statement "Mrs. Jones is a good teacher" because we feel that she is an outstanding teacher.

Likert-type scales provide great flexibility because the descriptors on the scale can vary to fit the nature of the question or statement. Here are examples:

Science is:

_____	_____	_____	_____	_____
Critical	Very important	Important	Somewhat important	Very unimportant

How often is your teacher well organized?

_____	_____	_____	_____	_____
Always	Most of the time	Sometimes	Rarely	Never

How would you rate Cindy's performance?

_____	_____	_____	_____	_____
Very poor	Poor	Fair	Good	Excellent

Indicate the extent to which your performance was a success or failure.

_____	_____	_____	_____	_____
Extreme success	Success	OK	Failure	Extreme failure

Indicate how you feel about your performance:

_____	_____	_____	_____	_____
Immense pride	Some pride	Neither pride nor shame	Some shame	Immense shame
Very happy	Somewhat happy	Neither sad nor happy	Somewhat sad	Very sad

Other scales include:

_____	_____	_____	_____	_____
Definitely True	True	Unsure	False	Definitely False
Definitely Yes	Probably Yes	Uncertain	Probably No	Definitely No
Very hard to understand	Hard to understand	Not too easy or too hard to understand	Easy to understand	Very easy to understand

Researchers sometimes wonder whether the undecided or neutral choice should be included in a true Likert scale. Although both forms are used, it is generally better to include the middle category. If the neutral choice is not included and that is the way the respondent actually feels, then the respondent is forced either to make a choice that is incorrect or not to respond at all. The forced-choice format may lead to some frustration by respondents. However, the argument for deleting the undecided or neutral choice has merit in instances in which respondents have a tendency to cluster responses in that middle category.

It is also important to allow participants to select *not applicable* if the question or stem may include something that the respondents are not familiar with. Similarly, most observation schedules need to include a *not observed* category.

A variation of the Likert scale is the **semantic differential**. This scale uses adjective pairs, with each adjective as an end or anchor in a single continuum. On this scale, there is no need for a series of descriptors; only one word or phrase is placed at either end. The scale is used to

Semantic differential: choice between paired extreme adjectives

elicit descriptive reactions to a concept or object. It is an easily constructed scale and can be completed quickly by respondents. The examples that follow illustrate typical uses:

Math

Like ___ ___ ___ ___ ___ ___ ___ Dislike	
Tough ___ ___ ___ ___ ___ ___ ___ Easy	

My teacher

Easy ___ ___ ___ ___ ___ ___ ___ Hard
Unfair ___ ___ ___ ___ ___ ___ ___ Fair
Enthusiastic ___ ___ ___ ___ ___ ___ ___ Unenthusiastic
Boring ___ ___ ___ ___ ___ ___ ___ Not Boring

Reading

Unimportant ___ ___ ___ ___ ___ ___ ___ Important

Or for young children:

Questions that focus on how often a behavior has occurred are better than Likert items in many circumstances. Consider the following two examples:

I believe that doing mathematics homework is important:
Strongly Disagree, Disagree, Neutral, Agree, Strongly Agree

How often do you do mathematics homework?
Every day, Four days a week, Two or three days a week, One day a week.

The second question is less abstract, more behavioral. It provides more specific and objectively evaluated information. Note in Excerpt 9.1 that the researchers used a behavioral Likert-type scale.

Ranked Items   One problem with using a Likert scale or a semantic differential is that all the answers can be the same, making it difficult to differentiate between items. If a Likert scale is used to investigate the importance of each of five ways of spending money by a university department, for instance, a respondent can mark *very important* for each one. This result would do little for the researcher's efforts to prioritize expenditure of funds. If, however, the respondents are asked to *rank order* the five ways in sequential order, from most to least important, then the researcher can gather more valuable information on ways to spend the money. A **rank-order** assessment of the above example might look like this:

Rank-order: listing from highest to lowest

Rank order the following activities with respect to their importance as to ways our research fund should be allocated this year. Use 1 = most important, 2 = next most important, and so forth until 5 = least important.
_____ Annual colloquium   _____ Computer software
_____ Individual research projects   _____ Student assistantships
_____ Invited speakers

Respondents should not be asked to rank order more than about eight statements, however.

EXCERPT 9.1   Behavioral Likert-Type Scale

To measure the degree to which early childhood educators promote language and literacy activities in their centers, a 23-item survey was developed. The survey began with the following questions: "In my early childhood program, we. . ." Participants were then instructed to respond to a series of statements indicating how often they engage children in specific activities. . . . Response options for each of the 23 items ranged from 1 (Never) to 5 (Always).

Source: From Green, S. D., Peterson, R., & Lewis, J. R. (2006). Language and literacy promotion in early childhood settings: A survey of center-based practices. *Early Childhood Research & Practice*. Retrieved May 20, 2009, from http://ecrp.uiuc.edu/v8n1/green.html.

Checklist Items   A checklist is simply a method of providing the respondent with a number of options from which to choose. The item can require a choice of one of several alternatives (e.g., "Check one: The biology topic I most enjoy is _____ ecology, _____ botany, _____ anatomy, _____ microbiology, or _____ genetics."), or the item can ask respondents to check as many words as apply—for instance:

Check as many as apply. The most enjoyable topics in biology are
_____ botany   _____ ecology
_____ comparative anatomy   _____ microbiology
_____ genetics   _____ zoology

Checklists can also be used in asking respondents to answer *yes* or *no* to a question or to check the category to which they belong—for example:

Are you married? _____ yes _____ no

If no, check the appropriate category:
_____ single   _____ separated
_____ never married   _____ divorced
                                        _____ widowed

Item Format

There are several ways to present items and answers to items. The clearest approach is to write the item on one line and to place the response categories below, not next to, the item. It is also advisable to use boxes, brackets, or parentheses, rather than a line, to indicate where to place the check mark—for example:

Have you ever cheated?

☐ yes
☐ no

is better than

Have you ever cheated? _____ yes _____ no

With Likert and semantic differential scales, using continuous lines or open blanks for check marks is not recommended, because check marks may be entered between two options.

Sometimes when a researcher asks a series of questions, answering one question in a certain way directs the respondent to other questions. These are called *contingency questions* and are illustrated below:

Have you used the *Mathematics Curriculum Guide?*

☐ yes
☐ no

If yes: How often have you used the activities suggested?

☐ 0–2 times
☐ 3–5 times
☐ 6–10 times
☐ more than 10 times

Did you attend the State Conference on Testing?

☐ yes (please answer questions 17–20)
☐ no (please skip to question 21)

If several questions will use the same response format, as is typical with Likert scale items, it is often desirable to construct a matrix of items and response categories. An example of a matrix is illustrated in Figure 9.2.

For questions 1–8 use the following response scale:

1	2	3	4	5	6
Not At All	Very little	Some	Quite a bit	Extensively	Completely

To what extent were the final first semester grades of students in your class based on:

1. including 0s in the determination of final percentage correct if students failed to complete an assignment? 1 2 3 4 5 6
2. disruptive student behavior? 1 2 3 4 5 6
3. laudatory behavior of the student? 1 2 3 4 5 6
4. student attitudes toward learning? 1 2 3 4 5 6
5. improvement of performance since the beginning of the semester? 1 2 3 4 5 6
6. low student effort to learn? 1 2 3 4 5 6
7. high student effort to learn? 1 2 3 4 5 6
8. degree of effort of low-ability students? 1 2 3 4 5 6

FIGURE 9.2 **Question Matrix**

General Format

The general layout and organization of the questionnaire are very important. If it appears to be carelessly done or confusing, respondents are likely to set it aside and never respond. A well-done format and appearance provide a favorable first impression and will result in cooperation and serious, conscientious responses. The following rules should be adhered to:

To practice developing survey items, go to MyEducationLab for Research at www.myeducationlab.com. Click on the topic "Survey Research" and then select the Activities and Applications activity titled "Constructing Survey Items."

1. Carefully check grammar, spelling, punctuation, and other details.
2. Make sure that the print is clear and easy to read.
3. Make instructions brief and easy to understand.
4. Avoid cluttering the questionnaire by trying to squeeze many items on each page.
5. Avoid abbreviated items.
6. Keep the questionnaire as short as possible.
7. Provide adequate space for answering open-ended questions.
8. Use a logical sequence, and group related items.
9. Number the pages and items.
10. Use examples if the items may be difficult to understand.
11. Put important items near the beginning of a long questionnaire.
12. Be aware of how the positioning and sequence of the questions may affect the responses.
13. Print the response scale on each new page.
14. Put selected-response items before constructed-response items.

When surveying a large number of respondents, a scantron form is typically developed so that the answers can be accurately and quickly scored by a computer and entered into a database. Whereas in the past the format of scantron forms was standard, forms are now typically individualized for particular studies. An example of items on a scantron form is illustrated in Figure 9.3.

There is also widespread use of the Internet for gathering questionnaire responses, which also allows quick and accurate scoring. Some surveys will mix different response scales on the same questionnaire. This is fine as long as the directions are clear and respondents are careful in changing the basis for their responses. The use of different scales is illustrated in Excerpt 9.2.

In studies that use long questionnaires or a series of questionnaires, the researcher may use what is called *matrix sampling*. In **matrix sampling** each student responds to only some of the questions. That is, random sampling is used to form "equivalent" groups, and each group

Matrix sampling: each respondent answers some questions

EXCERPT 9.2 Combining Different Scales

The STARS Needs Assessment was developed from existing ECE and ECSE literature about effective practices with young children with disabilities in inclusive settings. . . . Part I includes five items concerning beliefs about including young children with disabilities in EDE settings, ranked on a five-point Likert scale (1 = Always, 2 = Usually, 3 = Sometimes, 4 = Rarely, and 5 = Never). Part II includes 16 skill-based items focusing on assessment and instructional band behavioral practices, as well as on working with families and professionals in inclusive settings (1 = Strongly agree, 2 = Agree, 3 = Neutral, 4 = Disagree, and 5 = Strongly disagree). Part III provides six choices of training needs and asks respondents to identify their top three needs. (p. 233)

Source: From Bruns, D. A., & Mogharrenban, C. C. (2007). The gap between beliefs and practices: Early childhood practitioners' perceptions about inclusion. *Journal of Research in Childhood Education, 21*(3), 229–242.

76. Your state-mandated testing program influences the amount of the time you spend on. . .

	Strongly Agree	Agree	Disagree	Strongly disagree
• Whole group instruction	○	○	○	○
• Critical thinking skills	○	○	○	○
• Individual seat work	○	○	○	○
• Basic skills	○	○	○	○
• Students working together in small groups (cooperative learning)	○	○	○	○
• Concept development using manipulatives or experiments	○	○	○	○
• Problems that are likely to appear on the state-mandated test	○	○	○	○

Background Information

77. How many years of teaching experience do you have, including this year?

○ 1   ○ 4–8   ○ 13–20
○ 2–3   ○ 9–12   ○ Over 20

78. What is your gender?

○ Female   ○ Male

79. Please mark the appropriate range for your age?

○ 20–30   ○ 41–50   ○ 61+
○ 31–40   ○ 51–60

80. Mark ALL of the following categories that best describe you.

○ African American

○ American Indian or Alaskan Native

○ Asian

○ White

○ Pacific Islander

○ Hispanic

○ Other, please specify:

FIGURE 9.3 **Example of Questionnaire Items on Scantron Form**

Source: From *Teacher Survey on the Impact of State Mandated Testing Programs,* 2000, Boston, MA: National Board on Educational Testing and Public Policy, Boston College. Copyright © 2000 by National Computer Systems, Inc. All rights reserved. Reprinted by permission.

EXCERPT 9.3 Matrix Sampling

We used a matrix sampling design to reduce the time required to complete the questionnaire, thus reducing time taken from instruction. Each subject-area questionnaire was divided into three forms that were distributed randomly in each classroom. A student received only one form containing 12 to 15 Likert items and two to three constructed-response items. . . . The three forms were uniformly distributed within each classroom to help ensure that students' samples across forms were equivalent. (p. 311)

Source: From Parke, C. S., & Lane, S. (2007). Students' perceptions of a Maryland state performance assessment. *The Elementary School Journal, 107*(3), 305–324.

is asked to complete a different set of items so that, when combined, all items are surveyed. Note in Excerpt 9.3 that three forms were used. Matrix sampling can also be used with cognitive measures.

Conduct a Pretest

Once you have developed a set of possible items, it is important to conduct a pretest by asking some thoughtful individuals to read and respond to the questions. Once they complete their responses, you will need to ask them about the clarity and wording of the questions, including the following:

Were the items clearly worded?
Was the meaning of the items clear?
Was there any difficulty understanding the items?
Were there any spelling or grammatical errors?
Were the response scales appropriate?
What suggestions are there for making improvements to the items?

Based on the responses to these questions, the items are revised. Often researchers will begin with more items than will eventually be used. Also, at this stage, items may be sent to content experts to gather evidence for validity. The experts will be asked whether the items match the areas intended, whether additional items will be needed to cover the construct (construct underrepresentation), and whether items not associated with the construct need to be deleted (construct irrelevant variance). (See de Leeuw, Borgers, and Smits [2004] for guidelines on developing questionnaires for children and adolescents.)

Conduct a Pilot Test

Once the items have been revised, the researcher will create and format the actual draft questionnaire, with headings and directions. At this point, it is important to conduct a pilot test. Excerpt 9.4 shows how an instrument was modified based on data gathered during the

EXCERPT 9.4 Revision of an Instrument Based on Pilot Testing

As a result of initial analysis of the items and open-response questions, several modifications were made to the pilot instrument. First, items that did not load on a factor (<.30) were eliminated. Second, in an effort to improve the clean item clustering on each scale, items that loaded onto more than one scale were revised. Third, items that either contained unclear language or contained two ideas were rewritten. Fourth, all five negatively worded items loaded onto a single factor . . . suggesting that there were some possible conceptual misconceptions among the respondents. These five items were either rewritten or deleted. Finally, several items that more comprehensively represented the literature and feedback from the open-response items—items pertaining to the mathematical task in particular—were added. (p. 76)

Source: From Casa, T. M., McGivney-Burelle, J., & DeFranco, T. C. (2007). The development of an instrument to measure preservice teachers' attitudes about discourse in the mathematics classroom. *School Science and Mathematics, 107*(2), 70–80.

TABLE 9.4 Do's and Don'ts of Writing Questionnaires

Do	Don't
• Use short, simple, clear directions and items.	• Use open-ended items.
• Label all points on a scale.	• Use "Other" as a category.
• Make the questionnaire professional looking.	• Use double-barreled questions.
• Use "Almost always" rather than "Always."	• Use negative items.
• Spell out acronyms.	• Use more than 6 or 7 points on a scale.
• Ask only for information you will use.	• Clutter the questionnaire.
• Draw attention to important terms (e.g., use bold type).	• Use ranking items with a long list.
• Put items into logically coherent sections.	• Use jargon.
• Put important items near the beginning.	• Squeeze as much text as possible on each page.
• Number all items and pages.	• Use terms that are biased.
	• Use leading questions.

pilot testing stage. The aim of the research was to develop an instrument that could be used to measure preservice teachers' attitudes regarding discourse used in the teaching of mathematics.

It is best to locate a sample of subjects with characteristics similar to those that will be used in the study. Although the size of the sample should be greater than 20, it is better to have only 10 subjects than to have no pilot test. The administration of the questionnaire should be about the same as that to be used in the study, and the pilot test respondents should be given space to write comments about individual items and the questionnaire as a whole. The researcher wants to know whether it takes too long to complete, whether the directions and items are clear, and so on. If there are enough pilot test subjects, an estimate of reliability may be calculated, and some indication will be given of whether there is sufficient variability in the answers to investigate various relationships.

Table 9.4 summarizes the do's and don'ts of writing questionnaires.

INTERVIEW SCHEDULES

Interviews in quantitative studies are essentially oral questionnaires (except for those used to assess cognitive learning). The major steps in constructing an interview are the same as those in preparing a questionnaire: justification, defining objectives, writing questions, deciding general and item format, and pretesting. The obvious difference is that the interview involves direct interaction between individuals, which has both advantages and disadvantages as compared with the questionnaire.

The interview technique is flexible and adaptable. It can be used with many different problems and types of persons, such as those who are illiterate or too young to read and write, and responses can be probed, followed up, clarified, and elaborated to achieve specific accurate responses. Nonverbal as well as verbal behavior can be noted in face-to-face interviews, and the interviewer has an opportunity to motivate the respondent. Interviews result in a much higher response rate than questionnaires, especially for topics that concern personal qualities or negative feelings. For obtaining factual and less personal information, a questionnaire is preferable.

The primary disadvantages of the interview are its potential for subjectivity and bias, its higher cost and time-consuming nature, and its lack of anonymity. Depending on the training and expertise of the interviewer, the respondent may be uncomfortable in the interview and unwilling to report true feelings; the interviewer may ask leading questions to support a particular point of view; or the interviewer's perceptions of what was said may be inaccurate. Because interviewing is labor intensive, it is costly and time-consuming (with the possible exception of telephone interviews), which usually results in sampling fewer subjects than could be obtained with a questionnaire. Because an interview involves one person talking with another, anonymity is not possible. Confidentiality can be stressed, but there is always the potential for faking or for being less than forthright and candid, because the subjects may believe that sharing certain information would not be in their best interest.

To mitigate potential bias, the interviewer should be thought of as a neutral medium through which information is exchanged. If this goal is attained, then the interviewer's presence will have no effect on the perceptions or answers of the respondent. In other words, if the interview is done correctly, it does not matter who the interviewer is; any number of different interviewers would obtain the same results. This aspect of interviewing is essentially one of reliability. If two or more interviewers agree on the way most of the responses to the questions should be classified, then the process will be reliable, as assessed by inter-rater agreement.

A good approach that can be used to increase the accuracy of the interview is to allow the respondent an opportunity to check the interviewer's perceptions. This can be accomplished if the interviewers write their perceptions of the answer to each question and send these written perceptions to the respondents. The respondents can then read the answers and make additions and corrections where appropriate. An additional advantage to this approach is that it helps build a positive relationship between the interviewer and respondents. This is helpful if the interviewer will be following up initial interviews or will be involved in a continuing evaluation or study.

Preparing the Interview

Once the researcher has decided to use an interview to collect data, an interview schedule is constructed. The schedule lists all the questions that will be asked, giving room for the interviewer to write answers. The questions are related directly to the objectives of the study and follow a given sequence that will be adhered to in each interview. In most cases, the written questions are exactly what will be asked orally, with appropriate probing questions. The questions are usually in one of three forms: structured, semistructured, or unstructured.

Structured questions: choices provided

Semistructured questions: some choices provided

Unstructured questions: broad questions asked in any order

Structured questions (also called *limited-response* or *selected-response* questions) are followed by a set of choices, and the respondent selects one of the choices as the answer—for example, "Would you say the program has been highly effective, somewhat effective, or not at all effective?" **Semistructured questions** have no choices from which the respondent selects an answer. Rather, the question is phrased to allow for individual responses. It is an open-ended question but is fairly specific in its intent—for example, "What has been the most beneficial aspect of your teacher training program?" **Unstructured questions** allow the interviewer great latitude in asking broad questions in whatever order seems appropriate. In quantitative educational studies, most interviews use a combination of structured and semistructured questions. This provides a high degree of objectivity and uniformity yet allows for probing and clarification.

After the questions have been written, a pilot test is necessary as a check for bias in the procedures, the interviewer, and the questions. During the pilot test, the procedures should be identical to those that will be implemented in the study. The interviewer should take special note of any cues suggesting that the respondent is uncomfortable or does not fully understand the questions. After the interview, the respondent can evaluate the questions for intent, clarity, and so on. The pilot test provides a means of assessing the length of the interview and will give the researcher some idea of the ease with which the data can be summarized.

A final consideration in preparing the interview is to think about the way personal characteristics of the interviewer may influence the responses (see Table 9.5). Many educational studies use naive or inexperienced interviewers. In this situation, not only will the personal characteristics of the interviewer provide possible bias, but there will be a potential for error simply because the interviewer is unskilled at handling interviews. If novices are used, it is best to provide training and supervision. This can be expensive and time-consuming but will increase the validity and reliability of the study. For details on training interviewers, see Babbie (2007), Gall, Gall, and Borg (2007), and the *Interviewer's Manual* (1999).

TABLE 9.5 Interviewer Characteristics

Variable	Effect on the Interview
Age of interviewer	• Rapport is high for young interviewers with middle-aged respondents. • The least inhibition in responding occurs with young persons of the same sex. • Most inhibition in responding occurs with persons of the same age but different sexes. • Interviewers between 26 and 50 years of age generally do the best job of interviewing.
College major	• Interviewers trained in the behavioral sciences are rated as being more accurate than those trained in the physical sciences; lowest rated are those who majored in fine arts, business, law, and the humanities.
Experience in interviewing	• Interviewers' accuracy increases as their experience in interviewing increases.
Racial background	• Responses of blacks differ, depending on whether they are interviewed by whites or blacks.
Gender	• Male interviewers tend to obtain fewer responses than females.

During the Interview

Appearance is very important. It is best for the interviewer to dress according to existing norms or in a fashion similar to that of the respondents, not in a way that may lead the respondent to think that the interviewer represents a particular point of view. The interviewer should be friendly, relaxed, and pleasant, and he or she should appear interested in the welfare of the respondents. To provide honest answers to questions, the respondent must feel comfortable with the interviewer. Appropriate appearance and demeanor provide a basis for establishing a comfortable relationship and rapport. The interviewer should spend a few minutes with small talk in order to establish a proper relationship.

Before asking specific questions, the interviewer should briefly explain the purpose of the interview and ask whether the respondent has any questions or concerns. The questions should then be addressed as indicated on the interview schedule. The questions should be read without error or stumbling in a natural, unforced manner. To accomplish this, the interviewer should be very familiar with the questions and should practice asking them aloud.

As the subject responds to the questions, the interviewer needs to record the answers. The recording is usually done by tape or digital recording and/or by means of written notes. Taped answers can be analyzed by several judges and used to estimate reliability. Recording the answers is generally most useful with open-ended questions. The recorder will obviously collect the information more completely and objectively than notes, but the mere presence of a recorder may disrupt the interview and affect the responses, especially if personal questions are asked. If the questions are highly structured, there is little need for recorded responses.

The most common method used to record responses is to take notes based on the answers. There are two extremes with notetaking. At one extreme, the interviewer can try to write the exact response as it is given; at the other, the interviewer can wait until the interview is over and then reconstruct the answer to each question. The problem with taking verbatim notes is that it takes much time during the interview; on the other hand, information is lost when interviewers rely solely on their memories to write answers after the interview. Most interviewers compromise between these extremes and during the interview take abbreviated notes that can be expanded on after the interview is completed.

Probing for further clarification of an answer is a skill that, if misused, can lead to incomplete or inaccurate responses. The interviewer should allow sufficient time for the respondent

Probing: questioning for further clarification

EXCERPT 9.5 Using Probes in Interviews

The "funnel" interview technique was used, in which initial broad questions encourage students to make extended statements about a topic. . . . Probing then begins with follow-up questions asking (if necessary) for clarification or elaboration of these initial statements. Finally, more specific questions are asked (if necessary) to call students' attention to aspects of the topic that they did not address spontaneously. . . . Interviews typically lasted 20–30 minutes. They were conducted in small offices or other locations outside the students' classrooms. To facilitate rapport and make sure that responses were preserved verbatim, the interviews were tape-recorded. (p. 429)

Source: From Brophy, J., & Alleman, J. (2002). Primary-grade students' knowledge and thinking about the economics of meeting families' shelter needs. *American Educational Research Journal, 39*(2), 423–468.

TABLE 9.6 Do's and Don'ts of Interviewing

Do	Don't
• Assure the respondent of confidentiality.	• Ask the complex questions first.
• Build rapport.	• Talk more than the respondent.
• Explain the benefits of the study.	• Dress in an intimidating manner.
• Ask questions that contain single ideas.	• Hint at expected responses.
• Use simple probes.	• Cross-examine the respondent.
• Be friendly and nonthreatening.	• Waste the respondent's time.
• Dress in an appropriate professional manner.	• Make respondents feel anxious.
• Conduct the interview in a quiet place.	• Be inflexible.
• Make respondents feel comfortable and relaxed.	• Rephrase questions too much.
• Listen more than talk.	• Use leading questions.
• Keep respondents focused.	• Interrupt the respondent.
• Tolerate silence.	• Debate the respondent.

to answer and should avoid anticipating and cuing a potential answer. Probes should also be neutral so as not to affect the nature of the response. If the initial question usually results in probing, then it is useful to list some probes next to the question. This allows time to develop the best probe and standardizes the probes for all interviews. A good example of using probes is illustrated in Excerpt 9.5. In this study, K–grade 3 students were interviewed individually to determine their understanding of economics and cultural universals.

Table 9.6 lists do's and don'ts for using interviews to collect quantitative data.

OBSERVATION SCHEDULES

In a sense, all techniques for gathering data involve observation of some kind. As a general term, then, the word *observation* is used to describe the data that are collected, regardless of the technique employed in the study. Observational research methods also refer, however, to a more specific method of collecting information that is very different from interviews or questionnaires. As a technique for gathering information, the observational method relies on a researcher's seeing and hearing things and recording these observations, rather than relying on subjects' self-report responses to questions or statements.

Complete observer: detached from the setting

The role of the observer in most quantitative research is to remain detached from the group or process and thus act as a **complete observer**. A researcher may, for example, want to study the adjustment of college freshmen to campus life by observing their behavior in various settings as an outsider, not participating but simply recording information.

A good example of a quantitative study that used observation focused on the self-regulatory behaviors of second-grade students (Stright & Supplee, 2002). In this study, the observers

EXCERPT 9.6   Observation

We trained two educational psychology doctoral students (observers) with experience as elementary school classroom teachers to use the classroom coding system over a 2-month period by coding together in third-grade classrooms not participating in the study. The coders were blind to the purpose of the study. Only one coder observed in a classroom unless data for intercoder agreement was being collected. . . . The headphones and the observers' manner minimized attempts by students and teacher to interact with the observers and to reduce disruptive effects of their presence. . . . The observers coded each child in his or her third-grade classroom for 12 five-min observation periods spaced evenly throughout the school year. . . . The observers immediately coded each child's self-regulatory behaviors after observing for a 5-min interval. . . . Data were collected for each child using at least four classroom visits. . . . To assess the intercoder agreement for the coding system, once data collection began, the two coders observed together and then independently coded 155 of the 624 5-min intervals of data collected (25%). Observations to assess agreement were spaced out equally across the school year. For the three codes assessed during a 3-point rating scale, Pearson's correlations of the two coders ranged from .94 to .98, and a version of Cohen's Kappa designed for ratings . . . ranged from .85 to .95. (p. 237)

Source: From Stright, A. D., & Supplee, L. H. (2002). Children's self-regulatory behaviors during teacher-directed, seat-work, and small-group instructional contexts. *Journal of Educational Research, 95*(4), 235–244.

recorded the frequency of such behaviors as "seeking assistance" and "fails to follow instruction" and used a 3-point scale (i.e., "Not at all," "slightly," "moderately") for rating listening, reading, and organization. Excerpt 9.6 is taken from this article. In reviewing it, note the careful attention to establishing intercoder agreement for reliability.

The role of observer also depends on the degree of inference or judgment that is required. At one extreme, the observer makes **high-inference** observations, which are judgments or inferences based on observed behaviors. What is recorded with high-inference observations is the judgment of the observer. For example, a high-inference observation of a teacher would be a rating made by the principal on factors such as classroom management and enthusiasm. The principal would observe the class and make a rating of excellent, good, fair, or poor in each of the two areas. **Low-inference** observations, on the other hand, require the observer to record specific behaviors without making judgments in a more global sense. Thus, the principal might record the number of rebukes or cues used by the teacher as information that is used subsequently to judge classroom management. Low-inference observation usually is more reliable, but many would argue that it is necessary to make judgments, based on the complexity and multitude of variables in a classroom, for valid observations. An in-between role for the observer is to make judgments (high inference) and then record the specific behaviors and context that led to the inference implied in the judgment.

High-inference: recording of judgment of the observer

Low-inference: recording of specific behaviors

Justification

The primary advantages of using observational methods are that the researcher does not need to worry about the limitations of self-report bias, social desirability, and response set and the information is not limited to what can be recalled accurately by the subjects. Behavior can be recorded as it occurs naturally. The second advantage is very important for research designed to study what occurs in real life, as opposed to in highly contrived or artificial settings. However, observational research is expensive and difficult to conduct reliably for complex behavior. It is relatively easy and straightforward to record simple behavior objectively, but most studies focus on more complex behavior that is difficult to define and assess through observation. There is also the problem of how the observer affects the behavior of subjects by being present in the setting.

Defining Observational Units

The first step in developing an observational study is to define in precise terms what will be observed. Beginning with the research problem or question, the variables that need to be observed are ascertained. If the problem or question is general, such as "How long are students engaged academically?" then the researcher must narrow the purpose to obtain specific, measurable units that can be observed. Because it is impossible to observe everything that occurs, the researcher must decide on the variables or units of analysis that are most important and then define the behavior so that it can be recorded objectively.

Recording Observations

Once the researcher has defined the behavior to be observed, the recording procedure is selected. There are five types: duration recording, frequency-count recording, interval recording, continuous observation, and time sampling.

Duration recording: how long a behavior is observed

Duration Recording   In **duration recording**, the observer indicates the length of time a particular kind of behavior lasts. Often a stop watch is used to keep track of the duration of the behavior. The researcher thus simply looks for a type of behavior (e.g., out of seat, talking to other students) and records the length of time this type of behavior occurs within a given time span.

Frequency-count recording: how often a behavior occurs

Frequency-Count Recording   **Frequency-count recording** is used when the observer is interested only in the frequency with which the behavior occurs, not how long it persists. Generally, the observer has a list of several kinds of behavior that will be recorded and keeps a running tally to indicate how often each occurs. Obviously, this type of recording is best when the duration of the behavior is short (i.e., one to five seconds).

Interval recording: behaviors occurring in a short period of time

Interval Recording   In **interval recording**, a single subject is observed for a given period of time and the behaviors that occur are recorded. The observer may indicate that each kind of behavior either does or does not occur, or he or she may record how many times it occurs within each interval.

Continuous observation: description of behaviors over an extended period

Continuous Observation   In **continuous observation**, the observer provides a brief description of the subject's behavior over an extended period. The description is written in chronological order, and the observer must decide which kind of behavior is important.

Time sampling: random or fixed schedule for observing specific behaviors

Time Sampling   In **time sampling**, the observer selects, at random or on a fixed schedule, the time periods that will be used to observe particular kinds of behavior. This procedure is used in conjunction with each of the four previously mentioned procedures. If possible, it is best to locate existing observational schedules that have been standardized to some degree. Virtually hundreds of schedules have been developed, and because they have been pilot tested and used in previous studies, they are more likely than new schedules to demonstrate good validity and reliability.

An example of time sampling in a large-scale observational study is illustrated in Excerpt 9.7.

Training Observers

The most important limitation of complete observation is with the person who records what is seen and heard—the observer. The difficulty lies in obtaining observations that are objective, unbiased, and accurate in the sense that the observer has avoided influencing the behavior of the subjects. The objectivity of the observer depends to some degree on the specificity of the behavior.

EXCERPT 9.7   Time-Sampling Recording

Observation of classrooms complements student test performance as a measure of quality in the educational system and can document opportunities to learn that are reflected in students' performances on tests. We observed first, third, and fifth grades. First we coded the presence of 44 behavioral events for 90 one-minute intervals. In a given school day, intervals were clustered into eight 10-minute cycles of coding, in which 30-second periods of observation alternated with 30-second periods of recording. Next, we rated nine dimensions of the quality of the emotional and instructional climate on the basis of 20 minutes of observation, again across eight cycles during the day. We used these codes and ratings to assess opportunities to learn. (p. 1795)

Source: From Pianta, R. C., Belsky, J., Houts, R., & Morrison, F. (2007). Opportunities to learn in America's elementary classrooms. *Science, 315,* 1795–1796.

EXCERPT 9.8 Interobserver Agreement

Interobserver agreement on the ESI was assessed on a randomly selected 38% of all 326 assessment tapes. Agreement was checked by a second person who independently recorded the same videotaped session simultaneously with the primary observer. The two observers' frequency counts for key elements and composite scores were examined for interobserver agreement and measurement reliability.

Pearson *r* was used to calculate the correlation between observers' estimates and the paired *t*-test was used to test for mean differences. Strong to very strong correlation and the lack of a statistically significant difference between two observers' estimates served as evidence of reliability and agreement. (pp. 99–100)

Source: From Carta, J. J., Greenwood, C. R., Luze, G. J., Cline, G., & Kuntz, S. (2004). Developing a general outcome measure of growth in social skills for infants and toddlers. *Journal of Early Intervention, 26*(2), 91–114.

EXCERPT 9.9 Using an Observational Rating Scale

To evaluate and determine the level of counseling skill development of the study participants, a team of six counselor educators was trained to use The Global Scale for Rating Helper Responses. . . . The instrument requires observers to score participants' counseling responses on a 4-point

scale indicating that the counseling response was the following: 1 = *not helpful: harmful*, 2 = *not helpful: ineffective*, 3 = *helpful: facilitative*, 4 = *helpful: additive*. This scale has been widely used in research studies as a measure of interpersonal communication skills. (p. 179)

Source: From Hayes, B. G., Taub, G. E., Robinson, E. D., III, & Sivo, S. A. (2003). An empirical investigation of the efficacy of multimedia instruction in counseling skill development. *Counselor Education and Supervision, 42*(3), 177–188.

That is, a kind of behavior described as "teasing other students" is much less specific and subject to error in interpretation than something as specific and objective as "raises hand" or "leaves chair."

Bias is a factor in observational research to the extent that the idiosyncratic perceptions and interpretations of the observer, influenced by previous experiences, affect the recording of behavior. Although it is almost impossible to eliminate bias, it can be controlled. One way to control bias is by carefully choosing observers. Obviously, it would be a bad idea to choose as an observer of the effects of authentic assessment an advocate of that kind of education, just as it would be unfair to choose a known opponent, because his or her preconceived notions could easily bias his or her observations. A second approach to controlling bias is to use carefully trained observers, comparing their observations with each other's in similar and different situations. Third, bias can be mitigated by using two observers in each setting during the study. As long as the observers agree independently, there is less chance that bias will be a confounding factor. A final type of bias that needs to be considered is contamination, which may occur if the observer is knowledgeable about the specifics of the study. For example, in a study of the differences between so-called good and poor teachers, if the observer knows before making the observations which teachers are supposedly good and which are poor, this knowledge is likely to bias the observations. It is thus best for the observers to have little or no knowledge of the purpose of the study. Their job is to observe and record in an objective, detached manner.

Excerpt 9.8 shows how researchers typically report interobserver agreement, and Excerpt 9.9 illustrates how observation as the instrument is described.

UNOBTRUSIVE MEASURES

Questionnaires, interviews, and direct observation are intrusive or reactive in the sense that the participants realize they are being questioned or watched. A major difficulty with subjects' awareness that they are participants is that their behavior may be affected by this knowledge. A type of measurement that is considered to be **nonreactive**, in which subjects are asked or required to do nothing out of the ordinary, is called *unobtrusive*. **Unobtrusive measures** provide data that

Nonreactive: not interfering with subjects

Unobtrusive measures: subjects unaware of data collection are uninfluenced by subjects' awareness that they are participants or by an alteration in the natural course of events. The major types of unobtrusive measures include physical traces, such as worn floors, books, and computers; documents, reports, and letters; and observations in which the subject is unaware of being researched (see Webb, Campbell, Schwartz, & Sechrest, 2000).

There are both strengths and weaknesses with each of the five major types of data collection techniques discussed in this chapter, as summarized in Table 9.7. Researchers need to consider these in selecting appropriate methods of gathering information.

TABLE 9.7   Strengths and Weaknesses of Data Collection Techniques

Technique	Strengths	Weaknesses
Paper-and-pencil tests	Economical	Norms may be inappropriate
	Standard questions	Standardized tests may be too broad and general
	Commercial tests strong in technical qualities	Standard scores may distort differences
	Objective tests easy to score	Standardized tests may give false sense of validity
	Standardized tests provide uniform procedures for all subjects and standard scores	Locally developed tasks often technically weak
		Test anxiety
		Restricted to subjects who can read
Alternative assessments	Provides direct, holistic measure of skills	Subjective ratings result in low reliability
	Closely aligned to instruction	Poor sampling of larger domain of skills
	Uses more authentic contexts	Costly
		Time-consuming
Questionnaires	Economical	Response rate of mailed questionnaires
	Can be anonymous	Inability to probe and clarify
	Standard questions and uniform procedures	Scoring open-ended items
	Usually easy to score	Faking and social desirability
	Provides time for subjects to think about responses	Restricted to subjects who can read and write
		Biased and ambiguous items
		Response set
Interviews	Flexible	Costly
	Adaptable	Time-consuming
	Ability to probe and clarify	Interviewer bias
	Ability to include nonverbal behavior	Not anonymous
	High response rate	Subject effects
	Used with nonreaders	Effect of interviewer characteristics
		Requires training
		Leading questions
Observations	Captures natural behavior	Costly
	Mitigates social desirability, response set, and subject effects	Time-consuming
	Relatively unobstrusive	Effect of observer on subjects
	Reliable for low-inference observations	Observer bias
		Requires training
		Reliability difficult for complex behavior and high-inference observations
		Inability to probe and clarify
		Usually not anonymous
		Interpretation of high-inference observations

Sources for Locating and Evaluating Existing Instruments

In conducting research, the researcher should choose an instrument that has established the reliability and validity he or she needs and that will provide sufficient variability of scores. Although reliability and validity are the most important considerations in selecting an instrument, there are other considerations, such as purchasing costs, availability, simplicity of administration and scoring, copyright limitations, level of difficulty, and appropriateness of norms.

Although it is often difficult to find an instrument that will meet all of the criteria a researcher might have, there are thousands of instruments, and it is probable that one is available that can be used intact or modified to meet a specific purpose. There are two primary ways to identify and evaluate existing instruments and those used by other researchers: (1) review the literature to see what other researchers have used for the same or similar constructs and (2) use sources that summarize information on possible measures. The sources in the following list are widely used and accessible:

One way to locate an existing instrument is to read about it in a published article. Practice evaluating one such article by going to MyEducationLab for Research at www.myeducation-lab.com. Click on the topic "Survey Research" and then select the Building Research Skills exercise titled "Evaluating a Survey Study."

Tests in Print, Volume 7, published periodically by the Buros Institute of Mental Measurement (Murphy, Spies, & Plake, 2006): Provides a summary of tests reviewed in all preceding mental measurement yearbooks.

Handbook of Research Design and Social Measurement, 6th ed. (Miller & Salkind, 2002): Reviews and critiques popular social science measures.

Index to Tests Used in Educational Dissertations (Fabiano, 1989): Describes tests and test populations used in dissertations from 1938 to 1980; keyed by title and selected descriptors.

Commissioned Reviews of 250 Psychological Tests (Maltby, Alan, & Hill, 2000): Contains brief reviews of tests published in the 1990s. Provides variable measured, description, sample tested, reliability, validity, where test can be found, and evaluative comments.

Directory of Unpublished Experimental Mental Measures, Volume 8 (Goldman & Mitchell, 2002): Describes nearly 1,700 experimental mental measures that are not commercially available. Includes references, source, and purpose on topics ranging from educational adjustment and motivation to personality and perception.

ETS Test Collection and *Testlink Test Collection Database:* The Educational Testing Service (ETS) has developed several sources that describe more than 25,000 tests and instruments. The database covers published and unpublished measures in several areas, including achievement, attitudes and interests, personality, special populations, and vocation/occupation. Each of over 200 separate bibliographies describes instruments and appropriate uses and can be ordered from ETS. *Tests in Microfiche* lists unpublished research instruments, also in a wide variety of areas.

Tests: A Comprehensive Reference for Assessments in Psychology, Education, and Business, 6th ed. (Maddox, 2007): Provides descriptions of over 3,100 published and unpublished tests, including purpose, cost, scoring, and publisher.

Test Critiques, Volumes 1–10 (Keyser & Sweetland, 1984–1994): Gives in-depth evaluations of widely used, newly published, and recently revised instruments in psychology, education, and business. Contains user-oriented information, including practical applications and uses, as well as technical aspects and a critique by a measurement specialist. The companion, *Test Critiques Compendium,* reviews 60 major tests from *Test Critiques* in one volume.

Mental Measurements Yearbook (MMY; Buros Institute of Mental Measurement): Provides reviews of commercially available tests in several areas, including character and personality, achievement, and intelligence. References for most of the tests facilitate further research. The MMY has been published periodically for 60 years. The Buros Institute website (http://www.unl.edu/buros) includes *Test Reviews Online,* which allows electronic searches of the Buros database.

Tests and Measurements in Child Development: Handbooks I and II (Johnson, 1976): Two volumes describe about 900 unpublished tests and instruments for children through age 18.

A Sourcebook of Mental Health Measures (Comrey, Backer, & Glaser, 1973): Describes about 1,100 instruments related to mental health, including juvenile delinquency, personality, and alcoholism.

Handbook of Family Measurement Techniques (Touliatos, Perlmutter, Straus, & Holden, 2001): A three-volume set provides overviews and reviews of hundreds of instruments used to measure family variables.

Socioemotional Measures for Pre-School and Kindergarten Children: A Handbook (Walker, 1973): Describes instruments to measure attitudes, personality, self-concept, and social skills of young children.

Handbook for Measurement and Evaluation in Early Childhood Education (Goodwin & Driscoll, 1980): A comprehensive review of affective, cognitive, and psychomotor measures for young children.

Dictionary of Behavioral Assessment Techniques (Hersen & Bellack, 2002): Provides descriptions of approximately 350 instruments that assess psychological and behavioral traits.

Given the capabilities of the Internet, it is also useful to simply Google the title of an instrument. Also, ERIC has an option to limit searches to Tests/Questionnaires, which will target measures in areas you have selected. This kind of search will reveal studies that have used the instrument, as well as studies related to technical qualities.

CHAPTER SUMMARY

This chapter introduced techniques that are commonly used to collect descriptive, quantitative data. These techniques are used in basic, applied, and evaluation research and can be used in experimental or nonexperimental research. The major points in the chapter are the following:

1. Standardized tests provide uniform procedures for administration and scoring.
2. Norm-referenced test results are based on comparing a score with the scores of a reference or norming group.
3. Criterion-referenced test results compare a score with an established standard of performance.
4. Aptitude tests predict behavior.
5. Achievement tests measure current knowledge.
6. Alternative assessments, which include performance-based and portfolio assessments, provide a direct, constructed-response measure of skills.
7. Noncognitive instruments measure personality, attitudes, values, opinions, and interests.
8. Written questionnaires are economical, ensure anonymity, and permit use of standardized questions.
9. Existing questionnaires probably have better reliability and validity than those developed by a researcher.
10. Items in a questionnaire should be based on specific objectives and be clear, relevant, short, and uncluttered. Biased items and terms should be avoided.
11. Items are in a closed or open format, depending on the objectives and nature of the information desired.
12. Scaled items, such as Likert and semantic differential items, use gradations of responses.
13. Questionnaires are economical and can be anonymous.
14. Interview schedules provide flexibility and the ability to probe and clarify responses; they note nonverbal as well as verbal behavior. They provide high response rates but are costly and more susceptible to bias.
15. Interview questions are structured, semistructured, or unstructured. Each type has advantages and disadvantages.
16. Observational procedures can record naturally occurring behavior and avoid some of the disadvantages associated with questionnaires and interviews.
17. Establishing and maintaining reliability and validity in observational research is difficult.
18. Low-inference observations stress objective recording of behavior, whereas high-inference observations require greater subjective judgments of observers.
19. Recording procedures in direct observation include duration, frequency, interval, continuous, and time sampling.
20. Unobtrusive measures are nonreactive and can be used to collect data without disruption of a naturally occurring event

APPLICATION PROBLEMS

1. For each of the following cases, indicate whether the questionnaire, interview, or observation technique would be most appropriate and justify your answer.
   a. Reasons that 1,500 couples believe they have problems in their marriages
   b. The attitudes of seventh-grade students toward mainstreamed children
   c. Knowledge of parents regarding the school curriculum
   d. Average age and experience of school principals
   e. The effects of watching violent TV programs on aggressive behavior
   f. College students' perceptions of the effectiveness of residence hall advisors
   g. Attitudes of preschool children toward their parents
   h. Attitudes of teachers toward competence-based instruction

2. Indicate what is wrong with each of the following questionnaire items:
   a. What do you think about open education?
   b. Rank the statements from most important to least important.
   c. Senior and junior high school teachers need more training in ways to motivate students.

Strongly agree	Agree	Disagree	Strongly disagree
____	____	____	____

   d. Mrs. Jones is a good teacher.

Strongly agree	Agree	Disagree	Strongly disagree
____	____	____	____

3. It is important for teachers to observe and record indications that their students are studying and trying to learn assigned material. If a third-grade teacher came to you and asked how such observations could be made with the least amount of disruption to the normal routine, what suggestions would you have?

4. Construct a short questionnaire that could be used to measure college students' attitudes toward research. What type of item and item format will you use? How will you score the results? What will be a good plan for collecting evidence for validity and reliability?

ANSWER TO APPLICATION PROBLEMS

1. a. Questionnaire, to enhance confidentiality of sensitive topics and keep expenses low
   b. Observation, because self-report measures would be susceptible to social desirability
   c. Phone interview, to ensure representative responses
   d. Questionnaire, because the information is simple and easily obtained
   e. Observation, to keep the situation as natural as possible
   f. Interview, because there would be a need to probe
   g. Interview; most small children are honest and are unable to respond to questionnaires
   h. Questionnaire or interview, depending on the specificity of the information needed. An interview is useful for generating specific items that can then be used on a questionnaire.

2. a. Ambiguity of the term *open education*
   b. No information about how to rank; is 1 or 10 most important?

   c. Use of both senior and junior high school teachers creates ambiguity; should ask about either senior or junior high school teachers but not both
   d. Ambiguity permitting a respondent who thinks "she's not just good, she's great" to answer "strongly disagree"

3. a. Alternate individual work sessions and group activities, and observe during individual work sessions
   b. Teach students to observe themselves (i.e., record the time taken to complete assignments)
   c. Use unobtrusive measures, such as number of requests from students for help, pencil shavings in pencil sharpener, detail and care in assignments, and amount of eraser that is used

4. (individual student response)

Nonexperimental Research Designs, Surveys, and Secondary Data Analysis

From Chapter 10 of *Research in Education: Evidence-Based Inquiry*, 7/e. James H. McMillan. Sally Schumacher.

Nonexperimental Research Designs, Surveys, and Secondary Data Analysis

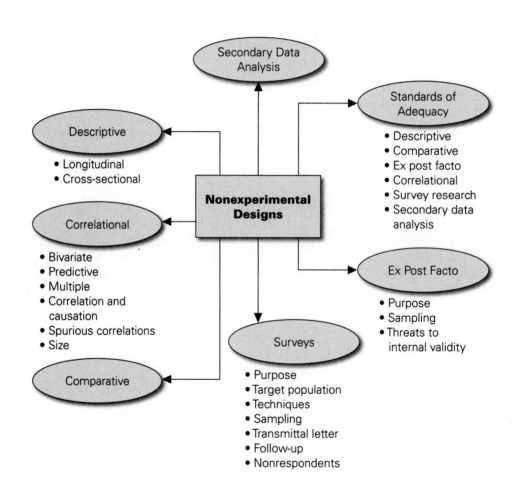

KEY TERMS

longitudinal
cross-sectional
comparative research
ex post facto research
bivariate
prediction study
predictor variable
criterion variable
bivariate regression
multiple regression
regression coefficient
beta weights

coefficient of multiple correlation
logistic regression
odds ratio
path analysis
structural equation modeling
spurious correlation
attenuation
restriction in range
coefficient of determination
survey research
secondary data
secondary data analysis

WHAT YOU WILL LEARN

Study this chapter and you will:

- Recognize research designs that are used for nonexperimental studies.
- Understand the advantages and disadvantages of longitudinal and cross-sectional designs.
- Know the design features of comparative studies.
- Know the design features of correlational studies.
- Be able to interpret correlational findings and not ascribe causation.
- Understand the effect of outliers on correlations.

- Distinguish between bivariate, prediction, and multiple regression analyses.
- Know the principles of conducting survey research.
- Know the steps in conducting survey research.
- Learn how to assure a high response rate and examine nonrespondents.
- Know the advantages and disadvantages of online survey research.
- Know what research questions and sampling are appropriate for secondary data analysis.

SIMPLE DESCRIPTIVE DESIGNS

Descriptive designs are used to summarize the current or past status of something. This type of research simply describes achievement, attitudes, behaviors, or other traits of a group of subjects. A descriptive study asks What is? or What was? It reports things the way they *are* or *were*. There is no intervention.

Simple descriptive designs provide very valuable data, particularly when first investigating an area. For example, there has been much research on the nature of classroom climate and its relationship to student attitudes and learning. A first step in this research was to describe adequately what is meant by *classroom climate*. Climate surveys—which assess characteristics such as how students talk and act toward one another, how they feel about the teacher, and feelings of openness, acceptance, trust, and respect—are used to understand the atmosphere of the classroom. Once this descriptive understanding has been achieved, various dimensions of climate can be related to student learning and teacher satisfaction, and ultimately climate can be controlled to examine causal relationships. For many teachers, simply describing the climate can be very useful in understanding the nature of the class.

Suppose you want to study the relationship between leadership styles of principals and teacher morale. Again, a first step is to describe principal leadership styles. The appropriate descriptive question might be "What are the leadership styles of principals?" Here are some additional examples of descriptive research questions:

How much do college students exercise?
What are the attitudes of students toward mainstreamed children?

How often do students cheat?

What do teachers think about merit pay?

How do students spend their time during independent study?

What are the components of the gifted program?

Excerpt 10.1, which is from a study of student bullying, illustrates the importance of simple descriptive research. Note how the authors indicate the need to develop a measure that adequately documents the dimensions of student bullying.

Excerpts 10.2 and 10.3 illustrate how results are reported for nonexperimental descriptive designs. In Excerpt 10.2 the researchers wanted to document the level of inclusion of multicultural education materials and activities in kindergarten classes. Based on a questionnaire that kindergarten teachers responded to, frequencies and percentages are reported. Excerpt 10.3 shows how researchers report descriptive results for a study on early childhood practitioners' perceptions about inclusion, for both Head Start and public prekindergarten teachers. The purpose is not, however, to compare these different groups of teachers. Rather, the researchers wanted to know if there were gaps between beliefs and practices among these groups.

Longitudinal: collecting quantitative data over time

Once a phenomenon has been described adequately, developmental, difference, and relationship questions can be addressed. **Longitudinal** studies investigate changes in participants over time. The same group or similar groups of subjects may be studied over some length of time on factors such as cognitive, social-emotional, or physical variables. For example, a longitudinal study of adult development would begin by identifying a group of adults as subjects; measure dependent variables such as interests, goal satisfaction, friendship patterns, and the like; and then continue to measure these variables for the same subjects every five years.

EXCERPT 10.1   Simple Descriptive Research

We began the exploration of bullying in schools by attempting to develop empirical indicators of student bullying. Thus, we report the results of two pilot studies. The first study maps the domain of the construct of student bullying and the second study refines the measure and meaning of bullying and examines teacher and school characteristics related to bullying. (p. 313)

Source: From Smith, P. A., & Hoy, W. K. (2004). Teachers' perceptions of student bullying: A conceptual and empirical analysis. *Journal of School Leadership, 14,* 308–324.

EXCERPT 10.2   Simple Descriptive Design Results

To get an overview on how teachers structured their classrooms, the participants in this study were asked how their classrooms were arranged and how themes were selected. Of the 477 respondents, 336 (70.4%) indicated that their classrooms were arranged in centers. Four hundred and thirteen (86.58%) had children working in small groups in centers while 240 (50.31%) had children working in small groups in centers most of the time. (pp. 4–5)

Source: Gayle-Evans, G. (2004). It is never too soon: A study of kindergarten teachers' implementation of multicultural education in Florida's classrooms. *The Professional Educator, 26*(2), 1–15.

EXCERPT 10.3   Simple Descriptive Design Results

Participants agreed with approximately half of the 16 statements about inclusive practices. For example, both groups of professionals agreed that they had the ability to arrange the classroom environment to meet all children's needs. Over 80 percent in both groups agreed that they could effectively observe children with and without disabilities to learn about their development skills and needs. (p. 233)

Source: From Bruns, D. A., & Mogharrenban, C. C. (2007). The gap between beliefs and practices: Early childhood practitioners' perceptions about inclusion. *Journal of Research in Childhood Education, 21*(3), 229–241.

EXCERPT 10.4 Trend Study Results

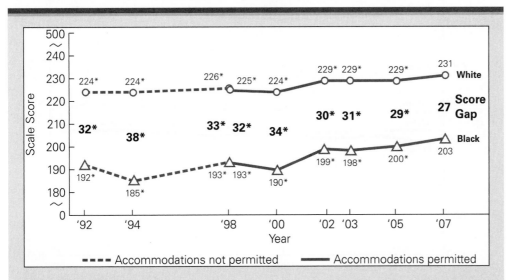

FIGURE 5 **Trend in fourth-grade NAEP reading average scores and score gaps, by selected racial/ethnic groups**

*Significantly different ($p < .05$) from 2007.
Note: Black includes African American, and Hispanic includes Latino. Race categories exclude Hispanic origin.
Score gaps are calculated based on differences between unrounded average scores.

Source: From *The Nation's Report Card* (2007). Washington, DC: U.S. Department of Education (p. 11).

There are variations of longitudinal designs, depending on the subjects who are samples or are used to make up the groups. In a *trend* study, a general population is studied over time; the subjects are sampled from the population each year or at other times of data collection. In recent years there has been much interest in trend studies that document changes in test scores for different groups of students. Each year the U.S. Department of Education publishes *The Condition of Education*. These reports are available online. They show, for example, how female and male school and college enrollment change over time. The reports effectively illustrate the trends with figures. For example, in Excerpt 10.4, differences between white and black fourth-grade students on reading are graphed with a figure that shows how the scores of each group changed from 1992 to 2007. In a *cohort* longitudinal study, the same population is studied over time, and in a *panel* study, the same individuals are surveyed each time data are collected. A good example of the procedures used in a panel longitudinal study is presented in Excerpt 10.5. The study was a panel investigation in which the same 50 teachers were interviewed over three years. In a **cross-sectional** study, different groups of subjects are studied at the same time—for example, as in our study of adult 20-, 25-, 30-, 35-, 40-, and 45-year-old groups, all of whom are surveyed in the same year.

> **Cross-sectional:** assessment of different groups at one time

An obvious advantage of a panel study is that because the same group is studied over time, comparability of subjects is assured. Another advantage is that the subjects respond to present

EXCERPT 10.5 Panel Longitudinal Study

Overall, the round of interviews that we conducted in 1999 revealed how many factors come into play as teachers consider whether to remain in teaching, and the data underscored the role of school-site conditions in teachers' ultimate career decisions. Follow-up interviews conducted during the summer of 2001 enabled us to track these new teachers' experiences and choices and to explore how they weighed various factors in deciding whether to stay in public school teaching, remain in their schools, or move to new ones. (p. 588)

Source: From Johnson, S. M., and Birkeland, S. E. (2003). Pursuing a "sense of success": New teachers explain their career decisions. *American Educational Research Journal, 40*(3), 581–617.

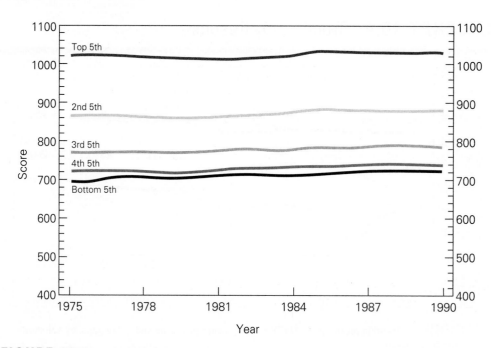

FIGURE 10.1 **Average SAT by High School Class Rank**

Source: From *Perspectives on Education in America*, 1991, Albuquerque, NM: Sandia National Laboratories. Reprinted by permission.

circumstances, attitudes, beliefs, and so on rather than trying to recollect the past. A disadvantage of trend studies is that the population of interest may change from one year to the next, which could affect the results. A good example of this is the trend analysis of SAT scores from 1975 to 1990. Although it is true that the average SAT score for all students taking the test declined, this decline was more a function of who took the test than the performance of the students. As illustrated in Figures 10.1 and 10.2, the so-called decline was really caused by more students who were less able taking the test. The actual finding, when SAT scores were analyzed for different levels of high school performers, was that the scores remained relatively stable; they clearly did not show a decline.

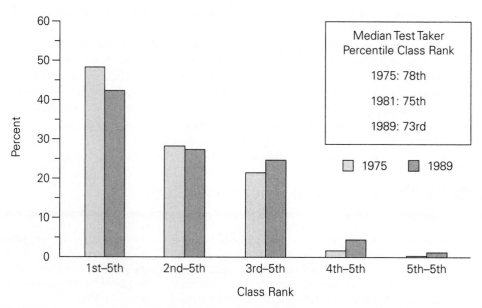

FIGURE 10.2 **Percentage of Students Taking SAT by Class Rank**

Source: From *Perspectives on Education in America*, 1991, Albuquerque, NM: Sandia National Laboratories. Reprinted by permission.

238

Major disadvantages of longitudinal research are that it takes a long time to complete and that it involves significant commitments of the researcher's time, money, and resources. It is also difficult to keep track of subjects and maintain their cooperation for an extended period. Researchers involved in cross-sectional studies can study larger groups at less cost, all at the same time. Thus, they do not need to wait years to complete the research. The major disadvantage of cross-sectional research is that selection differences between the groups may bias the results.

In conducting descriptive research, it is important to pay close attention to the nature of the subjects and the instruments. You should know, for example, whether the sample is made up of volunteers and whether results could have been different if other subjects had been included. Data collection techniques need to address reliability and validity, and procedures for collection information should be specified. You need to indicate when the data were collected, by whom, and under what circumstances. For example, the description of a classroom may well differ, depending on whether the observer is a teacher, parent, or principal.

A WORD ABOUT *RELATIONSHIPS* IN NONEXPERIMENTAL RESEARCH

Before examining comparative and correlational designs, the nature of "relationships" among variables needs clarification. All quantitative research that is not simply descriptive is interested in *relationships*. A relationship, or association, is found when one variable varies systematically with another variable. This can be accomplished either by comparing different groups or with correlations.

A relationship established by comparing different groups is illustrated in Figure 10.3, where the variables of interest are grade level and self-concept. There is a relationship between grade level and self-concept because there are progressively fewer students with a high self-concept as grade level increases. In this case, the relationship is negative, because as grade level increases, the number of high-self-concept students decreases. This same research question could be examined by computing a correlation coefficient between grade level and self-concept scores.

Relationships are important in our understanding of teaching and learning for several reasons. First, relationships allow us to make a preliminary identification of possible causes of important

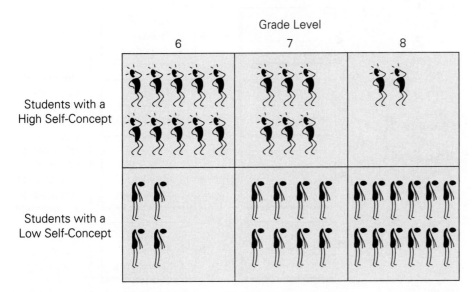

FIGURE 10.3 Relationship between Grade Level and Self-Concept

Source: From McMillan, James H., *Educational Research: Fundamentals for the Consumer, 5th ed.* Published by Allyn and Bacon/Merrill Education, Boston, MA. Copyright © 2008 by Pearson Education. Reprinted by permission of the publisher.

educational outcomes. Second, relationships help us identify variables that need further investigation. Third, relationships allow us to predict one variable from another. As we will see later in this chapter, prediction is needed for a variety of purposes.

COMPARATIVE DESIGNS

Comparative research:
investigates differences
between groups

The purpose of comparative studies is to investigate the relationship of one variable to another by examining whether the value of the dependent variable in one group is different from the value of the dependent variable in the other group. In other words, **comparative research** examines the differences between two or more groups on a variable. Here are some examples of difference questions:

Is there a difference between eighth-grade and ninth-grade attitudes toward school?
What are the differences between students attending private schools and students attending public schools?
How are new teachers different from experienced teachers?
Is there a difference between second-, third-, and fourth-grade self-concept scores?

In each case, the researcher makes a comparison based on descriptive data.

A simple example of comparative research is a study of the relationship between gender and school grades. A sample of female students' grades could be compared to the grades of a sample of male students. The results would show how differences in one variable, gender, relate to differences on another variable, grades. If the results showed that females have a higher grade-point average (not surprising!), this would indicate that there is a relationship between the two variables. Note, however, that this would not be a *causal* relationship. Although we can predict grades by knowing gender, we do not know why being male or female affects grades.

Another example is a study of the relationship between race/ethnicity and achievement. Suppose there are four race/ethnicity categories and a measure of reading achievement. A sample of students representing each group can be obtained, and the average reading score for each group can be compared. If we find that some group is associated with higher reading achievement, then there is a relationship, although, as in the example of gender and grades, it cannot be concluded that race/ethnicity caused the achievement. This hypothetical study is diagramed in Figure 10.4.

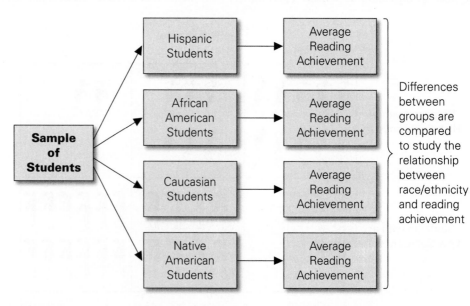

FIGURE 10.4 **Diagram of a Relationship Study Comparing Different Groups**

Source: From McMillan, James H., *Educational Research: Fundamentals for the Consumer, 5th ed.* Published by Allyn and Bacon/Merrill Education, Boston, MA. Copyright © 2008 by Pearson Education. Reprinted by permission of the publisher.

EXCERPT 10.6   Comparative Research Design

[The table] highlights the significant differences in self-reported cheating behaviour. . . . A larger share of the Russian students reported cheating at some point. While 55% of the American students reported they had cheated at some point during college, 64% of the Russian students reported having cheated. Russian students also were much more likely to report cheating in the class in which the data were collected. In fact, only 2.9% of the American students acknowledged cheating in the class where the data were collected, whereas 38.1% of the Russian students admitted to cheating in the class. (p. 21)

Source: From Lupton, R. A., & Chapman, K. J. (2002). Russian and American college students' attitudes, perceptions, and tendencies towards cheating. *Educational Research, 44,* 17–27.

A good example of a published study that uses comparisons is an investigation that examined differences between American and Russian business college students' attitudes, perceptions, and tendencies toward cheating (see Excerpt 10.6). A single independent variable, student nationality, had two levels, and there were several dependent variables. This is very typical of comparison studies. Samples of students from each country were given scenarios about different aspects of cheating and the percentages of possible responses were compared. For example, 68.5 percent of American students responded "yes" to the question "Have you given a student in a later section information about an exam?", whereas 91.9 percent of Russian students responded "yes" to the same question. (*Note:* As you might surmise, selecting the samples from each country was critical to the credibility of this study.)

Excerpt 10.7 is from the study about teachers' perceptions of student bullying that compared male to female teachers. In Excerpt 10.8 the authors summarize the comparisons that were calculated based on the number of part-time hours of working high school students (independent variable of "work intensity," with four levels). These comparisons were made for several dependent variables, including educational aspirations and engagement in school. Note that the researchers decided to use a certain number of hours worked to define the different levels of intensity. Another researcher might come up with a different operationalized independent variable. Also note the title of the study, which uses the word *effects*. Many studies of this kind may be based on the logic of "what is the effect of . . . ?" but this is nonexperimental, and causal

EXCERPT 10.7   Comparative Research Design

Do male and female teachers perceive bullying differently? To begin to answer this question, we compared the mean scores of men and women teachers on our measures of bullying. There were no significant differences between men ($n = 40$) and women ($n = 53$) on the two measures. For student bullying, men had a mean of 3.36 and women 3.59 ($t = -.15$, ns) and for teacher protection, men had a mean of 3.62 and women 3.79 ($t = -.76$, ns). (p. 318)

Source: From Smith, P. A., & Hoy, W. K. (2004). Teachers' perceptions of student bullying: A conceptual and empirical analysis. *Journal of School Leadership, 14,* 308–324.

EXCERPT 10.8   Comparative Research Design

To further understand the differences in school factors on the basis of work intensity, we divided working students into four categories according to the number of hours worked per week: (a) less than or equal to 10 hr (low work intensity), (b) between 11 to 20 hr (moderate work intensity), (c) between 21 to 30 hr (high work intensity), and over 31 hr (very high work intensity). . . . There were significant differences among students who worked different numbers of hours. . . . For example, students who worked less than 10 hours had significantly higher educational aspirations than did the high intensity and very high intensity groups ($M = 4.24$ versus 4.04 and 3.96, respectively). (p. 17)

Source: From Kusum, S., Chang, M., & Dika, S. (2007). Effects of part-time work on school achievement during high school. *The Journal of Educational Research, 101*(1), 12–23.

conclusions, like "effect," can only be made with caution. In this case, there may be other reasons that students in these four categories report different aspirations and engagement.

There is one type of comparative design that is structured to allow tentative causal conclusions, despite its inability to actively control the intervention. This design is often called *ex post facto*, or *causal-comparative*. In these studies, the purpose of the research is to examine how an identified independent variable affects the dependent variable, but the circumstances in which the research is conducted do not allow an experimental design. Consider the following list of research questions. In each case, the implied cause-and-effect relationship rules out experimental manipulation of the independent variable:

> What is the effect of attendance at day-care facilities on the social skills of children?
> What is the effect of single parenting on achievement?
> Do teachers who graduate from liberal arts colleges have greater longevity in the teaching field than teachers who graduate from colleges of education?
> What is the relationship between children's participation in extracurricular activities and self-concept?

It is simply impossible, unethical, and infeasible to manipulate variables such as single or couple parenting, day-care attendance, and choice of college by students, as well as many other variables such as race, socioeconomic status, and personality. A researcher would probably have some difficulty assigning children on a random basis to either attend or not attend day care! Although it is desirable to study cause-and-effect relationships in such situations, the circumstances of the research are such that manipulation of the independent variable cannot be carried out.

Ex post facto research: comparative study of previously implemented interventions

The purpose of **ex post facto research** is to investigate whether one or more pre-existing conditions have possibly caused subsequent differences in the groups of subjects. In other words, the researcher identifies conditions that have already occurred (*ex post facto* is Latin for "after the fact") and then collects data to investigate the relationship of these varying conditions to subsequent behavior. In ex post facto research, the investigator attempts to determine whether differences between groups (the independent variable) have resulted in an observed difference on the dependent variable.

Ex post facto designs are easily confused with experimental designs because they both have a similar purpose (to determine cause-effect relationships), group comparisons, and the use of similar statistical analyses and vocabulary in describing the results. In experimental and quasi-experimental studies, however, the researcher deliberately controls the effect of some condition by manipulation of the independent variable, whereas in ex post facto research, there is no manipulation of conditions because the presumed cause has already occurred before the study is initiated. In ex post facto designs, therefore, there is usually an *intervention* group and a *control* group—a factor that can further confuse the research with experimental approaches. Ex post facto designs are also confused with comparative and correlational research, because all three involve no manipulation and there are similar limitations in interpreting the results.

Several procedures are used in planning ex post facto research that limit plausible rival hypotheses. The first step is to formulate a research problem that includes possible causes of the dependent variable. The choice of possible causes is based on previous research and on the researcher's interpretation of observations of the phenomena being studied. Suppose, for example, the researcher wants to investigate the effect of class size on achievement, and it is impossible to assign students randomly to classes of different sizes to conduct a true experiment. The researcher's interest may be based on correlational research that shows a negative relationship between class size and achievement and observations that students in smaller classes seem to do better. The research problem, then, is this: What is the effect of class size on achievement?

A second step is to identify plausible rival hypotheses that might explain the relationship. For instance, the researcher might list as possible causes of better achievement in smaller classes several factors such as the following: smaller classes have better teachers; students with higher ability are in smaller classes; students with stronger motivation are in smaller classes; more students from high socioeconomic backgrounds attend smaller classes than do students from low socioeconomic backgrounds; and perhaps teachers of smaller classes use a different type of instruction than those of larger classes use. Each of these factors might be related to the reason students in smaller classes achieve more than students in larger classes.

The third step is to find and select the groups that will be compared. In our example of class size and achievement, the researcher will first need to define operationally *large* and *small* class size as well as *achievement*. A *small* class could have fewer than 15 students and a *large* class more than 25. *Achievement* could be defined as the gain in knowledge of the students while in the class. The researcher also needs to identify grade levels and locations. Suppose, in this case, the researcher is interested in elementary grade levels and the accessible population is a single school district. Once the variables have been defined, groups must be selected that are as homogeneous as possible in the characteristics that constitute rival hypotheses and that are different with respect to the independent variable. In our example, then, the researcher will select groups that differ with respect to class size but that are similar in such factors as ability, socioeconomic background, teaching methods, quality of teachers, and student motivation. Matching is a good approach to forming groups that will be as homogeneous as possible in factors affecting the dependent variable. In our example of class size, the researcher could match and select students on the basis of initial ability so that only students with about the same level of ability are included in the analysis, even though other students would be contained in the classes.

The fourth step is to collect and analyze data on the subjects, including data on factors that may constitute rival hypotheses. Data analysis is very similar to procedures used for experimental and quasi-experimental studies in that groups are compared on the variables of interest. In our proposed study of class size, for example, all achievement scores in the small classes would be averaged and compared with the average achievement scores in large classes. Data from the extraneous variables would also be compared and incorporated into the statistical analyses to help make judgments about plausible rival hypotheses.

In interpreting the results of ex post facto research, cause-and-effect statements must be made cautiously. In our example of large and small classes, if a difference in achievement is found between the groups, then the researcher can conclude that there is a relationship between class size and achievement. The results do not mean, unequivocally, that being in either a small or large class had a causative effect on achievement. There may be a cause-and-effect relationship, but this depends on the researcher's ability to select comparison groups homogeneous on all important variables except being in small or large classes and on the confidence with which other plausible rival hypotheses can be ruled out. If, for example, it turned out that all the small classes came from one school and all the large classes from another, then policies or procedures unique to the schools and unrelated to class size (e.g., stress on basic skill attainment or a special training program for teachers) may constitute plausible rival hypotheses.

Like descriptive studies, comparative research needs to provide a clear description of subjects, instrumentation, and procedures. Also, as in descriptive research, causal conclusions can only be made in rare circumstances. The best that can be concluded is that there is a difference or relationship. This principle is easily overlooked because some comparative studies seem to logically establish a causal connection between the independent and dependent variables. For example, suppose it is reported that students from private charter schools outperform students from public schools. It is tempting to conclude that the reason, or cause, of the difference is the nature of the school. However, there are many other possible explanations, such as differences in parental involvement or in the socioeconomic status of the students.

Often, comparative research results are presented in graphs. Sometimes a visual image does not match well with the actual data. When interpreting such graphs, be sure to examine the actual numbers or scales on which the graph is based and be alert to distortions.

CORRELATIONAL DESIGNS

You should already be familiar with the correlation coefficient. This chapter uses the basic idea of correlation as a way to conceptualize research problems and report results. Simple relationship studies are presented first, then more complex multifactor prediction and explanatory research, and finally cautions in interpreting correlations.

Bivariate Correlational Studies

Bivariate: two variables

In a bivariate correlational study, researchers obtain scores from two variables for each subject and then use the pairs of scores to calculate a correlation coefficient. The term **bivariate** or *zero-order* means that two variables are correlated. The variables are selected because theory, research, or experience suggests that they may be related. Then a sample is selected and data are collected from the sample.

It is important in correlational studies that researchers select the subjects to provide a range of responses on the variables. If the subjects are homogeneous with respect to either variable, a relationship between the variables is unlikely. Similarly, it is important to select instruments that are reliable and will provide a range of responses. Various instruments can be used, including tests, questionnaires, interviews, and observations. Regardless of the type of instrument, it is best to conduct a pilot test or have previous data from similar subjects to ensure reliability and variability in responses. For instance, it is often difficult to relate student ratings of professors to other variables because of a ceiling effect in such ratings, which results in most professors being highly rated. Similarly, norm-referenced achievement scores of gifted students are unlikely to correlate with other variables because the scores may have a restricted range. (We will discuss restricted range in more detail later in the chapter.)

In some relationship studies, bivariate correlations of several variables may be reported. In fact, an advantage of correlational research is that it permits the simultaneous study of several variables. However, it is possible for some researchers, without reasonable justification, to measure a large number of variables to find some significant relationships. This is called the *shotgun* approach, and it is used inappropriately in the hope that some of the many correlations calculated will indicate significant relationships.

An example of how the results from a bivariate correlational study are presented is illustrated in Excerpt 10.9. In this study, bivariate correlations were calculated to explore relationships between adolescents' and mothers' attitudes toward science, intrinsic value of science, peer support, available science activities, grades, science grade-point average, and preference for future science careers.

Prediction Studies

There are many situations in education in which we need to make predictions. Teachers predict student reactions in making certain assignments. Principals predict teacher behavior on the basis of the criteria used for evaluation of teacher effectiveness. Teachers counsel students to focus on particular majors on the basis of occupational interest or aptitude test results. Students are selected for special programs because teachers predict that they will do better than other students.

Prediction study: using one or more variables to indicate what will occur

We conduct a **prediction study** to provide a more accurate estimation of what is likely to occur. Suppose you are the director of admissions at a small, selective college. A large number of students apply to the college each year, many more than can be admitted. How will you decide which students will be admitted? You could draw names from a hat randomly, but then some students will be admitted who may flunk out, while some well-qualified students will be rejected. You decide that it would be best if you could *predict,* on the basis of already established characteristics, which students are most likely to succeed. Because it seems reasonable that prior achievement will predict later achievement, you see whether there is a correlation between high school grade-point average (GPA) (prior achievement) and college GPA (later achievement). When you discover that these two variables correlate .70, you have information that can be used to select students. Other things being equal, high school students with high GPAs are more likely to have high college GPAs than high school students with low GPAs.

Predictor variable: comes before the outcome

Criterion variable: is determined by the predictor variable

In this case, high school GPA is a **predictor variable** and college GPA is a **criterion variable**. The predictor variable is determined *before* the criterion variable. Thus, in prediction studies, outcomes such as GPA, dropping out, success as a leader or manager, effectiveness of a drug to cure a disease, and the like are related to behaviors that occurred prior to the criterion. To make this prediction, it is necessary to have data on the subjects that span some length of time. This can be done retrospectively through records on subjects, or it can be done longitudinally by first collecting predictor variable data, waiting an appropriate amount of time, and then collecting the criterion variable data.

EXCERPT 10.9 Presentation of Bivariate Correlation Results

Zero-Order Correlations between Perceived Motivational Context Variables and Indexes of Alienation

Independent Variables	1	2	3	4	5	6	7	8	9
1. Science GPA	1.0								
2. Grade in school	.02	1.0							
3. Friends' support	.16	.05	1.0						
4. Number of science/math activities	.21*	−.15	.20*	1.0					
5. Number of nonscience activities	.21*	.02	.08	.23**	1.0				
6. Mothers' perceptions of child's science ability	.56**	−.05	.10	.17*	.07	1.0			
7. Mothers' valuing of science for females	.13	−.01	.09	.19*	.03	.30**	1.0		
8. Adolescents' interest in biology	.28**	.02	.19*	.36**	.14	.29**	.16	1.0	
9. Adolescents' interest in physical science	.29**	.08	.08	.29**	.23**	.39**	−.24**	.47**	.10

*$p < .05$. **$p < .01$.

Source: From Jacobs, J. E., Finken, L. L., Griffin, N. L., & Wright, J. D. (1998). The career plans of science-talented rural adolescent girls. *American Educational Research Journal, 35*(4), 681–704. Copyright © 1998 by the American Educational Research Association. Reproduced with permission of the publisher.

For example, suppose you need to select the best new teachers for a school division. Essentially, you are predicting that the new teachers you choose will be effective. In your state, all prospective teachers take the Teacher Examinations (TE), so you are able to study the predictive relationship of the TE to teacher effectiveness (measured by principal and supervisor evaluations). Once you have established the predictive power of the TE with one group of teachers, you would test the predictive relationship with another group of new teachers. In testing the prediction, the researcher uses the values of the predictor variables from a new group of prospective teachers—in this example, scores on the TE— and then weights each score by a factor calculated from the original prediction equation. This will indicate how well the researcher can expect the TE to predict teacher effectiveness. The tested relationship will be lower than the one originally used to establish a prediction equation.

When researchers make predictions based on two variables, the statistical procedure that they use is called **bivariate regression**. Bivariate regression is similar to *bivariate correlation* in that both are used with two variables in the analysis. Whereas a simple correlation describes the relationship between variables, a regression determines how well scores from the independent variable predict scores on the dependent variable. Unlike simple correlation, bivariate regression establishes a regression equation that can be used to make predictions.

Excerpt 10.10 is an example of predictive research using high school dropout as the criterion variable. In this study, the extent of students' leisure boredom is used to predict whether students would drop out.

Bivariate regression: use of one predictor and one criterion variable

EXCERPT 10.10 Predictive Research

This prospective cohort study investigated whether leisure boredom predicts high school dropout. . . . The original cohort of grade 8 students ($n = 303$) was followed up twice at 2-year intervals. Of the 281 students at the second follow up, 149 (53.0%) students had dropped out of school. . . . Leisure boredom was a significant predictor of dropout. (p. 421)

Source: From Wegner, L., Flisher, A. J., Chikobvu, P., Lombard, C., & King, G. (2008). Leisure boredom and high school dropout in Cape Town, South Africa. *Journal of Adolescence, 31*(3), 421–431.

Multiple regression: use of two or more predictor variables

It may occur to you that by having several predictor variables, you would be able to make a more accurate prediction. Suppose that in our example of predicting effective teaching, we also had information such as college GPA, references, results of an interview, and a statement by each applicant in addition to the TE scores. Each subject would receive a score for each variable. (The references, results of the interview, and statement would be judged and scored according to a rating system.) All of the predictor variables could be combined to form what is called a **multiple regression** prediction equation. This equation adds together the predictive power of several independent variables. Each predictor variable could be represented by X_1, X_2, X_3, and so on, and the criterion variable by Y. Thus, in our example:

$$Y = X_1 + X_2 + X_3 + X_4 + X_5$$

where Y = teaching effectiveness
X_1 = TE score
X_2 = college GPA
X_3 = rating on references
X_4 = rating on interview
X_5 = rating on applicant's statement

Regression coefficient: multiplier for a predictor variable

To obtain a predicted teacher effectiveness score, values on each of the five predictor variables would be placed in the equation and each would be weighted by a number, called a **regression coefficient**, to determine the contribution of each factor to predicting teacher effectiveness. Because the units of each predictor variable are different (i.e., ratings might range from 0 to 10, GPA from 0 to 4), the regression coefficients in the equation cannot be compared directly. To compare the predictive power of the variables, the regression coefficients are converted to **beta weights**, which can be compared directly. Thus, in our example, the relative contribution of each variable can be compared. If the beta weight for TE is .32 and the beta weight for GPA is .48, then GPA is contributing more than TE in predicting teaching effectiveness. The combined effect of the independent variables, in terms of predictive power, to the dependent variable is represented by R, the coefficient of multiple correlation. The **coefficient of multiple correlation** can be thought of as a simple correlation of all the independent variables together with the dependent variable.

Beta weights: standardized multipliers for a predictor variable

Coefficient of multiple correlation: correlation of all independent variables together with the dependent variable

When planning a predictive study, the researcher should keep in mind several factors that will affect the accuracy of the prediction. One is the reliability of the measurement of the predictor and criterion variables. More reliable measures will result in more accurate predictions. Another factor is the length of time between the predictor and criterion variables. In most cases, predictions involving short time spans (e.g., weeks or months) are more accurate than those in which there is a long time between the predictor and criterion variables (e.g., years). This is because of the general principle that the correlation between two variables decreases as the amount of time between them increases; also, with more time, there is more opportunity for other variables to affect the criterion variable, which would lower the prediction. Finally, some criterion variables, such as success in college, leadership, and effective teaching, are more difficult to predict because they are influenced by so many factors. Relatively simple criterion variables, such as success on the next mathematics test and being admitted to at least one college, are much less difficult to predict.

Explanatory Studies

Multiple regression is a versatile data analysis procedure that is used for many different kinds of studies, not just prediction research. It can be used with comparative and even experimental studies and with variables that are nominal, ordinal, or interval in nature. Regression is often used to explain *why* subjects have different scores on the dependent variable. For example, if you were interested in what variables explain why students differ in their level of motivation to learn science, several independent variables—such as past success in science, parental support and involvement, motivation of peers, and self-efficacy—could be used in a regression for explanation. However, it is important in such studies to differentiate between *why* and *what caused* something. Regressions are excellent for explaining, but causal conclusions may not be warranted. For example, showing that parental support and involvement explains some of a student's motivation does not necessarily mean that this support actually caused the motivation. At the same time, parental support may indeed be causally linked to motivation. It's just that other variables, some not included in the design, may be the actual causal agents.

One of the most useful features of multiple regression is that it allows researchers to "control" for selected variables to determine the relationship between the remaining independent variables and the dependent variable. For example, if a study is investigating the relationship between class size and achievement, a measure of socioeconomic status could be entered first in the regression so that it is controlled, allowing a conclusion about the relationship without having to worry about socioeconomic status being confounded with class size (e.g., smaller classes have higher-socioeconomic-status students). It is as if variability in achievement due to socioeconomic status is removed, allowing the remaining variability in achievement to be related to class size.

The next three excerpts, 10.11, 10.12, and 10.13, illustrate the use of multiple regression analyses. In Excerpt 10.11 you will recognize the study on part-time work in high school. This part of the study used multiple regression to determine the predictive power of part-time work "controlling" for other variables, such as, in this case, family background. The excerpt shows that variables were "added" to examine changes in how much variability is accounted for in the relationship between the independent variables and grades. This is common language used to gauge the impact of the control variables. As long as a control variable makes a significant contribution, it is kept in the overall equation. Here the intent is to provide an explanation of the impact of part-time work on grades, with other variables being controlled or accounted for. This procedure is helpful in pinpointing explanatory factors, but it still uses correlational data and

EXCERPT 10.11 Use of Multiple Regression to "Control" Variables

The most important question that we addressed is the effect of part-time work on school achievement. . . . we regressed students' self-reported grades on family background variables. Parents' education, educational aspirations and mother's and father's educational occupations together explained 20.8% of the variance. . . . Second, we added educational aspirations of the student to the model. The beta = .319, and the addition of educational aspirations resulted in a significant change in R. . . . Controlling for all prior factors, working part-time had a significant negative effect. (p. 18)

Source: From Kusum, S., Chang, M., & Dika, S. (2007). Effects of part-time work on school achievement during high school. *The Journal of Educational Research, 101*(1), 12–23.

EXCERPT 10.12 Explanatory Use of Multiple Regression

The second research question asked, "What are the educator or programmatic characteristics that are significantly associated with the promotion of language and literacy activities in early childhood centers?" To arrive at an answer to this question seven independent variables were entered into a multiple regression equation, including the early childhood educator's race/ethnicity, years of experience in the profession, literacy training received, . . . perceptions of literacy training adequacy . . . [and] number of children cared for by the educator and the availability of print materials at the center. . . . The following variables were found to significantly influence early childhood educators' efforts to promote language and literacy activities in their centers: availability of children's books and other print material (beta = .52), perceived adequacy of basic literacy skills training (beta = .36), and the number of children cared for by the early childhood educator (beta = .17).

Source: From Green, S. D., Peterson, R., & Lewis, J. R. (2006). Language and literacy promotion in early childhood settings: A survey of center-based practices. *Early Childhood Research & Practice, 8*(1). Retrieved August 22, 2008, from http://ecrp.uiuc.edu/v8n1/green.html.

EXCERPT 10.13 Multiple Regression

We performed regression analyses using hierarchical entry of independent variables to test a sequence of hypotheses about the factors influencing reading engagement, attitude, and learning. . . . The three independent variables were entered in separate steps to test their relative contributions in accounting for the outcome measures. At Step 1, topic interest was entered. At Step 2, situational interest was entered. Finally, at Step 3, choice was added to the equation to determine whether it made any additional contribution to prediction of the outcome over and above the effects of the two interest measures. (p.101)

Source: From Flowerday, T, Schraw, G., & Stevens, J. (2004). The role of choice and interest in reader engagement. *Journal of Experimental Education, 72*(2), 93–114.

the measures used are typically imperfect, so saying that something is controlled is not exactly correct because it is not as if it has no influence or is no longer a concern. *Adjusted for* is a better way to phrase this aspect of multiple regression.

In Excerpt 10.12, multiple regression is used to investigate the extent to which "educator or programmatic characteristics . . . are . . . associated with the promotion of language and literacy activities in early childhood centers." Note the different beta weights reported. These suggest that the most important determinant of promotion activities is the availability of reading materials, and that this was much more important than the number of children cared for.

In Excerpt 10.13, regression is used to assess the relative contributions of variables that are entered sequentially to predict engagement in reading.

Logistic Regression

Logistic regression: predicts a dichotomous criterion

A procedure called **logistic regression** is becoming more and more prevalent in educational research. Like other types of regression, it involves one dependent variable, and typically two or more independent variables. In contrast to bivariate and multiple regression, in logistic regression, the dependent variable is dichotomous. For example, logistic regression could be used to predict whether a student drops out of high school or passes or fails a test. A unique aspect of logistic regression is in the nature of the findings. Central to reporting results is the concept of **odds ratios.** The odds ratio allows the researcher to show for each independent variable the probability that it will be related to determining the difference in the dependent variable. Suppose you are studying high school dropouts and find that the number of failing grades is related to whether a student does or does not drop out. The results would allow you to conclude something like "Students who fail three classes are twice as likely to drop out as students who do not fail any classes." Language such as "half as likely," "five times more likely," and "less likely" is used, which is more easily interpreted by many in comparison to other statistical findings. Odds ratios are calculated for each independent variable.

Odds ratio: likelihood of occurrence

Excerpt 10.14 shows how logistic regression results are reported. In this study, the dependent variable was high or low participation in sports in young adulthood.

EXCERPT 10.14 Logistic Regression

The first logistic regression model examined sports participation in young adulthood as the dependent variable with the following independent variables: gender, sports participation in childhood, family structure, parental education, young adult education level, young adult SES, young adult marital status, young adult parental status, and sports participation in adolescence. Gender and sports participation in adolescence were found to be significant predictors of sports participation in young adulthood. . . . According to the odds ratio, men have twice the odds of participating in sports as young adults than women. . . . Those who participated in a medium amount of sports as adolescents are 3.67 times more likely to participate in sports as young adults than those who rated their adolescent sports participation low. (pp. 508–509)

Source: From Perkins, D. F., Jacobs, J. J., Barber, B. L., & Eccles, J. (2004). Childhood and adolescent sports participation as predictors of participation in sports and physical fitness activities during young adulthood. *Youth and Society, 35*(4), 495–520.

EXCERPT 10.15 Use of LISREL Structural Equation Modeling

I formulate a LISREL model to gauge the ultimate impact of college racial composition on blacks' self-esteem and self-efficacy. The model assumes that the racial makeup of colleges potentially influences post-college self-esteem and efficacy both directly and indirectly. College racial composi-tion in turn is deemed a correlate of institutional selectivity and a likely function of attributes of the individual's background and personality. These attributes include socioeconomic background, standardized test performance, quality of the high school, and pre-college attitudes toward self. (p. 19)

Source: From St. Oates, G. L. (2004). The color of the undergraduate experience and the black self-concept: Evidence from longitudinal data. *Social Psychology Quarterly, 67*(1), 16–32.

Although the vast majority of correlational research is concerned only with relationships, some statistical techniques use multiple correlations to investigate cause-and-effect questions. One technique, **path analysis**, uses the correlations of several variables to study causal patterns. A causal model is established, based on theory, which shows by arrows the cause sequences that are anticipated. The correlations between the variables in the model provide empirical evidence of the proposed causal links.

Path analysis: pattern of corre-lations

A relatively new technique that investigates relationships among many variables is called **structural equation modeling** (SEM). SEM is a powerful and increasingly popular analysis that suggests causal effects from the nature of relationships obtained that test a theoretical model. Typically, a factor called a *latent trait* or *latent variable* is used. The latent trait results from com-bining multiple measures, which enhances reliability. One extensively used SEM procedure is called LISREL. Excerpt 10.15 uses LISREL in a study of the impact of institutional racial com-position on African American students' self-concept by first controlling for various precollege attributes and institutional selectivity.

Structural equation modeling: specified pattern of correlations

Although these techniques are useful for examining causal relationships, they are sophisti-cated statistically and are difficult to use. Also, they have the same fundamental limitations as all correlational data. Unmeasured variables related to both the independent and dependent vari-ables are always a source of potential alternative causal explanations, and the direction is not always clear.

Interpreting Correlational Research

Correlation coefficients are widely used in research and appear to be simple, straightforward indices of relationship. There are, however, several limitations with the use of correlation that need to be understood fully. Most concern an overinterpretation—making too much of a meas-ured relationship. In this section, we present some important principles that will help you under-stand the meaning of results of correlational research.

Correlation and Causation   You may be familiar with the well-known injunction "Never infer causation from correlation." This principle is virtually drilled into the minds of students, and for good reason, because it is probably the most frequently violated principle of measures of relationship.

There are two reasons correlation does not infer causation: First, a relationship between X and Y may be high, but there is no way to know whether X causes Y or Y causes X; and second, there may be unmeasured variables that are affecting the relationship. With respect to the direc-tion of possible causation, consider this example: A researcher finds a high positive correlation between self-concept and achievement. Does this mean that improving self-concept will cause an improvement in achievement? Perhaps, but it would be equally plausible for improved achieve-ment to result in a higher self-concept. If we find that school dropout rates are negatively asso-ciated with teacher salaries, should we assume that higher teacher pay will cause fewer dropouts?

Unaccounted-for variables are also important to consider in interpreting correlations. Let us say that there is a positive relationship between attending church-related schools and hon-esty. Although the schools may help cause greater honesty, there are many other variables, such as family beliefs, parental attitudes, and methods of discipline, that would be more plausibly related in a causal way. Or what about the finding that schools that spend more per pupil have higher achievement? It would be a mistake to pump money into poor schools with the expectation that this will cause better achievement, because family background, an unmeasured variable, would more likely be a much larger factor in achievement than per pupil expenditure.

These two limitations seem straightforward enough, but correlations are still misinterpreted. Consider the *fact* that there is a strong positive relationship between body weight and reading achievement. Unbelievable? Examine the explanation that follows (adapted from Halperin, 1976).

1. Plot the body weight and scores of a group of first-graders.

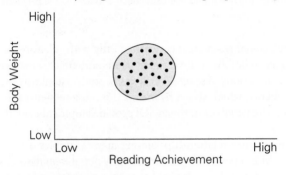

2. Next, add the scores of second-graders.

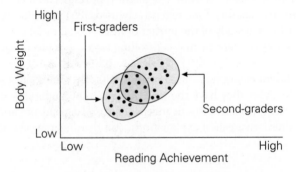

3. Finally, add the scores of pupils in grades 3 through 6.

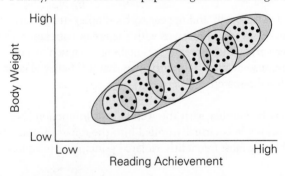

Voila! We have now demonstrated a positive relationship between body weight and reading achievement by stringing together a series of near-zero correlations. Why? Because a third variable that was not included, age, happens to be related to body weight, and obviously, there is a positive relationship between age and reading achievement. If the reader believes that correlation did mean causation, then reading achievement could be improved by fattening up students! (Or improving reading achievement would lead to fatter students.)

Spurious Correlations   When a correlation overrepresents or underrepresents the actual relationship, it is called a **spurious correlation**. Spurious correlations that overestimate relationships are obtained if there is a common variable that is part of both the independent and the dependent variables. For example, if a researcher has pretest and posttest data and measures the

Spurious correlation: higher or lower than the actual relationship

relationship between posttest scores and the gain scores from pretest to posttest, the correlation would be spuriously high because the posttest score would be included in both variables. Obviously, when something is correlated with itself, the relationship will be very high! Similarly, if there were a third unmeasured variable that is common to both variables, as with our example of reading achievement and body weight, the correlation would be spuriously high. Such a result would occur when height is correlated with weight, because a third factor, age, would be common to both.

Correlations obtained from two measures that are imperfectly reliable will result in coefficients lower than the true relationship between the measures. This lowering of the coefficient is referred to as **attenuation**, and occasionally, researchers will compute a correction for attenuation to estimate what the correlation might have been if the measures were more reliable. A researcher will use this correlation most commonly with pilot studies in which the measures used have low reliability.

Attenuation: lowering of the correlation coefficient

Another situation in which the correlation coefficient is lower than the actual relationship is one in which the range of scores on one of the variables is confined to a representation of only part of the total distribution of that variable. This problem is called **restriction in range**, and it results in a lowering of the correlation. Suppose, for example, that a researcher wants to investigate the relationship between aptitude test scores and achievement of students in a program for the gifted. Figure 10.5 shows why the researcher would probably find only a small positive relationship between these two variables. Note that the figure illustrates the hypothetical aptitude and achievement scores for all students (A and B), along with the sample of students in the gifted program (B).

Restriction in range: little variability of scores

In this case, the range of aptitude scores is thus limited or restricted to a small part of the total range of aptitude scores. If the full range of scores is utilized, then the correlation is highly positive. Restriction in range explains in part the usually modest relationship between college admissions tests and achievement in college: The range is restricted to students who have high test scores on the admissions tests. Under certain conditions, a correction for restriction in range can be applied in these cases in order to indicate what the correlation might have been if a large sample had been available.

Another situation that can lead to spurious correlations is one in which the sampling procedures result in a more heterogeneous or more homogeneous sample than is actually present in the population. This sampling bias would lead to either a high spurious correlation, if the sample were more heterogeneous, or a low spurious correlation, if the sample were more homogeneous. For example, if a researcher investigating the relationship between effective teaching behavior and student achievement for all students oversampled high achievers, resulting in a more homogeneous group than the population, the correlation would be spuriously low. If, however, the population had mostly gifted students but the procedures undersampled these gifted students, then the correlation would be spuriously high.

Finally, spurious correlations may be reported if outlier data are included in the calculations. Figure 10.6 shows two scatterplots to illustrate the effect an outlier can have

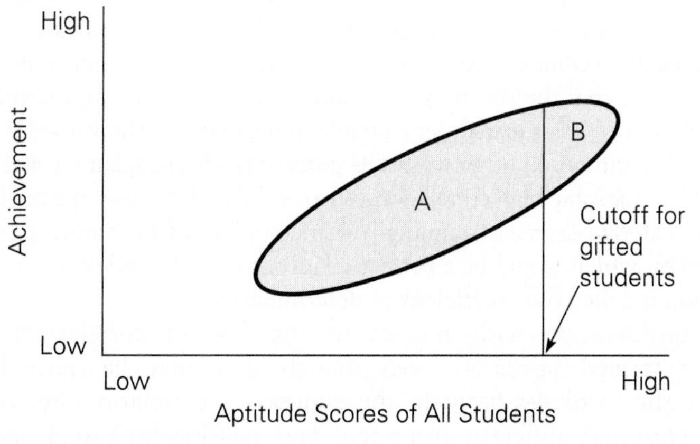

FIGURE 10.5 **Restriction of Range**

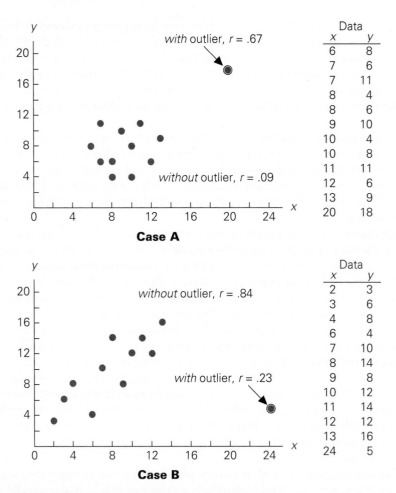

FIGURE 10.6 The Effect of Outliers on Correlation Coefficients

Source: Adapted from Stevens, J. (1996). *Applied Multivariate Statistics for the Social Sciences* (3rd ed.) Mahwah, NJ: Lawrence Erlbaum Associates. Reprinted by permission.

on either increasing or decreasing the correlation coefficient so that the correlation misrepresents the data. Correlations have been calculated both with and without the outliers. As you can see, the difference in results obtained is dramatic with a relatively low number of subjects.

Size of Correlation Coefficients Correlations such as .86, .95, and −.89 are high; .43, −.35, and .57 are moderate; and .07, −.01, and .12 are small, but these words only hint at the magnitude of the relationship. Because correlation coefficients are expressed as decimals, it is easy to confuse the decimal with a percentage. The coefficient is a mathematical way of expressing the degree to which there is covariance between the variables, not an indication of the degree to which the variables share common properties or characteristics. To obtain an estimate of the proportion of the variance that the two measures share or have in common, the coefficient must be squared. A correlation of .40, squared, for example, indicates that the variables have 16 percent of their variance in common. In other words, 84 percent is left unexplained or unpredicted by the .40 correlation. Even for some high correlations, such as .70 and .80, the square of the correlations thus results in a moderate degree of common variance (49 and 64 percent, respectively, out of a total of 100 percent, which would be a perfect relationship). The index that results from squaring the correlation is called the **coefficient of determination**.

Coefficient of determination: variance in common

Another consideration with respect to the size of correlations is that many correlations are termed *significant* even though they may be quite low (.15, .08). Researchers use the word *significant* in the context of correlations to indicate that the coefficient is *statistically* different from zero (no relationship) at a specified level of confidence. If a study has a very large number of subjects (more than 1,000), then

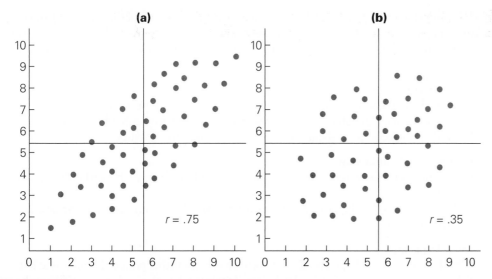

FIGURE 10.7 Scatterplots Indicating Different Correlations (*N* = 50)

small correlations can be significant but only in a statistical sense. We know that a simple correlation of .30, if significant, accounts for only 9 percent of the common variance, so our interpretation needs to reflect the 91 percent of the variance that the findings do not account for. For research in which prediction is the primary goal, such low correlations, even though statistically significant, are of little practical significance. Generally, in studies investigating relationships only, correlations as low as .30 or .40 are useful, but in prediction studies or estimates of reliability and validity, higher correlations are needed. In educational research, if a very high correlation is reported, such as .99, or .98, then the reader should suspect spurious results caused by methodological, design, or calculation inadequacies. As a final illustration of the power of correlations, inspect the scatterplots in Figure 10.7. These figures show what actual correlations look like when graphed. Take the score of 5.5 on the horizontal axis in Figure 10.7 and look at the large range of scores it predicts. For scatterplot (a), which is a high correlation of .75, predicted scores range from 3 to 8. This isn't nearly as precise, then, as .75 might imply. The predicted range for scatterplot (b) (*r* = .35) is wider because the correlation is lower.

Finally, with respect to interpretation, the usefulness of correlations varies, depending on whether the investigation is focusing on groups or on individuals. Generally, a much larger correlation is needed for use with individuals than groups. For correlations below about .35, only a small relationship is shown; this is of value in some exploratory research but has little value in predictions concerning individuals or groups. In the middle range, from .35 to .75, crude group predictions can be made, and if several moderate correlations can be combined, they can be used with individual predictions. Above .75, both individual and group predictions are useful with a single measure of correlation.

Now that you have read about different research approaches, practice identifying different types of studies. Go to MyEducationLab for Research at www. myeducationlab.com and practice identifying causal-comparative, correlational, or experimental research. Click on the topic "Causal-Comparative Research" and then select the Activities and Applications activity titled "Identifying Causal-Comparative Research."

SURVEY RESEARCH

What Is Survey Research?

In **survey research**, the investigator selects a sample of respondents from a target population and administers a questionnaire or conducts interviews to collect information on variables of interest. Questionnaires are distributed by mail, in person to a captive group of subjects, or via the Internet. Interviews are conducted either by phone or face to face. Surveys are used to learn about people's attitudes, beliefs, values, demographics, behavior, opinions, habits, desires, ideas, and other types of information. They are used frequently in business, politics, government, sociology, public health, psychology, and education because accurate information can be obtained for large numbers of people with a small sample.

Survey research: collecting sample information using interviews or questionnaires

Most surveys describe the incidence, frequency, and distribution of the characteristics of an identified population. In addition to being descriptive, surveys can be used to explore relationships between variables, or in an explanatory way. Consider these examples of topics in each of the three categories:

Descriptive
What is the average length of time that teachers take to prepare a lesson?
What are the most popular counseling techniques used by high school counselors?
What do principals think about inclusion of students with disabilities?

Exploring a Relationship
Do teachers who favor tenure try innovations less often than teachers who disapprove of tenure?
Is there a relationship between teacher attitude toward discipline and student satisfaction with the class?

In an Explanatory Way
Why do some principals send regular letters to parents and other principals rarely send letters?
Why are the students in one school achieving better than similar students in another school?

Survey research is very popular in education, primarily for three reasons: versatility, efficiency, and generalizability (Schutt, 1996). Surveys are versatile because they can be used to investigate almost any problem or question. Many doctoral dissertations use surveys; state departments of education use surveys to determine levels of knowledge and to ascertain needs in order to plan programs; schools use surveys to evaluate aspects of the curriculum or administrative procedures; governmental agencies use surveys to form public policy.

Surveys are popular because credible information from a large population can be collected at a relatively low cost, especially if the survey is distributed and collected by mail, during a phone interview, or through the Internet (as long as the response rate is good). Surveys are also efficient because data on many variables can be gathered without substantial increases in time or cost. Also, small samples can be selected from larger populations in ways that permit generalizations to the population. In fact, surveys are often the only means of obtaining a representative description of traits, beliefs, attitudes, and other characteristics of the population. Surveys also allow for generalizability across the population, in which subgroups or different contexts can be compared.

Conducting Survey Research

The following sequence of steps is used to conduct survey research:

1. *Define the purpose and objectives.* The first step is to define the purpose and objectives of the research. This should include a general statement and specific objectives that define in detail the information that needs to be collected. The objectives should be as clear-cut and unambiguous as possible. This is not always as easy as it sounds. An objective such as "The purpose of this research is to determine the values of college students" is quite vague. What is meant by *values*? Which college students are included? Another way to evaluate the objectives is to ask whether there are specific uses for the results. Often data are collected with the idea that either "It would be nice to know" or "Let's see what the results are and then decide how to use the data." Either notion is a weak reason to collect data. The researcher needs to know before the data are collected exactly how the results will be used. Careful consideration of objectives also helps determine what to emphasize and what to treat in a more cursory way.

2. *Select resources and the target population.* It is necessary to make decisions about the total amount of time, money, and personnel available before designing the specific methodology to gather the data. A locally developed questionnaire might be best, for example, but financial constraints may make it necessary to use an instrument that has established reliability and validity. The amount of money available will also affect the size of the sample that can be drawn. The objectives of the study may also need to be modified to reflect the financial constraints. It is better to do a small study well than a large study poorly.

It is also important to define the population or target group to which the researcher intends to generalize. The definition is a list of characteristics or boundaries to clarify external validity and specify the group from which the data are collected. If the population is too broad, such as "all teachers" or "all students," then it will be difficult and expensive to obtain a representative sample. If the population is too narrow, such as "male special education teachers with between 5 and 10 years' teaching experience," then the external validity of the study will be weak.

3. ***Choose and develop techniques for gathering data.*** The written questionnaire, telephone interview, and personal interview are the most frequently used techniques for collecting data, although Internet-based surveys are becoming increasingly popular. Consider the advantages and disadvantages of each technique for reaching the objectives and then select the approach that will provide the most credible information given available resources.

4. ***Instructions.*** It is important to develop clear instructions for the respondent. There can be no ambiguity about how, where, and when participants will respond. For example, does the respondent check a box, circle the correct answer, or make checks on a continuum? If there is a separate answer sheet (which generally is not recommended; if you intend to use a scantron form, it is best to have the questions printed right on the form), be clear about "bubbling," using a pencil if needed (some scantron forms only need a darkened area, not necessarily in pencil), and administer the survey in person rather than via the mail. Instructions should also clearly indicate how the participant should return the questionnaire. You can point this out in the letter of transmittal, at the beginning of the survey, or at the end of the survey. The best policy is to have the instructions for completing and returning the survey on the survey itself.

5. ***Sampling.*** Most surveys use probability sampling in order to ensure adequate representation of the population. The random sampling is often stratified on some variables, such as sex, grade level, ability level, and socioeconomic status. When researching a relationship, be sure that the sample will provide variation in responses. Use the largest possible number of subjects for probability sampling that resources will allow.

6. ***Letter of transmittal.*** In the case of mailed and Internet-based questionnaires, the nature of the cover letter or letter of transmittal is crucial in determining the percentage of subjects who return completed forms. The letter should be brief and establish the credibility of the researcher and the study. This is accomplished by including the following: the names and identifications of the investigators; the purpose and intention of the study without complete details; the importance of the study for the respondent and profession; the importance of the respondent for the study; the protection afforded the respondent by keeping the identities of the respondents confidential; a time limit for returning a written survey that is neither too long nor too short (usually a week or less); endorsements for the study by recognized institutions or groups; a brief description of the questionnaire and procedure; mention of an opportunity to obtain results; a request for cooperation and honesty; and thanks to the respondent. Naturally, if the letter is neat, professional in appearance, and without grammatical and spelling errors, the respondent will be more likely to cooperate. It is best if the letter establishes that the research is being conducted by an organization that is recognized by the respondent as credible. If possible, letters of transmittal should be personalized. Figures 10.8 and 10.9 show sample letters illustrating these points. Figure 10.8 shows a letter sent to parents. Figure 10.9 illustrates a letter sent directly to participants.

7. ***Pilot test.*** It is critical to pilot test both the instructions and the survey before distributing them to the identified sample. This pilot should be done with respondents similar to those in the sample. Generally, the pilot can be successful in identifying needed changes if as few as 10 individuals are willing to complete it and provide suggestions to improve the clarity and format. The pilot test also gives you an estimate of the amount of time it will take to complete the survey. Finally, the pilot test provides an initial idea of the pattern of responses that are likely and whether revisions need to be made to avoid ceiling or floor effects. Occasionally, an initial informal pilot test will be conducted, followed by a more formal pilot test with a larger sample.

Cover letters are an important part of survey research. Practice writing one by going to MyEducationLab for Research at www.myeducationlab.com. First, click on the topic, "Survey Research" and then select the Activities and Applications activity "Designing a Cover Letter."

February 1, 2009

Dear Parent/Guardian:

The Richmond area superintendents of schools are jointly sponsoring a study with VCU School of Education faculty to gather information about how teachers grade and measure student progress and students' opinions about motivation and engagement. We hope that the study will identify educational practices that enhance student motivation and engagement and will contribute to improved academic success. We hope to learn about what influences students' motivation, the amount of effort they put into classwork, and their academic goals. In addition, we want to understand how these issues are related to teaching practices. Your student's class has been invited to participate in this study, and we would like permission to survey him/her. We ask that you read this letter, discuss it with your student and call or email us if you have any questions.

> Importance of study

If you and your student agree to participate in the study, the teacher will ask participants to assent in their class indicating that they understand the study. The teacher will read information to them that describes the purpose of the study, informs students that their answers are confidential, states that they can stop taking the survey at any time, and that their participation is voluntary. Your student will then complete a short survey in class which will take about 15 minutes. The survey includes approximately 35 questions about the student's motivation, goals, academic effort, and the grading practices used in the class. Some of the questions will ask students about how often they complete assignments on time, if they volunteer to answer questions in class, and how important learning new information and skills is to them. In keeping with established practice, the survey forms will be kept secure for five years after the study is complete. We will keep the information received from your student confidential and do not foresee any risks associated with this study. Students are also cautioned to protect the confidentiality of their answers by not discussing them with anyone else. Although students will gain no personal benefit from this study, their participation may have a long-term benefit by identifying the grading and assessment practices associated with greater levels of motivation and engagement.

> Consent procedure

> Description of questionnaire

> Minimal risk

> Importance of study

In an effort to understand the relationship among grading practices, student motivation and engagement, and achievement the school district will provide SOL test scores to the VCU research team for each student that participated in the survey. The scores will be provided to the VCU researchers without any identifying information. Individual student names and other identifiers will not be attached to any SOL information. Again, this information will be confidential.

> Description of study

> Assurance of confidentiality

If you and/or your student choose not to participate in the pilot study they will remain in the classroom and complete an alternative activity during the survey administration.

> Alternate activity

Please understand that participation is strictly voluntary, and you or your student may withdraw from the study at any time, for any reason, without any consequence from VCU or your child's school. Any questions or concerns about the study and your student's participation can be directed to us. Finally, VCU's Office of Research Subjects Protection wants you to know that you should contact them at 828-0868 if you have any questions concerning your student's rights as a research participant.

> Voluntary

> Contact information

Sincerely,

Dr. Jim McMillan
Professor of Education
MERC Project Director

FIGURE 10.8 **Letter of Transmittal**

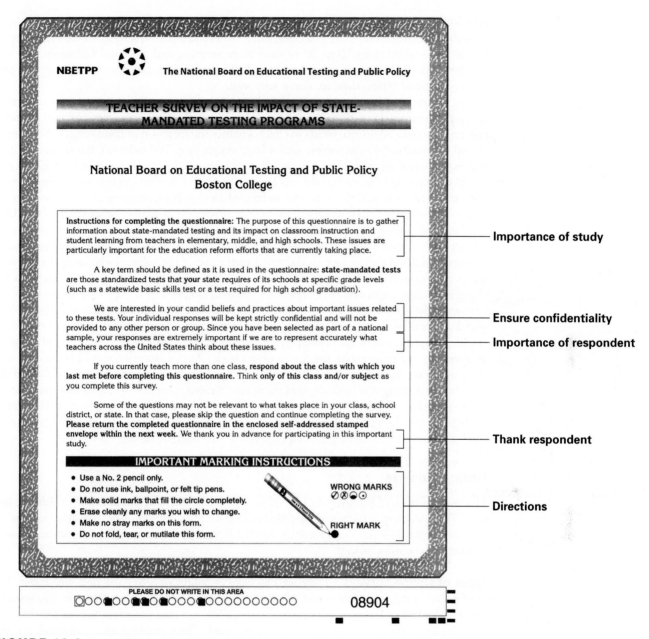

FIGURE 10.9 Letter of Transmittal

Source: From Teacher survey on the impact of state-mandated testing programs, National Board on Educational Testing and Public Policy, Boston: Boston College Press. Reprinted by permission.

8. *Mail survey follow-up.* The initial mailing of the letter of transmittal, questionnaire, and stamped return-addressed envelope will usually result in a response rate of from 40 to 60 percent—that is, 40 to 60 percent of the sample will typically return the questionnaires. This rate is higher for short questionnaires of obvious importance and lower for long questionnaires on an obscure or highly personal topic. The standard procedure for follow-up is to first send a reminder postcard about 10 days to two weeks after receipt of the initial mailing. For nonrespondents, a follow-up letter is sent about three to four weeks after the initial mailing, which includes another copy of the survey. If the return rate is still low and resources permit, a certified letter with yet another copy of the survey is sent six to eight weeks after the initial mailing. In the case of surveys that have assured anonymity, it is impossible to know who has or has not returned the questionnaire. In this case, researchers can use one of several procedures: They can send a follow-up letter or postcard to everyone, indicating that those who did return the questionnaire may ignore the follow-up; they can code the

questionnaires without the knowledge of the subjects in order to identify respondents; or the subjects can send separate postcards when they return their questionnaires. The postcard follow-up usually brings 10 to 30 percent more returns, and a second follow-up may add another 5 to 10 percent to the return rate. If the researchers can obtain a total return rate of 70 percent or better, they are doing very well.

9. *Nonrespondents.* In most survey studies, there will be a percentage of subjects who fail to return the completed questionnaire. These subjects are called *nonrespondents,* and the researcher may need to make additional efforts to check whether the inclusion of these subjects would have altered the results. For most surveys with a large sample (e.g., 200 or more), the nonrespondents will probably not affect the results in an appreciable way if the return rate is at least 70 percent. However, as pointed out by Sarndal and Lundström (2005), it is always best to examine respondents to search for bias. If the results are to be used for important decisions or if the nature of the questions might cause a certain type of subject not to respond, then the nonrespondents should be checked. The suggested approach for investigating the possibility of a biased group of respondents is to somehow obtain a random sample of the nonrespondents. If possible, these individuals should be interviewed and their responses compared with those of the subjects who completed written questionnaires. If the responses are the same, then the researcher is safe in concluding that the obtained written questionnaires represent an unbiased sample. If it is impossible to interview the randomly selected nonrespondents, the next best procedure is to compare them with the subjects who did respond with respect to demographic characteristics. If either the responses or the demographic characteristics of the nonrespondents are different, then this difference should be noted in discussing and interpreting the results of the study. Special attention should be focused on a study with a relatively low rate of return (lower than 70 percent) and without an analysis of the way nonrespondents may have changed the results. Research has demonstrated that the response rate to mailed surveys can be substantially increased by the use of monetary gratuities (Hopkins & Gullickson, 1992). A $1.00 gratuity may increase response rate by an average of 20 percent. A good approach for determining nonresponse bias is illustrated in Excerpt 10.16.

Online Surveys

The pervasiveness of the Internet has led researchers to this medium as a way to conduct surveys. These kinds of surveys may be called online *electronic surveys, e-surveys, email surveys,* or *Internet surveys.* The common feature is that the Internet is used to send the survey and usually to receive the results, as well.

Types of Online Surveys There are two types of online surveys: email and Web-based. The most common type of online survey in education is one in which respondents are contacted by email and asked to complete an attached survey. Two software programs, Survey Monkey and Inquisite, make the process simple and straightforward. These programs are economical, are easy to use for constructing and formatting questions, and can be purchased with some simple reporting of results. They are simple to construct and distribute, particularly when all the subject needs to do is check the appropriate responses and use the "Reply" function to return the completed survey. Email can also be used with an attachment that needs to be printed and then completed and returned by mail to assure confidentiality. (Of course, this places a greater burden on the respondent to obtain an envelope, address it, and mail it.) Following up with email is easy and inexpensive.

EXCERPT 10.16 Determining Nonresponse Bias

Additionally, we contacted 20 nonrespondents by telephone and asked them to complete the inventories. All of the individuals agreed to complete the inventory. . . . Comparative analysis on the composite scale scores of each of the inventories . . . revealed that there were no statistically significant differences in the mean responses of respondents and nonrespondents. (p. 124)

Source: From Nelson, J. R., Maculan, A., Roberts, M. L., & Ohlund, B. J. (2001). Sources of occupational stress for teachers of students with emotional and behavioral disorders. *Journal of Emotional and Behavioral Disorders, 9*(2), 123–130.

A Web-based Internet survey uses a specific website for respondents to access the survey. Individuals may be invited to the website by email or letter, or a sample can be drawn from those individuals who access the website. For example, the American Educational Research Association may want to survey its members about themes for the annual meeting. To do so, it could send out email to members, solicit their participation in journals, or provide a link on the organization's homepage to the survey for members to access it. Web-based surveys can have more advanced graphics and can utilize multimedia. This versatility, however, comes with increased cost in terms of technical assistance.

One of the authors received a letter in January 2004 requesting his participation in a national study of postsecondary faculty and instructional staff. A letter of transmittal was received that emphasized confidentiality:

> Your responses will be secured behind firewalls and will be encrypted during Internet transmission. All identifying information is maintained in a separate file for follow-up purposes only. Your responses . . . [will] not be disclosed, or used, in identifiable form for any other purpose.

The letter also gave simple directions to find the questionnaire on the Web:

- Go to: https://surveys.nces.ed.gov/nsopf/.
- Type in the study ID and password (see below) on the Home/Login page.
- Press "Enter" or "Login" to begin the questionnaire.

Advantages and Disadvantages of Using Online Surveys   Online surveys offer a number of advantages compared to paper, telephone, or personal interview techniques, and in the right circumstances, these advantages far outweigh the associated disadvantages. The main advantages are obvious: reduced cost and time, quick response, easy follow-up, and the ability to survey a large population. The main disadvantages are also obvious: limited sampling (i.e., those with computer access), lack of confidentiality and privacy, and low response rate. These disadvantages are less serious when the samples are Internet savvy, such as teachers, principals, and college faculty, and the nature of the topic is professional, not personal.

Depending on the topic and the sample surveyed, response rates for online surveys can fluctuate widely, from rates in single digits to higher rates comparable to those of mail surveys. Email response rates are better than Web-based response rates, but in either case, obtaining a sufficient response rate is difficult. Research has shown that mail surveys typically result in about a 20 percent higher return rate but nearly a 40 percent cost savings with simple surveys that do not require much technical expertise (Schonlau, Fricker, & Elliott, 2002). However, the nature of the sample and of the questions can significantly affect the return rate and cost. The response rate can be improved by making follow-up contacts with nonrespondents, by making personalized contacts, and by using a preliminary contact prior to receiving the survey (Cook, Heath, & Thompson, 2000). Table 10.1 provides a comprehensive list of the advantages and disadvantages of using online surveys.

Online Survey Design   Many of the rules of effective questionnaire design are also appropriate for online surveys; however, there are additional considerations related to the technology. Essentially, it is important to have a simple, clear layout of easily answered questions. These further guidelines for the design of online surveys are provided by Best and Krueger (2004), Dillman (2000), and Ritter and Sue (2007):

- Use a few short items that are simple and direct.
- Show one or just a few items per screen.
- Avoid excessive scrolling.
- Use simple graphics.
- Limit the use of matrix questions.
- Use specific error/warning messages.
- Password protect Web surveys.
- Indicate progress in completing the survey.
- Use hypertext and color to enhance presentation and understanding.

Online surveys are now ubiquitous, and most professionals are adept at using them. With the right sample, there is no question that this kind of survey can be the most effective with both response rate and reaching a high number of participants.

TABLE 10.1 Advantages and Disadvantages of Online Surveys	
Advantages	**Disadvantages**
Less expensive	Participants must have online access and skills to
Quick response	navigate the Web
Less time to distribute	Low response rate
Each question directly and easily	Lack of confidentiality
answered	Potential for information overload if the survey is
Can use enhanced presentation (e.g.,	too long
color and graphs)	Difficult to communicate ethical principles
Immediate database construction	Difficult to use incentives
Convenient	Inabillity to know definitely who has responded
Less error in responses	
Easy follow-up	
Easy access to distant participants	

Before leaving the topic of surveys, we need to emphasize that survey research is not simple to prepare and conduct. There are many factors related to item format, positioning of questions, wording, sampling, and other variables that need to be considered. For an excellent review of these problems, see Schuman and Presser (1996), and for additional information on developing and conducting surveys, see *The Survey Kit*, a series of volumes published by Sage Publications that covers question development, conducting surveys, data analysis, and reporting.

We now turn to an approach to research that has recently become very popular—*secondary data analysis*.

SECONDARY DATA ANALYSIS

With Kirsten Barrett

Secondary data: already collected and in a database

Secondary data analysis: statistically examining secondary data

Secondary data, simply put, are data that have already been collected. These data are different from primary data in that the data user had no involvement in the data collection effort. When a researcher analyzes data that have been collected by some other organization, group, or individual at some prior time, the work is called **secondary data analysis**. Examples include a local school administrator analyzing decennial census data to better understand the socioeconomic status of parents in the community, a principal examining trends in high-stakes testing from a state database, and a parent analyzing achievement test scores across a number of schools to inform decisions about family relocation.

Reasons for Using Secondary Data

A researcher may choose to use secondary data for a number of reasons. Five of the most significant are the benefits of time efficiency, cost effectiveness, data quality, increased sample size, and, in many cases, lack of need to obtain IRB approval.

Using secondary data can save considerable time. The researcher does not need to spend time designing the research study and collecting primary data. When using secondary data, this work has already been done. Time savings can be a significant benefit when a person or an organization needs to make program or policy decisions within a short period of time. Also, students completing coursework, master's theses, or doctoral dissertations can often expedite their efforts by using secondary data.

Using secondary data also can be cost effective. Cost savings are realized because the researcher does not need to fund the primary data collection. Costs related to photocopying,

TABLE 10.2 Key Sources of Secondary Data	
Source	**Internet Address**
Inter-University Consortium for Political and Social Research (ICPSR)	http://www.icpsr.com
National Center for Education Statistics	http://nces.ed.gov
U.S. Census Bureau	http://www.census.gov
National Center for Health Statistics	http://www.cdc.gov/nchs
State-level departments of education	*Examples:*
	Virginia: http://www.pen.k12.va.us/VDOE/Publications
	Texas: http://ritter.tea.state.tx.us/research
	Maine: http://www.maine.gov/education/

postage, telecommunication charges, personnel time, and data entry are minimized as well. Also, many secondary datasets are freely available in electronic format from reputable organizations. Further, state-level department of education websites often contain accessible, downloadable data pertaining to, among other things, achievement and accountability test scores, graduation rates, and disciplinary actions. Table 10.2 lists the key sources of secondary data and the Internet address for each.

A third benefit is data quality. Depending on the dataset being used, the findings that result from secondary analyses may well have a high degree of validity and reliability. Reputable data collection organizations have the fiscal and human resources necessary to develop and extensively test surveys prior to implementing them. These organizations also have the resources necessary to field surveys using sampling methods and sample sizes that allow for reliable and valid population estimates.

Secondary datasets usually provide very large samples. With increased sample size comes greater flexibility in examining identified subgroups (especially small segments of the population), improved reliability, and generally credible results. However, large samples can also result in producing statistically significant findings that have little practical significance.

Finally, many researchers find that it is easy to use secondary source data because there is usually no need for IRB review and approval. This is definitely the case with publicly available databases that are organized so that it is impossible to connect individual participants with their responses.

Considerations for Using Secondary Data

A number of factors should be considered when deciding if secondary data and secondary data analyses are appropriate to answer a research question or to test a research hypothesis:

1. *Does the dataset contain variables that will allow the research question to be answered or the research hypothesis to be tested?* If the answer is *no* or *probably not*, then the dataset is not appropriate. If the dataset does contain the variables of interest, the researcher needs to determine how the data were collected. That is, how were the questions worded, and what response categories were made available to the respondents? The potential data user needs to determine how the variables of interest were operationally defined. Information about variables can usually be found in the technical documentation and code book that accompanies the dataset. If these documents do not exist or exist only in part, the researcher should be wary about using the dataset.

2. *Were data collected from the population of interest?* A survey may yield a dataset containing the variables of interest, but the data may not have been collected from a sample that is representative of the population the researcher is interested in. For example, if a researcher is interested in children in a specific age bracket, the dataset should contain data collected from children in the age bracket of interest. Sampling for secondary analysis studies is illustrated in Excerpts 10.17 and 10.18.

EXCERPT 10.17   Secondary Databases and Subject Selection

In 1998, the Early Childhood Longitudinal Survey–Kindergarten cohort . . . published data on a nationally representative sample of 21,399 children at the start of kindergarten. . . . Of those children, slightly over half (10,956) were boys. The sample can be considered representative of kindergarten boys in the United States in 1998. We used all of the boys in the sample for the full hierarchical linear modeling (HLM) analysis, then trimmed the sample to exclude cases in which there was only 1 boy in a given site, leaving a sample of 8,945 boys in 963 schools. (p. 333)

Source: From Smith, J., & Niemi, N. (2007). Exploring teacher perceptions of small boys in kindergarten. *The Journal of Educational Research, 100*(6), 331–336.

EXCERPT 10.18   Secondary Databases and Subject Selection

The data for this study came from a restricted-use version of the National Center for Education Statistics Baccalaureate and Beyond Longitudinal Study (B & B). . . . The B & B was especially suited for this study because it elicited data on each individual's status by 1997 in the "teacher pipeline," a useful way to describe progress toward becoming a teacher. . . . [I]n addition, the B & B has measures of academic proficiency to proxy for teacher quality, such as SAT and American College (ACT) scores. . . . From these data, a teacher was defined as someone who had taught at the elementary or secondary levels at any time between graduating from college up to the spring term when the follow up survey was administered. (p. 159)

Source: From Bacolod, M. (2007). Who teaches and where they choose to teach: College graduates of the 1990's. *Educational Evaluation and Policy Analysis, 29*(3), 155–168.

3. **When were the data collected?** The researcher should consider the time period in which the data were collected. If the research has implications for current practice, the data used for the analyses should be relatively current. If the research is historical in nature or examines change over time, then the dataset may be older or may contain data collected over a number of years. Also, the researcher should consider the timing of data collection relative to major social or political events. For example, data from a survey about attitudes toward women in sport conducted prior to the passage of Title IX should not be used to make inferences about current attitudes toward women in sport.

4. **Is there adequate computing capacity to work with the secondary dataset?** This consideration relates both to computer software and to computer storage capacity and processor speed. Many secondary datasets from reputable data repositories are derived from surveys that involved complex multistage sampling designs. Some researchers may not have access to the statistical software necessary to analyze such data, or they may not have the expertise needed to use the software appropriately.

5. **Are the data easily accessible?** Some secondary datasets can be downloaded from the Internet, whereas others need to be ordered. If a dataset needs to be ordered, it is important to determine how it will be provided to the end user. Will it be sent via email as an attachment or provided on a CD, DVD, or diskette? Also, in what format will the data file be provided? Does the end user have the skills to manipulate the data file? Data provided as hard copy (i.e., printed pages) can be useful but will require scanning or manual data entry.

6. **Is documentation about the dataset available?** It is important for the researcher to have technical documentation that describes what data were collected through what method(s) and in what time interval(s). The technical documentation should provide the end user with the variable names, their locations in the data file, the associated survey question and response categories, and, ideally, the number of respondents for each response category.

7. **What is the structure of the data file?** This is an important and more technical consideration. Some secondary datasets contain data at different levels—say, an individual, a family, and/or a household. Figure 10.10 is an example of a dataset that contains data at a number of different levels. In this example, although there are 10 records, only 5 unique households are represented (i.e., 100, 200, 300, 400, and 500). Household 100, comprised of three people (Person Numbers 1, 2, and 3), contains two families. This could be a husband and wife (Record IDs 1 and 2) and a nonrelated renter (Record ID 3). Contained within the dataset are two variables: age and household income. Age is a person-level variable, whereas Household Income is a household-level variable. As can be seen in the figure, all people with a Household Number of

Record ID	Household Number	Family Number	Person Number	Age	Household Income
1	100	1	1	42	$45,650
2	100	1	2	45	$45,650
3	100	2	3	32	$45,650
4	200	1	1	21	$32,000
5	300	1	1	35	$48,200
6	300	1	2	32	$48,200
7	400	1	1	54	$43,250
8	500	1	1	36	$35,750
9	500	2	2	42	$35,750
10	500	2	3	46	$35,750

FIGURE 10.10   Example of Dataset with Household, Family, and Person Records

100 have the same household income. This distinction is important. Suppose that the researcher wants to report average household income by household. It would be incorrect to simply add all 10 household income values and divide by 10. If this were done, the average household income would appear to be $41,585. To determine the average household income by household, the researcher should add the household incomes of all the households and divide by 5, since there are five households in the file. The result would be an average household income of $40,970.

What is important with data file structures is to recognize that care needs to be taken to ensure that analysis is done at the appropriate level (household, family, and/or person) and that the interpretations are accurate based on the file structure and the variables used.

8. *Is technical assistance available relative to the dataset and its use?* When working with secondary data, researchers may come across unanticipated problems, such as frequency counts that do not match those identified in the technical documentation, difficulty applying sample weights, or a lack of knowledge about how best to account for a complex sample design. When such a situation arises, support from the individual or organization providing the data is needed. If support is not available, the researcher should find someone who has used the dataset previously and seek his or her help.

Protecting Human Subjects

Secondary data that are publicly available, whether free or at cost, are usually coded so that the identification of any single individual is not possible. Thus, research involving the collection or study of existing data, documents, or records in which subjects cannot be identified—directly or through identifiers linked to them—usually does not need the subjects' informed consent.

However, not all secondary datasets are devoid of identifying information about participants. It is therefore important to look beyond the obvious identifiers, such as name, Social Security number, and address information. Sometimes, through a combination of variables in the dataset, an individual can be identified. For example, consider a small dataset of 200 individuals living in a small community. In the dataset is information about individuals' jobs, types of cars, and numbers of people in households, as well as information about age, race, and marital status. This information, in combination, could be enough to allow for the identification of an individual person. Although no one variable would serve to identify an individual, combining variables could allow for identification. Reputable federal statistical agencies and data repositories address this issue by ensuring that there is an adequate number of respondents for key variables in the dataset prior to its release.

Combining Secondary Data with Primary Data Collection

Using a combination of primary and secondary data can often strengthen research findings. Not only can analyzing existing data inform primary data collection efforts, but it can also lead to discovering new research questions, to refining existing research questions, and to informing primary data collection efforts. For example, if a researcher is analyzing secondary data and finds that a high percentage of the respondents refused to answer a particular question, he or she may use this information in developing new survey instruments.

Secondary data also can provide a context for interpreting the findings that result from primary data collection efforts. Consider the issue of school consolidation. When school leaders are making decisions about consolidating students and closing schools, they often solicit feedback from key stakeholders, including parents and teachers. School leaders could survey parents and teachers in order to learn about their attitudes about school consolidation, and the survey data could be augmented with data about student enrollment over time based on analysis of school administrative records. In this example, the survey data would be the primary data and the school administrative data would be the secondary data.

Secondary data can be used to help researchers identify where members of the target population are most likely to be located. An example would be a survey of households in which there are children under the age of 18. Decennial census data could be used to identify at very small levels of geography areas with the highest proportion of households with children under 18. Once this was determined, the sampling methods could be targeted so that these areas would be maximally surveyed and other areas would be surveyed to a lesser extent.

After data have been collected, there is a chance that the sample will be distributed in ways that are inconsistent with what is known about the target population. For example, in a hypothetical survey of a local community, 50 percent of the respondents have less than a high school education, 30 percent are married, and 20 percent have at least one child under the age of 18. However, through secondary analysis of decennial census data, you determine that the true percentages in the community in each of these categories are 35 percent, 50 percent, and 15 percent, respectively. The discrepancy identified through the secondary data analysis suggests that the researcher should apply statistical weighting procedures so that the sample will better represent the target population. This is one method of enhancing external validity.

Research Articles and Secondary Data

For the most part, journal articles written by researchers who have used secondary data follow the same form as journal articles written by researchers conducting primary data collection. However, when describing the sampling and data collection methods, researchers using secondary data write about what was done by the individual or group that initially collected the data. Researchers who conduct primary data collection write about what they did to collect the data used in the study yielding the findings being reported.

The following should be included in the research methods section of a journal article written by a researcher using secondary data:

- The name of the dataset and its source should be clearly identified.
- If more than one dataset is used and they are linked, the names of all datasets should be provided and their sources identified.
- The time period in which the data were collected should be identified. If the data were pooled over a number of years, this should be stated as well.
- The sampling methods and the characteristics of the sample should be described.
- If the researcher is interested in a subset of cases in a dataset, any procedures used to limit the dataset to select cases should be identified in sequence.
- The key variables used in the analysis should be identified and, in some cases, the specific survey questions identified.

STANDARDS OF ADEQUACY

In judging the adequacy of the descriptive, comparative, ex post facto, correlational, survey, and secondary analysis research designs, it will be helpful to keep the following questions in mind. The questions are organized to focus your attention on the most important criteria in designing and evaluating these types of research:

Descriptive Designs

1. Is the research problem clearly descriptive in nature?
2. Is there a clear description of the sample, population, and procedures for sampling?
3. Will the sample provide biased or distorted results?
4. Are the scores resulting from the instrumentation reliable and valid?
5. Do graphic presentations of the results distort the findings?
6. Are inappropriate relationships or causal conclusions made on the basis of descriptive results?
7. If the design is cross-sectional, do subject differences affect the results?
8. If the design is longitudinal, is loss of subjects a limitation?
9. Are differences between groups used to identify possible relationships?

Comparative Designs

1. Does the research problem clearly indicate that relationships will be investigated by comparing differences between groups?
2. Is the description of subjects, sampling, and instrumentation clear?
3. Do sampling procedures bias the results?
4. Is there sufficient evidence for reliability and validity?
5. Are inappropriate causal inferences made?

Ex Post Facto Designs

1. Was the primary purpose of the study to investigate cause-and-effect relationships?
2. Have the presumed cause-and-effect conditions already occurred?
3. Was the independent variable manipulated?
4. Were the groups being compared already different with respect to the independent variable?
5. Were potential extraneous variables recognized and considered as plausible rival hypotheses?
6. Were causal statements regarding the results made cautiously?
7. Were threats to external validity addressed in the conclusions?

Correlational Designs

1. Does the research problem clearly indicate that relationships will be investigated?
2. Is there a clear description of the sampling? Will the sample provide sufficient variability of responses to obtain a correlation?
3. Are the scores resulting from the instrumentation valid and reliable?
4. Is there a restricted range on the scores?
5. Are there any factors that might contribute to spurious correlations?
6. Is a shotgun approach used in the study?
7. Are inappropriate causal inferences made from the results?
8. How large is the sample? Could sample size affect the significance of the results?
9. Is the correlation coefficient confused with the coefficient of determination?
10. If predictions are made, are they based on a different sample?
11. Is the size of the correlation large enough for the conclusions?

Keeping in mind the standards of adequacy, take a few moments to evaluate a survey study. Go to MyEducationLab for Research at www.myeducationlab.com and practice evaluating an actual study. Click on the topic "Survey Research" and then select the Building Research Skills activity "Evaluating a Survey Study."

Survey Research

1. Are the objectives and purposes of the survey clear?
2. Is it likely that the target population and sampling procedure will provide a credible answer to the research question(s)?
3. Is the instrument clearly designed and worded? Has it been pilot tested? Is it appropriate for the characteristics of the sample?
4. Is there assurance of confidentiality of responses? If not, is this likely to affect the results?
5. Does the letter of transmittal establish the credibility of the research? Is there any chance that what is said in the letter will bias the responses?
6. What is the return rate? If it is low or borderline, has there been any follow-up with non-respondents?
7. Do the conclusions reflect the return rate and other possible limitations?

Secondary Data Analysis

1. Does the database contain variables that match the objectives of the study?
2. Does the database sample match the objectives of the study?

3. Are there significant missing data?
4. Is documentation of the nature of the database available?

CHAPTER SUMMARY

This chapter has provided a review of descriptive, correlational, survey, and ex post facto research, stressing design principles that affect the quality of the research. The main points in the chapter include the following:

1. Descriptive research is concerned with the current or past status of something.
2. Developmental studies investigate changes of subjects over time and are longitudinal or cross-sectional.
3. Comparative relationship studies examine differences between groups.
4. Ex post facto designs are used to study potential causal relationships after a presumed cause has occurred.
5. In ex post facto research, subjects are selected on the basis of the groups they were in at one time; there is probably no random assignment of subjects to different groups; and there is no active manipulation of the independent variable.
6. Correlational relationship studies use at least two scores that are obtained from each subject.
7. Comparative and correlational studies should clearly define sampling, instrumentation, and procedures for gathering data.
8. The selection of subjects and instruments in correlational research should ensure a range of responses on each variable.
9. In predictive research, the criterion variable is predicted by a prior factor as measured by the independent variable.
10. Bivariate regression predicts the dependent variable from a single independent variable.
11. Multiple and logistic regression combine several independent variables in relating all to the dependent or criterion variable.
12. Correlation should never infer causation because of third nonmeasured variables and the inability to assess the causal direction between the two variables.
13. Spurious correlations overrepresent or underrepresent the actual relationship between two variables.
14. The coefficient of determination is the square of the correlation coefficient, and it estimates the variance that is shared by the variables.
15. Correlation coefficients should be interpreted carefully when they are statistically significant, with low relationships and a large number of subjects.
16. Decisions for individuals require higher correlations than do decisions for groups.
17. Survey research uses questionnaires and interviews to describe characteristics of populations.
18. Surveys are used for descriptive, relationship, and explanatory purposes.
19. The nature of the letter of transmittal in a mail survey is crucial to obtaining an acceptable response rate of 70 percent or greater.
20. Online surveys can be one of two types: email or Web based.
21. With the right kind of sample and purpose, an online survey is more economical than a paper survey or interview.
22. Low response rate is a significant disadvantage of online surveys, depending on the question and sample.
23. Secondary data analysis studies use previously gathered data from sources existing at the time of data collection.
24. There are many large databases readily available for secondary analysis, although special skills may be needed to understand and extract the data needed.
25. Secondary data analysis may be efficient and cost effective, with large numbers of participants.
26. It is important to review the structure of the data files, dataset documentation, and accessibility, as well as whether technical assistance is available.
27. Secondary data analysis can be used with primary data to strengthen and extend findings.

APPLICATION PROBLEMS

1. In a study of motivation and learning, a teacher employed the following research strategy: Students were asked what teaching methods were most motivating. The teacher then looked back at her test scores to investigate whether the test scores were higher for the more motivating sessions compared with the less motivating sessions. The teacher found that, indeed, student achievement rose as the teacher used more and more motivating methods. From this result, she decided to use the more motivating methods all the time. Was her decision to use more motivating methods correct? Why or why not?

2. For each description below, indicate whether the research is descriptive, comparative, correlational, predictive, or ex post facto.
   a. A researcher finds that there is a positive relationship between grades and attendance.
   b. A researcher finds that students who are more lonely have more permissive parents than students who are less lonely.

c. The dean of the school of education uses SAT scores to identify students who may have trouble with National Teacher Examinations.

d. Children in supportive, loving homes have a higher self-concept than children in rejecting homes.

e. The majority of faculty at U.S.A. University favor abolishing tenure.

f. Researchers find that graduate students who attended small colleges have stronger writing skills than students from large universities.

3. Identify a topic in your area of study that would be appropriate for an online survey. Write some questions for the survey as well as a letter of transmittal. Design the screen pages, at least in the form of rough sketches. Considering the advantages and disadvantages of using online surveys, would your proposed survey be best done on the Internet? Why or why not?

4. Read the study presented in the example below for understanding and analysis. What kind of nonexperimental research is this study? What are the independent and dependent variables? Judge the research according to the standards of adequacy presented in this chapter, as well as the criteria for judging the research question and review of literature. Do the conclusions seem warranted? What could be done to improve the research?

EXAMPLE Example of a Nonexperimental Study

Individual and Social Factors Related to Urban African American Adolescents' School Performance

Cheryl L. Somers *Wayne State University*   Delila Owens *Wayne State University*

Monte Piliawsky *Wayne State University*

The purpose of this study was to examine factors related to the academic success of urban, African American youth. Participants were 118 African American male and female ninth graders from a large urban high school in the Midwest. A majority of students at the school receive free or reduced lunch. Factors studied were social support from five sources (parent, peer, teacher, classmate, close friend) and six educational attitudes and behaviors (educational intentions, educational behavior, personal control, persistence, and understanding of the personal and financial value of educational attainment). The major purpose of this study was to examine the role of these various sources of social support in the educational attitudes and behaviors and academic achievement of this sample of African American youth. Results indicated that social support was mildly correlated with better grades, with parent and peer support relatively the more important forms of support. Moderate and strong correlations were found between the five support variables and most of the educational attitudes and behaviors variables, with support from parents, teachers, and peers most strongly related. The combination of all predictors explained a large proportion of variance in achievement, with educational intentions and personal persistence the strongest contributors. Detailed results and implications of the results are discussed.

Introduction

It was projected that by the year 2003, students of color would comprise approximately 40% of the total school population of the United States (U.S. Department of Education, 2003). They would represent over 70% of the population in large cities in states such as California, Michigan, New York, and Texas (U.S. Department of Education, 2003). Given the above statistic, it is important that educators understand how to support the academic development of students of color.

There is a growing body of literature that documents the achievement gap (Thernstrom & Thernstrom, 2003; Ferguson, 2002). Unfortunately, African Americans are habitually the students who fall short of meeting the educational standards in America (Ford & Moore, 2004; National Governors Association, 2003; Ogbu, 2003). Although the numbers are more striking in urban school districts (Cooper & Jordan, 2003; Council of Great City Schools, 1999), there is empirical evidence that, when compared to their White counterparts, African American students are not performing as well as other children in America's schools (Barnett, 2004; Ferguson, 2002; Ogbu, 2003). Thus, African American youth are the focus of this study.

It is imperative that educators continue to address the unique issues faced by urban African American children. Many urban children are from low income families, which are not only economically poor, but also socially underserved. There are a variety of reasons why African American youth do not perform well in school and/or eventually drop out. Dropping out of high school is a symptom of the larger issues affecting youth.

Youth living in urban areas are often faced with violence, poverty, and racism to name a few of the issues. These factors can hinder them both academically and emotionally (Baur, Sapp, & Johnson, 2000). A link between poverty and school drop out has been identified (Guo, Brooks-Gunn, & Harris, 1996). Because of their impoverished environments and surroundings, some African American children fail to draw the correlation between academic success and later adult career success. In addition, African American children are keenly aware of the stereotypes associated with their

(continued)

race. This awareness can have an effect on the self-concepts of African American children, thus having an effect on their school performance (Cokley, 2003).

To understand the achievement gap, in an effort to begin to close it, a closer look at the historical background of African American children is crucial. Improving the educational and employment opportunities of urban youth is vital. Thus, it is important to understand factors that contribute to or hinder their academic success. Gallagher (1998), as cited in *Socio-Economic Conditions and Student Achievement*, highlighted outside factors that will contribute to student's academic success. He contended that:

> *"We need to face the unpleasant reality that education, by itself, is a weak treatment. It is clear that there are other variables within the family, within the culture, and within the physical environment, plus limitations within the genetic makeup of the individual, which will have a greater influence on student achievement than our 'improved educational program' for that student."*

The role of individual perceptions and social support in educating these youth must be considered. Furthermore, the environment that is related to the schooling process is often not examined. School culture communicates to students how the school views them and their ethnic group (Banks & Banks, 2001). When the school culture promotes value, respect, and collegiality, students are often more positive. Healthy school climates have an identified impact on the success of students (Karpicke & Murphy, 1996). African American students sometimes abandon the educational process all together because they are not supported by the school system. Clearly, school culture can have an effect on students' academic achievement (Moore, 2006).

There are additional factors that contribute to an adolescent's academic achievement besides traditional curriculum (e.g., mathematics, english, science). School mobility and school environment have been found to be additional factors that are related to student achievement (Swanson & Schneider, 1999). It is important to understand how other variables will affect achievement for African American adolescents, especially for those students who are struggling academically. Thus, it is beneficial to explore factors that contribute to adolescents' perceptions, attitudes, and behaviors toward their academic performance.

The Role of Peers

Research has indicated that peer influence plays a momentous role in adolescents' dispositions toward school (Berndt & Keefe, 1995; Ogbu, 2003; Wentzel, 1994). Academic support from peers is positively related to the pursuit of academic pro-social goals (Wentzel, 1994). However, African American students in particular may receive negative sanctions from their peer group for succeeding academically (Ford & Moore, 2006). African American students who excel academically could be ridiculed by their peers as "acting white" (Fordham & Ogbu, 1986; Grantham & Ford, 2003). Although some adolescents may want to succeed academically, lack of approval from their peers could serve as a barrier. In spite

of the ridicule, some African American students succeed academically because they have developed a positive racial identity that serves as a coping strategy to fight off negative performance expectations (Constantine & Blackmon, 2002).

The Role of Parents

Additionally, parental support plays a role in the academic success of students. Karavasilis, Doyle, and Margolese (1999), wrote that encouraging and supportive relationships with parents fostered a greater sense of autonomy in adolescence. Students in these types of families are able to comfortably explore their environments and return to the family for emotional support. Research has also shown that parental involvement is particularly crucial for minority children (Epstein, 2001; Henderson & Mapp, 2002; Xu, 2002). Trusty (1998) found that parental involvement and parental attempts to integrate into their child's schooling was predictive of student academic achievement. Thus, teachers and administrators may promote the academic success of African American students by exploring avenues to get parents involved in their schooling. Additionally, broader social support, discussed next, has been linked to academic success for students.

The Role of Social Support

Social support for adolescent school retention is also important (Guest & Biasini, 2001). Four important factors have been identified as influencing the academic success of African American adolescents. School, parents, peers, and neighborhood environment all play roles in African American students' academic success (Newman, Myers, Newman, Lohman, & Smith, 2000). Some students may be expected to succeed academically, while others may not. These expectations can vary by context.

Other social variables may also account for the academic success of African American students as well as their task engagement in the classroom. Broader conceptions of social factors that may influence direct task engagement in classroom activities have been offered. For example, Owens, Hamm, Jaynes, and Rawls (2007) found that urban low-income African American youth reported extracurricular activities such as babysitting, childrearing, and after-school employment as social influences that were related to their task engagement in classroom assignments. All activities reportedly had both positive and negative associations with youth outcomes. However, all students indicated that despite their environmental influences, obtaining an education was extremely important (Owens, et al., 2007).

Ecological Theory and The Transition to High School

Much research has examined academic achievement among urban African American students in grades K-12 in the last two decades. This research has focused on the issues African American students face in pursuit of academic success (e.g., Flowers, Milner, & Moore, 2003; Howard, 2003; Ogbu, 2004). Results have shown that there are a variety of factors that influence academic success among urban African American students. Many studies only examined a few variables at a time.

The ecological perspective advanced by Bronfenbrenner (1979) is likely to explain a larger portion of variance in academic success because it considers multiple levels of contexts in a child's life. For example, the roles of family, self, and peers are considered in the ecological model, as well as the roles of outside influences such as parents' jobs, societal values and dynamics, etc.

Also, little empirical data exists regarding the transition from middle school to ninth grade. However, existing literature indicates that for freshmen, the transition to high school can be anxiety-producing. For some ninth graders, the transition to high school brings negative consequences such as low grades and poor school attendance (Barone, Aguirre-Deandreis, & Trickett, 1991). Researchers such as Eccles, Midgley, Wigfield, & Buchanan (1993) have demonstrated that school transitions are related to decreased academic performance, lower self esteem, less involvement in activities, and greater feelings of anonymity. Coupled with the challenges of the period of adolescence in general, school performance can substantially suffer. For this reason, we focus specifically on ninth grade students in the current study.

Purpose of the Study

Based on the aforementioned literature review, the purpose of this study was to examine how factors from several life contexts were related to the school success of urban, African American youth. The end goal was to broaden our understanding of how we may intervene to more effectively assist them. The specific study variables were social support from five sources (parent, peer, teacher, classmate, close friend), six educational attitudes and behaviors (educational intentions, educational behavior, personal control, persistence, and understanding of the personal and financial value of educational attainment), and academic achievement in the fall of 9th grade. The primary research questions were: 1) what is the role of social support in the educational attitudes and behaviors of these youth?; and, 2) what are the combined and comparative roles of both social support and educational attitudes and behaviors in predicting academic achievement for this sample of African American youth?

Method

Participants

The participants in this study were 118 African American students (43 males, 75 females) in the ninth grade of a large, urban, public school in the Midwest. The school has a 65% free and reduced lunch rate, and thus, a majority of students are likely to be economically disadvantaged. This data was not collected on individual study participants. The school student racial/ethnic demographic is 96% African American. The community surrounding the school is best characterized as working-class homeowners. The city is also one of the nation's poorest cities with one in three children living below the federal poverty level (Kantor, 2000). The students participating in the study came from several sections of general education science classes, which all 9th graders have to take.

No parents refused their children's participation, and most all students were administered the survey. Thus, it is expected that this sample well represents the school's 9th grade population.

Measures

Social support

The following five measures were taken from the Children and Adolescent Social Support Scale (CASSS) (Malecki, Demaray, & Elliott, 2000). Participants responded to items using a six-point scale, ranging from 1 = "never," to 6 = "always." Malecki et al. (2000) reported Cronbach's alphas of .89 to .95 in previous research. Below, Cronbach's alphas for the current sample are reported. The items on these five measures utilized 6-point subscales and answered ("never" to "always"). The measures are as follows:

1. Parent support (9 items, a = .90, e.g., "My parents show they are proud of me");
2. Teacher Support (12 items, a = .92, e.g., "My teacher takes time to help me learn something well");
3. Classmate support (8 items, a = .92 e.g. "My classmates give me ideas when I don't know what to do");
4. Close friend support (items, a = .96; "My close friends give me ideas when I don't know what to do");
5. General school support (12 items, a = .97; "People at school listen to me when I need to talk").

Educational attitudes and behaviors

The following six measures were used to assess students' educational attitudes and behaviors. Measures six through nine, listed below, were derived from Somers & Piliawksy (2004), and were found to have adequate reliability. Participants responded to items using a 5-point scale ranging from 1 = "strongly disagree" to 5 = "strongly agree". Cronbach's alphas were computed to the current sample and are reported for each instrument below as appropriate.

6. Educational Intentions (4 items, a = 72; e.g., "I plan to finish high school");
7. Educational Commitment Behavior (3 items, a = .60; e.g., " I work hard on my school grades");
8. Identification of Financial Value of Education (1 item, e.g. "It will be very easy for me to make money without a high school diploma");
9. Identification of Personal Value of Education (1 item, e.g."I am motivated to finish high school for my own personal satisfaction").

The 10th measure was responded to using a 5 point scale ("always true" to "never true").

10. Belief in Personal Control Scale (Berrenberg, 1987) (45 items, a = .67; e.g., "If I just keep trying, I can overcome any obstacle").

(continued)

e x a m p l e *(c o n t i n u e d)*

The final instrument was responded to using a "yes/no" format.

11. Persistence Scale for Children (Lufi & Cohen, 1987) (40 items, a = .70; e.g. "I often do not complete many activities I begin").

Grades

School grade point averages were obtained at the first report card marking in the fall of ninth grade. Grades used a 4.0 scale, with 4.0 being the highest possible GPA.

Procedure

Participants were recruited from several classrooms within the school on a voluntary basis. Any child or parent who was interested was permitted involvement. The potential benefit expressed to parents was that they would have the opportunity to attend a free lecture about the study results, including a summary of the research on which factors best predicted these students' academic success. Instruments were administered in classrooms under the supervision of the teachers and researchers. Although students were informed of their freedom to leave any items blank, response rates were nearly 100%.

Results

The purpose of this study was to better understand which factors are related to the school success of urban, African American youth, so to broaden how professionals could more effectively assist them. Table 1 includes descriptive information about all variables included in the study.

First, a multiple linear regression analysis was run with the five support variables entered as the predictor variables (parents, classmates, teachers, close friends, and school) and GPA as the criterion. These support variables at the beginning of 9th grade were not significantly predictive of their GPAs that fall. However, the Pearson correlation coefficients indicated that there were mild statistically significant relations between each of the social support variables and fall GPA (range of r = .18–.26, p < .05; See Table 2).

Next, correlations were run between the five support variables and the six education-related attitudes and behaviors. Moderate and strong correlations were found between the five support variables and most of the educational attitudes and behaviors variables (range of r = .22–.56, p < .01). See Table 2.

Support from parents, teachers, and peers were consistently correlated with these attitudes and behaviors. Specifically, they were correlated wth educational intentions to complete school and pursue further schooling, educational commitment behavior, and identification of the personal value of an education. Only parent support was related to identification of the financial value of an education.

However, support from best friends and schools were only minimally correlated with educational attitudes and behaviors. Additionally, correlations were run between social support and belief in personal control, as well as persistence. Only parent support was related to greater persistence levels and belief in personal control for the adolescents in this study.

TABLE 1 Descriptive Statistics for all Variables

Variable	Mean	*SD*	Min.	Max.
Parent support	4.52	1.15	1.00	6.00
Teacher support	4.17	1.34	1.00	6.00
Classmate support	3.71	1.22	1.00	6.00
Close friend support	4.70	1.24	1.00	6.00
School support	3.41	1.57	1.00	6.00
Educational intentions	4.65	0.56	2.00	5.00
Educational commitment behavior	4.11	0.56	2.00	5.00
Identification of financial value of education	3.52	0.56	2.00	5.00
Identification of personal value of education	4.70	0.52	2.00	4.00
Belief in personal control	3.11	0.33	2.00	4.00
Persistence	1.57	0.11	1.35	1.88
GPA – beginning of 9th grade	1.89	0.77	0.40	3.67

Note. B = Standardized beta coefficient. * = p < .05.

Finally, using hierarchical linear regression analyses to predict GPA in the fall of ninth grade, the five support variables were entered on step one and the six attitudinal and behavioral variables were entered on step two (educational intentions, educational commitment behavior, personal value of education, financial value of education, persistence, and belief in personal control). This was done in order to examine the individual and combined contributions of the 11 predictor variables selected for this study. GPA in the fall of ninth grade was entered as the criterion variable. Results revealed that this combination of predictors provided a statistically significant explanation of variance in fall GPA (R^2 = .569, p < .05). Beta weights revealed that only educational intentions to finish high school and personal persistence significantly contributed to the equation above and beyond the others (respectively b = .688 and .391). See Table 3.

Discussion

The main goal of this study was to explore the role of factors from several life contexts in the school success of African American ninth grade youth who live in an urban setting. The unique contribution of this study is that it considers a host of ecological factors that are related to school success. The data indicate that this group of adolescents varied widely in their academic success in the transition to 9th grade, with many of them receiving below average grades. Thus, it appeared especially important to better understand what factors predict higher achievement.

TABLE 2 Correlations Between Social Support and GPA and Educational Behaviors and Attitudes

Behavior/Attitude	Source of Social Support				
	Parents	Teachers	Classmates	Close Friends	School
Educational intentions	.454***	.386***	.367	.118	.218*
Educational commitment behavior	446***	.456***	.296**	.173	.314**
Identification of financial value of education	.225*	.022	.035	–.078	.088
Identification of personal value of education	.557***	.355***	.313**	–.011	.194
Belief in personal control	.301*	.231	.223	.237	–.076
Persistence	.347**	.221	.191	.147	.141
Achievement					
GPA – start of 9th grade	.258*	.202*	.238*	.229*	.173

Note. *** = $p < .001$, ** = $p < .01$, * = $p < .05$.

TABLE 3 Regression Analysis predicting Beginning 9th Grade GPA

Predictor Variables	Multiple R^2	Sig. of R^2	B-weight	Sig. of B
Step 1	.318	.034*		
Parent support			.314	.131
Teacher support			.259	.294
Classmate support			–.117	.635
Close friend support			.322	.092
School support			–.012	.959
Step 2	.569	.015*		
Educational intentions			.688	.033*
Educational commitment behavior			–.185	.232
Identification of financial value of education			–.514	.142
Identification of personal value of education			–.089	.622
Belief in personal control			.081	.596
Persistence			.391	.032*

Note. B = Standardized beta coefficient. * = $p < .05$.

Overall, certain variables appear to be more related to adolescents' achievement than others. The five types of social support alone were not predictors of grades, but they were correlated with grades. Parents and peers were most strongly correlated, teachers next, and peers and schools least strongly correlated. Interestingly, social support was correlated with educational intentions, educational behavior, and identification of the personal and financial value of education, some of which were predictive of grade point average. Personal control, but not persistence, was correlated with positive outcomes as well.

Social support, from each of the sources studied here, is clearly an important factor in school success, both in terms of GPA and positive educational attitudes and behaviors. Social support and academic success has been routinely studied in the literature. It is important to consider the role of social support, why it is important, what it means, and what we could/should be doing in schools and with parents. Research has shown that the most consistent predictor of academic achievement and students' attitudes toward learning is parental expectations (Reynolds et al., 1993). The data here suggest that social support is important in a child's academic success. Schools should be looking at creative ways to facilitate discussions between parents and teachers.

The source of social support found to be most related to academic success is important to consider. The correlation between support from parents and peers and grade point average supports previous literature. African American parents generally want their children to excel academically. Education is seen as a valued commodity in the African American community. Therefore, many African American parents actively encourage their children to excel academically and do well in school (Boyd-Franklin, 1989; Coleman, 1986; Hill, 1972). Hara (1998) wrote that continual parental involvement will increase academic achievement among high school students. Jeynes (2000) found that parental involvement does affect academic achievement in students from minority groups. However, he also wrote that there is a greater need to understand the

(continued)

varied aspects of parental involvement in students' education, and thus, socio-economic status should also be considered.

There is a tendency for lower socio-economic status families to be unaware of their rights and roles in the school for a number of reasons. Oftentimes, lower income parents are reluctant to get involved in their child's education because they may not see themselves as part of their children's educational process. Parents may not feel adequate enough to contribute to school success, and school environments may not be welcoming to some parents (Hoover Dempsey & Sandler, 1997). Much more education needs to occur in order to help these parents realize their potential power to help children succeed. Perhaps legislation is needed to ensure that school districts develop policies to engage all families. One example of such legislation is Senate Bill 307, passed in Michigan in 2004, which mandated that schools develop parental involvement policies and procedures.

Similarly, our finding that peer support was related to grade point average is consistent with the literature. Adolescents typically spend more time with their peer group than their parents. They are oftentimes with their peer group without supervision (Brown, 1990). Historically, research has found that peer influence is more prevalent in early adolescence versus late adolescence (Berndt, 1979; Collins and Thomas, 1972). Researchers have found that on the whole, African American students may not receive academic support from their peers (Steinberg, Dornbusch, & Brown, 1992). Fordham and Ogbu (1986) wrote that African American students who excel academically may be perceived by their peers as "acting white." These findings suggest that some African American students may not perform to their fullest potential for fear of losing the acceptance of their peer group. The school should be involved in efforts to break down such stereotypes about who can allow themselves to be successful.

In addition to social support, other factors must be considered in understanding academic success. Although many of the relations found in these analyses reflect small to moderate strength correlations, educational intentions or aspirations to complete high school was the variable that emerged as significant above and beyond the rest for this sample of adolescents. Although there was a small degree of inter-correlation (multi-collinearity) among the independent variables that were simultaneously entered into the regression analysis, this variable nonetheless contributed significant explanation of variance in GPA. Those students with intentions to complete high school are likely motivated to achieve by future possibilities. It is also likely that social support has helped them to feel motivated to aspire for high school completion and beyond. It seems important to help all adolescents, especially those at risk of dropping out, to see the relevance of what they are learning, and to realize the long term effects of their educational behavior today.

This help could be achieved through interventions designed to help adolescents feel more personal control and power over their long-term plans and outcomes. Interestingly, belief in personal control was significantly related to

outcomes, along with social support. This may at least partially explain why educational intentions to finish high school were so important in explaining variance in GPA.

Also, it was notable that in this study none of the social support variables were related to personal persistence. It may be that personal persistence is an enduring personality trait that is not necessarily linked to lack of success. Although persistence clearly has benefits for success, it may not necessarily be cause for drastic concern when a child fails to be as persistent as we might prefer. Instead, these children may simply require more extrinsic motivators to ensure that they follow a successful path, at least until they develop more intrinsic habits.

Given our findings, it is important that young adolescents are involved with long term programs that offer social support. Both prevention and intervention efforts are important, considering all contexts of adolescents' lives. Multimodal interventions are important, tapping family, community, school, and individual levels. We can start at the individual child and adolescent level, but each child's entire support network also needs to scaffold their educational goals, plans, and daily progress toward meeting goals.

Overall, results of this study revealed that for this sample of urban, African American children, social support from classmates, parents, teachers, close friends, and schools all were significantly correlated with their 9th grade GPAs and educational intentions. Given the findings, there are several implications for educators. Even though the correlations between school and teacher support and GPA were small, they were still significant and necessitate the role of educators in the interventions needed. Clearly, teacher relationships with students can have a positive association with academic success. The implications for educators also include the need for further examination of broader research that examines parental relationships with schools and why parents become involved. In addition, schools and community organizations must develop strategies and policies to broaden parental involvement in schools. A theoretical model that examines the parental involvement process in schooling practices and a definition of what it means for parents to be involved is imperative.

There are several limitations that could be improved for future research, including sample size and more precise or inclusive measurements of achievement than GPA alone. Cross-cultural research would also provide information about whether or not these dynamics are unique to African American, urban populations. Nonetheless, these findings both support previous literature and contribute new information about urban, African American adolescents as they make the sometimes turbulent transition to ninth grade. These findings can be used to drive not only future research questions but applied prevention and interventions efforts as discussed above.

References

Banks, J. A., & Banks, C. A. M. (2001). Multicultural education/Issues and perspectives. (5th ed.). Boston: Allyn and Bacon.

Baur, S., Sapp, M., & Johnson, D. (2000). Group Counseling Strategies for Rural At-Risk High School Students. *High School Journal, 83*. 41–51.

Barnett, W. S. (2004). Better teachers, better preschools: Student achievement linked to teacher qualifications. In *Preschool Policy Matters, 2,* 1–11. New Brunswick, NJ: National Institute for Early Education Research, Rutgers.

Barone, C., Aguirre-Deandreis, A. I., & Trickett, E. J. (1991). Mean-ends problem-solving skills, life stress, and social support as mediators of adjustment in the normative transition to high school. *American Journal of Community Psychology, 19* (2), 207-225.

Berrenberg, J. L. (1987). The belief in personal control scale: A measure of God-mediated and exaggerated control. *Journal of Personality Assessment, 51,* 194–206.

Berndt, T. (1979). Developmental changes in conformity to peers and parents. *Developmental Psychology, 15,* 606–616.

Berndt, T., & Keefe, K. (1995). Friends' influence on adolescents' adjustment to school. *Child Development, 66* (5), 1312–1329.

Boyd-Franklin, N. (1989). *Black families in therapy: A multi-systems approach.* NY: Guildford Press.

Bronfenbrenner, U. (1979). *The ecology of human development.* Cambridge, MA: Harvard University Press.

Brown, B. B. (1990). Peer groups and peer cultures (pp.171–196). In S. S. Feldman and G. R. Elliott (Eds), *At the threshold: The developing adolescent.* Cambridge, MA: Harvard University Press.

Cokley, K. O. (2004). What do we know about the motivation of African American students? Challenging the 'anti-intellectual' myth": Correction. *Harvard Educational Review, 73* (4), 524–558.

Coleman, B. P. (1986). The Black educator: An endangered species. *Journal of Negro Education, 55*(3), 326–334.

Collins, J. K., & Thomas, N. T. (1972). Age and susceptibility to same-sex peer pressure. *British Journal of Educational Psychology, 42,* 83–85.

Constantine, M. G., & Blackmon, S. M. (2002). Black adolescents' racial socialization experiences: Their relations to home, school and peer self-esteem. *Journal of Black Studies, 32,* 322–335.

Cooper, R., & Jordan, W. J. (2003). Cultural issues in comprehensive school reform. *Urban Education, 38,* 380–397.

Council of Great City Schools (1999). *Closing the achievement gaps in urban schools: A survey of academic progress and promising practices in the great city schools.* Washington, DC: Author.

Eccles, J. S., Midgley, C., Wigfield, A., Buchanan, C. M. (1993). Development during adolescence: The impact of stage environment fit on young adolescent's experiences in schools and families. *American Psychologist: Special Issue: Adolescence, 48* (2), 90–101.

Epstein, J. (2001). *School, family, and community partnerships.* Boulder: Westview Press.

Ferguson, R. E. (2002). *Addressing racial disparities in high-achieving suburban schools.* Retrieved from http://ww.ncrel.org/policy/pubs/html/pivol113/dec2002b.htm, February 17, 2005.

Flowers, L. A., Milner, H. R., & Moore III, L. (2003). Effects of locus of control on African American high school seniors' educational aspirations: Implications for preservice and inservice high school teachers and counselors. *The High School Journal, 87,* 39–50.

Ford, D. Y., & Moore III, J. L. (2004). The achievement gap and gifted students of color. *Understanding Our Gifted, 16,* 3–7.

Ford, D. Y., & Moore III, J. L. (2006). Eliminating deficit orientations: Creating classrooms and curricula for gifted students from diverse cultural backgrounds. In D. W. Sue and M. Constantine (Eds.), *Racism as a barrier to cultural competence in mental health and educational settings.* Indianapolis, IN: John Wiley and Sons.

Fordham, S., & Ogbu, J. U. (1986). Black students' school success: Coping with the "burden of acting White." *The Urban Review, 18* (3), 176–206.

Gallagher, J. J. (July 8, 1998). Education, alone, is a weak treatment. Education Week, www.edweek.org. In *Socio-Economic Conditions and Student Achievement.* Retrieved http://www.weac.org/greatschools/Issuepapers/socioconditions.htm (11/21/04).

Grantham, T. C., & Ford, D. Y. (2003). Beyond self-concept and self-esteem: Racial Identity and gifted African American students. *The High School Journal, 87,* 18–29.

Guest, K. C., & Biasini, F. J. (2001). Middle childhood, poverty, and adjustment: Does social support have an impact? *Psychology in the Schools, 38* (6), 549–560.

Guo, G., Brooks-Gunn, J., & Harris, K. M. (1996). Parents' labor force attachment and grade retention among urban black children. *Sociology of Education, 69* (3), 217–236.

Hara, S. R. (1998). Parent involvement: The key to improved student achievement. *School Community Journal, 8,* 9–19.

Henderson, T. A. & Mapp, K. L. (2002). A new wave of evidence: The impact of school, family and community connections on student achievement. Metairie, LA: Southwest Educational Development Laboratory, National Center for Family and Community Connections with Schools.

Hill, R. (1972). *The strengths of Black families.* Washington, DC: National Urban League.

Hoover-Dempsey, K. V., & Sandler, H. M. (1997). Why do parents become involved in their children's education? *Review of Educational Research, 67* (1), 3–42.

Howard, T. C. (2003). "A tug war for our minds": African American high school students' perceptions of their academic identities and college aspirations. *The High School Journal, 87,* 4–17.

Jeynes, W. (2000). Assessing school choice: A balanced perspective. *Cambridge Journal of Education, 30* (2), 223–241

Kantor, P. (2000). Can Regionalism Save Poor Cities? *Urban Affairs Review,* Vol. 35, No. 6, 794–820.

Karavasilis, K., Doyle, A. B., & Margolese, S. K. (1999). *Links between parenting styles and adolescent attachment.* Poster presented at the biennial meetings of the Society for Research in Child Development, Albuquerque, NM.

Lufi, D., & Cohen, A. (1987). A scale for measuring persistence in children. *Journal of Personality Assessment, 51,* 178–185.

Malecki, C. K, Demaray, M. K., & Elliott, S. N. (2000). The child and adolescent social support scale. Dekalb, IL: Northern Illinois University.

Moore III, J. L. (2006). A qualitative investigation of African American males' career trajectory in engineering: Implications for teachers, school counselors, and parents. *Teachers College Record, 108,* 246–266.

National Governors Association. (2003). *Ready for tomorrow: Helping all students achieve secondary and postsecondary success.* Washington, DC: Author.

Newman, B., Myers, M. C., Newman, P. R., Lohman, B. J., & Smith, V. L. (2000). The transition to high school for academically promising, urban, low-income African American youth. *Adolescence, 35,* 45–66.

Ogbu, J. U. (2003). *Black American students in an affluent suburb: A study of academic disengagement.* Mahwah, NJ: Lawrence Erlbaum.

Ogbu, J. U. (2004). Collective identity and the burden of "acting white" in Black history, community, and education. *The Urban Review, 36,* 1–35.

Owens, D., Hamm, D., Jaynes, C., & Rawls, G. (2004). Factors affecting task engagement in urban African American adolescents. A pilot study. Ohio Journal of Professional Counseling. http://www.ohiocounselingassoc.com

Reynolds, A. J., Mavrogenes, N. A., Hagemann M., & Bezruczko, N. (1993). *Schools, families, and children: Sixth year results from the longitudinal study of children at risk.* Chicago: Chicago Public Schools, Department of Research, Evaluation, and Planning.

Somers, C. L., & Piliawsky, M. (2004). Drop-out prevention among urban, African American adolescents: Program evaluation and practical implications. *Preventing School Failure, 48* (3), 17–20.

Steinberg, L., Dornbusch, S. M., & Brown, B. B. (1992). Ethnic differences in adolescent achievement: an ecological perspective. *American Psychologist, 46*(6), 723–729.

Swanson, C. B., & Schneider, B. (1999). Students on the move: Residential and educational mobility in America's schools. *Sociology of Education, 72*(1), 54–67

Thernstrom, S. & Thernstrom, A. (2003). *No excuses: Closing the racial gap in learning.* New York: Simon and Schuster.

Trusty, J. (1998). Family influences on educational expectations of late adolescence. *The Journal of Educational Research, 91,* 260–270.

U.S. Department of Education. (2003). *Overview of public elementary and secondary schools and districts: School year 2001–02: Statistical analysis report.* NCES 2003–411. Retrieved on May 3, 2005 from http://nces.ed.gov/pubs2003/2003411

Wentzel, K.R. (1994). Relations of social goal pursuit to social acceptance, classroom behavior, and perceived social support. *Journal of Educational Psychology, 86*(2), 173–182.

Xu, J. (2002). *Middle school family involvement in urban settings: Perspectives from minority students and their families.* Paper presented at the annual meeting of the American Educational Research Association, Seattle, WA.

ANSWER TO THE APPLICATION PROBLEMS

1. Her decision may have been correct, but her inference that the methods caused the achievement is incorrect because it is possible that other events occurred at the same time as the methods to cause greater achievement. This is an example of inferring causation from correlation.

2. a. correlational
    b. comparative
    c. predictive
    d. comparative
    e. descriptive
    f. ex post facto

3. (individual student response)

4. This is an example of both a comparative and a correlational study. The independent variables were participation/no participation in service learning, previous work experience, and level of training. The dependent variables were self-efficacy and state anxiety. The description of the sample was not complete, because characteristics of each group were not documented. This is a serious limitation, because other differences between the groups, in addition to whether they did service learning, could account for the findings. The group that did not participate in service learning was small. The measures are fairly well described, although more detail would be helpful in evaluating the information. Reliability and validity are addressed, although it would be best to have evidence from their subjects. There is good range of scores. Correlation and coefficient of determination, here reported as R^2, are reported separately. A shotgun approach was not used. Spurious correlations could easily result if other factors at the schools affected self-efficacy and anxiety. Causal conclusions are not presented. Overall credibility is not strong.

Experimental, Quasi-Experimental, and Single-Subject Designs

From Chapter 11 of *Research in Education: Evidence-Based Inquiry*, 7/e. James H. McMillan. Sally Schumacher.

Experimental, Quasi-Experimental, and Single-Subject Designs

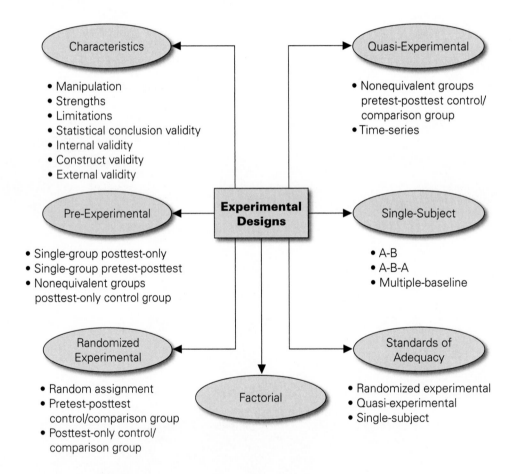

KEY TERMS

randomized experimental research

intervention, experimental or
  treatment group

control or comparison group

fidelity of intervention

pre-experimental designs

single-group posttest-only design

single-group pretest-posttest design

nonequivalent groups posttest-only design

randomized pretest-posttest control
  group design

randomized groups pretest-posttest
  comparison group design

randomized posttest-only control and
  comparison group designs

quasi-experimental designs

nonequivalent groups pretest-posttest
  control or comparison group designs

time-series design

abbreviated time-series design

single-group interrupted time-series design

control group interrupted time-series design

abbreviated time-series design

factorial designs

interaction

single-subject designs

A-B design

A-B-A design

reversal, removal, or withdrawal design

multiple-baseline designs

WHAT YOU WILL LEARN

Study this chapter and you will:

- Understand the key elements of experimental research.
- Identify the strengths and weaknesses of experimental designs.
- Recognize and understand the importance of random assignment.
- Plan experimental studies.
- Apply internal, construct, statistical conclusion, and external validity threats to different experimental designs.
- Understand the difference between possible and plausible threats to internal validity.

- Understand essential differences between pre-experimental, randomized experimental, and quasi-experimental designs.
- Know how key components of each experimental design affect the plausibility of rival hypotheses.
- Know how to read and interpret experimental studies.
- Understand the key components of single-subject designs and threats to internal validity.

INTRODUCTION TO EXPERIMENTAL RESEARCH

Experiments are making a comeback in educational research! For the past 20 years, there has been a steady, justified emphasis on qualitative methods. Now, due primarily to changes in policy at the U.S. Department of Education, experimental designs must be employed, where possible, when investigating cause-and-effect relationships.

This chapter considers the conduct of experiments in detail. It focuses on four major categories of experimental designs that are used to make causal inferences about the relationship between independent and dependent variables: pre-experimental, randomized experimental, quasi-experimental, and single-subject designs.

The term *experiment*, like many other terms, can have different meanings. Defined in a general way, an experiment is simply a way of learning something by varying some condition and observing the effect on something else. In other words, we change something and watch for the effect. As humans, we use natural experiments constantly to learn. For instance, young children experiment with a host of tactics to see which one will affect Mom or Dad most; teachers try a new approach to discipline to see whether it works; and students vary study techniques to see which ones seem to result in the best grades. Each of these simple trial-and-error behaviors is an attempt to show causation, which is the primary purpose of an experiment. The difference between these casual experiments and highly sophisticated experiments is the extent to which the researcher can be certain that the varied conditions caused the observed effect. It is the interpretation *of causation*, then, that is a key element in experimental research.

Keep in mind four criteria for making causal conclusions (Schneider, Carnoy, Kilpatrick, Schmidt, & Shavelson, 2007):

1. ***Causal Relativity.*** In education it is rarely the case that an intervention is compared to a control group that received no intervention. Almost always, choices are made about which of several alternative interventions are most effective. It is not simply a matter of showing that an intervention is effective; the relative causality of one intervention needs to be compared to that of other interventions.
2. ***Causal Manipulation.*** The independent variable that is used to make causal conclusions must be *manipulated*, or controlled, by the experimenter, unlike assigned independent variables such as age or gender.
3. ***Temporal Ordering.*** There must be a specified time interval during which the intervention is administered. That is, there is an ordering of aspects of the study that occur in sequence—preintervention, intervention, and postintervention. The intervention is something that is planned ahead to follow from what is known before the intervention.
4. ***Elimination of Alternative Explanations.*** Good experiments are designed so that there are no plausible rival explanations of what caused postintervention differences. Outcomes need to be attributed to the intervention and not to other variables or influences.

Characteristics of Experimental Research

Traditionally defined experimental research—that is, the type of design that is based on the gold standard in medical research—has six distinguishing characteristics:

1. theory-driven research hypotheses
2. statistical equivalence of subjects in intervention and control and/or comparison groups (achieved through random assignment)
3. researcher-controlled interventions independently and uniformly applied to all subjects
4. measurement of each dependent variable
5. use of inferential statistics
6. rigorous control of conditions and extraneous variables

These characteristics are usually present in physical and biological science experimental research, including medical and agricultural, but such conditions can rarely be achieved completely in educational research. This does not, however, diminish the importance of the experimental method for education. Much research in education approximates most of these characteristics, and we need to understand the way different methods of conducting research that investigates causal relationships affect the interpretation of the results. That is what Campbell and Stanley (1963) had in mind in writing their classic and still influential chapter "Experimental and Quasi-Experimental Designs for Education." The following quotation leaves little doubt about their perspective.

> This chapter is committed to the experiment: as the only means for settling disputes regarding educational practice, as the only way of verifying educational improvements, and as the only way of establishing a cumulative tradition in which improvements can be introduced without the danger of a faddish discard of old wisdom in favor of inferior novelties. (p. 2)

We need to distinguish, then, between what can be labeled **randomized experimental research** (sometimes called *true* or *pure* experimental research), in which the previous six characteristics are completely present, and the experimental method of research more broadly, in which the characteristics are partially present. This is particularly important because so many agencies and organizations now have an increased interest in conducting

Randomized experimental research: random assignment with intervention experiments, especially for determining policy. Attention has been focused on research that contains the six characteristics mentioned earlier. Here are some terms commonly used to communicate the nature of the randomized experiment:

    randomized trials of uniform treatment
    randomized controlled experiment
    randomized controlled trials (RCTs)
    random trials
    randomized experiments
    randomized field trials (RFTs)

Clearly, the emphasis is on the design feature of being *randomized*, but there is also an intent to have more rigorous designs from which cause-and-effect relationships can be established. Although all of these terms are used in the broader literature, we will define experimental research in which the six characteristics are mostly present, as *randomized experiments*.

The first characteristic, having theory-driven research hypotheses, explains why there are cause-and-effect findings and provides a clear indication of how the findings should be generalized. Because specific hypotheses are postulated, the range of possible outcomes is restricted and the likelihood that chance is a factor is reduced.

Achieving statistical equivalence of individuals in groups that are compared, the second characteristic, is essential for ruling out the many possible variables that could invalidate causal conclusions. That is, the researcher wants to make the groups under comparison as similar as possible so that no subject characteristics or experiences can be said to explain the results.

Whether or not randomization is implemented in educational research depends on many factors, including the willingness to use students as subjects and to expose them to alternate interventions that might have a negative impact or to a control group that has no intervention at all. It would not be ethical to withhold a treatment known to have a positive impact. Randomization should be implemented when the demand for a program or service outstrips the supply and when a program or service cannot be introduced to all subjects at the same time (e.g., perhaps for financial reasons).

Researcher-controlled interventions, or direct manipulation of the intervention, is perhaps the most distinct feature of experimental research. *Manipulation*, in this sense, means that the researcher decides on and controls the specific intervention, treatment, or condition for each group of subjects. The independent variable is manipulated in that different values or conditions (levels) of the independent variable are assigned to groups by the experimenter. Suppose, for example, that a research team is interested in investigating whether the order of difficulty of items in a test makes a difference in student achievement. The study might have one independent variable, order of items, with two levels: items ordered from easiest to most difficult and items ordered from most difficult to easiest. These are the conditions that are manipulated by the researchers, who would probably divide a class into two groups, randomly, and give all students in each group one of the two types of item order.

The fourth characteristic, measurement of dependent variables, means that experimental research is concerned with outcomes that can be assigned a numerical value. If the results of the study cannot be measured and quantified in some way, then the research cannot be experimental.

Another characteristic that involves numbers is the use of inferential statistics. Inferential statistics are used to make probability statements about the results. This is important for two reasons: (1) because measurement is imperfect in education and (2) because we often want to generalize the results to similar groups or to the population of subjects.

The final characteristic of experimental research is perhaps the most important from a generic point of view because the principle of control of extraneous variables is not unique to experimental research. What is unique to experimental research is that there is a determined effort to ensure that no extraneous or confounding variables provide plausible rival hypotheses to explain the results. We control extraneous variables either by making sure that they have no effect on the dependent variable or by keeping the effect the same for all groups.

Strengths and Limitations of Experimental Research

The experimental method is clearly the best approach for determining the causal effect of an intervention. This is primarily because of the potential for a high degree of control of extraneous and confounding variables and the power of manipulation of variables. The careful control that characterizes good experimental research becomes a liability for the field of education, however. Control is most easily achieved with research on humans only in restrictive and artificial settings. As pointed out by Hess and Henig (2008), educational experiments cannot be conducted in restrictive and artificial ways if the results are able to provide generalized guidance to actual complex settings.

Here is an example of this dilemma: Suppose that the problem to be investigated is whether an individualized approach or a cooperative group discussion is the best method for teaching science concepts to fourth-graders. The objective is to find the method of teaching that gives the best results in achievement. An experimental approach is selected because the problem is clearly one of causation, and presumably the method of instruction—the independent variable—can be manipulated easily. To maximize control of extraneous variables, the experiment might be arranged as follows: (1) At the beginning of one schoolday, all fourth-graders report to a special room, where they are randomly divided into individualized and cooperative groups. (2) To remove any effect the present teachers might have, graduate assistants from the universities act as the teachers. (3) To remove any effect of different rooms, all of the groups of students are taken to similar rooms in different locations. (4) To control possible distractions, these rooms have no windows. (5) To ensure that directions are uniform, the teachers read from specially prepared scripts. (6) The science material selected has been carefully screened so that it will be new information for all students. After studying the material for an hour, the students are tested on the concepts. The results compare the achievement of the groups, and because the design has controlled for most extraneous variables, this difference can be attributed to the independent variable: the method of instruction.

What do we do with this knowledge? Because one approach seemed best in this experiment, does it mean that Mr. Jones—in his class, with his style of teaching, in his room, with students that may have particular learning strengths and weaknesses—should use the supposedly proven method? Perhaps, but the difficulty that is illustrated is one of generalizability, a common problem for experiments that are able to exhibit tight control over extraneous variables. On the other hand, if we want to maximize external validity, then we need to design the experiment right in Mr. Jones's class, as well as in the classes of other teachers, and somehow design the study to control as many variables as possible without disrupting the natural environment of the class. The researcher would need to select the variables most likely to affect achievement, such as aptitude, time of day, and composition of groups, and control these as much as possible. This approach makes it more difficult to show that one or the other method of teaching is more effective, but the results will be more generalizable to normal classrooms. The real challenge is to design the procedures so that the results obtained can be reasonably generalized to other people and environments—that is, balancing internal and external validity in a design.

In the end, we need to realize that the nature of the causal evidence varies from strong to weak. In an idealized experiment, there are certain characteristics that lead to strong evidence and assurance of causality. In educational field settings, however, the characteristics of the design do not allow strong evidence. Look at the characteristics of strong and weak evidence in Table 11.1. Clearly, field studies can at best lead to tentative causal conclusions. In other words, the nature of the causal evidence in field settings is compromised. This means that results of field experiments, even when random assignment is used, need to be supplemented with other kinds of evidence of impact (Chatterji, 2007). In the end, it is a matter of being *reasonable* in the nature of the conclusions that can be drawn, incorporating all evidence as well as more anecdotal observations.

We hope that the use of the word *reasonable* is not confusing. The simple fact is that we approximate randomized experimental designs as well as we can because such designs convincingly determine causation. In the final analysis, however, because we are working with human

TABLE 11.1 Ideal and Actual Characteristics of Strong and Weak Evidence in Experimental Research

Ideal—Leading to Strong Evidence	Actual—Leading to Weak Evidence
Restricted, controlled environment	Complex, uncontrolled environment
Results clearly attributed to intervention	Factors other than the intervention may affect results
Random assignment of subjects	Subjects rarely randomized
Sufficiently large sample	Due to nesting within classes and schools, small unit of analysis
Completely separate experimental and control groups	Interaction between experimental and control groups
Tightly controlled administration of the intervention	Messy, difficult-to-control implementation
Conducted with sufficient time to allow intervention effects	Tends to be conducted over shorter periods of time
Experimental and control group environments are the same	Experimental and control group environments are different

beings in complex situations, we must almost always use professional judgment, or reason, in making conclusions on the basis of observed results. Knowledge of the designs covered in this chapter and threats to internal and external validity help us in applying this judgment.

A useful resource for examining interpretation of experiments is provided by the What Works Clearinghouse (WWC; http://ies.ed.gov/ncee/wwc/). This federally funded center examines the effectiveness of educational interventions and assesses the rigor of the research evidence based on design and procedures. The WWC uses a systematic review process in which each study is placed in one of three categories: (1) meets evidence standards, (2) meets evidence standards with reservations, and (3) does not meet evidence standards. A study will meet standards when it is a well-controlled, randomized control trial that does not have problems with randomization or subject attrition. Studies that meet standards with reservations are quasi-experimental, with adequate control of group characteristics.

What is interesting about the WWC reviews is the number of experiments that fall into each of these categories. Table 11.2 shows the results for recent reviews that were available on the WWC website. Note the large percentage of studies that fall in the "does not meet evidence standards" category. This may give the impression that most experimental research in education is poorly conducted. What is presented, though, is no doubt a function of the fact that educational experiments are rarely conducted as "ideal," as summarized in Table 11.1, and many of the studies in the "does not meet" category can provide important information and insights.

The American Educational Research Association (AERA) adopted a resolution in 2003 that recognizes the importance of randomized designs. The resolution also stressed that research

TABLE 11.2 WWC Reviews

Program or Product	Meets Evidence Standards	Meets Evidence Standards with Reservations	Does Not Meet Evidence Standards
To enhance beginning reading	27	24	836
Elementary school math curricula	2	7	227
Dropout prevention programs	7	9	43

questions should guide the selection of method of inquiry from many alternatives. The resolution states:

> Council recognizes randomized trials among the sound methodologies to be used in the conduct of education research and commends increased attention to their use. . . . However, the Council of the Association expresses dismay that the Department of Education . . . is devoting singular attention to this one tool of science, jeopardizing a broader range of problems best addressed through other scientific methods. (www.aera.net/meeting/councilresolution03.htm)

Planning Experimental Research

The first steps in planning experimental research are to define a research problem, search the literature, and state clear research hypotheses. It is essential that experimental research be guided by research hypotheses that state the expected results. The actual results will either support or fail to support the research hypotheses.

Next, the researcher selects subjects from a defined population and, depending on the specific design used, usually assigns subjects to different groups. A simple experimental study involves two groups, one called the **intervention, experimental, or treatment group** and the other called the **control or comparison group**. Each group is then assigned one level (intervention) of the independent variable. Technically, a control group receives no treatment at all (e.g., when comparing people who smoke with people who do not), but in most educational research, it is unproductive to compare one group receiving a treatment with another group receiving nothing. It would be like comparing children who received extra individual tutoring with children who did not and then concluding on the basis of the results that children need individual tutoring. It is also unrealistic in school settings to expect that one group will be doing nothing while another group receives a special treatment. For these reasons, it is most common to conceive of the two groups in experimental research as the treatment and comparison groups or as a design with two interventions.

In assigning the treatments, as indicated by levels of the independent variable, the researcher determines the nature of the value, forms, or conditions each group receives. This could be a simple assignment, such as lecture versus discussion, loud reprimands versus soft reprimands, or high or low effort assignments, or there could be more than two levels, with varying degrees of the condition in each level of the independent variable. For example, if a researcher were interested in the effect of different types of teacher feedback on student attitudes, then feedback, the independent variable, could be represented in four levels: grade only, grade plus one word only, grade plus one sentence, and grade plus three sentences. Hence, the researcher would form four levels by randomly assigning subjects to four groups. The researcher would arrange appropriate control so that any difference in attitude could be explained as caused by different types of feedback.

One of the difficulties in planning experimental research is knowing whether the interventions will be strong enough—that is, if the treatment condition is providing feedback to students, will the feedback make enough of an impact to affect students' attitudes? Would feedback given over several consecutive days make a difference? Maybe the feedback has to be given for a month or more. In other words, either the treatment should be tested in advance to ensure that it is powerful enough to make an impact or sufficient time should be allocated to give the treatment a chance to work. This can be an especially difficult problem in much educational research because many factors (e.g., achievement, attitudes, motivation, and self-concept) may affect the dependent variables, and it is hard to single out a specific independent variable that will have a meaningful, unique effect, given all other influences. Finally, experimental treatments are sometimes insufficiently distinct from treatments given comparison groups for a statistical difference to be possible. In a study of different counseling techniques, for example, if the only difference between the experimental and control conditions was the distance the counselor sat from the clients (say, four feet or six feet), it is unlikely, given all the other influences, that a researcher will obtain a difference in results.

Another important consideration in designing an experiment is to be sure that the treatment or intervention has occurred as planned, which is called **fidelity of intervention**. To

Intervention, experimental, or treatment group: subjects who receive the intervention

Control or comparison group: subjects who do not receive the targeted intervention or receive a different intervention

Fidelity of intervention: actual implementation of the planned intervention

EXCERPT 11.1   Fidelity of Implementation

Three lessons . . . were filmed in each intervention classroom to obtain data on the fidelity of implementation of the treatment at each site. The tapes were subsequently coded to reflect the degree to which the teacher correctly implemented the key elements of the lesson plan. . . . They were summed per lesson per teacher to provide a single indicating fidelity of implementation. Six of the nine teachers implemented over 70% of key lesson elements over the three weeklong observations. . . . The three teachers with the highest fidelity enhanced the implementation with additional elements that were consistent with its design, and none of the six high implementers committed any errors of implementation. (p. 194)

Source: From Carl, M. S., August, D., Mclaughlin, B., Snow, C. E., Dressier, C., Lippman, D. N., Lively, T. J., & White, C. E. (2004). Closing the gap: Addressing the vocabulary needs of English-language learners in bilingual and mainstream classrooms. *Reading Research Quarterly, 39*(2), 188–215.

EXCERPT 11.2   Fidelity of Implementation

To measure whether the intervention curricula were implemented with fidelity, descriptive statistics were computed . . . there were few notable differences . . . total fidelity scores were acceptably positive . . . there is no evidence that they changed over time, were different in the two intervention groups, or interacted with program type. (pp. 466–467)

Source: From Clements, D. H., & Sarama, J. (2008). Experimental evaluation of the effects of a research-based preschool mathematics curriculum. *American Educational Research Journal, 45*(2), 443–494.

determine if the intervention was implemented as designed, five criteria can be used (O'Donnell, 2008):

1. *Adherence*—whether each component of the intervention is delivered as designed
2. *Duration*—whether the intervention was implemented with a sufficient length and number of sessions
3. *Quality of delivery*—whether the techniques, processes, and procedures as prescribed are delivered
4. *Participant responsiveness*—whether participants are engaged in and involved with program activities and content
5. *Program differentiation*—whether features that distinguish the intervention from other programs are present

Essentially, the researcher gathers data from the participants and monitors the intervention to assure fidelity. This is very important in field studies, where extraneous variables can affect not only the results but also the nature of the intervention. Other words and phrases that refer to fidelity of implementation include *integrity, adherence,* or *quality of program delivery, adherence to program model standards, closeness of implementation as compared to what was intended* (*program as planned* and *program as delivered*), and *degree to which specified components are implemented* (O'Donnell, 2008). Examples of how researchers address fidelity of implementation are illustrated in Excerpts 11.1 and 11.2.

EXPERIMENTAL VALIDITY

Consider four types of experimental validity: statistical conclusion, internal, construct, and external. Each of these is considered here, with particular implications for experimental designs.

Statistical Conclusion Validity

Five of the seven threats to statistical conclusion validity address why a study may not provide valid conclusions of "no difference" or "no relationship." In an experiment, this may mean that

TABLE 11.3 Summary of Threats to Statistical Conclusion Validity

Threat	Description
Low statistical power	The design does not have enough subjects or a powerful enough intervention to detect a difference.
Violated assumptions of statistical tests	Assumptions such as having a population with a normal distribution and equal variances are not met, leading to incorrect support or incorrect nonsupport of the research hypotheses.
"Fishing" and the error rate problem	A statistically significant difference has been found with one of many statistical tests on the same data.
Unreliability of measures	The presence of measurement error makes it difficult to obtain a significant difference.
Restriction of range	Small variances or ranges make it difficult to obtain significant relationships.
Unreliability of intervention implementation	Differences in the administration of an intervention to different individuals or groups result in underestimating the effect of the intervention.
Extraneous variance in the experimental setting	Differences in the settings in which the interventions took place inflate the error rate, making it more difficult to find a relationship or difference.

a conclusion such as "The intervention of technology did not significantly affect achievement" may be wrong if there are plausible threats to statistical conclusion validity. This is one of two ways in which a research hypothesis is considered against the findings: Either it is or is not supported by the data. When it is not supported by the data, the researcher must be sure that none of the five threats is present. The threat of "fishing" and the error rate problem is one in which support for the research hypothesis can be found because many statistical tests are done (one of which is significant). Threats to statistical conclusion validity are summarized in Table 11.3.

Internal Validity

The internal validity of a study is a judgment that is made concerning the confidence with which plausible rival hypotheses can be ruled out as explanations for the results. It involves a deductive process in which the investigator must systematically examine how each of the threats to internal validity, which constitute rival alternative hypotheses, may have influenced the results. If all the threats can be reasonably eliminated, then the researcher can be confident that an observed relationship is causal and that the difference in treatment conditions caused the obtained results.

Internal validity is rarely an all-or-none decision. Rather, it is assessed as a matter of degree, depending on the plausibility of the explanation. As will be pointed out, some designs are relatively strong with respect to internal validity because most rival hypotheses can be ruled out confidently, whereas designs that lend themselves to a host of plausible rival explanations are weak in internal validity. It cannot be stressed too much that, in the final analysis, researchers must be their own best critics and carefully examine all threats that are possible. It is important, then, for consumers of research, as well as for those conducting research, to be aware of the common threats to internal validity and of the best ways to control them. Researchers need to be *anthropologists* of their study, knowing well that threats to internal validity can be identified.

A useful way to think about threats to internal validity is to distinguish what is *possible* from what is *plausible*. A possible threat is clearly not controlled by the design, but to be considered seriously, the possible threat needs to be plausible in two respects. First, the factor needs to be something that affects the dependent variable. For example, there can be differences between compared groups in eye color, but that is not likely to be related to

TABLE 11.4 Summary of Threats to Internal Validity

Threat	Description
History	Unplanned or extraneous events that occur during the research may affect the results.
Selection	Differences between the subjects in the groups may result in outcomes that are different because of group composition.
Statistical regression	Scores of groups of subjects take on values closer to the mean due to respondents' being identified on the basis of extremely high or low scores.
Pretesting	The act of taking a test or responding to a questionnaire prior to the treatment affects the subjects.
Instrumentation	Differences in results are due to unreliability, changes in the measuring instrument, or observers.
Attrition	The systematic loss of subjects affects the outcome.
Maturation	An effect is due to maturational or other natural changes in the subjects (e.g., being older, wiser, stronger, tired).
Diffusion of intervention	Subjects in one group learn about interventions or conditions for different groups.
Experimenter effects	Deliberate or unintended effects of the researcher influence subjects' responses.
Intervention replications	Number of replications of the intervention is different from the number of subjects.
Subject effects	Changes in behavior result in response to being a subject or to being in an experiment.

the dependent variable! Second, the factor needs to be systematically related to one group. That is, it needs to affect one group more than the other group. If a factor affects both groups equally, then it is not a threat to internal validity.

Threats to internal validity are summarized in Table 11.4 in order to help you commit each one to memory. They will be discussed again in the context of each of the designs summarized in the chapter, both in the text and in Tables 11.7 through 11.9, which provide overviews of the threats that are controlled by each design.

Construct Validity

Consider the notion of construct validity in research design. In experiments, the term *construct validity* describes how well measured variables and interventions represent the theoretical constructs that have been hypothesized (i.e., construct validity of the *effects* and *causes*, respectively). That is, how well is the theory supported by the particular measures and treatments? Table 11.5 lists three threats to construct validity that may, if not controlled, restrict causal conclusions and implications.

External Validity

External validity is the extent to which the results of an experiment can be generalized to people and environmental conditions outside the context of the experiment. That is, if the same intervention conditions were replicated with different subjects, in a different setting, would the results be the same? We conclude that an experiment has strong external validity if the generalizability is relatively extensive and has weak external validity if we are unable to generalize very much beyond the actual experiment. Table 11.6 summarizes the sources of threats to external validity.

It is difficult to view external validity in the same way that we view internal validity because most experiments are not designed specifically to control threats to external validity.

TABLE 11.5 Summary of Threats to Construct Validity

Threat	Description
Inadequate explication of the constructs	Invalid inferences are made about the constructs because they have not been sufficiently described and supported by theory.
Mono-operation bias	Only a single type of intervention or dependent variable is used when using multiple types would lead to more assurance that the more abstract theory is supported.
Mono-method bias	Implementing the intervention or measuring the dependent variable in only one way restricts inferences to just those methods as well as to the hypothesized theoretical relationships.

Researchers consciously control some threats to internal validity by using a particular design, but most threats to external validity are a consideration regardless of the design. In only a few designs can it be concluded that sources of external validity are controlled. Under the ecological category, for example, such threats as description of variables, novelty effect, setting/treatment interaction, and time of measurement treatment interaction, are not controlled with any particular experimental design. These threats are more a function of

TABLE 11.6 Summary of Threats to External Validity

Threat	Description
Population	
Selection of subjects	Generalization is limited to the subjects in the sample if the subjects are not selected randomly from an identified population.
Characteristics of subjects	Generalization is limited to the characteristics of the sample or population (e.g., socioeconomic status, age, location, ability, race).
Subject/treatment interaction	Generalization may be limited because of the interaction between the subjects and the intervention (i.e., the effect of the intervention is unique to the subjects).
Ecological	
Description of variables	Generalization is limited to the operational definitions of the independent and dependent variables.
Multiple-treatment interference	In experiments in which subjects receive more than one intervention, generalizability is limited to similar multiple-intervention situations because of the effect of the first intervention on subsequent treatments.
Setting/treatment interaction	Generalization is limited to the setting in which the study is conducted (e.g., room, time of day, others present, other surroundings).
Time of measurement/treatment interaction	Results may be limited to the time frame in which they were obtained. Interventions causing immediate effects may not have lasting effects.
Pretest-posttest sensitization	The pretest or posttest may interact with the intervention so that similar results are obtained only when the testing conditions are present.
Novelty or disruption effect	Subjects may respond differently because of a change in routine, and generalization may be limited to situations that involve similar novelty or disruption (e.g., an initially effective intervention may become ineffective in time as the novelty wears off).

procedures and definitions than of design, and in most studies, the reader decides whether any of the threats are reasonable.

Two of the ecological threats—multiple-treatment interference and pretest-posttest sensitization—are present only in particular designs. Multiple-treatment interference is a consideration only if more than one intervention is applied in succession. Pretest sensitization is a serious threat when investigating personality, values, attitudes, or opinions, because taking the pretest may sensitize the subject to the treatment.

Educational researchers are often confronted with the difficult dilemma that as internal validity is maximized, external validity may be sacrificed. High internal validity requires strict control of all sources of confounding and extraneous variables, a type of control that may mean conducting the study under laboratory-like conditions. The more the environment is controlled, however, the less generalizable the results will be to other settings. This is a constant dilemma for educators. Although research that cannot be used with other populations in other settings contributes little to educational practice, there must be sufficient control for making reasonable causal conclusions. Without internal validity, of course, external validity is a moot concern. Most research strives to balance the threats of internal and external validity by using sufficient rigor to make the results scientifically defensible and by conducting the study under conditions that permit generalization to other situations. One good approach to solving the dilemma is to replicate tightly controlled studies with different populations in different settings.

An important implication of external validity is that the results may be limited to the context of the study. That is, the effect is causal, but only in certain conditions. As you may surmise, field conditions are more influential in this regard than conditions in a tightly controlled, laboratory-like study. The term *causal conditionals* is used to describe this principle. This is also a factor in taking interventions that are successful within a small, specific context "to scale," because what works well in the more constricted context may not work very well when it is employed more generally.

SINGLE-FACTOR PRE-EXPERIMENTAL DESIGNS

The three designs summarized in this section are termed **pre-experimental designs** because they are without two or more of the six characteristics of experimental research listed earlier. As a consequence, few threats to internal validity are controlled. This does not mean that these designs are always uninterpretable, nor does it mean that the designs should not be used. There are certain cases in which the threats can be ruled out on the basis of accepted theory, common sense, or other data. Because they fail to rule out most rival hypotheses, however, it is difficult to make reasonable causal inferences from these designs alone. They are best used, perhaps, to generate ideas that can be tested more systematically.

It should be noted that the designs in this section and the next two use a single independent variable. Most studies use more than one independent variable. These designs are called *factorial*.

Pre-experimental designs: no comparison group or no pretest with the comparison group

Notation

In presenting the designs in this chapter, we will use a notational system to provide information for understanding the designs. The notational system is unique, although similar to that used by Campbell and Stanley (1963), Cook and Campbell (1979), and Shadish, Cook, and Campbell (2002). Our notational system is as follows:

R	Random assignment
O	Observation, a measure that records pretest or posttest scores
X	Intervention conditions (subscripts 1 through n indicate different interventions)
A, B, C, D, E, F	Groups of subjects or, for single-subject designs, baseline or treatment conditions

Single-Group Posttest-Only Design

In the **single-group posttest-only design**, the researcher gives a treatment and then measures the dependent variable, as is represented in the following diagram, where A is the intervention group, X is the intervention, and O is the posttest.

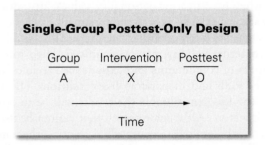

Although not all threats to internal validity are applicable to this design because there is no pretest and no comparison with other treatments, valid causal conclusions are rare. Without a pretest, for example, it is difficult to conclude that behavior has changed at all (e.g., when testing a method of teaching math to students who know the answers to the final exam before receiving any instruction). Without a comparison or control group, it is also difficult to know whether other factors occurring at the same time as the intervention were causally related to the dependent variable. Even though only five of the threats to internal validity are relevant to this design, the above weaknesses are so severe that the results of research based on this design alone are usually uninterpretable (see Table 11.7). The only situation in which this design is reasonable is when the researcher can be fairly certain of the level of knowledge, attitude, or skill of the subjects before the intervention, and can be fairly sure that history is not a threat. For example, let's say that an instructor in an introductory research methods class wants to conduct a study of how much students have learned about statistical regression. It seems reasonable to conclude that they did not know much about regression before the course began and that it is unlikely that they will learn about it in other ways—say, during party conversations! Consequently, the single-group posttest-only design may provide valid results.

Single-Group Pretest-Posttest Design

This common design is distinguished from the single-group posttest-only design by one difference—the addition of an observation that occurs before the treatment condition is experienced (pretest).

In the **single-group pretest-posttest design**, one group of subjects is given a pretest (O), then the treatment (X), and then the posttest (O). The pretest and posttest are the same, just given at different times. The result that is examined is a change from pretest to posttest. (This design is popularized as the *pretest-posttest design*.) Although the researcher can at least obtain a measure of change with this design, there are still many plausible rival hypotheses that are applicable.

Single-Group Pretest-Posttest Design

Group	Pretest	Intervention	Posttest
A	O	X	O

Time

Consider this example: A university professor has received a grant to conduct inservice workshops for teachers on the topic of inclusion. One objective of the program is to improve the attitudes of the teachers toward including children with disabilities in their "regular" class.

To assess this objective, the professor selects a pretest-posttest design, administering an attitude pretest survey to the teachers before the workshop and then giving the same survey again after the workshop (posttest). Suppose the posttest scores are higher than the pretest scores. Can the researcher conclude that the cause of the change in scores is the workshop? Perhaps, but several threats to internal validity are plausible, and until they can be ruled out, the researcher cannot assume that attendance at the workshop was the cause of the change.

The most serious threat is history. Because there is no control or comparison group, the researcher cannot be sure that other events occurring between the pretest and posttest did not cause the change in attitude. These events might occur within the context of the workshop (e.g., a teacher gives a moving testimonial about exceptional children in a setting unrelated to the workshop), or they might occur outside the context of the workshop (e.g., during the workshop, an article about inclusion appears in the school paper). Events like these are uncontrolled and may affect the results. It is necessary for the researcher, then, to make a case either that such effects are implausible or that if they are plausible, they did not occur. Data are sometimes used as evidence to rule out some threats, but in many cases, it is simply common sense, theory, or experience that is used to make this judgment.

Statistical regression could be a problem with this design if the subjects are selected on the basis of extremely high or low scores. In our example with the workshop, for instance, suppose the principal of the school wanted only those teachers with the least favorable attitudes to attend. The pretest scores would then be very low and, because of regression, would be higher on the posttest regardless of the effect of the workshop.

Pretesting is often a threat to research carried out with this design, especially in research on attitudes, because simply taking the pretest can alter the attitudes. The content of the questionnaire might sensitize the subjects to specific problems or might raise the general awareness level of the subjects and cause them to think more about the topic. Instrumentation can also be a threat. For example, if the teachers take the pretest on Friday afternoon and the posttest the next Wednesday morning, the responses could be different simply because of the general attitudes that are likely to prevail at each of these times of the day and week.

Attrition can be a problem if, between the pretest and posttest, subjects are lost for particular reasons. If all the teachers in a school begin a workshop, for example, and those with the most negative attitude toward inclusion drop out because they do not want to learn more about it, then the measured attitudes of the remaining subjects will be high. Consider another example. To assess the effect of a schoolwide effort to expand favorable attitudes toward learning, students are pretested as sophomores and posttested as seniors. A plausible argument—at least one that would need to be ruled out—is that improvement in attitudes is demonstrated because the students who have the most negative attitudes as sophomores never become seniors; they drop out. In this situation it is not appropriate to use all students taking the pretest and all students taking the posttest and then compare these groups. Only students who completed both the pretest and the posttest should be included in the statistical analysis. Attrition is especially a problem in cases with transient populations, with a long-term experiment, or with longitudinal research.

Maturation is a threat to internal validity of this design when the dependent variable is unstable because of maturational changes. This threat is more serious as the time between the pretest and posttest increases. For instance, suppose a researcher is investigating the self-concept of middle school students. If the time between the pretest and posttest is relatively short (two or three weeks), then maturation is probably not a threat, but if a year elapses between the pretest and posttest, changes in self-concept would probably occur regardless of the treatment because of maturation. Maturation includes such threats as being more tired, bored, or hungry at the time of test taking, and these factors might be problems in some pretest-posttest designs. In the example of the workshop on mainstreaming, it is unlikely that maturation is a serious threat, and it would probably be reasonable to rule out these threats as plausible rival hypotheses.

Intervention replications may be a threat, depending on the manner in which the treatment is administered. Experimenter effects, subject effects, and statistical conclusion threats are possible in any experiment, and these would need to be examined.

From this discussion, it should be obvious that there are many uncontrolled threats to the internal validity of a single-group pretest-posttest design. Consequently, this design should be used only under certain conditions that minimize the plausibility of the threats (e.g., use reliable instruments

EXCERPT 11.3 Single-Group Pretest-Posttest Design

An eight-week summer program was designed and implemented to prevent high-risk adolescents from dropping out of school. Identified by their high school counselors as being at high risk for dropping out, participants were provided a total immersion curriculum that included academic and vocational instruction, as well as personal counseling services. . . . The results of the two administrations of the Coopersmith Self-Esteem Inventory . . . [revealed] significant differences . . . between pretest and posttest self-esteem total scores. (p. 432)

Source: From Wells, D., Miller, M., Tobacyk, J., & Clanton, R. (2002). Using a psychoeducational approach to increase the self-esteem of adolescents at high risk for dropping out. *Adolescence, 37,* 431–434.

and short pretest-posttest time intervals) and when it is impossible to use other designs that will control some of these threats.

Several modifications can be made to the single-group pretest-posttest design that will improve internal validity, including the following:

- Adding a second pretest
- Adding a second pretest and posttest of a construct similar to the one being tested (i.e., to show change in the targeted variable and no change in the other variable)
- Following the posttest with a second pretest/posttest with the intervention either removed or repeated and determining if the pattern of results is consistent with predictions

Excerpt 11.3 is an example of a study that used a single-group pretest-posttest design. Note how the targeted students suggest that regression to the mean may be a plausible rival hypothesis.

Nonequivalent Groups Posttest-Only Design

Nonequivalent groups posttest-only design: no pretest with a control or comparison group

This design is similar to the single-group posttest-only design. The difference is that in a **nonequivalent groups posttest-only design,** a group that receives no intervention or a different intervention is added to the single-group posttest-only design. The design with a control group is diagrammed below.

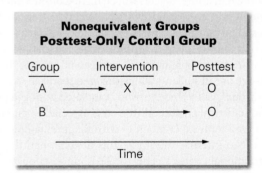

The procedure followed in this design is to administer the intervention to one group and then assess the dependent variable (via the posttest), and then to give only the posttest to another group at the same time the posttest is administered to the first group. The term *nonequivalent groups* is used for the design because selection is the most serious threat to the internal validity of the results.

Notice that there is no random assignment of subjects to each group. Differences in the groups of subjects may therefore account for any differences in the results of the posttests. The more different the groups are, the more plausible selection becomes as a reason for the results. Suppose, for example, that the professor conducting the inclusion workshop wanted to get a comparison group and located a school willing to help. Even if the posttest scores of the treatment group were better than the scores of the comparison group, it is untenable to conclude that the better scores were due to the workshop. It may be that the teachers in the experimental school had more favorable attitudes to begin with and that the workshop had little effect on the attitudes of teachers there.

There are also other, less serious threats to the internal validity of research based on this design. These threats occur when the basic design includes alternate interventions, as indicated below.

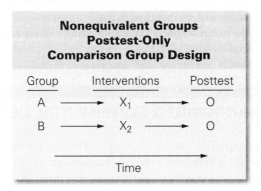

This design is used when a researcher wants to compare two or more interventions but cannot give a pretest or randomize the assignment of subjects to each group. In this case, internal or within-group history is a threat, because what might occur within each group, unrelated to the interventions, could affect the posttest. External history is not usually a threat unless selection differences expose subjects outside the context of the study to different conditions that affect the results. Regression may be a threat even though only one observation is made. Pretesting is not a threat because there is no pretest, but instrumentation could be a threat if there are differences in how the posttest assessments are made for each group (e.g., an observer's being more alert for one group than the other). Attrition is a threat because subject loss, due either to the initial characteristics of the subjects (selection) or to different interventions, may cause certain subjects to drop out. Maturation may also be a threat, depending on selection characteristics. If the subjects in each group are aware of the intervention given the other group, it is possible for diffusion of interventions to be a threat. Experimenter effects, subject effects, intervention replications, and statistical conclusion threats are also possible. The nonequivalent groups posttest-only design is relatively weak for testing causation. If this design is used, a researcher should make every effort to use comparable groups in order to decrease the selection threat.

The possible sources of invalidity for research carried out by the three pre-experimental designs are summarized in Table 11.7. Because different designs control different factors and also have unique weaknesses, the researcher chooses the best design on the basis of the research conditions. If, for example, the researcher can reasonably argue that two groups are about the same

TABLE 11.7 Threats to Internal Validity of Pre-Experimental Designs

Design	History	Selection	Statistical Regression	Pretesting	Instrumentation	Attrition	Maturation	Diffusion of Intervention	Experimenter Effects	Intervention Replications	Subject Effects
Single-group posttest only	–	–	?	NA	?	?	–	NA	?	?	?
Single-group pretest-posttest	–	?	?	–	?	?	–	NA	?	?	?
Nonequivalent groups posttest only	?	–	?	NA	?	?	?	?	?	?	?

Note: In this table, and in Tables 11.8 and 11.9, a minus sign means a definite weakness, a plus sign means the factor is controlled, a question mark means a possible source of invalidity, and NA indicates that the threat is not applicable to this design.

with respect to important variables (e.g., socio-economic status, achievement, age, experience, motivation), then the strongest design will be the posttest-only with nonequivalent groups. In any event, all these designs are relatively weak for use in testing causal relationships, but with sufficient foresight, they usually can be modified slightly to permit more reasonable causal inferences. (See Shadish, Cook, and Campbell [2002] for ways to improve nonequivalent groups posttest-only designs.)

SINGLE-FACTOR RANDOMIZED EXPERIMENTAL DESIGNS

This section presents two designs that have been called *randomized experimental designs*. Both include procedures for ruling out group differences through randomization of subjects to groups. These designs represent what is now considered the gold standard for educational research and evaluation.

Randomized Pretest-Posttest Control Group Design

Randomized pretest-posttest control group design: random assignment with a control group, pretest, and posttest

The **randomized pretest-posttest control group design** is an extension of the single-group pretest-posttest design in two ways: A second group is added, called the *control group*, and subjects are assigned randomly to each group. This design is represented below. Group A is the experimental group, and R represents randomization of subjects.

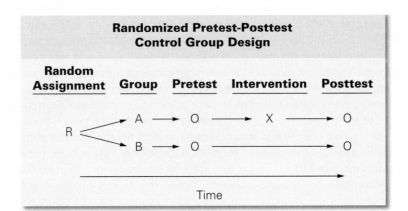

The first step is random assignment of the subjects to the experimental group and the control group. In studies with a relatively small number of subjects, it is usually best to rank order the subjects on achievement, attitudes, or other factors that may be related to the dependent variable. Then, in the case of a two-group design, pairs of subjects with similar characteristics are formed; the researcher randomly assigns one subject from each pair to the experimental group and the other subject to the control group.

The purpose of random assignment is to enable the researcher to reasonably rule out any differences between the groups that could account for the results. With a small group of subjects, it is less likely that the groups will be the same. If only 10 subjects are randomly assigned to two groups, for example, there is a good chance that even though the assignment is random, there will be important differences between the groups. If 200 subjects are randomly assigned, however, there is a very small chance that the groups will differ. Generally, educational researchers like to have at least 15 subjects in each group in order to assume statistical equivalence, and they have more confidence in the results if there are 20 to 30 subjects in each group. In Excerpt 11.4, the researchers indicate that data are used to argue that there were no systematic differences between the groups even though there was random assignment. Excerpt 11.5 illustrates how researchers report statistically significant results indicating no difference between the groups helps assure that selection is not a threat to internal validity. These descriptive data are also helpful in considering external validity. Note in Excerpt 11.6 how random

EXCERPT 11.4 Checking for Statistical Equivalence between Randomized Groups

All grade 6 teachers were assigned randomly to the treatment or control group . . . at the time of the pretest, we also administered other measures to test the equivalency of the groups . . . we also included other teacher background measures. (p. 54)

Source: From Ross, J., & Bruce, C. (2007). Professional development effects on teacher efficacy: Results of a randomized field trial. *The Journal of Educational Research, 101*(1), 50–61.

EXCERPT 11.5 Checking for Statistical Equivalence between Randomized Treatment and Control Groups

The participants were randomly assigned to either an experimental treatment group receiving advance planning strategy instruction or a comparative treatment group receiving a modified version of process writing instruction. Separate *t*-tests were performed to determine if there were significant differences between the two groups with respect to chronological age, IQ, reading and writing achievement, or number of years enrolled in special education. No significant differences between the groups were found. (p. 293)

Source: From Troia, G. A., & Graham, S. (2002). The effectiveness of a highly explicit, teacher-directed strategy instruction routine: Changing the writing performance of students with learning disabilities. *Journal of Learning Disabilities, 35*(4), 290–305.

assignment is made by class and not by student. This would be considered a pre-experimental posttest-only design, which means there would be many potentially serious threats to internal validity. Students are not, as implied, randomly assigned to interventions. In Excerpt 11.7, matching is used with random assignment to ensure the statistical equivalence of the groups being compared.

The second step is to pretest each group on the dependent variable. (In some designs, the pretest is given first, followed by random assignment.) The third step is to administer the intervention to the experimental group but not to the control group, keeping all other conditions the same for both groups so that the only difference is the manipulation of the independent variable. Each group is then posttested on the dependent variable.

EXCERPT 11.6 Random Assignment of Intact Groups

Students from three classrooms at a local elementary school participated in this study . . . Each of the three intact classrooms was randomly assigned to one of the three classroom evaluations structure conditions. Twenty-five fifth-grade students were assigned to the token economy condition, 18 fourth-grade students to the contingency contract condition, and 28 fifth-grade students to the control condition. (p. 108)

Source: From Self-Brown, S. R., & Mathews, II, S. (2003). Effects of classroom structure on student achievement goal orientation. *Journal of Educational Research, 97*(2), 106–111.

EXCERPT 11.7 Random Assignment with Matching

Within each class, the remaining students were matched in terms of abilities and then randomly assigned to three experimental conditions: (a) mastery learning only, (b) accuracy-oriented overlearning, and (c) fluency-oriented overlearning. (p. 775)

Source: From Peladeau, N., Forget, J., & Gagne, F. (2003). Effect of paced and unpaced practice on skill application and retention: How much is enough? *American Educational Research Journal, 40*(3), 769–801.

Randomized Pretest-Posttest Comparison Group Design

In the diagrammed control group design, there is no intervention at all for the control group. As indicated previously, it is more common and usually more desirable to have comparison rather than control groups. A comparison design uses two or more variations of the independent variable and can use two or more groups. Suppose, for example, that a teacher wants to compare three methods of teaching spelling. The teacher randomly assigns each student in the class to one of three groups, administers a pretest, tries the different methods, and gives a posttest. This **randomized groups pretest-posttest comparison group design** would look like the following:

Randomized groups pretest-posttest comparison group design: random assignment with a comparison group, pretest, and posttest

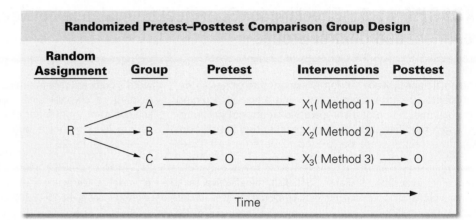

It would also be possible to combine several different treatments with a control group, as follows:

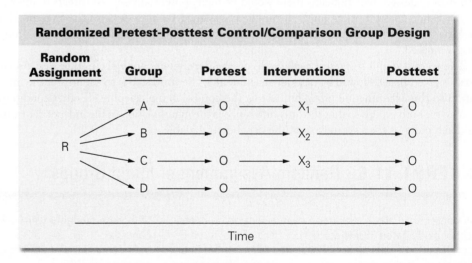

The pretest-posttest control group design controls four sources of threats to internal validity, as indicated in Table 11.8. Threats related to history are generally controlled insofar as events that are external to the study affect all groups equally. The reason for the question mark in the category, however, is that it is always possible that unique events may occur within each group to affect the results. Selection and maturation are controlled because of the random assignment of subjects. Statistical regression and pretesting are controlled, because any effect of these factors is equal for all groups. Instrumentation is not a problem when the same standardized self-report procedures are used, but studies that use observers or raters must be careful to avoid observer or rater bias (e.g., knowing which students are receiving which treatments, or using different observers or raters for each group). Attrition is not usually a threat unless a particular treatment causes systematic subject dropout.

Diffusion of interventions may be a source of invalidity in experiments in which subjects in one group, because of close physical proximity to or communication with subjects in another group, learn about information or interventions not intended for them. Because the conditions that were intended for one group, then, are transmitted to other groups, the effect of the intervention is dispersed. For example, if a researcher compares two methods of instruction, such as cooperative group instruction and individualized instruction, and conducts the experiment within a single fourth-grade class by randomly assigning half of the class to each method, it is likely that students in one group will know what is occurring in the other group. If the students in the individualized group feel left out or believe they have a less interesting assignment, they may be resentful and may not perform as well as possible. Diffusion might also occur if students in the cooperative group learn to help others and then assist students in the individualized group.

Experimenter effects comprise another threat, depending on the procedures of the study. If the individuals who are responsible for implementing the treatments are aware of the purpose and hypotheses of the study, they may act differently toward each group and affect the results. If a teacher is involved in a study to investigate the effect of differential amounts of praise on behavior (i.e., more praise, better behavior) and understands what the hypothesized result should be, then he or she may act more positively toward the students receiving more praise (e.g., be closer physically, use more eye contact, offer less criticism) and thus contaminate the intended effect of amount of praise.

Similarly, subject effects could be important if subjects in different groups respond differently because of their treatment. For example, subjects who know they are in the control group may try harder than they otherwise would, or they may be demotivated because they were not selected for the special intervention, or those in the special intervention may feel an obligation to try harder or give better responses. Treatment replications may be a threat, depending on how the interventions were administered, and statistical conclusion is always a possibility.

Excerpt 11.8 is another example of the randomized pretest-posttest design. It shows how two researchers described their experimental procedures. This study examined the effect of a classroom assistant on student achievement, as illustrated in Figure 11.1. Note that they used three interventions, a control group, and a single posttest administered twice.

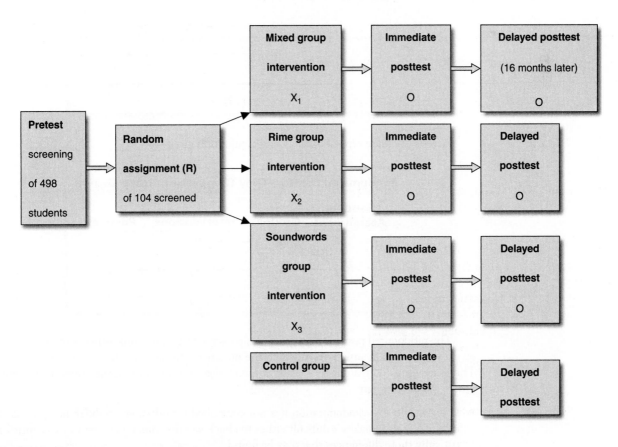

FIGURE 11.1   Diagram of the Savage and Carless 1 × 4 Experimental Study (Excerpt 11.8)

EXCERPT 11.8   Randomized Pretest-Posttest Design

The original intervention study was carried out in three phases: a pretest screening phase, an intervention phase, and an immediate posttest phase. All of these three phases took place in the first year of formal teaching when children were aged six. This was augmented in the present study by a 16-month follow-up of performance of the children—termed a delayed posttest. . . . Within each school, children were randomly allocated to a CA-delivered intervention condition . . . or to a control condition. (pp. 366, 368)

Source: From Savage, R., & Carless, S. (2008). The impact of early reading interventions delivered by classroom assistants on attainment at the end of year 2. *British Educational Research Journal, 34*(3), 363–385.

Randomized Posttest-Only Control and Comparison Group Designs

The purpose of random assignment, as indicated previously, is to equalize the experimental and control groups before introducing the intervention. If the groups are equalized through randomization, is it necessary to give a pretest? Although there are certain cases in which it is best to use a pretest with random assignment, if the groups have at least 15 subjects each, the pretest may not be necessary—that is, it is not essential to have a pretest in order to conduct a true experimental study. The **randomized posttest-only control and comparison group designs** are the same as the randomized pretest-posttest control and comparison group designs except that there is no pretest on the dependent variable. The posttest-only control group design can be depicted as follows, with R representing the pools of subjects:

Randomized posttest-only control and comparison group designs: random assignment with no pretest

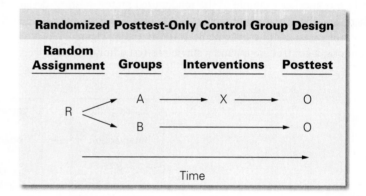

Here is the same type of design using comparison groups.

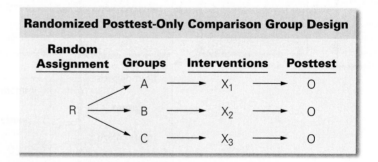

The randomized posttest-only group design is used when it is unfeasible or inconvenient to give a pretest and in situations in which the pretest might have an effect on the intervention. There are four disadvantages to using a randomized posttest-only rather than a randomized pretest-posttest design:

- It is possible that randomization has not controlled for initial group differences or that the lack of a pretest makes it difficult either to check whether differences exist or to control statistically those differences that may be found.

EXCERPT 11.9 Randomized Posttest-Only Control and Comparison Group Design

We randomly assigned the 84 participants to one of six experimental conditions or a practice-only control group, with 12 girls in each group. The experimental conditions were based on the three types of goal setting (process goal, outcome goal, and shifting process-outcome goal), and two variations in self-recording (present or absent). . . . As a check for effectiveness of random assignment, we compared the NEDT English usage of girls in the six experimental groups at baseline and found no significant differences. . . . All girls were posttested in order for attributions, self-efficacy, writing skill, self-reaction, and intrinsic interest. The experimenter began and terminated each section of the study and recorded the posttest scores. (pp. 244–245)

Source: From Zimmerman, B. J., & Kitsantas, A. (1999). Acquiring writing revision skill: shifting from process to outcome self-regulatory goals. *Journal of Educational Psychology, 91*(2), 244–250.

- The researcher is unable to form subgroups on the basis of the pretest for investigating effects of the intervention on different subgroups.
- The researcher is unable to determine whether differential attrition has occurred.
- The statistical analysis is less precise and less likely to show a difference between the groups.

The pretest-posttest design may be preferable in these situations:

- There are subtle, small differences between intervention conditions.
- Differential mortality is possible.
- Subgroup analysis is desirable.
- Anonymity is unnecessary.
- Pretesting is a normal part of the subjects' routine.

The advantages of the posttest-only design are that it allows experimental evidence when it is impossible to give a pretest, it avoids the reactive effect of pretesting, and it makes ensuring anonymity easier. This design is especially good, then, for attitude research for two reasons: The use of an attitude questionnaire as the pretest may well affect the treatment, and attitudes are generally reported more honestly if anonymity can be ensured.

The posttest-only control group design controls for almost the same sources of invalidity as the pretest-posttest control group design. Table 11.8 summarizes the sources of invalidity.

In Excerpt 11.9, a randomized posttest-only control/comparison design is used to investigate the effect of several sentence-combining revision strategies on writing skill, self-motivation, and intrinsic interest in writing. There were six experimental conditions and a control group.

TABLE 11.8 Threats to Internal Validity of Randomized Experimental Designs

Design	History	Selection	Statistical Regression	Pretesting	Instrumentation	Attrition	Maturation	Diffusion of Intervention	Experimenter Effects	Intervention Replications	Subject Effects
Pretest-posttest control and/or comparison group	?	+	+	+	?	?	+	?	?	?	?
Posttest-only control and/or comparison group	+	+	NA	NA	?	?	+	?	?	?	?

Note: In this table, and in Tables 11.7 and 11.9, a minus sign means a definite weakness, a plus sign means the factor is controlled, a question mark means a possible source of invalidity, and NA indicates that the threat is not applicable to this design (and is also, then, not a factor).

Occasionally, a situation arises in which the researcher needs to rule out the effect of the pretest on the intervention. The design used for this purpose is a combination of the posttest-only control group and pretest-posttest control group design and is called the *Solomon four-group design*. Although this design controls for the effects of mortality and pretest-treatment interactions, it is difficult to carry out in education because it requires twice as many subjects and groups as other designs.

SINGLE-FACTOR QUASI-EXPERIMENTAL DESIGNS

True experimental designs provide the strongest, most convincing arguments of the causal effect of the independent variable because they control for the most sources of internal invalidity. There are, however, many circumstances in educational research in which it is not feasible to design randomized experiments or in which the need for strong external validity is greater than the need for internal validity. The most common reasons that true experimental designs cannot be employed are that random assignment of subjects to experimental and control groups is impossible and that a control or comparison group is unavailable, inconvenient, or too expensive.

Quasi-experimental designs: no random assignment

Fortunately, there are several good designs that can be used under either of these circumstances. They are termed **quasi-experimental designs** because, although not true experiments, they provide reasonable control over most sources of invalidity and are usually stronger than the pre-experimental designs. Although there are many quasi-experimental designs (Cook & Campbell, 1979; Shadish, Cook, & Campbell, 2002), we will discuss only the most common ones.

Nonequivalent Groups Pretest-Posttest Control or Comparison Group Designs

Nonequivalent groups pretest-posttest control or comparison group designs: no random assignment with a pretest and posttest

Nonequivalent groups pretest-posttest control or comparison group designs are very prevalent and useful in education, because it is often impossible to randomly assign subjects. The researcher uses intact, already established groups of subjects, gives a pretest, administers the intervention condition to one group, and gives the posttest. The only difference between this design, then, and the randomized pretest-posttest control group design is the lack of random assignment of subjects. The design is as follows:

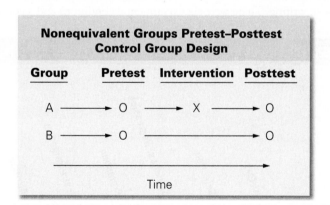

The most serious threat to the internal validity of research conducted with this design is selection. Because the groups may differ in characteristics that affect the dependent variable, the researcher must address selection and provide reasonable arguments that this threat is not a plausible rival hypothesis. Suppose a researcher is interested in studying the effect of three different methods of changing the attitudes of student teachers toward computer-assisted instruction. The researcher has three classes of student teachers to work with, and it is impossible to assign students randomly within each class to each of the three methods. The researcher therefore uses each class intact and gives each class a different treatment. The design would be as follows:

Class	Pretest	Method	Posttest
A $\longrightarrow$	O $\longrightarrow$	X_1 $\longrightarrow$	O
B $\longrightarrow$	O $\longrightarrow$	X_2 $\longrightarrow$	O
C $\longrightarrow$	O $\longrightarrow$	X_3 $\longrightarrow$	O

Time

The interpretation of the results will depend largely on whether the groups differed on some characteristic that might reasonably be related to the independent variable. This decision is made by comparing the three groups on such characteristics as gender, time the groups meet, size of groups, achievement, aptitude, socioeconomic status, major, and pretest scores. For instance, if Class A comprises all elementary majors and Classes B and C secondary majors and the results showed that Class A gained more than B and C, the gain may be attributable to the values and backgrounds of elementary majors compared with those of secondary majors. On the other hand, if the classes are about the same in most characteristics, then it would be reasonable to assume that selection differences probably would not account for the results. Consequently, if the researcher knows in advance that randomization is impossible, the groups should be selected to be as similar as possible. The pretest scores and other measures on the groups are then used to adjust the groups statistically on the factor that is measured. Another approach to controlling selection when intact groups such as classrooms must be used is to use a large number of groups and then randomly assign entire groups to either control or intervention conditions. This procedure then changes the study to a true experimental design. This is, in fact, the preferred approach when diffusion of intervention or local history threats are viable.

The threats of maturation and statistical regression are the only other differences between this design and the pretest-posttest control group design. Regression is a problem if one of the groups happens to have extremely high or low scores. For example, if a study to assess the impact of a program on gifted children selected gifted children who score low and normal children who score high as comparison groups, then statistical regression will make the results look like a difference in posttest scores when nothing has actually changed. Maturation effects (e.g., growing more experienced, tired, bored) will depend on the specific differences in characteristics between the groups.

A nonequivalent groups pretest-posttest design is illustrated in Excerpt 11.10. This was a study to determine the effect of an earth systems science course on preservice elementary teachers' mathematics and science teaching efficacy. Note the term *nonrandom* in the description of how the sample was obtained and the difference in the number of teachers in each group, which is a tip that a nonrandom procedure was used.

Quasi-experimental designs that use either control or comparison groups can be strengthened by taking the following measures:

EXCERPT 11.10 Nonequivalent Groups Pretest-Posttest Design

The design of this study was a nonrandomized control group pretest-posttest design. . . . The instruments were administered . . . on the first day of class (pretest) and at the end of the semester (posttest). . . . Participants in this study included two convenient nonrandom groups of preservice elementary teachers. . . . The experimental group consisted of 20 students who participated in an earth systems science course . . . [and] the control group consisted of 42 students who . . . did not participate in the earth systems science course. (p. 5)

Source: From Moseley, C., & Utley, J. (2006). The effect of an integrated science and mathematics content-based course on science and mathematics teaching efficacy of preservice elementary teachers. *Journal of Elementary Science Education, 18*(2), 1–12.

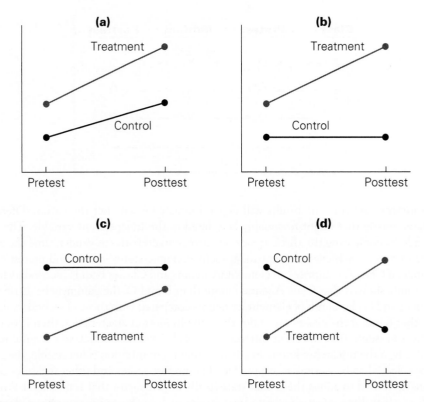

FIGURE 11.2 **Possible Outcomes of Two-Group Quasi-Experimental Pretest-Posttest Designs**

- Adding a second pretest
- Replicating the treatment with another group at another time with the same pretest
- Using a comparison group that reverses the effect of the targeted intervention

The plausibility of threat to internal validity for quasi-experimental nonequivalent groups designs depends in part on the pattern of pretest differences between the groups, predicted outcomes, and posttest differences. Figure 11.2 shows four possible patterns of findings. In pattern (a), the intervention group's pretest score is higher than the control group's pretest score, and the results suggest that the intervention group is simply maturing at a different rate. In (b), it is possible that the intervention group's posttest score will be higher, since its pretest score was initially higher than that of the control group. Patterns (c) and (d) show relatively strong findings, because improvement is demonstrated for the intervention group even though its pretest score was lower.

Time-Series Designs

Time-series design: intervention with many observations before and after

In the single-group pretest-posttest design, a single group of subjects usually receives only one pretest and one posttest. If the group is repeatedly measured before and after the intervention, rather than once before and once after, a **time-series design** or *abbreviated time-series design* is created. Time-series designs are especially useful when there are continuous, naturally occurring observations of the dependent variable over time and there is a sudden or distinct intervention during the observations. These designs offer significant improvement over the pretest-posttest design because with a series of preobservations and postobservations, patterns of stability and change can be assessed more accurately.

Single-group interrupted time-series design: one group, one intervention, with many observations before and after

Single-Group Interrupted Time-Series Design The **single-group interrupted time-series design** requires one group and multiple observations or assessments before and after the intervention. The observations before the intervention can be thought of as repeated pretests, and those after the intervention can be thought of as repeated posttests. The single-group interrupted time-series design can be diagrammed as follows:

Single-Group Interrupted Time-Series Design				
Group	**Preobservations**	**Intervention**	**Postobservations**	
A	O O O O O O	OXO	O O O O O O	

Time

Several conditions should be met in employing this design. First, the observations should be made at equal time intervals and conducted with the same procedures in order to reduce the threat of instrumentation. Second, the intervention introduced should be a distinctive, abrupt intervention that is clearly new to the existing environment. Third, there should be some evidence that the subjects involved in each observation are the same (i.e., have low attrition). A variation of using the same subjects for each measurement is to use different but very similar groups. Fourth, there should not be any kind of change affecting the subjects occurring at about the same time as the intervention. A new curriculum could be assessed very well with a time-series design. For example, sixth-grade student achievement could be plotted for several years with the old curriculum, and then achievement scores could be recorded for several years after the new curriculum was introduced. The key element in this design is that the characteristics of the sixth-grade students must be about the same year after year. Obviously, if there is an immigration of brighter students over the years, achievement will increase regardless of the curriculum.

Some possible outcomes for the study are indicated in Figure 11.3. If Outcome A is achieved, then the researcher may conclude that the curriculum had a positive effect on achievement. Outcome B indicates a steady improvement of scores, so it is difficult to interpret the effect of the curriculum, and Outcome C indicates little change over the time span. In interpreting these results, however, the researcher should look for alternate explanations. If there happened to be a change in the student population, such as migration from city to suburban schools, then the observations would be expected to change. The testing instrument would need to be the same (e.g., there should be no change in the norming group). Perhaps the most serious threat to validity is history. It is possible that events other than the treatment—in this case, the curriculum—occurred at about the same time and affected the posttest observations; for example, maybe in the same year the curricula were changed, the teachers also changed. Other threats include seasonal variation (e.g., self-concept scores may be lower in winter than in spring) and pretesting (e.g., the effect of the pretesting on the intervention).

Control Group Interrupted Time-Series Design   In this design, a control or comparison group is added to the single-group interrupted time series. The addition of a control group

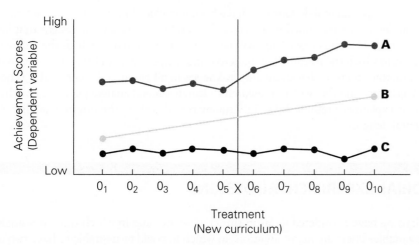

FIGURE 11.3 **Possible Outcome Patterns of Achievement Over Time for Time-Series Designs**

strengthens the design considerably, since the major threat of history is eliminated. Instrumentation is also a less likely explanation, and if random assignment is included, then selection is not a threat to validity. Since a control group is present, however, diffusion of intervention becomes a threat. The **control group interrupted time-series design** is represented below:

Control group interrupted time-series design: intervention and control groups

Control-Group Interrupted Time-Series Design			
Group	**Preobservations**	Intervention ↓	**Postobservations**
A	O O O O	X	O O O O
B	O O O O		O O O O

Time →

There are many variations of the basic time-series design. An intervention can be removed rather than added, for example, and multiple interventions can be compared, either with one group or several groups. Some variations are illustrated in the next diagram. In Situation 1, three different interventions are compared and three groups of subjects are used. In Situation 2, only one group of subjects is used and two interventions are compared, and in Situation 3, the same intervention is compared in two groups at different points in time. Note that in Situation 3 there are only three pre- and posttests. This could be called an **abbreviated time-series design**, which is very useful in situations where random assignment is not possible.

Abbreviated time-series design: only a few pre- and post measures

Situation 1	A O O O O O X_1O O O O O	
	B O O O O O X_2O O O O O	
	C O O O O O X_3O O O O O	
Situation 2	A O O O O X_1O O O O X_2O O O O	
Situation 3	A O O O X_1O O O O O O O	
	B O O O O O O X_1O O O	

Time →

The quasi-experimental designs that have been introduced in this chapter are simple, basic designs that are usually expanded in actual studies, and there are several designs that have not been mentioned. The choice of design will depend on the variables studied, the circumstances of the setting in which the research is conducted, and the plausibility of threats to internal validity. The important point is that there are weaknesses in all research designs, and it is necessary for the investigator and the reader of research to search out and analyze plausible rival hypotheses that may explain the results. Table 11.9 summarizes threats to the internal validity of quasi-experimental designs.

FACTORIAL EXPERIMENTAL DESIGNS

Factorial designs: two or more independent variables analyzed together

The designs we have considered so far in this chapter are ones in which there is a single independent variable. There are many situations in which it would be desirable to have two or more independent variables and use what is called a **factorial design**. Factorial experimental designs

TABLE 11.9   Threats to Internal Validity of Quasi-Experimental Designs

Design	History	Selection	Statistical Regression	Pretesting	Instrumentation	Attrition	Maturation	Diffusion of Intervention	Experimenter Effects	Intervention Replications	Subject Effects
Nonequivalent groups pretest-posttest design	?	–	?	–	?	?	–	?	?	?	?
Single-group interrupted time-series	–	?	+	?	?	?	+	NA	+	?	?
Control group interrupted time-series	+	?	–	+	?	?	+	?	?	?	?

Note: In this table, and in Tables 11.7 and 11.8, a minus sign means a definite weakness, a plus sign means the factor is controlled, a question mark means a possible source of invalidity, and NA indicates the threat is not applicable to this design (and is also, then, not a factor).

are extensions of single-factor designs that study a single independent variable. Factorial designs are used for two primary purposes: (1) to see if the effects of an intervention are consistent across characteristics of the subjects (e.g., age, aptitude, or gender) and (2) to examine the unique effect of the independent variables together (this is called an *interaction*).

Suppose a researcher is interested in whether there is a difference between small-group and individualized counseling on students' well-being, and also wonders if the effect of the interventions is the same for students in different grades (9, 10, and 11). This study would have two independent variables, one with two levels and one with three levels. One of the variables is an intervention; the other is an assigned variable. The levels of the independent variables are designated by the notation, as illustrated in Figure 11.4. This notation system used with factorial designs tells you how many independent variables are included and the number of levels of each

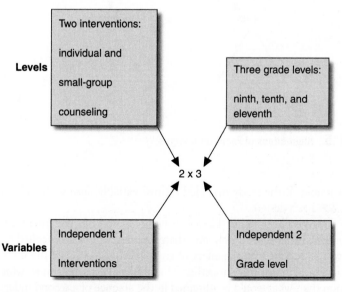

FIGURE 11.4   Interpreting a 2 × 3 Experimental Design

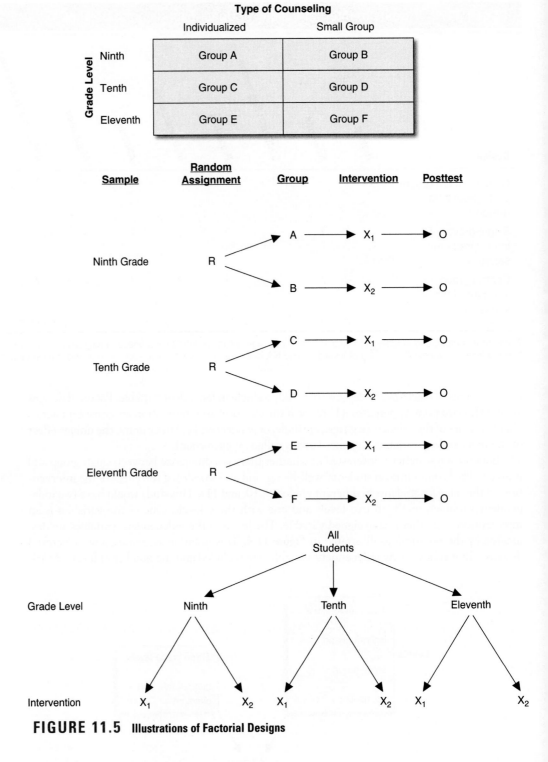

FIGURE 11.5 Illustrations of Factorial Designs

independent variable. If the study included a third variable, also with two levels, it would be described as a $2 \times 2 \times 3$ design.

The 2×3 design is illustrated in different ways in Figure 11.5. The intent is to study the effect of each independent variable separately, and then together, with what is called an *interaction*. That is, the results will be reported for the effect of grade level, the effect of the intervention, and the effect of grade level and intervention together. This results in three outcomes, which provides much more information than what would be obtained in the absence of a second independent variable.

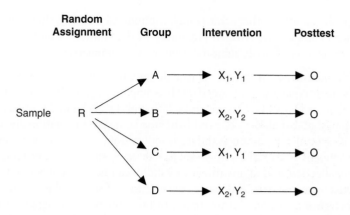

Where

X_1 = graphed; X_2 = not graphed; Y_1 = growth information; Y_2 = no growth information

FIGURE 11.6 Illustration of a 2 × 2 Factorial Experimental Design with Two Interventions

An **interaction** occurs when the effect of one variable is not the same across levels of the second variable. That is, the effect of the intervention may not be consistent for each category of the second independent variable. In our example in Figures 11.4 and 11.5, which illustrates a posttest-only randomized design, an interaction would exist if the effect of type of counseling on student well-being was unique for students in different grades. For example, you might find that individualized counseling is best for ninth-grade students and small-group counseling is best for tenth- and eleventh-graders. If there is no interaction, then the effects of the interventions would be the same for all three grades.

Interaction effects are very important in educational research due to the effect of individual characteristics on the impact of different interventions. Think about some of the variables that could be included in a study to investigate interactions, such as gender, aptitude, and socioeconomic status. There are also many circumstances in which there is more than one intervention. Suppose you wanted to determine the effect of different ways of presenting test results on teachers' planning. You decide to vary whether the results are graphed and whether they include growth information. This could be a 2 × 2 design, with four different groups of teachers, as illustrated in Figure 11.6. If the groups are all randomly assigned, it would be true experimental; if intact groups of teachers are used, it would be quasi-experimental as long as there was a pretest.

Interaction: effect of combining levels of independent variables

SINGLE-SUBJECT DESIGNS

The experimental designs that have been discussed are based on groups of subjects. We are typically interested, for example, in fourth-grade students' attitudes in general or in whether a particular method of reading is generally best for a group of subjects. There are, however, many circumstances in which it is either undesirable or impossible to use groups of subjects, such as when examining instructional strategies to be used with individual students. In these situations, **single-subject designs** are often employed to provide rigorous causal inferences for the behavior of one, two, or a few individuals. The term *single subject* actually refers to the way the results are presented and analyzed—that is, by individual subject—as contrasted with group designs, which use average scores. The basic approach is to study individuals in a nonintervention condition and then in an intervention condition, with performance on the dependent variable measured continually in both conditions. The continuous measurement of the targeted behavior is conceptually like a time-series design. There must be several measures in each phase of the study to establish a dependable pattern.

Single-subject designs: one or a few subjects with an intervention

The design characteristics that achieve high internal validity with single-subject designs are somewhat different from those covered previously in the context of group designs. The most important characteristics of single-subject designs can be summarized as follows:

1. *Reliable measurement* Single-subject designs usually involve many observations of behavior as the technique for collecting data. It is important that the observation conditions, such as time of day and location, be standardized; that observers be well trained and checked for reliability and bias; and that the observed behavior be defined operationally. Consistency in measurement is especially important as the study moves from one condition to another. Because accurate measurement is crucial to single-subject designs, the researcher typically reports all aspects of data collection so that any threat to validity can be reasonably ruled out.

2. *Repeated measurement* A distinct characteristic of single-subject designs is that a single aspect of behavior is measured many times, in the same way, throughout the study. This is quite different from measurement in many group studies, in which there is a single measure before or after the intervention. Repeated measurement controls for normal variation that would be expected within short time intervals and provides a clear, reliable description of the behavior.

3. *Description of conditions* A precise, detailed description of all conditions in which the behavior is observed should be provided. This description allows application of the study to other individuals in order to strengthen both internal and external validity.

4. *Baseline and intervention condition; duration and stability* The usual procedure is for each condition to last about the same length of time and contain about the same number of observations. If either the length of time or number of observations varies, then time and number of observations become confounding variables that complicate the interpretation of the results and weaken internal validity. It is also important that the behavior be observed long enough for the establishment of a stable pattern. If there is considerable variation in the behavior, then it will be difficult to determine whether observed changes are due to natural variation or to the intervention. During the first phase of single-subject research, the target behavior is observed under natural conditions until stability is achieved. This period of time is called the *baseline*. The intervention phase occurs with a change in conditions by the researcher and also must be long enough to achieve stability.

5. *Single-variable rule* It is important to change only one variable during the intervention phase of single-subject research, and the variable that is changed should be described precisely. If two or more variables are changed simultaneously, the researcher cannot be sure which change or changes caused the results.

A-B Design

In order to distinguish single-subject designs from traditional group designs, a unique notational convention is used. In it, the letters stand for conditions instead of groups of subjects. That is, A stands for the baseline condition and B for the intervention condition.

A-B design: baseline and intervention comparison

The **A-B design** is the most simple and least interpretable single-subject design. The procedure in using it is to observe the target behavior until it occurs at a consistent, stable rate. This condition is the baseline, or A condition. An intervention is then introduced into the environment in which baseline data have been collected, and that condition is labeled B. The design can be diagrammed as follows:

A-B Single-Subject Design	
Intervention	
Baseline Data **A**	**Intervention Data** **B**
	X X X X X X
O O O O O O	O O O O O O

Time

The interpretation of the results is based on the premise that if no intervention were introduced, the behavior would continue as recorded in the baseline. If the behavior does change during the intervention condition, it may be attributed to the intervention introduced by the researcher. Other factors, however, such as testing and history, often cannot be ruled out reasonably in this design, so it is relatively weak in internal validity.

A-B-A Design

A more common design in single-subject research is the **A-B-A design**, also called a **reversal, removal, or withdrawal design,** in which a second baseline period is added after the intervention period. In this design, which is represented below, the researcher establishes a baseline (A), introduces the intervention (B), and then removes the intervention to re-establish the baseline condition (A).

A-B-A design: baseline, intervention, and baseline comparison

Reversal, removal, or withdrawal design: adding an intervention and then taking it away

```
          A-B-A Single-Subject Design

  Baseline        Intervention        Baseline
     A                  B                 A
                 │ X  X  X  X  X │
 O O O O O │ O  O  O  O  O  O │ O  O  O  O

 ─────────────────────────────────────────▶
                    Time
```

This design allows strong causal inference if the pattern of behavior changes during the intervention phase and then returns to about the same pattern as observed in the first baseline after the intervention is removed. As a hypothetical example, suppose a teacher is interested in trying a new reinforcement technique with John, a fifth-grader, in the hope that the new technique will increase the time John spends actually engaged in study (i.e., time on task). The teacher first records the average amount of time on task for each day until a stable pattern is achieved. Then the teacher introduces the reinforcement technique as the intervention and continues to observe time on task. After a given length of time, the teacher stops using the reinforcement technique to see whether the on-task behavior returns to the baseline condition. Figure 11.7 illustrates the results of this hypothetical study, which provides good evidence of a causal link between the reinforcement technique and greater time on task.

Further evidence of a change in behavior that is caused by the intervention may be obtained if the A-B-A design is extended to reinstitute the intervention, or become A-B-A-B. Not only does the A-B-A-B design provide stronger causal inference than the A-B-A design, but it also ends with the intervention condition, which, for ethical reasons, is often more favorable for the subject. If the pattern of results fails to support the effect of the intervention, then

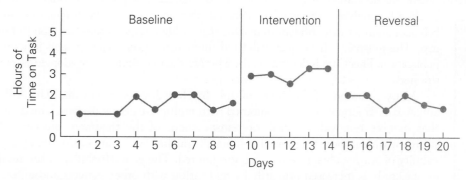

FIGURE 11.7 Results from a Hypothetical Study Using an A-B-A Design

the interpretation is less clear. If the behavior is changed during the intervention but fails to return to the baseline condition once the intervention is ended, the researcher does not know whether factors other than the intervention caused the change, or perhaps the intervention was so effective that it could be removed and still have an impact on behavior.

Multiple-Baseline Designs

Multiple-baseline designs: more than one subject, variable, or context

When it is impossible or undesirable to remove an intervention condition or when the effects of an intervention extend into a second baseline phase, strong causal inference can be made by using **multiple-baseline designs** rather than a simple A-B design. Multiple-baseline designs employ the A-B logic, but rather than using one subject and one kind of target behavior, the researcher collects data on two or more actions, subjects, or situations or some combination of actions, situations, and subjects.

Multiple Baselines across Behavior
In this design, baseline measurements are recorded on two or more discrete, independent behaviors for one subject. After a stable baseline has been established for all behaviors, the intervention is first applied to one behavior and then, after a constant time interval, it is applied to the second behavior, and so forth until all have received the intervention.

Strong causal inference can be made as to the effect of the intervention if performance shows consistent change only after the intervention has been introduced for each type of behavior. To provide a meaningful comparison, it is necessary to begin the interventions at different times for each one. In this way, behavior remaining at the baseline condition provides control for that receiving the intervention condition. The most troublesome problem with this design occurs when using two or more behaviors that are so similar that the first time the intervention is introduced, it affects both.

Multiple-Baselines across Situations
In this design, a single type of target behavior of one individual is observed in two or more settings. A teacher might, for example, be interested in investigating whether a student will respond the same way to individualized feedback in math, science, and English. The basic design is the same as in the multiple-baselines-across-behaviors design except that situation replaces types of behavior as the condition that is varied (e.g., learning behavior in both a classroom and a grocery store or a classroom and a cafeteria).

Multiple Baselines across Individuals
This design uses two or more individuals and holds the behavior and the situation constant. After a stable baseline has been observed for one subject, the intervention is introduced for that subject only. After a given interval, the second subject receives the intervention, and so forth. This design is effective as long as the subjects involved are uninfluenced by one another because one of them has received the intervention (e.g., with students in the same class or with siblings). A good use of this type of design would be to have a teacher employ the same intervention procedure with individual students in four different classes.

A unique feature of single-subject designs is that the analysis of the results consists of a visual analysis. There are no statistical tests. Essentially, the data are graphed and conclusions are reached by analyzing the graphs. Although this approach has been much debated, behavior analysts are confident in making reasonable interpretations based on its findings. The judgments have been validated through the peer-review process in journal publication. Effect size is determined by whether the new findings are adopted by practitioners.

Many variations of the three multiple-baseline designs are possible. The A-B-A and A-B-A-B formats can be combined with multiple-baseline designs. The designs that involve removal, reversal, or reinstatement of the treatment are generally strongest with respect to internal validity. As might well be suspected, the external validity of single-subject designs is quite limited. The generalizability of the results of one study is increased primarily by replication with other subjects and different settings.

To practice selecting a single-subject design, go to MyEducationLab for Research at www.myeducationlab.com. Click on the topic "Single-Subject Experimental Research" and then select the Activities and Applications activity "Selecting a Single-Subject Design."

STANDARDS OF ADEQUACY

In judging the adequacy of the designs that have been presented in this chapter, you should focus your attention on a few key criteria. These criteria are listed here in the form of questions that should be asked for each type of design.

Randomized Experimental Designs

1. Was the research design described in sufficient detail to allow for replication of the study?
2. Was it clear how statistical equivalence of the groups was achieved? Was there a full description of the specific manner in which subjects were assigned randomly to groups?
3. Was a true experimental design appropriate for the research problem?
4. Was there manipulation of the independent variable?
5. Was there maximum control over extraneous variables and errors of measurement?
6. Was the intervention condition sufficiently different from the comparison condition for a differential effect on the dependent variable to be expected?
7. Were potential threats to internal validity reasonably ruled out or noted and discussed?
8. Was the time frame of the study described?
9. Did the design avoid being too artificial or restricted for adequate external validity?
10. Was an appropriate balance achieved between control of variables and natural conditions?
11. Were appropriate tests of inferential statistics used?

Quasi-Experimental Designs

1. Was the research design described in sufficient detail to allow for replication of the study?
2. Was a true experiment possible?
3. Was it clear how extraneous variables were controlled or ruled out as plausible rival hypotheses?
4. Were all potential threats to internal validity addressed?
5. Were the explanations ruling out plausible rival hypotheses reasonable?
6. Would a different quasi-design have been better?
7. Did the design approach a true experiment as closely as possible?
8. Was there an appropriate balance between control for internal validity and for external validity?
9. Was every effort made to use groups that were as equivalent as possible?
10. If a time-series design was used, (a) Was there an adequate number of observations to suggest a pattern of results? (b) Was the intervention introduced distinctly at one point in time? (c) Was the measurement of the dependent variable consistent? (d) Was it clear, if comparison groups were used, how equivalent the groups were?

Single-Subject Designs

1. Was the sample size one or just a few?
2. Was a single-subject design most appropriate, or would a group design have been better?
3. Were the observation conditions standardized?
4. Was the behavior that was observed defined operationally?
5. Was the measurement highly reliable?
6. Were sufficient repeated measures made?
7. Were the conditions in which the study was conducted fully described?
8. Was the baseline condition stable before the treatment was introduced?
9. Was there a difference between the length of time or number of observations between the baseline and intervention conditions?
10. Was only one variable changed during the intervention condition?
11. Were threats to internal and external validity addressed?

Take a moment to evaluate a single-subject study design. Go to MyEducationLab for Research at www.myeducation-lab.com. Click on the topic "Single-Subject Experimental Research" and then select the Building Research Skills exercise titled "Evaluating a Single-Subject Design Study."

CHAPTER SUMMARY

The purpose of this chapter has been to introduce designs that permit investigation of the causal effect of one variable on another. The challenge for most researchers is to use the design that, given the conditions of the research, is best suited to their goal. The major points of the chapter can be summarized as follows:

1. Experimental research involves manipulating experimental variables in order to investigate cause-and-effect relationships.
2. Classic experimental research is characterized by random assignment of subjects to intervention and control groups, manipulation of independent variables, and tight control of extraneous variables.
3. Strict control of extraneous variables in experimental educational research may lead to limited generalizability of results.
4. Planning experimental research involves the creation of experimental and comparison groups, manipulation of the factor of the group to receive the intervention, and assessment of the effect of the intervention on behavior.

5. The key element in interpreting experimental studies is to rule out plausible rival hypotheses.
6. Pre-experimental designs control for very few threats to internal validity.
7. Randomized experimental designs control the threats to internal validity, but some threats, such as local history and diffusion of the intervention, may still constitute plausible rival hypotheses.
8. Quasi-experimental designs are often employed because of the difficulties in conducting randomized experiments.
9. Factorial designs study the effect of two or more independent variables.
10. Time-series designs, in which many observations are made before and after the intervention, are especially useful in cases where periodic testing is a natural part of the environment.
11. Single-subject designs provide techniques for making strong causal inferences about the effect of an intervention on a single individual or group.

APPLICATION PROBLEMS

For each of the following cases, identify the design that is being used and represent it graphically using the notation system discussed in the chapter.

1. A researcher wants to test the effectiveness of three methods of teaching typing to a group of eleventh-grade students. The researcher locates a school willing to cooperate and a teacher who says that the researcher can use three of his classes. The researcher administers a pretest to all students, each class receives a different method of teaching for two weeks, and then the researcher gives all students a posttest.
2. A teacher is interested in determining the effect of using a point system with students in order to control misbehavior. The teacher decides to record the amount of misbehavior of two students, a boy and a girl who seem to have more problems than the other students. For two weeks, the teacher records the misbehavior of the students. At the end of the second week, the teacher begins using the point system with the boy and at the same time continues to

record misbehavior for another two weeks. The girl does not receive the point treatment until the end of the third week.
3. A researcher is interested in whether the order of questions in a multiple-choice test affects the number of items answered correctly. The researcher makes three forms of the test: one with easy items first and difficult items last; another with easy items last, difficult ones first; and a third with no order at all, easy and difficult items mixed together. The test is given to a class of 60 students. The tests are organized into 20 piles, with each pile containing Forms 1, 2, and 3. The 20 piles are then put together, and the tests are passed out to the students. The researcher then compares the average scores of students taking each form of the test.
4. Use the standards of adequacy presented in this chapter to evaluate the Box and Little article, a study of the effect of a specific type of cooperative learning on students' self-concept and achievement.

EXAMPLE Example of an Experimental Study

Cooperative Small-Group Instruction Combined with Advanced Organizers and Their Relationship to Self-Concept and Social Studies Achievement of Elementary School Students

Jeanie A. Box and David C. Little

Research has shown that the use of small-group instruction in the classroom may positively affect student self-concept, as well as academic achievement. The purpose of this study was to determine if the use of the Jigsaw cooperative learning approach incorporated with social studies materials presented in the form of advance organizers could positively affect the self-concept and academic achievement of elementary school students. Five third-grade social studies classes served as the subjects of the study, four experimental and one control. Three assessment instruments were used: the Piers-Harris Children's Self-Concept Scale, the Teacher Inferred Self-Concept Scale, and a researcher developed social studies test based on information contained within the third-grade textbook. The students' self-concepts increased in three of the experimental classes and in the control class; however, a significant decline occurred in teacher perceptions of student self-concept in the control class, as opposed to the experimental classes. Finally, the social studies test scores revealed considerable gains in all five classes. In conclusion, the researchers believe that teachers should consider the use of cooperative small groups with advance organizers as a method of improving self-concepts and social studies achievement of their students.

Numerous articles have explored the relationship between academic achievement and the self-concept of children. A study by Aspy and Buhler (1975) supports the influence of general self-concept in learning situations. A study by Lyon (1993) also reveals data in support of academic self-concept as a powerful predictor of academic achievement.

Research has shown that the use of small-group instruction in the classroom may affect student self-concept. Aronson, Blaney, Rosenfield, Sikes, and Stephan (1977) conducted an experiment using a cooperative form of small grouping along with regular classroom instruction. Results of the study indicated that students who received only small-group instruction gained in self-esteem. A decrease in self-esteem occurred in the control groups.

Aronson and his associates (Aronson, Blaney, Sikes, Snapp, and Stephan, 1975) developed a method of classroom instruction that incorporated the beneficial aspects of small-group cooperation and peer teaching into the tightly structured environment of the traditional classroom. With this Jigsaw approach, teachers are no longer the major source of instruction within the classroom. In time, students, through teaching and listening in cooperative learning situations, depend on each other for instruction. Peer teaching is essential to the concept of cooperative learning. Aronson has indicated that four to six students form into small groups to study assigned *instructional* material. Members of each group are assigned questions or activities about the material being studied. Then each student is placed in a subgroup composed of members from each of the other groups who are responsible for studying the same material. After completing their specific questions in subgroups, all members return to their regular groups to share the answers to the assigned questions.

Ausubel (1963), in his theory of meaningful verbal learning, advocated the use of advance organizers to facilitate the learning of written material. Ausubel reasoned that advance organizers presented students an overview of the more detailed material being studied. This could facilitate learning when presented before the actual presentation of material to be learned. Advance organizers, as defined by Barnes and Clausen (1975), are written materials that serve the function of facilitating the incorporation and retention of reading material. The use of chapter summaries, outlines, key terms, and chapter questions, as introductions to more detailed text are examples of advance organizers.

The purpose of this study was to determine if the use of the Jigsaw cooperative learning approach coupled with social studies materials presented in the forms of advance organizers could positively affect the self-concept and academic achievement of elementary school students. Also measured within this study was the effect of the two treatments on teacher-inferred self-concept toward the students being taught.

Methodology

The subjects of the study included members of five third-grade social studies classes at a suburban elementary school located in the Southeast. Third grade was chosen because developmentally third grade is when children's self-regulatory skills become more proficient (Alexander, Cart, & Schwanenflugel, 1995). Approximately twenty-five students were assigned to each class and were heterogeneously grouped.

Three assessment instruments were used in the study. The Piers-Harris Self-Concept Scale (Harris & Piers, 1969) measured student reported self-concept with a pretest to posttest design. The Teacher Inferred Self-Concept Scale measured the pre- to post assessments of students'

(continued)

self-concepts as reported by their classroom teachers (McDaniel, 1973). The researchers developed a social studies test based on information contained within the third-grade textbook used in the study to assess the pre- to posttest social studies achievement of the students.

Four experimental third-grade classes received social studies instruction in small groups instructionally designed according to Aronson's Jigsaw cooperative learning approach. In addition, one of the four types of advance organizers used in the study was randomly assigned to each experimental group.

A fifth third-grade class served as the control group. In this class, the teacher taught using traditional, large-group instruction techniques. Small groups or advance organizers were not included in the *instructional* design of the control group.

Data Analysis

The raw scores from the self-concept scales and the social studies test were analyzed by using a two-way analysis of variance (ANOVA). Analyses of the simple main effects and Tukey's KSD test results were conducted to determine if significant differences existed between pre- and posttest mean scores on the three assessment instruments. An alpha level of $p < .05$ represented the criterion for statistical significance.

Results

The results of the study were varied. Observation on the differences between pre- and post evaluation mean scores for the Piers-Harris Children's Self-Concept Scale revealed gains in three of the experimental classes concerning students' self ratings of self concept. The evaluation of the mean scores for the fourth experimental group showed a decline in the Piers-Harris Children's Self-Concept Scale scores from pre- to posttest. On the other hand, significant gains in self-concept occurred in the control class.

Observations of the differences between pre- and post evaluations mean scores for the Inferred Self-Concept Scale revealed significant gains in three of the experimental classes concerning teacher rating of self-concept. A fourth experimental class revealed a slight decline in the mean scores from pre- to posttest. In the control class, a significant decline occurred in teacher perceptions of student self-concept.

Observations of the differences between pre- and post evaluation mean scores for the social studies test revealed significant gains in the four experimental classes. A significant gain was also reported for the social studies scores of the control class.

Discussion

The advantages of the Jigsaw Small-Group Approach combined with advance organizers could be placed in two categories: Academic and psychological. First, the researchers noted that the use of the Jigsaw approach combined with advance organizers was effective in improving the self-concepts of students as measured by the Piers-Harris Children's Self-Concept Scale. The teacher-inferred self-concept as measured by the Inferred Self-Concept Scale was also found to be effective.

Second, the researchers noted that the *instructional* procedures used in all five classrooms were effective in improving the social studies achievement of the third-grade students. While no clear cause for this outcome is evident, the researchers believe that the results may indicate that the students and teachers who participated in the study possessed a high level of motivation.

Third, of major concern is the significant decline in scores for the control group on the Inferred Self-Concept Scale. The question could be asked if the continuous teaching of students in large groups could negatively affect how the teacher views the self-concepts of the students in the class.

Overall, the researchers believe that the results of the study support the use of cooperative small-group instruction and advance organizers in teaching classes. It should be emphasized, however, that the use of such small groups and advance organizers should serve as a supplement to conventional instruction, rather than an alternative to it.

References

Alexander, J. M., Cart, M., & Schwanenflugel, P. J. (1995). Development of metacognition in gifted children: Directions for future research. *Developmental Review, 15,* 1–37.

Aronson, E., Blaney, N., Sikes, J., Snapp, M., & Stephen, C. (1975). Busing and racial tension: The jigsaw route to learning and liking. *Psychology Today, 8*(9), 43–50.

Aronson, E., Blaney, N. T., Rosenfeld, D., Sikes, J., & Stephan, C. (1977). Interdependence in the classroom: A field study. *Journal of Educational Psychology, 69*(2), 121–128.

Aspy, D. N., & Buhler, J. H. (1975). The effect of teachers' inferred self concept upon student achievement. *Journal of Educational Research, 68,* 386–389.

Ausubel, D. P. (1963). *The psychology of meaningful verbal learning.* New York: Grune and Stratton.

Barnes, B. R., & Clauson, E. U. (1975). Do advance organizers facilitate learning? Recommendations for further research based analysis of 32 studies. *Review of Educational Research, 45,* 637–659.

Harris, D. B., & Piers, E. V. (1969). *The Piers-Harris children's self-concept scale.* Los Angeles: Western Psychological Services.

Lyon, M. (1993). Academic self concept and its relationship to achievement in a sample of junior high students. *Educational and Psychological Measurement, 53,* 201–209.

McDaniel, E. L. (1973). *Inferred self-concept scale.* Los Angeles: Western Psychological Services.

Source: From Box, J. A., & Little, D. C. (2003). Cooperative small-group instruction combined with advanced organizers and their relationship to self-concept and social studies achievement of elementary school students. *Journal of Instructional Psychology, 30*(4), 285–288. Reprinted by permission.

ANSWERS TO APPLICATION PROBLEMS

1. Nonequivalent groups pretest-posttest comparison group design

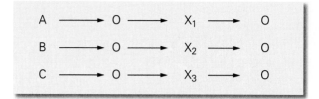

2. Multiple baseline across subjects design

3. Randomized posttest-only comparison group design

Randomization	Group	Treatment	Posttest
60 students	A	X_1	O
	B	X_2	O
	C	X_3	O

4. a. Much more detail about the design is needed—for example, time frame, how instruments were administered, how the intervention condition was administered.

b. It is not possible to use a randomized design in this setting, even if students could be randomly assigned to classes, because the intervention was done by class and groups within classes.

c. There was no discussion of potential threats to internal validity.

d. No. Several key threats were not addressed, including selection, treatment replications, diffusions of treatment, subject effects, and experimenter (teacher) effects.

e. No explanations were provided.

f. This design is the best that could be used in this school.

g. No, because there was an inadequate effort to show that the classes did not differ with respect to student characteristics, and control of the implementation of the intervention was not examined.

h. There was little indication of any emphasis on external validity.

i. No. Other procedures, such as matching, could be used to ensure group equivalency.

Understanding and Reporting
Inferential Data Analyses

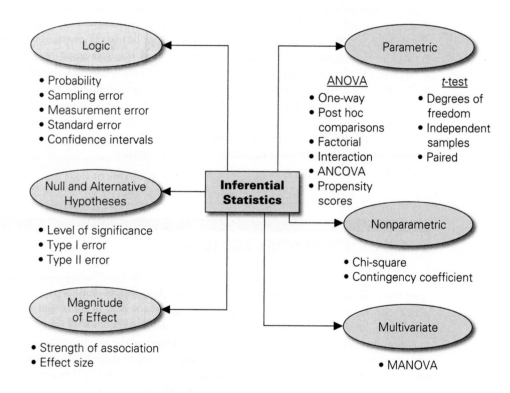

KEY TERMS

probability
sampling distribution
standard error
confidence interval
statistical hypothesis
null hypothesis
alternative hypothesis
level of significance
alpha level
Type I error
Type II error

statistically significant
single-sample *t*-test
independent samples *t*-test
degrees of freedom
paired *t*-test
analysis of variance
   (ANOVA)
post hoc comparisons
planned comparisons
factorial ANOVA
interaction

analysis of covariance
   (ANCOVA)
propensity score matching
parametric
nonparametric
chi-square
multivariate
magnitude of effect
effect size

WHAT YOU WILL LEARN

Study this chapter and you will:

- Understand the logic of statistics and probability.
- Understand how sampling and measurement error affects results.
- Know the differences between null and research hypotheses.
- Explain how significance testing is applied to inferential statistics.
- Be able to interpret inferential analyses.
- Know how to interpret level of significance.
- Understand different parametric statistical tests and how to apply them to specific research designs.

- Know how *t*-tests are different from ANOVA.
- Be able to interpret inferential statistical data presented in tables and report narratives.
- Understand that nonparametric statistics, such as chi-square, can also be used to provide inferential analyses.
- Understand how interaction is important in factorial designs and analyses.
- Understand what effect size is and why it is important in reporting data results.

LOGIC OF INFERENTIAL STATISTICS

This is the part of research books that many readers dread. The term *inferential statistics* can send waves of anxiety and fear into students already concerned about the so-called more simple descriptive data analysis procedures! Although it is true that the actual mathematical computations associated with inferential statistics are complicated, you do not need to learn equations or complete calculations to understand and use the results of these procedures. Learning the principles of inferential statistics requires study and application, but it is more a matter of understanding logic than of mathematical calculations. We'll begin with logic and then move on to other inferential principles and guidelines.

In some ways, it would be very nice if we could be certain in predicting outcomes. When we go to see a movie, how sure are we that we will enjoy it? When a teacher uses a particular grouping procedure, how sure is he or she that it will work? How confident is a patient that an operation will be successful? Are farmers certain that there will be sufficient rain for their crops?

We could ask any number of questions like these because it is in our nature to try to predict the future. However, the degree to which we can be certain about the predictions varies greatly. There are very few things in our world that we can be absolutely certain about, and in the social sciences and education, there is usually a fair amount of uncertainty. In making statements about investigated phenomena, we use language that reflects the probabilistic nature of the case. The numbers, concepts, and terms used in inferential statistics provide this language. Although there are many inferential statistical procedures, many quite complicated, the purpose is always the same: to determine in a precise way the probability of something.

Probability

Probability is a scientific way of stating the degree of confidence we have in predicting something. Consider dice rolling as an example. With one die, there is a total of six possible cases. If the favorable case is rolling a four, the probability of actually rolling a four would be 1/6, or .17; that is, if a die is rolled 100 times, about 17 fours will be rolled. If we have two dice, what is the probability of rolling a seven? Because there is a total of 36 different combinations for throwing two dice (1 and 1; 1 and 2; 1 and 3; and so on) and only six of these equal 7 (1 and 6; 2 and 5; 3 and 4; 6 and 1; 5 and 2; and 4 and 3), the probability of rolling a seven is 6/36, or .17. What about throwing boxcars (two sixes)? There is only one combination of numbers that will give you boxcars, so the probability is 1/36, or .03.

This logic is applied to more complicated situations in research. How sure, for example, can pollsters be that their predictions are accurate? What is the probability of being right or wrong? When teachers use positive reinforcement, how sure are they that the desired behavior will increase in frequency? In these situations, we make probability statements that are influenced by the amount of error possible in measuring variables and sampling subjects.

Error in Sampling and Measurement

Sampling is a technique for studying a portion from the population of all events, observations, or individuals under consideration. The *population* is the larger group to which the researcher intends to generalize the results obtained from the sample. As a subgroup of the population, the *sample* is used to derive data, and then inferential statistics are used to generalize to the population. Let us assume, for example, that a researcher is interested in assessing the self-concept of fourth-graders in a school district. The researcher could measure the self-concept of every fourth-grader, but that would be time-consuming, expensive, and probably unnecessary. Rather, the researcher should take a sample of the fourth-graders and measure each child's self-concept. Then the researcher could *infer* what the self-concept of all fourth-graders is from the results of the sample chosen. The group of all fourth-graders is the population, and the researcher uses descriptive statistics (i.e., mean and standard deviation) from the sample to estimate the characteristics of the population.

Where does probability enter this process? When a sample is drawn, the resulting statistics represent an imperfect estimate of the population. There is error in drawing the sample, and probability relates to our confidence in the fact that the sample accurately represents the population. Even if the researcher uses a random sample, the mean and variance of the particular sample drawn would be slightly different from those of another sample. A third sample would also be different, as would a fourth, a fifth, and so on. The sample descriptive statistics only estimate the population values, so the inferences made must take into account what possible sample statistics could have been generated.

Consider the following example (see Figure 12.1). Let us say that a researcher is interested in determining the reading level of ninth-graders of a school district. A random sample is selected and the mean of the sample is, say, 65, with a standard deviation of 2.5 (Figure 12.1a). Now let's say that the researcher draws another random sample, and this time the mean is 66. Now there are two means (Figure 12.1b). Which one is correct? He or she decides to take five more samples and gets means of 64, 63.5, 64.5, 65.7, and 65.2 (Figure 12.1c). Now which one is correct? The researcher decides to really find out and takes 30 more samples. Surely that will do it! Different sample means are drawn, but when the means are put together, they begin to look like something familiar—a normal curve (Figure 12.1d).

In fact, if 100 samples were drawn, the sample means, when put together, would constitute a normal curve, with its own mean and standard deviation. The resulting distribution is called the **sampling distribution**, and the standard deviation of this distribution is termed the **standard error** or *standard error of the mean*. Thus, when we imagine that multiple samples are extracted

Probability: degree of certainty

Sampling distribution: array of scores obtained from the sample

Standard error: variance of sample means

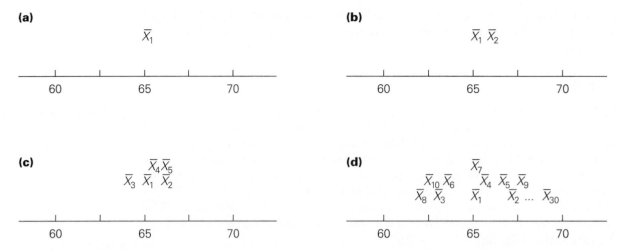

FIGURE 12.1 Random Sample with (a) One Mean, (b) Two Means, (c) Several Means, and (d) the Means Showing a Normal Curve

from the population and scored, the standard error is the standard deviation of this sampling distribution. That is, the standard error is the measure of variability when multiple samples are drawn from the population. The *mean of means*, then, and the standard error of the sampling distribution can be calculated. The researcher can use this information to know not what the population mean is but what the probability is of its having a certain value based on the properties of the normal curve. That is, about two-thirds of the means drawn would be within one standard error of the mean of means, and 96 percent of the means would be within two standard errors. This allows the researcher to describe a range of probable means and be fairly certain of the range, even though individual sample means will be slightly different.

In reality, researchers only take one sample, but from the mean and variance of that sample, the range of sample means that could be drawn, can be calculated. Here, then, is where probability is integrated with inferential statistics. Inferential statistics are used to estimate the probability of a population mean being within a range of possible values. The researcher is able to say, to infer, that 68 times out of 100, the population mean will be within one standard error of the mean of means and that 96 times out of 100, it will be within two standard errors.

Confidence interval: range of likely population means

An important related concept is that of *confidence interval*. The **confidence interval** is a range of numerical values in which the actual value of the population probably lies. The upper and lower boundaries of the confidence interval are called the *confidence limits*. Typically, researchers report a 95 or 99 percent confidence interval, which means that the probability of the population value being between the confidence limits is 95 or 99 percent, respectively. For example, if it is reported that the 99 percent confidence interval from a statewide poll is .435 to .492, this means that from the sample it can be inferred that there is a 99 percent chance that between 43.5 and 49.2 percent of the population is in favor of a particular proposal. Thus, it is highly likely that the majority of the population is against the proposal. If the 99 percent confidence interval was completely above .50, then a majority would probably favor the proposal.

Suppose a researcher is not interested in taking a sample from a population but rather includes the entire population as the sample. Would this mean that the researcher could ignore the principles of sampling error and inferential statistics in obtaining a result that represents the entire group? While sampling error is not a concern, measurement error is. Recall that whenever we assess variables in education, the measurement is never perfect. There is always some degree of error. Thus, we *infer* a real or true value on a variable from the imperfect measure. This could be thought of as a type of sampling error in the sense that the one measure obtained is a sample estimating the true value. Consequently, in all educational research, there is definitely measurement error, and in some research, there is also sampling error.

In most research, however, we are interested in much more than estimating populations from samples. We usually want to compare population means with each other or with some established value. The next section discusses how these comparisons are made.

NULL AND ALTERNATIVE HYPOTHESES

Let us assume that a researcher wants to compare the attitudes of sixth-graders toward school to those of fourth-graders. The researcher randomly selects samples of sixth- and fourth-graders and finds the mean of each group. The mean is 30 for fourth-graders and 37 for sixth-graders. Can the researcher then assume that sixth-graders have more positive attitudes than fourth-graders? Perhaps, but this conclusion must take into account sampling and measurement error. The population means are thus estimated and compared to find the probability that the *possible* population means of each group are different. The probabilities are formalized by statements that are tested. These statements are referred to as *hypotheses*. Research hypotheses have already been introduced as the research prediction that is tested. (In this example, the research hypothesis might be that sixth-graders have more positive attitudes than fourth-graders.)

When we refer to probability in terms of sampling and measurement error, the statement used is called the **statistical hypothesis**. Statistical hypotheses are stated in either the *null* or *alternative* form. The **null hypothesis** states that there is no difference between the *population* means of the two groups. That is, the population means are the same. The researcher employs an inferential statistical test to determine the probability that the null hypothesis is untrue. If the null is false, then there is a high probability that there is a difference between the groups. The null hypothesis in our example would be that attitudes of sixth- and fourth-graders toward school are the same. If we can show that there is a high probability of being correct in rejecting the null, then we have found evidence of a difference in the attitudes.

The null hypothesis is indicated by the symbol H_0, which is followed by population means that are compared. The population means are symbolized by u. Thus, a typical null hypothesis would be $H_0: u_1 = u_2$, where u_1 is the mean of one population and u_2 is the mean of a second population. If four populations are compared, the null hypothesis will be $H_0: u_1 = u_2 = u_3 = u_4$.

Theoretically, we know that the population range of means of both groups can be estimated, and if there is little overlap in those ranges, then it is likely that the population means are different. This case is diagramed in Figure 12.2. Note that there is virtually no overlap between the two normal curves. This means that we can be confident of being correct in rejecting the null hypothesis.

The reason null hypotheses are used with inferential statistics is that we never prove something to be true; we only fail to disprove it. Failure to disprove is consistent with the reality of probability in our lives. If we cannot find compelling evidence that two things are different, the most plausible conclusion is that they are the same.

It should be pointed out that failure to reject the null hypothesis does not necessarily mean that the null is true. It is especially difficult to accept null hypotheses as reality in studies that use a small number of subjects or that use instruments with low reliability. The fact that the null hypothesis was not rejected may be due to a large sampling error or measurement error.

The **alternative hypothesis**, which is designated as H_a or H_1, is the opposite of the null hypothesis. It states the research or experimental hypothesis in statistical terms. The alternative hypothesis can be either directional or nondirectional. A *directional* alternative hypothesis states that one population mean is either greater than or less than the other population mean (e.g., $H_a: u_1 > u_2$). A *nondirectional* alternative hypothesis states that the means are not the same (e.g., $H_a: u_1 \neq u_2$). Because the directional alternative hypothesis postulates one outcome, it is often referred to as *one-tailed* or *one-sided*. The nondirectional alternative hypothesis, which is used

Statistical hypothesis: expectations based on statistical results

Null hypothesis: no difference in population means

Alternative hypothesis: difference in population means

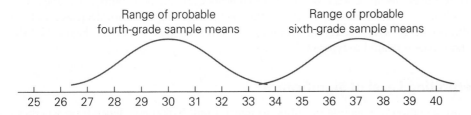

Range of probable
fourth-grade sample means

Range of probable
sixth-grade sample means

25 26 27 28 29 30 31 32 33 34 35 36 37 38 39 40

FIGURE 12.2 **Range of Population Means of Two Groups**

much more frequently than the directional one, only predicts a difference without specifying whether one mean is greater than or less than another mean. This is called a *two-tailed* or *two-sided alternative hypothesis*. The directional/nondirectional nature of the alternative hypothesis is used to make decisions about whether the null hypothesis can be rejected.

Level of Significance

Because the basis of inferential statistics is the probability of estimation, rejecting the null hypothesis is also related to probability or chance, rather than being a dichotomous decision. That is, because of error in sampling and measurement, we can only give the probability of being correct or incorrect in rejecting or not rejecting the null. To put it differently, we can be fairly sure that a certain number of times out of 100, the sample means we *could* draw would not be the same.

Level of significance: probability of being wrong in rejecting the null hypothesis

The **level of significance** is used to indicate the probability that we are wrong in rejecting the null. Also called *level of probability*, or *p* level, it is expressed as a decimal and tells us how many times out of 100 or 1,000 we would be wrong in rejecting the null, assuming the null is true. (In other words, it tells us how often we would expect no real difference even though we rejected the null.) The logic of level of significance is that we assume that the null hypothesis is correct, and then we see what the probability is that the sample means we have calculated would be different by chance alone. If we find that there is a probability of only 1 in 100 that we would find a particular difference in the means by chance or random fluxations ($p = .01$), then we would probably reject the null because it is quite probable that the null is false. In other words, the level of significance tells us the chance probability of finding differences between the means. The smaller the level of significance, therefore, the more confidence we have that we are safe in rejecting the null. After all, for example, if we find a difference of five points between two means that, through our null hypothesis, we assume to be the same, and our statistics tell us that there is only 1 chance in 1,000 of finding a five-point difference by chance ($p = .001$), then it is logical to assume that the null hypothesis is false and reject it (or say that we are very, very lucky!). We reject the null hypothesis in favor of the research, or alternative, hypothesis.

Alpha level: used to accept or fail to accept the null hypothesis

Some researchers will use a slightly different approach to hypothesis testing, in which a given level of significance is determined prior to data collection to act as a criterion for accepting or failing to accept the null hypothesis. This critical value is called the **alpha level (α)**, and it determines the conclusion based on the numbers generated from the results.

Errors in Hypothesis Testing

The purpose of using inferential statistics, null hypotheses, and levels of significance is to make a decision, based on probability, about the nature of populations and real values of variables. It is possible that the decision is wrong. When the decision is to reject the null hypothesis when in fact the null hypothesis is true, the researcher has made what is called a **Type I error**. The probability of making this type of error is equal to the level of significance: That is, with a significance level of .05, there is a probability of 5 times out of 100 that the sample data will lead the researcher to reject the null hypothesis when it is in fact true. A researcher consequently avoids a Type I error to the degree that the level of significance is high. (That is, a .001 level is better than .01 for avoiding Type I errors.)

Type I error: reject a true null hypothesis

Another type of wrong decision occurs when the null hypothesis is not rejected when, in fact, the null hypothesis is actually wrong. This is referred to as a **Type II error**. Although there is no direct relationship between the level of significance and the probability of making a Type II error, as the level of significance increases, the likelihood of Type II error decreases. A level of significance of .10 is thus better for avoiding a Type II error than .05 or .01. Figure 12.3 shows how error type is related to types of decisions.

Type II error: failure to reject a false null hypothesis

Interpreting Level of Significance

The interpretation of rejecting or failing to reject a null hypothesis depends on whether the researcher is interested in avoiding a Type I or Type II error and in whether a predetermined

True Nature

	Null hypothesis is true	Null hypothesis is false
Reject null hypothesis	Type I error	Correct decision
Fail to reject null hypothesis	Correct decision	Type II error

(Left axis label: **Action Taken**)

FIGURE 12.3 Relationship of State of Nature, Decisions, and Error in Hypothesis Testing

alpha level is set. If a predetermined value is stated, such as .05 or .01 for a Type I error, then the researcher rejects the null by comparing the computed level of significance with the predetermined level. If the calculated significance is less than the predetermined level (e.g., .01 < .05), then the null hypothesis is rejected.

In many research studies, there is no predetermined alpha level. In these studies, statisticians use a general rule for rejecting a null hypothesis. If the *p* value is the same as or less than .05, then the null is rejected and the statement is made that there is a **statistically significant** difference (though more accurately, it is always a difference at some level of confidence). A *p* value between .05 and .10 is usually thought of as *marginally* significant, and anything greater than .10 is labeled a nonsignificant difference. We are saying, then, that if there is more than 1 chance out of 10 of being wrong in rejecting the null (1 chance in 10 that the means are the same), then that is too much risk to take in saying that the means are different. The results may be due more to error than to a treatment or real difference.

It is best to report the specific *p* level for each statistical test because the conventions for rejecting the null hypothesis are general rules of thumb. Individual researchers and consumers, depending on the circumstances, may differ with respect to what constitutes a statistically significant difference. A level of .05, for example, generally agreed to be statistically significant, would probably be unacceptable if the test concerned usage of a drug that might cause death (i.e., 5 times out of 100, the researcher is wrong in saying no death will occur).

Another important point in interpreting *p* levels and corresponding conclusions is that although it is common for researchers to fail to reject the null (e.g., *p* = .20), the failure to find a statistically significant difference or relationship does not necessarily mean that in *reality* there is no difference or relationship. Only when the circumstances of the research warrant (in which there is *adequate power* in the test) is a nonsignificant finding taken as evidence that there is no relationship. The reason a nonsignificant finding is usually uninterpretable is that many factors, such as low reliability, diffusion of the intervention, insufficient number of subjects, and so forth, can cause the nonsignificance. Thus, a significant finding indicates that a real relationship exists, but the opposite is not necessarily true. Recently, there has been considerable criticism of the use of null hypothesis significance testing. Most arguments focus on placing too much emphasis on using the so-called magical .05 level of significance to determine conclusions (e.g., as if there is a meaningful difference between .05 and .06). See Wainer and Robinson (2003) for a review of these criticisms.

Statistically significant: rejection of the null hypothesis based on the alpha level

ANALYZING ONE OR TWO MEANS: THE *t*-TEST

One of the most commonly used statistical procedures is the *t*-test. There are actually three variations of the *t*-test that we will consider: (1) single-sample, (2) two-sample with different groups, and (3) two-sample with the same group. In each case, there is a comparison between two values to see if they are different (think about it as t[ea] for two!).

EXCERPT 12.1 Single-Sample *t*-Test

To address our first aim, single-sample *t*-tests were used to compare the CES-D scores reported in this sample (mean = 15.9) with those of samples from three studies (Abbeduto et al. 2004; Eisenhower et al. 2005; Blacher & McIntyre 2006). . . . Consistent with expectations and previous research, our sample reported more depressive symptoms than [those for] mothers raising children with Down syndrome and Fragile X syndrome (Table 3). The present sample reported more depressive symptoms than [those for] the sample of mothers raising children with cerebral palsy (CP) in Eisenhower et al. (2005), although there were no significant differences in depressive symptoms between the current sample and [the] CP sample reported in Blacher & McIntyre (2006). As expected, the present sample reported depressive symptoms similar to [those of] all three ASD comparison groups. (p. 603)

Source: From Schwichtenberg, A., & Poehlmann, J. (2007). Applied behaviour analysis: Does intervention intensity relate to family stressors and material well-being? *Journal of Intellectual Disability Research, 51*(8), 598–605.

Single-Sample *t*-Test

Single-sample *t*-test: involves one group

The **single-sample *t*-test** is used to either describe the nature of the population confidence intervals or compare the group mean to a specified value. To establish confidence intervals, the mean and standard error of the mean are calculated and confidence intervals are established, typically at 95 or 99 percent. This gives the researcher "confidence" that the true mean of the population is between the endpoints of the interval. A single mean can also be compared to a specified value. In this case, the researcher tests the null hypothesis that there is no difference between the sample mean and the fixed numerical value. For example, a researcher could draw a sample of high school students' SAT scores, calculate the mean, and then compare the sample mean to the national average. In this way, conclusions about whether the sample of students was significantly above or below the national norm can be determined. The *z*-test (not to be confused with the *z*-score) is sometimes used for this purpose when the sample size is less than 30. It is also used to test whether a correlation coefficient is different from zero. Excerpt 12.1 shows how the single-sample *t*-test was used to compare a sample of children with autism spectrum disorder to means from previous studies to confirm few differences.

Two-Sample *t*-Test with Independent Groups

Independent samples *t*-test: involves two groups

This is the most common use of the *t*-test. It is usually referred to as an **independent samples *t*-test**. The purpose of this procedure is to determine if there is a statistically significant difference in the dependent variable between two different populations of subjects. The mean and standard deviation of each sample are calculated and used to determine the *t*-statistic, which is the difference between the sample means divided by the standard error of the mean (the denominator is calculated from the standard deviations). The formula is

$$t = \frac{\overline{X}_1 - \overline{X}_2}{S}$$

where X_1 = mean of group 1
X_2 = mean of group 2
S = standard error of mean differences

One way of thinking about this formula is that the variation (difference) *between* the groups is divided by the variation that exists both between groups and *within* groups. Researchers may refer to this as simply *variation between divided by variation within*. As the distance between the group means gets larger and as the standard error gets smaller, the *t* statistic gets larger.

The calculated *t* value is a three- or four-digit number with two decimal places (e.g., 2.30, 3.16, 8.72, or 1.85). To determine the level of significance, the researcher compares this number with theoretical *t* values in a table. The table is called *distribution of t* or *critical values for the t-test* and is shown in Table 12.1. The researcher uses the table by locating two numbers: the *degrees of freedom (df)* and the level of significance desired. The term **degrees of freedom** is a mathematical concept that denotes the number of independent observations that are free to vary. For each statistical test, there is a corresponding number of degrees of freedom that is calculated, and then this

Degrees of freedom: number of units that are free to vary

TABLE 12.1 *t* Distribution

df	Level of Significance for a One-Tailed Test				
	.05	.025	.01	.005	.0005
	Level of Significance for a Two-Tailed Test				
	.10	.05	.02	.01	.001
1	6.314	12.706	31.821	63.657	636.619
2	2.920	4.303	6.965	9.925	31.598
3	2.353	3.182	4.541	5.841	12.924
4	2.132	2.776	3.747	4.604	8.610
5	2.015	2.571	3.365	4.032	6.869
6	1.943	2.447	3.143	3.707	5.959
7	1.895	2.365	2.998	3.499	5.408
8	1.860	2.306	2.896	3.355	5.041
9	1.833	2.262	2.821	3.250	4.781
10	1.812	2.228	2.764	3.169	4.587
11	1.796	2.201	2.718	3.106	4.437
12	1.782	2.179	2.681	3.055	4.318
13	1.771	2.160	2.650	3.012	4.221
14	1.761	2.145	2.624	2.977	4.140
15	1.753	2.131	2.602	2.947	4.073
16	1.746	2.120	2.583	2.921	4.015
17	1.740	2.110	2.567	2.898	3.965
18	1.734	2.101	2.552	2.878	3.922
19	1.729	2.093	2.539	2.861	3.883
20	1.725	2.086	2.528	2.845	3.850
21	1.721	2.080	2.518	2.831	3.819
22	1.717	2.074	2.508	2.819	3.792
23	1.714	2.069	2.500	2.807	3.767
24	1.711	2.064	2.492	2.797	3.745
25	1.708	2.060	2.485	2.787	3.725
26	1.706	2.056	2.479	2.779	3.707
27	1.703	2.052	2.473	2.771	3.690
28	1.701	2.048	2.467	2.763	3.674
29	1.699	2.045	2.462	2.756	3.659
30	1.697	2.042	2.457	2.750	3.646
40	1.684	2.021	2.423	2.704	3.551
60	1.671	2.000	2.390	2.660	3.460
120	1.658	1.980	2.358	2.617	3.373
∞	1.645	1.960	2.326	2.576	3.291

Source: From Fisher, R. A., and Yates, F. (1974). *Statistical Tables for Biological, Agricultural and Medical Research,* Table III, 6th Ed. London: Pearson Education Limited. Copyright © 1974 by Pearson Education Limited. Reprinted by permission of the authors and publisher.

number is used to estimate the statistical significance of the test. In the distribution of a *t*-table, the number at the intersection of the degrees of freedom row and the level of significance column is the relevant theoretical value of *t*. If this critical *t* is less than the *t* value calculated by the *t*-test equation, it means that the observed difference in means is greater than could have been expected under the null hypothesis, so the hypothesis can be rejected at that level of significance.

EXCERPT 12.2 Independent Samples *t*-Test

The composite mean scores for students on this dimension were consistently lower than the teacher scores for both science and social studies. Across grades, teacher data were approximately at 3.00, whereas the student data were approximately at 2.50. An independent-samples *t*-test showed that the difference between teacher and student composite mean scores was significant: science, $t(526) = 18.96$, $p = .001$; social studies, $t(585) = 21.23$, $p = .001$. This suggested that teachers were more likely to indicate that their science or social studies classroom instruction had a greater emphasis on the state standards and reform-oriented classroom tasks. (p. 316)

Source: From Parke, C. S., & Lane, S. (2007). Student perceptions of a Maryland state performance assessment. *The Elementary School Journal, 107*(3), 305–324.

Notice that at the top of the table, there are two rows: the top row for what is called a *one-tailed* and the other for a *two-tailed* test of significance. The *tails* refer to the ends of the normal sampling distribution that are used in the significance test. *One-tailed* means that one of the two ends of the distribution is used as the region of rejection, so that if the *p* value is .05, that 5 percent is all at one end of the distribution. In a *two-tailed* test, the region is divided between both ends of the distribution; for example, for a *p* value of .05, .025 percent is at either end of the distribution. The one-tailed test is more liberal and should be used only when the researcher is very confident that a result that is opposite the research hypothesis will not be obtained. Unless otherwise stated, significance tests can be assumed to be two-tailed.

Excerpts 12.2 and 12.3 are examples of how the results of independent samples *t*-tests are reported. Note that in Excerpt 12.2 the authors chose to report the results in a narrative, indicating the approximate means of each group. In Excerpt 12.3 more complete information is provided in the tables.

EXCERPT 12.3 Independent Samples *t*-Test

The independent samples *t*-tests for MAT pre-test mean scores for groups E1 and C1 were not significantly different (Table I), implying that the groups had similar characteristics and were therefore suitable for the study. The independent samples *t*-test of pre-test scores on MAT based on gender showed that the mean scores for male and female students were not significantly different (Table II). (pp. 448–449)

TABLE I Independent Samples *t*-Test of Pretest Scores on MAT Based on Groups E and C

Variable	Group	N	Mean	SD	F-value	p-value
MAT	E	32	10.49	4.0		
	C	36	9.19	5.85	1.003	0.320 ns

TABLE II Independent Samples *t*-Test of Pretest Scores on MAT Based on Groups E and C

Variable	Gender	N	Mean	SD	F-value	p-value
MAT	M	41	10.24	5.72		
	F	27	9.04	3.91	1.034	0.305 ns

Source: From Githua, B. N., & Nyabwa, R. A. (2008). Effects of advance organizer strategy during instruction on secondary school students' mathematics achievement in Kenya's Nakuru district. *International Journal of Science and Mathematics Education, 6*(3), 439–457.

EXCERPT 12.4 Paired-Samples *t*-Test

The purpose of this study was to use a larger sample size ($N = 20$) to see if these two tests, when given on the same day by the same tester, produce comparable results for people with IQs less than 80. . . . Each participant took both the RIAS and WAIS-III. To control for any order effect, half of the people took the WAIS-III first and the other half took the RAIS first. . . . [A] *t* test showed no significant difference between tests given first and tests given second, $t(20) = -0.24$, $p = .99$ (two tailed). (pp. 230–231)

Source: From Umphress, T. B. (2008). A comparison of the low IQ scores from the Reynolds Intellectual Assessment Scales and Wechsler Adult Intelligence Scale—Third Edition. *Intellectual and Developmental Disabilities, 46*(3), 229–233.

Paired *t*-Test with Dependent Groups

The third form of the *t*-test can be referred to by several different names, including *paired, dependent samples, correlated,* or *matched t-test.* This *t*-test is used in situations in which the subjects from the two groups are paired or matched in some way (see Excerpt 12.4). A common example of this case is the same group of subjects tested twice, as in a pretest-posttest study. Whether the same or different subjects are in each group, as long as there is a systematic relationship between the groups, it is necessary to use the **paired *t*-test** to calculate the probability of rejecting the null hypothesis.

A more concrete explanation of using the *t*-test is the following example. Suppose a researcher is interested in finding out whether there is a significant difference between blue-eyed and brown-eyed sixth-graders with respect to reading achievement. The research question would be: Is there a difference in the reading achievement (the dependent variable) of blue-eyed fourth-graders compared with brown-eyed fourth-graders (the independent variable)? The null hypothesis would be: There is no difference between blue-eyed and brown-eyed fourth-graders in reading achievement. To test this hypothesis, the researcher would randomly select a sample of brown- and blue-eyed fourth-graders from the population of all fourth-grade students. Let us say that the sample mean of blue-eyed students' reading achievement is 54 and the sample mean for brown-eyed fourth-graders is 48. Because we assume the null hypothesis—that the population means are equal—we use the *t*-test to show how often the difference of scores in the samples would occur if the population means are equal. If our degrees of freedom is 60 and the calculated *t* value is 2.00, we can see by referring to Table 12.1 that the probability of attaining this difference in the sample means, for a two-tailed test, is .05, or 5 times out of 100. We reject the null hypothesis and say that there is a statistically significant difference between the reading achievement of blue-eyed and brown-eyed fourth-graders.

Finally, we need to point out that some researchers may calculate an *F* statistic rather than a *t* statistic when comparing two means or comparing a mean with a fixed number. The results will be the same. We'll take up the *F* statistic in the next section with designs that must use the *F* formula rather than the *t*.

Paired *t*-test: one group with two measures

COMPARING TWO OR MORE MEANS: ANALYSIS OF VARIANCE (ANOVA)

One-Way Analysis of Variance

If a study is done in which three or more sample means are compared on one independent variable, then to test the null hypothesis, the researcher would employ a procedure called single-factor or *one-way analysis of variance* (abbreviated *ANOVA*). ANOVA is simply an extension of the *t*-test. Rather than the researcher's using multiple *t*-tests to compare all possible pairs of means in a study of two or more groups, ANOVA allows the researcher to test the differences between all groups and make more accurate probability statements than are possible when using a series of separate *t*-tests. It is called **analysis of variance** because the statistical formula uses the variances of the groups and not the means to calculate a value that reflects the degree of differences in the means. Instead of a *t* statistic, ANOVA calculates an *F* statistic (or *F* ratio). The *F* is analogous to the

Analysis of variance (ANOVA): involves two or more groups

t. It is a three- or four-digit number that is used in a distribution of *F* table with the degrees of freedom to find the level of significance that the researcher uses to reject or not reject the null. There are two degrees of freedom. The first is the number of groups in the study minus one, and the second is the total number of subjects minus the number of groups. These numbers follow the *F* in reporting the results of ANOVA. For example, in reporting $F(4,80) = 4.25$, the degrees of freedom mean that there are five group means that are being compared and 85 subjects in the analysis.

ANOVA addresses the question *Is there a significant difference between the population means?* If the *F* value that is calculated is large enough, then the null hypothesis (meaning there is no difference among the groups) can be rejected with confidence; the researcher is correct in concluding that at least two means are different. Let us assume, for example, that a researcher is comparing the locus of control of three groups—high-, medium-, and low-achieving students. The researcher selects a random sample from each group, administers a locus of control instrument, and calculates the means and variances of each group. Let us further assume that the sample group means are A (low achievement) = 18, B (medium achievement) = 20, and C (high achievement) = 25. The null hypothesis that is tested, then, is that the population means of 18, 20, and 25 are equal or, more correctly, that these are different only by sampling and measurement error. If the *F* was 5.12 and $p < .01$, then the researcher can conclude that at least two of the means are different, and that this conclusion will be right 99 times out of 100.

Sometimes the results from an ANOVA are presented in a summary table, as illustrated in Excerpt 12.5. Excerpts 12.6 and 12.7 demonstrate a more typical reporting of ANOVA results. Note in Excerpt 12.6 that there was a 1 × 4 ANOVA, and that the results of several single-factor ANOVAs were summarized in Excerpt 12.7.

EXCERPT 12.5 ANOVA Summary Table

A one-way ANOVA procedure was used to establish whether there was a statistically significant difference in mean scores among the four groups. The results indicated that differences in mean scores among the four groups were statistically significant at the $\alpha = .05$ level. (p. 450)

TABLE IV One-Way ANOVA of the Post-Test Scores on the MAT

	Sum of squares	Df	Mean square	F-value	p-value
Between groups	898.751	3	299.582	6.57	0.000
Within groups	6,290.326	138	45.582		
Total	7,189.077	141			

Source: From Githua, B. N., & Nyabwa, R. A. (2008). Effects of advance organizer strategy during instruction on secondary school students' mathematics achievement in Kenya's Nakuru district. *International Journal of Science and Mathematics Education, 6*(3), 439–457.

EXCERPT 12.6 Reporting ANOVA Results with Post Hoc Tests

We conducted separate analyses to examine differences among working students on the basis of work hours (Table 4). We used ANOVA to examine differences on school factors among low intensity (*n* = 325), moderate intensity (*n* = 316), high intensity (*n* = 160), and very high intensity (*n* = 96), followed by post hoc comparisons. There were significant differences among students who worked different numbers of hours (see Table 4). For example, students who worked less than 10 hr had significantly higher educational aspirations than did the high-intensity and very high intensity groups (*M* = 4.24 versus 4.04 and 3.96, respectively). The two low-intensity groups were not different from one another in terms of educational aspirations. . . . we conducted post hoc comparisons with Tukey's HSD method and controlled for the Type 1 error rate. Table 4 shows details on all significant differences. (p.18)

Source: From Singh, K., Chang, M., & Dika, S. (2007). Effects of part-time work on school achievement during high school. *The Journal of Educational Research, 101*(1), 12–23.

EXCERPT 12.7 Reporting ANOVA Results with Post Hoc Tests

To determine if there were significant differences in the composite mean scores among grade levels for teachers and for students, we conducted analyses of variance. There were no significant teacher grade-level differences in either subject. However, for students, we found a significant grade-level difference in science, $F(3, 524) = p < .001$, but not in the social studies. Tukey HSD post hoc analyses were then conducted to identify which grades differed. Of the six possible pair-wise comparisons of grades, three were significant. The science composite mean score for grade 8 students was significantly higher than the scores for each of the other three grades, meaning that grade 8 students were more likely to report a greater emphasis on the science standards. (p. 317)

Source: From Parke, C. S., & Lane, S. (2007). Student perceptions of a Maryland state performance assessment. *The Elementary School Journal, 107*(3), 305–324.

Post Hoc and Planned Comparison Procedures

When a researcher uses ANOVA to test the null hypothesis that three means are the same, the resulting statistically significant F ratio tells the researcher only that two or more of the means are different from each other. Usually, the researcher needs to employ further statistical tests that will indicate which of the means are different. These tests are called **post hoc comparisons**. Other terms that are synonymous for post hoc comparisons include *a posteriori test, follow-up test,* and *multiple-comparison test*. Another procedure, called the *Bonferroni technique*, is also used as a post hoc test, although it is more commonly used when researchers are investigating many dependent variables to adjust the level of significance to reduce the chance of finding a significant difference because of multiple statistical tests.

Post hoc comparisons: done after ANOVA to indicate which means are different

Post hoc comparisons are designed to test each possible pair of means. There are five common multiple comparison tests: Fisher's LSD, Duncan's new multiple range test, the Newman-Keuls, Tukey's HSD, and the Scheffé's test. All of the tests are used in the same way, but they differ in the ease with which a significant difference is obtained; for some tests, that is, the means need to be farther apart than for other tests for the difference to be statistically significant. Tests that require a greater difference between the means are said to be *conservative,* whereas those that permit less difference are said to be *liberal*. The listing of the tests above is sequential, with Fisher's test considered most liberal and Scheffé's test most conservative. The two most common tests are the Tukey (pronounced "too-key") and Scheffé tests, but different conclusions can be reached in a study, depending on the multiple comparison technique employed.

Excerpts 12.6 and 12.7 are examples of one-way ANOVA and post hoc tests.

Planned comparisons are similar to post hoc tests in that pairs of means are compared, but the procedure is used with specific comparisons that are identified prior to completing the research. Usually, a few of the possible pairs of means, those that are of particular interest, are included in the analysis. Because the pairs are identified before rather than after the ANOVA, it may also be referred to as an *a priori* test.

Planned comparisons: specified before ANOVA and done afterward

Factorial Analysis of Variance

Single-factor ANOVA has been introduced as a procedure that is used with one independent variable and three or more levels identified by this variable. It is common, however, to have more than one independent variable in a study. In fact, it is often desirable to have several independent variables because the analysis will provide more information.

For example, if a group of researchers investigates the relative effectiveness of three reading curricula, they would probably use a 1 × 3 ANOVA to test the null hypotheses that there is no difference in achievement between any of the three groups (that is, $\overline{X}_1 = \overline{X}_2 = \overline{X}_3$). If the researchers were also interested in whether males or females achieved differently, gender would become a second independent variable. Then there would be six groups, because for each reading group, males and females would be analyzed separately. If X is the reading curriculum and

M/F is gender, then the six groups are X_1M; X_1F; X_2M; X_2F; X_3M; and X_3F. This situation is diagrammed as follows:

First independent variable:
Reading curriculum groups

Second independent variable: Gender

$$X_1 \quad X_2 \quad X_3$$
$$M \quad F \quad M \quad F \quad M \quad F$$

Another way to illustrate the study is to put each independent variable on one side of a rectangle as follows:

Reading curriculum

	X_1	X_2	X_3
Gender M			
F			

Factorial ANOVA: analysis of two or more independent variables together

In this hypothetical situation, then, there are two independent variables analyzed simultaneously and one dependent variable (achievement). The statistical procedure that would be used to analyze the results would be a two-way ANOVA (*two-way* because of two independent variables). *Factorial* means more than one independent variable. **Factorial ANOVA**, then, is a generic term that means that two or more independent variables are analyzed together. The more specific term, such as *two-way* or *three-way* ANOVA, tells the exact number of independent variables. Researchers can be even more precise in indicating what the analysis is by including the levels of each independent variable. As pointed out earlier, *levels* refers to the subgroups or categories of each independent variable. In the example cited earlier, *reading curriculum* has three levels and *gender* two levels. The levels can be shown by numbers that precede the ANOVA abbreviation. In our reading example, it is a 2×3 ANOVA. (For a three-way ANOVA, there would need to be three numbers, such as $2 \times 2 \times 3$ ANOVA. This means that there are two levels in two of the variables and three levels in one variable.)

Using this notation, a researcher can concisely communicate a lot of information. The number of factors is usually two or three, and the number of levels can be any number greater than one (though rarely above five). Each number shows how many levels there are in each dependent variable. In the hypothetical example above, if there were four reading curriculums and the researcher was interested in the way each curriculum affected high, low, and medium achievers, then the resulting analysis would be a 3×4 ANOVA. It would still be a two-way ANOVA, but the number of levels would be different. This situation can be illustrated with the following diagram:

Reading curriculum

		X_1	X_2	X_3	X_4
	High				
Ability level	Medium				
	Low				

Here is another hypothetical example to clarify the tests of significance that result from a two-way ANOVA: A teacher is interested in whether using specific techniques to aid retention is effective in improving the achievement of high-anxiety and low-anxiety students. The teacher has developed two techniques, one with mnemonics and the other with distributed practice in memorizing the material. The teacher also has a control group. Thus, there are two independent variables, one with two levels (anxiety: high and low), the other with three levels (intervention techniques: mnemonics, distributed practice, and control group). This would constitute a 2×3 ANOVA design, as illustrated in Figure 12.4.

Within each square in the diagram is a mean for that group. These squares are called *cells*. The number 50 in the upper-right-hand cell ($\overline{X}_5$) thus refers to the mean of highly

Treatment Techniques

		Mnemonics	Distributed practice	Control	Column means
Anxiety	High	$\overline{X}_1 = 62$	$\overline{X}_3 = 50$	$\overline{X}_5 = 50$	$\overline{X}_7 = 54$
	Low	$\overline{X}_2 = 44$	$\overline{X}_4 = 59$	$\overline{X}_6 = 59$	$\overline{X}_8 = 54$
		$\overline{X}_9 \cong 53$	$\overline{X}_{10} \cong 55$	$\overline{X}_{11} \cong 55$	Row means

FIGURE 12.4 Hypothetical 2 × 3 Anova

anxious subjects who served as the control group. The 2 × 3 ANOVA tests three null hypotheses: that there is no difference between high- and low-anxiety students; that there is no difference between the treatment and control conditions; and that there is no interaction between the two factors. (*Interaction* is defined in the next paragraph.) The first two hypotheses are similar in interpretation to one-way ANOVAs. They tell the researcher whether any differences occur for each of the factors independent of each other. These are termed *main or simple effects* in a factorial ANOVA. There is a main (not necessarily significant) effect for anxiety and another main effect for treatment technique. In computing the 2 × 3 ANOVA, there will be a separate *F* ratio for each main effect, with corresponding levels of significance. In our example, the main effect for anxiety is tested by comparing $\overline{X}_7$ with $\overline{X}_8$. These row means disregard the influence of the techniques and address anxiety only. Because $\overline{X}_7$ and $\overline{X}_8$ both equal 54, the null hypothesis that $\overline{X}_7 = \overline{X}_8$ would not be rejected; examining anxiety alone, that is, there is no difference in achievement between high- and low-anxiety students. For the main effect of technique, $\overline{X}_9$, $\overline{X}_{10}$, and $\overline{X}_{11}$ are compared. Again, it appears that there is little difference in achievement between the three technique groups. The first two null hypotheses could have been tested by using separate one-way ANOVAs, but the 2 × 3 ANOVA is more accurate, more powerful in detecting differences, and more parsimonious than two one-way ANOVAs. In addition, the 2 × 3 ANOVA allows the researcher to test the third null hypothesis. This hypothesis is concerned with what is called an *interaction* between the independent variables.

An **interaction** is the effect of the independent variables together; that is, the impact of one factor on the dependent measure varies with the level of a second factor. Stated differently, it is the joint effect of the independent variables on the dependent variable. An interaction is evident if the differences between levels of one independent variable are inconsistent from one level to another of the other independent variable. In other words, an interaction exists if the effect of one variable differs across different levels of the second variable. In our example, if we look at the difference between $\overline{X}_1$ and $\overline{X}_2$ (62 − 44 = 18) and compare that difference with $\overline{X}_3 - \overline{X}_4$ (−9) and $\overline{X}_5 - \overline{X}_6$ (−9), we find that there is a large difference between high and low anxiety as we move across each of the treatment techniques. This is visual evidence of an interaction. Statistically, an *F* ratio is reported for the interaction with a corresponding level of significance. This statistical test is called the *interaction effect*.

Interaction: effect of the independent variables together

Now it is clear how a factorial ANOVA can provide more information than one-way ANOVAs. In our example, it is evident that intervention techniques do make a difference for high- or low-anxiety students. High-anxiety students do better with mnemonics than with distributed practice or with no intervention, while low-anxiety students do better with distributed practice or with no intervention, than they do with mnemonics. This finding would be statistically significant even though neither of the main effects by themselves was significant.

It is common to present a graph of a statistically significant interaction, which shows the nature of the interaction more clearly than cell means do. The graph is constructed by placing values for the dependent variable along the vertical axis (ordinate) and the levels of one independent variable on the horizontal axis (abscissa); all the cell means are located within the graph and identified with the second independent variable. For our hypothetical example, the interaction is illustrated in Figure 12.5. In the figure, lines are used to connect the cells' means. If the lines are parallel, then there is no interaction. If the lines cross, the interaction is said to be *disordinal*.

See if you can understand the results of a study. Read the research plan provided on MyEducationLab for Research at www. myeducationlab.com. Click on the topic, "Inferential Statistics," and then select the Activities and Applications activity titled, "Understanding the Results of a Study."

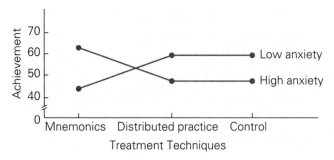

FIGURE 12.5 Interaction for Hypothetical Study

Excerpt 12.8 shows a complete reporting of results for a study that investigated two independent variables, each with two levels and two dependent variables. In Table 1 of the excerpt, the column and row means are presented under the heading Overall. In the figures, two significant interactions are illustrated. The interaction shows that with a low evaluative threat test anxiety does not matter, but it does in the high evaluative condition.

EXCERPT 12.8 Factorial ANOVA

Results

Means, standard deviations, and sample sizes for the achievement and motivation levels by treatment group are reported in Table 1. The results of the ANOVA in which achievement level was the dependent variable and test anxiety and evaluative threat were the independent variables are given in Table 2. The main effect for test anxiety was not significant, $F(1, 57) = 3.49$, $p > .05$. Students with high test anxiety did not obtain a significantly lower mean score $(M = 90.00$, $SD = 4.40)$ in achievement than did students with low test anxiety $(M = 91.77$, $SD = 3.09)$. However, there was a significant main effect for evaluative threat, $F(1, 57) = 6.39$, $p < .05$. Individuals in the high evaluative threat group demonstrated a significantly lower average level of achievement $(M = 89.71$, $SD = 4.14)$ than did their peers in the low evaluative threat group $(M = 92.07$, $SD = 3.26)$. The magnitude of difference or effect size between the high and low evaluative threat groups as calculated with Cohen's d (Hedges & Olkin, 1985) was 0.57.

Furthermore, there was a statistically significant interaction, $F(1, 57) = 4.67$, $p < .05$ (see Figure 1), revealing an effect on students' achievement of the combination of independent variables. Specifically, high test anxiety students in the high evaluative threat condition obtained a significantly lower mean score $(M = 87.94$, $SD = 3.86)$ in achievement than did high test anxiety students in the low evaluative threat condition $(M = 92.20$, $SD = 3.95$; $t = 3.04$, $p < .05)$ and low test anxiety students in both the high evaluative threat condition $(M = 91.60$, $SD = 3.67$; $t = 2.71$, $p < .05)$ and the low evaluative threat condition $(M = 91.93$, $SD = 2.52$; $t = 3.39$, $p < .05)$.

TABLE 1 Means, Standard Deviations, and Sample Sizes of Achievement and Motivation Levels

| | Threat of evaluation | | | | | | | | |
| | Low | | | High | | | Overall | | |
Treatment group	*M*	*SD*	*n*	*M*	*SD*	*n*	*M*	*SD*	*n*
Achievement									
Low test anxiety	91.93	2.52	15	91.60	3.67	15	91.77	3.09	30
High test anxiety	92.20	3.05	15	87.94	3.86	16	90.00	4.40	31
Overall	92.07	3.26	30	89.71	4.14	31	90.87	3.89	61
Motivation									
Low test anxiety	17.33	1.99	15	17.00	2.27	15	17.17	2.10	30
High test anxiety	17.73	2.12	15	14.63	2.16	16	16.13	2.63	31
Overall	17.53	2.03	30	15.77	2.49	31	16.64	2.42	61

TABLE 2 2 × 2 Analysis of Variance of Effects of Test Anxiety and Threat of Evaluation on Achievement

Variable	SS	df	MS	F
Test anxiety (TA)	43.93	1	43.93	3.49
Threat of evaluation (TE)	80.46	1	80.46	6.39*
TA × TE	58.18	1	58.18	4.67*
Residual	717.871	57	12.59	

*$p < .05$.

TABLE 3 2 × 2 Analysis of Variance of Effects of Test Anxiety and Threat of Evaluation on Motivation

Variable	SS	df	MS	F
Test anxiety (TA)	14.86	1	14.86	3.26
Threat of evaluation (TE)	45.14	1	45.14	9.89*
TA × TE	29.34	1	29.34	6.43*
Residual	260.02	57	4.56	

*$p < .05$.

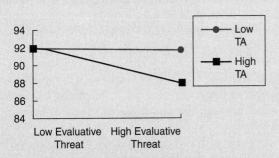

FIGURE 1 Test Anxiety (TA) and Threat of Evaluation on Achievement

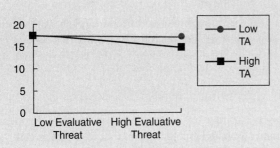

FIGURE 2 Test Anxiety (TA) and Threat of Evaluation on Motivation

The results of the ANOVA in which motivation level was the dependent variable, and test anxiety and evaluative threat were the independent variables, are reported in Table 3. As with achievement, the main effect for test anxiety was not significant, $F(1, 57) = 3.26$, $p > .05$. Students with high test anxiety did not obtain a significantly lower mean score ($M = 16.13$, $SD = 2.63$) in motivation to learn than did students with low test anxiety ($M = 17.17$, $SD = 2.10$). However, there was a significant main effect for evaluative threat, $F(1, 57) = 9.89$, $p < .05$. Individuals in the high evaluative threat group demonstrated a significantly lower average level of motivation ($M = 15.77$, $SD = 2.49$) than did their peers in the low evaluative threat group ($M = 17.53$, $SD = 2.03$), with an effect size of 0.71.

Furthermore, there was a statistically significant interaction, $F(1, 57) = 6.43$, $p < .05$ (see Figure 2), revealing an effect on students' motivation of the combination of independent variables. Specifically, high test anxiety students in the high evaluative threat condition obtained a significantly lower mean score ($M = 14.63$, $SD = 2.16$) in motivation than did high test anxiety students in the low evaluative threat condition ($M = 17.73$, $SD = 2.12$; $t = 4.04$, $p < .05$) and low test anxiety students in both the high evaluative threat condition ($M = 17.00$, $SD = 2.27$; $t = 2.99$, $p < .05$) and the low evaluative threat condition ($M = 17.33$, $SD = 1.99$; $t = 3.63$, $p < .05$). (pp. 287–288)

Source: From *Journal of Educational Research, 94*(5), 284–290, Reprinted with permission of the Helen Dwight Reid Educational Foundation. Published by Heldref Publications, 1319 Eighteenth St., NW, Washington, DC 20036–1802. Copyright © 2001.

Analysis of Covariance

Analysis of covariance (ANCOVA) is a statistical procedure used in cases similar to ones in which a one-way or factorial ANOVA is used. ANCOVA has two major purposes: (1) to adjust initial group differences statistically on one or more variables that are related to the dependent variable but uncontrolled and (2) to increase the likelihood of finding a significant difference between group means.

For the first purpose, consider the following example. A researcher uses two classes to investigate whether cooperative or individualized instruction is more effective. On the basis of a pretest, the researcher knows that one class has greater knowledge of the dependent variable (achievement in mathematics) than the other group. (For example, the cooperative group pretest

Analysis of covariance (ANCOVA): adjusts for initial group differences

mean is 12 and the individualized group pretest mean is 10.) If a posttest is given and it is found that the cooperative group mean is 24 and the individualized group mean is 20, the researcher might be tempted to conclude that the cooperative group achieved more than the individualized group. This would be likely to happen if the pretest scores were ignored.

An alternative approach would be to look at pretest-posttest gain scores and use a *t*-test to determine whether the gain scores are significantly different. This approach would result in comparing 12 (24 − 12) to 10 (20 − 10). Although this approach is theoretically better than not using the pretest scores, for reasons beyond the scope of this book, there are technical problems with comparing gain scores. The best method of analyzing the data in this circumstance is to use ANCOVA. ANCOVA would statistically adjust the posttest scores by the differences that existed between the groups on the pretest. In this example, the posttest score of the cooperative group would be lowered by one point, because this group's mean was higher by one point than the mean of both groups on the pretest. Similarly, because the individualized group pretest mean is one point lower than the mean of the two pretests, the posttest score of 20 would be raised by one point to 21. Instead of comparing 20 to 24, ANCOVA would thus compare 21 to 23.

The variable that is used in ANCOVA to adjust the scores (in the above example, the pretest) is called the *covariate* or *concomitant variable*. Covariates are often pretest scores or results from achievement, attitude, or aptitude tests that would be related to the dependent variable. IQ scores and scores on prior standardized achievement tests, for instance, are commonly used as covariates.

The second purpose of covariance analysis is to increase the power of the statistical test to find differences between groups. A full explanation of the concept of power is beyond the scope of this book. Briefly, power is the probability of detecting a significant difference. It is useful to increase power when the sample size is low or when the researcher has reason to believe that the differences between the groups will be small.

ANCOVA can be used in several situations: with two groups and one independent variable in place of a *t*-test; with one independent variable that has more than two groups in place of one-way ANOVA; and with factorial analysis of variance. Studies can also use more than one covariate in a single ANCOVA procedure. The reporting of ANCOVA is very similar to the reporting of ANOVA. Excerpt 12.9 presents results from a 2 × 3 ANCOVA, using fall test scores as the covariate.

Because ANCOVA is used frequently with intact groups, without random assignment, it should be noted that the interpretation of results should weigh the possibility that other uncontrolled and unmeasured variables are also related to the dependent variable and hence may affect the dependent variable. In other words, although statistical adjustment of the effect of the covariate can be achieved, the researcher cannot conclude that the groups are equal in the sense of random assignment.

Propensity score matching: matching to adjust for group differences using several variables

An alternative to covariance analysis is using what are called *propensity scores*. **Propensity score matching** is a procedure to statistically match subjects from different groups using several variables. It results in a matched pairs design, in which control or comparison group subjects are matched with the intervention group so that the groups are as similar as possible. Only matched subjects are used for the analysis (either one-to-one or one-to-many matched subjects). More technically, propensity scores are the predicted probability, using several

EXCERPT 12.9   ANCOVA

The fall and spring standard scores for the "English only" and the "other language" children in the three subject groups are also shown in Table 2. In order to examine the effect of the interaction between group and home language on spring standard scores, a two-way analysis of covariance (ANCOVA) was conducted, controlling for fall scores. The results indicated a significant main effect for group $F(1, 267) = 15.74$, $p < .001$ language . . . a significant main effect for language $F(2, 267) = 9.22$, $p = .003$ . . . and a significant interaction between group and language $F(2, 267) = 5.41$, $p = .05$. (p. 141)

Source: From Schechter, C., & Bye, B. (2006). Preliminary evidence for the impact of mixed-income preschoolers on low-income children's language growth. *Early Childhood Research Quarterly, 22*(1), 137–144.

EXCERPT 12.10   Use of Propensity Score Matching

In this study, propensity score techniques were used to match a probability sample of Head Start participants in Georgia with a group of children who were eligible for Head Start but who attended the state prekindergarten program in Georgia. . . . This study indicates that economically disadvantaged children who attended Georgia's universal prekindergarten entered kindergarten at least as well prepared as similar children who attended Head Start. (p. 77)

Source: From Henry, G. T., Gordon, C. S., & Rickman, D. K. (2006). Early education policy alternatives: Comparing quality and outcomes of Head Start and state prekindergarten. *Educational Evaluation and Policy Analysis, 28*(1), 77–99.

covariates, of group membership. Logistic regression is used for the analysis. Using propensity scores is especially useful with large databases that have extensive demographic information on the subjects.

Rudner and Peyton (2006) illustrate the power of using propensity scores to compare different groups. The authors examined the college admission test scores of two groups of students, one group taking the test near the time of graduation and planning to enroll later, and one group taking the test after graduation and planning to enroll soon afterward. A very large database existed to compare the groups. This is what they found using *unmatched* groups:

	Near Graduation	**After Graduation**
Test Score:	$\bar{X} = 532$	$\bar{X} = 505$

Their dataset also included several background variables, including gender, major, undergraduate GPA, citizenship, and intended enrollment, that could be used to calculate propensity scores. When the analysis was done with these propensity scores, the results looked very different. After controlling for the differences found on the background variables, this was the result:

	Near Graduation	**After Graduation**
Test Score:	$\bar{X} = 532$	$\bar{X} = 513$

Adjusting for the background variables changed the degree of difference between the two groups.

An example of using propensity scores is shown in Excerpt 12.10. In this study the investigators "started" with 353 pre-K and 134 Head Start children. Using propensity scores resulted in samples of 201 pre-K children and 106 Head Start children.

NONPARAMETRIC TESTS

In our discussion of statistical tests up to this point, we have been concerned with procedures that use sample statistics to estimate characteristics of the population. These characteristics of the population are called *parameters*, and the statistical procedures are referred to as **parametric** procedures. Parametric statistics are used when the researcher can assume that the population is normally distributed, has homogeneity of variance within different groups, and has data that are interval or ratio in scale, though often parametric tests are used with ordinal data with large samples.

Parametric: normality, equal variances, interval-level data assumed

As long as the assumptions upon which parametric statistics are based are met, for the most part, the researcher uses a *t*-test, ANOVA, ANCOVA, or some other parametric procedure. If these assumptions are not met—for example, if the data are not interval or ratio or are not distributed normally—the researcher should consider using a **nonparametric** analog to the parametric test. For most parametric procedures, there is a corresponding nonparametric test that can be used. The interpretation of the results is similar with both kinds of tests. What differs is the computational equation and tables for determining the significance level of the results. Both procedures test a hypothesis and report a level of significance for rejecting the null. In contrast to parametric tests, however, nonparametric tests do not test hypotheses about the characteristics of a population. Rather, nonparametric procedures test hypotheses

Nonparametric: parametric assumptions not met

TABLE 12.2 Parametric and Nonparametric Procedures*

Parametric	Nonparametric
Pearson product-moment correlation coefficient	Spearman rank correlation coefficient
Independent samples *t*-test	Median test
Dependent samples *t*-test	Mann-Whitney *U* test
Single-factor ANOVA	Sign test:
	Wilcoxon rank test
	Median test
	Kruskal-Wallis one-way ANOVA of ranks
Factorial ANOVA	Friedman two-way ANOVA

*For further information on nonparametric tests, see Siegel (1956), Marascuilo and McSweeney (1977), and Gibbons (1993).

about relationships between categorical variables, shapes of distributions, and normality of distribution. Whereas parametric procedures use means, nonparametric techniques are concerned with frequencies, percentages, and proportions. The parametric tests are generally more powerful in detecting significant differences and are used frequently even when all assumptions cannot be met.

Table 12.2 gives the names of nonparametric tests that are analogous to parametric tests we have already discussed.

Chi-square (pronounced "kī square") is a common nonparametric procedure that is used when the data are in nominal form. This test is a way of answering questions about association or relationship based on frequencies of observations in categories. The frequencies can be in almost any form—people, objects, votes—and are simply counted in each category. The researcher thus forms the categories and then counts the frequency of observations or occurrences in each category. In the single-sample chi-square test, the researcher has one independent variable that is divided into two or more categories. For example, a college administrator may be interested in the number of freshman, sophomore, junior, and senior students who attended the counseling center, or in other words, the relationship between year in college and use of counseling services. The independent variable is year in college, with four categories. The researcher might select a random sample of 50 students from each category and record the number of students in each category who attended the counseling center. The statistical test compares the reported, or observed, frequencies with some theoretical or expected frequencies. In our example, the college administrator might expect that the frequencies in each category would be the same. Then the null hypothesis that is tested is that there is no difference in the number of students attending the counseling center among the four categories. The following table illustrates this example.

Chi-square: tests frequencies of observations in categories

	Freshmen	Sophomores	Juniors	Seniors
Observed	30	25	15	30
Expected	25	25	25	25

To obtain the level of significance, the researcher computes a formula to obtain a chi-square value (χ^2), uses the appropriate degrees of freedom, and refers to a chi-square table (see Appendix D) in order to determine the level of significance in rejecting the null. In our example, it appears that the test would be significant, showing that freshmen and seniors attend the counseling center more than sophomores and juniors and that juniors attend less than any other class.

If the researcher has more than one independent variable, the *independent samples chi-square test* can be used to analyze the data. In our example above, if the administrator was also interested in differences between males and females at each class level, then the analysis would be like a factorial ANOVA. In this case, it would be a 2 × 4 contingency table.

EXCERPT 12.11 Chi-Square

Chi-square analyses indicated statistically significant differences between athletes and nonathletes in reported use of 4 of the 12 substances. In terms of recreational drugs, significantly more nonathletes than interscholastic athletes have smoked cigarettes, χ^2 (1, $N = 520$) = .7.455, $p < .01$. Nonathletes also reported using cocaine, χ^2 (1, $N = 59$) = 11.491, and psychedelics, χ^2 (1, $N = 171$) = 18.382, $p < .001$, with greater frequency. One ergogenic aid, creatine, was used significantly more by athletes than nonathletes (1, $N = 115$) = 7.455, $p < .01$. Athletes were less likely to use marijuana, amphetamines, and barbiturates than were nonathletes, although the differences fell just short of being statistically significant.

Source: From Naylor, A. H., Gardner, D., & Zaichkowsky, L. (2001). Drug use patterns among high school athletes and nonathletes. *Adolescence, 36*(144), 627–639.

There are many uses for the chi-square test. It can be used in attitude research if the researcher categorizes responses as favorable or unfavorable; with high-, low-, and medium-ability students displaying on-task behavior; in special education research with frequencies of appropriate behavior; and in many other problems. Researchers may report a generic measure of relationship with the chi-square results. These measures would be termed *phi coefficient* or *contingency coefficient* and would be interpreted in about the same way as a Pearson product-moment correlation coefficient. Excerpt 12.11 is an example of reporting chi-square test results.

MULTIVARIATE ANALYSES

Our discussion of inferential statistics would be incomplete without *multivariate analyses*. Social scientists have realized for many years that human behavior in complex situations can be understood best by examining many variables simultaneously, not by dealing with one or two variables in each study. The statistical procedures for analyzing many variables at the same time have been available for many years, but only since the availability of computers have researchers been able to utilize these procedures. Today, these more complex statistics are commonly reported in journals.

The term **multivariate** refers to methods that investigate patterns among many variables or to studies that involve two or more related dependent variables for each subject. Many researchers will refer to *multiple regression* as a multivariate procedure, and some researchers use the term *multivariate* to describe the analysis in any study of many variables. In contrast, designs that employ *t*-tests, ANOVA, and ANCOVA with a single dependent would clearly be classified as *univariate*.

Multivariate: tests of patterns among many variables or more than one dependent variable

All of the statistical procedures discussed to this point have only one dependent variable. Yet there are many instances in which the researcher is interested in more than one dependent variable. For example, if a researcher is studying attitudes toward science, many aspects of a general attitude toward science would be of interest, such as enjoying science as well as valuing science, for chemistry as well as biology, for dissection as well as field trips, and so on. In fact, many attitude instruments have subscales that reflect feelings and beliefs more specifically and accurately than one general score can. The researcher could combine all these different aspects and consider the attitude as a general disposition, but it is usually better to look at each aspect separately. Why not use a separate univariate analysis for each dependent variable? That is, why not compute as many ANOVAs or *t*-tests as there are dependent variables? The reason is that as long as the dependent variables are correlated, the use of separate univariate analysis will increase the probability of finding a difference simply because so many tests are employed. It is similar to the reason that in ANOVA, we use post hoc tests rather than many *t*-tests. Multivariate analyses are also more parsimonious—that is, more direct and quicker, with fewer separate calculations.

Although the computation and interpretation of multivariate tests are quite complex, the basic principle of rejecting null hypotheses at some level of significance is the same as for all inferential statistics. The difference is that all the dependent variables are considered together

TABLE 12.3 Multivariate Analogs

Univariate Test	Multivariate Test
t-test	Hotelling's T^2
ANOVA	MANOVA (multivariate analysis of variance)
ANCOVA	MANCOVA

EXCERPT 12.12 Multivariate ANCOVA

The first set of analyses compared post-intervention achievement and course enrollments in math and science for each of the three groups (coeducational boys, coeducational girls, and single-sex girls). A multivariate analysis of covariance (MANCOVA) was run for the four achievement and course-enrollment outcomes . . . with class condition entered as the grouping variable and with parental education, perceived parental expectations, perceived teacher effectiveness, school, and pre-high school math achievement entered as covariates. . . . The effect of class condition for this MANCOVA was significant. . . . In all of the four univariate follow-up analyses, it was also significant. That is, achievement in math, achievement in science, and average course enrollment in math and science differed as a function of educational group. (p. 945)

Source: From Shapka, J. D., & Keating, D. P. (2003). Effects of a girls-only curriculum during adolescence: Performance, persistence, and engagement in mathematics and science, *American Educational Research Journal, 40*(4), 929–960.

in one analysis. For most of the procedures previously discussed that have one dependent variable, a multivariate analog can be used when there is the same independent variable or variables but more than one dependent variable.

Table 12.3 summarizes some multivariate tests that correspond to procedures used with one dependent variable. Excerpt 12.12 illustrates use of a 1 × 3 MANCOVA to analyze the effects of single-sex education.

MAGNITUDE OF EFFECT

One of the most important issues that creates confusion in interpreting statistics is the decision about whether the results are meaningful. That is, how much will the results make a difference in the real world? Are the results *educationally* significant, not just statistically significant? The statistical test tells only that there is a difference, but the worth or importance of a finding must also be judged. When a finding is reported to be statistically significant, the reader should examine the reported means to see how different they are or the magnitude of the correlations. Meaningfulness is related to the specifics of a situation. For example, there may be a statistically significant difference in reading achievement among first-graders who use curriculum X as opposed to curriculum Y, but that does not mean that curriculum X should be purchased. It is possible that the difference represents only one percentile point and that curriculum X costs several thousand dollars more than curriculum Y. Only the reader can judge what is meaningful.

One of the reasons that statistically significant *p* values can be misleading is that the value that is calculated is directly related to sample size. Thus, it is possible to have a very large sample, a very small difference or relationship, and still report it as significant. For example, a correlation of .44 will be statistically significant at the .05 level with a sample as small as 20, and a sample of 5,000 will allow a statistically significant .05 finding with a correlation of only .028, which is, practically speaking, no relationship at all.

The American Psychological Association (2001), and many research journals now strongly recommend or require that investigators report appropriate indicators that illustrate the strength or magnitude of a difference or relationship along with measures of statistical significance. These **magnitude of effect** measures, as they are called, are either measures of strength of association

Magnitude of effect: measures of practical significance

or effect size. Measures of association are used to estimate proportions of variance held in common, such as the coefficient of determination, (r^2), R^2, eta-squared (η^2), or omega-squared (ω^2). **Effect size (ES)** is more commonly used. It is typically reported in a generalized form as the ratio of the difference between the group means divided by the estimated standard deviation of the population. This is referred to as the *standardized mean difference*, and it is represented by the following equation:

Effect size: difference between two means in standard deviation units

$$d = \frac{\overline{X}_1 - \overline{X}_2}{SD_p}$$

where

d = Cohen's ratio for effect size

$\overline{X}$ = the mean

SD_p = the standard deviation of the population

According to Cohen (1988), the *effect size index* may then provide an indication of the practical or meaningful difference. Effect size indexes of about .20 are typically regarded as small effects, those of about .5 as medium or moderate effects, and those of .8 and above as large effects. However, these interpretations are arbitrary. According to the What Works Clearinghouse, a d as small as .25 has practical significance. It is best to evaluate practical significance in the context in which the research is conducted and upon considering the intended use of the results.

Examples of reporting effect size in a journal are illustrated in Excerpts 12.13 and 12.14. Clearly, measures of effect magnitude, along with confidence intervals, provide much better information than a simple rejection of the null hypothesis.

Roadmaps of Statistical Tests

Hundreds of statistical tests have been developed and used for determining statistical inferences. In Figures 12.6 and 12.7, two *roadmaps* are designed to help you connect the nature of a

EXCERPT 12.13 Reporting Effect Size

On the basis of Cohen's categories of small, medium, and large effect sizes (Buzz, 1995), a power analysis revealed that most of the effect sizes for sex differences in this study were small to medium (see Table 3). (p.133)

TABLE 3 Summary of Sex Equity Findings

Dependent Measure	Males		Females		F	df	p	Effect Size	Cohen's Category
	M	*SD*	*M*	*SD*					
Instructor calling on students	0.2480	0.2425	0.2034	0.2608	0.71	1, 22	.4131	0.18	Small
Student volunteering	1.1000	1.0615	0.9548	1.3027	0.45	1, 22	.5081	0.12	Small
Instructor interacting with students	1.3274	1.2999	1.5623	1.6247	0.55	1, 22	.5078	0.11	Small
Students raising their hands	0.1835	0.1469	0.1334	0.1155	1.70	1, 22	.2055	0.38	Medium
Staying after class	0.1440	0.0534	0.1066	0.0612	3.18	1, 22	.0885	0.58	Medium
Seat location	1.2496	1.4105	0.3891	0.0571	1.65	1, 28	.2101	1.17	Large

Note: The means presented here are in ratio form. Each female student mean is based on averages of the female response divided by the number of women in the class. Each male student mean is based on averages of the male response divided by the number of men in class. Men and women are compared on the basis of their actual participation rates, taking into consideration the proportion of women to men in class.

Source: From Brady, K. L., & Eisler, R. M. (1999). Sex and gender in the college classroom: A quantitative analysis of faculty-study interactions and perceptions, *Journal of Educational Psychology, 91*(1), 127–145. Reprinted by permission.

EXCERPT 12.14   Reporting Effect Size

There has been a shift from considering only results of statistical significance testing to the inclusion of measures of practical significance (Leven, 1993). Statistical significance is concerned with whether a research result is due to chance, whereas practical significance is concerned with whether the result is useful in the "real world" (Cohen, 1988; Levin, 1993).

Tables 5 and 6 detail the effect size results for the outcomes in the presented study. Effect size results ranged between .15 and .45, reflecting a modest effect for all short-term social and emotional competency outcomes. . . . The largest ES was in the social adjustment in school by age 7 (d = .45) and social adjustment in school at ages 8–9 (d = .33).This result suggests that the CPC preschool group did almost one-half standard deviation better than the comparison group, respectively. . . . [T]he overall pattern of findings . . . helps identify meaningful effects that are worthy of policy intervention for social and emotional development.

Source: From Niles, M. D., Reynolds, A. J., & Nagasawa, M. (2006). Does early childhood intervention affect the social and emotional development of participants? *Early Childhood Research & Practice, 8*(1). Retrieved September 15, 2008 from http://ecrp.uiuc.edu/v8n1/index.html.

Using the skills you have learned in this chapter and the research roadmaps provided, test your understanding of inferential statistics used in a real article. Go to MyEducationLab for Research at www.myeducationlab.com and click the topic, "Inferential Statistics." Then, select and complete the Building Research Skills exercise titled, "Understanding Inferential Statistics."

study with the appropriate statistical procedure. These don't include all possibilities, by any means, but we think it will be helpful in providing some guidelines for matching statistical analysis with design. The roadmaps are designed to show how to start with features of the research questions and design and, through a number of decision points, reach the correct analysis.

The roadmap in Figure 12.6 is for nonexperimental studies. It is organized by whether the research question and logic are correlational or focused on differences between groups. Then the number of independent variables is considered to identify the correct analysis. In Figure 12.7, for experimental studies, the first determining characteristic is the number of independent variables. Then levels of independent variables are used to determine the analysis.

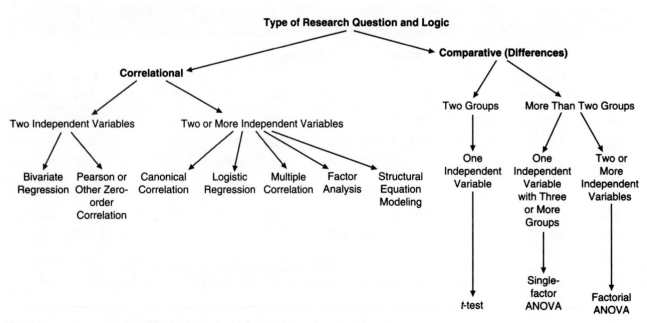

FIGURE 12.6   **Decision Tree to Determine Statistical Analyses for Nonexperimental Studies**

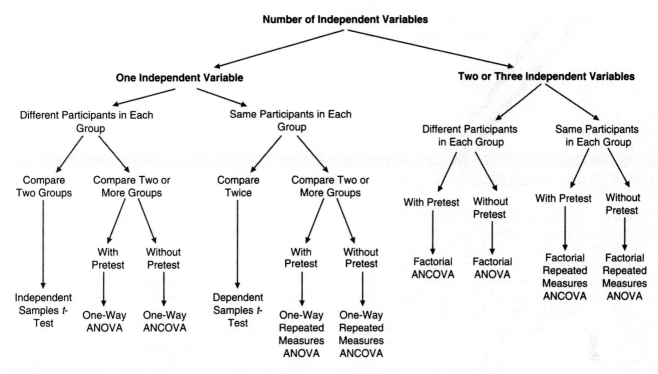

FIGURE 12.7 Decision Tree to Determine Statistical Analyses for Experimental Studies

CHAPTER SUMMARY

This chapter has introduced the logic of inferential statistics and described some of the more common statistical procedures researchers use to analyze data. The following points summarize the concepts presented:

1. Inferential statistics are used to make inferences based on measured aspects of a sample about the characteristics of a population.

2. In conducting research, probability is a concern because of the error involved in sampling and measurement.

3. Sample statistics represent imperfect estimates of the population.

4. Inferential statistics estimate the probability of population characteristics being within a certain range of values. Confidence levels are commonly reported.

5. The null hypothesis is used to test the assumption that there is no difference between population values.

6. Researchers attempt to reject the null hypothesis by using inferential statistics to indicate the probability of being wrong in rejecting the null.

7. The level of significance of the statistical test tells the researcher the probability of making a Type I error in rejecting the null hypothesis.

8. Most researchers use a *p* level of .05 or less (< .05) to indicate statistical significance.

9. The single-group *t*-test tests differences between the mean and a fixed value.

10. The *t*-test is used to compare two means, and depending on the nature of the research, it uses an independent samples equation or a dependent samples equation to calculate the *t*-value.

11. Single-factor ANOVA tests the difference between levels of one independent variable, whereas factorial ANOVA examines more than one independent variable.

12. Post hoc and planned comparison tests are designed to locate significant differences among pairs of means in ANOVA.

13. An interaction is examined in factorial ANOVA as the unique effect of the independent variables acting together to affect the dependent variable results.

14. Parametric tests assume ratio, or interval level data, homogeneity of variance, and a normal distribution. Nonparametric tests can be used in cases in which the assumptions are violated and the test is not robust for that violation.

15. ANCOVA is used to adjust differences between groups on a covariate variable that is related to the dependent variable.

16. The chi-square test is a frequently encountered nonparametric test that is used when the researcher is examining frequencies of occurrences.

17. Multivariate analyses are used in cases in which there are several related dependent variables.

18. Effect magnitude measures, such as effect size, indicates the magnitude of differences and relationships and should be reported with statistical significance.

APPLICATION PROBLEMS

For each of the problems below, select the statistical procedure that would best analyze the data.

1. A researcher is interested in the way three different approaches to discipline work with fifth-graders. Student teachers were assigned randomly to one of three groups. Each group received instruction in a different approach to handling discipline problems. Each student teacher was then observed over a three-week period, and the frequency and duration of discipline problems were recorded.

2. A teacher is interested in whether her sixth-graders' attitudes toward sex will change following a four-week sex-education course. To assess the impact of the program, the teacher measures the students' attitudes before and after the course.

3. The teacher in problem 2 now decides to test her program more thoroughly and is able to assign each of her students randomly to one group that receives a control condition. The teacher also analyzes the effects on boys and girls.

4. A counselor wants to know if there is a relationship between the self-esteem of eleventh-graders and the frequency of visits to the counseling center.

5. A doctoral student is interested in studying the attitude differences between high- and low-achieving students who receive different kinds of teacher feedback following their performance on tests. Four types of teacher feedback are designed for the study, and there are eight attitudes, such as attitude toward teacher, toward the subject studied, toward learning, and so on.

6. Calculate the approximate effect size for each of the following:

   a. The difference between two means is 14 and the standard deviation of the population is 7.

   b. The mean for Group A is 32 and that for Group B is 22. The standard deviation of the population is 10.

   c. The group that received individualized counseling obtained a mean score of 76 on the measure of self-concept, whereas the group that received no counseling obtained a mean score of 52. The standard deviation of the population was 15.

   d. Group A showed the following scores: 4, 5, 7, 7, 8, 10. Group B had scores of 12, 12, 13, 13, 14, 16. The standard deviation of the population was 6.

7. Summarize in words each of the following findings:

   a. Group A = 52, Group B = 63, $t = 4.33$, $p < .02$.

   b. Group A's mean SAT score was 558; Group B's was 457; Group C's was 688; $F = 4.77$, $p < .001$.

   c. The Tukey test was significant at .01 for two groups (A and E).

ANSWER TO APPLICATION PROBLEMS

1. There are three groups in this study. The researcher would hence use one-way ANOVA or an appropriate nonparametric analog, depending on the nature of the dependent variables. Most likely, means would be reported for the groups, and the parametric procedure would be acceptable, followed by post hoc comparisons if necessary.

2. Because the same group of students is assessed twice, a dependent samples t-test is the statistical procedure. If there were more than one dependent variable (i.e., several facets to sex education), then the teacher should employ a multivariate test.

3. The teacher should now use a 2 × 2 ANOVA (group × gender). The analysis will provide a test for each main effect and a test for the interaction between group and gender.

4. There would be two ways to analyze this data: First, a correlation could be computed between self-esteem and frequency of visits and tested by a t-test to see whether the correlation is significantly different from zero; or second, groups of students could be identified (e.g., high, low, medium self-esteem) and a 1 × 3 ANOVA computed on the mean frequencies of each group.

5. There are two independent variables and eight related dependent variables, resulting in the need for a 2 × 4 MANOVA, with appropriate post hoc tests if necessary.

6. a. 2
   b. 1
   c. 1.6
   d. 1.08

7. a. There was a statistically significant difference between Group A and Group B. Or Group B demonstrated significantly greater scores than Group A. Or there is a 1/50 probability that the researcher is wrong in concluding that Group B was significantly higher than Group A.

   b. There was a statistically significant difference in SAT scores among Groups A, B, and C. Or there is 1 chance out of 1,000 that the researcher is wrong in concluding that there is a significant difference in SAT scores among Groups A, B, and C. Or, depending on post hoc analyses, Group C had SAT scores that were significantly higher than those of Groups A and B.

   c. In a comparison of five groups, there was a statistically significant difference between Group A and Group E. Or there is 1 chance in 100 that the researcher is wrong in concluding that there is a difference between Group A and Group E.

Designing Qualitative Research

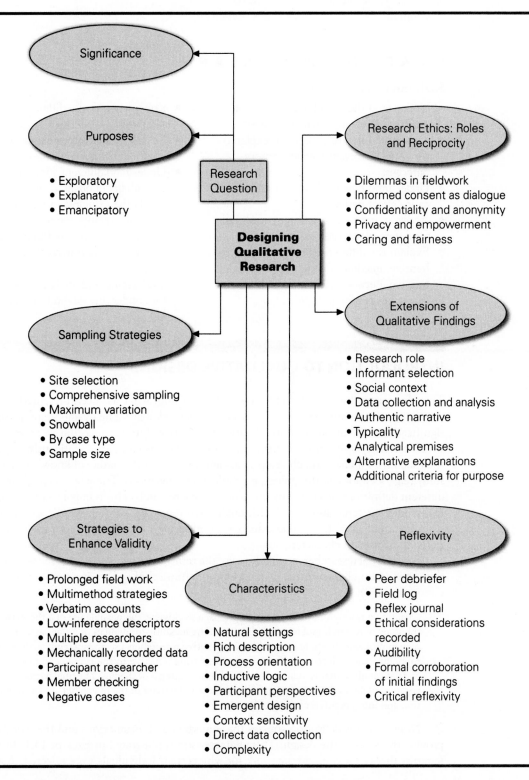

Significance

Purposes
- Exploratory
- Explanatory
- Emancipatory

Research Question

Designing Qualitative Research

Research Ethics: Roles and Reciprocity
- Dilemmas in fieldwork
- Informed consent as dialogue
- Confidentiality and anonymity
- Privacy and empowerment
- Caring and fairness

Extensions of Qualitative Findings
- Research role
- Informant selection
- Social context
- Data collection and analysis
- Authentic narrative
- Typicality
- Analytical premises
- Alternative explanations
- Additional criteria for purpose

Sampling Strategies
- Site selection
- Comprehensive sampling
- Maximum variation
- Snowball
- By case type
- Sample size

Strategies to Enhance Validity
- Prolonged field work
- Multimethod strategies
- Verbatim accounts
- Low-inference descriptors
- Multiple researchers
- Mechanically recorded data
- Participant researcher
- Member checking
- Negative cases

Characteristics
- Natural settings
- Rich description
- Process orientation
- Inductive logic
- Participant perspectives
- Emergent design
- Context sensitivity
- Direct data collection
- Complexity

Reflexivity
- Peer debriefer
- Field log
- Reflex journal
- Ethical considerations recorded
- Audibility
- Formal corroboration of initial findings
- Critical reflexivity

KEY TERMS

context sensitivity

inductive reasoning

participant perspectives

emergent design

site selection

comprehensive sampling

maximum variation
   sampling

snowball sampling

sampling by case type

triangulation

member checking

negative case

discrepant data

reflexivity

positionality

field log

reflex journal

authenticity

typicality

discrepant data

WHAT YOU WILL LEARN

Study this chapter and you will:

- Understand the key characteristics of qualitative research that affect design.
- Know the differences between explanatory, exploratory, and emancipatory purposes.
- Understand how purpose and significance affect design.
- Apply appropriate sampling procedures for different purposes.
- Explain the differences between comprehensive, maximum variation, comprehensive, network, snowball, and case-type sampling.

- Know when to use different kinds of sampling.
- Be able to indicate the phases of conducting qualitative studies.
- Understand different strategies to enhance the validity of qualitative research.
- Apply the principle of reflexivity to designing qualitative research.
- Know the criteria used to describe the extensions and transferability of qualitative findings.
- Understand and apply ethical standards for conducting qualitative studies.

INTRODUCTION TO QUALITATIVE DESIGNS

This chapter marks a decided change of direction from what has been presented for quantitative designs. Qualitative research is an accepted methodology for many important questions, with significant contributions to both theory and practice. Unlike quantitative research designs, which are fairly uniform in structure, qualitative designs can vary significantly, depending on the theoretical framework, philosophy, assumptions about the nature of knowledge, and field of study (e.g., sociology, anthropology, psychology, or education). These factors result in somewhat different definitions of what constitutes qualitative research. This is important because there are many different terms associated with qualitative research, including *field research*, *naturalistic*, *ecological*, *constructivist*, *case study*, and *ethnomethodology*, each with its own traditions, assumptions, and common characteristics.

Educational researchers are likely to use the term *qualitative* in a generic sense as an approach that has certain characteristics. An excellent definition of qualitative research is provided by Creswell (2007):

> Qualitative research begins with assumptions, a worldview, the possible use of a theoretical lens, and the study of research problems inquiring into the meaning individuals or groups ascribe to a social or human problem. To study this problem, qualitative researchers use an emerging qualitative approach to inquiry, the collection of data in a nature setting sensitive to the people and places under study, and data analysis that is inductive and establishes patterns or themes. The final written report or presentation includes the voices of participants, the reflectivity of the researcher, and a complex description and interpretation of the problem. (p. 37)

Note that this definition stresses the importance of assumptions and the worldviews that provide the basis of the design. This characteristic is illustrated in Excerpt 13.1. In this study, feminist theory provides a framework for why certain individuals were selected. Assumptions

EXCERPT 13.1 Connection Between Assumptions and Research Design

The group of participants was limited to mothers who identified themselves as being working class or having low incomes . . . reliance on the mothers' self-identification aligns with the feminist methodological principles that emphasize the importance of self-definition. The research approach further affirms the notion that class is subjective and fluid (Bullock & Limbert, 2003). (p. 496)

Source: From Cooper, C. W. (2007). School choice as "motherwork": Valuing African American women's educational advocacy and resistance. *International Journal of Qualitative Studies in Education, 20*(5), 491–512.

and worldviews used in qualitative studies are definitely different from those of quantitative research but are also different among variations or types of qualitative studies. Although some of these differences are accounted for by considering the five types of qualitative research covered in this book, it is still important to understand the approaches taken and what they mean for the design of the study, data collection, and reporting of results.

Characteristics of Qualitative Research

Here we go into more detail about some prominent characteristics of qualitative research. We refer to these as nine *key characteristics* (see Table 13.1). We want to stress that these characteristics are typically present *to some degree* in any qualitative study, and not all of them may be evident. Furthermore, it is helpful to distinguish between qualitative research and qualitative data analysis. Qualitative analysis strategies are sometimes used in quantitative studies and, of course, are used in mixed-method studies. As with the term *experimental*, there are variations. Perhaps it would be helpful to label some as *quasi-qualitative*, although to our knowledge, this term is not in the literature. The term does stress, however, the nature of many qualitative studies that do not contain all the following characteristics.

Natural Settings A distinguishing characteristic of qualitative research is that behavior is studied as it occurs naturally. There is no manipulation or control of behavior or settings, nor are there any externally imposed constraints. Rather, the setting is an actual classroom, school, clinic, or neighborhood. This is why qualitative research is often described as *field* research; it

TABLE 13.1 Key Characteristics of Qualitative Research

Characteristic	Description
Natural settings	Study of behavior as it occurs or occurred naturally
Context sensitivity	Consideration of situational factors
Direct data collection	Researcher collects data directly from the source
Rich narrative description	Detailed narratives that provide in-depth understanding of behavior
Process orientation	Focus on why and how behavior occurs
Inductive data analysis	Generalizations are induced from synthesizing gathered information
Participant perspectives	Focus on participants' understanding, descriptions, labels, and meanings
Emergent design	The design evolves and changes as the study takes place
Complexity of understanding and explanation	Understandings and explanations are complex, with multiple perspectives

EXCERPT 13.2 Natural Setting

During the first year of the study, my colleagues and I spent 50–75 days observing formal and informal settings in the eight schools, interviewing teachers and administrators, and shadowing school leaders during the school day. In addition, we observed 105 predominantly second- and fifth-grade classroom lessons (involving 47 different teachers). (p. 291)

Source: From Diamond, J. B. (2007). Where the rubber meets the road: Rethinking the connection between high-stakes testing policy and classroom instruction. *Sociology of Education, 80,* 285–313.

takes place out in the field or setting. For example, a qualitative approach to studying beginning teachers would be to conduct the research in a few schools and classrooms in which these individuals are teaching. In contrast, a quantitative approach might use a questionnaire to gather the perceptions, beliefs, and practices of a sample of beginning teachers. Qualitative researchers believe that behavior is best understood as it occurs without external constraints and control.

Excerpt 13.2 describes the natural setting for an extensive study of connections between high-stakes testing and instruction. Note the great deal of time that was invested by the researchers.

Context sensitivity:
understanding the effect of the immediate and larger contexts

Context Sensitivity The situational context is very important in understanding behavior. This is based on the belief that human actions are strongly influenced by the settings in which they occur. Essentially, it is assumed that an explanation of behavior that does not take into account the context is incomplete. Thus, qualitative researchers need to have **context sensitivity**. The larger context in which the research is conducted is also important. The understanding is that meaning is bound by social, political, gender-based, racial, class, and technological factors. These factors form a "lens" through which the researcher interprets behavior (Corbin & Strauss, 2007).

Direct Data Collection In qualitative studies the investigator usually acts as an observer in the setting that is being studied, either as the interviewer, the observer, or the person who studies artifacts and documents. Qualitative researchers want to have information directly from the source. They do this by spending a considerable amount of time in direct interaction with the settings, participants, and documents they are studying. They essentially constitute the instrument. There is a reluctance to use other observers or quantitative measuring techniques because the researchers are then not as "close" to the data as they need to be for a full understanding. Direct data collection is illustrated in Excerpt 13.3.

Rich Narrative Descriptions Qualitative researchers approach a situation with the assumption that nothing is trivial or unimportant. Every detail that is recorded is thought to contribute to a better understanding of behavior. The descriptions are in the form of words or pictures rather than numbers, although simple numerical summaries are used in some qualitative studies. The intent is to provide "rich" descriptions that cannot be achieved by reducing pages of narration to numbers. Rather, the descriptions capture what has been observed in the same form in which they occurred naturally in a particular context. Nothing escapes scrutiny or is taken for granted. This detailed approach to description is necessary to obtain a complete understanding of the

EXCERPT 13.3 Direct Data Collection

Furthermore, qualitative research is intended to build, rather than test, understanding and theory (Newman & Benz, 1998). To implement such research, the first author immersed herself in a setting without preconceived hypotheses. She acted as the evidence-collection instrument. Qualitative research required her to use her subjective interpretation of the phenomena that she observed and recorded. (p. 39)

Source: From Andrews, L., & Ridenour, C. S. (2006). Gender in schools: A qualitative study of students in educational administration. *The Journal of Educational Research, 100*(1), 35–44.

setting and to accurately reflect the complexity of human behavior. To accomplish these goals, the studies may extend over a long period of time and require intense involvement. Typically, they culminate in very extensive written reports.

Process Orientation   Qualitative researchers want to know how and why behavior occurs. In contrast to most quantitative studies, qualitative studies look for the *process* by which behavior occurs as well as explanations, not just the outcomes or products. For example, whereas quantitative research can document the impact of teachers' expectations on students' achievement, qualitative studies are appropriate for understanding *how* teachers' expectations affect students' achievement and behavior. The emphasis is on how expectations are formed and how they are played out in the nature of teachers' interactions with students. The emphasis on process allows for conclusions that explain the reasons for results. For instance, suppose a state is interested in how staff development impacts student achievement. A quantitative approach would be to simply record students' behavior following the staff development, whereas a qualitative inquiry would focus on how the teachers changed as a result of the staff development and how this change affected students' achievement. This approach would provide a greater understanding of what it was about the staff development that was most important.

Inductive Data Analysis   Qualitative researchers do not formulate hypotheses and gather data to prove or disprove them (deduction). Rather, the data are gathered first and then synthesized inductively to generate generalizations. The emphasis is on **inductive reasoning**. Theory is developed from the ground up, or bottom up from the detailed particulars, rather than from the top down. This approach is important because the qualitative researcher wants to be open to new ways of understanding. Predetermined hypotheses limit what will be collected and may cause bias. In other words, qualitative researchers create a picture from the pieces of information obtained. The process is like a funnel. In the beginning, the data may seem unconnected and too extensive to make much sense, but as the researcher works with the data, progressively more specific findings are generated.

Inductive reasoning: synthesis of data

Participant Perspectives   Qualitative researchers try to reconstruct reality from the standpoint of **participant perspectives**, *as the participants they are studying see it.* They do not apply predetermined definitions or ideas about how people will think or react. For example, a quantitative researcher may assume that a teacher's praise is interpreted by a student in a certain way, whereas a qualitative researcher would be interested in how the participant (student) interpreted the praise. The goal in qualitative research is to understand participants from their own point of view, in their own voice. In other words, there is a focus on the meaning of events and actions as expressed by the participants. This approach involves multiple realities as different people construct meaning from the same event. In this sense, *reality* is the subjective meanings of the participants. As a result, much of what is reported in qualitative studies consists of participants' perspectives. Thus, in a qualitative study of what motivates students, it would be important to describe motivation using the words and actions of the students, not the researcher.

Participant perspectives: views expressed by participants

Emergent Design   Like quantitative researchers, qualitative researchers have a plan or design for conducting the research. The difference is that in a qualitative study the researchers enter the investigation "as if they know very little about the people and places they will visit. They attempt to mentally cleanse their preconceptions" (Bogdan & Biklen, 2007, p. 54). Because of this perspective, they do not know enough to begin the study with a precise research design. Rather, they use an **emergent design**. As they learn about the setting, the people, and other sources of information, they are better able to know what needs to be done to fully describe and understand the phenomena being studied. Thus, a qualitative researcher will begin the study with *some* idea about what data will be collected and what procedures will be employed, but a full account of the methods is done *retrospectively*, after all the data have been collected. The design is emergent in that it evolves during the study. It often results in changes in the questions asked, the sites in which observations take place, and the documents that need to be reviewed.

Emergent design: design that evolves

Complex Understanding and Explanation   Central to qualitative research is the belief that the world is complex and that there are few simple explanations for human behavior. Behavior results from the interaction of multiple factors. It follows, then, that the methods that investigate behavior, as well as the explanations, need to be sufficiently complex to capture the true meaning of what has occurred. This leads researchers to examine multiple perspectives. At the same time, though, qualitative researchers realize that it is not possible to account for all of the complexity present in a situation.

Research Questions

Every study begins with an appropriate research question or purpose. From a design standpoint, it is helpful to think about purpose and significance. Once these aspects of the research are identified, features of the design will follow.

Purpose

Historically, qualitative researchers cited two major purposes of a study: *to describe and explore* and *to describe and explain*. Similar terms could be *to examine* or *to document, to understand*, and *to discover or generate*.

Exploratory studies add to the literature by building rich descriptions of complex situations and by giving directions for future research. Other qualitative studies are explicitly explanatory. They show relationships between events and meanings as perceived by participants. These studies increase readers' understanding of the phenomena. Other purposes address action, advocacy, or empowerment, which are often the ultimate goals of critical studies (critical, feminist, postmodern, and participatory research). Although researchers can claim empowerment and taking action as part of the study's purpose, realistically, they can only note how the inquiry may offer opportunities for informed empowerment (see Table 13.2).

TABLE 13.2   Research Purpose and Illustrative Research Questions

Research Purpose	Illustrative Research Questions
Descriptive Exploratory	
To examine new or little-understood phenomena	What is occurring in this social situation?
To discover themes of participants' meanings	What are the categories and themes of participants' meanings?
To develop in detail a concept, model, or hypothesis for future research	How are these patterns linked for propositions/assertions?
Descriptive Explanatory	
To describe and explain the patterns related to the phenomena	What events, beliefs, attitudes, and/or policies impact on this phenomenon?
To identify relationships influencing the phenomena	How do the participants explain the phenomenon?
Emancipatory	
To create opportunities and the will to initiate social action	How do participants describe and explain their problems and take positive action?

Source: Designing Qualitative Research, 3rd edition by Marshall & Rossman. Copyright 1998 by Sage Publications Inc Books. Reproduced with permission of Sage Publications Inc Books in the formats Textbook and Other Book via Copyright Clearance Center.

Significance

Planning a case study design involves selecting the general research question and incorporating components that add to the potential contributions and significance of the study. Qualitative research can be designed to contribute to theory, practice, policy, and social issues and action. We describe each of these in addition to other justifications.

Contributions to Theory   Case study design is appropriate for exploratory- and discovery-oriented research. An *exploratory study*, which examines a topic about which there has been little prior research, is designed to lead to further inquiry. The purpose is to elaborate a concept, develop a model with its related subcomponents, or suggest propositions. Some studies provide an understanding of an abstract concept, such as school-based management, from the participants' social experience. Other studies link participants' perceptions to social science and suggest propositions about humans in general, rather than link the findings to an educational concept. The concepts, models, or hypotheses are *grounded theory* because they are based on observations rather than deduced from prior theories.

Contributions to Practice   Qualitative studies can provide detailed descriptions and analyses of particular practices, processes, or events. Some studies document happenings, and other studies increase participants' own understanding of a practice to improve that practice. A series of qualitative studies over a span of years may contribute to knowledge through the preponderance of evidence accumulated. Specific areas of education for which *quantitative* designs have proven inadequate have begun to accumulate case study evidence. Until quantitative design difficulties can be resolved, knowledge based on a preponderance of evidence cannot easily be ignored.

Contributions to Policy   Qualitative research employing a case study design also contributes to policy formulation, implementation, and modification. Some studies focus on the informal processes of policy formulation and implementation in settings with diverse cultural values to explain the outcomes of public policy. These studies frequently identify issues that suggest the need to modify statutes or regulations and to help policy-makers anticipate future issues.

Contributions to Social Issues and Action   Critical studies often aim at historical revision and transformation, erosion of ignorance, and empowerment. Some studies focus on the lived experiences of racial and ethnic groups, social classes, and gender roles. Researchers examine qualities such as race, ethnic group, social class, homosexual, and female in a more holistic social context to critique their ideological aspects and the political/economic interests that benefit from a given situation. Studies frequently express the so-called culture of silence experienced by various groups; others describe forms of resistance and accommodation of groups that develop their own values as a force for cohesion and survival within the dominant culture.

Other Justifications   *Feasibility issues* related to obtaining valid data can justify a qualitative case study design. Qualitative research is typically done when the nature of the situation or the individuals do not permit use of an instrument. Qualitative strategies, for example, are appropriate with persons who are extremely busy, are expressive nonverbally, or use a second language. When the topic is controversial or confidential or occurred within an institution that has maintained minimal documentation, qualitative inquiry should be chosen. In some situations, an experimental study cannot be done for practical or ethical reasons.

QUALITATIVE SAMPLING STRATEGIES

The sources of information used by qualitative researchers include individuals, groups, documents, reports, and sites. Regardless of the form of the data, purposeful sampling is used. *Qualitative sampling*, in contrast to *probabilistic sampling*, is "selecting information-rich cases for study in-depth" (Patton, 2002, p. 242) when one wants to understand something about those cases without needing or desiring to generalize to all such cases. Qualitative sampling is done to increase the utility of information obtained from small samples. It requires that information be obtained about variations among the sub-units before the sample is chosen. The researcher then searches for *information-rich* key informants, groups, places, or events to study. In other words, these samples are chosen because they are likely to be knowledgeable and informative about the phenomena the researcher is investigating.

The power and logic of qualitative sampling is that a few cases studied in depth yield many insights about the topic, whereas the logic of probability sampling depends on selecting a random or statistically representative sample for generalization to a larger population. Probability sampling procedures such as simple random or stratified sampling may be inappropriate when (1) generalizability of the findings is not the purpose; (2) only one or two subunits of a population are relevant to the research problem; (3) the researchers have no access to the whole group from which they wish to sample; or (4) statistical sampling is precluded because of logistical and ethical reasons.

Types of qualitative sampling are summarized in Table 13.3. Prior to sampling, a site is identified.

Site Selection

Site selection: determining the best sites to gather data

Site selection, in which a site is selected to locate people involved in a particular event, is preferred when the research focus is on complex microprocesses. A clear definition of the criteria

TABLE 13.3 Qualitative Sampling Strategies

Sample Strategy	Description
Site selection	Select a site where specific events are expected to occur.
Comprehensive sampling	Choose the entire group by criteria.
Maximum variation sampling	Select to obtain maximum differences of perceptions about a topic among information-rich informants or group members.
Snowball sampling	Each successive person or group is nominated by a prior person as appropriate for a profile or attribute.
Sampling by case type	
Extreme case	Choose extreme cases after knowing the typical or average case—e.g., outstanding successes, crisis events.
Intense case	Select cases that are dramatic but not extreme illustrations—e.g., below-average students.
Typical case	Know the typical characteristics of a group and sample by cases—e.g., selection of a typical high school principal would eliminate women, persons too young or too old, and single men.
Unique case	Choose the unusual or rare case of some dimension or event—e.g., the implementation of a new federal policy mandate.
Reputational case	Obtain the recommendation of knowledgeable experts for the best examples—e.g., a principal nominates competent teachers or state officials identify effective schools.
Critical case	Identify the case that can illustrate some phenomenon dramatically—e.g., the real test case or the ideal case.
Concept/theory-based	Select by information-rich persons or situations known to experience the concept or to be attempting to implement the concept/theory—e.g., a school implementing site-based management, teacher burnout.
Combination of purposeful sampling strategies	Choose various sampling strategies as needed or desired for research purposes, especially in large-scale studies and lengthy process studies.

for site selection is essential. The criteria are related to and appropriate for the research problem and design. For example, if the initial problem is phrased to describe and analyze teachers' decision making regarding learning activities or students' perspectives regarding classroom management, then the site selected should be one in which these viewpoints or actions are likely present and can be studied.

Comprehensive Sampling

Comprehensive sampling, in which every participant, group, setting, event, or other relevant information is examined, is the preferred sampling strategy. Each subunit is manageable in size and so diverse that one does not want to lose possible variation. For example, a study of inclusion with autistic children in one school division would probably require observation of all autistic children. Suppose a study of high school student interns in an external learning program had 35 different sites. Each work setting was so diverse—a hospital speech clinic, a community newspaper, a labor union, two legislative offices, an animal shelter, and others—that comprehensive selection would be necessary. Because groups are rarely sufficiently small and resources are seldom plentiful, researchers use other sampling strategies.

Comprehensive sampling: involves all participant groups

Maximum Variation Sampling

Maximum variation sampling, or *quota sampling*, is a strategy to illuminate different aspects of the research problem. For instance, a researcher may divide a population of elementary school teachers by number of years of service into three categories and select key informants in each category to investigate career development. This is not a representative sample because the qualitative researcher is merely using this strategy to describe in detail different meanings of teacher career development for individuals with different years of service.

Maximum variation sampling: involves divergent participant groups

Snowball Sampling

Snowball sampling, also called *network sampling*, is a strategy in which each successive participant or group is named by a preceding group or individual. Participant referrals are the basis for choosing a sample. The researcher develops a profile of the attributes or particular trait sought and asks each participant to suggest others who fit the profile or have the attribute. This strategy may be used in situations in which the individuals sought do not form a naturally bounded group but are scattered throughout populations. Snowball sampling is frequently used for in-depth interview studies rather than participant observation research.

Snowball sampling: one participant leading to another

Sampling by Case Type

Other sampling strategies are used when a study requires an examination of a particular type of case. *Case* refers to an in-depth analysis of a phenomenon and not the number of people sampled. Examples of **sampling by case type** are extreme-case, intensive-case, typical-case, unique-case, reputational-case, critical-case, and concept/theory-based sampling. Each of these sampling strategies is defined in Table 13.3. A researcher may choose combinations of case types as needed, especially in large-scale studies and lengthy process studies. (See Patton [2001] for additional case-type sampling.)

Sampling by case type: type of sampling

Qualitative sampling strategies employed in a study are identified from prior information and are reported in the study to enhance data quality. In addition, the persons or groups who actually participated in the study are reported in a manner to protect confidentiality of data. When sampling documents or records, researchers specify the public archives and private collections used and frequently refer to each document or court case in explanatory footnotes. In this manner, researchers using noninteractive techniques to study the past reduce threats to design validity.

Excerpts 13.4–13.6 illustrate different case-type sampling procedures as described in published articles. In each case there is justification for why certain individuals were selected.

EXCERPT 13.4 Typical Case Sampling

Interviewees of these two community colleges were identified through a purposeful sampling strategy to target adults who (a) were at least 30 years of age, (b) were in good academic standing according to their institution's criteria, (c) were in a college transfer program, and (d) had completed at least 15 hours of academic coursework beyond developmental studies. (pp. 6–7)

Source: From Kasworm, C. (2005). Adult student identity in an intergenerational community college classroom. *Adult Educational Quarterly, 56*(1), 3–20.

EXCERPT 13.5 Extreme Case Sampling

The perceptions of the meaning of care as experienced by the participants in their interactions with one another was the primary focus. At each of the two sites, a teacher who was identified by the principal as being particularly caring was purposely selected. (p. 249)

Source: From Alder, N. (2002). Interpretations for the meaning of care: Creating caring relationships in urban middle school classrooms. *Urban Education, 37*(2), 241–266.

EXCERPT 13.6 Intense Case Sampling

In order to obtain a homogeneous sample for this study . . . participants were limited to 40 social studies students. . . . Because the students' academic performance in the class could affect their strategy use and I was interested in students who were academically successful . . . I only interviewed students who had an "A" or "B" average in their social studies classes. (p. 65).

Source: From Martin, L. A. (2004). Use of cognitive strategies by high school social studies students. *Action in Teacher Education, 26*(4), 62–78.

Sample Size

Qualitative inquirers view sampling processes as dynamic, ad hoc, and phasic rather than static or a priori parameters of populations. Although there are statistical rules for probability sample size, there are only guidelines for qualitative sample size. Thus, qualitative samples can range from 1 to 40 or more. Typically, a qualitative sample seems small compared with the sample needed to generalize to a larger population.

The logic of the sample size is related to the purpose, the research problem, the major data collection strategy, and the availability of information-rich cases. The insights generated from qualitative inquiry depend more on the information richness of the cases and the analytical capabilities of the researcher than on the sample size.

The following are guidelines for determining sample size:

1. *Purpose of the study.* A case study that is descriptive/exploratory may not need as many persons as a self-contained study that is descriptive/explanatory. Further, a phenomenological study usually has fewer informants than are needed in grounded theory to generate dense concepts.
2. *Focus of the study.* A process-focused study at one site may have fewer participants than an interview study using network sampling.
3. *Primary data collection strategy.* Qualitative researchers are guided by circumstances. For instance, a study may have a small sample size, but the researcher may be continually returning to the same situation or the same informants, seeking confirmation. The number of days in the field is usually reported.
4. *Availability of informants.* Some informants are rare and difficult to locate; others are relatively easy to identify and locate.

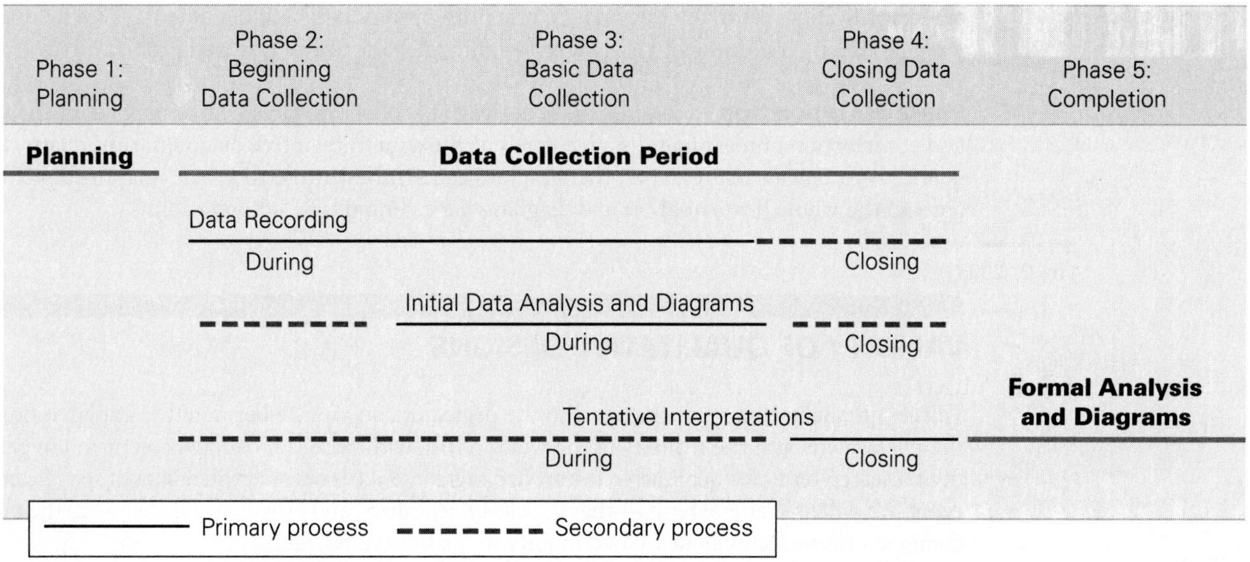

Phase 1: Planning	Phase 2: Beginning Data Collection	Phase 3: Basic Data Collection	Phase 4: Closing Data Collection	Phase 5: Completion

Planning | **Data Collection Period**

Data Recording
During — — — — Closing

Initial Data Analysis and Diagrams
During — — — Closing

Formal Analysis and Diagrams

Tentative Interpretations
During — — Closing

———— Primary process   — — — — Secondary process

FIGURE 13.1   **Phases of Qualitative Research**

5. *Redundancy of data.* Would adding more individuals or returning to the field yield any new insights?
6. *Researchers submit the obtained sample size to peer review.* Most qualitative researchers propose a *minimum* sample size and then continue to add to the sample as the study progresses.

PHASES OF DATA COLLECTION AND ANALYSIS STRATEGIES

The qualitative phases of data collection and analysis are interwoven and occur in overlapping cycles. They are not called *procedures* but *strategies*—that is, techniques that depend on each prior strategy and the resulting data. Figure 13.1 illustrates the five research phases: planning (Phase 1), data collection (Phases 2, 3, 4), and completion (Phase 5). Each phase will be discussed in this section.

Phase 1: Planning   Analyzing the problem statement and the initial research questions will suggest the type of setting or interviewees that would logically be informative. In Phase 1, the researcher locates and gains permission to use the site or network of persons.

Phase 2: Beginning Data Collection   This phase includes the first days in the field, in which the researcher establishes rapport, trust, and reciprocal relations with the individuals and groups to be observed (Wax, 1971). Researchers obtain data primarily to become oriented and to gain a sense of the totality for purposeful sampling. Researchers also adjust their interviewing and recording procedures to the site or persons involved.

Phase 3: Basic Data Collection   The inquirer begins to *hear* and *see* what is occurring, which goes beyond just *listening* and *looking*. Choices of data collection strategies and informants continue to be made. Tentative data analysis begins as the researcher mentally processes ideas and facts while collecting data. Initial descriptions are summarized and identified for later corroboration.

Phase 4: Closing Data Collection   The researcher "leaves the field," or conducts the last interview. Ending data collection is related to the research problem and the richness of the collected data. More attention is given to possible interpretations and verifications of the emergent findings with key informants, remaining interviews, and documents. The field may yield more data but does *not* yield more insights relevant to the research problem.

Phase 5: Completion   Completion of active data collecting blends into formal data analysis and construction of meaningful ways to present the data. Integrative diagrams, time charts, frequency lists, process figures, and other graphics can synthesize a sense of the relationship of the parts to the whole. Data analysis and diagrams are essential for interpretations.

VALIDITY OF QUALITATIVE DESIGNS

Validity, in qualitative research, refers to the degree of congruence between the explanations of the phenomena and the realities of the world. Although there is broad agreement to use pertinent research terms for qualitative research, disagreement occurs over the names of specific concepts. We will use general terms—that is, *validity*, *reflexivity*, and *extension of findings*—as the most common criteria for evidence-based inquiry in qualitative research.

Validity addresses these questions: Do researchers actually observe what they think they see? Do inquirers actually hear the meanings that they think they hear? In other words, *validity of qualitative designs* is the degree to which the interpretations have *mutual meanings* between the participants and the researcher. Thus, the researcher and participants agree on the description or composition of events and especially on the meanings of these events.

Strategies to Enhance Validity

Claims of validity rest on data collection and analysis techniques. Qualitative researchers use a combination of any 10 possible strategies to enhance validity, as listed and described in Table 13.4.

TABLE 13.4   Enhancing Design Validity: Data Collection Strategies to Increase Agreement on the Description by Researcher and Participants

Strategy	Description
Prolonged and persistent fieldwork	Allows interim data analysis and corroboration to ensure a match between findings and participants' reality
Multimethod strategies	Allows triangulation in data collection and data analysis
Participant language; verbatim accounts	Obtain literal statements of participants and quotations from documents
Low-inference descriptors	Record precise, almost literal, and detailed descriptions of people and situations
Multiple researchers	Agreement on descriptive data collected by a research team
Mechanically recorded data	Use of tape recorders, photographs, and videotapes
Participant researcher	Use of participant-recorded perceptions in diaries or anecdotal records for corroboration
Member checking	Check informally with participants for accuracy during data collection; frequently done in participant observation studies
Participant review	Ask participant to review researcher's synthesis of interviews with participant for accuracy of representation; frequently done in interview studies
Negative or discrepant data	Actively search for, record, analyze, and report negative or discrepant data that are an exception to patterns or that modify patterns found in data

As many strategies as possible are used to ensure design validity. Choosing from among strategies involves issues of feasibility and ethics. Strategies are added as appropriate to maintain the least amount of intrusion while increasing the quality of the data.

Prolonged and Persistent Fieldwork   Participant observation and in-depth interviews are conducted in natural settings to reflect lived experience. The lengthy data collection period provides opportunities for interim data analyses, preliminary comparisons, and corroboration to refine ideas and to ensure the match between evidence-based categories and participant reality.

Multimethod Strategies   Most qualitative researchers employ several data collection techniques in a study but usually select one as the central method—either participant observation or in-depth interviews. To some extent, participant observation, open observation, interviewing, and documents are an interwoven web of techniques. How each of these strategies is used varies with the study. Multimethod strategies permits **triangulation** of data across inquiry techniques. Different strategies may yield different insights about the topic of interest and increase the credibility of findings. In its broad sense, *triangulation* also can refer to use of multiple researchers, multiple theories, or perspectives to interpret the data; multiple data sources to corroborate data, and multiple disciplines to broaden one's understanding of the method and the phenomenon of interest (Janesick, 1998).

Triangulation: obtaining convergent data using cross-validation

Participant Language and Verbatim Accounts   Interviews are phrased in the informant's language, not in abstract social science terms. Researchers are also sensitive to *cultural translators*—that is, informants who translate their words into social class terms. For example, when "tramps" were asked "Where is your home? What is your address?" they interpreted the question as referring to a middle-class residence and said "I have no home." An ethnographer could find that men labeled as *homeless* by social scientists did, in fact, have *"flops,"* which could function for them as homes.

Low-Inference Descriptors   Concrete, precise descriptions from field notes and interview elaborations are the hallmarks of qualitative research and the principal method for identifying patterns in the data. *Low inference* means that the descriptions are almost literal and that any important terms are those used and understood by the participants. Low-inference descriptions stand in contrast to the abstract language of a researcher.

Multiple Researchers   The use of multiple researchers is one method to enhance validity. The use of more than one researcher is handled in different ways: (1) extensive prior training and discussion during fieldwork to reach agreement on meanings, (2) short-term observations for confirmation at different sites, and (3) more commonly, an arrangement by which each field observer is independently responsible for a research site and periodically meets with the team to share emerging ideas and strategies. Qualitative research based on a large group team approach, however, is infrequently done; most studies involve only two researchers as a team.

Mechanically Recorded Data   Tape recorders, photographs, and videotapes provide accurate and relatively complete records. For the data to be usable, situational aspects that affected the data record are noted—for instance, failure of equipment, angles of videotaping, and effects of using technical equipment on the context (see Excerpt 13.7).

Participant Researcher   Many researchers obtain the aid of an informant to corroborate what has been observed and recorded, interpretations of participants' meanings, and explanations of overall processes. Participants may keep diaries or make anecdotal records to share with the researcher (see Excerpt 13.7).

Member Checking   Researchers who establish a field residence frequently confirm observations and participants' meanings with individuals through casual conversations in informal situations. **Member checking** can also be done within an interview as topics are rephrased and probed to obtain more complete and subtle meanings (see Excerpt 13.7).

Member checking: verification by participants

EXCERPT 13.7 Mechanically Recorded Data, Participant Researcher, and Member Checking

Data collection . . . occurred over a 10-month period by the first two authors and Millie, Jeffrey's mother. The procedures included semi-structured interviews and an audiojournal. The first two authors conducted five of the six . . . interviews with Millie, Bob, and Chris. Millie conducted the final interview with her husband, Bob. . . . Millie maintained a[n] audiojournal where she recorded her feelings and perceptions of the support process and subsequent changes in Jeffrey's behavior and family functioning. . . . Establishing credibility occurred with member checks, . . . periodically offering Millie the opportunity to respond to the accuracy of the data and . . . coding. (p. 200)

Source: From Fox, L, Vaughn, B., Dunlap, G., & Bucy, M. (1997). Parent-professional partnership in behavioral support: A qualitative analysis of one family's experience. *JASH: Journal of the Association for Persons with Severe Handicaps, 22*(4), 198–207.

Participant Review   Researchers who interview each person in depth or conduct a series of interviews with the same person may ask the person to review a transcript or synthesis of the data obtained from him or her. The participant is asked to modify any information from the interview data for accuracy. Then the data obtained from each interviewee are analyzed for a comprehensive integration of findings.

Negative case: opposite findings

Discrepant data: findings not consistent with emerging themes

Negative and/or Discrepant Data   Researchers actively search for, record, analyze, and report negative cases or discrepant data. A **negative case** is a situation, a social scene, or a participant's view that contradicts the emerging pattern of meanings. **Discrepant data** present a variant to the emerging pattern. For example, a school ethnographer may find that faculty interact freely among themselves in six situations. No negative situations are found. Discrepant data, however, may suggest that faculty interactions are free in five situations and only semifree in the sixth situation, depending on who is present.

REFLEXIVITY IN QUALITATIVE RESEARCH

Reflexivity: rigorous self-examination of the researcher

Reflexivity is a broad concept that includes rigorous examination of one's personal and theoretical commitments to see how they serve as resources for selecting a qualitative approach, framing the research problem, generating particular data, relating to participants, and developing specific interpretations. Further, all data are processed through and reconstructed in the researcher's mind as the report is written.

In other words, reflexivity is rigorous self-scrutiny by the researcher throughout the entire process. The researcher's very act of posing difficult questions to himself or herself assumes that he or she cannot be neutral, objective, or detached. Reflexivity is an important procedure for establishing credibility. Qualitative researchers thus do not deny human subjectivity, but rather take it into account through various strategies.

Interpersonal Subjectivity and Reflexivity

Qualitative research depends to a great extent on the interpersonal skills of the inquirer, such as building trust, maintaining good relations, being nonjudgmental, and respecting the norms of the situation. Researchers use all their personal experiences and abilities of engagement, balancing the analytical and creative through empathetic understanding and profound respect for participants' perspectives. Interpersonal emotions in fieldwork are essential in data collection activities because of the face-to-face interaction.

The progress of the study often depends primarily on the relationship the researcher builds with the participants. The interactive process is relatively personal; no two investigators observe,

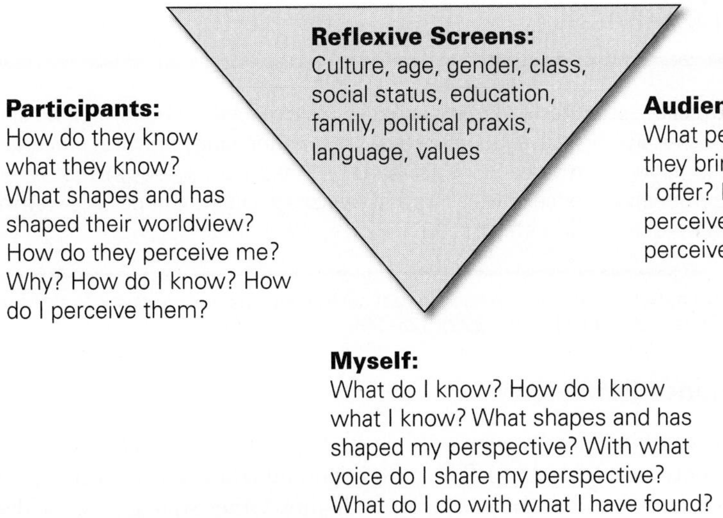

FIGURE 13.2 Reflexive Questions
Adapted from M. Q. Patton. (2002), p. 66.

interview, or relate to others in exactly the same way. These issues are handled primarily within the actual study to enhance reflexivity.

Data obtained from informants are valid even though they may represent particular views or have been influenced by the researcher's presence. Such data are problematic only if they are claimed to be representative beyond the context. Potential researcher bias can be minimized if the researcher spends enough time in the field and employs multiple data collection strategies to corroborate the findings. Providing sufficient details about the design, including reflexivity strategies, is necessary.

What exactly is *reflexivity*? Pillow (2003) suggests these four validated strategies of reflexivity:

1. Reflexivity as recognition of self—personal self-awareness
2. Reflexivity as recognition of the other—capturing the essence of the informant, or "letting them speak for themselves"
3. Reflexivity as truth gathering—the researcher's insistence on getting it right or being accurate
4. Reflexivity as transcendence—the researcher, by transcending his or her own subjectivity and cultural context, works to be released from the weight of (mis)representation for accuracy in reporting

Reflexivity also involves discomfort as researchers seek to minimize predispositions through self-questioning. Patton (2002) suggests this questioning focus on several screens that the researcher uses for self, audience, and participants (see Figure 13.2).

Some critical studies may require the use of additional strategies. Critical researchers are wary that their empirical work will be viewed as an ideological discourse and are fearful of duplication of social, racial, ethnic, and gender biases in their studies. For example, one difficult question relates to *voice*: Were all the voices allowed to emerge, especially those of the socially silenced, whose perspectives are often counter to the situation?

Another reflex strategy is **positionality**, which assumes that only texts in which researchers display their own positions (standpoints) and contextual grounds for reasoning can be considered good research. Critical researchers often write in the introduction their individual social, cultural, historical, racial, and sexual location in the study (see Excerpt 13.8).

Positionality: researcher's lens

In participatory research, the inquirer includes in the data his or her own actions. The complicated dual role of researcher and participant requires scrutiny of both the role and the resulting data. This is not an easy task, nor should it be taken lightly.

EXCERPT 13.8   The Researcher's Stance

My status as a White, European American, male college professor would play an important role as a researcher in Mr. Wilson's class. . . . I hoped to break down the hegemonic relationships that form when a White, European American male college professor enters the classroom of a

Black, African American male teacher. I began keeping a reflexive journal before I started the study in which I recorded my reactions to readings I had completed on the experience of Muslims and Africans in United States. This was the first step. (p. 131)

Source: From Case, R. (2004). Forging ahead into new social networks and looking back to past social identities: A case study of a foreign-born English as a Second Language teacher in the United States. *Urban Education, 39*(2), 125–148.

Strategies to Enhance Reflexivity

Qualitative researchers combine any of seven possible strategies to monitor and evaluate the impact of their subjectivity (see Table 13.5). The most important strategies are keeping a field log and a field (reflex) journal and documenting for audibility. Other strategies are added as needed to obtain valid data.

Peer Debriefer   A *peer debriefer* is a disinterested colleague who discusses the researcher's preliminary analysis and next strategies. Such a discussion makes more explicit the tacit knowledge that the inquirer has acquired. The peer debriefer also poses searching questions to help the researcher understand his or her own posture and its role in the inquiry. In addition, this dialogue may reduce the stress that normally accompanies fieldwork.

Field log: documentation of fieldwork, including a chronological record

Field Log   A **field log** documents the persistent fieldwork and provides a chronological record by date and time spent in the field, including getting access to sites and participants. The field log also contains, for each entry, the places and person involved.

Reflex journal: recording of decisions made during the emergent design

Reflex Journal   A **reflex journal** is a continuous record of the decisions made during the emergent design and rationale. This allows for justification, based on the available information at the time, of the modifications of the research problem and strategies. The reflex journal also contains assessments of the trustworthiness of each dataset. A reflex journal traces the researcher's ideas and personal reactions throughout the fieldwork.

TABLE 13.5   Strategies to Enhance Reflexivity: Strategies to Monitor and Evaluate Researcher Subjectivity and Perspective

Strategy	Description
Peer debriefer	Select a colleague who facilitates the logical analysis of data and interpretation; frequently done when the topic is emotionally charged or the researcher experiences conflicting values in data collection
Field log	Maintain a log of dates, time, places, persons, and activities to obtain access to informants and for each dataset collected
Field (reflex) journal	Record the decisions made during the emerging design and the rationale; include judgments of data validity
Ethical considerations recorded	Record the ethical dilemmas, decisions, and actions in the field journal, as well as self-reflections
Audibility	Record data management techniques, codes, categories, and decision rules as a "decision trail"
Formal corroboration of initial findings	Conduct formal confirmation activities such as a survey, focus groups, or interviews
Critical reflexivity	Self-critique by asking difficult questions; positionality

Ethical Considerations Recorded   Researchers make strategy choices in the field, some of which are based primarily on ethical considerations. A record of ethical concerns helps to justify choices in data collection and analysis.

Audibility   *Audibility* is the practice of maintaining a record of data management techniques and decision rules that document the chain of evidence or decision trail. That record includes the codes, categories, and themes used in description and interpretation as well as drafts and preliminary diagrams. Thus, the chain of evidence will be available for inspection and confirmation by outside reviewers.

Audibility criteria can be met with or without an outside reviewer—that is, an *auditor* who submits a reviewer's appraisal. An alternative is to place a list of files, codes, categories, and decision rules in an appendix for readers' perusal.

Formal Corroboration of Initial Findings   Surveys, focus groups, and in-depth interviews with those not selected originally may be used for formal confirmation, especially when the findings depend on a few informants. As a corroboration activity, the data must be completely analyzed first. Confirmation activities ensure that the patterns found have not been unduly contaminated by the researcher.

EXTENSION OF QUALITATIVE FINDINGS

Qualitative researchers provide for the logical extension of findings, which enables others to understand similar situations and apply the findings in subsequent research or practical situations. Knowledge is produced by the preponderance of evidence found in separate case studies over time.

Authenticity is the faithful reconstruction of participants' perceptions. In other words, readers can relate to or connect with informants and situations. Some studies, such as grounded theory, cite the theoretical frameworks for other researchers. Other studies are more contextual for practical implications. A study that is idiosyncratic and has a minimum of design description has limited usefulness for future inquiry.

Authenticity: actual participants' voices

Design Components to Generate Extension of Findings

Ten design components can affect logical extensions; those actually employed should be described. The components are research role, informant selection, social context, data collection strategies, data analysis strategies, authentic narrative, typicality, analytical premises, alternative explanations, and other criteria associated with a particular research purpose (see Table 13.6).

Research Role   The importance of the inquirer's social relationship with the participants necessitates a description of his or her role and status within the group or at the site. The preferred research role is that of a person who is unknown at the site—in other words, an *outsider*. Researchers often cite personal or professional experiences that enable them to empathize with the participants—that is, they recognize more readily the observed processes and subtle participant meanings than those who lack such experiences. Participatory research requires planning the dual role of participant and researcher, which usually limits extension of the findings.

Informant Selection   The rationale and the decision-making process for choosing the participants are described. Future studies will require researchers to contact individuals similar to those used in the prior study. If a particular person is not cooperative or not available, researchers will search for other informants until a pattern emerges. Increasing the number of sites or persons does not aid the extension of findings; the criterion is information-rich individuals or social scenes (see Excerpt 13.9).

TABLE 13.6 Design Components to Generate Extension of Findings

Strategy	Adequate Description in the Study
Research role	The social relationship of the researcher with the participants
Informant selection	Criteria, rationale, and decision process used in qualitative sampling
Social context	The physical, social, interpersonal, and functional social scenes of data collection
Data collection strategies	The multimethods employed, including participant observation, interview, documents, and others
Data analysis strategies	Data analysis process described
Authentic narrative	Thick description presented as an analytical narrative
Typicality	Distinct characteristics of groups and/or sites presented
Analytical premises	The initial theoretical or political framework that informs the study
Alternative explanations	Retrospective delineation of all plausible or rival explanations for interpretations
Other criteria by research approach (after study completion)	
Ethnography	Comprehensive explanation of the complexity of group life
Phenomenology	Understand the essence of lived experience; generates more research questions
Case study	Understand the practice; facilitates informed decision making
Grounded theory	Concepts or propositions relate to social science; generates verification research with more structured designs
Critical traditions	Informs or empowers participants about their situation and opportunities; generates further research; action stimulus

Social Context   The social context influences data content and is described physically, socially, interpersonally, and functionally. Physical descriptions of the people, the time, and the place of the events or the interviews all assist in data analysis. The purpose of group meetings, such as inservice training or official business, requires other researchers to find similar social contexts for further study.

Data Collection Strategies   Using the study for future inquiry will be impossible without precise descriptions of data collection techniques: the varieties of observational and interview-

EXCERPT 13.9   Informant Selection

Participants: Richness of professional background and willingness to participate in a series of personal in-depth interviews were the primary considerations in identifying participants for the study. . . . A male superintendent, who had supervised two women principals at different times and in different districts, suggested their names to the first author. A family friend of the first author suggested a third choice. . . . This study included 3 participants, all African American women who had been principals in urban school settings. (p. 149)

Source: From Bloom, C., & Erlandson, D. (2003). African American women principals in urban schools: Realities, (re)constructions, and resolutions. *Educational Administration Quarterly, 39*(3), 339–369.

ing methods and data recording techniques used. How different strategies were employed is noted as well. For example, if the primary interest was observing a group process, then individual interviews and documents would be corroborative data collection strategies.

Data Analysis Strategies   Simply asserting that data analysis was done carefully or citing that a certain software program was used is insufficient. The researcher must provide retrospective accounts of how data were synthesized and identify the general analytical strategies used. Frequently, the categories used in data analysis and their decision rules are listed in an appendix.

Authentic Narrative   Most qualitative studies contain thick description in the narrative, interspersed with brief quotations representing participants' language. A good narrative is one that may be read and lived vicariously by others. A narrative is authentic when readers connect to the story by recognizing particulars, by visioning the scenes, and by reconstructing them from remembered associations with similar events. It is the particular, not the abstract, that triggers emotions and moves people. Stories stand between the abstract and the particular by mediating the basic demands of research along with the personal aspects.

Typicality   Another design component is the extent of **typicality** of the phenomenon—that is, the degree to which it may be compared or contrasted along relevant dimensions with other phenomena. Qualitative researchers' virtual obsession with describing the distinct characteristics of groups studied is, in fact, an appreciation of the importance of this information for extension of findings. The attributes of groups and sites can include socioeconomic status, educational attainment, age range, racial or ethnic composition, time period, and contextual features of the location. Unique historical experiences of groups and cultures may limit extension, but few groups' experiences are totally ethnocentric. Once typicality has been established, a basis for extension will be evident and can be used to provide insights across time frames and situations.

> **Typicality:** comparison with other contexts and participants

Analytical Premises   The choice of conceptual framework made by one researcher for a given study will require other researchers to begin with similar analytical premises (see Excerpt 13.10). Because one major outcome of qualitative research is the generation and refinement of concepts, inquirers contrast their findings to those of prior research. When discrepancies are presented, researchers cite the attributes of the group, time period, and settings. This alerts other researchers when they use these same findings. Much qualitative research, however, is nontheoretical.

Alternative Explanations   During data analysis, qualitative researchers search for negative evidence and discrepant data to challenge or modify emerging patterns. Negative and discrepant data are useful for identifying alternative explanations. Observers and interviewers actively search for informants and social scenes that appear to vary from or disagree with prior data. A major pattern becomes an explanation only when alternative patterns do not offer reasonable explanations related to the research problem. Major and alternative explanations are discussed in the study because both might generate further research.

EXCERPT 13.10   Analytical Premises and Prior Research

Not surprisingly, then, the girls whose families were *not* like the television families thought the television families were more unrealistic. Following McRobbie's (1991) culturalist approach, the girls were interpreting and assessing media based on their own lived experiences. Greenberg and Reeves (1996) also find that children's personal experiences affect their perceptions of reality on television. Children in general do not have multiple reference points regarding family life, so the girls in this study saw any family as deviating from those they know as unrealistic. This data also empirically supports Greenberg and Reeves's prediction that television content is perceived as more like real life if the child's attitudes and behaviors, or in this case, family dynamics, are consistent with the television content. (pp. 398–399)

Source: From Fingerson, L. (1999). Active viewing: Girls' interpretations of family television programs. *Journal of Contemporary Ethnography, 28*(4), 389–418.

Other Criteria by Research Approach (After Study Completion)   In addition to providing adequate descriptions of the general components mentioned, specific qualitative approaches may emphasize additional criteria. For example, phenomenology, grounded theory, and critical studies have slightly different effects on research communities, readers, and participants. An *ethnography* provides a comprehensive understanding of the complexity of group life, which leads to further case studies. A *phenomenological study* increases the understanding of lived experiences by readers and others. A *case study* promotes better understanding of a practice or issue and facilitates informed decision making. A *grounded theory study*, however, usually leads to more structured designs to test a concept or to verify a proposition. Some forms of critical traditions not only inform through historical revisionism but also empower and stimulate action. Thus, the researcher frequently has a meeting with the major informants or all participants, reviews the findings, and initiates a dialogue. The researchers also may provide additional resource information to foster personal and group empowerment.

When qualitative researchers appropriately address the issues of design validity, reflexivity, and extension of findings, as noted previously, their work is regarded as credible by other qualitative investigators. Many design issues are handled by planning and conducting studies based on the appropriate criteria for evidence-based research.

QUALITATIVE RESEARCH ETHICS: ROLES AND RECIPROCITY

Qualitative research is more likely to be personally intrusive than quantitative research. Thus, ethical guidelines include policies regarding informed consent, deception, confidentiality, anonymity, privacy, and caring. Fieldworkers, however, must adopt these principles in complex situations.

Ethical Dilemmas in Fieldwork

A credible research design involves not only selecting informants and effective research strategies but also adhering to research ethics. Qualitative researchers need to plan how they will handle the ethical dilemmas in interactive data collection. Some qualitative researchers, for example, have collected data after gaining the confidence of persons potentially involved in illegal activities. Other researchers have investigated controversial and politically sensitive topics. When researchers study, say, drugs on campus, lesbian and gay youth, and violence in schools or families, profound ethical dilemmas arise.

Researchers may also be drawn unexpectedly into morally problematic situations. Some typical questions that a qualitative inquirer may face are: Do I observe this abuse, or do I turn away from it? Do I record this confession, and if I do record it, do I put it in a public report? If I see abuse or neglect, do I report it to the officials? Am I really seeing abuse or projecting my own values into the situation? If I promised confidentiality when I entered the field, am I breaking my bargain if I interfere? These questions suggest that it is difficult to separate research ethics from professional ethics and personal morality.

Most qualitative researchers devise roles that elicit cooperation, trust, openness, and acceptance. Sometimes, researchers assume helping roles, dress in a certain manner, or allow themselves to be manipulated. When people adjust their priorities and routines to help a researcher or even tolerate his or her presence, they are giving of themselves. A researcher is indebted to these persons and should devise ways to reciprocate, within the constraints of research and personal ethics. Some researchers prefer to collaborate with their informants and share authorship. Reciprocity can be the giving of time, feedback, attention, appropriate token gifts, or specialized services. Some inquirers, upon completion of the report, become advocates for a particular group in the larger community, including policy-making groups.

Research Ethics in Fieldwork

Most qualitative researchers use discussion and negotiation to resolve ethical dilemmas in fieldwork. Negotiations revolve around obtaining consensus on situational priorities.

Informed Consent as a Dialogue   In gaining permission, most researchers give participants assurances of confidentiality and anonymity and describe the intended use of the data. Institutional review boards (IRBs) require a protocol for informed consent to be signed by each participant. As Malone (2003) demonstrates, the typical protocol is usually not accurate for most qualitative research because one cannot anticipate what may be intrusive for each participant.

Many researchers view informed consent as a dialogue with each new participant. However, in some situations, such a dialogue is impossible—for instance, in a sudden and unexpected trauma that brings persons to the scene during the observation or the observation of public behavior in a crowd. Usually, the time required for participation and the noninterfering, nonjudgmental research role is explained. Informants select interview times and places. Because researchers need to establish trusting relationships, they plan how to handle the dialogue. Most participants can detect and reject insincerity and manipulation.

Confidentiality and Anonymity   The settings and participants should not be identifiable in print. Thus, locations and features of settings are typically disguised to appear similar to several possible places, and researchers routinely code names of people and places. Officials and participants should review a report before it is finally released. Researchers have a dual responsibility: to protect the individuals' confidences from other persons in the setting and to protect the informants from the general reading public.

However, the law does *not* protect researchers if the government compels them to disclose matters of confidence. The report, the field notes, and the researcher can all be subpoenaed. For example, one researcher was asked to be an expert witness in a school desegregation case. The researcher initiated the "ethical principle of dialogue" (L. M. Smith, 1990, p. 271) in presenting the dilemma to several school officials for mutual problem solving. Finally, a top official said that the lawyer would not call the researcher as a witness because it violated the confidentiality commitments.

Privacy and Empowerment   Deception violates informed consent and privacy. Although some well-known ethnographers have posed as hobos, vagrants, and even army recruits, they claim that no harm to informants resulted from their research. However, even informed persons who cooperate may feel a sense of betrayal upon reading the research findings in print.

Fieldworkers negotiate with participants so that they understand the power that they have in the research process. This power and the mutual problem solving that results from it may be an exchange for the privacy lost by participating in a study (Lincoln, 1990).

Feminist researchers may focus on communitarian ethics rather than the normal research ethics (Denzin, 1997). The mission of social science is to enable community life to transform itself. From this perspective, qualitative research is "authentically sufficient when it fulfills three conditions: represents multiple voices, enhances moral discernment, and promotes social transformation" (Christians, 2000, p. 145). These inquirers focus on general morality rather on than professional ethics per se.

Caring and Fairness   Although physical harm to informants seldom occurs in qualitative research, some persons may experience humiliation and loss of trust. Justifying the possible harm to one individual because it may help others is unacceptable. A sense of caring and fairness must be part of the researcher's thinking, actions, and personal morality.

Many inquirers argue for *committed relativism* or *reasonableness* in particular situations. Open discussions and negotiation usually promote fairness to the participants and to the research inquiry.

STANDARDS OF ADEQUACY

Qualitative designs are judged by several criteria. Following are the questions readers typically ask about a qualitative design before accepting the study as evidence-based inquiry:

1. Is the one phenomenon investigated clearly articulated and delimited?
2. What characteristics of qualitative research are present? How would this affect the credibility of the study?

3. Are the research questions focused and phrased to discover and describe the hows and whys of the phenomenon?

4. Which purposeful sampling technique(s) were selected to obtain information-rich informants or sites? Are the informants described and is the type of site obtained identified? If potentially useful groups were not selected, is a rationale presented?

5. Did the sample size seem logical, given the research purpose, time, and resources?

6. Is the design presented in sufficient detail to enhance validity? That is, does it specify essential strategies such as prolonged fieldwork, collection of verbatim accounts with descriptive data, and negative case search? If the design was modified during data collection, is justification presented for the change?

7. Which multimethod data collection strategies were employed to ensure agreement between the researcher and informants? Did the researcher have knowledge of and experience with the primary strategy used? How were different data collection strategies employed?

8. If multiple researchers or participant researchers collected data, how were issues of data quality handled?

9. Which strategies did the researcher employ to enhance reflexivity? Did these seem appropriate to the study?

10. Which design components were included to enhance the usefulness and the logical extensions of the findings? Could others have been incorporated into the study? If so, which ones?

11. Does the researcher specify how informed consent, confidentiality, and anonymity were handled? Was any form of reciprocity employed? If any design decisions were made due to ethical considerations, is the justification reasonable?

CHAPTER SUMMARY

The following statements summarize the major aspects of qualitative research design:

1. Key characteristics include natural settings, context sensitivity, direct data collection, rich narrative description, process orientation, induction, participant perspectives, emergent design, and complexity.

2. Qualitative researchers study participants' perspectives—feelings, thoughts, beliefs, ideals—and actions in natural situations.

3. Qualitative researchers use interactive strategies to collect data for exploratory, explanatory, and emancipatory studies.

4. Qualitative researchers employ emergent designs.

5. Qualitative sampling is selecting small samples of information-rich cases to study in depth without desiring to generalize to all such cases.

6. Types of qualitative sampling include comprehensive sampling, maximum variation sampling, network sampling, and sampling by case type.

7. Sample size depends on the purpose of the study, the data collection strategies, and the availability of information-rich cases.

8. Data collection and analysis are interactive and occur in overlapping cycles.

9. The use of research strategies rather than procedures allows for flexibility to study and corroborate each new idea as it occurs in data collection.

10. The five phases of qualitative research are planning, beginning data collection, basic data collection, closing data collection, and formal data analysis and diagrams.

11. The validity of a qualitative design is the degree to which the interpretations and concepts have mutual meanings between the participants and researcher.

12. Qualitative researchers enhance validity by making explicit all aspects of their designs.

13. Data collection strategies to increase validity are a combination of the following strategies: prolonged fieldwork, multimethod, verbatim accounts, low-inference descriptors, multiple researchers, mechanically recorded data, participant researcher, member checking, participant review, and negative case reporting.

14. Qualitative researchers employ interpersonal subjectivity to collect data and reflex strategies or evidence-based inquiry.

15. Qualitative studies aim at extension of findings rather than generalization of results. Generalizability is usually not the intent of the study.

16. Design components that enhance the extension of findings are specification of the researcher role, informant selection, the social context, data collection and analysis strategies, authentic narrative, typicality, analytical premises, and alternative explanations.

17. Field researchers employ dialogue and reciprocity while following ethical and legal principles when interacting with participants.

APPLICATION PROBLEMS

1. The director of an inner-city preschool program wants to obtain parents' perspectives of the program. She is especially interested in this year's innovation in one class: a parent education program. Materials are sent home twice a week for a parent or guardian to work with the child, and records of teacher-parent contacts are made. There are 12 children in the preschool class. Four children live with a single parent, six live with both parents, and two children live with one parent and their grandparents.
   a. What type of sampling is appropriate and why? (probability or qualitative)
   b. How should the sampling be done?
   c. Which qualitative strategies would be appropriate?
2. A researcher is interested in how principals make decisions about retention of elementary schoolchildren. How would you design this study?
3. A researcher wants to understand the concept of site-based school management. He has located a school district that has spent one year in planning and writing guidelines

for site-based management at six selected schools. The researcher is primarily interested in how a site-based management team operates and whether this affects the role of the principal and the school's relationship to the district's central management. A site-based management team consists of six members from the community and three teachers plus the principal as an ad hoc member. A central office facilitator frequently attends the monthly meetings after conducting six orientation sessions. How would you design the study?
   a. Which type of sampling is appropriate and why? (probability or qualitative)
   b. How should the sampling be done?
   c. Which qualitative methods would be appropriate?
4. For Problem 1, which research strategies could increase design validity, enhance reflexivity, and encourage extension of findings?
5. For Problem 3, which research strategies could enhance design validity, enhance reflexivity, and foster extension of findings?

ANSWERS TO APPLICATION PROBLEMS

1. a. Purposeful sampling is appropriate because the interest is only in *these* parents and *this* program. There is no interest in generalizability.
   b. Comprehensive sampling is appropriate because there is only a director, 1 teacher of the class, and 12 households. The 12 households are also maximum variation sampling because there are three types of households. The researcher needs to determine within each household who is actually attending the child and his or her schooling in the parent education program.
   c. Interview, documents of the program, records of parent/teacher contracts, and materials sent to the parent.
2. Elementary school principals are the key informants. The research question focuses on how, which suggests obtaining information on the process of decision making, who is consulted, which records are used, and copies of school and district guidelines for retention. The design would require use of in-depth interviews and documents analysis. A purposeful sample should be used, but the sample size will depend on locating principals who have had experience with making retention decisions.
3. a. Purposeful sampling is appropriate because the focus is on understanding a concept and a process.
   b. Reputational sampling. Knowledgeable central office personnel who planned, selected the six schools, and

did the orientation sessions could select the school where a team is operating on a regular basis. Other cases could be added—such as a negative case or a typical case—depending on the information obtained from this site.
   c. Field observations of the monthly team meetings, in-depth interviews with the principal and the facilitator, and documents (e.g., records of all meetings, district guidelines, and others).
4. a. Extension of findings can be enhanced by specifying the researcher role, informant selection, multimethods employed, and data analysis strategies in the report. Data collection strategies that could increase extension are obtaining verbatim accounts, using low-inference descriptors, having the teacher keep records (participant researcher), and participant review.
   b. Strategies to minimize threats to validity are use of participant language, visiting the households and the program, and techniques to enhance reflexivity.
   c. The researcher needs to specify how typical these households are and the common and contrasting features of this parent education program in relation to other programs.

5. a. Validity can be enhanced by specifying in the study the researcher role, site selection, social context of the team meetings, data collection and analysis strategies, and analytical premises—concept of site-based school management. Data collection strategies that could increase validity are verbatim accounts, low-inference descriptors, mechanically recording data, and member checking with team members and others.

   b. To minimize threats to validity, the researcher can collect data on team meetings for a year, use the language of the site, do all data collection in the field, and keep a reflex journal. Obtaining baseline data is important in a process study.

   c. The researcher needs to describe the typicality of the school and the contrasting dimensions of site-based management with that of other management approaches. Of interest is this district's definition of site-based management in contrast to that of other districts and to the theory of site-based school management. Because prior research has been done on site-based school management, the results of this study can be contrasted to those of prior research.

Collecting Qualitative Data

Collecting Qualitative Data

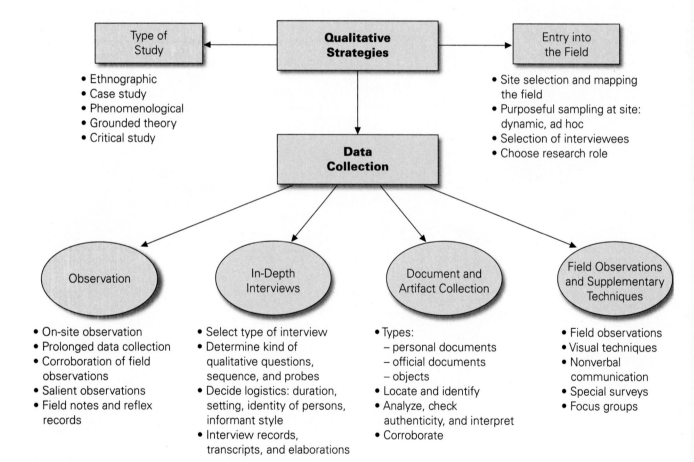

Type of Study

- Ethnographic
- Case study
- Phenomenological
- Grounded theory
- Critical study

Qualitative Strategies

Entry into the Field

- Site selection and mapping the field
- Purposeful sampling at site: dynamic, ad hoc
- Selection of interviewees
- Choose research role

Data Collection

Observation

- On-site observation
- Prolonged data collection
- Corroboration of field observations
- Salient observations
- Field notes and reflex records

In-Depth Interviews

- Select type of interview
- Determine kind of qualitative questions, sequence, and probes
- Decide logistics: duration, setting, identity of persons, informant style
- Interview records, transcripts, and elaborations

Document and Artifact Collection

- Types:
  – personal documents
  – official documents
  – objects
- Locate and identify
- Analyze, check authenticity, and interpret
- Corroborate

Field Observations and Supplementary Techniques

- Field observations
- Visual techniques
- Nonverbal communication
- Special surveys
- Focus groups

KEY TERMS

ethnography	phenomenological	field notes
culture	grounded theory	gatekeeper
realist ethnography	critical studies	mapping the field
case study	research role	reflex records
intrinsic case	complete outsider	in-depth interviews
instrumental case	complete insider	artifacts
collective case	participant observer	focus group interview

WHAT YOU WILL LEARN

Study this chapter and you will:

- Understand how ethnography, case study, phenomenological, grounded theory, and critical studies designs emphasize different data collection strategies.
- Distinguish between intrinsic, instrumental, and collective case study designs.
- Understand the importance of in-depth interviews for phenomenological studies.
- Distinguish between different types of grounded theory designs.
- Understand the importance of gaining appropriate entry into the field.
- Know the steps taken to conduct qualitative observations.
- Understand the dynamic interplay between design and ongoing findings.

- Understand why most qualitative observation involves partial participation.
- Understand the importance of prolonged and intensive observations.
- Distinguish between different researcher roles while in the field.
- Know the steps taken to conduct qualitative interviews.
- Distinguish between different types of interviews and interview questions.
- Know how to take notes during observations and interviews.
- Know how to use documents and artifacts.
- Understand how focus groups can be used as a qualitative data collection strategy.

CHOOSING QUALITATIVE DATA COLLECTION STRATEGIES

Data collection and other aspects of methodology follow from the research questions. In quantitative studies, methods align well with questions that address description, comparisons, correlations, and experimental and single-subject approaches to gathering and analyzing the data. In qualitative research there are five major methods for gathering data: observation, interviews, questionnaires, document review, and use of audiovisual materials. How do you match these methods with research questions so that the best data for answering the question will be gathered and analyzed? We believe a good approach is to first determine which of the five major qualitative traditions will be used. When this decision is combined with the research questions, you will be well on your way to knowing which methods of data collection are most appropriate.

Ethnography

An ethnographic qualitative study, or **ethnography**, is an in-depth description and interpretation of cultural patterns and meanings within a specified culture or social group. Educational ethnography is rooted in cultural anthropology. Anthropologists have used ethnographic techniques to study primitive and contemporary cultures, focusing on such factors as religious beliefs, social relations, child rearing, marriage, and language. The primary strategies for gathering data in these studies have been observation over a long period of time, interaction and interviews with members of the culture, and analysis of documents and artifacts. Although educational ethnographies are typically not as time-consuming, resource

Ethnography: in-depth study of a culture

369

intensive, and complex as the studies of anthropologists, the fundamental tenets of educational ethnography are based on cultural anthropology.

Culture: shared norms

Culture can be defined as shared patterns of beliefs, thinking, language, expectations and behaviors, and meanings. The emphasis is on what is characteristic for the overall group and for the culture that is shared by members of the group. This can include beliefs, rituals, economic structures, communication styles, mores, and forms of interaction. The "group" can be relatively narrowly defined (e.g., two students needing remediation, married doctoral students, tenure-track education faculty, student-athletes, academic departments) or defined more broadly (e.g., a school, a church, college dormitories, a liberal arts college).

The key concept for understanding culture is that it is what is *shared* that is most important. A group establishes its culture after having interacted for a sufficient period of time to establish shared patterns of thinking and behavior. This typically involves several weeks, months, or years. There is continued interaction, on a regular basis, that promotes a shared pattern of thinking and behaving.

The goal of data collection in ethnographies is to gather the best information to address a specific cultural theme or trait. These themes and traits are generalizations that are formed from the data through inductive reasoning. For example, a theme could be the induction of beginning teachers, student-teacher relationships, persistence of athletes, or teacher decision making about how to use formative assessment. There must be some purpose that goes beyond a simple description of something.

In determining what data need to be collected for an ethnography, it is helpful to determine which type of ethnography is best suited to the researcher's intent and research problem. Although there are as many as 10 variations of ethnography research (Creswell, 2008), we focus here on the one that is most common in educational studies—realist ethnography.

Realist ethnography: detailed description

A **realist ethnography** is a relatively straightforward, detailed description of a cultural group. The researcher is "outside" of the culture, not participating in it. There is heavy reliance on observation. What is reported is an "objective account of the situation" (Creswell, 2008, p. 475). The goal is to report on what is documented. With a realist ethnography, the researcher stays detached from the culture and does not include personal reflections about the data as they are collected. The ethnography is focused on showing a deep understanding of the targeted theme. The researcher's interpretation is separate from the account describing the culture and theme.

This kind of ethnography, then, is primarily a detailed description, answering questions such as the following:

- How do beginning teachers modify their initial classroom management techniques?
- What transpires in teacher-parent conferences?
- What is the nature of faculty participation in faculty meetings?
- What is the nature of fifth-grade students' engagement in learning?
- How do teachers use formative assessment feedback to increase student achievement?

Because the primary purpose is description, there is an emphasis on observations over an extended period of time. Interviews and document analysis are also used, but they have less influence on the description that is provided. For example, suppose a researcher wants to describe patterns of interaction between the principal and counselors in a high school. There would be need to observe these interactions over an entire semester, perhaps by shadowing the principal in meetings with the counselors and reviewing email communications between the principal and counselors. The researcher would need to specify what a *pattern of interaction* means and how it is carried out in the setting. Then observational and other forms of data collection can be specified.

Case Study

Case study: examination of a single entity

A **case study** is an in-depth analysis of a single entity. It is a choice of what to investigate, identified as a single case or *the case* (Stake, 2008). Creswell (2008) refers to a case study as "an in-depth exploration of a bounded system (e.g., an activity, event, process, or individuals) based on extensive data collection" (p. 476). Being *bounded* means being unique according to place, time, and participant characteristics. Whether we use the term *system, event,* or *case*, the emphasis is on a single instance of something or a single entity, not on methodology. Thus, a case study can be quantitative and/or qualitative. In our use of the term here, we are considering a qualitative case study. Some authors may actually classify case study as a type of ethnographic study. Although case study research shares many of the characteristics of ethnography, we believe it is best studied as a separate type of qualitative research.

There are several types of cases. A case can be an individual, group, activity, or event, or it could be a process, such as how graduate students navigate their way through their program. Stake (2008) distinguishes between intrinsic and instrumental cases. An **intrinsic case** is one in which the focus is on the case itself. Typically, intrinsic case studies investigate unusual or unique individuals, groups, or events (e.g., an unusually gifted athlete, a new advanced placement class, a charter school, a political election). An **instrumental case** provides insight into a specific theme or issue. Here the focus is on in-depth understanding of the entity, issue, or theme. The case study is used to elucidate that entity, issue, or theme (e.g., teenage sexual activity by studying students in a single school; teacher retention by investigating teachers in a single school district). Instrumental case studies are illustrated in Excerpts 14.1 and 14.2. In Excerpt 14.1, the authors justify the use of a case study by explaining that they are interested in studying a single phenomenon, student-initiated retention programs. They use two instances of such programs as cases. In Excerpt 14.2, the authors explain why a qualitative case study is appropriate for their investigation of how kindergarten teachers balance the demands of new academic mandates with meeting the developmental needs of students. In this study two cases are utilized.

When a number of different cases are combined in a single study, the investigation may be called a *collective*, *multiple*, or *multisite* case study. With a **collective case** study more than one example or setting is used. For example, you could study, describe, and compare the effect of new admissions procedures used in four specialty high schools. Each high school is considered a case.

With case studies data collection is extensive and varied, depending on the question and situation. Essentially, the researcher needs to gather whatever information is required to provide

> **Intrinsic case:** case-focused study

> **Instrumental case:** theme-based study

> **Collective case:** two or more cases

EXCERPT 14.1 Instrumental Case Study

We chose case study as a research method for the obvious reason that we needed to develop a holistic understanding of SIRPs [Student-Initiated Retention Project]. Yin (1989) described case study research as a flexible form of inquiry best suited for studying a particular phenomenon within its natural context. Such studies . . . through the use of interviews and observations, seek to develop "thick descriptions" of the setting or phenomenon in question. . . . Accordingly, we relied on formal structured interviews, informal interviews (with key informants), observations, and key documents. (p. 615)

Source: From Maldonado, D. E. Z., Rhoads, R., & Buenavista, T. L. (2005). The student-initiated retention project: Theoretical contributions and role of self-empowerment. *American Educational Research Journal, 42*(4), 605–638.

EXCERPT 14.2 Instrumental Case Study

To examine kindergarten teachers' experiences balancing the responsibility to meet the developmental needs of their students with the expectations for academic achievement and accountability that accompany the new mandates and policies, and to explore teachers' perceptions of the challenges they face as a result, I engaged in qualitative case study research (Yin, 1994) . . . it was an ideal method for investigating the impact of policy on practice. This method enabled me to position my participants' experiences, perceptions, and decisions in relation both to the specific demands presented by their school and district requirements as well as to the state and national legislation that shaped those requirements. In addition, the case studies are intended to provide detailed, specific accounts of particular circumstances rather than offering broad, generalizable findings (Stake, 1995). Employing a case study design allowed me to use narrative vignettes depicting the participants' practices to provide compelling and rich representations for the different instructional strategies participants used to accommodate the competing demands shaping their work. (p. 381)

Source: From Goldstein, L. S. (2007). Embracing pedagogical multiplicity: Examining two teachers' instructional responses to the changing expectations for kindergarten in U.S. public schools. *Journal of Research in Childhood Education, 21*(4), 378–400.

an in-depth understanding. Typically, case studies use multiple methods to collect data. There is less emphasis on observation compared to ethnographic studies.

Phenomenological Study

Phenomenological: participant perspectives of an event

The purpose of a **phenomenological** study is to describe and interpret the experiences of participants regarding a particular event in order to understand the participants' meanings ascribed to that event. This can be thought of as capturing the essence of the experience *as perceived by the participants*. The basis of phenomenology is that there are multiple ways of interpreting the same experience and that the meaning of the experience for each participant is what constitutes reality. This is akin to the previously mentioned characteristic of *participant perspectives*. Although all qualitative studies have this orientation, a phenomenological study focuses much more on the consciousness of human experiences. Typically, there is a search for essential or invariant structure in the meanings given by the participants. The researcher needs to suspend, or "bracket," any preconceived ideas about the phenomenon to elicit and better understand the meanings given by the participants.

The research problem for a phenomenological study is focused on what is essential for elucidating the meaning of the event, episode, or interaction. It is also focused on understanding the participants' voice. This can be stated directly, such as "What is the nature of student conferences with counselors?" or less directly, such as "What is the relationship between a school counselor and a student really like?"

The data collection mainstay of a phenomenologist is the personal in-depth, unstructured interview. These interviews are typically long, and the researcher may have several interview sessions with each participant. Because of the heavy reliance on this single method of data collection, it is very important for the researcher to be skilled at interviewing. On the one hand, some structure is required to stay on topic, but the researcher also needs considerable skill in listening, prompting when appropriate, and encouraging participants to reflect, expand, and elaborate on their remembrances of the experience. The interviews usually last for about an hour, though two-hour interviews are also used. The interviews are almost always tape recorded for analysis. In addition, some phenomenological studies use the depictions of interviews by other researchers as drawn from the literature.

In Excerpt 14.3 the researcher explains why he used a phenomenological approach to studying students' out-of-school science experiences.

Grounded Theory

Grounded theory: uses data to explain phenomena

The intent of a **grounded theory** study is very specific: to discover or generate a theory that explains central phenomena derived from the data. The theory is essentially an abstract schema, or set of propositions, that pertain to a specific experience, situation, or setting. The context of the phenomenon being studied provides the basis for a grounded theory study. In this sense, the theory is "grounded" in the field data. The interpretations and conclusions of the research are made inductively, with constant reference to the data. Grounded theory may provide a better explanation than an existing theory and may suggest changes to the theory. Grounded theory is also used to describe and explain actions of individuals or groups.

EXCERPT 14.3 Rationale for a Phenomenological Study

This study used a phenomenological approach to investigate the recollections of participants of an out-of-school science program. Phenomenology seeks clarification and understanding of people's perceptions and experiences, especially the meanings they give to events, concepts, and issues (Mabry, 2000). This process examines the experience of each participant and recognizes that these experiences have a relationship with the phenomenon (in this case the out-of-school science experience). (p. 46)

Source: From Knapp, K. (2007). A longitudinal analysis of an out-of-school science experience. *School Science and Mathematics, 107*(2), 44–52.

EXCERPT 14.4 Grounded Theory Study

This research study used grounded theory in an attempt to explain how 10th grade public school students in average and advanced classes used strategies to learn material in their high school social studies classes. This study sought to understand the strategies that students used to learn information, the frequency of their strategy use, and the students' method of acquiring these strategies. The results suggested that cognitive strategy use involves the students' knowledge of cognitive strategies, a need to use the strategies, and a motivation by the students to use the strategies. (p. 63)

Source: From Martin, L. (2005). Use of cognitive strategies by high school social studies students. *Action in Teacher Education, 26*(4), 63–73.

Creswell (2008) identifies three types of grounded theory designs: systematic, emerging, and constructivist. The *systematic* approach is used extensively in education. It involves the methodical use of a rigorous set of procedures and techniques in which there is careful coding of the data. The coding is "open" in the sense that the data drive the categories that are used rather than using pre-existing categories. With an *emerging* design the procedure for coding and categorization is less structured and prescribed. There is more flexibility both in the process used and in the determination of categories, themes, and theories. The *constructivist* design focuses on the perspectives, feelings, and beliefs of the participants. The findings tend to reflect "active" codes that emphasize how participants have changed their perceptions and insights.

The participants for a grounded study are selected on the basis of their ability to contribute to the development of the theory. Often a homogeneous sample is selected first, one in which each individual has had a similar experience. Once the theory is developed, a heterogeneous sample, consisting of individuals who have had different experiences, may be selected to confirm or disconfirm tenets of the theory. Typically, 20 to 30 interviews may be needed with a homogeneous sample to reach a point where no new important information related to the theory is obtained (this is referred to as *saturation*).

As in phenomenological studies, the individual interview is the primary method of data collection. Some grounded theory studies also use observation and document analysis, but the main source of data is the individuals interviewed. The interviews are open-ended and searching. The researcher needs to learn as much as possible from the participants about their perceptions of the nature and impact of the experiences as related to a possible theory.

Excerpt 14.4 is taken from a grounded theory study that examined what cognitive strategies students use, how much the strategies are used, and how they are acquired. Forty-two open-ended audio-recorded interviews and some observations were conducted over a nine-week period to collect data.

Critical Studies

Critical studies, sometimes operationalized as *critical ethnographies*, are distinguished by the researcher's use of an advocacy role to respond to important themes of marginalized individuals or groups. These studies are focused on systems of power and control, privilege, inequity, dominance, and influence on groups based on race, gender, and socioeconomic class. The struggles of these groups become the central issue. Often the researcher is involved in empowering members of these groups and changing society so that participants have more power and influence. It is an emancipation of the group from the more dominant culture, reducing inequality. For example, critical perspectives could be integrated into a study of how students with learning disabilities are marginalized by their inclusion in regular classes. Data would be gathered to challenge the status quo and to support these students in an effort to influence changes in the school. Concepts such as dignity, dominance, oppressed, authority, empowerment, inequality, and social justice are emphasized. The critical researchers not only study groups, they advocate for them by stimulating changes.

Critical studies use all means of data collection, concentrating on whatever will document the manner in which the participants are marginalized. Methods related to ethnography, such as observation and interviewing, are used most often. The key is to gather the right kind of infor-

Critical studies: focus on inequality and injustice

EXCERPT 14.5 Critical Study

This study's use of qualitative methods allowed mothers to define how they make meaning of their educational view, choices and experiences, and how these are shaped by socioeconomic and cultural factors. I also examined how the mothers perceive school contexts, policies and other sociopolitical conditions as hindering or empowering them within an urban educational marketplace, and I learned how they use strategies to help empower themselves within this setting. . . . In accordance with feminist methodological standards, the interviews were open-ended and conversational, which is a naturalistic format intended to strengthen research-participant rapport. (pp. 487–488)

Source: From Cooper, C. W. (2007). School choice as 'motherwork': Valuing African-American women's educational advocacy and resistance. *International Journal of Qualitative Studies in Education, 20*(5), 491–512.

mation that will support the advocacy desired. In Excerpt 14.5 a critical study using interviews was conducted with African American mothers. Note how critical study concepts are used in describing the study.

ENTRY INTO THE FIELD

An important characteristic of qualitative research is that it is typically conducted in the *field*, on the participants' turf. These places are called *natural settings*, in which participants exhibit normal behavior. They may include schools, classrooms, universities, churches, homes, and other places where the participants spend their time in work or play. This natural characteristic is most important in ethnographic and observational studies. Even interviews and document analysis, though, are usually done in the field. An exception would be much focus group research, in which participants leave their field and come together at a central meeting location. If nothing else, researchers attempt to collect all qualitative data in a way that allows the participants to respond naturally and honestly.

Entry into the field, then, is a critical step in gathering data. Once the site is selected and mapped, access to the site is needed. Once access is approved, data collection can be planned and executed.

Research role: position in relation to participants

Complete outsider: detached and uninvolved

Complete insider: researcher as participant

In the field, those collecting data develop a **research role**, which establishes the position of the investigator and his or her relationships with others in the situation. At one extreme, the researcher is a **complete outsider**, totally detached from the naturally occurring behavior and activities of the participants. He or she essentially has no involvement in what occurs in the setting. The researcher is detached—coming in, collecting data, and then leaving. A **complete insider**, on the other hand, is a researcher who has an established role in the setting in which data are collected, engaging in genuine and natural participation. For example, to study the life of a college freshman, the complete insider would become a college student, directly experiencing everything other freshmen experience. Or, if a teacher in a school studies the learning styles of students in that school, the role would be that of a complete insider. This is essentially what anthropologists do in some of their studies—they become a member of the culture.

Most fieldworkers' roles are between these extremes, using what could be labeled *insider/outsider* or *partial participation*. These individuals participate to some extent in the setting, rather than just sit on the sidelines, but they are not full participants. This would occur, for example, if a researcher spends time in a school and actually does some teaching. Also, a parent volunteer could participate to some extent. Some level of researcher participation is good to help establish rapport with the participants. Such rapport helps participants continue their natural behavior and helps establish trust.

Qualitative researchers often change their role as data are collected. The nature and duration of different roles are determined in part by the situation. As situations change, roles may also change. When first entering a site, the researcher takes on primarily an outsider role; as the study progresses, more of an insider role could develop. This happens frequently with ethnographic studies. Resources and available time could also be a factor. In studies with a limited time frame, it is more difficult for a researcher to become an active participant.

	Complete Insider ←	Partial Participation	→ Complete Outsider
Examples			
Observation	Counselor observes students participating in small groups.	Researcher from outside the school helps counselors run small groups.	Researcher from outside the school observes students in small groups.
Interview	Principal interviews teachers in his/her school.	Researcher from outside the school helps teachers carry out some instruction.	Researcher from outside the school interviews teachers.
Document Review	Teacher reviews memorandums concerning formative assessment practices in his/her department.	Teacher from another department reviews memorandums.	Researchers from outside the school review memorandums.

FIGURE 14.1   Researcher Roles

Figure 14.1 illustrates different roles with examples, depending on the strategy used. These differences will be explored further as each strategy is considered.

The research role is really many roles as the fieldworker acquires language fluency with the participants, interacts to obtain data, establishes social relationships, and moves from role sets appropriate for one group (or person) to different role sets for other groups (or persons). The research role may vary with the degree and intensity of interaction. For example, in many ethnographic studies, case studies, and grounded theory approaches, the interactions are quite widespread but the researcher is less intrusive in collecting data. In phenomenological studies, the interaction is more intrusive, close, and personal. Unlike mechanical recording devices, fieldworkers are able to raise additional questions, check out hunches, and move deeper into the analysis of the phenomenon.

Valid data result when the events unfold naturally and the participants act in typical fashion in the reseacher's presence. Because the research role affects the type of data collected, the primary role and the various roles assumed in data collection are stated in the study.

Decisions regarding data collection strategies are usually revised after site selection, entry into the field, and initial mapping of the field. Initial plans are reviewed and refined. Information originally planned to be obtained by observation may be available primarily through interviewing; preliminary findings from interview data may have to be substantiated through researcher-constructed questionnaires or artifact analysis. Analysis of documents or unexpected events may suggest new directions for observing or interviewing. Choosing data collection strategies is a process of deciding among available alternatives for collection and corroboration of data and modifying one's decisions to capture the reality of the phenomenon (see Excerpt 14.6).

EXCERPT 14.6   Multiple Data Collection Strategies

Our year-long ethnography employed participant observation, formal and informal interviewing, and document review. . . . Participant observation in the school milieu allowed us to unobtrusively and systematically obtain data and interact socially with informants. . . . We visited the school at least once a week. On the days of our visits, we participated in the school, shadowing the principal, visiting classrooms, and talking to parents and staff in the halls. We observed teachers, students and staff during the regular course of the school day and during special events. (p. 161)

Source: From Zollers, N. J., Ramanathan, A. K., & Yu, M. (1999). The relationship between school culture and inclusion: How an inclusive culture supports inclusive education. *Qualitative Studies in Education, 12*(2), 157–174.

EXCERPT 14.7 Nonparticipant Observation

My role during the field observations was that of a non-participant observer. I did not participate in class activities, offer suggestions about how to provide instruction or interact with the students. I chose that form of observation because it allowed me to closely document each student's performance. I believed that if I acted as a participant observer, I might have engaged in activities that distracted me from my data collection or limited what I saw. Finally, I believed that if I interacted with the students, classmates, or teachers, I might have affected their decisions with text and influenced the validity and reliability of the study. (p. 135)

Source: From Hall, L. A. (2007). Understanding the silence: Struggling readers discuss decisions about reading expository text. *The Journal of Educational Research, 100*(3), 132–142.

OBSERVATIONS

Observation is a way for the researcher to see and hear what is occurring naturally in the research site. It is the mainstay of qualitative research, an essential data collection strategy for ethnographic studies, and used frequently with other types of qualitative studies. Often, observation is prolonged. By observing naturally occurring behavior over many hours or days, the researcher hopes to obtain a rich understanding of the phenomenon being studied. Typically, the nature of the observation is comprehensive in the sense that it is continuous and open to whatever may be significant. It facilitates a deep understanding of the context and the participants' behavior, which allows collection of a more complete set of data to reflect the importance of the effect of the context.

In observational studies, the researcher who is a complete insider is often called a *participant observer*. A **participant observer** is one who completes the observations as he or she takes part in activities as a regular member of the group. In Excerpt 14.7 the role is described as that of a "nonparticipant" observer, in contrast to a participant observer. Note too that the choice of role was influenced by the nature of the setting and participants.

Participant observer: researcher who both observes and takes part in group activities

Steps in Conducting Observations

The steps that are followed for doing qualitative observations are summarized in Figure 14.2. Once the site is selected, the researcher identifies an initial role to guide the first sets of observations. Entry to the site is completed, followed by relatively brief, initial, and fairly general observations of the field. Here the researcher "eases" into the site, building rapport and familiarity with the setting. With preliminary data collected, the researcher identifies in greater detail the specifics of more intense observations and adjusts his or her role as needed. At this point, more extensive, targeted observations are conducted. These observations will occur over time and will also change from the initial plan as needed. During and immediately after the observations, the researcher takes **field notes** to record not only what is seen and heard, but

Field notes: recordings of observations and reflections on them

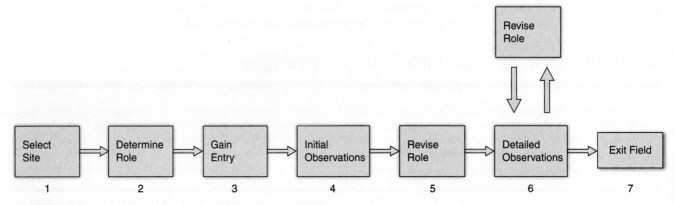

FIGURE 14.2 **Steps in Conducting Qualitative Observations**

also reflections on what has occurred. Following these observations, it may be necessary to change the role and conduct further observations. Field notes are then used as data that will be analyzed. Finally, the observer leaves the field.

Site Selection and Mapping the Field

Choosing a site is a negotiation process to obtain freedom of access to a site that is suitable for the research problems and feasible for the researcher's resources of time, mobility, and skills. The field researcher usually obtains information in advance through informal channels. Useful information includes the identities, power alignments, and interests of the principal actors; the general history, routines, and social system of the site; and the activities of the site. Information regarding the site and its potential suitability is obtained from a variety of sources: documents, present and prior associates, and public information. Much depends on the researcher's good judgment, timing, persistence, and tact in gathering information informally.

After the researcher identifies a possible site, contact is made with a person who can grant permission for access to the setting and participants. This person is called the **gatekeeper**. Some researchers make a formal contact after informal confirmation that the research proposal will be positively reviewed. Typically, researchers prepare a brief written statement that specifies the site, the participants and activities, the length of time for the entire study, and the research role. The statement also provides information about the researcher, the sponsor or organizational affiliation, and the general uses of the data, including the protection of the rights of human subjects. Formal authorization is essential for research ethics and for proceeding to enter the field and establish a research role. Once authorization has been granted, the researcher gives up leadership of the site to map the field, conduct purposeful sampling, and establish a research role.

Gatekeeper: gives access to the field

Mapping the Field Gaining entry into the field requires establishing good relations with all individuals at the research site. Research permission comes without a guarantee that the participants will behave naturally before an outsider who takes field notes or that the participants will share their perceptions, thoughts, and feelings with the observer. The inquirer's skill is reflected in whether the participants see the researcher as an interested, respectful, nonjudgmental observer who maintains confidentiality or as a rude, disruptive, critical observer who cannot be trusted. The researcher must attend to maintaining the trust and confidentiality of the participants constantly throughout the data collection period. At any time, the participants may decline to share their perceptions, feelings, and thoughts with the researcher.

Mapping the field is acquiring data on the social, spatial, and temporal relationships in the site to gain a sense of the total context. A *social map* notes the number and kinds of people, the organizational structure, and the activities people engage in. A *spatial map* notes the locations, the facilities, and the specialized services provided. A *temporal map* describes the rhythm of organizational life, the schedules, and the unwritten routines.

Mapping the field: aquiring data on social, spatial, and temporal structures

Qualitative Sampling at the Site Once researchers have initially mapped the field, they selectively choose the persons, situations, and events most likely to yield fruitful data about the evolving research questions. Initially, researchers search for information-rich informants, groups, places, and events from which to select subunits for more in-depth study. This is a purposeful sampling strategy of choosing small groups or individuals likely to be knowledgeable and informative about the phenomenon of interest. Furthermore, most researchers do not know in advance whether potentially information-rich cases will yield valid data until they have completed an interim data analysis. As new questions emerge during data collection, participant observers change (through additional qualitative sampling) the observation times and locations in order to collect valid data (see Excerpt 14.8).

Prolonged Data Collection

Data collection continues until the logical termination of a naturalistic event or until the situation changes so dramatically that the site is not relevant for the research focus. For instance, the natural boundary for data collection may be the entire three-week period of a state-sponsored summer school arts program. The natural boundary for a study of nursing clinical instruction will

EXCERPT 14.8   On-Site Participant Observer, Additional Qualitative Sampling

I observed the class over 30 times, interviewed the teachers both individually and together, and attended a number of related school events. I soon became aware that their collaboration was connected to school wide efforts to enhance sensitivity to diversity, this in response to a wave of neo-Nazi hate literature on campus. . . . I broadened my investigation, attending committee meetings related to diversity (the Multicultural Advisory Committee, the Multicultural Non-Sexist Committee, etc.) and asking questions about these efforts in interviews with administrators and teachers.

Data collection spanned the fall semester. . . . [I conducted] 19 hour-long interviews, observed 53 school events, gathered school and community artifacts, and maintained the fieldwork log and journal. (p. 308)

Source: From DiPardo, A. (2000). What a little hate literature will do: "Cultural Issues" and the emotional aspect of school change. *Anthropology and Education Quarterly, 37*(3), 306–332.

EXCERPT 14.9   Prolonged Field Time

During the first year of the study, my colleagues and I spent 50–70 days observing formal and informal settings in the eight schools, interviewing teachers and administrators and shadowing school leaders during the school day. In addition, we observed 105 predominantly second- and fifth-grade classroom lessons (involving 47 different teachers). . . . Each lesson in these schools was approximately 50 minutes long. (p. 291)

Source: From Diamond, J. B. (2007). Where the rubber meets the road: Rethinking the connection between high-stakes testing policy and classroom instruction. *Sociology of Education, 80,* 285–313.

be the length of the rotation, or 10 weeks. When the examined situation is no longer relevant to the research foci, the field residence terminates. Data collection might also end with the unexpected promotion or resignation of a key person, which, of course, would remove him or her from the site. See Excerpt 14.9 for an example of prolonged involvement.

Intensive Observation

Participant observation enables the researcher to obtain people's perceptions of events and processes expressed in their actions, feelings, thoughts, and beliefs. These perceptions or constructions take three forms: verbal, nonverbal, and tacit knowledge. It is crucial that the researcher acquire the particular linguistic patterns and language variations of the individuals observed to record and to interact with them. Field observation is an active process that includes *nonverbal cues*—facial expressions, gestures, tone of voice, body movements, and other unverbalized social interactions that suggest the subtle meanings of language. *Tacit knowledge* is personal, intuitive knowledge that is difficult or impossible for the individual to articulate; instead, the person demonstrates this knowledge by actions or by the use of created objects. Some cultures are called *expressive* because meanings are conveyed more in the nonverbal and tacit modes than in the verbal mode. Participants' stories, anecdotes, and myths—such as are found in the daily gossip in the teachers' lounge or among student groups in hallways—indicate the content of their world and how they perceive it.

Listening is also a demanding task; researchers listen with all their senses. Listening involves being able to take on the role of the other person, to see the world as the participant does. The fieldworker listens for the words *is* and *because*. *Is* reveals perceptions of things, people, events, and processes that appear real or factual to a person. *Because* reveals the *whys* and *wherefores*, the beliefs, thoughts, feelings, and values—in essence, the logic about the content of a person's perceptions. To listen intently requires the researcher to put aside his or her own thoughts and seek first those of the participants.

Salient Field Observations

Because the interactive social scene is too complex and too subtle to observe or record everything, researchers do *not* seek to capture everything that happens. Rather, they rely on the prolonged field residences to develop skills in deciding what should be included and what can be excluded. Researchers observe and record the phenomena salient to the foreshadowed problems, their broader conceptual frameworks, and the contextual features of the interactions. These elements explain

EXCERPT 14.10 Salient Field Observations

In its early phases, the study focused on how district leaders and school principals thought about and led districtwide reform in elementary literacy. As the district added mathematics to its agenda, the study shifted to include interviews and observations with principals, district leaders, and teachers surrounding ways in which they saw the mathematics work as both similar [to] and different from the literacy work. (p. 425)

Source: From Stein, M. K., & Nelson, B. S. (2003). Leadership content knowledge. *Educational Evaluation and Policy Analysis, 25*(4), 423–448.

the diversity of field notes cited in ethnographies despite the commonalities on the methodology (see Excerpt 14.10).

What do fieldworkers observe? Most record descriptive details about *who, what, where, how,* and *why* an activity or social scene occurred. This information then can be used to obtain more subtle information. See Table 14.1 for an observation grid. Although no one addresses all these questions at once in studying a group scene, the framework does indicate major areas of observation foci.

TABLE 14.1 Participant Observation Grid

Observation	Description
1. *Who* is in the group or scene?	How many people are present? What are their kinds or identities? How is membership in the group or scene acquired?
2. *What* is happening here?	What are the people in the group or scene doing and saying to one another?
a. *What* behaviors are repetitive and irregular?	In what events, activities, or routines are people engaged? How are activities organized, labeled, explained, and justified?
b. *How* do the people in the group behave toward one another?	How do people organize themselves or relate to one another? What statuses and roles are evident? Who makes what decisions for whom?
c. *What* is the content of their conversations?	What topics are common and rare? What languages do they use for verbal and nonverbal communication? What beliefs do the contents of their conversations illustrate? What formats and processes do the conversations follow? Who talks and who listens?
3. *Where* is the group or scene located?	What physical settings form their contexts? What natural resources and technologies are created or used? How does the group allocate and use space and physical objects? What sights, sounds, smells, tastes, and feelings are found in the group contexts?
4. *When* does the group meet and interact?	How often and how long are these meetings? How does the group conceptualize, use, and distribute time? How do participants view their past and future?
5. *How* do the identified elements interrelate—from either the participants' or the researcher's perspective?	How is stability maintained? How does change originate, and how is it managed? What rules, norms, or mores govern this social organization? How is this group related to other groups, organizations, and institutions?
6. *Why* does the group operate as it does?	What meanings do participants attribute to what they do? What symbols, traditions, values, and worldviews can be found in the group?

Recording Data

As noted earlier, data are recorded as field notes—observations of what occurs while the researcher is in the field. Field notes are dated and the context is identified. The notes are often filled with idiosyncratic abbreviations and are difficult for others to read without editing. Researchers record detailed descriptive fields that are not vague or judgmental. Following are hypothetical examples of vague notes contrasted to the actual field notes in a study of adult beginning readers (Boraks & Schumacher, 1981, pp. 76, 86):

Vague Notes	Descriptive Field Notes
1. Bea misreads *wood* for *would*.	"(OBS: Intensity of Bea is demonstrated by her heavy breathing, even swearing during the reading. There is little doubt she is trying hard.) Sometimes she cues herself, when reading: 'Would you believe I would not do it again,' Bea read *would* as *wood*. The tutor says would. Bea tries again to reread, then says, 'Oh, I missed the point, would he.'"
2. June retells few parts of a story and only the parts that relate to herself. She elaborates on these parts.	"June is a tall, thin, talkative woman. A staff member said she was referred by a treatment center and was considered mentally retarded and emotionally disturbed. When asked to tell a story from the text cue, she had to be prompted. For example, her story about an accident: *June:* 'My hair caught on fire.' *Tutor:* 'How did your hair catch fire? Can you tell me more?' *June:* 'I was smoking a cigarette and my lighter went up. I had the lighter close to my ear and it carried to my hair and my whole head was in flames.' *Tutor:* 'Can you tell me anything more?' *June:* 'And they told me I looked like a Christmas tree all lit up.'"

Reflex records: researcher comments and interpretations immediately after leaving the site

Reflex records, written immediately after leaving the site, synthesize the main interactions and scenes observed and, more important, assess the quality of the data and suggest questions and tentative interpretations. In both the field notes and reflex records, the tentative interpretations are separated from the actual observations (data). Sometimes these insights have the quality of free associations: They may cite analogies, use metaphors and similes, or note theories and literature that may be useful in subsequent data analysis.

Typically, part of the reflex records is the researcher's critical self-monitoring for potential biases. Often stated as "Self in Research" in the study, the researcher reports biographical sources of subjectivity and strategies to minimize the influence on data collection and analysis (see Excerpt 14.11).

EXCERPT 14.11   Reflex Notes

Rather than make a futile attempt to eliminate this subjectivity, Horvat engaged in a "formal systematic monitoring of self" throughout the course of the data collection which enabled her to manage her own subjectivity. . . . To this end she wrote self-reflective memos, shared manuscripts of analyzed data with study participants, and discussed emerging themes with colleagues familiar with the project.

Moreover we believe that our backgrounds shape our roles as researchers. Horvat is a married white woman in her early thirties who grew up in . . . the area. . . . She comes from a privileged background. . . . She attended a private secondary school similar to Hadley. The second author . . . is a Filipino male who was raised by immigrant parents. . . . Socioeconomically his upbringing is somewhat dissimilar from that of the majority of the informants in the study. . . . As research collaborators, we took advantage of our different backgrounds by actively engaging each other with challenges to possible biases. (p. 320)

Source: From Horvat, E. M., & Antonio, A. (1999). Hey, those shoes are out of uniform: African American girls in an elite high school and the importance of habitus. *Anthropology and Education Quarterly, 30*(3), 317–342.

IN-DEPTH INTERVIEWS

In-depth interviews use open-response questions to obtain data on participants' meanings—how individuals conceive of their world and how they explain or make sense of the important events in their lives. Interviewing may be the primary data collection strategy or a natural outgrowth of observation strategies. Field interviews vary in formats, specialized applications, question content, question sequence, and the logistics of conducting and recording interviews.

In-depth interviews:
extensive, long, probing

Types of Interviews and Specialized Applications

Qualitative interviews may take several forms: the informal conversational interview, the interview guide approach, and the standardized open-ended interview. These forms all vary in the degree of structure and planning and the comparability of responses in data analysis.

In the *informal conversation interview*, the questions emerge from the immediate context and are asked in the natural course of events; there is no predetermination of question topics or phrasing (see Excerpt 14.12). Informal conversations are an integral part of participant observation. In the *interview guide approach*, topics are selected in advance, but the researcher decides the sequence and wording of the questions during the interview (see Excerpt 14.13). Both the informal conversation and the interview guide approach are relatively conversational and situational. In the *standardized open-ended interview*, participants are asked the same questions in the same order, thus reducing interviewer flexibility. Furthermore, standardized wording of questions may constrain and limit the naturalness and relevancy of the response (see Table 14.2).

Selection of the interview strategy depends on the context and purpose: (1) to obtain the present perceptions of activities, roles, feelings, motivations, concerns, and thoughts; (2) to obtain future expectations or anticipated experiences; (3) to verify and extend information obtained from other sources; and/or (4) to verify or extend hunches and ideas developed by the participants or researcher. Specialized applications of the interview strategy are key informant interviews, career and life history interviews, elite interviews, and phenomenological interviews.

Key informant interviews are in-depth interviews of individuals who have special knowledge, status, or communication skills that they are willing to share with the researcher. They are usually chosen because they have access to observations unavailable to the ethnographer. They are often atypical individuals and must be selected carefully from among possible key informants.

Career and life history interviews, which elicit life narratives of individuals, are used by anthropologists to obtain data about a culture. Educational ethnographers use this interview technique to obtain career histories or narratives of professional lives. For example, when an examination

EXCERPT 14.12 Informal Conversation Interview

Finally, approximately 45 hours of spontaneous interactions among ESL students and their teacher or his assistants in the classroom, as well as interactions among ESL friendship groups inside and outside the school, were recorded on audiocassette. (p. 52)

Source: From Olivo, W. (2003). "Quit talking and learn English!": Conflicting language ideologies in an ESL classroom. *Anthropology and Education Quarterly, 34*(1), 50–71.

EXCERPT 14.13 Semistructured Interviews

Semistructured interviews of 1–2 hours in length were conducted following a predetermined interview guide. [Sexually assaulted] women were asked to describe the nature of the attack that they endured, their immediate reactions to the assault, and the negative effects that they continued to experience up to the time of the interview. (p. 174)

Source: From Regehr, C. R., Marziali, E., & Jansen, K. (1999). A qualitative analysis of strengths and vulnerabilities in sexually assaulted women. *Clinical Social Work Journal, 27*(2), 171–183.

TABLE 14.2 Types of Interviews

Type of Interview	Description
Informal conversation	Questions emerge from the immediate context. There are no predetermined topics or wording.
Interview guide	Topics are outlined in advance. The researcher decides the sequence and wording during the interview. Interview probes can increase comprehensiveness.
Standardized open-ended	The exact wording and sequence of questions are predetermined. Questions are completely open-ended.

of female secondary school teachers' notion of *career* differed from prior research about male teachers' notion of *career*, the researcher suggested that the concept of career should be extended to encompass professional women. Career and life history research of educators frequently requires two- to seven-hour interviews, and it may take considerable time to locate the informants if the shared social experience occurred years ago.

Elite interviews are a special application of interviewing that focus on persons considered to be influential, prominent, and well informed in an organization or a community. Elites are usually familiar with the overall view of the organization, its relations to other organizations, and especially the legal and financial structure of the organization. The researcher must rely on sponsorship, recommendations, and introductions to obtain appointments with elites. Frequently, elites prefer a more active interplay with the interviewer, and much variation will occur in the degree of interview control. Elites respond well to inquiries in broad areas of content and to provocative, intelligent questions that allow them freedom to use their knowledge. Elites often contribute insights and meaning because they are comfortable in the realm of ideas, policies, and generalizations.

A *phenomenological interview* is a specific type of in-depth interview used to study the meanings or essence of a lived experience among selected participants (see Excerpt 14.14). The strategy may be a single, long, comprehensive interview with each person or three separate interviews with each of the individuals. Phenomenological studies investigate what was experienced, how it was experienced, and, finally, the meanings that the interviewees assign to the experience. The experience studied is usually something that has affected the individual significantly, such as recalling a teenage pregnancy or childhood incest or acquiring a physical disability. Before interviewing, the researcher writes a full description of his or her own experience with the phenomenon of interest. Phenomenological interviews permit an explicit focus on the researcher's personal experience combined with the experiences of the interviewees. Educators frequently apply phenomenological interviewing in a general manner to obtain the multiple meanings of an experience.

Qualitative Questions, Probes, and Pauses

Question content varies because of different research purposes and problems, theoretical frameworks, and the selection of participants. Adopting questions from prior research will probably *not* produce valid interview data; however, the examination of different alternatives is essential

EXCERPT 14.14 Phenomenological Interviews

Following a phenomenological perspective, we want to understand the insider's viewpoint. . . . Semistructured interviews were conducted. The semistructured format guaranteed that we asked each principal open-ended questions where the researchers had little control over the principals' responses. All interviews were audio taped with participants' permission, and transcribed. Data analysis was ongoing and iterative. (p. 477)

Source: From Goldring, E., Crowson, R., Laird, D., & Berk, R. (2003). Transition leadership in a shifting policy environment. *Educational Evaluation and Policy Analysis, 25*(4), 473–488.

TABLE 14.3 Types of Interview Questions

Type	Description and Illustration
Experience/behavior	To elicit what a person does or has done—descriptions of experiences, behaviors, actions, activities during the ethnographer's absence: "If I had been here that day, what experiences would I see you having?"
Opinions/values	To elicit what the person thinks about his or her experiences, which can reveal a person's intentions, goals, and values: "What would you like to see happen or what do you believe about . . . ?"
Feelings	To elicit how the person reacts emotionally to his or her experiences: "Do you feel anxious, happy, afraid, intimidated, confident about . . . ?"
Knowledge	To elicit factual information the person has or what the person considers as factual: "Tell me what you know about . . ."
Sensory	To elicit the person's descriptions of what and how he or she sees, hears, touches, tastes, and smells in the world. "What does the counselor ask you when you walk into her office? How does she actually greet you?"
Background/demographic	To elicit the person's descriptions of himself or herself to aid the researcher in identifying and locating the person in relation to other people: Routine information on age, education, occupation, residence/mobility, and the like.

Note: Questions may be phrased in past, present, or future tense. See Patton (2002).

in interview script construction. Interview questions can focus on experiences or behaviors, opinions and values, feelings, knowledge, sensory perceptions, and the individual's background or demographic information (see Table 14.3). Each of these question topics can be phrased in a present, past, or future time frame.

Qualitative interviewing requires asking truly open-ended questions. Novice researchers often begin with the data they want to obtain and phrase questions in a manner that enables interviewees to infer the desired responses. These are *dichotomous-response questions*, which elicit yes/no answers or short phrases in response. When these occur, the interview assumes an interrogative rather than a conversational tone.

Qualitative in-depth interviews are noted more for their *probes* and *pauses* than for their particular question formats. Establishing trust, being genuine, maintaining eye contact, and conveying through phrasing, cadence, and voice tone that the researcher hears and connects with the person elicit more valid data than a rigid approach. After a series of interviews, researchers usually feel at ease in adjusting the interview to each person.

Techniques to ensure good qualitative questions include interview script critiques by experienced interviewers, interview guide field testing, and revision of initial questions for final phraseology (see Excerpt 14.15). Following are examples of initial phrasing with the field-test responses and the final phrasing of an interview guide (Schumacher, Esham, & Bauer, 1985, pp. 150–153):

EXCERPT 14.15 Interview Protocol Piloted

A 17-page [interview] protocol was piloted. The protocol consisted of six sections: general information, general university climate, mentor relationships, other faculty relationships, peer relationships, and influential factors. . . . [We] used items which emerged consistently from the literature that validated the experiences of African Americans in graduate programs. (p. 277)

Source: From Kea, C. D., Penny, J. M., & Bowman, L. J. (2003). The experiences of African American students in special education master's programs at traditionally white institutions. *Teacher Education and Special Education, 26*(4), 273–287.

Initial Dichotomous-Response Questions	Final Qualitative Questions
Q: Did teachers have difficulty in seminars? *R:* Yes.	*Q:* What did you expect teachers to have difficulties with in the seminar?
Q: Did teachers change? *R:* Some of them did.	*Q:* How did participation in the seminar affect the teachers?
Q: Did you learn anything in teaching the seminars? *R:* Yes.	*Q:* What did you learn about the teaching strategies you presented to this group?
Q: Did you identify any problems the planning committee should address? *R:* Yes.	*Q:* What would you like to see the planning committee do?

Although this is an extreme example of responses to initial dichotomous-response questions, it is obvious that the qualitative questions would (and did) generate different data, revealing multiple meanings of the seminars.

Dichotomous-response questions can be *leading questions*, which imply a preferred response. Such questions may frame a "devil's advocate" or a *presupposition question*, a query that implies a deliberate assumption designed to provoke a complex or elaborate response. In the examples that follow, those in the left column are dichotomous-response leading questions that were rephrased as presupposition leading questions in the right column (Schumacher, 1984, pp. 75–82):

Dichotomous-Response Leading Questions	Presupposition Leading Questions
Were inservice teachers enthusiastic about taking a class after school hours?	"What were the most difficult aspects [of the program] to implement?" (Presupposition: Many difficulties.)
Did you expect the teachers to be different from having participated in the seminars?	"How did you expect the teachers to be different from having participated in the seminars?" (Presupposition: There was an immediate change.)
Do you know of any unexpected results or spillover effects?	"How did the planning committee handle unanticipated opportunities?" (Presupposition: There were unexpected opportunities.)

Some researchers emphasize the general ineffectiveness of questions preceded with the interrogative *why*. *Why* questions are usually assumptive, frequently ambiguous, and often too abstract to elicit concrete data. In some situations, however, beginning with the interrogative *why* enables the researcher to elicit cause-and-effect processes or relationships that are potentially informative by revealing assumptions of the person.

Question Sequence

Effective interviewing depends on efficient probing and sequencing of questions, as suggested in these guidelines:

1. **Interview probes** elicit elaboration of detail, further explanations, and clarification of responses. Well-designed interview scripts are field tested to identify the placement and wording of probes necessary to adjust topics to the variation in individuals' responses. Broad questions are often phrased more specifically as probes. The researcher should talk less than the respondent; the cues the respondent needs can usually be reduced to a few words during the interview.

2. **Statements of the researcher's purpose and focus** are usually made at the outset. Assurances of protection of the person's identity and an overview of the possible discussion topics are also given at this time (see Excerpt 14.16). The information communicated is the importance of the data, the reasons for that importance, and the willingness of the interviewer to explain the

EXCERPT 14.16   Interview Protocol and Interviewee Language

The interview protocol with the Mexican mothers included open-ended questions to initiate the conversation and to explore the mothers' values and personal experiences in relation to the schools and their children's education. [Footnote 2: *I am a Puerto Rican native speaker of Spanish and . . . conducted the interviews in Spanish.*] I asked: Have you had an experience in which you had to make a decision about the education of your children and you did not know what to do? How did you solve the problem? If you were to advise Mexican mothers newly arrived in Chicago about the education of their children, what would you advise them? Do you find that it is more difficult to raise your children here or in Mexico? (p. 378)

Source: From Olmedo, I. M. (2003). Accommodation and resistance: Latinas struggle for their children's education. *Anthropology and Education Quarterly, 34*(4), 373–395.

EXCERPT 14.17   Semistructured Questions with Funneling

A semistructured schedule emerged from the work of Chipuer et al. (1999). . . . Consistent with a funneling technique questions were initially more general in nature and then gradually became more specific (Smith, 1995). An example of a more general question is "Tell me about your school community." These questions were used to probe the children's understanding of their school community using a conversational technique. . . . This style was utilized to minimize the power differential between the interviewer and child to minimize its effect on the process and subsequent outcome of interviewing [these] children. (p. 90)

Source: From Pooley, J. A., Breen, L., Pike, L. T., Cohen, L., & Drew, N. M. (2008). Critiquing the school community: A qualitative study of children's conceptualizations of their school. *International Journal of Qualitative Studies in Education 21*(2), 87–98.

purpose of the interview out of respect for the interviewee. Researchers provide explanations or shifts in the interview focus for informants to adapt their thinking along new areas.

3. **Order of questions** varies, although most researchers make choices that enable them to obtain adequate data for each question from the informant efficiently. Rigid sequencing may ensure comprehensiveness, but it may also produce both informant and interviewer fatigue and boredom. Generally, questions are grouped by topic, but in many instances, interviewers ignore the script sequence as people voluntarily elaborate on earlier replies.

4. **Demographic questions** may be spread throughout the interview or presented in the concluding remarks. Some researchers prefer to obtain this data at the beginning of the interview to establish rapport and focus attention.

5. **Complex, controversial, and difficult questions** are usually reserved for the middle or later periods in the interview, when the informant's interest has been aroused. Some interviewers prefer to begin interviews with descriptive, present-oriented questions and move to more complex issues of beliefs and explanations.

Often qualitative interviews will be semistructured, beginning with general questions and then probing with more specific questions. This type of questioning is illustrated in Excerpt 14.17.

Interview Logistics

Researchers choose interview topics and questions while planning the general logistics that influence an interview session. Five contingencies that affect an interview session are (1) *duration,* or length of session; (2) *number,* or how many separate interviews are required to obtain the data; (3) *setting,* or location of the interview; (4) *identity of the individuals* involved and the number present in the session; and (5) *informant styles,* or communication mores of the interviewees. Some research designs plan for periodically scheduled interviews; other designs require interviewing only after important events.

Interviewers vary their interactive styles. The interactive mode can be adversarial, emotionally neutral but cognitively sophisticated, or empathetic. Specific techniques can be used for pacing, keeping control of the interview, and using support and recognition appropriately.

EXCERPT 14.18 Interview Transcripts—Selected Quotations

[Principals' experiences with shared governance in their schools]

- "You always wonder if you're really needed. . . . A lot of times you start to question, Could this place just run without me? Then a parent calls, one who wouldn't talk with the teacher anymore, and I know I'm needed."
- "I don't think the teachers always realize how much they need me; sometimes they think that if I was out of the picture, they wouldn't have all these limitations. Now I have more of a community relations role, and I spend more time on community involvement. . . ."
- "I'm growing. Learning to become more of a partner. . . . You get a lot more accomplished working with a group than trying to work by yourself. . . ."
- "Personally and professionally, [shared governance] has given me a great sense of satisfaction." (pp. 83, 85)

Source: From Blase, J., & Blase, J. (1999). Shared governance principals: The inner experience. *NASSP Bulletin, 83*(606), 81–90.

Most qualitative interviewers prefer a conversational tone to indicate empathy and understanding while conveying acceptance to encourage elaboration of subtle and valid data.

Interview Records, Transcripts, and Elaborations

The primary data of qualitative interviews are verbatim accounts of what transpires in the interview session. Tape or digital recording the interview ensures completeness of the verbal interaction and provides material for reliability checks. These advantages are offset by possible respondent distrust and mechanical failure. The use of a tape recorder does *not* eliminate the need for taking notes to help reformulate questions and probes and to record nonverbal communication, which facilitates data analysis. In many situations, handwritten notes may be the best method of recording. Interviewer recording forces the interviewer to be attentive, can help pace the interview, and legitimizes the writing of research insights (i.e., beginning data analysis) during the interview. Neither notetaking nor tape recording, however, should interfere with the researcher's focusing his or her full attention on the person.

Immediately following the interview, the researcher completes and types the handwritten records or transcribes the tape. Typed drafts will need to be edited for transcriber/typist error and put into final form. The final record contains accurate verbatim data and the interviewer's notation of nonverbal communication with initial insights and comments to enhance the search for meaning. Interviewer notations and comments are usually identified by the interviewer's initials. The final form also includes the date, place, and informant identity or code. Excerpt 14.18 illustrates data obtained from in-depth interviews.

The researcher writes an *interview elaboration* of each interview session—self-reflections on his or her role and rapport, the interviewee's reactions, additional information, and extensions of interview meanings. This activity is a critical time for reflection and elaboration to establish quality control for valid data. Many initial ideas developed at this time are subsequently checked out through other data collection activities. As a rule of thumb, for every hour of interviewing, a researcher usually allows three hours of further work to produce the final record or transcript and the additional elaborations.

Practice identifying research questions and data collection approaches for a study involving observation. Go to MyEducationLab for Research at www.myeducationlab.com, click on the topic "Qualitative Data Collection," and select the Activities and Application activity titled "Collecting Data through Observation."

DOCUMENTS AND ARTIFACT COLLECTION

Artifact collection is a noninteractive strategy for obtaining qualitative data with little or no reciprocity between the researcher and the participant. It is less reactive than interactive strategies in that the researcher does not extract the evidence. During field residence in school settings, for example, the ethnographer must interact with individuals—even if only nonverbally—and become, to some degree, a participant. This is *not* an impediment if the researcher notes the consequences of this interactive role. In contrast, artifact collection strategies are noninteractive but may require imaginative fieldwork to locate relevant data.

TABLE 14.4 Documents and Artifact Collections

Type	Examples	Used For
Personal documents	Diaries	Personal perspective
	Personal letters	
	Anecdotal records	
Official documents	Internal papers	Informal or official perspective within the organization
	External communication	Official perspective for the public
	Student records and personnel files	Institutional perspective on a child or employee
	Statistical data (enumeration)	Suggests trends, raises questions, corroborates qualitative findings, describes rituals and values
Objects	Symbols	Suggests social meanings and values
	Objects	Suggests social meanings and values

Artifacts are tangible manifestations that describe people's experience, knowledge, actions, and values. Qualitative researchers studying current groups have adopted the techniques of historians who analyze documents and of archaeologists who examine objects created by ancient peoples.

Artifacts: documents and relics

Types of Artifacts

Artifacts of present-day groups and educational institutions may take three forms: personal documents, official documents, and objects (see Table 14.4).

Personal Documents   A personal document is any first-person narrative that describes an individual's actions, experiences, and beliefs. Personal documents include diaries, personal letters, and anecdotal records. These documents are usually discovered by the researcher, but sometimes, an ethnographer will ask a participant to make anecdotal records such as a log, a journal, notes on lesson plans, or a parent's development record of a child. Documents also can surface during an interview or participant observation.

Official Documents   Official documents are abundant in organizations and take many forms. Memos, minutes of meetings, working papers, and drafts of proposals are *informal* documents that provide an internal perspective of the organization. These documents describe functions and values and how various people define the organization. Internal documents can show the official chain of command and provide clues about leadership style and values. Documents used for *external communication* are those produced for public consumption: newsletters, program brochures, school board reports, public statements, and news releases. These documents suggest the official perspective on a topic, issue, or process. School board minutes from 1915 to 1980, for example, were an important source in the study of an innovative school 15 years after an ethnographic study, and the original job applications of the school staff provided demographic clues to locate these persons for interviews.

Existing archival and demographic collections may be located during field residence and are usually readily available to the researcher. Institutions also keep individual records on each student and employee; in order to gain access to these records, parental, student, or employee permission is usually required. *Student and personnel files* can become quite elaborate over time and may contain a variety of records and reports. A student's file may have records of testing, attendance, anecdotal comments from teachers, information from other agencies, and a family profile. Researchers use a file not so much for what it tells about the student but rather for what it suggests about the people who make the records. The file represents different perspectives (e.g., psychologists', teachers', counselors', administrators') on the student.

Statistical data can be demographic information about a group or population, dropout rates, achievement scores, number of acts of violence and suspension, attendance records, student eligibility lists for certain federal programs, the number of athletic injuries, and other numerical computations. Qualitative researchers use statistical data in several ways: (1) to suggest trends, (2) to propose new questions, and (3) to corroborate qualitative data. Qualitative researchers are more interested in what the statistics tell about the assumptions of the people who use and compile the data—that is, how statistics reveal people's thinking and commonsense understandings. Routinely produced numerical data describe the rituals and social values of an organization. Fieldworkers seldom take statistical data at face value but instead question the social process that produced the data and how the data have been used.

Objects *Objects* are created symbols and tangible entities that reveal social processes, meanings, and values. Examples of symbols are logos and mascots of school teams and clubs, such as athletic letters and trophies, posters, and award plaques. In a study of institutional collaboration, a symbolic record was a newly created logo that combined parts of the emblems of the university and of the school system to represent a new relationship between the two organizations. Interactive data revealed the difficulties surmounted to obtain official approval to use institutional emblems in a new form. The data obtained the following year described the use of the new logo. Qualitative researchers may investigate teachers' value of students' work by periodically checking bulletin board displays in elementary classrooms and corroborate this finding with other field data.

Analysis and Interpretation of Artifact Collections

Collecting and analyzing artifacts requires the use of these five strategies:

1. **Location of artifacts** begins with entering the field and continues for the duration of the study. Researchers anticipate the artifacts and proceed to locate and obtain documents and objects. Participants also offer documents and artifacts.
2. **Identification of artifacts** requires placing the artifact in retrievable form and cataloging for access. Documents are photocopied, and objects are photographed, filmed, or taped. Identifications are made by noting the category of artifact, a brief description of the artifact, a history of its use and owners/successors, and data on frequency and representativeness.
3. **Analysis of artifacts** requires descriptive data about the production or acquisition of the artifact by the group. Important questions concern who uses it, how it is used, where it is used, and the purpose of its use.
4. **Criticism of artifacts** is the determination of its authenticity and accuracy to identify the meanings of the artifact in the social setting.
5. **Interpretation of artifact meanings** must then be corroborated with observation and interview data. Artifact interpretation for subtle meanings depends on the social context and other data.

SUPPLEMENTARY TECHNIQUES

A technique fundamental to all qualitative research is *field observation*—direct eyewitness accounts of everyday social actions and settings that take the form of field notes. A variety of supplementary techniques are also employed in most studies. They are selected to help interpret, elaborate, and corroborate data obtained from participant observation, in-depth interviews, and documents and artifacts.

Supplementary techniques include visual techniques, analysis of nonverbal communication, special surveys, and focus groups. Each of these is a separate, specialized method with its own methodological literature. The qualitative researcher, however, selectively uses these techniques as a generalist to corroborate initial findings and to raise additional questions.

EXCERPT 14.19 Creating a Photographic Archive

Between 1996 and 2001, I visited 30 field sites throughout Eastern Europe that have been designated as memorial spaces to commemorate violent acts against Jews both during the war and immediately after. . . . I chose photography as a means of data gathering at the Holocaust sites. Photography facilitated the construction of a portable database that could be transferred from the emotion-laden research setting (the Holocaust site) to the comparatively safe haven of my office in the [United States]. . . . I videotaped the interior of concentration camps . . . and I took photographs of . . . displays and artifacts of women that I could analyze when I returned. (pp. 225, 227–228)

Source: From Jacobs, K. L. (2004). Women, genocide, and memory: The ethics of feminist ethnography in Holocaust research. *Gender and Society, 78*(2), 223–238.

Visual Techniques The use of films and photographs of a current social scene comprises visual techniques. Films are especially useful for validation, as they document nonverbal behavior and communication and can provide a permanent record. Films also can be problematic, however, in terms of interpretation. One must consider the technical intrusion, the selective lens view, and the expense. Excerpt 14.19 describes the use of photographs for documentation.

Analysis of Nonverbal Communication This technique is very important in most qualitative studies. The study of body motion and its messages is called *kinesics*. The recording of facial expressions, gestures, and movements can be triangulated with verbal data. An interviewer can trust participants' responses more if their body language is congruent with their verbal statements. It is important to note that many gestures have different meanings in different cultures.

Another issue is personal space. The study of the people's use of space and its relationship to culture is called *proxemics*. Studies have been conducted on the use of interpersonal space in public places and the identification of territorial customs of certain cultures. Qualitative researchers may note how others react to space and invasion of privacy (i.e., personal territory), for example, in assigned classroom seats, functioning in a crowded work area, and selecting seats in a formal meeting. Caution must be used in interpreting nonverbal communication, and interpretations should be corroborated with other data.

Special Surveys Survey instruments may take the forms of confirmation surveys, participant-constructed instruments, and even projective techniques using photographs, drawings, and games. Data on preservice teacher induction activities, obtained through nine months of participant observation, for example, could be corroborated with a questionnaire administered to principals and participant-constructed instruments administered during planning retreats and workshops.

Focus Groups A variation of an interview is the **focus group interviews** that are used to obtain a better understanding of a problem or an assessment of a problem, concern, new product, program, or idea. That is, a qualitatively sampled group of people is interviewed, rather than each person individually. By creating a social environment in which group members are stimulated by one another's perceptions and ideas, the researcher can increase the quality and richness of data through a more efficient strategy than one-on-one interviewing. Participant observers and in-depth interviewers use focus group interviewing as a confirmation technique. Case study research and critical studies may use focus groups as one of several techniques. Focus groups also can be the primary evidence-based technique used in evaluation and policy studies.

The group leader or facilitator should be skilled in both interviewing and group dynamics. The group typically consists of 8 to 12 persons who are relatively homogeneous but unknown to each other. For complex topics, smaller groups of five to seven are recommended. A typical session lasts for one and a half to two hours. Noticeable differences in education, income, prestige, authority, and other attributes can lead to less than optional group dynamics. The leader facilitates discussion by posing initial and periodic questions. Usually, an assistant observes body language, tape records the session, and assists in interpreting the data.

Ideally, the participants in focus groups will be homogeneous in characteristics that are related to the purpose of the research. For example, in researching faculty members' thinking

Focus group interview: involves a small, homogeneous group gathered to study or assess

EXCERPT 14.20   Focus Group Interview

The three student focus groups represented Praire High's diverse student population, but the groups selected by faculty and staff were stratified by race. The "at risk" group was comprised entirely of African American and newcomer Latino students . . . The "average" students focus group was equally divided among African American, Latino, and White students. The "honors" group was all White. (p. 7)

Source: From Patterson, J. A., Hale, D., & Stessman, M. (2007). Cultural contradictions and school leaving: A case study of an urban high school. *High School Journal, 91*(2), 1–16.

about a possible vision for their school, it would be better to place untenured professors and tenured professors in different groups rather than having a heterogeneous group including both tenured and untenured faculty. With common traits, members of each group are encouraged to think more deeply about the topic and are in a better position to question each other to arrive at a group result. Group interviews that consist of a series of standardized questions and recording of how each participant responded are not considered focus groups. In Excerpt 14.20, the researchers used three homogeneous groups of students.

The addition of supplementary techniques to a study can increase not only the validity of the initial findings but also the credibility of the entire study. However, most qualitative researchers are not formally trained in each supplementary method and should not use them exclusively for obtaining their data.

STANDARDS OF ADEQUACY FOR COLLECTING QUALITATIVE DATA

Many qualitative studies are published as books or reports rather than as journal articles. With the increasing acceptance of the methodology, more journals are publishing qualitative manuscripts. The studies published in journals may be highly synthesized, or only one of many findings is reported to fit the journal format. The typical journal article may also reduce the methodological procedures that would be explicit in the full study. Considering the following questions will aid the reader in reviewing such studies:

Entry into the Field

1. Did the foreshadowed research problem provide sufficient selection criteria for the site to be observed or suggest a profile for the individuals to be interviewed?
2. Is the research role that has been assumed clearly articulated and appropriate for the research questions?
3. How did the research role affect data collection? How does the researcher address her or his potential influence?

Observation

1. Is the rationale given for the qualitative sampling choices made during the fieldwork a reasonable one?
2. Was the length of data collection at the site detailed and reasonable?
3. Are descriptive field notes presented as data? Is there evidence of a reflex record?

In-Depth Interviewing

1. Are the qualitative sampling strategies used with obtained interviewees described and are they reasonable?
2. Was each person screened by the attribute or profile developed for the study before proceeding with the interview?
3. Was the type of interview selected appropriate for the research problem?
4. Do the data presented indicate the use of appropriate interview questions and probes?

To practice describing and identifying qualitative data collection techniques in studies, go to MyEducation-Lab for Research at www.myeducationlab.com and complete the Building Research Skills exercise "Collecting Data for a Qualitative Study." Click on the Topic "Qualitative Data Collection" and select "Collecting Data for a Qualitative Study."

Supplementary Techniques

1. Were the supplementary techniques employed appropriate for the study, and did they yield valid data?

CHAPTER SUMMARY

The following statements summarize the major characteristics of qualitative strategies:

1. Data collection involves multimethod strategies, but a primary method is selected for a given study, such as participant observation or in-depth interviewing.
2. Data collection strategies follow from the type of qualitative study: ethnographic, case study, phenomenological, grounded theory, or critical study.
3. The role of the researcher includes complete insider, complete outsider, and partial participant.
4. Entry into the field allows the researcher access to informative sites and participants.
5. Site selection is guided by the criteria implied in the foreshadowed problems and by concerns of suitability and feasibility.
6. The qualitative researcher first maps the field to obtain a sense of the total context and to ensure qualitative sampling, thereby producing a selection of information-rich informants and social scenes.
7. Observation involves conducting prolonged fieldwork to obtain and corroborate salient observations of different perspectives, which are recorded as field notes and reflex records.
8. In-depth interviews vary in terms of format, the kinds of questions posed, the question sequence, and interview logistics.
9. Interview records include field notes, tape recordings, transcripts, and interview elaborations.
10. Artifact collections include personal documents, official documents, and objects, all of which must be corroborated with other evidence.
11. Supplementary techniques include visual techniques, nonverbal communication records, specialized surveys, and focus groups.

APPLICATION PROBLEMS

1. To help make a decision about implementing a new science curriculum across the school district, a superintendent asked a researcher to observe how one elementary school implemented the new curriculum. The researcher easily established rapport with the science supervisor and the principal at that school and observed the teaching of five of the school's six teachers. The sixth teacher, who seemed to oppose the innovation, only related her experiences with the new curriculum. She skillfully managed to avoid teaching the curriculum when the ethnographer was present. What should the ethnographer do?
2. A researcher is living in a student dormitory for the purpose of studying how high school students attending a state summer school program develop creativity through photography. Although the researcher originally thought that observation of the photography classes and the evening program would be sufficient, she found that participating in student social activities during free time and extracurricular activities on the weekends influenced students' photographic productions. Should the researcher observe and record these informal happenings? Would student products (i.e., photographs) be a useful source of data?
3. During data collection, an adult education program director overhears negative remarks made by some adults about the program and sees the researcher recording them. The director explains to the researcher that such remarks, if made public, could create a poor image for the program and asks the researcher to destroy those particular field notes. How should the researcher handle this situation?
4. Rephrase the following interview guide questions to make them suitable qualitative questions, and then place the questions in a sequence that would be appropriate for eliciting teachers' perceptions regarding evaluation by their building principal.
   a. Do you think that teachers, as professionals, should be evaluated by their principal?
   b. Did your principal visit your classroom several times before he or she did your annual evaluation?
   c. Does your principal hold a conference with you after each visit?
   d. Is the principal's evaluation of your teaching fair?

ANSWERS TO APPLICATION PROBLEMS

1. The researcher can collect data by observations and casual conversations with the other teachers and school personnel. Rapport can be maintained with the sixth teacher by indicating interest without demanding that she use the curriculum in the researcher's presence. Sufficient data about the curriculum can be obtained from other sources. Further, for confidentiality of the data, the ethnographer should not tell other district officials of the teacher's reluctance.

2. A researcher tries to observe all the happenings, formal and informal, in the setting, although the major foci may be on the processes within the photography class and the evening programs. Thus, social activities, meals, and extracurricular activities are also potential sources of data. Student photographs are sources of data as well. Field notes of all observations and conversations should be made because the ethnographer will not know what is important at the time it occurs.

3. The researcher can remind the director of the agreement established at entry into the field—that all data are confidential and all names and places will be coded. Second, the ethnographer does not know what the remarks mean or if the remarks will be reported in the findings, which will reflect only patterns established through cross-checking with other sources. Third, the ethnographer could use the occasion to encourage the director to talk more about these adults so that the researcher could assess the trustworthiness of the adult testimony. The ethnographer could also use the occasion to have the director talk about her concerns regarding the public image of the adult education program.

4. The question may be as follows:
   a. How do you feel when your principal visits your class?
      Probe: Could you tell me why?
   b. Principals usually have a conference with teachers after observing their instruction. Can you tell me what these conferences are like?
   c. Do you think that your principal's evaluation of your teaching is fair?
      Probe: Why is it fair or unfair?
   d. How do you think evaluation relates to your idea of being a professional teacher?
      Probe: What type of evaluation would be most appropriate? Why?

Qualitative Data Analysis and Narrative Structure

From Chapter 15 of *Research in Education: Evidence-Based Inquiry*, 7/e. James H. McMillan. Sally Schumacher.

Qualitative Data Analysis and Narrative Structure

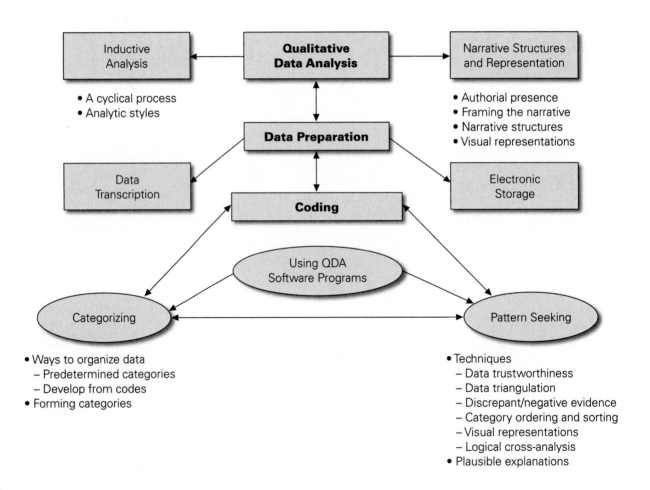

- Inductive Analysis
  - A cyclical process
  - Analytic styles

- Qualitative Data Analysis

- Narrative Structures and Representation
  - Authorial presence
  - Framing the narrative
  - Narrative structures
  - Visual representations

- Data Preparation

- Data Transcription

- Electronic Storage

- Coding

- Using QDA Software Programs

- Categorizing
  - Ways to organize data
    - Predetermined categories
    - Develop from codes
  - Forming categories

- Pattern Seeking
  - Techniques
    - Data trustworthiness
    - Data triangulation
    - Discrepant/negative evidence
    - Category ordering and sorting
    - Visual representations
    - Logical cross-analysis
  - Plausible explanations

KEY TERMS

inductive analysis	*in vivo* code	triangulation
crystallization	categories	visual representation
segment	recursive	
code	pattern	

WHAT YOU WILL LEARN

Study this chapter and you will:

- Know the steps that are taken to analyze qualitative data.
- Understand the differences between data segments, codes, and categories.
- Understand the constant, recursive nature of qualitative data analysis.
- Know how to organize data for analysis.
- Know how to code qualitative data.

- Know how to create categories from codes.
- Know how to create general patterns from categories.
- Understand the strengths and weaknesses of using software to help analyze qualitative data.

INDUCTIVE ANALYSIS: AN OVERVIEW

Qualitative data analysis is primarily an inductive process of organizing data into categories and identifying patterns and relationships among the categories. Although analytic styles vary among researchers, the general inductive processes and techniques that they use are universal.

In qualitative studies there is usually a great amount of data to be analyzed, summarized, and interpreted. Pages of field notes or interview transcripts must be critically examined and synthesized. One characteristic that distinguishes qualitative research from quantitative research is that the analysis is done *during data collection* as well as after all the data have been gathered. Analysis is an ongoing part of the study. Data collection and analysis are interwoven, influencing one another. This process is illustrated in Figure 15.1, with arrows pointing in both directions. It means that fieldwork leads to data but also that data may influence fieldwork. Following coding there may be a need for further data. In other words, the process is iterative and recursive, going back and forth between different stages of analysis.

Inductive analysis is the process through which qualitative researchers synthesize and make meaning from the data, starting with specific data and ending with categories and patterns. In this way, more general themes and conclusions emerge from the data rather than being imposed prior to data collection. Although computer programs can assist with this process, we want to emphasize that nothing takes the place of the researcher's inductive analysis of the raw data.

Inductive analysis: moving from specific data to general categories and patterns

The Process of Inductive Analysis

Qualitative analysis is a relatively systematic process of coding, categorizing, and interpreting data to provide explanations of a single phenomenon of interest. The general process of data analysis is represented in Figure 15.1 as having four overlapping phases. As researchers move to more abstract levels of data analysis, they constantly double-check and refine their analysis and interpretation. And unless certain elements are present in the data, the analysis will not proceed smoothly. Researchers negotiate permission to return to the field, if necessary, to seek additional data and to validate emerging patterns.

Most qualitative researchers have learned that there is no set of standard procedures for data analysis or for keeping track of analytical strategies. Making sense of the data depends largely on the researcher's intellectual rigor and tolerance for tentativeness of interpretation until the analysis is completed.

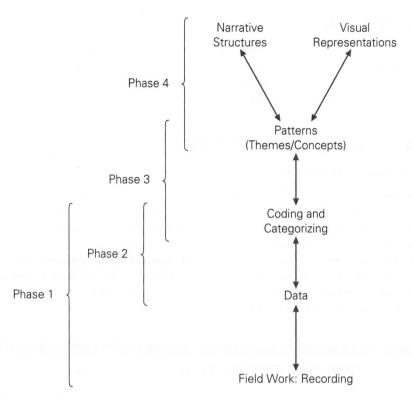

FIGURE 15.1 **General Process of Inductive Data Analysis**

Analytical Styles

Qualitative researchers develop analytical styles, but they rarely make explicit all of their data analysis strategies. Figure 15.2 shows a continuum of idealized analytic styles, from prefigured technical to emergent intuitive.

At the objectivist (i.e., left-hand) end of the continuum is the *technical and quasi-statistical style*, in which the researcher decides the categories in advance. The categories are thus predetermined and rigid. This style is often used in linguistic analyses. A *template analysis style* logically applies derived sets of codes and categories to the data; however, these classifications are frequently revised during data analysis. The initial codes or categories may be derived from the research questions, the interview guide, or the data, and this initial set may or may not be retained in the final analysis. The *editing analysis style* is less prefigured; the interpreter searches the data for parts to illustrate categories of meaning and writes memos during the process. Although there is little or no use of codes, the analyst must group descriptive memos that illuminate major interpretations. At the subjectivist (i.e., right-hand) end of the continuum is the *immersion/crystallization style*, in which the researcher collapses coding, categorizing, and pattern seeking into an extensive period of intuition-rich immersion in the data. The process of **crystallization** seeks to open the analyst to maximum experiences within the analytic style; the researcher may conduct intensive reflexive analyses simultaneously. This style often involves reliving each field experience and persistently questioning the data for subtle nuances of meaning. Patterns are identified by iterative reflection.

Crystallization: in-depth immersion in data

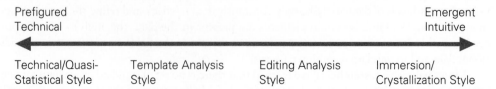

FIGURE 15.2 **Continuum of Analytic Styles**
Source: Adapted from Marshall & Rossman (1999, p. 151).

Most qualitative researchers lean more toward the interpretivist/subjectivist style than the technical/objectivist style. Even so, analyzing qualitative data is an eclectic activity. There is no one right way; data can be analyzed in any number of ways. Each analyst must find his or her own style of intellectual craftsmanship. And although there are no strict rules that must be followed mindlessly, the researcher is not allowed to be limitlessly inventive. Qualitative analysis should be done artfully, but it also demands a great deal of methodological knowledge and intellectual competence.

The technique of *comparing and contrasting* is used in practically all intellectual tasks during analysis. Categories are tentative in the beginning, and they remain flexible, not rigid. The goal is to identify similarities. Our discussion will illustrate a combination of template (i.e., use of codes and categories) and editing styles that many researchers use. The *template style* can be easily adapted to computer-assisted analysis. We have chosen to use more general qualitative data analysis terms. Several general principles guide most researchers.

DATA PREPARATION

The steps in qualitative analysis are illustrated in Figure 15.3. This figure shows the iterative, inductive process that researchers follow. We'll consider each of these steps in greater detail.

Data Organization

An essential early step in analysis is to organize the large amount of data so that coding is facilitated. Some believe that at this point it is best to take a break from the study, to let it lie and come back to it fresh (Bogdan & Biklen, 2007). By creating some distance between the data and researcher, the data "sink in" and may lead to insights about organization, coding, or categorization.

Organizing the data separates it into a few workable units. The vast amount of data can seem overwhelming, and creating these units gives you confidence that you can make sense of it!

Where does a researcher get ideas for organizing data? More than likely, the researcher has some initial ideas for organizing the data from either his or her work in the field or preplanning. There are five sources that researchers use to get started:

1. The research question and foreshadowed problems or subquestions
2. The research instrument, such as an interview guide
3. Themes, concepts, and categories used by other researchers
4. Prior knowledge of the researcher or personal experience
5. The data themselves

Using Predetermined Categories　It is often easiest to use predetermined categories, especially with an interview guide, or the research questions or topics about which you are quite knowledgeable. These categories tend to be general and fairly broad. There are several kinds

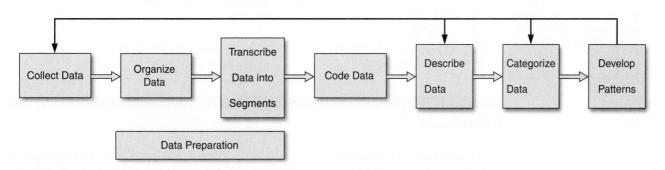

FIGURE 15.3　**Steps in Analyzing Qualitative Data**

(Bogdan & Biklin, 2007; Creswell, 2008; Patton, 2002) from general knowledge that can be readily adapted to a particular study:

1. **An evaluator** might use categories such as the setting and context, program description, administrator's expectations of the program, participants' perceptions of the program, critical incidents, processes, and perceived outcomes and unanticipated effects. The categories might also be those topics about which the person authorizing the evaluation desires information.
2. **A study of a school or classroom** might use the setting and context, the situation, participants' perspectives, participants' ways of thinking about people, objects and activities, processes, activities/events, instructional strategies, relationships, and social structure.
3. **A study of small-group meetings** might use the setting and context, purpose of the meeting, discussions, decisions, processes, relationships, and social structure.
4. **An interview study** might use the topics embedded in the questions asked. Each category is then divided into subcategories as the data are analyzed. For example, the category "Participants' perspectives" could contain subcategories for each different perspective or person. However, the use of predetermined categories provides only a starting point; they are provisionally applied and refined.

Most qualitative researchers implement a system for organizing the data. It could be by type of data collected (e.g., interview, observation, documents), site, participant, initial broad categories, date, or a combination of these. Some researchers still use index cards that can easily be arranged by meaningful characteristic. It may be possible to begin with an overall organizational approach and then make changes as data are collected. For example, suppose you have a set of taped transcriptions of counselors talking about how they use group counseling techniques with different types of students. An easy and obvious way to begin organizing would be by counselor. As the data are read and reread, it may be evident that organizing counselors by years of experience makes sense or that organizing by different grade levels is helpful.

Data Transcription

There are essentially three kinds of data in qualitative studies—notes taken during observation and interviewing, audiotape-recorded interviews, and visual images. Transcription is the process of taking these notes and other information and converting them into a format that will facilitate analysis. For field and interview notes, it is best to make brief summaries that can be expanded immediately after the observations or interview. We have had success scheduling a half hour to an hour that immediately follows the observation or interview. That provides an opportunity to fill in details and record the researcher's comments and insights. These handwritten notes are then typed for entry into a database or for manual review. Audiotape transcription of typed notes requires considerable time and resources. A general rule is that it takes two to four hours to transcribe one hour of audiotape, resulting in 20–30 single-spaced pages of written text.

Transcription will prepare the data for visual review. Here are some procedures to incorporate in the transcription so that the format and spacing facilitate the analysis process (Creswell, 2008):

- Use large margins for additional comments and coding.
- Leave space between interviewer questions and participant responses.
- Highlight as appropriate to show headers, questions, different participants, and comments.
- Type in words to record what was occurring during the session that could be important (e.g., [pause], [long silence], [cell phone call]).

Take a moment to practice reading text from a qualitative study and writing memos about it. Go to MyEducationLab for Research at www.myeducationlab.com. Click on the topic "Qualitative Research: Data Analysis and Interpretation" and select the Activities and Application activity titled "Reading and Memoing."

DATA CODING

Segment: data element that can be understood by itself

Data coding begins by identifying small pieces of data that stand alone. These data parts, called *segments*, divide the dataset. A data **segment** is text that is comprehensible by itself and contains one idea, episode, or piece of relevant information. Although a segment can be any size—a

TABLE 15.1 Types of Codes

Type	Description	Examples
Setting/Context	Describes the situation in which the research is conducted, both specific to the study and for larger cultural contexts. This includes participants' descriptions.	Low socioeconomic status school Morning classes After school Teacher-parent conference
Participants' Perspectives	The way participants communicate ideas about specific aspects of the setting.	Chapter tests Use of the computer Class rules
Participants' Thinking about People and Objects	The way participants use words to describe others and specific objects.	Students who are lazy Teachers who don't care Students who are immature
Process	Words and phrases that present sequences of events and changes or time.	Stages of teacher comfort with using technology Sequence of activities to promote applications to college
Activity	Regularly occurring behavior.	Lunch period Teacher meeting Lab work
Event	Specific activity occurring infrequently.	Called meeting for faculty Special program for students Election day
Relationship and Social Structures	How participants interact with each other, including groups, cliques, coalitions, enemies, bullies, and jocks.	Student athletes Student friendships Isolated students
Strategy	How participants accomplish things, including use of techniques, ploys, and tactics.	Student cheating Teacher system of classroom management

Source: Adapted from Bogdan and Bicklen (2007).

word, a sentence, a few lines of text, or several pages—it is typically one to three sentences. Segments are then analyzed to come up with *codes* so that each segment is labeled by at least one code (some segments have more than one code). A **code** is a name or a phrase that is used to provide meaning to the segment. Codes can be activities, quotations, relationships, context, participant perspectives, events, processes, and other actions or ideas (see Table 15.1). Labels that use participants' wording are called ***in vivo* codes**. *Emic* terms represent participants' views, coded as words, actions, and explanations that are distinctive to the setting or people. *Etic* terms provide a cross-cultural perspective from the researcher, showing the views, concepts, and social science ideas and phrases. The key in this process is to allow the data to suggest the codes. Most qualitative studies will include 30–50 initial codes.

Use the following steps to identify and refine data codes:

1. ***Get a sense of the whole.*** Read at least two datasets and write ideas about the data as you read. This will give you ideas about what the data segments will look like. It will also give you ideas about what to call different codes. Qualitative researchers need substantial uninterrupted periods of time to digest and think about the totality of the data. Keep a pad of paper handy to write notes and impressions.

2. ***Generate initial codes from the data.*** Read a segment and ask yourself What is this about? What word or words describe it? What were the participants doing or talking about? When done manually, each code is written in the margin (see Excerpt 15.1).

The following activity builds on the previous activity on writing memos. Go to MyEducationLab for Research at www.myeducationlab.com and practice dividing data into segments. Click on the topic "Qualitative Research: Data Analysis and Interpretation" and select the Activities and Application activity titled "Classifying Data."

Code: label for a segment

***In vivo* code:** labels consisting of participants' voices

EXCERPT 15.1 Initial Topics in Transcripts of Elementary School Principals' Practices of Grade Retention

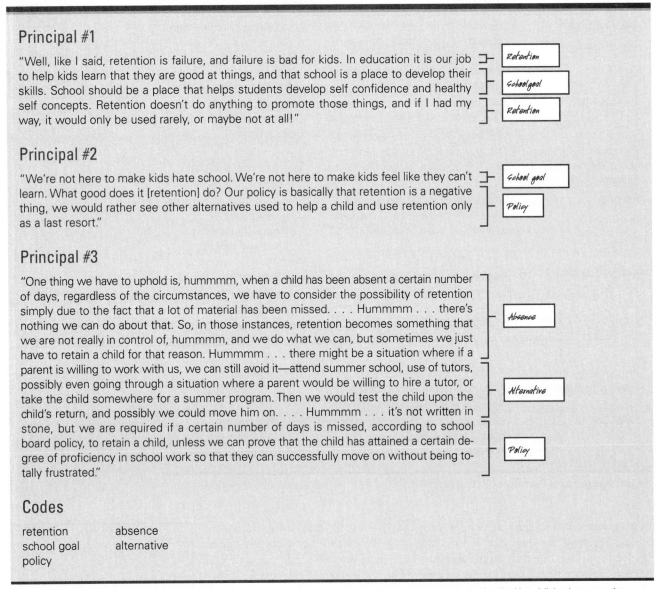

Principal #1

"Well, like I said, retention is failure, and failure is bad for kids. In education it is our job to help kids learn that they are good at things, and that school is a place to develop their skills. School should be a place that helps students develop self confidence and healthy self concepts. Retention doesn't do anything to promote those things, and if I had my way, it would only be used rarely, or maybe not at all!"

Retention
School goal
Retention

Principal #2

"We're not here to make kids hate school. We're not here to make kids feel like they can't learn. What good does it [retention] do? Our policy is basically that retention is a negative thing, we would rather see other alternatives used to help a child and use retention only as a last resort."

School goal
Policy

Principal #3

"One thing we have to uphold is, hummmm, when a child has been absent a certain number of days, regardless of the circumstances, we have to consider the possibility of retention simply due to the fact that a lot of material has been missed. . . . Hummmm . . . there's nothing we can do about that. So, in those instances, retention becomes something that we are not really in control of, hummmm, and we do what we can, but sometimes we just have to retain a child for that reason. Hummmm . . . there might be a situation where if a parent is willing to work with us, we can still avoid it—attend summer school, use of tutors, possibly even going through a situation where a parent would be willing to hire a tutor, or take the child somewhere for a summer program. Then we would test the child upon the child's return, and possibly we could move him on. . . . Hummmm . . . it's not written in stone, but we are required if a certain number of days is missed, according to school board policy, to retain a child, unless we can prove that the child has attained a certain degree of proficiency in school work so that they can successfully move on without being totally frustrated."

Absence
Alternative
Policy

Codes

retention	absence
school goal	alternative
policy	

Source: From Reed, J. S. (1991). Ethnographic study of the practice of grade retention in elementary schools. Unpublished manuscript.

3. **Compare codes for duplication.** Make a list of the codes, with one column for each dataset. Compare the codes for duplication and overlapping descriptions. See Figure 15.4 for a visual image of this process. Using a list of all the codes, check for duplication. Group similar codes and recode others to fit the description. At this point, some researchers write out a definition of the code. Make lists of the *major codes*, the *important codes*, and the *minor codes*.

4. **Try out your provisional coding.** Using unmarked copies of each data set you have worked with so far, apply your organizing system. See Excerpt 15.2 for an illustration of recoded transcripts. Notice that some codes, such as "School goal" and "Retention," have gained subcomponents and that some initial codes have become categories. Notice that the single code of "Policy" is now two codes, "School policy" and "School Board policy," because the content of each differs. You can now tell how well the descriptive code name corresponds to the data and whether some codes in the data were initially overlooked on the first reading.

5. **Continue to refine your coding system.** As you collect more data, your initial system will be refined and perhaps more codes will be added. How many codes are essential? Consider

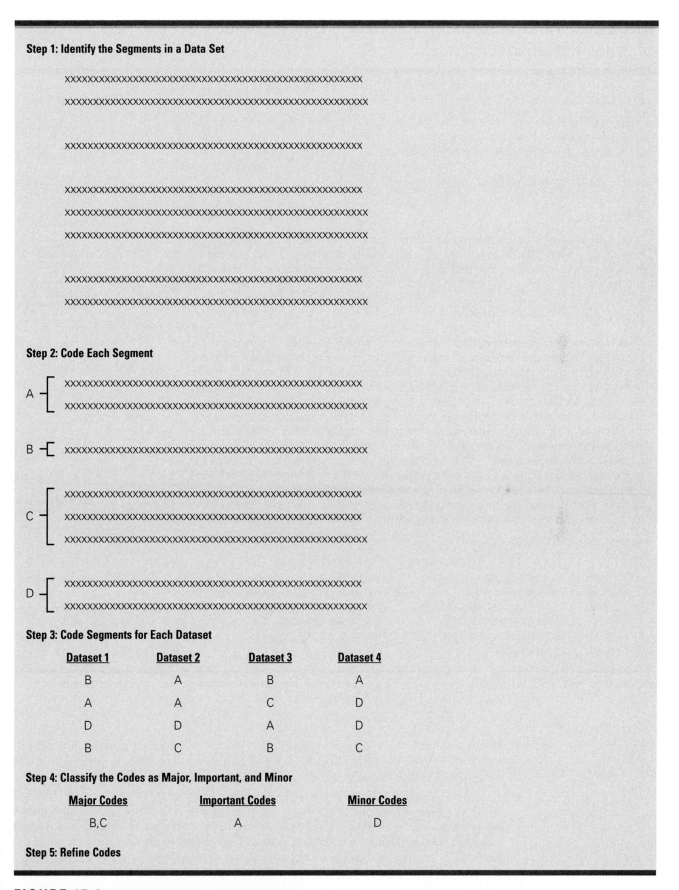

FIGURE 15.4 Steps in Developing and Applying Codes

EXCERPT 15.2 Recoded Transcripts of Elementary School Principals' Practices of Grade Retention

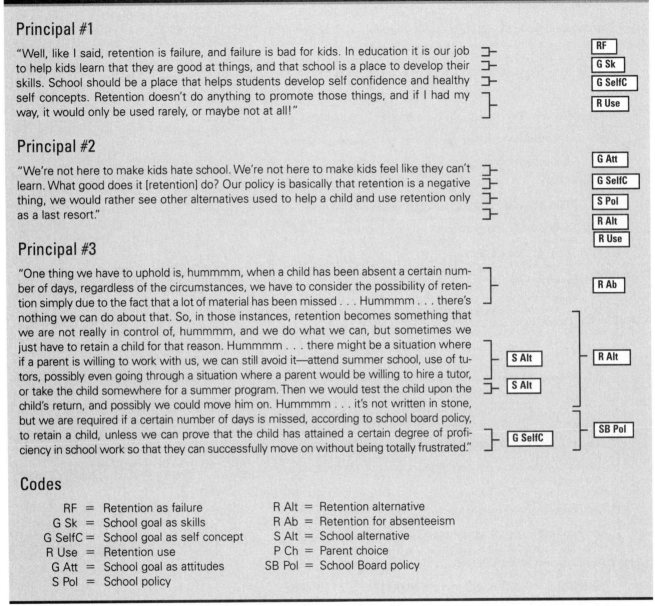

Principal #1

"Well, like I said, retention is failure, and failure is bad for kids. In education it is our job to help kids learn that they are good at things, and that school is a place to develop their skills. School should be a place that helps students develop self confidence and healthy self concepts. Retention doesn't do anything to promote those things, and if I had my way, it would only be used rarely, or maybe not at all!"

RF
G Sk
G SelfC
R Use

Principal #2

"We're not here to make kids hate school. We're not here to make kids feel like they can't learn. What good does it [retention] do? Our policy is basically that retention is a negative thing, we would rather see other alternatives used to help a child and use retention only as a last resort."

G Att
G SelfC
S Pol
R Alt
R Use

Principal #3

"One thing we have to uphold is, hummmm, when a child has been absent a certain number of days, regardless of the circumstances, we have to consider the possibility of retention simply due to the fact that a lot of material has been missed . . . Hummmm . . . there's nothing we can do about that. So, in those instances, retention becomes something that we are not really in control of, hummmm, and we do what we can, but sometimes we just have to retain a child for that reason. Hummmm . . . there might be a situation where if a parent is willing to work with us, we can still avoid it—attend summer school, use of tutors, possibly even going through a situation where a parent would be willing to hire a tutor, or take the child somewhere for a summer program. Then we would test the child upon the child's return, and possibly we could move him on. Hummmm . . . it's not written in stone, but we are required if a certain number of days is missed, according to school board policy, to retain a child, unless we can prove that the child has attained a certain degree of proficiency in school work so that they can successfully move on without being totally frustrated."

R Ab
S Alt
S Alt
R Alt
G SelfC
SB Pol

Codes

RF = Retention as failure
G Sk = School goal as skills
G SelfC = School goal as self concept
R Use = Retention use
G Att = School goal as attitudes
S Pol = School policy

R Alt = Retention alternative
R Ab = Retention for absenteeism
S Alt = School alternative
P Ch = Parent choice
SB Pol = School Board policy

Source: From Reed, J. S. (1991). Ethnographic study of the practice of grade retention in elementary schools. Unpublished manuscript.

that researchers have to remember all the codes as they later look for patterns. It is difficult to remember more than 25 to 35 individual codes, so they will probably be grouped later into categories. These coding steps are illustrated in Excerpt 15.3.

As another illustration of coded information, Figure 15.5 shows results from a study of student resilience conducted by one of the authors. Students who had been at risk but who subsequently did well in school were interviewed. This phenomenological study sought to describe how students view their condition and reasons for their success. The numbers in the margin correspond to different codes. Figure 15.6 shows many of the codes that were used when the data were analyzed.

Some of the most detailed coding procedures for qualitative research are found in phenomenological studies. Because the focus is on shared meaning and consciousness, the researcher must be very careful in creating codes and concepts that form the basis for descriptions and meanings.

EXCERPT 15.3 Data Coding

I based the data-coding processes on the strategy specified by Merriam (2001). First, I printed out all the raw data. Then, I chose a part of my field notes and read it. While reading the notes line by line, I wrote down—both in the notes and on a separate memo—my reflections and the names of the categories that I created. I added, modified, or deleted the names of the categories on the list during this process. I re-peated this coding process several times until the tempo-rary coding of these notes was satisfactory. Then, I moved to another part of the field notes, transcripts, or documents. I repeated the process but also compared the previous data set with the current list, adding new category names to the latter accordingly. I repeated the process over and over un-til I finished coding all of my data. (p. 69)

Source: From Chen, C. H. (2008). Why do teachers not practice what they believe regarding technology integration? *The Journal of Educational Research, 102*(1), 65–75.

Interviewer: Is that something the school sponsored?

(1) #2: Yeah, and they have a divorce group where the parents are divorced and you go in there and talk about how, why your parents divorced, and how you feel about it.

Interviewer: That was last year, too?

(1) #2 I kind of got my act straight this year so I don't really need to go. I've been in all kinds of group things since the third grade so I kind of got used to it. I learned how to put up with it. I wasn't in anything this year. I think both groups are very good.

Interviewer: They're still here? You just didn't feel like you needed to participate?

#2: I'm not sure if they're in here or not.

Interviewer: Of all the people that you know or that you see on TV or public figures, is there anybody that you admire, any one person?

(12)
(16) #2: My sister—she was not the best teenager but she's 22 now and I spend every weekend with her because when my mom comes from North Carolina she stays with my sister in the house. My sister lives with my grandpa because ever since my grandma died he has been by himself. She's got a baby and a boyfriend, she's not married but she is an excellent person to look at and say "Hey, I want to be like that." When my grandma was alive, she took care of her. She fed her, she cooked for her. My grandma had lost both of her legs. My sister took care of all her needs. She was wonderful. She's the partying type, she likes to have a good time, but she really gets serious when she wants to. If she wants to get something done she doesn't give up. That's the way she is. She likes to do what she says she is going to do. I think I like my sister the best.

Interviewer: Does she work?

(12)
(16) #2: No. She stays home and takes care of grandpa. At one time she was taking care of both grandpa and grandma. She takes care of her baby and her boyfriend. She's like the center of attention in the house. She's wonderful.

Interviewer: Back to the question skipped earlier. Do you have some advice or something to say to other kids that need to turn it around as to how they might turn it around? What do they need to do?
(10)
#2: They need to think about it, some of the good things they do and some of the bad things they do, and com-pare them. It's not worth it.

(17) Interviewer: Last question—If you had three wishes, what would you wish for?

(2) #2: That's so easy—Honor roll first, parents, and then college. I want to go to college.

Interviewer: If you want to college, what would you like to study?

(2) #2: Psychology. I'm serious.

FIGURE 15.5 Research Data from a Study of Resilience

Source: Materials used in preparation of McMillan, J. H., & Reed, D. (1994). Resilient at-risk students' views about why they succeed. *The Journal of At-Risk Issues, 1*(2), 27–33.

FIGURE 15.6 **Codes and Categories Used for a Study on Student Resilience**
Source: From McMillan, J. H., & Reed, D. (1994). Resilient at-risk students' views about why they succeed. *The Journal of At-Risk Issues, 1*(2), 27–33.

Typically, the analysis begins with a description of the researcher's experiences with the phenomena. Next, statements that show how the participants are experiencing the phenomenon are identified in the interview. Meaningful units are then formed from the statements, using verbatim language from the participants as illustrations. Descriptions of what was experienced are separated from how it was experienced. The researcher may reflect on his or her own experiences to integrate them with those of the participants. Finally, an overall description of meaning of the experience is constructed. Individual as well as composite descriptions are written to show how the experiences fit with the meaning derived. Like ethnographies and case studies, the transcription, coding, organizing, and analyzing of the data may seem overwhelming at first.

FORMING CATEGORIES

Categories: grouped codes

Categories (or *themes*) are entities comprised of grouped codes. A single category is used to give meaning to codes that are combined. The categories represent major ideas that are used to describe the meaning of similarly coded data. Codes can be used in more than one category. For instance, in the study of student resilience the code "home conditions" was used in two categories—"outside of school" and "family" (see Figure 15.6). The complete set of categories in this study included these six:

1. Opinions about school
2. Personality
3. Current activities
4. Family
5. Outside of school
6. Goals

Categories represent the first level of induction by the researcher. Similar codes are put together to form the category, which is then labeled to capture the essence of the codes. Typically, qualitative studies will have between four and eight categories. Not all of the categories have the same level of importance. Some categories are coded "major" or "primary" because they represent a main idea. Others may be labeled "minor," "expected," or "outlier," depending on the type of information provided.

The process of identifying categories can be arduous. Before the development of computers, it was not unusual to have each coded piece of data written on cards, spread out, and then sorted into piles according to different categories. Imagine a room with five or six piles, each with several codes and primary data elements. This could be called the *dining room table* method of analysis. Now, of course, we have computer programs that help make the process more manageable, but those of us who used the dining room table approach still believe that this gives the researcher a familiarity with the data that may not be provided by electronic analysis. The sorting and rearranging that are needed are more controlled by the researcher when done by hand and hard copy.

When the researcher is engaged in forming categories, a very important process occurs. This could be described as *recursive*. The **recursive** process involving the repeated application of a category to fit codes and data segments. This could be called *constant comparison*, in which the researcher is continually searching for both supporting and contrary evidence about the meaning of the category. The recursive process is usually reported as part of data analysis. This is illustrated in Excerpts 15.4 and 15.5.

Recursive: occurring repeatedly

EXCERPT 15.4 Recursive Analysis

Moreover, iterative analytical methods were used to identify themes in the participant narratives. I fully transcribed each interview and read through the transcripts several times to pinpoint salient themes, patterns and relationships . . . I coded the transcripts while reading them, and I repeatedly reevaluated my coding scheme. I looked for consistency and contradictions with and across the mothers' narratives. Furthermore, I drafted three sets of memos that captured my preliminary analysis of the individual, school-based and cross-participant findings. Once I was confident of the trustworthiness and usefulness of my coding scheme, I clustered my data by code and did a final review. Inductive analytical methods were used to confirm or disconfirm the salience of my theoretical framework. (p. 498)

Source: From Copper, C. W. (2008). School choice as "motherwork": Valuing African-American women's educational advocacy and resistance. *International Journal of Qualitative Studies in Education, 20*(5), 491–512.

EXCERPT 15.5 Recoding and Forming Categories

My coding of participants' statements went through many iterations. For example, at various times each team member spoke of personal relationships, professional development and mutual improvement of benefits of teaming. Each assessed his or her own ability to work closely with a colleague. . . . [These] initially were given general codes with tentative categories assigned to them and were progressively grouped and regrouped until a more specific category was established. For instance, the final categories of "teacher choice" and "influences on practice" were derived from analysis of earlier designations, such as "teachers' self-perceptions" and "teachers as risk takers," which I evaluated as either too vague or as reflecting too much of my own preferences. (p. 70)

Source: From Murata, R. (2002). What does team teaching mean? A case study of interdisciplinary teaming. *Journal of Educational Research, 96*(2), 67–77.

DISCOVERING PATTERNS

Pattern: relationships among
categories

The ultimate goal of qualitative research is to make general statements about relationships among categories by discovering patterns in the data. A **pattern** is a relationship among categories. Pattern seeking means examining the data in as many ways as possible. In searching for patterns, researchers try to understand the complex links among various aspects of people's situations, mental processes, beliefs, and actions.

Pattern seeking starts with the researcher's informed hunches about the relationships in the data. It demands a thorough search through the data, challenging each major hunch by looking for negative evidence and alternative explanations. The researcher then shifts to a deductive mode of thinking—moving back and forth among codes, categories, and tentative patterns for confirmation. The researcher determines how well the data illuminate the research problem and which data are central.

Patterns can take different forms and levels of abstraction, depending on the purpose and use of the study. Patterns also relate to the conceptual framework selected for the inquiry. The major pattern(s) serves as the framework for reporting the findings and organizing the reports. This process is schematically represented in Figure 15.7. Notice that the number of segments (the x's) that a code represents varies. Some codes fit into more than one category, and other codes are not central to the research problem. Further, a category can fit into more than one pattern. This elasticity of code and category meanings allows *patterns of meanings* to emerge. The meanings of categories and patterns depend on both the content of each and the comparison made with that content—other categories or other patterns.

The process is usually a circular one of returning to the data to validate each pattern and then modifying or recasting the idea as part of a larger abstraction. Although some of the process is tedious and time-consuming, it also requires making carefully considered judgments about what is really important and meaningful in the data.

Techniques of Pattern Seeking

The following techniques facilitate pattern seeking. Researchers must select those that illuminate the patterns. Qualitative researchers are obligated to monitor and report their own analytical techniques and processes as fully as possible.

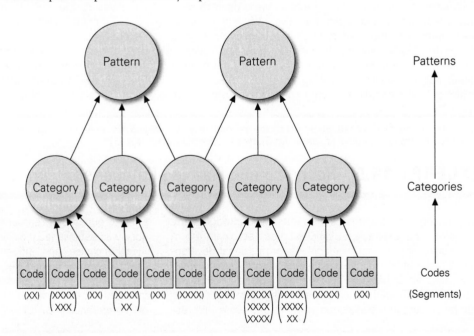

FIGURE 15.7   **Building Patterns of Meaning**

Source: Adapted from A. Vierra and J. Pollock. (1992). *Reading educational research* (2nd ed). Scottsdale, AZ: Gorsuch Scarisbrick, p. 262.

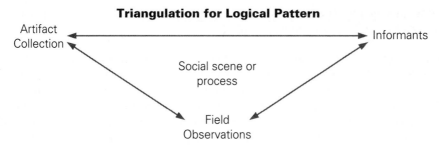

Triangulation for Logical Pattern

Artifact Collection — Informants

Social scene or process

Field Observations

FIGURE 15.8 Triangulation

Gauging Data Trustworthiness   Although gauging the trustworthiness of data is done at the time of each field experience and in reflex records, it is also important during pattern seeking. The researcher should select trustworthy evidence for pattern seeking by qualitatively assessing solicited versus unsolicited data, subtle influences among the people present in the setting, specific versus vague statements, and the accuracy of the sources (e.g., an observant person, a thoughtful person, an emotional person, a biased person). Selecting trustworthy data also involves an awareness of the researcher's assumptions, predispositions, and influence on the social situation.

Using Triangulation   Researchers use **triangulation**, which is the cross-validation among data sources, data collection strategies, time periods, and theoretical schemes. To find regularities in the data, the researcher compares different sources, situations, and methods to see whether the same pattern keeps recurring. A theme of *institutional collaboration*, for example, could be cross-checked by comparing data found in artifact collections (minutes, memos, official brochures, letters), informant interviews (project co-directors, teachers, principals), and field observations of project meetings. Figure 15.8 illustrates cross-method triangulation.

> **Triangulation:** convergence of findings

Researchers sense, however, that even though they directly observed, heard, or recorded only one instance, for some types of analysis a single incident is meaningful.

Evaluating Discrepant and Negative Evidence   Researchers actively search for discrepant and negative evidence that will modify or refute a pattern. Negative evidence is a situation, a social scene, or a participant's views that contradicts a pattern. In other words, there are two patterns rather than one. Discrepant evidence presents a variation of a pattern (see Excerpt 15.6). These exceptions are very useful because they make the original pattern more distinctive. For example, a pattern might be that a particular action occurs in almost all situations.

Ordering Categories for Patterns   Ordering categories can be done in several ways to discover patterns. One way is to place the categories in order of occurrence. Researchers might ask, Which situation or action came first? Did more than one belief accompany the event? What was the consequence or outcome? Arranging the categories in a sequence is useful for a process analysis to identify changes from one time to another time. A second way is to enlarge, combine, subsume, and create new categories that make empirical and logical sense—that is, they

EXCERPT 15.6   Analysis of Discrepant Data

Not surprisingly, gender issues were sometimes more salient for Native women whose pueblos prohibited or limited severely the participation of women in the political lives of their tribes than they were for individuals such as Kari, who experienced few, if any, obstacles as women. For example, contrast Kari's statement, above, with that of Karen, a pueblo activist: "I'm a woman caught between two worlds. I'm a professional outside but traditional and, I hate to use the word, submissive at home. For example, letting the men eat first, keeping your eyes down." (p. 603)

Source: From Prindeville, D-M. (2003). Identity and the politics of American Indian and Hispanic women leaders. *Gender and Society,* 77(4), 591–608.

go together in meaning. The logical sense in pattern seeking is that the meaning of a category is influenced by its relationship to a pattern.

Sorting Categories for Patterns   Researchers group categories in several ways to identify meanings. In a study of principals and unsatisfactory teachers, for instance, the category "Unsatisfactory teachers" was sorted first by types of unsatisfactory teachers and then by types of resolution. Each category was rearranged to see whether there was a pattern between type of unsatisfactory teacher and type of resolution. When no pattern was found, another category—"Methods of identification of unsatisfactory teachers"—was sorted with types of resolution. This sorting led to a pattern that related methods of unsatisfactory teacher identification to types of resolution.

Visual representation: organized assembly of information

Constructing Visual Representations   Researchers construct a **visual representation**, an organized assembly of information, such as figures, matrices, integrative diagrams, and flowcharts, which assist in the analysis. Most researchers are careful *not* to reach hasty closure in building integrative diagrams. Descriptive contextual data must accompany diagrams. Visual representations are *devices*; they are not reality per se. Diagrams assist researchers in moving to a more abstract analysis by allowing them to ask different questions about the data. Researchers attempt to balance respect for the complexity of reality with the need to simplify for analytical and communication purposes. Integrative diagrams, once finalized, serve as a visual representation of the entire study and are presented in the report.

Doing Logical Cross-Analyses   Usually presented in matrix format, categories are crossed with one another to generate new insights for further data analysis. These cross-categories reveal logical discrepancies in the already analyzed data and suggest areas in which data and patterns might be logically uncovered. However, the researcher should *not* allow these matrices to lead the analysis but rather should use them to generate hunches for further pattern seeking.

Plausibility of Patterns

As researchers build their categories and search for patterns, they need to search for other plausible explanations for links among categories. Alternative explanations always exist, but they may not be reasonably supported by the data. A pattern becomes an explanation only when alternative patterns do not offer reasonable explanations central to the research problem. Plausibility is a matter of judgment about the quality of the data within the design limitations. Plausibility is demonstrated by the presentation of the data and the rigor of the analysis.

Returning to our study of resilience, the final set of patterns that were developed is shown in Figure 15.9 as a visual diagram. You can see that there is a sequence that explains how the categories were related.

Working with the same transcript as in the previous activity, practice interpreting data by identifying patterns. Go to MyEducationLab for Research at www.myeducationlab.com. Click on the topic "Qualitative Research: Data Analysis and Interpretation" and select the Activities and Application activity titled "Data Interpretation."

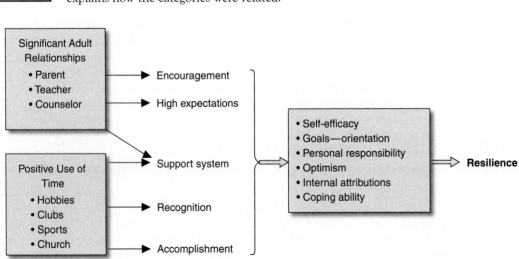

FIGURE 15.9   **Study of Resilience General Patterns**

EXCERPT 15.7   Case Study Data Analysis

To ensure validity, we worked separately and collaboratively, using an interpretive method coding (Ericson, 1986) to ascertain confirming and disconfirming evidence of assertions arising from our data sources. We independently read and coded the data following the open-coding techniques outlined by Strauss and Corbin (1994). All the texts were examined multiple times, looking for evidence of emotional struggle and navigation in each particular event taking place in Sara's classroom as well as in the events that took place as a whole across the semester and in Sara's reflections. Simultaneously, we looked for the ways emotions were operating in reciprocal transaction, being shaped by and shaping her practice and relationships. Building on this analysis, we interpreted the data by developing themes, categories, and tentative hypotheses. The themes that were developed in both of our analyses were explored in greater depth and were put into broader categories. The overarching themes and categories began to illustrate various aspects of the emotions related to the development of Sara's teaching practices for social justice. (pp. 291–292)

Source: From Chubbuck, S. M., & Zembylas, M. (2008). The emotional ambivalence of socially just teaching: A case study of a novice urban schoolteacher. *American Educational Research Journal, 45*(2), 274–318.

Excerpt 15.7 is taken from the analysis section of a case study of a teacher in an urban school district. Drawing from feminist and critical theory, the researcher examined emotional perspectives of teaching. Note how the sequence of analyzing codes, categories, and then general patterns was executed.

ELECTRONIC QUALITATIVE DATA ANALYSIS

Computer software programs have been available to facilitate qualitative data storage and analyses for at least 20 years, and currently there are at least 30 different software choices (for a listing, with brief descriptions, go to http://www.eval.org/Resources/QDA/htm, retrieved October, 20, 2008). Typically referred to as QDA (qualitative data analysis), these programs have become increasingly easy to use as well as more sophisticated. The most popular software products for educational researchers include the following:

- MaxQDA   http://www.Maxqda.com
- ATLAS.ti   http://www.atlasti.com
- Ethnograph   http://www.qualisresearch.com
- Nvivo   http://www.qsrinternaltional.com
- HyperRESEARCH http://www.researchware.com

An excellent source for comparing the programs is a book by Ann Lewins and Christina Silver, *Using Software for Qualitative Data Analysis: A Step-by-Step Guide* (2007). The comparisons are also available on the Internet as the CAQDAS Networking Project (http://caqdas.soc.surrey.ac.uk/). If you are thinking about using software, it is best to check the company websites; recommendations from others who have used it will also be very helpful. Software is constantly being updated.

The primary advantage of using software is that it is much easier to work with mounds of data—obtained with hundreds of pages of text. It is easier to store and organize large amounts of data than hard copy. Software also makes it easier to quickly search for and locate segments of data. This is similar to a content analysis, where single words and phrases can be located. Once data are coded, it is easy to pull all data segments for each code and each of the codes for categories. Retrieval of data is relatively easy, without the need to search pages and pages of text. Qualitative software is able to analyze and combine text, audio, and visual elements as well as different codes. Some software programs are also able to test propositions and hypotheses about the meaning of the data (patterns). In addition, some programs allow mapping of relationships among codes and categories, using visual diagrams to show the relationships.

On the negative side, learning to use the software may take considerable time. There is a temptation when using software to allow the computer to manage data analysis. These programs can assist in analysis, but the researcher still must do the coding and categorization. Too much reliance on the software may create an unhealthy distance between the researcher and the data. Finally, software programs may not have all the capabilities that are needed, so supplemental hands-on procedures are required.

NARRATIVE STRUCTURE AND REPRESENTATION

A hallmark of most qualitative research is the narrative presentation of evidence and the diversity of visual representations of data. Data are presented as quotations of participants' actual language for an evidence-based inquiry. However, not all data are reported in a single study, nor are they necessarily reported in the same format to all readers. There are four potential audiences: (1) academics, (2) participants in the study, (3) policy-makers, and (4) members of the general public. The narrative structure used will depend on the purpose of the research, the qualitative design, and the audience.

Qualitative authors recommend using an overall structure that does not blindly follow the standard quantitative format (Richardson, 1998). Methods can be called *procedures* or *strategies*, and results can be called *findings*. Subheadings often use participants' expressive language rather than social science rhetoric. The writing style might be personal, readable, and applicable for a broad audience, and the level of detail may make the narrative seem real and alive, carrying the reader directly into the world of the participants.

Audience and Authorial Presence

To write a report, the researcher must address issues such as encoding for specific audiences, preparing visual representations of findings, and acknowledging the author's presence (Creswell, 2007). *Encoding* is the use of literary devices to shape a report for a particular audience. For academic audiences and publications, it is appropriate to include the prominent display of the author's academic credentials; to include references, footnotes, and methodology sections; and to use academic metaphors. For moral/political audiences, it is appropriate to use highly connotated "in-group" words (e.g., *woman, women, feminist* in feminist writing), to provide the moral or active credentials of the author, and to use empowerment metaphors. For participants and policy-makers, there should be less literature and theory, an abbreviated methodological overview, and a detailed description of the practice, addressing practical concerns or issues and the use of commonsense metaphors.

The author's presence is acknowledged through various literary devices. First, the researcher's role is described. In addition, the author's presence can be acknowledged with reflective footnotes, interpretative commentaries, or an epilogue. In some critical studies, the researcher's political lens is usually stated in the introductory section.

Two aspects of a study are presented as data: the context and the quotations of participants. The researcher's task is to arrange these statements in a logical manner, making participants' meanings unmistakable to the reader.

Framing the Narrative and Presenting the Participants' Language

In most studies, framing the narrative is essential for readers to understand the study and for extending the findings to future research studies and practices. A study can be framed in several ways: (1) in the naturalistic context, (2) in the phenomenological experience, (3) by using selected theories, or (4) by using a political orientation. The context of a study is the situational description of people and events in which the phenomenon of interest occurred. How the researcher frames a given study varies with the choice of qualitative design: ethnography, phenomenology, case study, grounded theory, or critical study.

In ethnographic studies and case studies, the context is the setting, the participants, and the data collection time period. The holistic context in case study research is considered an important finding; the naturalistic setting is described and used to identify contextual elements that influence the cultural life, or the case. In a study of the first year of operation of an innovative school, for example, the context is the floorplan and details of the new school building, the entirely new faculty, and the faculty mandate for the academic year. Part of the context is also how the innovative school fits into larger systems—that is, the school system, the community, and the state education system.

The frame for a phenomenological study is the type of experience that has happened—for instance, being a working single parent, a female administrator who has voluntarily resigned, or a child who has experienced the death of a sibling. The naturalistic situation is used in descriptions of *what* happened and *how* the experience occurred.

Whereas the naturalistic context is very important in ethnographic and case study research, it is less important in grounded theory studies. In grounded theory, the identification of the theories that frame the study is crucial, and a brief description of the natural context (e.g., hospital wards, school playgrounds, cancer support groups) is part of the methodology. Because of the different types of critical studies, the narration may be framed by the naturalistic context or by a theoretical or political frame (e.g., the researcher's political orientation or standpoint).

Presentation of the participants' language is imperative because it is *the data*. Evidence can be presented in several formats: (1) using short, eye-catching quotations separated from the text, often bulleted or placed in a table; (b) embedding brief quotations within the narrative; and (c) including entire paragraphs of field notes and interview transcripts. The use of longer quotations requires guiding readers into and out of these quotations and focusing their attention on the controlling idea of the section. Lengthy quotations are usually set off from the narrative text and provide some identification of the original dataset, such as the date or the interviewee number.

Narrative Structures and Visual Representations

Narrative structures and visual representations vary among qualitative designs. We will discuss each evidence-based design with an emphasis on substantive research manuscripts:

1. *Ethnographic studies* provide description, analysis, and interpretation of the culture-sharing group. The holistic "thick description" is presented in chronological order or narrative order. The analysis may focus on critical incidents or selected social scenes with dialogue, or it may tell the story from different perspectives. The analysis may also compare and contrast across groups within the culture. Data, transformed as patterns or themes, are summarized and provide a *cultural portrait*, or synthesis of all aspects of the group life illustrating its complexity (Wolcott, 1999). The overall interpretation or meaning is discussed with the findings in terms of how it relates to wider scholarly issues or to current issues (see Excerpt 15.8).

2. *Phenomenological studies* of a lived experience emphasize textual descriptions of what happened and how the phenomenon was experienced. Because the experience is one that is common to the researcher and the interviewees, data are drawn from both the researcher's written record of his or her experience and records of the interviewees. The report includes a description of each participant's experience, including the researcher's, followed by a composite description and the essence of the experience.

3. *Case studies*, similar to ethnographic studies, contain description, analysis, and naturalistic summaries. Case studies typically use a report format that includes vignettes to provide vicarious experiences for the reader (Stake, 2000). Case studies can be 60 to 40 percent or 70 to 30 percent in favor of description versus analysis and interpretation. An extensive description

EXCERPT 15.8   Summary Statements and Recommendations

This study demonstrates that unshared sociolinguistic practices . . . are crucial aspects of communicative failure between hearing and deaf children in mainstream elementary school settings. . . . We suggest that just as deaf children are expected to develop skills for accommodating to hearing children, hearing children in classes with deaf children should be expected to develop comparable skills for interacting . . . to enrich peer interactions and enable the deaf students to have equal access to all learning opportunities. (p. 131)

Source: From Keating, E., & Mirus, G. (2003). Examining interactions across language modalities: Deaf children and hearing peers at school. *Anthropology and Education Quarterly, 34*(2), 115–135.

EXCERPT 15.9 Informing Educational Policy

In concluding, . . . [the] findings reported here might inform future educational policy. Judging from what second language researchers and those working with ESL students say about the importance of allowing language learners to practice speaking English, having a classroom environment that works to minimize opportunities for students to talk seems undesirable. (p. 67)

Source: From Olivo, W. (2003). "Quit talking and learn English!" Conflicting language ideologies in an ESL classroom. *Anthropology and Education Quarterly, 34*(1), 50–71.

EXCERPT 15.10 Grounded Theory Assertions

This study was a qualitative investigation of the knowledge and beliefs, roles, and guiding principles of two exemplary high school science teachers. . . . The findings of the study are summarized in the following assertions.

Assertion 1: The important knowledge and beliefs of each teacher are best represented as one cluster of teaching principles.

Assertion 2: Each teacher had multiple teaching roles, with each role described by a different role metaphor.

Assertion 3: The teaching roles of each teacher are consistent with his or her cluster of teaching principles.

Assertion 4: Each teacher had guiding principles that are overlying and constant.

Source: From Floyd, J. M. (1999). Knowledge and beliefs, roles, and guiding principles of two exemplary high school science teachers and model for teacher reflection. Unpublished doctoral dissertation, Virginia Commonwealth University, Richmond, VA.

is given of the case and its context, based on a wide variety of data sources. A few key issues are presented so that the reader can appreciate the complexity of the case. These issues are drawn from a collection of instances in the data to detect issue-relevant meanings. Finally, the researcher develops summaries (i.e., patterns) or "lessons learned," which are useful to participants or to readers when applied to similar cases (see Excerpt 15.9).

4. *Grounded theory studies* emphasize an analytic story; description is kept secondary to a theoretical scheme or concept density. The analytic story also specifies variations of the phenomenon and relevant conditions for multiple causes. A visual representation accompanies the culminating propositions of the grounded theory. Because of the emphasis on conceptual discussion and relating the grounded theory to theoretical literature, few readers fully appreciate the entire study (Charmaz, 2000). Other grounded theory studies present a descriptive narrative that connects the categories and advances concept density. Theoretical propositions can be presented in a narrative form or as a list of assertions (see Excerpt 15.10).

5. *Critical studies* include such diverse research methods as critical ethnography, feminist and ethnic research, narrative analysis, participatory action research, and action research. Most critical ethnographies and much feminist and ethnic research adopts the narrative structures of substantive research reports. However, researchers are particularly concerned about the multiple voices presented in the discourse, including that of the author. Visual representations may include tables, charts, and integrative diagrams. (Tables present verbatim statements.) Visual representations may also be matrices or models that identify context, causal conditions, and consequences. Directional arrows indicate the flow of initial events to consequences, as shown in Figure 15.9.

CHAPTER SUMMARY

The following statements summarize the process and techniques of qualitative data analysis:

1. In inductive analysis, the categories and patterns emerge from the data.

2. Analytic styles of qualitative data analysis include prefigured technical, template, editing, and crystallization styles.

3. Continual comparing and contrasting is used in practically all intellectual tasks during analysis.

4. Data must be organized in order to analyze them, either using predetermined categories or developing codes from the data.

5. Predetermined categories are derived from the research problem, an interview guide, literature, and personal or general knowledge.

6. A data segment (e.g., a word, sentence, paragraph, or page) is comprehensible by itself and contains one idea, episode, or piece of relevant information.

7. The term *code* is the descriptive name for a segment.

8. Researchers refine their provisional organizing system of codes (topics) throughout the study.

9. *Category* is an abstract term used to describe the meaning of similar codes.

10. Techniques to develop categories include refining analytic questions, making mental comparison of similar and unlikely situations, and analyzing "red flags."

11. A *pattern* is a relationship among categories.

12. Patterns are plausible explanations when they are supported by data and alternative patterns are not reasonable.

13. Techniques for pattern seeking include triangulation, ordering and sorting categories, analyzing discrepant or negative evidence, constructing visual representations, and conducting logical cross-analyses.

14. Data management comprises the use of a partially or completely electronic system to retrieve datasets and to assemble coded data in one place. Researchers can combine manual techniques with word-processing programs or use specially designed qualitative data analysis (QDA) software.

15. Deciding to use a QDA program begins with assessing one's needs, computer skills, and other factors. Choosing a specific QDA program requires investigating the available choices and knowing your analytical style to tailor the program to your research.

APPLICATION PROBLEMS

1. Below are published paraphrases of teachers' beliefs about kindergarten readiness and practices (Smith & Shepard, 1988, pp. 316–319). Identify the line numbers for categories of the following:
   - Beliefs about child development
   - Beliefs about the possibility of catching up
   - Beliefs about the possibilities of influencing a child's preparation for school
   - Beliefs about what teachers can do

   Also list any other categories you see in the data.

   ### Mrs. Willis:

   1. "Because development constitutes physiological unfolding, rates of
   2. development are smooth, continuous, with no spurts or discontinuities. The
   3. child who is 6 months behind in September will be 6 months behind in
   4. June. . . . There is little likelihood that a child who is developmentally behind
   5. his agemates would close the gap that separates them. . . . Intervention is
   6. futile with a developmentally unready child. Extra help or remediation
   7. causes pressure, frustration and compensation. Teachers cannot influence
   8. psychomotor abilities, ability to attend, social maturity, and so
   9. forth. . . . Teachers can provide the child with more time to mature; place the
   10. child in developmental kindergarten or preschool, send him home another
   11. year; place the child in a slow group in class; reduce instruction below [the]
   12. frustration level, lower expectations, boost self-concept, use

   13. manipulatives; retain in kindergarten; providing academic assistance is
   14. irrelevant and harmful."

   ### Miss Johnson:

   15. "Within broad limits of chronological age, children's readiness is a
   16. function of their experience, learning program, and environment. . . . A child
   17. who is less prepared than his peers can close the gap given the right
   18. educational circumstances; academic assistance is required. . . . The teacher
   19. can make a difference, as can the parent and other aspects of [the] environment;
   20. within a broad range of pupil abilities, what the pupil learns is largely a
   21. function of opportunities and experiences. . . . The teacher can provide
   22. additional academic help; accommodate differences in achievement; hold high
   23. expectations, reinforce and train; work hard and encourage the pupil to work
   24. hard."

2. Now, go back and look at the meaning of each category. Do certain beliefs occur with other beliefs? That is, does one category relate to another category to suggest a pattern? State any patterns you see in the data.

   An example of a published qualitative article follows. The margin notes are used to help you better understand the article. As you read it, think about the criteria for evaluating qualitative studies. What appears to be well done? What are some weaknesses? How could the study be modified to have more credibility?

EXAMPLE Reading Qualitative Research

Parents as Professionals in Early Intervention:
A Parent Educator Model

Peggy A. Gallagher, *Georgia State University*   Cheryl A. Rhodes, *Georgia State University*

Sharon M. Darling, *Boise State University*

One of the goals of a family-centered approach in early intervention is to equally involve family members as active partners with professionals. This article describes one state's model of family involvement using parents of young children with disabilities as parent educators in the Part C system. Qualitative focus group data were collected with the parent educators over 6 time periods and revealed their changing perceptions about their roles as parent educators, as well as their perceived challenges and successes. Parent educators ultimately came to see themselves as "professionals" working to bring a family perspective to the early intervention system.

[Abstract]

A hallmark of Part C of the Individuals with Disabilities Education Act (IDEA, 1990) is that parents of infants and toddlers with disabilities are partners with professionals in their children's development. The Part C Early Intervention (EI) system views family members as an integral component of the program through their participation in policy development, program implementation, training, and the Individualized Family Service Plan (IFSP) process. Bruder (2000) remarked that family-centered early intervention has become conceptualized around the values of family strengths (rather than deficits), the promotion of family choice, and the development of a collaborative partnership between the family members and the EI system and its professionals (Durst, Trivette, & Deal, 1994).

[Legislative background]

The goals of a family-centered philosophy are to equally involve parents as active partners and to recognize their central and long-term roles in the lives of their children with special needs (Mahoney et al., 1999). Controversy in the literature has focused on some of the terms used to involve families, such as "parent education," "parent involvement," and "parent support" (Durst, 1999). There has also been ongoing discussion of why family-centered care is not more easily implemented (Bruder, 2000). Bruder emphasized that parents must be given information in a supportive way so that they can parent their child with special needs and facilitate the child's learning without in any way threatening the family's self-confidence or cultural or religious traditions. McWilliam (2001) categorized these family supports as being emotional, informational, or instrumental/financial.

Winton and DiVenere (1995) outlined four ways that families of children with disabilities have been involved in early intervention to establish a broad base of parent support: parents as instructors, parents as practicum supervisors, parents as team participants in staff development, and parents as planners and policymakers. Winton and DiVenere stressed the value of having a wide variety of levels of involvement available because each family has unique circumstances and may (or may not) want to get involved at differing levels. Capone, Hull, and DiVenere (1997) described the partnerships that can develop between parents and professionals in EI systems. They suggested that parents are participating at both the preservice and inservice levels in various ways, including as members of task forces and advisory boards, as mentors for other families, as grant reviewers, as participants in quality improvement initiatives, and in personnel preparation.

[Literature: Family-centered approach]

A few empirical studies have validated the success of parents who were involved in EI programs beyond the traditional parenting role with their own children. Whitehead, Jesien, and Ulanski (1998) found that the consistent and regular presence of parents at planning and other meetings added a note of reality and shaped the entire complexion of the program in a more family friendly way. They recommended that programs include a parent of a child with a disability as a member of the core team. In doing so, program members would want to assure diverse representation in terms of ages of children, cultural backgrounds, and family composition of parents. Hanson, Randall, and Colston (1999) described a process involving parents of children with disabilities as advisors to the Department of Defense systems of services and in medical education. These parents served as advisors in many roles, such as making presentations at grand rounds or to service providers, writing items for surveys to evaluate a program, and coteaching courses. Bailey (2001) suggested that parent involvement and family support must be individualized, give parents every opportunity to be active partners in planning and working with professionals, and be organized such that families feel competent to learn and to become advocates for their child.

[Prior research]

Building on Winton and DiVenere's (1995) model of parental involvement, Turnbull, Blue-Banning, Turbiville, and Park (1999) discussed the idea of family members as educators of other professionals. They have viewed families from a strengths perspective (Allen & Petr, 1996), in which the expertise of parents and other family members is valued as a critical resource for professionals. They have called for research that focuses on the efficacy of parents as providers of education to other parents and professionals and maintain that if we truly value parents as resources, we need to help build an infrastructure

[Research needed]

that supports parents taking on traditional educational roles. The purpose of this study is to describe a model of parents as professionals in one state's EI system. Parent educators' progress was documented through quantitative and qualitative methods, including surveys from the families and EI personnel with whom they worked and focus groups in which parent educators shared their own perspectives.

General purpose of article

Description of Model

The Parent Educator model began in December 1995 with the hiring of a parent of a child with disabilities as the coordinator. Parent educators, parents of children who are or have been in the Part C program, were then hired on a part-time, flexible schedule to develop family-centered partnerships, collaborate with state and local EI staff and other agencies, and promote cultural sensitivity throughout the state's Part C program, known as Babies Can't Wait (BCW). The mission of the program is to actively promote family participation in the BCW program by disseminating current information so that families of children with disabilities have timely and easy access to needed resources and services.

Details of model

The Parent Educator model is a component of Project SCEIs (Skilled Credentialed Early Interventionists), a consortium of six universities created to implement the major components of Georgia's Comprehensive System of Personnel Development (CSPD) for the Part C Early Intervention system. Parents have been instrumental in policy development since the beginning of the EI program, and family-centered principles are found throughout SCEIs training activities including parents as authors of a handbook for other parents about the EI system and parents paid as trainers at all SCEIs workshops required for EI personnel. Thus, it was an easy progression to move to a Parent Educator model.

BCW parent educators develop and distribute parent education materials to families new to BCW; provide information to BCW families on specific topics, as requested; work with local EI personnel to plan and carry out activities and programs for families; serve on and encourage other families to be involved in local and state interagency coordinating councils and other policy committees; and work with EI personnel to publicize BCW in the community. They also help to identify family needs and inform families about parent resources available through BCW, including a parent handbook, a parent conference, and lending libraries. Parent educators also develop materials in which parents have expressed an interest, such as updates in local EI newsletters or information on specific issues such as extended hospitalizations.

Recruitment of parent education specialists (the original job title used) began in December 1995 with an announcement and job description that was sent throughout Georgia to EI coordinators, local interagency coordinating councils, and

Implementation process

disability organizations. The original job description specified overall job duties to "develop and conduct family training activities and materials on BCW program and policies" and to "collaborate with local EI coordinators, public schools, parent groups, and other community agencies about BCW services to families." Although the original job name of "parent education specialist" was changed to "parent educator," the overall job responsibilities remained the same over time, though more specific duties, such as providing parents with a general introduction to the BCW system or maintaining monthly status reports, were added. The title "parent educator" was adopted in 1998 at parent educators' request because they thought it more clearly described their role in teaching other parents about and supporting parents in the BCW program than did the original title. "Parent educator" is consistent with the term used by Winton, Sloop, and Rodriguez (1999), who suggested its use in situations when parents are educating professionals.

A statewide interview committee—which included the parent educator coordinator, project SCEIs director, an early intervention coordinator; and in some cases, the parent of a child with a disability who was working as a graduate research assistant—interviewed all candidates who passed the initial screening. Prior to hiring, all references were checked, and the prospective parent educator had an interview with the local EI coordinator. In most cases, the EI coordinator already knew the parent from his or her district.

Six parent educators were hired in February 1996. All had children who either were currently in or who had participated in EI. All had at least a bachelor's degree, a job requirement, and had held various jobs, including attorney, community volunteer, and teacher. Since March 1996, Georgia has had 24 parent educators, with a maximum of 14 at any one time. The average length of stay has been 2 years 11 months, with the shortest tenure being 4 months and the longest 7 years; two of the original parent educators are still employed. All of the parent educators have had a strong desire to work within the EI system to help families maximize their time in early intervention and to give back to the program that has meant so much to them and their families.

Currently, there are 13 parent educators serving in Georgia, 11 covering 80% of the state's health districts and 2 serving as statewide resources, 1 in cultural diversity. Parent educators have many

Current status

training opportunities, including a full-day orientation with Project SCEIs and BCW staff when they first begin. Parent educators receive a training manual containing BCW policies and procedures, definitions, a copy of the Parent Handbook for Success in Early Intervention, and resource and other useful materials. Specialized training also occurs at least once a year on such topics as IFSP development, transition planning, community resources, or natural environments. Parent educators also attend a service coordinator orientation and the six Project SCEIs training modules, which are designed for service coordinators and special instructors.

(continued)

Parent educators are paid a monthly salary that includes telephone and travel charges within their district. If

| Current status (continued) |

they have expenses or are asked to come to activities outside of their district, they are reimbursed for those activities. Parent educators are supervised locally by the individual EI coordinators in their districts but are paid and directly supervised by the Project SCEIs parent educator coordinator, who is the parent of a child with disabilities and a licensed professional counselor and licensed marriage and family therapist. Parent educators work out of their homes; some are given office space in their local district office as well. All parent educators have access to a home computer.

Evaluation of the Parent Education Component

The evaluation is multifaceted, with data gathered from consumers (parents at an annual Parent Conference and parents selected through an independent evaluator); from supervisors, including EI coordinators and selected service coordinators; from Project SCEIs' parent educator coordinator (through annual university evaluations); and from the parent educators themselves through role surveys, focus groups, and monthly reports. Quantitative data summaries of ratings from EI coordinators and service coordinators have consistently indicated high levels of satisfaction with key aspects of the parent educators' performance, including their assistance in getting information to families, their role in involving families in local inter-agency committees, and their responsiveness to requests from parents and EI personnel. Parents in the EI program, as well, have consistently reported that parent educators were helpful to them in giving information, answering questions, sharing resources, and making suggestions.

Monthly, quarterly, and annual reports show the number and type of parent educator contacts (telephone and in person), as well as the types of activities completed by the

| Purpose of *this* study |

parent educators. As the number of parent educators has increased, so have their telephone contacts with families. In 1997 and 1998, approximately 450 calls were made to families, whereas the 1999 and 2000 data showed approximately 700 calls per year with Georgia families in BCW. Data from 2001 and 2002 showed contacts with more than 1,000 families annually. The focus of this article is to present the qualitative data from six focus groups held with parent educators to document the perspective of the parent educators regarding their roles, challenges, and successes across time.

Qualitative Methodology

The focus group component of the evaluation of the parent educators used a qualitative research paradigm (Bogdan & Biklen, 1982). Data were collected longi-

| Defined focus group interview |

tudinally using a focus group format. A *focus group* is a "carefully planned dis-

cussion designed to obtain perceptions on a defined area of interest in a permissive and non-threatening environment" (Krueger, 1988, p. 18). The group interaction of a focus group is what differentiates it from other types of qualitative data collection (Morgan & Krueger, 1993). The qualitative data were gathered through a series of six focus groups held over a 5-year period. Themes and patterns emerged from the transcripts to reveal par-

| Prolonged data collection |

ent educators' perspectives on their evolving roles, challenges, and successes.

Participants

Nine parent educators participated in the focus groups; two of them participated in all of the six focus groups, two more participated in five of the groups, one participated in four of the groups, and one participated in three of the groups. The other three participated in one or two of the focus groups. The participants were all women; three of them

| Informant selection |

were African American, and six of them were White. Their ages varied; three of the parent educators were from 25 to 30 years of age, four of them were in the 30- to 35-year age range, and two were older than 35 years of age at the beginning of the focus groups. All had a child with a disability; one of them was currently served in the BCW program, and seven of them had children with disabilities who were preschool age when the mother started as a parent educator.

Procedures

Questioning the Focus Group. The appendix lists the

| Source of questions |

focus group probe questions, which were designed from a review of the literature regarding parent involvement and parents as partners, as well as focus groups in general. The intent of the qualitative study was to understand the perspectives of parents on

| Semi structured interviews |

their roles as parent educators, as well as factors that influenced their success as parent educators. To ensure consistency across time, the same questions were asked at each focus group meeting. The purpose of the study was outlined at the beginning of each session, and confidentiality discussed and informed

| Ethics |

consent obtained at the beginning of the study.

Conducting the Focus Groups. Five focus groups with

| Logistics |

the parent educators were held over a 2-year time period. A follow-up focus group with the three parent educators from the original group was held 5 years after the program began. Focus groups lasted from 45 to 90 minutes and were always held in conjunction with a meeting in which parent educators were in attendance. The focus groups were always held before any training or meeting occurred so that any discussion did not influence the answers. Table 1 shows the dates and number of participants for each focus group session.

The six focus group sessions were

| Roles of leaders |

conducted by a two-member research team

consisting of the moderator (first author) and an observer (second author). The moderator, who had been trained in focus group and structured interview methodologies, led each session based on the focus group questions, monitored discussion, probed for additional comments and insights, and kept field notes during the session and immediately afterwards. The observer audio-taped all of the sessions (with the permission of the participants), recorded extensive field notes during each session, and verified the field notes recorded by the moderator.

Data Collection and Analysis

Field notes and recordings were used to collect data from the

sessions. The tape recordings of each session were transcribed verbatim. The narrative data from all six sessions were analyzed using two levels of qualitative methods (Johnson & LaMontagne, 1993; Krueger, 1988; Lederman, 1990; Morgan, 1997): postdiscussion reflection and a code-category-theme process.

Immediate Postdiscussion. The observer verified the moderator's field notes. The moderator and observer

reviewed the field notes and documented the main themes at the end of each focus group session. They also discussed contextual elements, such as the overall tone and climate of the discussion, and noted any representative quotations from participants (Bogdan & Biklen, 1992).

Code-Category-Theme Process. The content of the focus groups was analyzed using a code-category-theme process

(McWilliam, Young, & Harville, 1996) in order to obtain comprehensive data analysis. At the end of the sessions, all transcripts and field notes were read at one sitting by the first author. Data reduction and content analysis procedures, as described later, were then conducted on each individual session, using each question as a separate entity. The first author then read and reread each individual question across the six time periods to check for accuracy of the original categories

generated. For example, the October 1996 data were analyzed using Questions 1, 2, 3, and so forth; and then Question 1 was analyzed using the transcripts from October 1996, February 1997, August 1997, and so forth.

Data Reduction in Three Phases. First, the lead author (and later a second rater, who was not the observer) looked at the individual narrative units (sentences) and reduced the narrative to a simple, descriptive content phrase.

For example, the sentences "I've done numerous workshops. I started over the summer with the program for children who were hearing impaired. And worked with that agency and bringing in the Babies Can't Wait component of it" were reduced to "conducted workshops." Second, these descriptive content units were categorized according to their underlying focus (Johnson & LaMontagne, 1993; Marchant, 1995; Morningstar, Turnbull, & Turnbull, 1996). For example "talking to parents on the phone" and "a lot of calling" and "call backs" were all used under the category of making and receiving phone calls. Representative quotations were also noted in the various response categories. Third, themes and patterns emerged from the data after additional reviews that looked at the data question by question, as well as by time period. This final phase, called "integrating categories and their properties," led to identifying themes by combining categories with similar properties (Glaser & Strauss, 1967, p. 105).

A second rater independently read and coded the data. This second rater was

used to verify the first author's categorizing and coding system and to check the accuracy of the themes and patterns that emerged. On the few occasions when discrepancies occurred, the transcripts were reread and evaluated by both raters, as well as the observer, in order to reach consensus among the three researchers.

Credibility

The credibility of the findings was verified through data triangulation (Webb, Campbell,

Schwartz, & Sechrest, 1965) by using several sources (field notes by two persons, verbatim transcripts), multiple raters

TABLE 1 Dates and Participants in Focus Group Sessions		
Focus Group Date	Time on Job	Parent Educators Present
10/21/96	7 mo.	7
2/27/97	1 yr.	7 (4 for 1 year; 2 for 3 months; 1 for 1 month)
8/18/97	almost 18 mo.	5 (1 had resigned; 1 not present)
2/19/98	almost 2 yrs.	7 (1 for 1 month)
11/23/98	2½ yrs.	4 (1 home with baby; 1 resignation; 1 not present)
5/25/01	5 yrs.	3 (original parent educators)

(continued)

example (continued)

Member checks (moderator, observer, second rater), member checks on the accuracy of notes, and stakeholder reviews (Brotherson, 1994; Brotherson & Goldstein, 1992; Morningstar et al., 1996; Patton, 2002). The data were verified through review with several of the parent educators during and after each session. Parent educators agreed with the data as presented after the sessions and clarified minor details, such as names specific to their districts. To further ensure credibility and accuracy of the data, a stakeholder review was conducted. A draft of the present article was sent to eight of the nine participating parent educators for review. One had moved out of the country with a military spouse and was not able to be contacted. Parent

Participant review educators were asked to either send in comments or respond to a follow-up phone call made to each parent in an effort to gather feedback on the content, tone, and accuracy of the article through questions such as, "Does the summary reflect what you think the group said?" Three of the eight parent educators responded; fortunately, the respondents had each attended at least five of the sessions. All of the respondents agreed that the content of the article accurately portrayed their experiences as parent educators across time. One of the respondents pointed out that she believed parent educators might be perceived differently in rural versus urban areas of the state, noting that rural parent educators have to travel long distances for meetings. Because data were not kept specific to respondents, this reply was noted as a limitation in the discussion section. She also noted that many of the focus groups had taken place in conjunction with the annual statewide parent conference.

Directly related to research purposes
Results

Results are presented relative to the three overall purposes of the study: perceived roles, challenges, and successes of the parent educators across time.

Synthesis of Theme 1 with short quotations
Roles

Four general themes emerged in response to the question describing roles and responsibilities. Parent educators described their roles as gathering, sharing, and disseminating information; linking families to resources, the EI system, and other families; representing the parent perspective at the local EI office and on local and state committees; and being sensitive to special issues such as cultural diversity, single parenting, or the special needs of teen mothers. At the beginning, parent educators responded to the question about their roles and responsibilities by describing their role as one of gathering and sharing information and trying to make the BCW process more parent friendly. Parent educators described themselves as a bridge, an information specialist, and a resource guide for parents and said, "We parents do have a bond—no one else understands."

Parent educators also talked about the value of communication and the linkages among EI coordinators, themselves, and the service coordinators. Parent educators saw their role as one of reassuring parents, with one woman stating that she had assured parents "they were not overreacting. As a parent, we have to make sure that we have explored every avenue in order to be able to sleep well at night." They also saw their role as one of educating the professionals regarding family issues. The value of communication and linkages was reiterated at several of the later focus groups when parent educators discussed how much they thought their role had changed; they were now seen as an integral part of the local Babies Can't Wait office, a "regular," if you will.

Parent educators also mentioned the importance of being a parent voice on committees, and one said, "I found that they really respect the parents' point of view." They described numerous ways they believed they represented the parent perspective through work at the local EI office and work on local and state committees, such as the finance committee or the cultural diversity committee of the state interagency coordinating council. Parent educators expressed the desire for more training in special issues such as cultural diversity, single parenting, or the special needs of teen mothers as they viewed themselves as needing to be sensitive to and educated on these issues.

In response to the question about what a typical day was like, parent educators listed making phone calls, attending meetings, helping with mailings to parents, and putting together materials as the major activities in fulfilling their roles. Making phone calls was overwhelmingly the number one activity across all sessions. One parent educator described part of her day as "brainwork . . . you think a lot when you are doing all these things—writing letters, getting resources together; answering questions." Several also mentioned copying materials and reading many materials on a typical day so that they could give more parent input "where you know parental input would be valuable." In later focus groups, participants also mentioned traveling as a predominant activity, indicating that they were serving on more state committees and traveling across the district to meetings with parents and providers. Parent educators in later groups also mentioned that they were spending quite a bit of time focusing on relationships. One woman mentioned that she was "trying to figure out where parents are coming from and then where everyone else is coming from and why some families might still feel alienated."

Several patterns emerged that outline the experiences of parent educators across time. Parent educators became more specific in expressing the nature of their role and in valuing their role and its unique importance over time. In a cyclical fashion, as they came to value and express the importance of their role, they wanted more information to share and wanted to be sure the information they had was adequate and up to date. A second pattern was that parent educators increasingly saw themselves as a bridge or a link between the EI program and families, in helping professionals to understand the needs and perspectives of families.

A third pattern was that parent educators saw themselves as having more and more public relations responsibilities. They expressed feeling successful in this role, and as they came to feel accepted as "professionals," they wanted to stay current on the information they were disseminating. Another pattern was that parent educators found it important to spend time connecting with the information and, increasingly, the people they saw so they could do "their job." This involved talking to others, gathering information, and building relationships with BCW and the community. Not surprisingly with the immense strides in technology over the time period of the focus groups, the parent educators expressed an increasing need for and appreciation of technology resources in their jobs.

| Synthesis of Theme 2 with direct quotations |

Challenges

Overall themes related to challenges included not being able to consistently connect with local families, due to either confidentiality issues or "gatekeeping" by professionals; the challenge of helping the local district become more friendly to families; and later, the challenge of balancing home and family life with the demands of being a parent educator. Participants had many questions at the beginning of focus groups such as "Should we go into homes?" and "How do we get into homes and learn who the families are?"—suggesting that a challenge was getting to know and communicating with the families they would work with. Connecting with local parents in their district remained a challenge for parent educators due to confidentiality guidelines. Later, permission forms used during intake allowed a parent educator to contact a parent if the parent wished to be contacted. A challenge mentioned in the third session was that even with release forms now available, all service coordinators were not necessarily distributing them; thus, initial contact with parents was still difficult. Parent educators also worried that their roles were not understood or appreciated by service coordinators. For instance, one service coordinator told a parent educator, "What parent educators do would not be of interest to the parents I work with." Thus, service coordinators may have been serving a "gatekeeping" function. In a final focus group, a parent educator mentioned that she had probably depended too much on her relationship with the early intervention coordinator in the district and that she should have, instead, spent time building relationships with the service coordinators who had direct access to the families.

Making activities and materials from the district office more "family friendly" was also a challenge. As one parent educator noted, "It is not conducive for parents to have meetings always from 11:30 to 1:00. We are here to make it parent friendly." Balancing the role of a parent educator with home and family life was a third challenge. Several parent educators mentioned the challenge of trying to balance managing phone calls in the evening as well as during the day. One mentioned that having to work in the evenings and on the weekends (as some parents requested contacts dur-

ing these times) was a challenge for her: "When you work in your home, you work all the time." Balance between job and family life was mentioned again by several parent educators during the last focus groups, with one reporting that balancing family life with the job was a constant challenge, and another saying, "I feel like I want to be mom, too." A related challenge to the balance of home and family life was one that emerged over time—that of storing and organizing information.

Successes

| Synthesis of Theme 3 with brief quotations |

Themes related to parent educator success included helping fellow parents; facilitating positive public relations about the EI program; educating professionals on the needs and perspectives of families, which leads to gaining the respect of professionals; and finally, feeling success at a personal level through contributing to the family income and from one's own growth as a professional.

At all sessions, most participants mentioned the success they felt when they helped a fellow parent, especially when "a parent calls me back and thanks me." By the later focus groups, parent educators again expressed success in their work with families, in "being able to answer their questions," and in "telling families in baby steps how the system works." During the final focus group, parent educators expressed how they liked to "help parents get what they need" and how successful they felt when parents told them they appreciated them.

At the beginning focus group session, parent educators felt that their greatest success was sharing the parent educator and Babies Can't Wait programs with others. This feeling of success continued to be mentioned as parent educators discussed work with community resources such as childcare centers. Parent educators also expressed success in educating professionals on the needs and perspectives of families. By the second session, they felt that they had a successful and comfortable relationship with the EI coordinator and could "walk in to the EI coordinator and say 'This is important and I think you need to know about it.'" Later, parent educators discussed the importance of educating the professionals about parents and expressed feeling that they had gained the "respect of other members of the special needs community." Parent educators agreed that real success was being taken seriously and having the trust and respect of the professionals with whom they worked. One stated, "People seek me out to ask questions, from parents to professionals. They understand that I am legitimate, that I know what I am talking about." One mentioned that she now realized "we have valuable information to give . . ." and that she sees the "big picture" of EI.

A final theme of success was noted on a personal level. Participants mentioned the success that being a parent educator had been to them on a personal level, by helping with their family's income and helping learn to conduct themselves in a more professional manner. One summed up her success by saying, "We know the top people in the state [and] they appreciate our involvement."

(continued)

example (continued)

Discussion

The Parent Educator model builds on a perspective of parental involvement in early intervention outlined by Winton and DiVenere (1995) and later by Turnbull et al. (1999), with a focus on family members as educators of other professionals. The model values the expertise of parents as a critical resource for professionals and for other parents. The progress of parent educators was documented through quantitative and qualitative methods, including surveys from the families and EI personnel they worked with and their own perspectives through focus groups. General themes emerged from the focus groups regarding the parent educators' perspectives on their roles, challenges, and successes.

The themes that emerged describing the roles and successes of the parent educators over time are consistent with the work of Capone et al. (1997) in documenting the partnerships that can develop between parents and professionals in an EI system. Interestingly, over time, parent educators asked for more for themselves, both financially, and emotionally (raises, retreats). This may be because they came to view themselves increasingly as "professionals" and reported that they were treated as such over time. According to Golin and Ducanis (1981), a *profession* is a group of people who have unique skills and knowledge that are established in stages, culminating in external recognition of the autonomy of the profession. In this study, parent educators came to value themselves more as professionals and were able to ask more for themselves and see the value they each had to offer. They came to view the expertise among the group members and began requesting teambuilding activities and retreats in an effort to grow and learn from each other. Across time, they continued to be optimistic and hopeful in working to meet their goals. Their tasks remained basically the same across time, although their challenges became more "personal," including balancing their own family and work issues, rather than issues of relationships with professionals or families in the BCW system. This points to the importance of building a model that is fluid and ever evolving for family participants.

Qualitative research methodology inherently warrants some cautions (York & Tundi-dot; 1995). First is a limitation involving participants. The participants in this study came from only one state; thus, the results cannot be assumed to generalize to other parent populations. The parent educators hired in this model were all mothers; consequently, the perspective of a male parent educator was not available. Additionally, although two of the participants remained the same across focus groups, new parent educators were added as participants, changing the makeup and dynamics of the group and, thus, possibly affecting the outcomes. Changing focus group members over time might have influenced the themes discussed. Another possible limitation is that the data were not kept specific to

| Relates findings to literature |

| Limitation 1 |

the urban or rural category of residence of the participants. It may be that parent educators from different parts of the state had different perspectives specific to the nature of their type of settings. At the same time, it is important to remember that qualitative research such as this brings a unique perspective of a critical stakeholder—to the parent—which is valuable (Johnson & LaMontagne, 1993) in generating future policy and research directions in EI.

Second, sampling bias may have occurred. Because participants had all voluntarily applied for the role of parent educator, this could have influenced their perceptions of their roles and responsibilities, challenges, or successes, or how they adapted to them. Other parents in such a position might react in a different manner. Facilitator bias can also be a limitation of focus group methodology. The first author (who also served as the focus group moderator) is a strong advocate of parents being fully involved and embedded in EI systems. She chose to study this issue to document the perceptions of the parent educators as they began a new role and followed them over time as they became more involved with families and professionals. It is possible that her biases might have affected the results. Although care was taken to optimize the reliability of the findings through the use of several sources and raters, the perspectives of the researchers involved are present and the potential exists for researcher bias during the data reduction phases. Finally, the same questions were used in each focus group session. It is possible that the repeated nature of the questions might have influenced the responses over time.

| Limitation 2 |

| Limitation 3 |

As programs continue to look at a focus on family members as leaders in public policy and system improvement, it is important to have effective models in place to promote their growth and development and to continually expand the ways to involve family members at their level of comfort. Future research may look at what strategies are effective in achieving outcomes for varying types of families or whether geographic differences between parents in urban or rural areas play a role in parent education. This focus group data provide a holistic understanding of the parent educator role from their own perspectives. Families of children in the program are the ultimate consumers of parent educator activities, and it is important to have their perspective in evaluating the overall program. In this case, families consistently rated the parent educators as being most helpful in the area of disseminating information, encouraging families to become involved in EI, and helping families feel like an important member of the EI team, supporting the perspectives of the parent educators regarding the value of their roles. The Parent Educator model brought families into the system at all levels, including locally with families and health district staff members and statewide in committees and policy development.

| Future research |

Authors' Note. Partial support for this project was provided by the Georgia Department of Human Resources, Division of Public Health, Babies Can't Wait Program. The opinions expressed herein do not necessarily reflect the policy of the granting agency, and no official endorsement by this agency should be inferred.

References

Allen, R. L., & Petr, C. G. (1996). Toward developing standards and measurements for family-centered practice in family support programs. In G. H. S. Singer, L. E. Powers, & A. L. Olson (Eds.), Redefining family support: Innovations in public-private partnerships (pp. 39–56). Baltimore: Brookes.

Bailey, D. B., Jr. (2001). Evaluating parent involvement and family support in early intervention and preschool programs. Journal of Early Intervention, 24, 1–14.

Bogdan, R. C., & Biklen, S. K. (1982). Qualitative research for education: An introduction to theory and methods. Boston: Allyn & Bacon.

Bogdan, R. C., & Biklen, S. K. (1992). Qualitative research for education: An introduction to theory and methods (2nd ed.). Boston: Allyn & Bacon.

Brotherson, M. J. (1994). Interactive focus group interviewing: A qualitative research method in early intervention. Topics in Early Childhood Special Education. 74(1), 101–118.

Brotherson, M. J., & Goldstein, B. L. (1992). Quality design of focus groups in early childhood special education research. Journal of Early Intervention, 16, 334–342.

Bruder, M. B. (2000). Family-centered early intervention: Clarifying our values for the new millennium. Topics in Early Childhood Special Education, 20, 105–115.

Capone, A., Hull, K. M., & DiVenere, N. J. (1997). Partnerships in preservice and inservice education. In P. J. Winton, J. A. McCollum, & C. Catlett (Eds.), Reforming personnel preparation in early intervention (pp. 435–449). Baltimore: Brookes.

Dunst, C. J. (1999). Placing parent education in conceptual and empirical context. Topics in Early Childhood Special Education, 19, 141–147.

Dunst, C. J., Trivette, C. M., & Deal, A. G. (Eds.). (1994). Supporting and strengthening families: Volume 1: Methods, strategies, and practices. Cambridge, MA: Brookline Books.

Glaser, B. G., & Strauss, A. L. (1967). The discovery of grounded theory strategies for qualitative research. New York: Aldine.

Golin, A., & Ducanis, J. (1981). The interdisciplinary team. Rockville, MD: Aspen.

Hanson, J. L., Randall, V. R, & Colston, S. S. (1999). Parent advisors: Enhancing services for young children with special needs. Infants and Young Children, 12(11), 17–25.

Individuals with Disabilities Education Act of 1990, 20 U.S.C. § 1400 et seq.

Johnson, L. J., & LaMontagne, M. J. (1993). Research methods: Using content analysis to examine the verbal or written communication of stakeholders within early intervention. Journal of Early Intervention, 17, 73–79.

Krueger, R. A. (1988). Focus groups: A practical guide for applied research. Newbury Park, CA: Sage.

Lederman, L. C. (1990). Assessing educational effectiveness: The focus group interview as a technique for data collection. Communication Education, 38(2), 117–127.

Mahoney, G., Kaiser, A., Girolametto, L., MacDonald, J., Robinson, C., Safford, P., et al. (1999). Parent education in early intervention: A call for a renewed focus. Topics in Early Childhood Special Education, 19(3), 131–140.

Marchant, C. (1995). Teachers' views of integrated preschools. Journal of Early Intervention, 19, 61–73.

McWilliam, R. A. (2001, April). Early intervention programs changing to focus on natural environments. Paper presented at the meeting of the Council for Exceptional Children, Kansas City, MO.

McWilliam, R. A., Young, H. J., & Harville, K. (1996). Therapy services in early intervention: Current status, barriers, and recommendations. Topics in Early Childhood Special Education, 16, 348–374.

Morgan, D. L. (1997). Focus groups as qualitative research (2nd ed.). Thousand Oaks, CA: Sage.

Morgan, D. L., & Krueger R. A. (1993). When to use focus groups and why. In D. L Morgan (Ed.), Successful focus groups: Advancing the state of the art (pp. 3–19). Newbury Park, CA: Sage.

Morningstar, M., Turnbull, A. P, & Turnbull, H. (1996). What do students with disabilities tell us about the importance of family involvement in the transition from school to adult life. Exceptional Children, 62, 249–260.

Patton, M. Q. (2002). Qualitative research and evaluation methods (3rd ed.). Thousand Oaks, CA: Sage.

Turnbull, A. P, Blue-Banning, M., Turbiville, V, & Park, J. (1999). From parent education to partnership education: A call for a transformed focus. Topics in Early Childhood Special Education, 19, 164–172.

Webb, E. J., Campbell, D.T., Schwartz, R. D., & Sechrest, L. (1965). Unobtrusive measures. Chicago: Rand McNally.

Whitehead, A., Jesien, G., & Ulanaki, B. K. (1998). Weaving parents into the fabric of early intervention interdisciplinary training: How to integrate and support family involvement in training. Infants and Young Children, 10(3), 44–53.

Winton, P. J., & DiVenere, N. (1995). Family-professional partnerships in early intervention personnel preparation: Guidelines and strategies. Topics in Early Childhood Special Education, 15, 296–313.

Winton, P. J., Sloop, S., & Rodriguez, P. (1999). Parent education: A term whose time is past. Topics in Early Childhood Special Education, 19, 157–161.

York, J., & Tundidor, M. (1995). Issues raised in the name of inclusion: Perspectives of educators, parents, and students. Journal of the Association for Persons with Severe Handicaps, 20(1), 31–44.

Appendix: Focus Group Questions

1. Describe your role as a parent educator. What are your responsibilities?
2. What is a typical day like for you?
3. What has been your biggest challenge in being a parent educator so far?
4. What has been your greatest success as a parent educator so far?
5. What training needs do you have? | Open-response questions
6. What do you wish you had more information on? What else do you need to know to be able to do your job?
7. What other resources and supports do you need?
8. If Georgia had just been given thousands of dollars to expand its parent education component for Part C or beyond, how would you suggest the money be spent?

Source: From Gallagher, P. A., Rhodes, C. A., & Darling, S. M. (2004). Parents as professionals in early intervention: A parent educator model. *Topics in Early Childhood Special Education, 24*(1), 5–13. Adapted with permission.

ANSWERS TO APPLICATION PROBLEMS

1. a. Beliefs about child development: lines 1–3, 15–16.
    b. Beliefs about the possibility of catching up: lines 4–5, 17–18.
    c. Beliefs about the possibility of influencing a child's preparation for school: lines 6–9, 19–21.
    d. Beliefs about what teachers can do: lines 10–14, 22–24.

2. Some patterns that need confirmation are as follow:
    a. Teacher beliefs about child development relate to beliefs about the possibility of catching up.
    b. Teacher beliefs about the possibility of influencing a child's preparation for school relate to beliefs about what teachers can do.
    c. Teacher beliefs about the possibility of catching up relate to beliefs about what teachers can do.

Mixed Method Designs

with Jessica Hearn

From Chapter 16 of *Research in Education: Evidence-Based Inquiry*, 7/e. James H. McMillan. Sally Schumacher.
Copyright © 2010 by Pearson Education. All rights reserved.

Mixed Method Designs
with Jessica Hearn

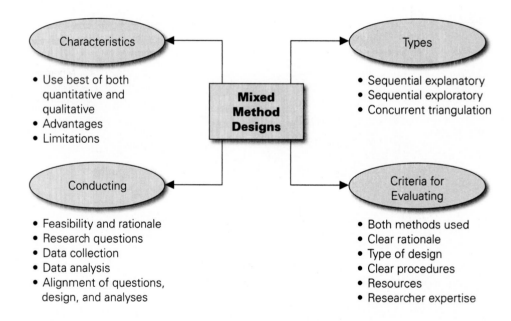

Characteristics
- Use best of both quantitative and qualitative
- Advantages
- Limitations

Conducting
- Feasibility and rationale
- Research questions
- Data collection
- Data analysis
- Alignment of questions, design, and analyses

Mixed Method Designs

Types
- Sequential explanatory
- Sequential exploratory
- Concurrent triangulation

Criteria for Evaluating
- Both methods used
- Clear rationale
- Type of design
- Clear procedures
- Resources
- Researcher expertise

KEY TERMS

mixed method designs
stratified purposeful sampling
purposive random sampling
concurrent triangulation sampling

multilevel mixed method sampling
sequential explanatory design
sequential exploratory design
concurrent triangulation design

WHAT YOU WILL LEARN

Study this chapter and you will:

- Understand that mixed method research substantially combines qualitative and quantitative approaches.
- Distinguish between mixed method studies and research that uses quantitative or qualitative methods superficially.
- Know both the advantages and disadvantages of mixed method research.
- Know how to write mixed method research questions.

- Know the sampling procedures for mixed method studies.
- Understand the differences between explanatory, exploratory, and triangulation designs.
- Know the essential steps in conducting mixed method studies.
- Know the standards of adequacy for mixed method research.
- Know how to read mixed method studies.

WHAT AND WHY OF MIXED METHOD RESEARCH

The development and use of **mixed method designs** have increased in recent years as researchers have realized that often the best approach to answering research questions is to use both quantitative and qualitative methods in the same study or when using solely a quantitative or qualitative method would be insufficient to provide complete answers that meet the goal or purpose of the study. For example, evidence gathered from teacher surveys might help a principal understand what teachers think about implementing a new curriculum, but these data may not adequately explain the barriers or resistance teachers perceive that would make it difficult to implement. Mixed method designs are also appropriate when there are individuals or a small group whose thinking differs significantly from that of the majority. Mixed method designs are very helpful in identifying issues, factors, and relevant questions that can become the focus of a quantitative study. Note in Excerpt 16.1 the justification the authors give for using a mixed method design.

Consider investigating whether there is a relationship between high-stakes testing and dropout rate when successful achievement is needed for graduation. On the surface, this question lends itself nicely to a nonexperimental, quantitative study in which characteristics of students, including their scores on graduation tests, can be entered into a regression model to determine if performance on the tests predicts dropping out once other variables have been controlled. On a deeper level, it would also be helpful to understand *why* students did not

Mixed method designs: both quantitative and qualitative

EXCERPT 16.1   Justification for Using a Mixed Method Design

The present investigation was based on a longitudinal mixed methodology case study of a large, high poverty district's experiences during a decade of accountability-focused reform efforts. A mixed method design was chosen in a pragmatic effort to capture the widest range of effects of accountability efforts (the what and so what of reform efforts together), with a range of participants' perspectives of how and why various reforms were attempted. (p. 50)

Source: From Stringfield, S. C., & Yakimowski-Srebnick, M. E. (2005). Promise, progress, problems, and paradoxes of three phases of accountability: A longitudinal case study of the Baltimore City Public Schools. *American Educational Research Journal, 42*(1), 43–75.

perform better on the tests and how having graduation tests affects students' motivation. These issues could be studied most effectively using interviews with students, teachers, and parents. By combining quantitative data with qualitative data, a more complete understanding of the relationship between high-stakes testing and dropping out can be developed.

Although the term *mixed method* has been used extensively to label research, only recently has it been given serious consideration by scholars. An indicator of this is the publication of the *Journal of Mixed Methods*, beginning in 2007 with the first volume. Consequently, you will find various types of studies referred to as *mixed method*, *mixed methodology*, and *multiple methods* in the literature. Other names, used less frequently, include *multimethod*, *multiple methodology*, *blended research*, *triangulated studies*, *hybrid*, and *integrative research* (Johnson, Onwuegbuzie, & Turner, 2007; Smith, 2006). According to Tashakkori and Creswell (2007), however labeled, these studies represent a variety of different qualitative and quantitative characteristics, which are manifest in language, philosophical assumptions, orientation, research questions, sampling, data collection procedures, types of data, types of data analysis, and conclusions.

You will find many different definitions of mixed method studies, and there is a trend toward using the term *mixed method* rather liberally to include any study that has some degree of both quantitative and qualitative methods. We believe that it is best to use the term *mixed method* for studies that include substantial contributions from each approach. We think the following definitions are especially good:

> research in which the investigator collects and analyzes data, integrates the findings, and draws inferences using both qualitative and quantitative approaches or methods in a single study or a program of inquiry. (Tashakkori and Creswell, 2007, p. 4)

> research . . . in which a researcher . . . combines elements of qualitative and quantitative research approaches (e.g., use of qualitative and quantitative viewpoints, data collection, analysis, inference techniques) for the broad purposes of breadth and depth of understanding and collaboration. (Johnson, Onwuegbuzie, & Turner, 2007, p. 123)

These definitions stress the need for the study to have an integrative character, although according to Bryman (2007), there are significant barriers that prevent this from occurring. It is more than simply using some quantitative and qualitative methods of gathering, analyzing, and reporting data separately in the same study. Rather, the definition indicates that mixed method studies combine qualitative and quantitative paradigms in meaningful ways. It is a convergence of philosophy, viewpoints, traditions, methods, and conclusions. This is how mixed method research is unique and is able to provide insights that are not possible when either the quantitative or qualitative approach is used independently. The result is enhancement and clarification.

You will find some studies that purport to be mixed method when in fact they only use both closed-ended and open-ended questions. The open-ended items may be referred to as *qualitative data*, but if that is the only qualitative characteristic, the study is hardly truly qualitative. For decades, survey data have included responses to open-ended questions, and these studies have been classified as quantitative because of the orientation and logic of the research questions and design.

Creswell and Plano Clark (2007) use the term *embedded design* to refer to a study in which "one data set provides a supportive, secondary role in a study based primarily on the other data type" (p. 67). The idea is that in some studies, using a single method is inadequate to completely answer the research questions. A good example is an experimental study that would include some open-ended interviews of participants to document the fidelity of the intervention. Here, a primarily quantitative study is supplemented by qualitative data. Our definition does not include such embedded designs, although sometimes it is difficult to distinguish between a mixed method study as we define it and an embedded mixed method design as presented by Creswell and Plano Clark.

There are both advantages and disadvantages to using a mixed method design (see Table 16.1). On the positive side, using both approaches allows the researcher to incorporate the strengths of each method. In this way, deficiencies in each method can be addressed. This provides for a more comprehensive picture of what is being studied, emphasizing quantitative outcomes as well as the process that influenced the outcomes. In addition, the nature of the data

TABLE 16.1 Advantages and Disadvantages of Mixed Method Research

Advantages	Disadvantages
Provides more comprehensive data	Researcher's training may not be adequate to conduct both types of research in a single study
Allows study of the process as well as the outcomes	One method may be used superficially
Compensates for limitations with use of a single method	Typically requires more extensive data collection
Allows investigation of different types of research questions	Typically requires more time and resources
Allows investigation of complex research questions	Difficulty in writing reports and forming conclusions
Enhances credibility of findings from a single method	May mislead readers if approach doesn't fully integrate both types of designs

collected is not confined to one type of method, which encourages the production of a more complete set of research questions as well as conclusions. It is also helpful to supplement a primarily quantitative or qualitative study with some data from the other method.

There are also some negatives to using mixed method designs. First, combining qualitative and quantitative methods in a single study typically requires that the researcher have competence in each type. Although it is relatively easy to gain an introductory understanding of both methodologies, greater depth of knowledge is needed to avoid less than credible findings. Second, a mixed method study requires extensive data collection and more resources than many studies using only a quantitative or qualitative approach. This suggests that it may not always be feasible to conduct a mixed method study. Finally, with the popularity of mixed methods, researchers may use one of the approaches superficially. For example, a researcher conducting a survey of school administrators about school climate could use both closed-ended (quantitative) and open-ended questions (presumably qualitative). Such a study would not be an example of a mixed method design as we have defined it, however, because the "qualitative" part would not include elements of an actual qualitative investigation. Similarly, if a researcher used random sampling to identify a group of counselors and then conducted in-depth interviews, it would be misleading to call this a mixed method study.

A mixed method study can be quickly identified by the title, methodology section, or research questions. Often, the title of the article will use the words *mixed method* or *quantitative and qualitative*. In the methodology section, there will be a clear indication of collecting both quantitative and qualitative data, usually in different sections or parts. Often, the research questions or purpose will include reference to using mixed methods or having both quantitative and qualitative purposes.

MIXED METHODS RESEARCH QUESTIONS

Good research begins with clear research questions. Most mixed method studies include both quantitative and qualitative questions and indicate the logic of the design. If both types of data are collected concurrently, the design may focus on the convergence of the information resulting from each method, giving equal priority to each. This may be called a *triangulation* type of study. If the logic of a study is more explanatory, quantitative questions will be followed by qualitative ones. An example of this kind of research problem is illustrated in Excerpt 16.2. Note the sequence of the questions—first quantitative, then qualitative. The qualitative data are used to explain the quantitative results.

EXCERPT 16.2 Sequential Explanatory Research Questions

The following research questions were addressed in this study:

1. To what extent do scores on an institutional ESL placement test . . . predict international graduate students' academic performance and their language difficulties in content courses during the first semester of their graduate education?

2. To what extent and in what ways do qualitative interviews with students and faculty members serve to contribute to a more comprehensive and nuanced understanding of this predictive relationship? (p. 369)

Source: From Lee, Y., & Greene, J. (2007). The predictive validity of an ESL placement test. *Journal of Mixed Methods Research, 1*(4), 366–389.

The sequence is the opposite for exploratory designs, in which the qualitative questions come first. Excerpt 16.3 shows three exploratory research questions that follow from a more general problem. The purpose of this study was to explain how political advertising affects college students' beliefs about the salience and relevance of the ads. Note how the stating of the research problem includes characteristics of the design. In Excerpt 16.4, three research questions are presented to frame a mixed methods study of kindergarten teachers' perceptions of retention.

One or more mixed method questions may follow the quantitative and qualitative questions. These questions address the integration of the methods in which qualitative and quantitative data are collected concurrently. In some mixed method studies, an overarching, integrated research question is presented, followed by more specific quantitative and qualitative questions. Questions that integrate the two methods are most typically found in studies in which the quantitative and qualitative data are collected and analyzed at about the same time. Less common

EXCERPT 16.3 Sequential Exploratory Research Problems and Questions

This study uses a mixed methods approach to explain how and why the political ads of the 2004 presidential candidates failed to engage young adults. Qualitative focus groups of college students examined how young voters interpret the salience of political advertising to them, and a quantitative content analysis of more than 100 ads from the 2004 presidential race focus[es] on why group participants felt so alienated by political advertising . . . three questions . . . are addressed:

- How does the interaction between audience-level and media-based framing contribute to college students'

interpretations of the messages found in political advertising?

- To what extent do those interpretations match the framing found in the ads from the 2004 U.S. presidential election?
- How can political ads be framed to better engage college students? (p. 186)

Source: From Parmelee, J. H., Perkins, S. C., & Sayre, J. J. (2007). "What about people our age?": Applying qualitative and quantitative methods to uncover how political ads alienate college students. *Journal of Mixed Methods Research, 1*(2), 183–199.

EXCERPT 16.4 Sequential Exploratory Research Problems and Questions

This study was designed to examine kindergarten teachers' perceptions of retention as an intervention. The following research questions guided the structure of the study:

1. What are kindergarten teachers' perceptions on kindergarten retention as an intervention?

2. Does a significant relationship exist between teachers' certification status and their perception of kindergarten retention?

3. Is there a significant relationship between teachers' teaching experience and their perception of kindergarten retention? (p. 402)

Source: From Okpala, C. O. (2007). The perceptions of kindergarten teachers on retention. *Journal of Research in Childhood Education, 21*(4), 400–406.

TABLE 16.2   Types of Mixed Method Research Questions

Type	Definition	Example	Method
Sequential Explanatory	Qualitative questions that provide explanations for findings from quantitative questions.	Teachers use zeros extensively in grading students. Why do teachers use zeros? How does this affect student motivation?	Teacher interviews followed by a survey of student motivation.
Sequential Exploratory	Qualitative questions asked first to generate information that is used in conducting the quantitative phase of the study.	What are teachers' grading practices? How do teachers determine how much weight is given to each component that determines the grades?	Survey of teachers' grading practices, followed by teacher interviews concerning reasons for the weight given each component.
Concurrent Triangulation	Quantitative and qualitative data collected concurrently to allow triangulation of the findings.	To what extent are zeros used in grading, and what is the effect on student motivation?	Concurrent interviews and surveys of both teachers and students.

are studies in which the research questions are developed as the study is conducted. Further examples of mixed method research questions are presented in Table 16.2.

SAMPLING IN MIXED METHOD RESEARCH

The selection of participants in a mixed method study includes both probability/nonprobability quantitative approaches to sampling and purposive qualitative approaches. Many studies use a convenience or available sample for the quantitative phase of the research, in which quantitative data are gathered. Teddlie and Yu (2007) have identified four types of probability sampling for mixed methods studies. The first is called **stratified purposive sampling**. In this kind of sampling, the quantitative approach of stratifying the population is followed by purposive selection of a small number of cases from each stratum that are studied intensely. For example, a researcher might stratify a sample of graduate students based on employment into three groups—fully employed, employed part-time, and not employed—and then select individuals from each of these groups who correspond to specific criteria.

Stratified purposeful sampling: targeted selection from a stratified sample

A variation of stratified purposive sampling is called **purposive random sampling**. This involves the random selection of a small number of cases from a larger population. For instance, in a study of the size of high schools, a researcher could select randomly from a population of, say, 350 high schools. Although the term *random* is used to describe the method of selecting the cases, it does not mean that the results can be generalized to the population. Rather, the strategy is used to provide qualitative results that complement quantitative findings. The sampling could occur either before or after the quantitative phase. It is more typical, however, for the sampling design to follow from the logic of the research questions. If the first question is clearly quantitative, then some kind of quantitative sampling process will be used, followed by a qualitative type of sampling. This is the most common sampling sequence in mixed method studies. Qualitative data may be gathered to help generate a survey that is administered to a large sample. In this case, qualitative questions precede the quantitative ones. There can also be *concurrent* qualitative and quantitative sampling. This strategy allows the researcher to *triangulate* the results, in which one component is used to corroborate, confirm, or cross-validate the findings.

Purposive random sampling: random selection of a small sample

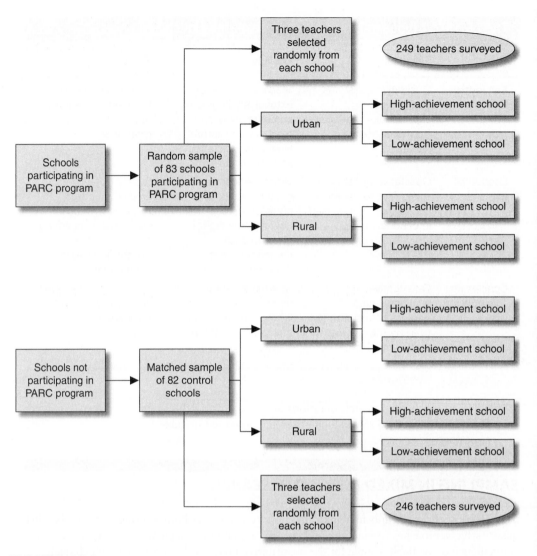

FIGURE 16.1 Concurrent Sampling for the Lasserre-Cortez (2006) Study

Concurrent triangulation sampling: systematic selection of a small sample

A good example of **concurrent triangulation sampling** in a mixed method design is illustrated in a study of characteristics of teachers and schools participating in action research group projects compared to control schools and the manner in which school climate impacted teacher effectiveness in working in small groups (Lasserre-Cortez, 2006). The researcher in this study used two sampling procedures at about the same time. A probability sample of 83 schools was selected using cluster sampling and matched with control schools. Three teachers were then selected randomly from each school and sent a survey. A sample of four intervention schools and four control schools was selected purposively from the larger group of 165 schools, using maximum variation sampling to document common patterns as well as differences. To obtain maximum variation, Lasserre-Cortez used two stratifying variables, achievement (high and low) and location (urban and rural). This resulted in four types of schools in both the intervention and control groups. The sampling in this study is illustrated in Figure 16.1.

Multilevel mixed method sampling: nested designs

The fourth type of sampling is called **multilevel mixed method sampling**. In this approach, the researcher selects cases that are representative of different levels of aggregation that comprise the overall population. Thus, in educational research, levels are represented by school districts, schools, teachers, and students. Depending on the research questions, appropriate probability and purposive sampling is used at each level. For example,

EXCERPT 16.5   Sampling in Mixed Method Research

One hundred of 110 international graduate students (91%) who took the university's English placement test . . .consented to participate . . . 55 questionnaires were returned for a response rate of 55%. . . . Interviews with 20 students [and] . . . 10 faculty members . . . were conducted individually. (pp. 370, 372)

Source: From Lee, Y., & Greene, J. (2007). The predictive validity of an ESL placement test. *Journal of Mixed Methods Research*, *1*(4), 366–389.

the Lasserre-Cortez study sampled schools and teachers randomly, then used purposive sampling to select the eight schools. Multilevel sampling is common in education because of three naturally occurring groups (districts, schools, and teachers) in each state. This type of situation is often called *nested*, because schools are located in specific districts and teachers are located in schools.

Note in Excerpt 16.5 how the authors described sampling in their mixed method study.

TYPES OF MIXED METHOD DESIGNS

Mixed method designs can differ to a great extent, depending on the purpose of the research, the sequence in which quantitative and qualitative methods are used, and the emphasis given to each method. We will consider the three major types of mixed method designs—sequential explanatory, sequential exploratory, and concurrent triangulation. See Creswell and Plano (2007) for additional designs.

Notation System

Creswell (2008) describes the following notation system to represent different mixed method designs:

- Uppercase letters (e.g., *QUAL* or *QUANT*) indicate a priority given to the method identified.
- Lowercase letters (e.g., *qual* or *quant*) show a lower priority given to the method.
- An arrow ($\rightarrow$) indicates the sequence of the collection of data.
- A + indicates the simultaneous collection of both quantitative and qualitative data.

Sequential Explanatory Designs

In a **sequential explanatory design**, quantitative and qualitative data collection is implemented in two phases, with the primary emphasis on quantitative methods. Initially, quantitative data are collected and analyzed. This is followed by qualitative data collection and analysis.

$$QUANT \longrightarrow qual$$

The qualitative data are needed to explain quantitative results or to further elaborate on quantitative findings.

Sequential explanatory design: quantitative followed by qualitative design

An explanatory design is generally used when quantitative data collection is clearly warranted but follow-up analysis—specifically, using qualitative methods—is necessary to elucidate the quantitative findings. For example, in a study comparing alternatively and traditionally prepared teachers, Miller, McKenna, and McKenna (1998) used three separate phases to answer their primary research question regarding differences in teaching practices between teachers who were traditionally certified and those who were alternatively certified (i.e., individuals who became teachers after having careers in other fields). The first two phases of the study were quantitative and utilized random sampling techniques and a

EXCERPT 16.6 Sequential Explanatory Research Design

In this study, we sought not only descriptions but also explanations of results, in this case teacher education outcomes. . . . The challenge in deciding on the design of the study was to reduce the complexity of the research objective without . . . unjustifiable simplifica-tions. . . . Written questionnaires were the chief instruments used to survey the whole sample. . . . We selected from all of the respondents a smaller number to form a representative subset . . . which was studied by . . . qualitative methods. (pp. 167, 171)

Source: From Brouwer, N., & Korthagen, F. (2005). Can teacher education make a difference? *American Educational Research Journal, 42*(1), 153–224.

Take a few moments to think about why you might use a mixed method approach in a real-life situation involving the assessment of preparatory programs for elementary school. Go to MyEducationLab for Research at www.myeducation-lab.com. Click on the topic "Mixed Methods Research" and then select the Activities and Applications activity "The Ready for School Los Angeles Program."

15-item rating scale to determine differences in teaching ability between the two groups. The last phase of the study used qualitative, in-person interviews to "gain insight into . . . teachers' perceptions of their teaching abilities" (p. 169). Although this study focused primarily on quantitative data, the qualitative interviews provided a richer understanding of the teachers' perceptions of their own abilities and how their training and certification program provided them with preparation for their teaching careers.

Another example of a mixed-method explanatory study was conducted by McMillan (2000). In this study, a large sample of teachers (850) was surveyed to determine the extent to which they used different factors in classroom assessment and grading. This provided a general overview of the teachers' practices. In the second phase, teachers were selected who represented high or low scores on the factors. Qualitative interviews were conducted with these teachers to determine why certain factors were emphasized. Thus, the qualitative phase was used to augment the statistical data to provide explanations for the practices.

See Excerpt 16.6 for an example of a study that used the sequential explanatory design.

Sequential Exploratory Designs

Sequential exploratory design: qualitative followed by quantitative design

A second type of mixed method research is the **sequential exploratory design**, in which qualitative data collection and analysis is followed by a quantitative phase. Generally, the purpose of a sequential exploratory design is either to use the qualitative data exploring a particular phenomenon to develop a quantitative instrument to measure that phenomenon or to use the quantitative portion of the study to explore relationships found in the qualitative data. If the main purpose is to test an instrument, there may be a greater emphasis on the quantitative part of the study:

$$Qual \rightarrow QUANT$$

If the quantitative portion of the study is used to confirm, determine, or expand on qualitative findings, then the qualitative part of the study will be emphasized:

$$QUAL \rightarrow quant$$

Using quantitative data to explore relationships found in qualitative studies allows the researcher to use in-depth information from participants to determine relationships. This can be achieved by listening during interviews or focus groups, determining if any of the themes appear to be related, and then following up with a quantitative measure to further explore those relationships, basically quantifying the connection established during the qualitative phase.

In developing a quantitative instrument from qualitative data, the researcher can use the language and emphasis of the participants in the wording of the items for the survey or scale. Doing so increases the validity of the scores from the newly developed instrument. For example, in a study by Rue, Dingley, and Bush (2002), the researchers utilized qualitative interviews

EXCERPT 16.7   Sequential Exploratory Mixed Method Design

The design began with a framing theory-based qualitative exploration of how college students interpret political ads, followed by quantitative investigation of the hypotheses that were generated as part of the qualitative study. (p. 186)

Source: From Parmelee, J. H., Perkins, S. C., & Sayre, J. J. (2007). "What about people our age?": Applying qualitative and quantitative methods to uncover how political ads alienate college students. *Journal of Mixed Methods Research, 1*(2), 183–199.

and language from many different participants with chronic health conditions to develop a quantitative instrument to measure the inner strength of women. This study relied heavily on participants' language and experiences with chronic conditions in order to develop items for a survey that could then quantitatively measure inner strength—a new concept in the field and one that had not previously been studied quantitatively.

Like explanatory designs, exploratory designs have both advantages and disadvantages. One advantage is that the quantitative portion of an exploratory study actually relies on the qualitative analysis to drive its direction, providing a greater understanding of the purpose of the quantitative data collection and analysis. However, like explanatory designs, exploratory designs require extensive data collection and analysis for both the qualitative and quantitative phases of the study. Moreover, it is sometimes difficult to indicate specifically how the qualitative findings were used to determine or influence the quantitative part of the study.

A sequential exploratory design is illustrated in Excerpt 16.7. The authors make it clear that the quantitative part of the study followed the qualitative part.

Concurrent Triangulation Designs

The third type of mixed method study is a **concurrent triangulation design** (also called an *integrative* or *convergent* design) in which the researcher simultaneously gathers both quantitative and qualitative data, merges them using both quantitative and qualitative data analysis methods, and then interprets the results together to provide a better understanding of a phenomenon of interest. Approximately equal emphasis is given to each method, even though one can follow the other:

$$\text{QUAL} + \text{QUANT} \text{ or } \text{QUANT} + \text{QUAL}$$

Or both can be conducted at the same time:

$$\text{QUANT} \\ + \\ \text{QUAL}$$

Concurrent triangulation design: quantitative and qualitative designs together

The interpretation of results is the key to this method, as it provides a convergence of evidence in which the results of both methods either support or contradict each other. When the results of different methods converge and support one another, researchers have *triangulated* the findings. In this case, the use of different methods results in very strong results. Often, the strengths of one method offset the weaknesses of the other, which allows for a much stronger overall design and thus more credible conclusions. Quantitative results enhance generalizability, and qualitative results help explain context. Consider a study that examined the relationship between working and family involvement in a child's education (Weiss et al., 2003). The researchers used concurrent quantitative and qualitative data collection and analysis to fully explore the relationship. They used data from an ongoing longitudinal study and also conducted interviews with working mothers and their children in order to determine the impact of working on family involvement in education. The researchers explain their methods in Excerpt 16.8.

Although giving equal priority to both methods is great for validity, triangulation requires that researchers have expertise to use both qualitative and quantitative methods. It is also a challenge to merge the qualitative and quantitative data so that there is a single study.

EXCERPT 16.8 Triangulation Mixed Method Design

For this study we employed a mixed method approach, using both quantitative and qualitative analyses. The added value of mixed method analysis has been documented in the literature, allowing, for example, better data triangulation and expansion of findings. We conducted the quantitative analyses in two phases: (a) We estimated the associations between demographic characteristics of mothers and their work/school statuses and their levels of school involvement; and (b) we estimated the association between mothers' work/school statuses and their levels of school involvement. Qualitative techniques supporting description and interpretation included reviewing ethnographic field notes, writing analytic memos, and systematically coding interviews. . . . Presented separately in the results below, these quantitative and qualitative analyses occurred in part on "parallel tracks." However, we also employed a "cross-over tracks" approach—an iterative mixed-method process, such that emergent findings from one method helped to shape subsequent analyses. (p. 886)

Source: From Weiss, H. B., Mayer, E., Kreider, H., Vaughan, M., Dearing, E., Hencke, R., & Pinto, K. (2003). Making it work: Low-income working mothers' involvement in their children's education. *American Educational Research Journal*, *40*(4), 879–901.

Table 16.3 summarizes the three major types of mixed method designs, including the purposes, advantages, and challenges in using each one.

CONDUCTING MIXED METHOD STUDIES

Which comes first? It is your turn to recommend the sequence for conducting a mixed method study. Go to MyEducationLab for Research at www.myeducationlab.com. Click on the topic "Mixed Methods Research" and then select the Activities and Applications activity "Reading Programs in the Chicago Public Schools."

Although the fundamental steps in conducting mixed method studies are similar to those used in a quantitative or qualitative study, there are some important differences. We will review seven essential steps. The sequence of steps is illustrated in Figure 16.2.

Step 1. *Determine the rationale.* It is important to identify the reasons for conducting a mixed method study and to determine whether these reasons provide sufficient justification. Researchers must be explicit about why a mixed method study is preferable to one that is entirely either quantitative or qualitative. This is best accomplished by incorporating mixed method literature.

Step 2. *Determine research questions.* While it is important to formulate a general purpose prior to establishing a design, at this point specific research questions can be formulated. Both quantitative and qualitative questions should be developed (although in an explanatory study, it may not be possible to establish qualitative questions until the quantitative questions have been addressed). Quantitative research questions should state expected relationships, while qualitative questions should be nondirectional.

Step 3. *Identify a data collection strategy and design.* It is also important to identify the extent to which each of the two methods will be used, whether priority will be given to one method, and in what sequence the two methods will be used. This information will be used to identify the design as exploratory, explanatory, or triangulation. It is helpful at this point to construct a diagram to show data collection

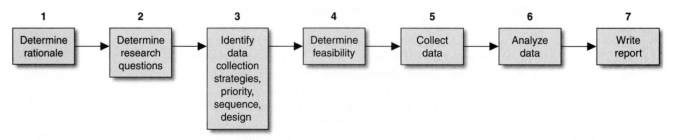

FIGURE 16.2 **Steps in Conducting Mixed Method Studies**

TABLE 16.3 Purpose, Advantages, and Challenges of Major Types of Mixed Method Designs

Type of Design	Purpose	Advantages	Challenges
Sequential Explanatory QUANT → qual	Qualitative data are used to elucidate, elaborate on, or explain quantitative findings. To follow up outliers or extreme cases.	• Straightforward implementation • Straightforward presentation of results. • Initial quantitative methods understood by researchers whose primary orientation is quantitative. Quantitative results can be used as a typology to identify themes in qualitative data.	• May require additional time for implementation and data collection compared to studies using only a quantitative or qualitative approach. • Decisions must be made about whether to collect data from the individuals, the same sample, or separate samples from the same population in each phase. • May be more difficult to obtain Institutional Review Board (IRB) approval because, prior to data collection, the nature of individuals sampled in the qualitative stage is not clear.
Sequential Exploratory QUAL → quant	Using qualitative data to establish groups to be compared; using quantitative data to explore relationships found in qualitative data. Use qualitative data to identify themes, scales, items, and variables that can be captured in quantitative measures.	• Separate phases make implementation straightforward. • Initial qualitative methods understood by researchers whose primary orientation is qualitative.	• May require additional time for implementation and data collection compared to studies using only a quantitative or qualitative approach. • Decisions must be made about whether the same individuals will serve as participants in both phases and whether additional participants are needed for the quantitative phase. • May be more difficult to obtain IRB approval because, prior to data collection, the sample used in the quantitative phase is not clear.
Concurrent Triangulation	Using both quantitative and qualitative designs and methods at about the same time. Used to compare quantitative to qualitative results and to combine results in order to identify themes and trends.	• Because the design is intuitive, it is easily understood; it is often the first choice of researchers new to mixed methods research. • Both types of data are collected and analyzed at the same time; data collection and analysis is efficient. • Well suited to collaborations or research teams.	• Because of the concurrent nature of data collection, additional effort and expertise in each method may be required. • Researchers may encounter situations where the results of the quantitative and qualitative data analyses diverge (do not agree or appear to tell different "stories"). This may require additional data collection or analyses.

Source: Adapted from McMillan (2008) and Creswell and Plano Clark (2007).

methods in the sequence used with assigned emphasis. Often, different phases are used to identify different stages of the design. Choosing how to weight the quantitative and qualitative methods in a study depends primarily on the purpose of the study and on what data collection and analysis methods are best suited to providing credible answers to the research questions. This will include a determination of whether one method is employed before the other and the time needed for each phase. In a sequential study, either the quantitative method is followed by the qualitative one or the opposite sequence is used. In concurrent studies, both methods are used together.

Step 4. ***Determine the feasibility of doing a mixed method study.*** Once the design is determined, the researchers need to think about whether resources and time are adequate to carry out the study. Feasibility is a function of the adequacy of training of study personnel and resources to collect and analyze the data. Sufficient time is needed to complete the data collection and analysis, and researchers must have expertise in both quantitative and qualitative methods. Limitations in terms of time and resources may force the researcher to prioritize and focus on one method more than the other. If researchers are uncomfortable or lack the expertise to implement both methods, then additional personnel should be added so that appropriate experience and knowledge can be used in the study. At this point, modifications to the design may be needed. Only what can be done well should be completed.

Step 5. ***Collect the data.*** The sequence for collecting data is determined by the design (i.e., exploratory, explanatory, or triangulation). This stage of the study will be lengthy, and appropriate principles for credible data collection for both the quantitative and qualitative phases should be followed.

Step 6. ***Analyze the data.*** The data are analyzed depending on the nature of the design. Data analyses for exploratory and explanatory designs are done separately. With a triangulation design, the quantitative and qualitative data are analyzed concurrently in an integrated fashion. In this case there is *data mixing*, in which quantitative and qualitative results are combined. In some cases, datasets are merged by transforming data of one type into the other. For example, qualitative data can be represented numerically based on frequency of occurrence, which can then be used in quantitative analyses. Statistical trends can be complemented by qualitative data.

Step 7. ***Write the report.*** The first important consideration in writing a mixed method study report or article is to frame the questions and methodology to be consistent with the design. It is helpful to be explicit about what design is used; don't assume that the reader will understand because the language of mixed method designs can vary from one researcher to another. The justification for a mixed method design should be summarized. It is also good to explain clearly how the design addresses the research questions. Results should be sequenced to be consistent with the design, matching the major or minor emphasis (e.g., QUANT or quant). Because of the logic of sequential designs, it is best to present and interpret results from the first analysis before reporting the second set of data.

STANDARDS OF ADEQUACY

What sets mixed method studies apart from other research designs is the intentional and substantial collection of both quantitative and qualitative data. This suggests that standards of adequacy for each of these studies by themselves would be appropriate. Thus, mixed method studies should be able to "hold their own weight" with regard to standards of rigor and quality checks for both quantitative and qualitative methods. In addition, there are several considerations that are unique. These are summarized in the following standards of adequacy.

1. Is it clear that both quantitative and qualitative methods were used? Is the study clearly identified as mixed method? Do the qualitative methods involve more than simple coding of open-ended responses?

2. Is there a clear rationale that states a convincing case for the type of mixed method design?
3. Are there multiple purposes and questions that justify the use of a mixed method design?
4. Is there a good match between research questions and methods?
5. Is the sequential nature of data collection reasonable?
6. To what extent has the researcher adhered to the criteria that define quality for both the quantitative and qualitative portions of the study?
7. Has the researcher addressed the tension between potentially conflicting demands of different paradigms in the design and implementation of the study?
8. To the extent possible, were there adequate resources to carry out the study?
9. Have appropriate limitations associated with the study been included?
10. Are appropriate criteria indicated for selecting participants for the qualitative aspect of the study?
11. Is the sampling strategy aligned with the research questions?
12. Are qualitative findings integrated with quantitative results?

Continue building your skills by evaluating a mixed method study. Go to MyEducationLab for Research at www.myeducationlab.com. Click on the topic "Mixed Methods Research" and then select the Building Research Skills exercise "Evaluating a Mixed Method Study."

CHAPTER SUMMARY

This chapter has presented an introduction to understanding and conducting mixed method research. The following key points summarize the chapter:

1. Mixed method designs combine quantitative and qualitative questions, methods, and analyses in a single study.
2. Mixed method studies incorporate the strengths of quantitative and qualitative designs to capture unique findings.
3. To use mixed method studies, researchers need to be competent in using both quantitative and qualitative methods.
4. There are three major types of mixed method designs: sequential explanatory, sequential exploratory, and concurrent triangulation.

5. In sequential explanatory designs, quantitative methods are employed first, followed by qualitative methods.
6. In sequential exploratory designs, qualitative methods are employed first, followed by quantitative methods.
7. In concurrent triangulation designs, quantitative and qualitative methods are used together.
8. Research questions, the sequence of methods, and the reporting of results should be clearly aligned.
9. Standards of adequacy for mixed method studies rely on quantitative and qualitative standards as well as the justification for and effectiveness of mixing the methods.

APPLICATION PROBLEMS

1. For each of the following descriptions, indicate the type of mixed method design being used.
   a. A doctoral student is interested in studying the effects of small-group counseling on students' self-esteem. Thirty students participate as subjects. The Coopersmith Self-Esteem Inventory is given as a pretest and a posttest, and interviews are used to follow up with students every month.
   b. Service learning is becoming very popular in both public schools and colleges and universities. However, relatively little is known about the perceptions of the beneficiaries of the services. A study is prepared to examine these perceptions using focus group interviews and a questionnaire to ask participants about the characteristics of effective volunteers.
2. Give an original example of each of the three types of mixed method designs.

3. A researcher has conducted a series of interviews about job stress and burnout with teachers of students with disabilities. Following the interviews, additional data could be collected to provide even more description of teachers' job stress and burnout as well as its effects on students. What procedures could be used to extend the study to be an exploratory design? What procedures could be used to extend the study to be a triangulation design?
4. In your own field of work and study, suggest an action research study that uses a mixed method design.
5. An example of a mixed method study follows. Identify the type of mixed method design that is used. What kind of sampling is used? Does it make sense to do the focus groups before the survey? To what extent are the standards of adequacy for mixed method studies met?

EXAMPLE

Perceptions of Parent Involvement in Academic Achievement

Jennifer DePlanty, Russell Coulter-Kern and Kim A. Duchane*
Manchester College, Indiana

ABSTRACT The authors sought to understand the types of parent involvement that teachers, parents, and students believe affect the academic achievement of adolescent learners at the junior high school level. Research that included focus groups, interviews, and surveys indicated that teachers and students believed that parent involvement at school was considered less important to a child's academic achievement than parent involvement in academics at home. In addition, parents rated themselves as more participatory in academics than did their children or junior high school teachers.

At the heart of the No Child Left Behind Act of 2001 is a promise to strengthen America's education system and raise the academic achievement of all students. Well-trained teachers can provide effective instruction so that students perform at their highest academic potential and that "no child is left on their behind." The law recognizes that parents are their children's first and most important teachers, and for students to succeed in school, parents must participate actively in their children's academic lives. Parents need to become involved early and stay involved throughout the school years. That is especially true during the adolescent years.

Many educational sociologists believe that adolescence is the most complex social period in the life of an individual. During adolescence, rapid physical, emotional, and intellectual changes occur, as well as an intense preoccupation with questions of personal identity, peer group expectations, and normative values (Fenwick, 1987). Throughout this critical time in a teenager's life, families and schools need to work together. Families provide the social, cultural, and emotional supports that youth need to function well in school. Schools provide opportunities for children's positive interactions with significant adults and other adolescents to enhance their home experiences and to support their continued development and related learning (Comer & Haynes, 1991). Our purpose in this study was to understand the types of parent involvement that teachers, parents, and students believe affect the academic achievement of adolescent learners at the junior high school level.

Parent Influences on Involvement

Adolescents tend to be affected positively when a relationship is sustained between their home and school environments. Involvement at home, especially parents discussing school activities and helping children plan their programs, has the strongest impact on academic achievement (SuiChu & Willms, 1996; VanVoorhis, 2003).

> Parents who are involved in their children's education in ways that create or reinforce direct experiences of educational success or verbal persuasion intended to develop attitudes, behaviors, and efforts consistent with school success, and create emotional arousal that underscores the personal importance of doing well in school are more likely to develop a strong, positive sense of efficacy for successfully achieving in school-related tasks than students whose parents are not involved. (Hoover-Dempsey & Sandler, 1995, p. 315)

Researchers have also found that parent-child discussion about school helps improve academic achievement and reduce problematic behavior (Epstein & Sheldon, 2002; McNeal, 1999; Sheldon & Epstein, 2005). Finally, the level of parent-school involvement is a better predictor of grades than are standardized test scores (Desimone, 1999). That finding strongly suggests that parent involvement is a valuable component of any student's education.

If the benefits of parent-school involvement are positive, then why are parents not becoming involved? Stevenson and Baker (1987) reported that as children grow older, parent involvement begins to decrease at home and in the school. Some parents believe that involvement in their children's education is not as important in Grades 7–12 as it was during the elementary school years. Parents also may think that adolescents desire and need independence, which causes the parents to decrease their level of involvement (Eccles & Harold, 1993).

Sheldon (2002) highlighted several other reasons why parents are not involved effectively. He suggested that the resources that parents gain through their social networks contribute to their involvement in their children's education. If parents have minimal social networks, they tend to be less involved. In addition, Sheldon noted that parents with access to more financial resources are more likely to be involved. He also reported that the more financially stable a family is, the more time that parents have for their children and the more concern they have for their education.

Another barrier to school involvement is the education level of the parent. Stevenson and Baker (1987) reported a positive correlation between the mother's education and the degree of parent involvement in school activities. The researchers stated that parents with more education are

* Address correspondence to Kim A. Duchane, 604 E College Avenue, MC Box PERC, North Manchester, IN 46962. (E-mail: kaduchane@manchester.edu)

more active in school activities, such as Parent-Teacher Association meetings and parent-teacher conferences. Parent involvement may also decrease as students move from elementary into junior high school because parents are less knowledgeable in some of the academic subject areas (Eccles & Harold, 1993). Those investigators suggested that parents with a higher education are better qualified than are less educated parents to help their children with homework. As a result, less educated parents might shift their attention away from school because they feel inadequate when helping their children with homework.

School Influences on Involvement

Schools also affect parent-involvement levels. Evidence shows that many parents want to become involved but are not encouraged or do not have the open communication or support from the school to do so. Epstein (1987) reported that large numbers of parents are excluded from the most common forms of communication with their children's school. Epstein (1987) concluded that (a) more than one third of all U.S. parents did not have a conference with a teacher during the school year, (b) over half of the parents had never talked with a teacher by telephone, and (c) most parents reported that they had never been involved in deep or frequent discussions with teachers about their children's program or progress. That finding was startling because 95% of the teachers interviewed said that they communicated with parents, suggesting a discrepancy between the experience of the teacher and that of the parents. Also, Epstein (1986) suggested that parents wanted teachers to more actively involve them in learning activities at home. About 58% of the parents in Epstein's 1986 study said that they rarely or never received requests from their children's teachers to become involved in learning activities at home. In addition, 16% of the parents said that they received no written correspondence from the teacher, over 35% of the parents had no parent-teacher conferences, and 60% never spoke to the teacher on the telephone.

Why do teachers not initiate more contact with parents? One reason why teachers do not send notes, have conferences, or call parents is because they believe that they do not have the time. Epstein and Becker (1982) reported that teachers think involving parents is extremely important, but time constraints limit their time to deal with parents. A quote by an anonymous teacher summarizes that point: "I believe both parents and students can benefit from parent involvement. However, I also know that it takes a great deal of training and explaining and coordination to have a good program. I've spent many hours doing just this. Frankly, I no longer feel like giving the many hours of extra time required to do this. We are not provided with time to do this type of training. It's all our own time. I no longer feel like giving my time without compensation." (p. 104)

Another barrier that often influences the involvement of parents is teacher efficacy. A teacher's sense of efficacy is a judgment about his or her capability to influence student engagement and learning, even among those students who may be difficult or unmotivated (Tschannen-Moran & Woolfolk Hoy, 2001). Epstein and Dauber (1991) reported that teachers who believe that they share similar beliefs with parents about involvement make more contacts with parents and conduct more types of activities to involve families. If a teacher has feelings of isolation or separateness, more than likely the teacher will not contact parents or try to get them to participate in at-home activities. Hoover-Dempsey, Bassler, and Brissie (1992) also reinforced a positive relationship between teacher efficacy and teacher reports of parent involvement. They speculated that higher efficacy teachers might invite and receive more parent involvement than do lower efficacy teachers.

Hoover-Dempsey and Sandler (1995) and the research studies previously highlighted have indicated a positive impact on a student's academic success when a relationship exists between the school and family. We undertook this study to collect information for a school improvement plan and to better understand the implicit beliefs of parents, teachers, and adolescent learners regarding the different types of parent-school involvement techniques that influence the academic success of junior high students. The following research questions guided this study:

1. Do teachers, parents, and students agree that parent-school relationships are important?
2. What do teachers, parents, and students believe is the ideal type of parent involvement that leads to academic success?
3. How often do parents participate in activities that they have identified as important?
4. How often do teachers and students think that parents participate in these activities?

Method

Participants

Twenty-two teachers and staff (counselor, librarian, paraprofessionals; 15 women and 7 men) from a junior high school in a rural county of a midwestern state participated in the study. They first attended our focus group meetings, then completed a survey. Two hundred and thirty-four junior high students (130 girls, 104 boys) participated by completing a survey given during their homeroom period. In addition to the junior high teachers, staff, and students, participants included 301 parents (165 women and 136 men) from a predominately Caucasian community.

We gathered the parent information from 185 surveys given during the scheduled parent-teacher conferences; one or both parents completed a survey for each family (see Table 1). From that data, we found that 82% of the junior high students were being raised in two-parent homes. Approximately 49% of the parent participants reported earning a high school diploma as their highest level of educational achievement, and 21% reported obtaining a bachelor's degree. The data also indicated that 84% of all parents were working full time outside of the home.

(continued)

example *(continued)*

TABLE 1 Demographic Information for Parent Participants		
Variable	**Frequency**	**%**
Gender		
Male	136	45
Female	165	55
Level of education		
No diploma	22	6
High school diploma	140	49
Some college	35	12
Professional degree	14	5
Undergraduate degree	63	21
Master's degree	22	6
Doctoral degree	5	1
Work status		
Full time	255	84
Part time	26	9
Does not work	20	7

Procedure

Interview To gain a better understanding of the levels of parent involvement in the school community, we initially interviewed the junior high principal. During that interview, discussion centered on the (a) importance of parent involvement in adolescent learning, (b) purpose of junior high education, (c) reasons that parents did or did not become involved, and (d) ideal levels of involvement. After obtaining the information, we developed focus group questions to help prompt discussion on parent involvement in junior high education. Examples of interview questions include:

Describe the ideal type and level of parent involvement at home, school, and in the community and how would you rate the parent involvement of your current students, and why?

Focus Groups Working in pairs, we conducted focus groups with junior high school teachers and staff. We asked the teachers and staff a series of questions regarding optimal levels of parent involvement, actual parent involvement, and ways that the school encouraged or inadvertently discouraged parent involvement. We then organized the data gathered from the junior high teachers and staff into themes that the faculty identified as important. We used the identified themes to develop a survey for the parents of the junior high school students.

Survey We developed the survey to provide an objective manner to measure the qualitative data obtained in the interviews and focus groups. Consistent with grounded theory methods (Strauss & Corbin, 1994), the findings that emerged from earlier data-collection methods provided the content assessed in the survey. The primary author constructed initial wording of items that the other authors reviewed for faithfulness to the parent-involvement themes

that emerged in interviews and focus groups. After professors involved in education research reviewed the items and made minor suggestions about content and wording, we revised the instrument.

In addition, we conducted a pilot study in which a class of 16 undergraduate research design students familiar with the project completed the survey and commented on its faithfulness to the themes identified in earlier data-collection methods. The students commented that the statements were clear, appropriate, and accurately reflected earlier themes on parent involvement. Because the criterion for assessing the validity of the instrument was the themes identified in the interviews and focus groups, we did not need to evaluate criterion or construct validity.

The authors established reliability (internal consistency) for the instrument by using coefficient alpha. The surveys were internally consistent with the following alpha coefficients: .82 for parents, .72 for teachers, and .90 for students. The survey asking parents to rate parent-involvement strategies that teachers identified as important at the junior high level and an informed consent form were given to parents following parent-teacher conferences: parents completed and returned 185 surveys. The survey also asked parents how often they participated in parent-involvement activities. Participating junior high teachers and students completed similar versions of the survey.

Results

In the initial stage of the study, we conducted an interview and focus groups with the teachers and staff. The need for parents to ensure that students completed their homework was one of the important themes that faculty identified. The faculty also indicated that parents' presence in the school was not important as long as parents emphasized the importance of education at home. Teachers and staff also stated that they believed that the level of parent involvement for their current students was low. When asked what type of involvement was most important for parents, the teachers indicated that involvement at home is far more important than is involvement in the school and community. When we asked the teacher participants why they thought that parents might not become involved, the majority stated cited "intimidation" as the overwhelming reason. The teachers and staff overwhelmingly believed that parents were intimidated by some aspect of the school or subject matter. During that stage in the investigation, we also explored elements of parent involvement, such as (a) ways to encourage it, (b) the relationship between academic success and parent involvement, and (c) information that teachers would like to acquire from parents.

We used the information gathered from focus groups to develop surveys, then administered them to the parents, teachers, and students at the junior high school. The surveys had two distinct sections. One section dealt with attitude about parent involvement, whereas the other section focused on behaviors that typified involvement. We calculated means and standard deviations, and parents, teachers, and students identified similar parent-involvement behaviors as important (see Table 2). All participants believed that ensuring that children attend school daily was the most important component of parent involvement. Parents and teachers also rated "observing child's classes" and "volunteering at school" as the least important activities. However, students believed that "talking with their friends' parents about school" and "limiting the time they watch television" were the least important activities. That finding could have resulted from the age and value differences between students and their parents, and students and their teachers.

Exploratory Factor Analysis

To determine the factor structure of the "importance items" from the surveys, we conducted a separate exploratory factor analyses on the instrument completed by parents and teachers, as well as on the instrument completed by students. We submitted the items assessing the importance of parent involvement on the parent and teacher survey to a principal-components factor analysis with varimax rotation and an eigenvalue greater than 1. The procedure yielded five factors; eigenvalues ranged from 1.69 to 2.74. We then evaluated each of the factors in terms of whether it was interpretable (i.e., made conceptual sense) and whether a large number of items (i.e., 10) had a factor loading greater than 0.40, or a small number of items (i.e., 4) had a factor loading greater than 0.60, as suggested by Guadagnoli and Velicer (1988). Although we did not meet the full criteria of those researchers because our intent was to understand the factor structure and we had to analyze the current data for potential future replication, we continued our analysis.

The procedure led to the retention of five factors, each comprising five, two, two, three, and three items with an eigenvalue of 2.74, 1.98, 1.79, 1.77, and 1.69, respectively. The five factors accounted for percentages of 18.27, 13.21, 11.94, 11.82, and 11.29 of the total variance, respectively; the remaining factors were not amendable to interpretation or had few items with factor loadings greater than .40. The resultant factors were labeled (a) School Involvement, (b) Time Management, (c) School Attendance, (d) Parent Structure, and (e) Supportive Home Environment. (See Table 3 for a list of items, factor loadings from the principal-component factor analysis, means, and standard deviations.) For future analysis, the stability of the factor structure should be further examined empirically with confirmatory factor analysis.

We submitted the student survey items concerning importance of parent involvement to a principal-components factor analysis by using the same criteria stated in the previous paragraphs. The procedure yielded three factors with eigenvalues ranging from 1.06 to 3.69. The factors each comprised 3, 4, and 3 items with eigenvalues of 3.69, 1.11, and 1.06, respectively. The three factors accounted for percentages of 33.53, 10.12, and 9.61 of the total variance, respectively. We labeled the factors (a) Parent Structure, (b) Time Management, and (c) School Attendance. Some variations in the factor structure existed between the combined parent and teacher scale and the student scale. However, that result would not be atypical given the 15 items on the parent and teacher version and 11 items on the student version. Although similar, there were several variations of item loadings on the Parent Structure, Time Management, and School Attendance factors between the parent and teacher version and the student version of the scale. (For student data, see Table 4 for a list of items, factor loadings from the principal-component factor analysis, means, and standard deviations.)

The second main section of the survey concerned the amount of time that parents were engaged in behaviors identified as important components of parent involvement. In this section, parents, teachers, and students ranked the participation of parent behaviors in a similar order. Of the various types of parent involvement, the three groups agreed that parent-teacher conferences was the activity that parents were involved in most (see Table 5). One intriguing element of this section was that teachers and students reported that parents engaged in parent-teacher conferences less than parents reported they did. Students even ranked parent participation in conferences lower than did teachers. There was a significant difference in the ways that parents perceived their behaviors and the manner in which teachers and students imagined parents' behaviors. Data reveal that teachers and students have a higher expectation for involvement than do parents. The parents might have been missing, or been uninformed of, the link that would make their involvement appear more successful to their children and to their children's teachers.

(continued)

example *(continued)*

TABLE 2 Participant Ratings of Importance of Items to Student Achievement

| | Participants | | |
| | Parents (N = 301) | | Teachers (N = 22) |
Item	M	SD	M
Making sure child is at school every day	3.88	0.36	4.00
Attending parent-teacher conferences	3.75	0.51	3.67
Regularly talking to child about school	3.65	0.53	3.86
Checking that child has done homework	3.64	0.60	3.57
Balancing schoolwork and school activities	3.63	0.58	3.86
Having a variety of reading materials in the house	3.49	0.69	3.57
Balancing schoolwork and time with friends	3.44	0.71	3.74
Having a set time for homework	3.37	0.70	3.57
Attending activities at school	3.35	0.73	3.57
Limiting the amount of time child watches TV	3.20	0.77	3.67
Reviewing child's weekly planner	3.19	0.82	3.38
Regularly talking with child's teacher	3.06	0.72	3.00
Talking to other parents about school	2.68	0.81	2.90
Observing child's classes	2.50	0.95	2.38
Volunteering at school	2.49	0.80	2.90

| | Participants | | |
| | | Students (N = 234) | |
Item	SD	M	SD
Making sure child is at school every day	0.00	3.44	0.79
Attending parent-teacher conferences	0.48	2.84	0.99
Regularly talking to child about school	0.35	2.88	0.88
Checking that child has done homework	0.91	2.56	0.97
Balancing schoolwork and school activities	0.35	—	—
Having a variety of reading materials in the house	0.60	—	—
Balancing schoolwork and time with friends	0.44	2.70	0.97
Having a set time for homework	0.67	3.41	0.76
Attending activities at school	0.50	2.69	0.99
Limiting the amount of time child watches TV	0.59	2.25	1.02
Reviewing child's weekly planner	0.90	2.43	0.96
Regularly talking with child's teacher	0.87	2.70	0.91
Talking to other parents about school	0.83	2.17	0.92
Observing child's classes	0.79	—	—
Volunteering at school	0.83	—	—

Note: Dashes indicate that items were included on the parent and teacher surveys but not on the student version.

TABLE 3 Factor Structure of Parent and Teacher Ratings of Importance of Items to Student Achievement

Subscale/item	Factor 1 loading	Factor 2 loading	Factor 3 loading	Factor 4 loading	Factor 5 loading	M	SD
School Involvement							
Volunteering at school	.810	.051	.034	.066	.254	2.52	0.80
Talking to other parents about school	.767	.205	.109	.038	.087	2.71	0.83
Regularly talking with my child's teachers	.642	−.078	.354	.275	.116	3.08	0.73
Observing my child's classes	.574	.284	.003	.354	−.041	2.48	0.93
Attending activities at school	.549	.353	.370	−.065	.024	3.38	0.72
Time Management							
Balancing schoolwork and time with friends	.180	.836	−.013	.180	.129	3.47	0.69
Balancing schoolwork and after-school activities	.200	.830	.157	.065	.145	3.65	0.58
School Attendance							
Attending parent-teacher conferences	.342	−.018	.721	.061	.039	3.75	0.49
Making sure my child is at school every possible day	−.117	.462	.581	.272	−.080	3.88	0.35
Parent Structure							
Checking to make sure my child has done homework	.035	.200	.012	.798	.029	3.65	0.59
Reviewing my child's weekly planner	.364	−.059	.373	.642	.085	3.22	0.83
Having a set time for homework	.133	.152	.063	.571	.478	3.39	0.70
Supportive Home Environment							
Limiting the amount of time child watches television	.088	.072	−.093	.135	.848	3.24	754
Regularly talking to my child about school	.081	.210	.557	.177	.566	3.68	0.53
Having a variety of reading materials in the house	.295	.092	.414	−.151	.533	3.39	0.70

TABLE 4 Factor Structure of Student Ratings of Importance of Items to Student Achievement

Subscale/item	Factor 1 loading	Factor 2 loading	Factor 3 loading	M	SD
Parent Structure					
Making sure you have done your homework	.796	.207	.033	2.58	0.958
Reviewing your school planner	.744	.033	.279	2.45	0.955
Having a set time for your homework	.621	.153	.281	3.43	0.733
Time Management					
Making sure your activities and time with friends are not interfering with schoolwork	.082	.790	.156	2.68	0.968
Your parents talking to you about classes and grades	.020	.698	.384	2.87	0.885
Limiting the time you watch television	.383	.641	−.185	2.23	1.007
Talking with your teacher about classes and grades	.293	.551	.386	2.71	0.904
School Attendance					
Attending other activities at school	.144	.026	.703	2.71	0.994
Talking with your friends' parents about school	.067	.199	.655	2.15	0.900
Making sure you are at school every day	.197	.097	.492	3.46	0.765
Attending student-led conferences	.365	.239	.414	2.83	0.985

(continued)

example *(continued)*

TABLE 5 Participant Responses for Frequency of Parent Engagement for Specific Behaviors

Item	Participant	Rank	*M*	*SD*
Attend parent-teacher conferences	Parent	1	3.84	0.43
	Teacher	1	3.62	0.50
	Student	1	3.39	0.91
Talk to child about school	Parent	2	3.59	0.56
	Teacher	2	3.00	1.00
	Student	2	2.97	0.93
Attend other activities at school	Parent	3	3.04	0.74
	Teacher	3	2.76	0.44
	Student	3	2.55	0.97
Review child's weekly planner	Parent	4	2.55	0.92
	Teacher	4	2.68	0.89
	Student	6	1.67	0.83
Talk with other parents about school	Parent	5	2.54	0.81
	Teacher	5	2.43	0.51
	Student	5	2.09	0.92
Talk to child's teacher	Parent	6	2.51	0.70
	Teacher	6	2.33	0.48
	Student	4	2.41	0.91

Discussion

Our purpose in the study was to understand the types of parent involvement that teachers, parents, and students believe affect the academic achievement of adolescent learners at the junior high school level so that no child is left on their behind. Researchers have identified parent involvement as an important factor for the academic success of children (Sheldon & Epstein, 2005; VanVoorhis, 2003). As the results suggest, teachers, parents, and students value the importance of parent involvement in education. Many similarities emerged regarding the behaviors that each group of participants perceived as being important. Parents displayed a link between attitude about parent involvement and their parent-involvement behaviors, which was indicated because behaviors with higher importance ranks reportedly occurred more often. Teachers and students also recognized the importance of parent-involvement behaviors, but consistently ranked parents' behaviors lower than did parents. Parents overestimated their involvement, but their motivation for doing so was unclear. That phenomenon warrants further investigation.

Researchers have noted that open communication between parents and teachers can benefit the academic success of junior high school students (Epstein, 1986; Epstein & Sheldon, 2002). Results from the surveys suggest that communication between the two groups was not as open as we expected. If mutual communication between school and home had occurred, then the results from the teachers,

parents, and students on the second portion of the survey, "How Often Parents Engage in the Following Behaviors," would have been more similar. The results from the first portion of the survey, "How Important Are Each of the Following to the Education of Students?," informed researchers that parents do know the behaviors in which they need to participate. As a result of these data, the goal of schools should be to persuade parents to participate in the activities that schools identify as important to the degree that teachers and students begin to notice a difference. The goal could be implemented through several means: (a) workshops focusing on the benefits of parent involvement and those parent behaviors that are the most important ones provided by the community or school, (b) brochures or pamphlets sent home informing parents about parent involvement, and (c) talks with parents about involvement during parent-teacher conferences.

We identified several important elements of parent involvement and generated many questions about parent perceptions of their involvement. Researchers could benefit by exploring the mismatch between parent behaviors perceived as important on the teacher, parent, and student surveys, and actual parent behavior. Thus, education leaders might gain a better understanding of why parents answered the way they did and whether parents believed that they were participating in activities that effectively supported the academic achievement of their child. Another advantage might originate from the teachers' reactions to the mismatch of rated importance and involvement. Researchers could clarify whether underlying issues at the school may explain the reasons that parents are not getting effectively involved. Also, it may prove helpful if researchers evaluate school programs that target parent involvement in ways that we identified as important.

Limitations

One must view the present study cautiously because of two limitations. The first limitation concerns the sample, which involved a small number of teachers from an intact group at one school. Because of the restricted range of participants, in similar studies, researchers should include a more diverse and representative sample of teachers.

The second limitation involved parent data being collected during parent-teacher conferences. Confounding reporting effects may have resulted if the parents offered what they perceived as socially acceptable responses. That problem is inherent in self-report instruments in which researchers rely on the truthfulness of participant responses.

Those limitations notwithstanding, we underscored the need for teachers to promote parent involvement so that students can achieve academically and succeed in school. We believe that the findings offer considerable insight into strengthening academic achievement in the nation's public and private schools.

Notes

The authors thank Jessica Hamlyn of Manchester College and Michael Stone of the Community Foundation of Wabash County for their contribution to this project.

This research was supported by a Scholarship of Engagement Faculty Grant from the Indiana Campus Compact.

References

Comer, J. P., & Haynes, N. M. (1991). Parents' involvement in schools: An ecological approach. *Elementary School Journal, 91,* 271–277.

Desimone, L. (1999). Linking parent involvement with student achievement: Do race and income matter? *The Journal of Educational Research, 93,* 11–30.

Eccles, J. S., & Harold, R. D. (1993). Parent-school involvement during the early adolescent years. *Teachers College Record, 94,* 568–587.

Epstein, J. L. (1986). Parents' reactions to teacher practices of parent involvement. *Elementary School Journal, 86,* 277–294.

Epstein, J. L. (1987). What principals should know about parent involvement. *Principal, 66,* 6–9.

Epstein, J. L., & Becker, H. J. (1982). Teachers' reported practices of parent involvement: Problems and possibilities. *Elementary School Journal, 83,* 103–113.

Epstein, J. L., & Dauber, S. L. (1991). School programs and teacher practices of parent involvement in inner-city elementary and middle schools. *Elementary School Journal, 91,* 289–305.

Epstein, J. L., & Sheldon, S. B. (2002). Present and accounted for: Improving student attendance through family and community involvement. *The Journal of Educational Research, 95,* 308–318.

Fenwick, J. J. (1987). Middle schoolers: Meeting the social needs. *Principal, 66,* 43–46.

Guadagnoli, E., & Velicer, W. F. (1988). Relation of sample size to the stability of component patterns. *Psychological Bulletin, 103,* 265–275.

Hoover-Dempsey, K. V., Bassler, O. C., & Brissie, J. S. (1992). Explorations in parent-school relations. *The Journal of Educational Research, 85,* 287–294.

Hoover-Dempsey, K. V., & Sandler, H. M. (1995). Parent involvement in children's education: Why does it make a difference? *Teachers College Record, 97,* 310–331.

McNeal, R. B. (1999). Parent involvement as social capital: Differential effectiveness on science achievement, truancy, and dropping out. *Social Forces, 78,* 117–144.

Sheldon, S. B. (2002). Parents' social networks and beliefs as predictors of parent involvement. *Elementary School Journal, 102,* 301–316.

Sheldon, S. B., & Epstein, J. L. (2005). Involvement counts: Family and community partnerships and math achievement. *The Journal of Educational Research, 98,* 196–206.

Stevenson, D. L., & Baker, D. P. (1987). The family-school relation and the child's school performance. *Child Development, 58,* 1348–1357.

Strauss, A., & Corbin, J. (1994). Grounded theory methodology: An overview. In N. K. Denzin & Y. S. Lincoln (Eds.), *Handbook of qualitative research* (pp. 273–285). Thousand Oaks, CA: Sage.

Sui-Chu, E. S., & Willms, J. D. (1996). Effects of parent involvement on eighth-grade achievement. *Sociology of Education, 69,* 126–141.

Tschannen-Moran, M., & Woolfolk Hoy, A. (2001). Teacher efficacy: Capturing an elusive construct. *Teaching and Teacher Education, 17,* 783–805.

U.S. Department of Education. (2001). Pub. L. No. 107-110, No Child Left Behind Act. Retrieved March 20, 2006, from http://www.ed.gov/policy/elsec/leg/esea02/index.html.

VanVoorhis, F. L. (2003). Interactive homework in middle school: Effect on family involvement and students' science achievement. *The Journal of Educational Research, 96,* 323–339.

ANSWERS TO APPLICATION PROBLEMS

1. a. Sequential explanatory
   b. Concurrent triangulation
2. (individual student response, e.g., exploratory—using teacher interviews to construct a survey given to teachers about math specialists; explanatory—observing students with special needs following a survey of teachers' perceptions; triangulation—assessing counselors' use of time with interviews and self-report surveys).

3. To extend the study to make it an exploratory design, the quantitative phase should be instituted and emphasized more than the qualitative phase. One way to accomplish this would be to use the findings of the interviews to create a quantitative survey that could be administered to a large group of teachers. A triangulation design could be implemented by asking each teacher to complete a survey right before or after his or her interview.
4. (individual student answer)

Concept Analysis and Historical Research

From Chapter 17 of *Research in Education: Evidence-Based Inquiry*, 7/e. James H. McMillan. Sally Schumacher.

Concept Analysis and Historical Research

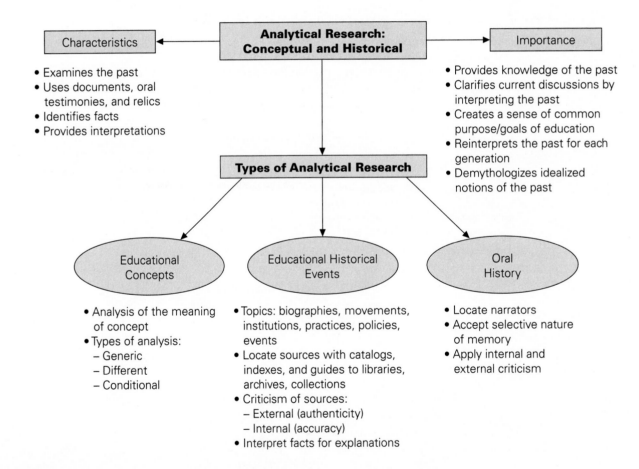

Characteristics	Analytical Research: Conceptual and Historical	Importance

Characteristics
- Examines the past
- Uses documents, oral testimonies, and relics
- Identifies facts
- Provides interpretations

Importance
- Provides knowledge of the past
- Clarifies current discussions by interpreting the past
- Creates a sense of common purpose/goals of education
- Reinterprets the past for each generation
- Demythologizes idealized notions of the past

Types of Analytical Research

Educational Concepts
- Analysis of the meaning of concept
- Types of analysis:
  - Generic
  - Different
  - Conditional

Educational Historical Events
- Topics: biographies, movements, institutions, practices, policies, events
- Locate sources with catalogs, indexes, and guides to libraries, archives, collections
- Criticism of sources:
  - External (authenticity)
  - Internal (accuracy)
- Interpret facts for explanations

Oral History
- Locate narrators
- Accept selective nature of memory
- Apply internal and external criticism

KEY TERMS

historiography	relics	internal criticism
concept analysis	primary source	facts
documents	secondary source	generalizations
oral testimonies	external criticism	oral history

WHAT YOU WILL LEARN

Study this chapter and you will:

- Know the characteristics of historical research and concept analysis.
- Know the different types of concept analysis.
- Know the sources from which data are collected in historical studies.

- Distinguish between primary and secondary sources.
- Understand how to develop external and internal criticism of data
- Know how to conduct oral histories.
- Know the standards of adequacy for evaluating analytical studies.

OVERVIEW AND PURPOSES OF ANALYTICAL RESEARCH

Several research techniques distinguish analytical studies from other kinds of educational research—namely, (1) selecting research topics related to the past, (2) applying internal and external criticism to primary sources, (3) identifying the facts, and (4) constructing interpretative explanations. The historical past may be as recent as the previous year or as distant as centuries ago. The evidence is usually written sources, many of which have been preserved in archives, manuscript collection repositories, and libraries. Sources include documents, oral testimonies, and relics.

Historiography is comprised of the techniques for discovering from records and accounts what happened during a past event or series of events, including revisions of prior history. Oral history, a form of historical research, records the spoken words and testimonies of eyewitness accounts to preserve a record before it is lost to future generations.

Historiography: a study of data collection methods

So, why study the past? What is the purpose of historical research? Why is so much time and money spent on preserving past records? Here are a few of the uses of analytical research:

1. *The analysis of educational concepts aids the selection of research problems, designs, and methodologies.* The analysis of the concept of *teaching* as different types of teaching acts, for example, could suggest research questions and aid in designing either quantitative or qualitative research on teaching. Such concepts as *behavioral objectives, alternative schooling,* and *problem solving* are not merely terms but elements of a language system that constructs a framework for planning a study.

2. *Historical research provides knowledge about the so-called roots of educational ideas, institutions, leaders, policies, and practices.* Knowledge of the past informs educational professionals, policy-makers, and members of general society about education and its role in U.S. society. By examining the results of past solutions to enduring problems, decision makers may become more realistic and moderate in their claims and more informed in their choices.

3. *Historical research clarifies present legal and policy discussions by interpreting the past with disciplined detachment and reasoned historical judgment.* Analytical research interprets the complexity of past collective educational, social, economic, legal, and political relationships. However, such research never claims that it *predicts* future actions.

4. *Historical research, in a broader and perhaps more philosophical sense, can create a sense of common purpose.* Although historical research can demythologize idealized notions about past events, most interpretations of such events reflect the fundamental belief that public education in the United States has served and can serve a common good. The role of education in U.S. society is often neglected in fragmented empirical research. Implicit in the purpose of analytical research, however, is the wish that the goals of education and educational practices benefit both the individual and society.

5. *Historical research is a dynamic area of educational inquiry because each generation reinterprets its past.* Educational historians, especially those termed *revisionists*, ask new questions, use a greater variety of sources, analyze the past with a wider range of social science concepts, and apply quantitative procedures when appropriate.

Historical research shares characteristics with qualitative methods, including a focus on natural behavior in actual events, interpretation based on context, and the importance of induction as an approach to analyzing data. Some researchers, in fact, categorize historical research as a type of qualitative research. But quantitative methods are also commonly used in historical research. This factor, along with the noninteractive nature of historical research and concept analysis, suggests that it is best to distinguish this kind of study as analytical, with aspects unique to data collection and analysis.

ANALYSIS OF EDUCATIONAL CONCEPTS

Concept analysis: examines the meaning of a concept

Concept analysis involves clarifying the meaning of a concept by describing its essential meaning, different meanings, and appropriate use. An analysis of the concept helps us explain the way people think about education. The focus is on the meaning of the concept, not on the researcher's personal values or on factual information.

Three types of analysis may be used to analyze such concepts as *education, literacy, knowledge, teaching, learning,* and *equal opportunity:*

1. *Generic analysis* identifies the essential meaning of a concept, isolating the elements that distinguish that concept from others. To clarify the concept of *academic discipline*, one might make a comparison with history, mathematics, and physics as clear standard examples and contrast home economics, animal husbandry, and water skiing as counterexamples in order to arrive at the generic meaning of the concept of *academic discipline*.

2. *Differential analysis* distinguishes among the basic meanings of a concept and suggests the logical domain that it covers. Differential analysis is used when a concept seems to have more than one standard meaning. To analyze the concept of *subject matter,* the analyst intuitively classifies concrete examples, such as *Silas Marner,* solar system, school subjects, knowledge, and skills. The distinguishing characteristics of each type of subject matter are then ascertained to clearly separate them, and a topology is developed.

3. *Conditions analysis* identifies the conditions necessary for proper use of a concept. Conditions analysis begins by providing an example that meets the necessary conditions of the concept but can easily be made a noninstance by changing the context. This forces either revision or rejection of the condition and leads to formation of a set of necessary conditions for correct use of the concept.

Critical to the analysis of educational concepts is the selection of typical uses and counterexamples. Examples should be drawn from generally accepted common uses of a given concept. Because different sets of examples are used frequently, the analysis of educational concepts may lead to reanalysis and further conceptual clarity.

Analysis of educational concepts is often used in historical research. For example, a study of the public school movement or technology in education since 1970 would first have to determine the meaning of *public school* or *technology,* respectively.

ANALYSIS OF HISTORICAL EVENTS IN EDUCATION

Historiography requires the systematic application of techniques to phrase a historical problem, locate and criticize sources, and interpret facts for causal explanations. The historian often proceeds in a circular fashion because of the interrelationships among the research questions, sources, criticisms, analysis, and explanations (see Figure 17.1).

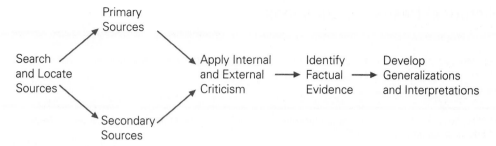

FIGURE 17.1 The Process of Historical Research

Topics and Justifications

Topics of Analysis   Topics of analysis include a wide range of new and recurring areas of interest. The following list illustrates the diversity of topics for historical investigation:

1. Movements—progressive education, lifelong learning
2. Institutions—public education, kindergarten, day care
3. Concepts—schooling, the child, literacy, professionalism
4. Biographies of educators—John Dewey, Phillis Wheatley, teachers
5. Comparative history of international education
6. Alternative forms of schooling—home instruction, distance education
7. Components of education—personnel, curriculum, administration, instruction
8. Cultural and minority education—gender, ethnic, minority, bilingual
9. Regionalism in U.S. education—geographic areas, state systems
10. Cultural influences—the family, professional associations, technology
11. Other topics—compilation (restoration) of documents with annotation

The historian begins with an initial subject, such as a historical period, person, idea, practice, institution, or policy. After initially reading widely to develop background knowledge, the historian will define the topic more exactly. Background knowledge will suggest the breadth of the subject, previous research on the problem, gaps in knowledge, and possible sources. The problem must be narrow enough to examine in detail but broad enough to allow identifying patterns for interpretation.

Background knowledge can be obtained from textbooks, monographs, encyclopedias and other reference works, dissertations, specialized journals, and of course, the Internet. General bibliographies cite secondary sources. Some bibliographies specifically useful to the historian, include *A Guide to Historical Literature*, *The Historian's Handbook: A Descriptive Guide to Reference Works*, and *A Bibliography of American Educational History*.

Limiting a topic and phrasing a problem statement about it are continuing efforts. The problem statement is expressed most succinctly and clearly at the end of the research, when the sources have been collected, analyzed, and interpreted. Considerations in limiting a topic are the availability and accessibility of primary sources; the historian's interests, specialized knowledge, time required to complete the study; and the type of study to be done. The statement of a historical problem indicates the particular event, person, institution, or policy under examination. The problem is delimited by the time period, geographic location, and viewpoint of the analysis (see Excerpt 17.1). Asking descriptive questions about the selected event is done in an

EXCERPT 17.1   The Historical Event and Selected Case

[Research examined] the story of how married women teachers gained tenure regardless of marital status . . . . While World War II saw the end of most hiring bans against married women, as the case of Rhode Island illustrated, legal discrimination in the form of denying them tenure survived until the mid 1960s. (p. 50)

Source: From Donahue, D. M. (2002). Rhode Island's last holdout: Tenure and married women teachers at the brink of the women's movement. *History of Education Quarterly, 42*(1), 50–74.

EXCERPT 17.2   Historical Research Questions

To what extent were the town officials who hired teachers actually influenced by beliefs about the masculine nature of schoolteaching? How did their hiring practices reflect and reinforce gender differences in power in early colonial society? (p. 351)

Source: From Preston, J. A. (2003). "He lives as a Master": Seventeenth-century masculinity, gendered teaching, and careers of New England schoolmasters. *History of Education Quarterly, 43*(3), 350–371.

EXCERPT 17.3   Justification for a Little-Known Topic

A noted but rarely explored axiom of the history of American education is that public school practices often originate in private sector settings. (p. 18)

Source: From Gold, K. M. (2002). From vacation to summer school: The transformation of summer education in New York City, 1894–1915. *History of Education Quarterly, 42*(1), 18–48.

EXCERPT 17.4   Problem Justification

Historians in recent decades have sought to recover the "lost voices" of teachers. . . . [This represents] a new field of inquiry . . . [as] predecessors . . . omitted frontline troops from the history of education . . . . Unless this gap could be filled, the historical record was incomplete and . . . very likely wrong-headed. (pp. 150–151)

Source: From Warren, D. (2004). Looking for a teacher, finding her workplaces. *Journal of Curriculum and Supervision, 19*(2), 150–168.

EXCERPT 17.5   Criticism of Prior Research

Footnote 58: Small, *Early New England Schools,* argues that schooldames sometimes served as the only town teacher as a cost-cutting measure. Since most of his evidence is derived from town records that can no longer be located, it is hard to verify the validity of his claim. (p. 371)

Source: From Preston, J. A. (2003). "He lives as a Master": Seventeenth-century masculinity, gendered teaching, and careers of New England schoolmasters. *History of Education Quarterly, 43*(3), 350–371.

effort to identify factual evidence, such as *who, what, where,* and *when.* Interpretations and explanations require evidence for how an event occurred and why (see Excerpt 17.2).

The significance of a historical topic is often stated in terms of completing the historical record, filling in gaps of knowledge about the past, exploring areas only alluded to in prior research, and opening a new field of inquiry. For instance, when the private papers of a well-known educator are made available for research years after his or her death, historians begin their task of understanding the person and his or her role in that era (see Excerpts 17.3 and 17.4). Moreover, when the interpretation of a prior study is seriously doubted, the topic is frequently re-examined from a revisionist viewpoint (see Excerpt 17.5).

Location and Criticism of Sources

Types of Sources   Historical evidence usually takes the form of written sources, many of which have been preserved in archives, manuscript collections, libraries, and personal collections.

Documents: records of past events

1. **Documents** are records of past events. They comprise both hand written and printed materials and may be official or unofficial, public or private, published or unpublished, prepared intentionally to preserve a historical record or prepared to serve an immediate practical purpose. As such, documents may be letters, diaries, wills, receipts, maps, autobiographies, journals, newspapers, court records, official minutes, proclamations, and regulations. Documents may also include statistical records (e.g., enrollment records).

TABLE 17.1 Types of Sources for Historical Research

Documents	Oral Testimonies	Relics
Letters	Participants in a historical event	Textbooks and workbooks
Diaries	Relatives of a deceased person	Buildings
Bills and receipts	Persons who are knowledgeable	Maps
Autobiographies	about an event	Equipment
Newspapers		Samples of student work
Journals and magazines		Furniture
Bulletins		Teaching materials
Catalogs		
Films		
Recordings		
Personal records		
Institutional records		
Budgets		
Enrollment records		
Graduation records		

2. **Oral testimonies** are records of the spoken word. The oral testimonies of persons who have witnessed events of educational significance are tape recorded, and verbatim transcripts are made. Oral testimonies relate to the event studied.

Oral testimonies: records of spoken words

3. **Relics** are objects that provide information about the past. Although relics may not be intended to convey information directly about the past, the visual and physical properties of these objects can provide historical evidence. Relics may be such diverse items as textbooks, buildings, equipment, charts, and examinations (see Table 17.1).

Relics: items from the past

Classification of Sources Sources can also be classified as primary and secondary. A **primary source** is the written or oral testimony of an eyewitness or participant or a record made by some mechanical device present at the event, such as a tape recorder, videotape, or photograph. Primary sources for a biography are the person's personal and public papers and the relics of his or her life (see Excerpt 17.6).

Primary source: direct record of eyewitness testimony

A **secondary source** is the record or testimony of anyone who was not an eyewitness to or a participant in the event. Thus, a secondary source contains information from someone who may or may not have lived through the event. Secondary sources include histories, biographies, and monographs that interpret other primary and secondary sources. As such, they provide insights and possibly facts for analysis.

Secondary source: account of a record

The classification of a source as primary or secondary depends on the research problem. The number of primary sources necessary for a study varies with the topic. To obtain primary sources, the historian thinks of the sources that would yield information on the topic and then investigates whether the applicable records were preserved and are accessible. A single study may use different kinds of sources, but primary sources must serve as the basis for documentation. (*Documentation* is the process of providing proof based on any kind of source, whether written, oral, or object.)

EXCERPT 17.6 Search for Sources

Footnote 23: Robert Patterson, "The Truth Cries Out," Association of Citizens' Council, Greenwood (MSU, Citizens' Council collection, folder 10); . . . Carroll, "Mississippi Private Education," 120–123; "How Can We Educate Our Children?," *The Citizen*, 10 (November, 1965), 7; William J. Simmons, "The Citizens' Councils and Private Education," *The Citizen,* 10 (February, 1966), 11. (p. 166)

Source: From Fuquay, M. W. (2002). Civil rights and private school movement in Mississippi, 1964–1971. *History of Education Quarterly, 42*(2), 159–180.

EXCERPT 17.7 Rationale for Choice of Primary Sources

Footnote 10: . . . The New York and Atlanta papers were chosen in particular because they represent . . . the closest to a "home town" paper available for Gibson and Coach- men. The black weeklies were selected . . . because of their prominence in the black community. (p. 249)

Source: From Lansbury, J. H. (2001). "The Tuskegee Flash" and "the Slender Harlem Stroker": Black women athletes on the margin. *Journal of Sports History, 28*(2), 233–252.

The use of primary sources is essential, but secondary sources may be used selectively and as necessary. Both primary and secondary sources should be subjected to techniques of criticism. The sources for a study are cited in the bibliography, and usually each source, fact, and quotation is footnoted. Criticism of sources may be found in the text of a study, the footnotes, or the appendices.

Location of Sources   The search for factual evidence begins with locating sources. The historian depends on sources that have been preserved; however, sources may or may not have been catalogued and identified for easy access. Locating sources is thus an exercise in detective work. It involves "logic, intuition, persistence, and common sense" (Tuckman, 1998, p. 258). The credibility of a study is determined partly by the selection of primary sources. The problem statement and limitations point to the necessary primary sources. For example, a study of the admissions policies of a university would be seriously flawed without institutional records (see Excerpt 17.7).

Documents can be located through specialized guides, catalogs, indexes, and bibliographies and through research centers. Examples of specialized reference works are *A Catalogue of Rare and Valuable Early Schoolbooks, Educational Periodicals during the Nineteenth Century, Selective and Critical Bibliography of Horace Mann,* and guides to national archives and private manuscript collections. *A Guide to Manuscripts and Archives in the United States* describes the holdings of 1,300 repositories, and the *Guide to Federal Records in the National Archives of the United States* (http://www.archives.gov/research/guide-fed-records/groups/243.html) indexes educational records of government agencies. The *National Union Catalogue of Manuscript Collections* (http://www.loc.gov./coll/nucmc/oclcsearch.html), published annually by the Library of Congress, cites the increasing number of educational collections made available to scholars. Archival research centers devoted to particular historical subjects often contain educational records, as well. Some online archives are the Urban Archives (http://www.library.temple.edu/urbana), the Education Policy Analysis Archives (http://www.epaa.asu.edu/epaa/arch.html), the Wilson Riles Archives and Institute for Education (WRAIE) (http://www.wredu.com~wriles/archive), and the Women's Studies Archives: International Women's Periodicals (http://www.womensperiodicals.psmedia.com/html).

Obtaining oral testimonies that are relevant to a topic requires preplanning. The researcher must decide which individuals are knowledgeable about the topic, and then locate them and collect data through interviews. The selection of informants for oral testimonies can be done with purposeful sampling procedures. Accessibility to the individuals, the importance of the presumed information, and feasibility (e.g., time, finances, and so on) are all considerations (see Excerpt 17.8).

Criticism of Sources   Techniques of *internal* and *external criticism* are applied to all sources: documents, oral testimonies, and relics. Even sources that are official publications or preserved in archives are subjected to criticism. As will be explained in detail later in this section, *external*

EXCERPT 17.8 Locating Oral Testimonies

Footnote 53: . . . I interviewed or corresponded with three teachers . . . who worked in Pawtucket in 1965. . . . [They] responded to my request . . . in the *Pawtucket Teachers Alliance* newsletter, for personal memories of the 1965 strike. (p. 67)

Source: From Donahue, D. M. (2002). Rhode Island's last holdout: Tenure and married women teachers at the brink of the women's movement. *History of Education Quarterly, 42*(1), 50–74.

EXCERPT 17.9   Limitations of Sources

Footnote 13: We know the highest level of education for hundreds more, but do not necessarily know what institution all attended. For example, we know of scores of the teachers who attended or graduated from a normal school or a normal course within a secondary school, but have not yet identified the institution. (p. 7)

Source: From Butchart, R. E. (2002). Mission matters: Mount Holyoke, Oberlin, and the school of southern blacks, 1861–1917. *History of Education Quarterly, 42*(1), 1–17.

criticism determines the authenticity of the source, and *internal criticism* determines the credibility of the facts stated by the source. Although the two types of criticism ask different questions about the source, the techniques are applied simultaneously. The criticism of sources may be provided in a methodological discussion, footnotes, or appendices (see Excerpt 17.9).

External criticism determines whether the source is the original document, a forged document, or a variant of the original document. Typical questions are Who wrote the document? and When, where, and what was the intention? The more specialized knowledge the analyst has, the easier it is to determine whether a document is genuine. The analyst needs knowledge about how the people in the era that produced the document lived and behaved, what they believed, and how they managed their institutions. An educational historian is less likely to deal with forged documents than is a social scientist who studies controversial political, religious, and social movements. Nonetheless, claims to a professional title or the date of an institution can be forged. Sometimes, it is impossible to determine the contribution of an individual to a government report or speech if there are multiple authors. The date and place of writing or publication can be established by means of the citation on the document, the date of the manuscript collection, and the contents of the document. However, working papers internal to an institution or a draft made by an individual may not contain any dates or may be insufficient for use if only the year is stated.

> **External criticism:** determines the authenticity of a document

The educational historian often finds *variant sources*—that is, two or more texts of the same document or two or more variant testimonies about the same event. For example, a newspaper account of the results of a state educational testing program may differ from the actual statistical report published by the state department of education, and both may differ from the separate drafts of the report (see Excerpt 17.10). In this situation, the newspaper account, the official report, and the separate drafts are all authentic sources of different texts. Oral testimonies by different individuals may also be authentic but variant sources.

Internal criticism determines the accuracy and trustworthiness of the statements in the source—for instance, answering the questions How accurate are the statements? and Are the witnesses trustworthy? *Accuracy* is related to a witness's chronological and geographical proximity to the event, his or her general competence, and his or her attention to the event. Obviously, not all witnesses equally close to the event are equally competent observers and recorders. *Competence* depends on expertness, state of mental and physical health, educational level, memory, narrative skill, and the like. It is well known that eyewitnesses under traumatic or stressful conditions remember selective parts of an event yet are convinced that because they were present, their accounts are accurate. Even though a witness may be competent, he or she may be an interested or biased party. Bias or preconceived prejudice causes a witness to habitually distort,

> **Internal criticism:** determines the accuracy of a record

EXCERPT 17.10   Using Collections of Primary Documents in Archives

[The following are the archives listed in the footnotes of one study:]

"1. American Jewish Archives. . . . 6. Philadelphia Jewish Archives. . . . 15. Chicago Historical Society. . . . 32. American Jewish Historical Society. . . . 36. National Association of Jewish Social Workers Papers. . . . 46. Jewish Museum of Maryland. . . . 51. Chicago Jewish Archives. (pp. 24–31)

Source: From Klapper, M. (2002). "A long and broad education": Jewish girls and the problem of education in America, 1860–1920. *Journal of American Ethnic History, 22*(1), 3–31.

EXCERPT 17.11   Need for Criticism of All Sources

Use oral history techniques and other personal memories, as I do, to help fill gaps left by the paucity of documents. Can memories be trusted? . . . All such sources require external evidence to establish plausibility. When contextualized, memory per se is not the problem. (p. 153)

Source: From Warren, D. (2004). Looking for a teacher, finding her workplaces. *Journal of Curriculum and Supervision, 19*(2), 150–168.

ignore, or overemphasize incidents. The conditions in which the statements were made may influence accuracy, as well. Literary style, the laws of libel, the conventions of good taste, and a desire to please may lead to exaggerated politeness or expressions of esteem.

Several techniques can be used to estimate the accuracy and dependability of a statement. Statements by witnesses that are made as a matter of indifference, those that are injurious to the people stating them, and those that are contrary to the personal desires of the people stating them are less likely to be biased than others. Likewise, statements that are considered common knowledge or incidental are less likely to be in error. Finally, other credible sources can confirm, modify, and reject statements (see Excerpt 17.11).

In a qualitative analysis, however, the simple agreement of statements from independent witnesses can be misleading, because the research depends only on preserved sources. Agreement with other known facts and circumstantial evidence will increase the credibility of a statement. The historian may cite the source by stating something like "According to the judge's opinion, . . ." "Horace Mann says, . . ." or "The Speaker of the House is our authority for the statement that . . ."

Applying internal and external criticism requires knowledge about the individuals, events, and behaviors of the period under study. The ability to put oneself in the place of historical individuals and to interpret documents, events, and personalities from their perspectives and standards is often called *historical mindedness.* Throughout the whole process, the researcher must remain skeptical of the sources and statements and not be easily convinced that the sources have yielded evidence as close to actual events as possible.

Facts, Generalizations, and Analytical Explanations

Facts: basic truths

Historians analyze **facts,** the most accurate parts of accounts in the most trustworthy and authentic sources. Facts provide the basis for making generalizations, interpretations, and explanations. The process is not simple, however. Criticism of sources may lead to rephrasing the problem and conducting a further search for sources and facts. Consider the following:

1. *Facts describe the who, what, when, and where of an event.* Most historians go beyond obtaining the descriptive facts and ask the interpretative questions of *how* and *why* a historical event occurred. The questions asked of sources are crucial to the entire process (see Excerpt 17.12). The skills used in questioning are similar to those of a detective looking for evidence and a scientist testing of evidence. Questions may be very specific, such as When did Henry Barnard die? or may be abstract, such as How did the scientific movement influence school administration practices? Methodological training and experience, both general and specialized knowledge, disciplined intuition, and logic all influence the analysis. The more questions asked of the sources about the topic, the more comprehensive and complex the analysis.

EXCERPT 17.12   Short Quotations of Facts from Primary Sources

Referring to her as "the lithe and muscular Miss Gibson," a "lanky jumping jack of a girl," and "tall and leggy,"[30] . . . they often used such physical attributes to explain the masculine power with which she played the [tennis] game. Gibson is "lean and her long arms are muscular." . . . "Althea's service gains power from her height."[31] (p. 242)

Source: From Lansbury, J. H. (2001). "The Tuskegee Flash" and "the Slender Harlem Stroker": Black women athletes on the margin. *Journal of Sports History, 28*(2), 233–252.

EXCERPT 17.13   Interpretations

Overall, summer education in New York highlights a number of important patterns of the early vacation schools and represents a standard piece of progressive school reform. First, . . . a response to a perceived social problem of the cities: the idleness of children. . . . Second, . . . push the public systems to lengthen school time. . . . Finally, the changes in . . . management . . . represented a fundamental shift . . . to modern summer schools. (p. 48)

Source: From Gold, K. M. (2002). From vacation to summer school: The transformation of summer education in New York City, 1894–1915. *History of Education Quarterly, 42*(1), 18–48.

When statements and facts conflict, additional information is sought to resolve the apparent differences. Eventually, however, the researcher must make a decision based on the most accurate information available. Facts are weighed and judged by consistency, the accumulation of evidence, and other techniques.

2. *Interpretations of the relationships between facts are generalizations.* Each generalization is subjected to analysis and then usually modified or qualified. Elements that often appear as facts in research articles are frequently generalizations of those facts that cannot be presented in the limited space. A **generalization** summarizes the separate facts that assert that an event took place (see Excerpt 17.13).

Generalizations: summaries of facts

3. *Analytical explanations are abstract syntheses of generalizations.* Explanations may be stated in the introduction as a thesis or in the closing as conclusions. Generalizations presented throughout the study are reanalyzed for context, internal consistency, documentation, accumulation of evidence, and logical induction. The process is cyclic, one of constantly returning to the facts and, if necessary, to the documents to derive meaning. A thesis stated in an introduction is a literary device of presenting an overview and not the researcher setting out to prove his or her personal notions. Consider that the introductory overview was probably the last section of the study to be written because the logic of the study must flow from it and the criteria for judging the quality of the study are derived from it. Conclusions synthesize generalizations that are previously documented in the study. In other words, conclusions are interpretative explanations. They may be stated in narrative form or as a brief list, followed by statements about the status of knowledge on the topic, identification of policy issues, and suggestions for further research.

When explanations are supported by facts stated in the study, the explanations are considered valid. A historian will say, "If you do not believe my explanation, take a closer look at the facts." Historians seldom claim, however, that they have all the facts. Instead, a given study contains a group of associated facts and ideas that leave no question unanswered *within* that presentation.

ORAL HISTORY

Historians have noted how much history has been written from the viewpoints of those in authoritative positions and how little is known of the daily experiences of everyday people in all walks of life (Berg, 2004). Oral history strategies allow researchers to avoid the inherent limitations of residual and official evidence in documents. That is, researchers can reconstruct moderately recent history from the memories of individuals, giving access to the past for as long as 80 to 90 years. The oral collection of historical materials goes back to ancient times, but formal associations began in the 1940s.

Conducting an **oral history** involves interviewing eyewitness participants in past events for the purposes of historical reconstruction (Grele, 1996). Oral histories provide empirical evidence about previously undocumented experiences and may empower social groups that have otherwise been hidden from history (Thompson, 1998). Oral history interviews are similar to other unstructured interviews and differ only in purpose. Oral history researchers proceed in much the

Oral history: interviews of eyewitnesses

EXCERPT 17.14   Oral History: Narrators

Footnote 4: I had forty-two responses from the newspaper/radio appeals, and found four other contributors by word of mouth. I interviewed twenty-seven people in all; the brief biographies . . . (names have been changed) are given. (p. 41)

Source: Clear, C. (2003). Hardship, help and happiness in oral history narratives of women's lives in Ireland, 1921–1961. *Oral History, 31*(2), 33–42.

same way as other historians but recognize that interviewing operates according to culturally specific communication norms.

Once the research topic has been selected and narrowed, the investigator locates individuals who have firsthand information on the subject. Such individuals can be located by using several strategies: (1) advertising a description of the type of person needed, (2) asking knowledgeable people for recommendations, (3) using records to obtain names and addresses, and (4) using an existing oral history archive (see Excerpt 17.14).

An *oral history archive* is a collection of individuals' narrations of their lives and historical events. Countless archives of this nature are available. Some have materials available only on audiotape (e.g., the Columbus Jewish Historical Society, http://www.columbusjewishhistoricalsociety.org/board.htm); others also have transcripts. There are numerous culturally related, religious, and political/economic oral history archives. Many of them can be accessed via the Internet and provide online audio versions of their materials and transcripts for downloading or printing. One of the most noted oral history archives is *Born in Slavery: Slave Narratives from the Federal Writers' Project, 1936–38*, which is housed at the Library of Congress and also available online. Many local and state oral history collections contain materials pertinent to research in education.

Like most historical studies, oral histories combine interview data with other sources of information. This is illustrated in Excerpt 17.15. Although the major source of data in this study is interviews with former women's college presidents, other documents are used.

Some of the methodological issues involved in conducting oral histories are as follow:

> Imagine a research topic of interest to you that might involve oral history. Describe your research plan, present an oral history, and identify other important data sources. Go to MyEducationLab for Research at www.myeducationlab.com. Click on the topic "Narrative Research" and select the Activities and Application activity titled "Collecting Narrative Data."

1. ***Locating informed and willing narrators*** Few scholars know the total number of persons who fit the desired profile and therefore do not know what percentage of the total group they have located. Because only those persons who are willing to participate can be recorded, their stories are not statistically representative of the subject. Volunteers can be biased as well.

2. ***Accepting that memories tend to be selective*** Researchers suggest that memory is best understood as a *social process*—that is, remembering in terms of experiences with others. Historians seek to understand how people's constructions of the past have been useful to them in the present. Cognitive psychologists suggest that people remember best what is normal, relevant, and consistent with their pre-existing knowledge. But in fact, individuals often remember best what is unexpected and bizarre. For a highly emotional event, the center is generally enhanced in memory, whereas the peripheral detail is lost. Memory repeatedly edits and revises the stories of people's lives.

3. ***Applying external and internal criticism*** Although oral historians can detect authenticity during an interview, they often work with variant recollections of the same

EXCERPT 17.15   Oral History Methodology

Using as its focal point the Women's College Coalition (WCC), a national organization founded in 1972 to represent the interests of such institutions, this work draws on archival sources and oral history interviews to consider the strategies by which women's college presidents collectively addressed their mutual concerns. (p. 565)

Source: From Thomas, A. D. (2008). Preserving and strengthening together: Collective strategies of U.S. women's college presidents. *History of Research Quarterly, 48*(4), 565–589.

event. Thus, internal criticism becomes very important. Scholars look for internal consistency of the interview, agreement with other interviewees, and consistency with documentary evidence.

STANDARDS OF ADEQUACY

The research process suggests criteria for judging the adequacy of historical research and oral history studies. Thus, the reader should judge a study in terms of the logical relationship among its problem statement, sources, facts, generalizations, and causal explanations. Implicit in the evaluation of a study is the question Did the analyst accomplish the stated purpose? If all the elements of the research are not made explicit, the study can be criticized as biased or as containing unjustifiable conclusions.

In evaluating adequacy, consider these questions:

1. Does the topic focus on the past or recent past, and is the problem justified?
2. Are primary sources relevant to the topic documented, authentic, and trustworthy? Was the selection and criticism of the sources appropriate?
3. Is factual evidence documented in detail? If conflicting facts are presented, is a reasonable explanation offered? If information is missing, is it noted and explained?
4. Are the generalizations reasonable and related logically to the facts?
5. Are the generalizations and explanations qualified or stated in a tentative manner?
6. Does the study address all the questions stated in the introduction—that is, does it fulfill the purpose of the study?

CHAPTER SUMMARY

The following statements summarize the major characteristics of analytical methodology and its application in studies of educational concepts, historical research, and oral histories:

1. Analytical research describes and interprets the past or recent past from relevant sources.
2. Historiography comprises the techniques for discovering from records and accounts what happened in the past.
3. Historical research provides knowledge of past educational events, clarifies present discussions with interpretations of the past with detachment, revises historical myths, and creates a sense of common purpose about education in U.S. society.
4. Concept analysis focuses on meaning within the language of education by describing the generic meaning, the different meanings, and the appropriate use of the concept.
5. Historical topics focus on biographies, movements, institutions, and practices. A historical problem is delimited by the time period, the geographic location, the specific event studied, and the viewpoint of the analysis.
6. Historical problems are justified by gaps in common knowledge and when new primary sources become available.
7. Sources include written documents, oral testimonies, and relics.

8. Primary sources are documents or testimonies of eyewitnesses to an event. Secondary sources are documents or testimonies of those who are not eyewitnesses to an event.
9. Specialized bibliographies and indexes locate the primary sources necessary for historical research; some catalogs of manuscripts and archives are available online.
10. External criticism determines whether the source is the original document, a forged document, or a variant of the original document. Internal criticism determines the accuracy and trustworthiness of the statements in the source.
11. Oral testimonies are in-depth interviews of participants used to supplement documents.
12. Historical studies make generalizations of the facts (*who, what, where,* and *when*) about an event and state interpretations and explanations that suggest multiple causes for any single event.
13. Oral history involves interviewing eyewitness participants in past events for the purpose of historical reconstruction. Oral histories provide empirical evidence about undocumented experience and may empower social groups.
14. Standards of adequacy for historical and oral history studies emphasize the logical relationship among the problem statement, selection and criticism of sources, and facts, generalizations, and causal explanations.

APPLICATION PROBLEMS

1. Suppose that a historian wants to study student discipline.
   a. How could this research problem be stated?
   b. Name at least one specialized bibliography or index.
2. Suppose that a historian is studying the life of Dr. Henry Daniel, who served as the chief state school officer from 1959 to 1979. The following article appeared in a newspaper reporting the remarks of various speakers given at a dinner to honor Dr. Daniel after 20 years of service as the state superintendent of education:

   > More than one hundred educational leaders throughout the state honored Dr. Henry Daniel last evening at the Hotel Johnson in the state capital. Following the remarks of several officials, an engraved plaque was presented to Dr. Daniel in recognition of his outstanding educational leadership to the state.
   >
   > The governor of the state noted that due solely to the efforts of Dr. Daniel, the state established a junior college system that has rapidly grown to meet important state needs in technical/vocational education for the state's industry, pro-

vided the only institutions of higher education in rural regions, and given a better general education to freshmen and sophomores than four-year colleges and universities.

   > The president of the state teachers' organization praised Dr. Daniel for his efforts to raise public school teachers' salaries and to maintain professionalism by expanding the requirements for certification of teachers. However, the president noted that salaries for public school teachers in the state still remained below the national average.
   >
   > The president of the state association for curriculum development and supervision stated that the efforts of Dr. Daniel alone established the state minimum competency testing program. This innovation has raised standards for all high school subjects and proved to the public that the high school diploma represented a high level of "educational competency."

   a. Why would the historian question the accuracy of the statements reported in this document?
   b. How could the historian corroborate the reported statements?

ANSWERS TO APPLICATION PROBLEMS

1. a. The research problem could be stated as follows: The research problem is to analyze the concept of the student in the past 50 years with references to moral development.
   b. Specialized bibliographies for history include *The Historian's Handbook: A Descriptive Guide to Reference Works* and *A Bibliography of American Educational History*.
2. a. A historical analyst would question the accuracy of statements made at a testimonial dinner. Considerations of good taste probably influenced statements such as (1) "due solely to," (2) the junior college sys-

tem meets state needs and provides a better general education, (3) "alone established" minimum competency testing, and (4) the innovation raised standards and so on.

   b. Other documents about the junior college system, teachers' salaries and certification requirements, and the minimum competency testing program from 1959 to 1979 would confirm, reject, or modify statements made in the newspaper account. The private oral testimonies of the dinner speakers and members of the educational agencies and associations might vary from the public statements.

Evaluation Research
and Policy Analysis
with Jessica Hearn

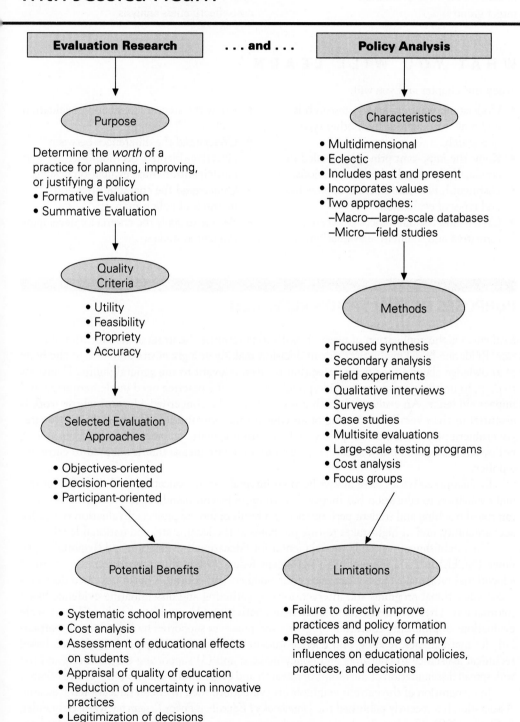

Evaluation Research   . . . and . . .   **Policy Analysis**

Purpose

Determine the *worth* of a
practice for planning, improving,
or justifying a policy
- Formative Evaluation
- Summative Evaluation

Quality Criteria

- Utility
- Feasibility
- Propriety
- Accuracy

Selected Evaluation Approaches

- Objectives-oriented
- Decision-oriented
- Participant-oriented

Potential Benefits

- Systematic school improvement
- Cost analysis
- Assessment of educational effects
  on students
- Appraisal of quality of education
- Reduction of uncertainty in innovative
  practices
- Legitimization of decisions
- Anticipation of policy issues
- Enlighten influential decision
  makers to anticipate issues

Characteristics

- Multidimensional
- Eclectic
- Includes past and present
- Incorporates values
- Two approaches:
  - Macro—large-scale databases
  - Micro—field studies

Methods

- Focused synthesis
- Secondary analysis
- Field experiments
- Qualitative interviews
- Surveys
- Case studies
- Multisite evaluations
- Large-scale testing programs
- Cost analysis
- Focus groups

Limitations

- Failure to directly improve
  practices and policy formation
- Research as only one of many
  influences on educational policies,
  practices, and decisions

KEY TERMS

evaluation	behavioral objectives
formative evaluation	decision-oriented evaluation
summative evaluation	participant-oriented evaluation
evaluation approach	responsive evaluation
stakeholder	policy analysis
objectives-oriented evaluation	multisite evaluation
target group	cost-effectiveness analysis

WHAT YOU WILL LEARN

Study this chapter and you will:

- Understand what evaluation research is and how it is different from other types of research.
- Know the important principles needed to conduct helpful and ethical evaluations.
- Distinguish between different approaches and types of evaluation.
- Understand the differences between formative and summative evaluation.

- Know the steps in conducting evaluation studies.
- Understand the differences between objective-oriented, decision-oriented, and participant-oriented evaluation designs.
- Understand the characteristics and methods of policy analysis.
- Be able to apply the criteria for developing evaluation studies.

PURPOSES OF EVALUATION RESEARCH

Evaluation is the application of research skills to determine the *worth* of an educational practice. Evidence-based evaluation aids in decision making at a given site and adds to the body of knowledge about a specific practice that is often relevant to the general public. Decisions to plan, to improve, or to justify widespread adoption of a practice need implementation and impact evidence. An *evaluator* is both a researcher and a concerned educator whose work is essential in the overall functioning of an educational organization. *Policy analysis* evaluates government policies to provide policy-makers with pragmatic recommendations from among policy alternatives. A *program* can be viewed as a specific means that is adopted to carry out a policy.

Evaluation activities have always been an integral part of education, and the need for formal evaluation in education has increased with more federal mandates to provide evidence of improved teaching and student performance as a result of funded projects. Evaluation is used for accountability, and in high-stakes testing programs at the local, state, and national levels.

The establishment of the National Center for Educational Evaluation and Regional Assistance (NCEE) in 2002 represented a significant federal policy shift toward the assessment of educational programs. The NCEE helps policy-makers and educators make informed decisions about educational programs and interventions by gathering and disseminating evidence-based information. The center engages in three major activities: (1) conducting unbiased large-scale evaluations of promising education programs and practices supported by federal funds, particularly for mathematics, reading, and science student achievement; (2) providing research-based technical assistance to educators and policy-makers; and (3) supporting the synthesis and the widespread dissemination of the results of research and evaluation throughout the United States.

In recognition of the current emphasis on evaluation, the American Educational Research Association has recently published the *Handbook of Education Policy Research* (Sykes, Schneider, & Plank, 2009). This handbook is a comprehensive source of theory and methodology for conducting educational policy research.

These resources and activities have had the effect of raising evaluation research to a very high level of visibility and influence. One important outcome of these initiatives is the emphasis on outcomes and approaches that feature rigor and appropriate methodological procedures. This often results in conducting experimental or quasi-experimental studies for evaluation, consistent with the principles of scientifically based research. It has also led to less emphasis on qualitative research.

Evaluation research is intended to present unbiased assessments of the effectiveness or merit of an educational program, product, procedure, or objective through systematic gathering of information. Often different methods are used in the same evaluation. These methods are based on quantitative, qualitative, and mixed method designs. However, evaluation goes beyond the reporting of results. The typical purpose is to provide evidence to aid decision making about what is best or most effective.

The American Evaluation Association (AEA) has outlined five principles to assist evaluators in their professional practice: systematic inquiry, competence, integrity/honesty, respect for people, and responsibility for general and public welfare. These principles support research that is used in the following ways:

1. to aid planning for the installation of a program
2. to aid decision making about program modification to enhance effectiveness
3. to aid decision making about program continuation or expansion
4. to obtain evidence to rally support for or opposition to a program
5. to contribute to the understanding of psychological, social, and political processes within a program, as well as external influences on the program

Evaluation requires a formal research design and procedures to collect and analyze data systematically for determining the worth of a specific educational practice. To say that a practice or program has *worth* means to examine it and to judge its value according to standards that are applied relatively or absolutely. The *value* of an educational practice may be intrinsic to it (e.g., reading programs value reading comprehension) or within a given site (e.g., community culture and values). *Educational practice* refers to a program, a curriculum, a policy or administrative regulation, an organizational structure, or a product. Most of the examples in this chapter, however, will be drawn from curriculum and program evaluation.

Evaluation: assessment of the worth of practice

There are two primary types of evaluation—formative and summative. **Formative evaluation** occurs while the program is being implemented. It is used to refine and improve the process to ensure that resources are being used effectively while work is progressing toward established goals. Typical questions are What parts of the program are working? and What needs to be changed and how? The evaluation results may lead to a decision to revise a curriculum, to extend the field testing to gather more data, or to abort further development in order not to waste resources on a program that ultimately may be ineffective. These studies, which are often done by internal evaluators, should be timed to be useful and should focus on variables over which educators have some control.

Formative evaluation: provides feedback for improvement

Summative evaluation occurs after a program has been implemented to determine its effectiveness or to compare it to other programs. A typical question is Which of several programs achieves these objectives most effectively and efficiently? Summative studies, which are typically conducted by external evaluators, can aid in purchase or adoption decisions of programs, products, and procedures.

Summative evaluation: focuses on the effectiveness of a program

Both formative and summative evaluations are essential because decisions are needed during program implementation to improve it and then again when it has been stabilized to judge its effectiveness. Table 18.1 summarizes the distinctions between formative and summative evaluation.

Standards for Judging the Quality of Evaluation Research

The second edition of *The Program Evaluation Standards* (1994) was published to continue the professionalization and specialization of evaluation research. The authoring group, the Joint Committee on Standards for Educational Evaluation, represented important national associations in education, research, evaluation, and measurement. The 30 standards they developed were intended to provide a conceptual framework for evaluation and a basis for self-regulation by professional evaluators.

TABLE 18.1 Formative versus Summative Evaluation

	Formative	Summative
Focus:	Provides feedback to improve the program	Determines worth and aids decisions about the future of a program; outcomes emphasized
Audience:	Program director	Funding agency, administrators, policy-makers, consumers
When:	During	After
Who does:	Internal and/or external evaluator	External evaluator
Examples:	Needs assessment	Outcome evaluation
	Evaluability assessment	Impact evaluation
	Structured conceptualization	Cost-effectiveness and cost-benefit analysis
	Implementation evaluation	
	Process evaluation	Secondary analysis
Types of questions asked:	What is working?	What were the outcomes?
	What needs to be revised?	Were objectives achieved?
	How can it be improved?	What were the costs and resources used?

The Joint Committee developed four criteria that a good evaluation study satisfies: utility, feasibility, propriety, and accuracy. Each criterion is described further in the following list, along with specific standards:

1. *Utility standards* ensure that an evaluation will serve the practical and timely information needs of given audiences. Eight standards are audience identification, evaluator credibility, information scope and selection, valuation interpretation, report clarity, report dissemination, report timeliness, and evaluation impact.
2. *Feasibility standards* ensure that an evaluation will be realistic, frugal, and diplomatic. Three standards are practical procedures, political viability, and cost effectiveness.
3. *Propriety standards* ensure that an evaluation will be conducted legally, ethically, and with due regard for the welfare of those involved in the evaluation and those affected by its findings. These standards are formal obligation, conflict of interest, full and frank disclosure, the public's right to know, the rights of human subjects, human interactions, balanced reporting, and fiscal responsibility.
4. *Accuracy standards* ensure that an evaluation will state and convey technically adequate information about the features of the practice studied that determine its value. Ten standards are object identification, context analysis, described purposes and procedures, defensible information sources, valid and reliable measurement, systematic data control, analysis of quantitative information, analysis of qualitative information, justified conclusions, and objective reporting.

The standards are a compilation of commonly agreed-on characteristics of good evaluation practice. In any specific formal evaluation situation, the choices and trade-offs relating to each standard are within the province of the evaluator. Furthermore, the standards serve as a guide to evaluators, officials who commission studies, and persons who use evaluation reports.

The Program Evaluation Standards were in the process of being updated in 2008–2009. The draft standards include a new area of evaluation called *meta-evaluation* activities. Just as a meta-analysis is a synthesis of research, a metaevaluation combines several evaluations to provide an overall conclusion about program effectiveness. Meta-evaluations can be formative or summative, and they can address both overall quality of evaluations and specific components, based on the needs of the stakeholders. To see the most recent version of these standards, go to http://www.wmich.edu/evalctr/jc/.

SELECTED APPROACHES TO EVALUATION

There are many different approaches to and types of evaluation. They are based on the purpose of the evaluation, what is being evaluated, and the orientation of the evaluation. Many aspects of education are evaluated, including curriculum materials, programs, instructional methods, educators, students, organizations, and management. The evaluation approach is based, then, on what information is desired and how that information will be used. It is also necessary to identify the entity to be evaluated (e.g., the group, product, method, organization, or management system). The evaluation approach chosen stems from these criteria.

An **evaluation approach** is a strategy to focus the evaluation activities and produce a useful report based on the purpose and types of information collected. Although there are many different approaches to evaluation, we will consider six commonly found in educational evaluations (see Table 18.2). The one that is chosen is based on the philosophy and values of the stakeholders. A **stakeholder** is a person, organization, or group that is interested in or impacted by the evaluation.

Each approach has prominent theorists, explicit rationales, discussions in the literature, a group of practitioners, evaluation studies, and critics (see Stufflebeam, Madeus, & Kellaghan, 2000). Each approach also has a different perspective on evaluation. Evaluators may borrow aspects from other approaches but typically will not mix approaches that are philosophically incompatible.

Three of the approaches most frequently used are objectives-oriented evaluation, decision-oriented evaluation, and participant-oriented evaluation. Together, these approaches illustrate the diversity of evidence-based evaluation.

Evaluation approach: focuses evaluation activities

Stakeholder: invested party

Objectives-Oriented Evaluation

Objectives-oriented evaluation determines the degree to which the objectives of a practice were attained by the target group. In other words, the evaluation measures the outcomes of the practice. The discrepancy between the stated objectives and the outcomes is the measure of success

Objectives-oriented evaluation: focuses on attainment of objectives

Evaluation Approach	Description
TABLE 18.2 Major Evaluation Approaches	
Objectives-oriented	Focus is on specifying goals and objectives and determining the extent to which they have been attained.
Consumer-oriented	Central issue is developing evaluative information on educational products, broadly defined, for use by educational consumers when choosing from among competing curricula, instructional products, and the like.
Expertise-oriented	Relies on the expertise of professionals to judge the quality of educational endeavors, especially resources and processes.
Decision-oriented	Emphasis is on describing and assessing educational change processes and outcomes to provide information to a decision maker to make or defend decisions.
Adversary-oriented	Presents arguments of evaluators both for and against a program or product, as in a trial.
Participant-oriented	Occurs when the stakeholders are involved as central determinants of the values, criteria, needs, and data for the evaluation.

of the practice. The practice may be a curriculum, inservice training, an inschool suspension program, parent education, or the like. The **target group**, or the group whose behavior is expected to change, may be students, parents, teachers, or others. We will illustrate the steps in conducting an objectives-oriented evaluation with curriculum evaluation (see Figure 18.1).

Target group: group whose behavior is expected to change

Behavioral objectives: terminal student behaviors that can be measured

Selection of Measurable Objectives   An evaluation study measures the objectives, not the abstract goals, of the practice. Curriculum *goals* are usually broad, general statements representing values of the society. *Objectives* are specific statements that are related logically to the goals and attainable through instruction.

Often, student outcomes are stated as **behavioral objectives**. The term *behavioral objective* is synonymous with *performance* or *measured objective*. Behavioral objectives are either terminal student behaviors or student products (e.g., a research paper, clay figurine, oral presentation) but *not* the process leading to terminal behaviors. The criteria for achievement of the objective may or may not be stated in the objective. Four examples of behavioral objectives that differ in level of generality are these:

- A student, on request, will be able to spell and capitalize his or her name correctly.
- A student will be able to compute correctly the answers to any division problems chosen randomly from the review exercises.
- A student will produce a drawing that is judged by three raters as creative by the criteria of originality, flexibility, and elaboration developed by the raters.
- At least 90 percent of the students will be able to answer correctly 70 percent of the questions in a competency test in mathematics.

The last example is a performance objective that states the minimal group performance of 90 percent and the minimal individual student performance of 70 percent. An analysis of the curriculum content coverage and emphasis will suggest the objectives that are most important.

If the objectives are stated in terms other than behavioral, the evaluator has three choices: (1) reword the objectives in behavioral terms without changing the intent, (2) ignore the nonbehavioral objectives, or (3) communicate to the client the fact that nonbehavioral objectives will not be measured but that these objectives could be described or appraised with other procedures.

Selection of Instruments and Design   Instruments include tests, questionnaires and self-report devices, rating scales, observation systems, and interview schedules. Evaluators frequently use data from routine testing programs.

Content-related evidence for validity can be determined logically by a panel of local experts by comparing the curriculum content with the test items. The validity and reliability of subtest scores may be considerably lower than those of the entire test. Other considerations are the appropriateness of the norms for the target group and the type of information sought. Most standardized norm-referenced tests provide only general information about students compared with those in the norm group.

Criterion-referenced or standards-referenced instruments may also be used to assess student outcomes. Criterion-referenced instruments must meet the requirements of any measurement procedure. If an evaluator or a local school system plans to develop a criterion-referenced instrument, knowledge of measurement and instrument development will be necessary. The instrument should be valid and reliable for the evaluation purposes, although the type of validity and reliability may differ from that associated with norm-referenced tests. Field testing is essential.

The most useful design in an objectives-based evaluation is a randomized or matched groups design; however, it may not be feasible. Quasi-experimental designs can also be used. Because most programs have both cognitive and affective objectives, a comprehensive evaluation would measure the different types of objectives if evidence for validity and reliability is adequate.

Interpretation of Results   The evaluation assesses the percentage of the target group that achieved the predetermined objectives, or it assesses which program, compared with others having similar objectives, is more successful in achieving the objectives. When the evaluator looks more closely at the objectives, he or she often finds that they are stated at different levels of specificity and that not all objectives can be evaluated. The methods for selecting the objectives for

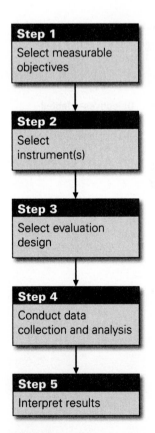

Step 1
Select measurable objectives

Step 2
Select instrument(s)

Step 3
Select evaluation design

Step 4
Conduct data collection and analysis

Step 5
Interpret results

FIGURE 18.1   **Steps in Conducting an Objectives-Oriented Evaluation**

formal evaluation are often inconsistent. Because only terminal outcomes are actually assessed, process evaluation is omitted. The results may suggest modifications of a practice but provide no specific directions for intervention to improve a practice, or the results may not provide the complete information necessary for adopting a practice at other sites.

Objectives-based evaluation is probably the most frequently used approach. Most educators would agree that the successful attainment of objectives indicates the worth of a practice. Educators can demonstrate accountability and the productive use of public funds when objectives are attained. Another advantage of the objectives-based approach is its highly definable methodology. The procedures for this approach have been worked out in great detail, a fact that appeals to many novice evaluators. No other approach has such an elaborate technology and scientific basis. Furthermore, the nonattainment of objectives or the attainment of only some objectives can lead to questioning programmatic components and a closer scrutiny of the practice.

Decision-Oriented Evaluation

Decision-oriented evaluation has a broad scope and implies a theory of educational change. Its primary purpose is to collect and analyze the data needed to make decisions. The evaluator and the administrator identify decision alternatives, which can be routine maintenance decisions (e.g., staff policies) or incremental decisions leading to systemwide change. **Decision-oriented evaluation** studies may thus be done at any point in a change process: needs assessment, program planning, implementation, or process and outcome evaluation. The types of evaluation studies with their subsequent decisions are summarized in Table 18.3 and below:

Decision-oriented evaluation: collecting and analyzing data to make decisions

1. *Needs assessment* compares the current status and values of an educational system with the desired outcomes. The evaluation identifies the context, provides baseline data on the accomplishments of the site, and identifies unmet needs. Needs can be stated by the students, the community, other groups, or society as a whole in relation to the system. Needs assessment leads to selection of a program to achieve specific objectives.

TABLE 18.3   Types of Decision-Oriented Evaluation

Needs Assessment

Evaluation	Current status contrasted with desired status—educational need
Decision	Problem selection

Program Planning and Input Evaluation

Evaluation	Kinds of programs that fit objectives derived from needs assessment and possible strategies
Decision	Program plan

Implementation Evaluation

Evaluation	Degree to which the program is implemented as planned
Decision	Program modification

Process Evaluation

Evaluation	Extent to which the program achieves its objectives and products
Decision	Program modification and improvement

Outcome or Product Evaluation

Evaluation	Worth of the program as reflected by the process and outcomes
Decision	Program certification and adoption

Source: Based on Stufflebeam et al. (1971), pp. 215–239.

2. *Program planning and input evaluation* involves examining alternative strategies, such as adoption of an available program or development of a new program, to achieve the new objectives. Researchers study available programs for their practicality, cost, and ease of reproducing components to achieve objectives. Researchers also examine the feasibility of developing a program locally. Program planning and input evaluation lead to the selection of a plan, including procedures, materials, facilities, equipment, schedule, staffing, and budgets for program development or implementation.

3. *Implementation evaluation* assesses the extent to which a program is developed or implemented as planned; it also identifies any defects in the program. Information with which to anticipate the changes necessary for continued program development and implementation is provided as well.

4. *Process evaluation* provides information on the relative success of the various components of a program and the extent to which the objectives and products are achieved. The evaluator plays the role of a so-called interventionist, collecting data that will lead to immediate decisions to improve the program. Data collection requires testing procedures and other methods. Process evaluation results in program modification.

5. *Outcome or product evaluation* assesses the extent to which the objectives were achieved. The data obtained include those from objectives-based evaluation and other information from earlier evaluations. This previously obtained information explains why the objectives were or were not achieved and helps the decision maker to eliminate, modify, retain, or expand the program for wider use. Outcome evaluation leads to program adoption.

Finally, the decision-oriented approach to evaluation focuses on gathering information by a variety of methods to aid in making decisions for program development and adoption or for wider use. Educational change is a logical, rational activity, and evaluation is an extension of it. Possible difficulties in using this type of evaluation lie in conflicting values and goal dissension within a complex educational system and between the educational organization and its constituencies. The decision-oriented approach assumes that the decision maker is sensitive to possible problems in bringing about educational change and is willing to obtain information regarding these realities. It is more difficult to specify and anticipate decisions to be served than it seems. Because the evaluator works closely with the decision maker, the impact of the evaluation effort depends as much on the skills of the evaluator as it does on the leadership of the decision maker.

Despite these difficulties, the decision-oriented approach allows for educational and methodological soundness in evaluation. Program evaluation is *not* based on an isolated outcome. The degree of program implementation is addressed before student outcomes are assessed. The approach is also flexible. It may be used for a formative purpose to guide decision making throughout an educational change process, or it may be used for a summative purpose to demonstrate accountability.

Participant-Oriented Evaluation

Educators have often expressed concerns about evaluations. Administrators have pointed out that (1) technically sophisticated instruments and reports often distract from what is really happening in education; (2) many large-scale evaluations are conducted without evaluators even once visiting some classrooms; and (3) report recommendations do not reflect an understanding of the phenomena behind the numbers, charts, and tables. Educators have further argued that the human element of everyday reality and the different perspectives of those engaged in education are missing. Hence, these approaches are called *participant-oriented evaluation*.

Participant-oriented evaluation is a holistic approach using a multiplicity of data to provide an *understanding* of the divergent values of a practice from the participants' perspectives (see Green, 2000; Guba & Lincoln, 1989). The literature and actual evaluation studies illustrate these commonalities:

1. Uses a *holistic approach,* which sees education as a complex human endeavor.
2. Accommodates and protects *value pluralism* by presenting or summarizing disparate preferences about the practice evaluated.
3. Reports a *portrayal,* as it has come to be called, of a person, classroom, school, district, project, or program that is placed in the broader context in which it functions.

Participant-oriented evaluation: use of many methods to understand a practice from participants' perspectives

4. Usually depends on *inductive reasoning*, which emerges from grassroots observation and discovery.
5. Uses a *multiplicity of data* from several different sources, usually within a qualitative methodology or by combining qualitative and quantitative data.
6. Uses an *emergent design* to give an understanding of one specific practice with its contextual influences, process variations, and life histories.
7. Records *multiple realities* rather than a single reality.

Stake (1975) notes that many evaluation studies are not used because the reports are irrelevant. According to Stake, "An educational evaluation is responsive evaluation if it orients more directly to program activities than to program intents; responds to audience requirements for information; and if the different value-perspectives present are referred to in reporting the success and failure of the programs" (p. 14). *Responsive evaluation* is an older alternative based on what people do naturally when they evaluate things: They observe and react. This approach responds to the natural ways in which people assimilate information and arrive at understanding. The evaluation design emerges from the issues and concerns expressed at the site.

Prominent Events: Informal Strategies Responsive evaluation is cyclical, including events that recur. Again quoting Stake, "Any event can follow any event, many events occur simultaneously, and the evaluator returns to each event many times before the evaluation is finished" (1975, p. 18). In Figure 18.2, the prominent events are presented as the face of a clock, emphasizing the cyclic nature of the approach.

The events can be expressed as research phases. In Phase 1 (noon to 5 o'clock), the evaluator talks with clients, program staff, and audiences—anyone directly or indirectly connected with the program—to get a sense of the different perspectives and values of the program. The evaluator also observes the program in operation. From these activities, the evaluator discovers the meaning of the purposes of the program and conceptualizes the issues and problems. In Phase 2 (5 to 9 o'clock), the evaluator ascertains the data needs and selects data collection methods. Although Stake expects observers and judges to be the primary method of data collection, instruments

Responsive evaluation: uses an emergent design to show how people learn and understand

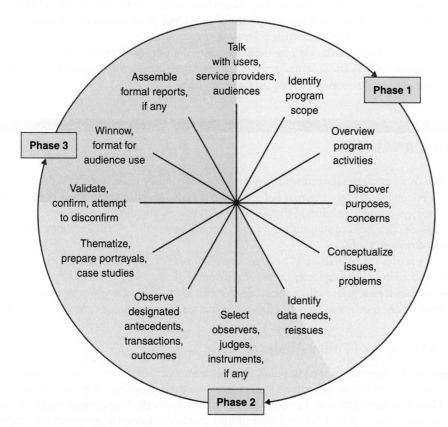

FIGURE 18.2 Responsive Evaluation
Source: Adapted from Stufflebeam, Madeus, and Kellaghan (2000).

may be appropriate. The data are organized as antecedents, transactions, and outcomes, including both intended and unintended outcomes. In Phase 3 (9 to 12 o'clock), the evaluator is concerned with communicating the findings in natural ways. Portrayals can be embodied in the conventional research report, but they usually will take the form of descriptive case studies, artifacts, round-table discussions, newspaper articles, graphics, or videotapes, depending on the audience. Only the primary concerns of each audience are reported to that audience. Last, the evaluator assembles formal reports and other types of reports.

Evaluator's Role Two aspects of participant-oriented evaluation—the evaluator's role and continuous feedback—distinguish this approach from the prior approaches discussed. The evaluator responds to audience concerns as they change throughout program development and stimulates ideas by trying out data-based insights and findings on the respondents. Negotiation and interaction are part of the method of ensuring accuracy and communication. Communication is a two-stage process in which findings are tried out on different audiences. This may lead to the evaluator's returning to the field for additional data or altering the way findings are stated in order to communicate more effectively. The results presented in the final report should not surprise any audience, because its content should have been thoroughly criticized before release.

In summary, participant-oriented evaluation recognizes that the concerns of different audiences about the same program represent different values and data needs. The evaluator must select the concerns and issues that are important and relevant within the limits of time and resources. The discovery of pluralistic values surrounding a program is made by the evaluator independent of any administrator. The source for the evaluation focus and questions is the various audiences. A variety of methodologies and designs can be used. The flexibility of responsive evaluation assures that it will be serviceable to the audiences.

Participant-oriented evaluation is usually a case study (Stake, 2000), and as with other subjective approaches, there are issues of credibility. Although most case studies differ in matters of emphasis, rather than truth or falsity, different observers emphasize different events. Ensuring methodological consistency while representing diverse interests remains a problem. Some believe that evaluators should balance the interests according to their own sense of justice; other evaluators take a disinterested and neutral position, providing descriptions and analyses but not recommendations. In addition, writing portrayals or case studies requires skill, training, and the handling of confidential data. Despite these difficulties, a well-constructed case study is a powerful evaluation and has the potential to be coherent, fair to people with diverse views, and accurate, especially about the inner workings of a program.

POLICY ANALYSIS

Policy analysis: evaluates government policies

Policy analysis evaluates government policies to provide policy-makers with pragmatic, action-oriented recommendations. *Policy* is both what is intended to be accomplished by government action and the cumulative effort of the actions, assumptions, and decisions of people who implement public policy. School administrators and teachers, in a real sense, make policy as they carry out their day-to-day jobs.

Policy analysis can focus on (1) policy formulation, especially deciding which educational problems to address; (2) implementation of programs to carry out policies; (3) policy revision; and (4) evaluation of policy effectiveness and/or efficiency. A program can be analyzed as separate from a policy, or it can be defined as a specific means adopted for carrying out a policy.

Characteristics of Policy Analysis

Two distinctive approaches used in policy analysis are a *macro approach*, which is based on economic models such as cost analysis and use of large-scale databases, and a *micro approach*, which is field-based to get the facts and emphasizes qualitative methods. Many policy studies are eclectic, combining both qualitative and quantitative methods. Depending entirely on statistical proof is seldom done in policy analysis for major policies.

Similar to evaluation research, policy analysis focuses on variables open to influence and intervention and is responsive to the users. The users may be numerous and vary in expectations, values, assumptions, and needs. The values of the users enter into the processes of defining the educational problem; formulating the research questions, design, and policy alternatives; and developing recommendations. Educational values are always embedded in the cultural context. These values often differ at the district level and at the state level. In addition, the normative values of society at large are considered.

Methods of Policy Analysis

Policy analysis incorporates a variety of methods to analyze problems of policy. These methods include focused synthesis, secondary analysis, field experiments, large-scale experimental or quasi-experimental evaluation, qualitative interviews, surveys, large-scale testing programs, case study analysis, cost analysis, and focus groups. The methods discussed in prior chapters and others are briefly defined here in the context of policy analysis:

- *Focused synthesis* is the selective review of written materials and prior research relevant to the policy question. A synthesis differs from a traditional literature review in that it discusses information obtained from a variety of sources beyond published articles—interviews with experts and stakeholders, records of hearings, anecdotal stories, personal experiences of the researcher, unpublished documents, staff memoranda, and published materials. An entire policy analysis study can employ this method.
- *Secondary analysis* is the analysis and reanalysis of existing databases. Rather than examine databases to determine the state of knowledge about an educational practice, secondary analysis generates different policy models and questions from which to examine the databases.
- *Field experiments* and quasi-experiments investigate the effect or change that results from policy implementation. Because experimental approaches explain existing educational conditions, the results are not useful in projecting into the future. Moreover, policy conditions may be so dynamic that the results are confined to that particular period of implementation.
- *Large-scale experimental or quasi-experimental evaluations* of major social and human services programs in the areas of health care, education, mental health, and public welfare can address several questions about the programs and sites. Large-scale quasi-experimental policy analysis of projects, usually funded for three to five years, is called **multisite evaluation.** Some reasons for conducting multisite evaluations include the following:

Multisite evaluation: large-scale field evaluations

- To determine the overall effect of the program after aggregating effects across all sites
- To evaluate the program in a sample of representative sites to estimate the effect of the program across all sites
- To determine if the program works under a variety of implementation conditions
- To study how the program interacts with specific site characteristics
- To compare program performance across sites to identify the most effective and ineffective ways of operating the program
- To facilitate cross-site sharing of effective practices and others

Because multiple sites have a number of different local administrative units, an effort must be made to do careful sampling and to standardize program implementation and procedures for collecting and analyzing data. The most widely agreed-upon purposes of multisite evaluations are to increase generalizability of findings, to maximize sample size to increase statistical power, and to respond to a variety of political and social concerns.

- *Qualitative interviews* of individual key informants help policy-makers anticipate the implications and consequences of proposed laws or policies. *Prospective studies* combine interviewing people who are knowledgeable in a field to solicit the latest and best thinking on a proposal with using existing government reports to identify trends.
- *Surveys* yield data on the present educational conditions of selected groups or situations. They can be in questionnaire or interview form and use purposeful or probability sampling.
- *Large-scale testing programs* at state and national levels reflect educational policies mandated by governments. Performance measurement and monitoring typically compares current

performance with either past performance or some predetermined goal or standard. Most performance-monitoring programs assess outcomes. In K–12 education, standards-based education centers on student achievement. These data, collected from multiple sites, can determine the overall effect of a program or policy when outcomes are aggregated.

- *Case study analysis* is frequently used for policy research because it can be designed to give a more global analysis of a situation. Case studies provide a more complete understanding of complex situations, identify unintended consequences, and examine the process of policy implementation, which is useful for future policy choices.

- *Cost analysis* focuses on policy effectiveness (i.e., Does the policy produce the desired results?) and policy efficiency (i.e., Were those results obtained at the smallest cost?). Four types of analysis are cost-benefit, cost-effective, cost-utility, and cost-feasibility analysis. The analysis typically done in education is cost-effective analysis. **Cost-effective analysis** compares program outcomes with the costs of alternative programs when the objectives of the different programs are similar and when common measures of effectiveness are used. *Effectiveness* could be measured by the results of standardized achievement test, psychological tests, or physical tests. Outcome measures need not be converted to monetary values, and the analysis is replicable. One drawback of cost-effective analysis, however, is that it fails to provide automatic policy choices between alternatives because nonquantifiable outcomes and constraints are not part of the analysis. It is difficult to incorporate multiple outcomes, rather than a single outcome, into the analysis.

- *Focus groups,* a method of obtaining qualitative data from a selected group of individuals, are frequently used for policy questions. The technique can be used to obtain reactions to planned or existing services, policies, or procedures or to learn more about the needs and circumstances of the participants. Focus groups can be employed in any phase of planning, implementation, or policy impact.

Cost-effective analysis: comparing the costs and outcomes of different programs with similar objectives and measures

EDUCATIONAL EVALUATION AND POLICY ANALYSIS: POTENTIAL BENEFITS AND LIMITATIONS

Evaluation studies and policy analysis offer many potential benefits to education, although they are not a panacea for all of the ills of education. Education is a complex activity that occurs within a larger and ever-changing society comprised of interdependent social, economic, and political systems. In this context, evaluation research and policy analysis bring a rational and empirical perspective to the arenas of educational decisions and policy-making.

The results of evaluation and policy studies are intended to be used. A study is considered utilized if the research is related to a discrete decision or enlightens decision makers about issues, problem definition, or new ideas for alternative actions. The latter type of research utilization—the psychological processing of a study—does not necessarily direct decisions or dictate action, however.

Some evaluators and analysts, with a realistic understanding of how policy is made, propose the types of research most likely to be used. For instance, studies using diverse criteria for worth and containing more comprehensive information, such as program context and implementation, have a good chance of being used. In addition, systematic, long-term studies are more likely to influence policy-makers, providing specifications of the full scope of issues and nontechnical summaries of findings.

Potential Benefits   The list of potential benefits will increase as more educators gain experience in conducting and using evaluation and policy studies. The most frequently mentioned potential benefits are these:

1. Allows planning and implementing school improvements on a systematic basis. Evidence of what works is important in program justification. Evidence of what does *not* work allows decision makers and those with influence over policy to recast alternatives considered as solutions.
2. Tests several popular myths about the effects of education on student development
3. Demonstrates professional responsibility by appraising the quality of educational programs
4. Reduces uncertainty about educational practices when experience is limited

5. Satisfies external agencies' requirements for reports to legitimize decisions and improve public image
6. Conducts cost-effectiveness analysis of programs and practices that require large expenditures
7. Enlightens influential persons in decision and policy arenas to enable them to better anticipate program and policy issues

Possible Limitations   The limitations most often cited are as follow:

1. Failure of many studies to improve educational practices and educaional policy formation. Studies frequently are conducted without first understanding the factors that affected the use of research information even when the studies were well done.
2. Lack of appreciation that research is only one of many influences on educational policies, practices, and decisions. Evaluation studies and policy analysis cannot *correct* problems, but they can identify strengths and weaknesses, highlight accomplishments, expose faulty areas, and focus on realistic policy alternatives. Correcting a problem is a separate step from using research results.

CREDIBILITY OF EVALUATION AND POLICY REPORTS

An evaluation or policy report is typically long and contains several chapters. The report consists of an introduction, stating the focus and design; the findings, organized by research questions or components of the practice; and a summary, which offers recommendations.

The criteria for judging the adequacy of a report emphasize two aspects: (1) the evaluation focus and design and (2) the findings, conclusions, and recommendations. Much of the report's credibility rests on proposing and conducting a study according to *The Program Evaluation Standards* (Joint Committee, 1994). The following questions illustrate typical criteria:

1. Is the evaluation focus stated, along with the context, objectives, and description of the practice or policy, the general purposes of the study, and the evaluation or policy approaches used?
2. Are the research questions stated and the data collection and analysis procedures specified? Are the procedures defensible?
3. Are the results reported in a balanced manner and with full and frank disclosure, including the limitations of the study?
4. Is the reporting objective to the extent that the findings are based on verified facts and free from distortion due to personal feelings and biases?
5. Are the conclusions and recommendations justified and is sufficient information presented to determine whether these conclusions and recommendations are warranted? Are plausible alternative explanations presented for findings, when appropriate?

CHAPTER SUMMARY

1. Evidence-based evaluation requires a formal design and procedures to determine the worth of a practice. Evaluation studies are used to plan, improve, and justify (or not justify) educational practices.
2. The worth of a practice is determined by making a judgment of its value according to standards applied, whether relatively or absolutely.
3. Formative evaluation helps revise a practice in a developmental cycle. Summative evaluation, which is conducted when a practice is established, determines the effectiveness of a practice compared with other competing practices.
4. A credible evaluation study satisfies the standards of utility, feasibility, propriety, and accuracy.
5. Major evaluation approaches include objectives-oriented, consumer-oriented, expertise, decision-oriented, adversary, and participant-oriented approaches.
6. Objectives-oriented evaluation focuses on terminal behaviors, or the extent to which the measurable objectives of a practice are attained by the target group.
7. Decision-oriented evaluation—such as needs assessment, program planning, implementation, and process and outcome assessment—provides information to decision makers during program or system change processes.
8. Participant-oriented evaluation is based on the concerns of the various stakeholders. Multiplicity of data, inductive

reasoning, and writing portrayals or a series of case studies characterize this approach.

9. Policy analysis evaluates government policies to provide policy-makers with pragmatic recommendations. Both macro (large-scale databases) and micro (field studies) approaches are employed.

10. Some policy analysis methods include focused synthesis, field experiments, large-scale multisite evaluations, qualitative interviews, surveys, large-scale testing programs, cost analysis, case studies, and focus groups.

11. The potential benefits of evaluation studies and policy analysis are systematic school improvements, cost analyses, assessment of educational effects on students, appraisal of the quality of education, reduction of uncertainty in innovative practices, legitimization of decisions, and enlightenment of policy-makers to better anticipate program and policy issues.

12. An evaluator, a client, and a user can each judge the adequacy of an evaluation proposal or report by using a checklist of criteria.

APPLICATION PROBLEMS

1. Analyze the following evaluation situation by identifying the problem and suggesting alternative procedures.

   A supervisor of instruction wanted to conduct an evaluation in order to compare a new independent study approach with the regular instructional approach in high school mathematics. A written formal agreement with the district evaluation staff stated the following arrangements:
   a. The evaluation was to help the high school mathematics department chairpersons decide whether to adopt the independent study approach districtwide.
   b. The procedures were to conduct a districtwide comparison of the two approaches, involving 20 percent of the high school's mathematics teachers and all of their students.
   c. Mathematics achievement, students' attitude, and teacher enthusiasm would be assessed.
   d. Teachers would be randomly selected and assigned to the two different approaches.

   The supervisor later decided that the evaluation should provide feedback to improve the new approach rather than to decide on adoption. She changed the procedure for assigning teachers and students to the project, which resulted in their not being assigned randomly. The evaluation staff—assuming that the evaluation focus and design, once agreed on, would remain the same—collected and analyzed data as originally planned.

   The evaluators found that students' attitudes toward both approaches were similar but that student achievement and teacher enthusiasm were significantly greater for the independent study approach. The report judged this approach as superior and recommended it for adoption.

   The supervisor was disappointed that the report did not help improve the independent study approach. The department chairpersons complained that the findings were not dependable for two reasons: (1) Many of the teachers assigned to the independent study approach were biased in favor of it before the study began, and (2) the students in the independent study classes were generally high achievers prior to entering the program.

2. Identify each of the following examples as either formative or summative evaluation.
   a. Tests were administered to see how much teachers' knowledge of mathematics improved.
   b. The goal of the evaluation of the new drama education series was to see if students' attitudes toward drama had changed.
   c. Project directors received regular communications from the evaluator throughout the implementation of a new curriculum.
   d. A new way of advising students was established in a school of education. Student data were obtained to conduct an evaluation of the effectiveness of the new system.
   e. A new evaluation design was implemented that included both internal and external evaluators.
   f. The data showed project directors how to improve the delivery of a new method of student learning.

3. Classify each of the following descriptions as objectives-oriented, decision-oriented, or participant-oriented.
   a. Mr. Green, principal of Midlothian High School, used a multimethod approach to the selection of a new book series for English instruction. He gathered students' perceptions from a pilot test and teacher ratings and also looked into the companies providing the different book series.
   b. Professional development of teachers to improve their assessment of student learning was implemented at James River High School. The results showed that 80 percent of the participating teachers had adopted new procedures that were emphasized in the training.
   c. Dr. Abrams recently conducted an evaluation of a new doctoral program. The evaluation consisted of obtaining multiple perspectives about the program, including those of faculty and students. She also observed faculty discussions of elements of the program, both before and after interviews that could be structured to confirm interpretations of the observations.

ANSWERS TO APPLICATION PROBLEMS

1. The evaluators should have monitored and noted the changes in purpose and procedures as they occurred. The evaluators could have met periodically with the supervisor to review the purposes and data needs and to check on the procedures that were not directly under their control. Near the end of the evaluation, the evaluation staff could have met with the supervisor and department chairpersons to consider the changed purpose and procedures in preparation for forming recommendations.

2. a. Summative
   b. Summative
   c. Formative
   d. Summative
   e. Formative
   f. Formative

3. a. Decision-oriented
   b. Objectives-oriented
   c. Participant-oriented

Action Research
with Lisa Abrams

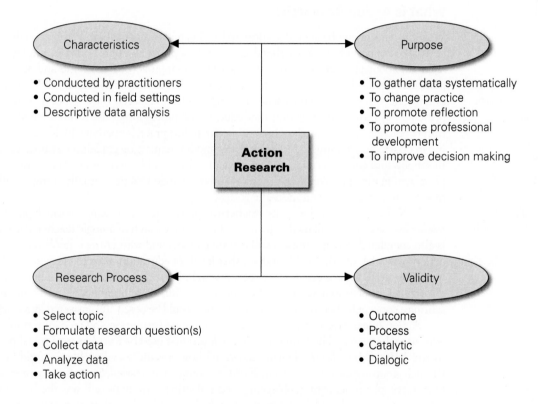

From Chapter 19 of *Research in Education: Evidence-Based Inquiry*, 7/e. James H. McMillan. Sally Schumacher.

WHAT YOU WILL LEARN

Study this chapter and you will:

- Know the characteristics of action research.
- Know how to state action research questions.
- Distinguish between action research and other kinds of educational research.
- Understand the strengths and weaknesses of action research.

- Know different types of action research.
- Know how to conduct action research.
- Know how to evaluate action research.
- Understand different types of action research validity.

ACTION RESEARCH

What Is Action Research?

With the current emphasis on data-driven decision making, educational professionals are increasingly asked to provide evidence that documents best practice. There is also an emphasis on *critical reflection* about practice that provides a systematic approach to gathering and analyzing information. It is the intersection, then, between systematic inquiry (i.e., research) and its use by practitioners that characterizes *action research*. **Action research** is the process of using research principles to provide information that educational professionals use to improve aspects of day-to-day practice. The research questions are rooted in practice, perhaps by K–12 teachers working in classrooms, administrators identifying and implementing guidelines, counselors practicing in schools and colleges, or faculty teaching at colleges and universities. Action research is simply a systematic approach to help professionals change practice, usually using a collaborative model that includes several individuals.

> **Action research:** systematic inquiry by practitioners

In K–12 education, the terms **teacher-researcher**, *teacher research*, *research practitioner*, and *teacher-as-researcher* are all used to focus on the action research of a single teacher. Action research is also completed in teams using a collaborative model and with entire schools (i.e., school-based action research). In other fields and at other levels of education, the broader term *applied* may be used to describe what is essentially action research. For example, teachers in a high school mathematics department may work together (or collaborate) to determine if a specific method of presenting a concept is effective, or the same question could be posed and answered by a single teacher.

> **Teacher-researcher:** teacher who conducts action research

Action research is an area that is gaining increased attention and recognition in the field of educational research. The term *action research* was first used by Kurt Lewin, a social psychologist, in the 1930s (Mills, 2007). Lewin recognized how specific social problems could be addressed through group discussions (Creswell, 2008). According to Creswell, Lewin's group process included four stages: planning, acting, observing, and reflecting. This approach was the basis for the current approaches and models of action research that emphasize a clear, systematic process, participation of various stakeholders, collaboration, and a focus on social change. The following are several definitions of action research that are related to Lewin's original intent of action research:

- An investigation conducted by the person or the people empowered to action concerning their own actions, for the purpose of improving their future actions (Sagor, 2005, p. 4)
- Any systematic inquiry conducted by teacher researchers, principals, school counselors, or other stakeholders in the teaching/learning environment to gather information about how their particular schools operate, how they teach, and how well their students learn . . . [it] is done by teachers for themselves (Mills, 2007, p. 5)
- A constructive inquiry, during which the researcher constructs his or her knowledge of specific issues through planning, acting, evaluating, refining and learning from the experiences . . . a

continuous learning process in which the researcher learns and also shares the newly generated knowledge with those who may benefit from it (Koshy, 2005, p. 9)

Action research is not limited to a specific methodology (although in most cases, there is at least some use of qualitative methods), and typically quantitative data are used descriptively (with little or no emphasis on inferential statistics). The goal is to introduce a more systematic process than what is typically employed, be it qualitative, quantitative, or mixed method. One important difference is that the intent of action research is only to address specific actions in a single context, whereas applied research seeks to have implications for the field more generally. However, that does not mean that action research does not have implications for the overall field. Because practitioners are involved throughout the study, action research promotes change in classrooms and schools, greater collaboration among those with a vested interest in the results, an integration of research with practice, and a willingness to test new ideas.

IMPLICATIONS OF ACTION RESEARCH FOR PRACTICE

Action research has a number of benefits. In the process of conducting it, teachers, counselors, and administrators collaborate with others and reflect meaningfully on why the results were obtained and what the results mean for their practice. This not only empowers teachers, it also helps them understand the benefits of existing literature in an area as well as those of evidence-based systematic inquiry. Action research engages individuals and acts as a powerful professional development activity. It models a way of thinking for students and changes the professional dispositions of teachers. Finally, action research can change the climate of a school to a more open, reflective atmosphere in which it is standard practice to openly examine instructional methods, take risks, and work collaboratively to design studies and to understand the usefulness of the results in a school-based context. Glanz (2003, p. 19) lists the following benefits of action research:

- Creates a systemwide mind-set for school improvement and a professional problem-solving ethos.
- Enhances decision making—provides greater feelings of competence in solving problems and making instructional decisions. In other words, action research provides for an intelligent way of making decisions.
- Promotes reflection and self-assessment.
- Instills a commitment to continuous improvement.
- Creates a more positive school climate in which teaching and learning are foremost concerns.
- Impacts directly to improve practice.
- Empowers those who participate in the process. For instance, educational leaders who undertake action research may no longer accept theories, innovations, and programs at face value without a critical review.

DIFFERENCES BETWEEN ACTION AND TRADITIONAL RESEARCH

Action research differs from traditional research in several ways. As discussed in this chapter, action research has a practical focus and can be conducted in a participatory or collaborative manner. The practical aspect of action research situates the focus of the investigation within a specific context such as a classroom or school. The results of the research are intended to inform a plan of action related to instructional decisions, curricular changes, or school policies, for example. As such, the sampling, data collection methods, analysis, and dissemination reflect this emphasis on practical and local problem solving. The results of action research studies are not intended to be broadly applicable beyond the specific context or problem that is the focus of the study. Action research encourages teachers and administrators to engage in reflective practice

TABLE 19.1	Characteristics of Action Research versus Traditional Research	
Characteristic	**Action Research**	**Traditional Research**
Who identifies the research question(s) and conducts the research	Practitioners: teachers, principals, counselors, administrators	Trained researchers; university professors, scholars, graduate students
Where the research is conducted	Schools, universities, daycare centers, and other institutions where the practice is implemented	Settings in which appropriate control can be implemented, from laboratories to field settings
Goal	Knowledge that is relevant to the local setting	Knowledge that can be generalized to the field
Literature review	Brief, with a focus on secondary sources	Extensive, with an emphasis on primary sources
Instrumentation	Use of instruments that are convenient and easy to administer and score	Measures are selected based on technical adequacy
Sampling	Convenient sampling of students or employees in the targeted setting	Tends to be random or representative
Data analysis	Descriptive	Descriptive and inferential
Dissemination	To the specific individual, classroom, or organization	To other professionals in different settings

Source: Adapted from Gall, Gall, and Borg (2003).

and is considered a form of professional development. These characteristics clearly distinguish action research from traditional research. Table 19.1 summarizes the differences between action research and traditional research. The reader should keep in mind, however, that there can be significant variability in the extent to which characteristics of traditional research are used in action research.

ACTION RESEARCH PROCESS

The process of conducting action research is an iterative, cyclical one in which theories of action are examined or tested and further evaluated until the desired outcome or goal is achieved. Figure 19.1 shows the cyclical nature of action research and how continued actions and evaluation can inform and improve reading instruction. Generally, action research is conducted in four phases: (1) selecting a focus, topic, or issue to study; (2) collecting data; (3) analyzing data; and (4) taking action based on the results. This four-stage process is illustrated in Excerpt 19.1, which describes an elementary science resource teacher's investigation of the effectiveness of an instructional unit on student learning of animal adaptations. Each stage of action research will be considered in more detail with some examples in the following section.

Selecting a Focus, Topic, or Issue to Study

The first step in any research endeavor is to determine the research question, goal, or purpose. A good topic is one that is important and relevant and that provides results that will immediately impact professional practice. Sometimes an informal needs assessment is used to identify a topic; sometimes a review of literature is used.

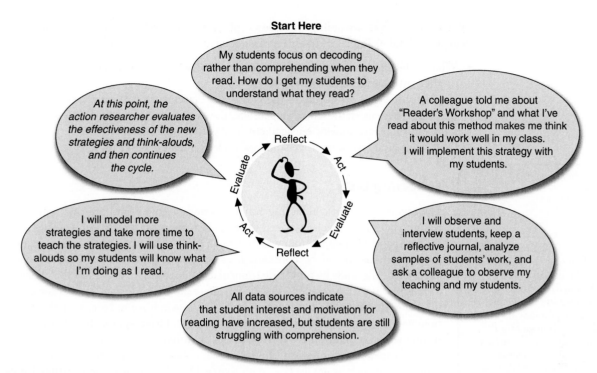

FIGURE 19.1 **The Action Research Process**

Source: From Cher C. Hendricks. *Improving Schools Through Action Research: A Comprehensive Guide For Educators, 1e.* Published by Allyn and Bacon/Merrill Education, Boston, MA. Copyright © 2006 by Pearson Education. Reprinted by permission of the publisher.

EXCERPT 19.1 Description of Action Research Process

In this paper, I describe the action research I conducted in my third-grade science classrooms over the course of two years. In order to gain an understanding of my third-grade students' ideas about animal adaptations and how the teaching of a unit on crayfish influenced these ideas, I used clinical interviews, observations, and written assessments. I did this research while working as a science resource teacher in a suburban elementary school. Their first year, I piloted the unit myself and then made changes to the unit based upon my findings. During the second year, the entire third-grade team taught the unit, and I co-taught with one of these third-grade classroom teachers. I found that students' ideas are developing and the connections to other parts of the science curriculum such as habitats, gases, and plants were necessary yet lacking. Teachers should be prepared to understand these connections themselves and to highlight them to students. Teachers should recognize that elementary students will not develop an understanding of adaptations from merely working with and observing animals in their habitats. Further research is needed to see if the students need specific lessons on adaptations, an understanding of evolution, and/or more experience and maturity in order to truly understand the concept of adaptation. (p. 33)

Source: From Endreny, A. (2006). Children's ideas about animal adaptations: An action research project. *Journal of Elementary Science Education, 18*(1), 33–43.

Usually, the experiences of the practitioner are used to identify topics for action research. School-based action research topics may address individual students, classrooms, group work, instruction, curriculum or general school improvement issues. Generally, the focus of action research among teachers and administrators is areas that concern improving teaching, learning, and the overall school atmosphere or functioning. Research is often suggested to address educational issues in an effort to gain understanding or solve problems. Once topics are identified, researchable questions need to be formulated to determine the appropriate methods of data collection. For example, the researchable question that guided the action research project described in Excerpt 19.1 was "What are the students' conceptions of the specific life science topics and how are they influenced by the teaching of a unit on crayfish adaptations?" (Endreny, 2006, p. 34). This question informed the selection and use of several different data collection methods, including interviews, observations, and written assessments. Here are some additional examples of questions characteristic of action research:

- What is the effect of assigning greater responsibility to students in completing the yearbook on their attitudes toward writing?
- How effective is peer tutoring in the Advanced Placement (AP) history course?
- In there a difference in the school climate after the introduction of a bullying-prevention program?
- How can I increase student engagement in classroom discussions?
- Does small-group work improve students' understanding of cell structure?

Take a moment to think about a hypothetical action research project in a high school setting. Go to MyEducationLab for Research at www.myeducationlab.com, identify appropriate data collection strategies for the research focus, and consider implications for practice. Click on the topic "Action Research" and then select the Activities and Applications activity titled "Action Research on the High School Science Club."

Experiencing: action research focused on observation

Enquiring: gathering new data

Collecting Data

The second phase of conducting action research is to collect data that will answer the research questions. Decisions need to be made about what type or types of data need to be collected and the sample from which data will be collected. Both quantitative and qualitative methods should be considered; using a variety of data collection tools usually strengthens the study by providing triangulation. Figure 19.2 illustrates the concept of triangulation in action research. As shown, there are multiple data sources for each of the three questions that are the focus of the action research study. Note that the data collections methods include both quantitative and qualitative approaches. For example, the second research question is "What changes occurred with our priority achievement targets?" To answer this question, the researcher collected quantitative measures of student achievement such as grades (i.e., data source 1) and qualitative observational notes and examples of student work or artifacts. Often, initial data gathering will lead to collecting additional data. For example, a teacher might begin to study the effectiveness of cooperative learning groups by first doing some informal observation while the groups are deliberating. From these data, a more structured observation could be developed, along with specific questions that students could be asked.

Typically, action researchers will use one of three approaches to data collection: experiencing, enquiring, and examining (Mills, 2007). **Experiencing** takes the form of observation, with a focus on understanding the variables, participants, and relevant phenomena. **Enquiring** occurs when the researcher needs to gather data that have not yet been obtained.

Research Question	Data Source 1	Data Source 2	Data Source 3
What did we actually do?	• Lesson plan book	• Attendance record	• Joann's portfolio of daily work
What changes occurred with our priority achievement targets?	• Grade book (quizzes, homework, journals, reflection papers, projects, tests, weekly assessments)	• Observational notes • Comments on her tests and papers	• Joann's portfolio of daily work • Joann's self-assessments
What was the relationship between the actions taken and changes in performance on the achievement targets?	• Contrast lesson plans with performance data from grade book.	• Correlate lesson plans with observation notes. • Correlate lesson plans with comments on papers.	• Correlate lesson plans with material in Joann's portfolio. • Correlate lesson plans with Joann's self-assessments.

FIGURE 19.2 **Triangulation Matrix**

Source: From Sagor, R. (2005), p. 98. *The Action research guidebook. A four-step process for educators and school teams.* Thousand Oaks, CA: Corwin Press.

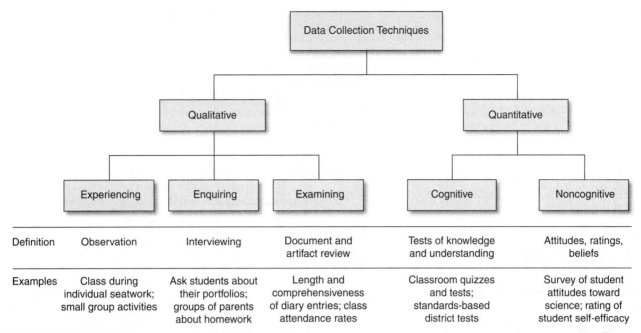

FIGURE 19.3 Examples of Different Types of Action Research

Source: From James H. McMillan. *Educational Research: Fundamentals for the Consumer, 5e.* Published by Allyn and Bacon/Merrill Education, Boston, MA. Copyright © 2008 by Pearson Education. Reprinted by permission of publisher.

This could involve interviews, questionnaires, and tests. **Examining** occurs when the researcher uses data that have already been collected. Whatever the approach, one challenge is to decide what data really need to be collected. The researcher does not want to be swamped with so much data that it will be difficult to analyze and summarize them. Figure 19.3 provides a summary of the types of quantitative and qualitative data collection approaches that are typical of action research. As suggested, action research often involves the use of both quantitative and qualitative data in an effort to understand issues of process or implementation as well as the impact on specified outcomes.

Examining: using already collected data

As in any research project, attention must be given to issues of credibility, transferability, dependability, validity, and reliability. Although highly technical conceptualizations will not be used (e.g., statistical calculations such as correlations and multiple raters), the *ideas* or notions of validity, reliability, and related principles must be addressed. This is often best accomplished by simply having others review the procedures and results to determine whether any factors could invalidate the findings or provide competing explanations. The ideas are more important than complex definitions, typologies of error, and statistical indices.

Analyzing Data

Next, the data need to be examined and interpreted. It is important that the data are clear and well organized. For qualitative analyses, action researchers will look for redundancy in what is being communicated *after* they have gained a complete understanding of what has been observed and recorded. Usually, some kind of categorization is utilized to organize the information. Quantitative data are summarized using simple descriptive statistics (e.g., frequencies, mean, mode, range) and graphs. It is helpful to ask others to review at least a portion of the data analyses, as well as the interpretations and conclusions, to help ensure that the analyses, interpretations, and conclusions make sense.

Action researchers often use the results from their initial data collection and analysis to change practice, which is evaluated, and then to suggest new research questions, which are followed by new data collection and analysis procedures. This is essentially a cyclical process, as illustrated in Figure 19.4. This process is essential to the action research project in Excerpt 19.2, in which college professors investigate the effect of using peer assessment in large classes.

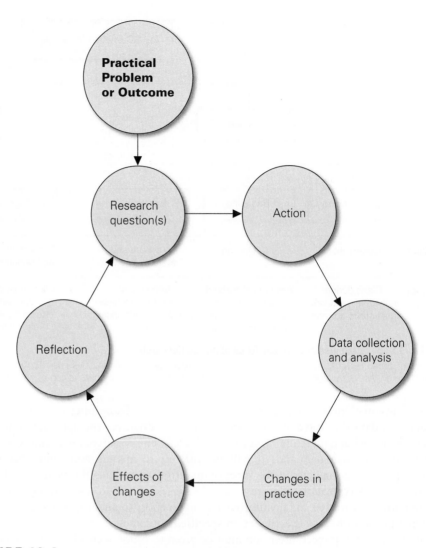

FIGURE 19.4 Cyclical Nature of Action Research

EXCERPT 19.2 Cyclical Process in Action Research

This study was conducted in three phases over a two-year period, and involved students and staff from three faculties of the Queensland University of Technology. A total of 1,654 students and 30 staff participated in the project. An action research process based on cycles of action and reflection . . . was used to develop peer assessment procedures that were responsive to student and staff needs and concerns. This process was participatory, collaborative and reflexive. (p. 430)

Source: From Ballantyne, R., Hughes, K., & Mylonas, A. (2002). Developing procedures for implementing peer assessment in large classes using an action research process. *Assessment and Evaluation in Higher Education, 27*(5), 427–441.

VALIDITY IN ACTION RESEARCH

Making a determination about the validity or credibility of the conclusions drawn from action research is dependent on the research design and data collection methods that were employed to conduct the investigation. As such, researchers should use the recommendations for ensuring the validity of interpretations of results set forth in previous chapters of the text related to quantitative and qualitative methods. In addition, to these recommendations Anderson, Herr,

Criteria	Question
Democratic validity	Have the multiple perspectives of all of the individuals in the study been accurately represented?
Outcome validity	Did the action emerging from the study lead to the successful resolution of the problem?
Process validity	Was the study conducted in a dependable and competent manner?
Catalytic validity	Were the results of the study a catalyst for action?
Dialogic validity	Was the study reviewed by peers?

FIGURE 19.5   **Criteria for Evaluating the Validity of Action Research**

Source: Adapted from Mills, G. (2007). *Action research: A guide for the teacher researcher.* Thousand Oaks, CA: Sage.

and Nihlen (1994) posited that action research requires a distinct system for judging the integrity or quality of the study. This system is based on five criteria: democratic validity, outcome validity, process validity, catalytic validity, and dialogic validity.

Democratic validity is concerned with representation of the stakeholders in either the process of conducting the action research or as data sources. For example, in an effort to ensure democratic validity, a researcher would want to gather multiple perspectives on an issue from the relevant groups that have a stake in the problem, such as students, other teachers, parents, and administrators. Also, a researcher may want to put together a collaborative research team that includes members from these various stakeholder groups. *Outcome validity* refers to the extent to which the action plan that emerges from the study is viable and effective. For example, the researchers would want to ask, Does the action plan address the problem? *Process validity* is related to concepts of internal validity in quantitative research and models of credibility (Maxwell, 1992) and trustworthiness in qualitative research. Process validity is concerned with the way in which the action research study was conducted. According to Mills (2007), "process validity requires that a study has been conducted in a 'dependable' and 'competent' manner" (p. 91). Enhancing process validity requires that action researchers take measures to ensure that their data collection methods are effective and appropriate for obtaining the information needed to answer the questions guiding the study.

Catalytic validity is based on the "action" component of action research. This concept of validity addresses the extent to which participants are compelled to take action, such as changing instruction, modifying the curriculum, or implementing new or altering existing school policies on the basis of the study findings. The final criterion, according to Anderson et al. (1994), *dialogic validity* is related to the dissemination of the study findings. Sharing the results of the action research investigation involves having a "conversation" or dialogue with colleagues through some type of public medium such as peer-review journals (see Excerpt 19.1), conferences, district-level professional development sessions, or websites. Figure 19.5 summarizes the model of validity in action research put forth by Anderson et al. (1994).

EVALUATING ACTION RESEARCH

The quality of action research is judged by criteria related to its primary purpose—that is, to change practice and solve the identified problem that prompted the study. It is in the usefulness of the action taken that credibility is assessed. This judgment is made by addressing the following questions:

- Is the research problem one that addresses the effectiveness of professional practice?
- Is the research question stated in a way that can be addressed empirically?
- Were sufficient data collected?

EXCERPT 19.3 Action Research Outcomes

A majority of students indicated that the alternative grading system did affect their academic preparation and performance in class (in a positive way), and that they had a more positive attitude toward the class. . . . We believe that the increased focus on personal learning, growth, and improvement that evolved from de-emphasizing grades made it less likely for students to fail and more likely for students to accept responsibility for their learning and to provide the evidence that they had learned. . . . By far the most rewarding part of working on an action research team was the opportunity to learn and grow with a small group of teacher colleagues. . . . By working with these colleagues consistently throughout the year, we were able to explore new ideas and take risks in the classroom. . . . We will continue to conduct action research. (pp. 101–102)

Source: From Mills, G. E. (2003). *Action research: A guide for the teacher researcher* (2nd ed.). Upper Saddle River, NJ: Merrill/Prentice Hall.

Practice evaluating action research by going to MyEducationLab for Research at www.myeducationlab.com and completing the Building Research Skills activity titled "Evaluating an Action Research Project." Click on the topic "Action Research" and select "Evaluating an Action Research Project."

- Could anything about the sampling, instrumentation, or procedures distort the findings?
- Were there multiple methods of data collection and analyses?
- Does the suggested action follow logically from the findings?
- Will the findings result in a change of practice?
- Has implementation of suggested changes improved the targeted participant outcomes?

Clearly, the evaluation rests as much, if not more, on the use of the results as on the technical adequacy of the research. This is in contrast to most other kinds of studies, in which details related to subject selection, instrument validity, and internal validity are stressed as the criteria for determining credibility. Consider Excerpt 19.3, in which four high school teachers implemented changes in the grading system to determine the effects on student effort, responsibility, and attitudes. Surveys, observations, and student interviews were used to collect data. Also consider the importance of collaboration among these teachers. Action research is usually most effective when teams of professionals work together on the same problem, issue, or practice.

CHAPTER SUMMARY

This chapter presented an introduction to action research. Following is a summary of the key points:

1. Action research is conducted by practitioners with the goal of changing actions in classrooms, schools, universities, and other settings.
2. Action research emphasizes the use of the data.
3. Action research is a systematic inquiry that may utilize both quantitative and qualitative methods.
4. Research is conducted in the settings in which changes in action are anticipated.
5. Data analyses are primarily narrative and descriptive, with the use of graphs when appropriate.
6. Highly sophisticated statistics and research principles are typically not employed, even though concepts such as validity and reliability must be considered to some extent to ensure production of credible results.
7. Action research often has a cyclical nature. Beginning with research questions, action leads to research, which leads to changes in practice, effects on targeted individuals, reflection, and further research questions.
8. Action research is evaluated primarily on the extent to which the investigation provided credible data that were used to successfully change practice.

APPLICATION PROBLEMS

1. Indicate whether each of the following is an example of action research.
   a. A researcher is interested in examining the correlation between high-stakes testing and grades. The test scores and grades are from 2000–2003.
   b. A teacher is interested in studying the effects of small-group counseling on her students' self-esteem. Thirty students participate as subjects. The Coopersmith Self-Esteem Inventory is given as a pretest and a posttest,

and interviews are used to follow up with students every month.

c. Service learning is becoming very popular in both public schools and colleges and universities. However, relatively little is known about the perceptions of the beneficiaries of the services. A study is prepared to examine these perceptions using focus group interviews and a questionnaire to ask participants about the characteristics of effective volunteers.

d. A principal is interested in knowing whether a new procedure for aligning classroom assessments with graduation requirements will result in more students graduating.

e. To compare student achievement in the United States with that of students in other countries, a professor bought and used a CD containing three years of relevant data.

2. For each of the following characteristics, indicate whether it is typical of action research or traditional research.

a. Tends to use mostly secondary sources

b. Is done in classrooms by teachers

c. Uses inferential statistics or qualitative software

d. Measures are selected to provide generalizability

e. Involves limited dissemination

f. Researcher bias is a particular concern

g. Findings are relevant for the field in general

3. In your own field of work and study, suggest an action research study that uses a mixed method design.

4. Suppose a teacher decides to study the impact of technology on the attention behavior of her fifth-grade students. She makes observations of students for three weeks before the technology is introduced and then continues her observations for the next three weeks while students use the technology. The results suggest that students pay increased attention when they use technology, so the teacher decides to use it for the rest of the semester.

a. What should the teacher do to ensure credible results?

b. How can teacher bias be controlled?

c. Is this an example of cyclical research? Why or why not?

ANSWERS TO APPLICATION PROBLEMS

1. b and d are examples of action research. In the other examples there is no explicit application to practice.

2. a. traditional
   b. action
   c. traditional
   d. traditional
   e. action
   f. action
   g. traditional

3. (individual student response)

4. a. Make arrangements to reduce teacher bias in observations; check to make sure that attention is measured the same way before and after the intervention; search for other reasons for increased student attention; analyze data to determine if increased attention is of practical significance; determine if technology is more effective for some types of students than others.

   b. The teacher could ask others to check her recording of behavior so that it is not biased; keep a log of anecdotal comments related specifically to bias; have others check her analysis to look for possible bias in the conclusions.

   c. This is not cyclical research because it does not include an action taken at the end of the teacher's study, nor is there an indication of reflection.

Guidelines for Writing Research Proposals

Guidelines for Writing Research Proposals

Writing a research proposal can be the most difficult yet satisfying step in the research process. In writing the proposal, the entire inquiry is synthesized into a specific form. Researchers demonstrate that they know what they are seeking, how they will seek and recognize it, and why the research is worthwhile. This appendix describes a general proposal format and provides guidelines for quantitative, qualitative, and mixed method proposals. The preparation and criticism of a proposal is also described.

QUANTITATIVE RESEARCH PROPOSALS

Quantitative research proposals generally follow this format:

I. **Introduction**
    A. General statement of the problem
    B. Review of the literature
    C. Specific research questions and/or hypotheses
    D. Significance of the proposed study
II. **Design and Methodology**
    A. Participants
    B. Instrumentation
    C. Procedures
    D. Data analysis and results
    E. Limitations of the design
III. **References**
IV. **Appendices**

I. Introduction   The *general problem statement* is a clear, precise statement of the research problem, which identifies for the reader the importance of the problem and the area of education in which it lies. A concise and direct statement of the problem is made very early in the introduction, ideally in the first paragraph, and is followed by a description of the background of the problem.

The *literature review* presents what is known about the problem from theoretical discussions and prior research, thus providing the background and the need for the study. The literature review concludes with a discussion of the knowledge to date on the problem and offers the researcher's insights, such as criticisms of designs of prior research and identification of gaps in the literature.

Specific research questions and/or hypotheses are stated next. They should clearly indicate the empirical nature of the investigation, such as the specific type of research design. Definitions—preferably operational definitions—of variables follow.

The *potential significance of the proposed study* notes the importance of the study in terms of (1) the development of knowledge and (2) general implications for further research and educational practices. The researcher discusses how the results of the study could add to theory and knowledge in the area of research. This summary could be located anywhere in the Introduction.

II. Design and Methodology   The design and methodology include the participants, instrumentation, procedures for obtaining the data, data analysis and presentation, and design limitations. The researcher also identifies the type of design to be used—survey, correlational, experimental, quasi-experimental, and the like. This orients the reader to expect certain design components to be discussed in the proposal.

The *participants* are identified by describing the population of interest and how the probability sample will be drawn from this population. The sample size is stated as well. A rationale for the sampling procedure and the sample size is given. Most proposals state how the protection of the rights of human subjects will be accomplished.

The *instrumentation* section of the proposal identifies the instrument(s) to be used and explains why the instrument was selected as the most appropriate operational definition of the variable(s). If the instrument is already established, then reliability and validity evidence are given. If the instrument must be developed, then the steps for obtaining validity and reliability data are outlined.

The *procedures* section describes how the study will be conducted, often providing a list of steps. This includes a description of the intervention for an experimental study.

The *data analysis and results* states the statistical techniques to be used and specifies how the data will be presented. The statistical test is stated for *each* research question and/or hypothesis and, if necessary, the rationale for the choice of the test.

The section about *limitations of the design* cites those issues that can be identified at this time: the scope of the study, the design, and/or the methodology. Stating the design limitations illustrates the researcher's knowledge of the threats to internal and external validity in the proposed design. Limitations are tempered with reasonableness and should not be so extensive that the study seems pointless or unimportant. Sometimes, the researcher may prefer to state the research assumptions that were made in order to conduct the study, rather than point out the limitations.

III. References   The references section lists the sources that the researcher actually used to develop the proposal and that are cited in the text of the proposal. That is, every source cited in the proposal must be included in the references, and every entry listed in the references must appear in the proposal.

IV. Appendices   The appendices provide supplementary materials that are needed for clarity and that allow for economical presentation. When these materials are placed in the appendices, the reader can refer to them as needed, rather than be distracted by them while attempting to follow the logical flow of the proposal. Included in the appendices may be such items as the following:

- Instructions to subjects
- Informed subject consent forms
- Letters of permission to conduct the study in an educational agency
- Pilot studies
- Copies of instruments
- Instructions for and training of data collectors
- Credentials of experts to be used in the study
- Diagrammatic models of the research design or statistical analysis
- Chapter outline for the final report
- Proposed time schedule for completing the study

QUALITATIVE RESEARCH PROPOSALS

The degree of specificity in a qualitative research proposal depends on the extent of preliminary work (i. e., gaining access to a site or persons to interview and previewing archival collections). Qualitative research proposals may be more tentative and open-ended than quantitative research proposals, allowing for an emergent design.

Qualitative research proposals generally follow this format:

I. Introduction
 A. General problem statement
 B. Preliminary literature review
 C. Foreshadowed problems
 D. Significance of proposed study

II. Design and Methodology
 A. Site or social network selection
 B. Research role
 C. Purposeful sampling strategies
 D. Data collection strategies
 E. Data management and analysis
 F. Limitations of the design

III.   References or Bibliography

IV.   Appendices

I. Introduction   The introduction consists of the general problem statement, the literature review, a description of foreshadowed problems, and a discussion of the potential significance of the proposed study.

The *general problem statement* is phrased as "to describe and analyze" an ongoing event, process, or concept in a discovery orientation. The direct statement of the problem is followed by a description of its background.

The *preliminary literature review* presents the initial conceptual frameworks used in phrasing foreshadowed problems/questions as well as the need for the proposed study by identifying gaps in knowledge. The literature review is not exhaustive but is rather a preliminary review that makes explicit the initial focus at the beginning of observing and interviewing. The literature review clearly justifies the need for an in-depth descriptive study.

The *foreshadowed problems* are stated as broad, anticipated research questions to be reformulated in the field. These problems are based on the researcher's general, preliminary information about what is likely to occur initially at the site or in interviews.

The *potential significance of the proposed study* describes how the study can (1) add to the development of knowledge and theory and (2) suggest general implications for further research and educational practices. Most qualitative proposals suggest further possibilities for research.

II. Design and Methodology   The design and methodology section includes the site or social network selected, the research role, purposeful sampling strategies, data collection strategies, data analysis, and design limitations. The researcher identifies the proposal design to orient the reader to expect certain design components to be discussed.

The *site selected* is described in terms that illustrate its suitability for investigating the phenomena. A description of the site characteristics is essential—for instance, a public or private agency, typical activities and processes, kinds of participants, and the like. The *selected social network* is described to justify that the group members are likely to be informed about the foreshadowed problems. There should be a logical relationship between the potential information to be elicited through personal contact and the foreshadowed problems.

The researcher states the *research role* to be assumed for data collection. The researcher, at this time, can describe the role only in general terms—for example, participant observer or interviewer.

The intent to use *purposeful sampling strategies* is stated in the proposal, and examples of possible strategies are given. Most proposals also state how the rights of human subjects will be protected.

Planned *data collection strategies* are stated next. Although specific data collection strategies will emerge in the field, the intent to use multiple methods should be stated explicitly to enable corroboration of the data. The researcher also states the expected length of fieldwork and the forms that the data will take, such as field notes and interview records. Finally, the researcher states how data will be catalogued, stored, and retrieved either manually or electronically.

The description of *data management and analysis* includes strategies to facilitate discovery in the field with interim analysis, coding and developing categories, and pattern-seeking techniques. Sometimes, the software programs for data management are stated.

The section on *limitations of the design* notes the limitations that can be identified at this time: the scope of the study, the methodology, and the design. Methodological limitations refer to possible difficulties in assuming the research role, in conducting purposeful sampling, and in conducting observations and interviews. Findings from a case study design are not generalizable, but without a case study design, other research purposes could not be achieved. Researchers discuss the strategies they intend to use to minimize threats to validity, researcher bias, and extension of results.

III. References or Bibliography   Researchers may use one of the two documentation styles: (1) that of the American Psychological Association, known as the *APA style* (APA, 2001) or (2) that of the *Chicago Manual of Style*, known as CMS style (2003).

IV. Appendices   The appendices in a qualitative proposal provide supplementary materials for clarity and economical presentation, as in a quantitative proposal. The items in the appendices may include the following:

- Letters of permission granting access to the site
- Agreements of informed rights of human subjects from key participants
- Protocols for obtaining informed consent in a social network
- Brief hypothetical examples of field notes and interview records
- A few pages of a coded transcript or field notes from a pilot study
- Lists of records and artifacts known to be available at the site or through a social network
- Proposed schedule for completing the study

MIXED METHOD PROPOSALS

Mixed method proposals have a format that is consistent with the logic and role of quantitative and qualitative aspects of the study.

I. **Introduction**
- A. General problem statement
- B. Review of the literature
- C. Research questions
- D. Significance

II. **Design and Methodology**
- A. Logic
- B. Participants and sampling strategies
- C. Research site or context
- D. Data collection
- E. Procedures
- F. Data analysis and results
- G. Limitations

III. **References**

IV. **Appendices**

Introduction   The introductory section will be much like those already described, with a need for a *general problem statement*, *review of the literature*, and *research questions* (both specific questions and more general foreshadowed problems). The *significance* of the study is often presented as a methodological need as much as a need to address the problem. That is, there is a need to justify why a mixed method approach is the best design rather than using either a quantitative or qualitative one.

Design and Methodology   An important starting point in this section is to explain the *logic* of the design as exploratory, explanatory, or triangulation. Once the logic is clear, the *participants,* appropriate *sampling, strategies, instrumentation, procedures,* and *data analyses* are presented, consistent with the nature of the design. Questions can also be divided as appropriate and referenced in the methods sections. The major emphasis of the study should be presented first, followed by the other facets of the study. Each major method will include information already summarized for both quantitative and qualitative methods sections. What is different is that there may not be as much detail as would be presented for a proposal that is either quantitative or qualitative.

The proposed *data analyses* and *presentation of results* will be in the same sequence as the nature of the design. It is important to match research questions to analyses so that it is clear how the questions will be answered. It is usually best to do all of each approach, either quantitative or qualitative, rather than to summarize both kinds of sampling, data collection, procedures, and analyses together.

Limitations should be noted for each phase of the study. Additional considerations should be directed to limitations due to using both quantitative and qualitative approaches together.

References   The references will be presented in one list for all aspects of the study, both quantitative and qualitative. That is, there is no separate reference list for the quantitative part and then a reference list for the qualitative part of the study.

Appendices   The appendix material is presented sequentially to match the order in which specific elements of the design are presented. For example, in an explanatory study, Appendix A could be a copy of a survey that will be used, and Appendix B could contain an example of a screening form that would be used to select participants for the qualitative part of the study. There would not be separate appendices for the quantitative and qualitative parts of the study.

PREPARATION AND CRITICISM OF A PROPOSAL

Most sponsoring institutions either have their own format and style manual or designate a style manual to be followed, such as the *Publication Manual of the American Psychological Association* (2001) and the *Chicago Manual of Style* (2003). *Format* refers to the organization of the proposal. *Style* refers to the rules of spelling, capitalization, punctuation, and word processing employed.

Reference style and format, the treatment of headings and sections, and writing style all differ from one manual to the other. Whereas APA style practically eliminates footnotes, CMS style provides for extensive use of explanatory footnotes to cite specific sources, methodological insights, and comments. And whereas an APA-style reference list contains only those sources that are cited in the text, a CMS-style list can include sources that provided background knowledge for the problem. The appropriate directions should be consulted for specific directions about these matters as well as grammar, use of personal pronouns, writing of numbers, and table presentations.

Format also addresses the preliminary pages of the proposal: the title page and the table of contents, including sections, references, and appendices. The same standards of scholarship are applied to the presentation of a proposal as to published articles. The final typed draft should be proofread carefully by the author.

After the final draft of a proposal has been completed, it is submitted to colleagues who read it critically in terms of research criteria, many of which were discussed in prior chapters.

For example, some questions that the reviewers could address would include the following:

Is the problem trivial?

Is the problem sufficiently delimited?

Is the methodology consistent with the research questions?

Is there sufficient justification for why it is quantitative, qualitative, or mixed method?

Does the proposed study meet the objectives of the course, program, or funding organization?

Guidelines for Writing Research Reports

Writing a good research report or article begins with a thorough understanding of the style, format, conventions, and requirements of the relevant journal, association, or audience. This is best accomplished by carefully reading and reviewing previously published reports and articles in whatever outlets the researcher is considering. For example, most journals that publish educational research use APA style and format, which are explained and illustrated in the *Publication Manual of the American Psychological Association* (2001). If the manuscript is targeted to a specific association, the researcher should check the association's website for directions regarding styles and formats and to review journals published by the association. For example, if the researcher is writing a manuscript for mathematics educators, he or she should check the National Council of Teachers of Mathematics (NCTM) website for guidelines and to obtain some examples of empirical studies in journals published by NCTM.

WRITING STYLE

Although the style of writing that is best will depend in part on whether the research is quantitative or qualitative, the goal is the same: to provide a clear and accurate report of what was done and what was found. By presenting different aspects of the study in an orderly manner, the researcher can lead readers logically from one aspect of the study to the next, which enhances their comprehension and understanding.

Although the style of writing in a research report should not be boring, it doesn't need to contain flowery adjectives and phrases. A research report is not a creative essay; it is a straightforward summary of what was planned, what happened, and what the results mean. The researcher should aim for an interesting and compelling writing style that will hold readers' attention and flow smoothly. Standard headings and parts should be used. In qualitative reports, the writing should be more personal and active, more elaborate, and more detailed to reflect the context and the participants' perspectives.

Table 1 shows some of the more popular conventions for effective writing of research reports.

PARTS OF THE MANUSCRIPT

Title Page   The title page should contain, at a minimum, the title, the author(s) name(s), the author's institutional affiliation, and the date. With multiple authors, the order of authors' names may be important in indicating which person is the primary author. When the order of authors is not alphabetical, the first person listed should be the primary author. When submitting an article for publication, the name of the journal is usually included. The title of the article should be a concise statement of the main idea of the research, written with a touch of style, avoiding redundancies such as "A study of" or "A quasi-experimental study of."

TABLE 1   Effective Writing Skills for Research Reports and Articles

Skill	Description	Examples Problematic	Examples Correct
Economy of Expression	Writing should be concise, and should avoid jargon, redundancy, and wordiness.	The socioeconomic status that pertained to most of the group A subjects who were in the control group was high.	Control group subjects had a high socioeconomic status. OR The socioeconomic status of the control group subjects was high.
Use of Pronouns	Limit the use of pronouns (e.g., *they, those, these,* and *it*).	Three methods were used. These developed as a result of the pilot test.	Three methods were used. These methods developed as a result of the pilot test.
Active Voice	Use active rather than passive voice.	The observation was conducted by all of the researchers.	We conducted the observations.
Past Tense	Use the past tense when reporting others' or your own results.	Jones (2008) presents the same finding.	Jones (2008) presented the same finding.
Subject-Verb Agreement	Singular and plural verbs must agree with subjects.	The data was gathered during the last three months.	The data were gathered during the last three months.
Gender Identification	Avoid using *he/she.*	When someone observes the teachers, he/she takes detailed notes.	When an individual observes the teacher, that person takes detailed notes. OR The observer takes detailed notes.
Race and Ethnicity Identification	Use currently acceptable language and capitalization.	The subjects included Afro-American and white students.	The subjects included Black and White students.
Disability Identification	Use language that equates the person with the disability; person first, then disability.	The learning-disabled subjects were assigned to three groups.	The subjects with learning disabilities were assigned to three groups.
Sexual Orientation Identification	Use *gay* or *lesbian* rather than *homosexual.*	The sample consisted of 100 homosexual adults.	The sample consisted of 60 gay and 40 lesbian adults.

Abstract   The abstract is typically 100 to 150 words. It should be dense with information yet concise, providing a summary of the purpose, participants, method, findings, and conclusions. Each sentence should provide information that is essential to understanding the research.

Introduction   The introduction should be one to several paragraphs and should summarize the purpose, background, and significance of the study. The author(s) should indicate why the study is important.

Review of Literature   The review is intended to provide a theoretical foundation and to summarize, critique, and relate other primary studies to the current one. The review should be an analysis and synthesis of previous research. Usually, the most closely related studies are reviewed last. The review should be written in the past tense. For qualitative studies, the review should be brief, and additional literature should be integrated into the paper as findings are presented.

Research Questions and/or Hypotheses   For quantitative research, specific research questions and/or hypotheses follow the review of literature. The questions and hypotheses should be consistent with the data analyses. It is usually not necessary to include null hypotheses.

Method—Participants   The methodology section should contain subsections with headings. The first subsection concerns the participants in the research or the data source. Using past tense, all participants are described using age, gender, socioeconomic status, grade level, aptitude, and other characteristics relevant to the study. The sampling procedure and assignment procedure are also described, if appropriate.

Method—Instrumentation   This section describes the data collection measures and procedures. For a quantitative study, it should contain a discussion of the validity and reliability of the obtained scores.

Method—Design   The design is the specific method (e.g., mixed method, quasi-experimental, longitudinal, nonexperimental).

Method—Procedure   This subsection is often combined with that on design and includes the steps taken to carry out the study. It also contains instructions to participants; how random assignment was done, if appropriate; how the researcher gained entry into the setting; and how interventions were carried out. Sufficient detail should be provided to enable other researchers to replicate the study. Past tense should be used.

Results   The results section contains a description of the techniques used to analyze the data collected and the findings from those analyses. Written in past tense, the results for quantitative studies should only present the findings, not analyze or interpret them. Presentation of the results should parallel the research questions, presenting sufficient detail to support the conclusions drawn. Individual scores are not usually included in quantitative studies. Self-explanatory tables and figures are often used; they should be uncluttered and provide detail that would be cumbersome to include in the narrative. Qualitative results are descriptive and often contain quotations from participants. Results from qualitative studies are also presented with tables and graphs, and findings are typically discussed when presented, integrating the relevant literature as appropriate. For quantitative studies, descriptive statistics should be included when presenting inferential analyses, along with confidence intervals and effect size measures.

Discussion   The discussion section includes an evaluation and interpretation of the findings, weaknesses or limitations of the study, conclusions, and implications for further research and professional practice. The findings are not simply repeated in this section. Interpretations are discussed in relation to previous studies, and theoretical implications are presented. Support for hypotheses is summarized, if appropriate. It is important in this subsection to avoid overgeneralizing the findings and to point out limitations and cautions in making inferences about the meaning of the results (e.g., alternative explanations). The importance of the study is often mentioned, as well.

References   An established style for references should be used—such as APA or CMS—and the conventions of that style should be strictly adhered to. The references list should contain only those sources that are actually cited in the paper. A bibliography can be added to indicate related sources, but that is not common in research. Sources are ordered alphabetically according to the first author's last name, and when there is no author, sources are alphabetized by the title of the document.

APPENDIX

Calculations for Selected Descriptive and Inferential Statistics

From Appendix D of *Research in Education: Evidence-Based Inquiry*, 7/e. James H. McMillan. Sally Schumacher.

Calculations for Selected Descriptive and Inferential Statistics

In this appendix, we will present a step-by-step guide for performing calculations for several simple statistical procedures.* Our intent is not to derive formulas but to show how the statistics are calculated. We believe that being able to apply these formulas assists greatly in understanding the meaning of the statistics.

MEASURES OF CENTRAL TENDENCY

Measures of *central tendency* are descriptive statistics that measure the central location or value of sets of scores. They are used widely to summarize and simplify large quantities of data.

The Mean

The *mean* is the arithmetical average of a set of scores. It is obtained by adding all the scores in a distribution and dividing the sum by the number of scores. The formula for calculating the mean is

$$\overline{X} = \frac{\Sigma X}{n}$$

where

$\overline{X}$ is the mean score
ΣX is the sum of the Xs (*i.e.* $X_1 + X_2 + X_3 \ldots X_n$)
n is the total number of scores

Example: Calculation of the Mean   If we have obtained the sample of eight scores—17, 14, 14, 13, 10, 8, 7, 7—the mean of this set of scores is calculated as

$$\Sigma X = 17 + 14 + 14 + \ldots + 7 = 90$$
$$n = 8$$

Therefore,

$$\overline{X} = \frac{90}{8} = 11.25$$

The Median

The *median* is the score in a distribution below which half of the scores fall. In other words, half of the scores are above the median and half are below the median. The median is at the 50th percentile.

*Statistical tables are located at the end of the appendix.

To calculate the median, the scores are rank ordered from highest to lowest; then one simply counts, from one end, one-half of the scores. In distributions with an odd number of scores, the median is the middle score, as illustrated here:

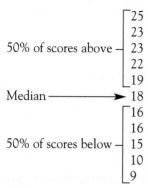

If the distribution has an even number of scores, the median is the average of the two middle scores. In this case, the median is a new score or point in the distribution, as shown here:

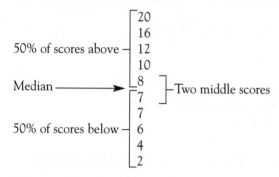

Thus, the median in this example is

$$7 + \frac{8}{2} = \frac{15}{2} + 7.5$$

The median is relatively easy to find in studies with a small number of subjects. As the number of scores increases, the calculation is done either by a formula or by grouping the scores into intervals of scores and using the intervals to make the calculations. Computers are able to apply these more complicated calculations easily, quickly, and reliably.

The Mode   The *mode* is simply the most frequently occurring score in a distribution, and it is found by counting the number of times each score was received. The mode in this distribution, for example, is 22:

23 ☐22 ☐22 ☐22 ☐20 ☐18 ☐18 ☐17 ☐16

MEASURES OF VARIABILITY

Measures of variability are used to show the differences among the scores in a distribution. We use the term *variability* or *dispersion* because the statistics provide an indication of how different, or dispersed, the scores are from one another. We will discuss three measures of variability: range, variance, and standard deviation.

The Range

The *range* is the simplest but also the least useful measure of variability. It is defined as the distance between the smallest and largest scores and is calculated by simply subtracting the bottom, or lowest, score from the top, or highest, score:

$$Range = x_H - x_L$$

where

x_H = the highest score

x_L = the lowest score

For the following scores, then, the range is $26 - 6 = 20$:

$$6 \;\square\; 8 \;\square\; 10 \;\square\; 11 \;\square\; 15 \;\square\; 20 \;\square\; 26$$

The range is a crude measure of variability and is unstable. Because the range can be biased, it is rarely used as the only measure of variability.

Variance

The *variance* (s^2 or σ^2) is a measure of dispersion that indicates the degree to which scores cluster around the mean. The variance provides the researcher with one number to indicate, in a sense, the average dispersion of scores from the mean. Computationally, the variance is the sum of the squared deviation scores about the mean divided by the total number of scores:

$$s^2 = \frac{\Sigma(X - \overline{X})^2}{N}$$

where

s^2 is the variance

$\Sigma(X - X)^2$ is the sum of the squared deviation scores

$(X - \overline{X})$ is the deviation score

N is the total number of scores

For any distribution of scores, the variance can be determined by following these five steps:

1. Calculate the mean: $(\Sigma X/N)$.
2. Calculate the deviation scores: $(X - \overline{X})$.
3. Square each deviation score: $(X - \overline{X})^2$.
4. Sum all the deviation scores: $\Sigma(X - \overline{X})^2$.
5. Divide the sum by N: $\Sigma(X - \overline{X})^2/N$.

These steps are illustrated with actual numbers as follows:

(1) Raw Scores	(2) $(X - \overline{X})$	(3) $(X - \overline{X})^2$	(4)	(5)
20	7	49		
15	2	4		
15	2	4		
14	1	1		
14	1	1	$\Sigma(X - \overline{X})^2 = 120$	$\dfrac{\Sigma(X - \overline{X})^2}{N} = 12$
14	1	1		
12	−1	1		
10	−3	9		
8	−5	25		
8	−5	25		

$\overline{\Sigma X = 130}$

$N = 10$

$\overline{X} = 13$

Substituting directly in the formula:

$$s^2 = \frac{120}{10} = 12$$

Here is another formula that can be used to calculate the variance that is computationally more simple:

$$s^2 = \frac{\Sigma \overline{X}^2 - N\overline{X}^2}{N}$$

Because the variance is expressed as the square of the raw scores, not the original units, it is not usually reported in research. To return to units that are consistent with the raw score distribution, we need to take the square root of the variance. Taking the square root of the variance yields the standard deviation.

Standard Deviation

The *standard deviation* (s, σ, or *SD*) is the square root of the variance. It is a measure of dispersion that uses deviation scores expressed in standard units about the mean; hence the name *standard deviation*. The standard deviation is equal to the square root of the sum of the squared deviation scores about the mean divided by the total number of scores. The formula is

$$s = \sqrt{\frac{\Sigma(X - \overline{X})^2}{N}}$$

where

s is the standard deviation
$\sqrt{}$ is the square root
$\Sigma(X - \overline{X})^2$ is the sum of the squared deviation scores
$(X - \overline{X})$ is the deviation score
N is the total number of scores

To calculate the standard deviation, simply add one step to the formula for variance: take the square root. In our example for variance, for instance, the standard deviation would be

$$s = \sqrt{\frac{\Sigma(X - \overline{X})^2}{N}} = \sqrt{\frac{120}{10}} = \sqrt{12} = 3.46$$

The standard deviation is commonly reported in research and, with the mean, is the most important statistic in research. It tells the number of scores (i.e., the percentage of scores) that are within given units of the standard deviation around the mean. This property of standard deviation is explained in the section called "Normal Distribution," which follows.

STANDARD SCORES

Standard scores are numbers that are transformed from raw scores to provide consistent information about the location of a score within a total distribution. They are numbers that are related to the normal distribution.

Normal Distribution

The *normal distribution* is a set of scores that, when plotted in a frequency distribution, result in a symmetrical, bell-shaped curve with precise mathematical properties. The mathematical properties provide the basis for making standardized interpretations. These properties include possessing a mode, mean, and median that are the same; having a mean that divides the curve into two identical halves; and having measures of standard deviation that fall at predictable places

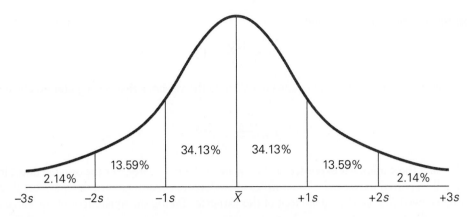

FIGURE 1   **Graph of the Standard Normal Distribution or Normal Curve**

on the normal curve, with the same percentage of scores between the mean and points equidistant from the mean.

This third characteristic is very important. We know, for example, that at $+1s$, we will always be at about the 84th percentile in the distribution. (The percentile score is the percentage of scores at or below the designated score.) This is because the median is at the 50th percentile, and $+1s$ contains an additional 34 percent of the scores ($50 + 34 = 84$). Similarly, the percentage of scores between $+1s$ and $+2s$ is about 14 percent, which means that $+2s$ is at the 98th percentile. These characteristics are illustrated in Figure 1, the graph of the standard normal distribution.

The pleasing aspect of this property is that for any raw score distribution with unique units, such as 1 or 2 as s, the interpretation is always the same. If one distribution has a mean of 10, therefore, and a standard deviation of 3, and a second distribution has a mean of 50 and a standard deviation of 7, a score of 4 in the first case is at about the same percentile (the second) as a score of 36 in the second case.

z-Scores

The most basic standard score is called a z-score, and it is expressed as a deviation from the mean in standard deviation units. A z-score of 1 is thus at one standard deviation, -1 is at minus one standard deviation, $+2$ is at two standard deviations, and so forth.

After the mean and standard deviation are calculated for a set of scores, it is easy to convert each raw score to a z-score, which then indicates exactly where each score lies in the normal distribution.

The formula for calculating a z-score is

$$z = \frac{X - \overline{X}}{s}$$

where

z is the z-score value
X is any particular score
$\overline{X}$ is the arithmetic mean of a distribution of scores
s is the standard deviation of that same distribution

Taking the scores used to illustrate variance and standard deviation, the z-scores would be found as follows:

$$\text{For the raw score of 20: } z = \frac{20 - 13}{3.46} = 2.02$$

$$\text{For the raw score of 14: } z = \frac{14 - 13}{3.46} = 0.29$$

$$\text{For the raw score of 10: } z = \frac{10 - 13}{3.46} = -0.87$$

Once the z-score has been calculated, it is easy to refer to conversion tables to find the percentile rank corresponding to each z-score.

T-Scores

One limitation of using z-scores is the necessity for being careful with the negative sign and with the decimal point. To avoid these problems, other standard scores are used by converting the z-scores algebraically to different units. The general formula for converting z-scores is

$$A = \overline{X}_A + s_A(z)$$

where

A is the new standard score equivalent to z
$\overline{X}_A$ is the mean for the new standard-score scale
s_A is the standard deviation for the new standard-score scale
z is the z-score for any observation

For T-scores, $\overline{X}_A = 50$ and $s_A = 10$. The equation for converting z-scores to T-scores is thus

$$T = 50 + 10(z)$$

For example, the T-scores for our earlier illustration would be as follows:

For the raw score of 20: $T = 50 + 10(2.02) = 70.2$
For the raw score of 14: $T = 50 + 10(0.29) = 52.9$
For the raw score of 10: $T = 50 + 10(-0.87) = 41.3$

Other Standard Scores

Other common standard scores include the following:

1. Normal Curve Equivalent (NCE) has a mean of 50 and s of 21.06. Thus, NCE = 50 + 21.06 (z-score).
2. IQ score has a mean of 100 and s of 15 or 16. Thus, IQ = 100 + 15 (z-score).
3. College Entrance Examination Boards (CEEB, such as SAT) use a mean of 500 and an s of 100. Thus, CEEB = 500 + 100 (z-score).
4. ACT (American College Testing Program) uses a mean of 20 and an s of 5. Thus, ACT = 20 + 5 (z-score).
5. Stanine. The stanine is also commonly reported. Stanines are standardized on a mean of 5 and s of 2, but unlike other standard scores, the numbers refer to intervals rather than to specific points on the normal distribution. Stanine 5 is located in the center of the distribution and includes the middle 20 percent of scores; stanines 4 and 6 include 17 percent of the scores; 3 and 7, 12 percent; 2 and 8, 7 percent; and 1 and 9, 4 percent.

MEASURES OF RELATIONSHIP

Measures of relationship are used to indicate the degree to which two sets of scores are related, or covary. We intuitively seek relationships by such statements as "If high scores on variable X tend to be associated with high scores on variable Y, then the variables are related" and "If high scores on variable X tend to be associated with low scores on variable Y, then the variables are related." The relationship can be either positive or negative and either strong or weak.

We use correlation coefficients as a statistical summary of the nature of the relationship between two variables. They provide us with an estimate of the quantitative degree of relationship. The numbers are almost always between -1.00 and $+1.00$. We will show how to calculate two common correlation coefficients: the Pearson product-moment and the Spearman rho correlations.

Pearson Product-Moment (Pearson *r*)

The *Pearson product-moment correlation coefficient* is the most widely used measure of relationship. The Pearson *r* is calculated to show the linear relationship between two variables. To compute the Pearson *r*, two measures on each subject are needed. Suppose, for example, we have a group of 10 subjects, and for each subject we have measures of self-concept and achievement. We can then calculate the Pearson *r* between self-concept and achievement for these 10 subjects using the following formula:

$$\text{Pearson } r = \frac{N\Sigma XY - (\Sigma X)(\Sigma Y)}{\sqrt{N\Sigma X^2 - (\Sigma X)^2} \cdot \sqrt{N\Sigma Y^2 - (\Sigma Y)^2}}$$

where

ΣXY is the sum of the XY cross-products
ΣX is the sum of the X scores
ΣY is the sum of the Y scores
ΣX^2 is the sum of the squared X scores
ΣY^2 is the sum of the squared Y scores
N is the number of pairs of scores

This formula may appear complex but is actually quite easy to calculate. The scores can be listed in a table, as follows. To use it, one simply finds the values for each summation in the formula, substitutes where appropriate, and performs the math indicated.

Subject	Self-Concept Score X	X^2	Achievement Score Y	Y^2	$X{-}Y$
1	25	625	85	7,225	2,125
2	20	400	90	8,100	1,800
3	21	441	80	6,400	1,680
4	18	324	70	4,900	1,260
5	15	225	75	5,625	1,125
6	17	289	80	6,400	1,360
7	14	196	75	5,625	1,050
8	15	225	70	4,900	1,050
9	12	144	75	5,625	900
10	13	169	60	3,600	780
	$\Sigma X = 170$	$\Sigma X^2 = 3{,}038$	$\Sigma Y = 760$	$\Sigma Y^2 = 58{,}400$	$\Sigma X \cdot Y = 13{,}130$
	$(\Sigma X)^2 = 28{,}900$		$(\Sigma Y)^2 = 577{,}600$		

To compute the Pearson *r*, follow these steps:

1. Pair each set of scores; one set becomes X, the other Y.
2. Calculate ΣX and ΣY.
3. Calculate X^2 and Y^2.
4. Calculate ΣX^2 and ΣY^2.
5. Calculate $(\Sigma X)^2$ and $(\Sigma Y)^2$.
6. Calculate $X \times Y$.
7. Calculate $\Sigma X \times Y$.
8. Substitute the calculated values into the formula.

$$\text{Pearson } r = \frac{10(131{,}300) - (170)(760)}{\sqrt{10(30{,}380) - 28{,}900} \cdot \sqrt{10(58{,}400) - 577{,}600}}$$

$$= \frac{131,300 - 129,200}{\sqrt{30,380 - 28,900} \cdot \sqrt{584,000 - 577,600}}$$

$$= \frac{2,100}{\sqrt{1,480} \cdot \sqrt{6,400}}$$

$$= \frac{2,100}{(38.47) \cdot (80)}$$

$$= \frac{2,100}{3,078}$$

$$= .68$$

The value of 0.68 shows a moderate positive relationship between self-concept and achievement for this set of scores. The levels of significance of correlation coefficients are indicated in Table 2 at the end of this appendix.

Spearman Rank (r ranks or Spearman rho)

The *Spearman rho* is used when ranks are available on each of two variables for all subjects. Ranks are simply listings of scores from highest to lowest. The Spearman rho correlation shows the degree to which subjects maintain the same relative position on two measures. In other words, the Spearman rho indicates how much agreement there is between the ranks of each variable.

The calculation of the Spearman ranks is more simple than the calculation of the Pearson *r*. The necessary steps are as follow:

1. Rank the X_s and Y_s.
2. Pair the ranked X_s and Y_s.
3. Calculate the difference in ranks for each pair.
4. Square each difference.
5. Sum the squared differences.
6. Substitute the calculated values into the formula.

The formula is:

$$\text{Spearman rho} = 1 - \frac{6\Sigma D^2}{n(n^2 - 1)}$$

For the data used in calculating the Pearson *r*, the Spearman rho would be found as follows:

Subject	Self-Concept Rank X	Achievement Rank Y	Difference D	D²
1	1	2	−1	1
2	3	1	2	4
3	2	3.5	−1.5	2.25
4	4	5.5	−1.5	2.25
5	6.5	8	−1.5	2.25
6	5	3.5	1.5	2.25
7	8	8	0	0
8	6.5	5.5	1	1
9	10	8	2	4
10	9	10	−1	1
				$\Sigma D^2 = 20$

Note: When ties in the ranking occur, all scores that are tied receive the average of the ranks involved.

$$r \text{ ranks} = 1 - \frac{6(20)}{10(100 - 1)}$$

$$= 1 - \frac{120}{990}$$

$$= 1 - 0.12$$

$$= .88$$

In most datasets with more than 50 subjects, the Pearson r and Spearman rank will give almost identical correlations. In the example used here, the Spearman is higher because of the low n and the manner in which the ties in rankings resulted in low difference scores.

CHI-SQUARE

Chi-square (χ^2) is a statistical procedure that is used as an inferential statistic with nominal data, such as frequency counts, and ordinal data, such as percentages and proportions. In the simplest case, the data are organized into two categories, such as *yes* and *no*, *high* and *low*, *for* and *against*. If, for example, a researcher is interested in the opinions of college professors about tenure and asks the question Should tenure be abolished? then all responses could be categorized as either *yes* or *no*. The total frequency in each category (observed frequencies) is then compared to the expected frequency, which in most cases is chance. This means that with two categories, half of the responses should be *yes* and half *no*. Assume the following results:

Should tenure be abolished?

	Yes	No
Observed	40	60
Expected	50	50

These values are then used in the following formula to calculate the chi-square statistic:

$$\chi^2 = \Sigma \frac{(f_o - f_e)^2}{f_e}$$

where

χ^2 is the chi-square statistic
Σ is the sum of
f_o is the observed frequency
f_e is the expected frequency

Inserting the values from the table, the result is

$$\chi^2 = \frac{(40 - 50)^2}{50} + \frac{(60 - 50)^2}{50}$$

$$= \frac{100}{50} + \frac{100}{50}$$

$$= 2 + 2$$

$$= 4.0$$

The obtained value, in this case 4, is then used with the degrees of freedom in the problem ($df = k - 1$, where k equals the number of categories; in our example, $df = 2 - 1$, or 1) to find the value of the chi-square in the critical values of chi-square table (Table 3 at the end of this appendix) to determine the level of significance of the results. By referring to the table and locating 4.00 within the table with 1 df, the result is significant at just less than a p value of .05.

Consequently, it would be appropriate to say that there is a significant difference in the number of professors responding *yes* as compared to the number responding *no*.

Suppose the researcher wanted to go a step further with this problem and learn whether administrators and professors differ in their responses to the question about abolishing tenure. The researcher would then have what is called a *contingency table*, which is a cross-tabulation of the frequencies for the combinations of categories of the two variables. A hypothetical contingency table is shown below for administrators and professors.

Should tenure be abolished?

	Professors	Administrators	Raw Totals
Yes	.40($p = 0.40$)	40($p = 0.80$)	80($p_a = 0.53$)
No	60($p = 0.60$)	10($p = 0.20$)	70($p_a = 0.47$)
	$n = 100$	$n = 50$	$n = 150$

Notice in the table that the proportion of responses in each response category (*yes* and *no*) is shown for both professors and administrators, and the total proportions are shown in the last column. These proportions are used in the following equation:

$$\chi^2 = \frac{\Sigma n(P - P_e)^2}{P_e}$$

where

χ^2 is the chi-square statistic
Σ is the sum of all cells in the problem (in our example, there are four cells)
n is the number of total observations in each column
P is the proportion of observed frequencies in each cell
P_e is the expected proportion for each row

For our example, therefore, the result would be

$$\chi^2 = 100\frac{(.4 - .53)^2}{.53} + 100\frac{(0.60 - .47)^2}{.47}$$

$$= 50\frac{(.80 - .53)^2}{.53} + 100\frac{(.20 - .47)}{.47}$$

$$= 100\frac{.017}{.53} + 100\frac{.017}{.47} + 50\frac{.07}{.53} + 50\frac{.07}{.47}$$

$$= 3.19 + 3.61 + 6.60 + 7.45$$

$$= 20.85$$

In contingency tables, the degrees of freedom are equal to $(r - 1)(c - 1)$, where r is the number of rows and c is the number of columns. In our example, the $df = (2 - 1)(2 - 1) = 1$. By locating 22.08 with 1 degree of freedom in the critical values of the chi-square table (Table 3), we note that the result is highly significant, $p < .001$. This result indicates that there is a significant association or relationship between the two variables (*professors* and *administrators*, and *yes* and *no*).

t-TEST

The *t*-test is used to indicate the probability that the means of two groups are different. We will present two common forms of the *t*-test: one used with independent samples and the other with dependent samples.

Independent Samples *t*-Test

The *independent samples t-test*, or *t*-test for independent groups, is used to determine whether the mean value of a variable on one group of subjects is different from the mean value on the same variable on a different group of subjects. It is important to meet three statistical assumptions: (1) that the frequency distributions of scores for both populations of each group are normal, (2) that the variances in each population are equal, and (3) that the observation of scores in one group is independent of the other group. If the sample size is greater than 30, violating the assumption of normality is not serious, and as long as the sample sizes are equal, violation of the assumption of homogeneity of variance is not a problem. It is crucial, however, that the observations for each group are independent.

The formula for calculating the *t*-test statistic is

$$t = \frac{\overline{X}_1 - \overline{X}_2}{s_{\overline{X}_1 - \overline{X}_2}}$$

where

t is the *t*-test statistic
$\overline{X}_1$ is the mean of one group
$\overline{X}_2$ is the mean of the second group
$s_{\overline{X}_1 - \overline{X}_2}$ is the standard error of the difference in means

The standard error of the difference in means is estimated from the variances of each distribution. This part of the formula is calculated by pooling the variances of each distribution to result in *s*. This is done using the following formula:

$$s = \sqrt{\frac{\Sigma x_1^2 + \Sigma x_2^2}{df_1 + df_2}}$$

Then,

$$s_{\overline{X}_1 - \overline{X}_2} = s\sqrt{\frac{1}{n_1} + \frac{1}{n_2}}$$

As an example, consider the following data:

Group x_1	Group x_2
$\overline{X}_1 = 18$	$\overline{X}_2 = 25$
$n_1 = 20$	$n_2 = 20$
$\Sigma X_1^2 = 348$	$\Sigma X_2^2 = 425$

From this point, we can calculate the *t*-test statistic using the following steps:

1. Calculate *s*:

$$s = \sqrt{\frac{348 + 425}{19 + 19}}$$

$$= \sqrt{20.34}$$

$$= 4.51$$

2. Calculate $s_{\overline{X}_1 - \overline{X}_2}$:

$$s_{\overline{X}_1 - \overline{X}_2} = 4.51\sqrt{\frac{1}{20} + \frac{1}{20}}$$

$$= 4.51\sqrt{\frac{1}{10}}$$

$$= 4.51(0.32)$$

$$= 1.44$$

3. Substitute into the t-test formula:

$$t = \frac{18 - 25}{1.44}$$

$$= \frac{7}{1.44}$$

$$= 4.86$$

Once the t-test statistic is calculated, it is found in the critical values for the t-table (Table 12.1) with corresponding degrees of freedom (which for the independent samples t-test is $n_1 + n_2 - 2$, or in our example, $20 + 20 - 2 = 38$) to determine the significance level of the results. In this example, the t-test statistic of 4.86, with 38 df, is significant at $p < 0.001$.

Here is another example of a computation with the t-test, beginning with raw data:

	Group 1		Group 2	
x^1	x_1^2	x_2	x_2^2
7	49	7	49
8	64	7	49
8	64	8	64
6	36	6	36
5	25	6	36
5	25	4	16
6	36	4	16
6	36	3	9
9	81	5	25
8	64	5	25
$\Sigma x_1 = 68$	$\Sigma x_1^2 = 480$	$\Sigma x_2 = 55$	$\Sigma x_2^2 = 325$
$n = 10$	$n = 10$	$\overline{X}_2 = 5.5$	
$\overline{X}_1 = 6.8$			

Following the three steps outlined earlier:

$$s = \sqrt{\frac{480 + 325}{9 + 9}} = \sqrt{44.72} = 6.69$$

$$s_{\overline{X}_1 - \overline{X}_2} = 6.69\sqrt{\frac{1}{10} + \frac{1}{10}} = 6.69\sqrt{\frac{1}{5}} = (6.69)(0.45) = 2.99$$

$$t = \frac{6.8 - 5.5}{2.99} = \frac{1.3}{2.99} = 0.43$$

In this case, the t-test statistic of 0.43, with 18 df, is not statistically significant. Even though the means for the groups are different, therefore, there is a good possibility that they can be different by chance alone.

Dependent Samples t-Test

When two groups that have been matched are being compared, as in a pretest-posttest design, the t-test formula must take into account the interrelationship between the groups: that is, the groups are not independent but rather related. The formula for this type of t-test is easier to calculate than for the independent samples t-test:

$$t = \frac{\overline{D}}{\sqrt{\dfrac{\Sigma D^2 - \dfrac{(\Sigma D)^2}{N}}{N(N-1)}}}$$

where

$\overline{D}$ is the mean difference for all pairs of scores
ΣD^2 is the sum of the squares of the differences
$(\Sigma D)^2$ is the square of the sum of the differences
N is the number of pairs of scores
$N-1$ is the degrees of freedom (one less than the number of pairs of scores)

Consider the following example and steps:

Subjects	Posttest Scores x_1	Pretest Scores x_2	$\overline{D}$	D_2
1	22	15	7	49
2	21	16	5	25
3	20	17	7	49
4	23	16	7	49
5	19	14	5	25
6	21	15	6	36
7	18	12	6	36
8	22	18	4	16
			$\Sigma D = 47$	$\Sigma D^2 = 285$

To perform the first step, calculate $\overline{D}$:

$$\overline{D} = \frac{\Sigma D}{N} = \frac{47}{8} = 5.9$$

To perform step 2:

$$(\Sigma D)^2 = 47^2 = 2{,}209$$

Finally, substitute into the formula:

$$t = \cfrac{5.9}{\sqrt{\cfrac{285 - \cfrac{2{,}209}{8}}{8(8-1)}}}$$

$$= \cfrac{5.9}{\sqrt{\cfrac{285 - 276}{56}}}$$

$$= \cfrac{5.9}{\sqrt{\cfrac{9}{56}}}$$

$$= \cfrac{5.9}{0.40}$$

$$= 14.75$$

The calculated t-test statistic (14.75) is located in the critical values of the t-table, with the degrees of freedom ($N - 1$, or in this example, $8 - 1 = 7$). The result from the table is that the group means are clearly different from each other and statistically significant at $p < .001$.

TABLE 1 Random Numbers

03 47 43 73 86	36 96 47 36 61	46 98 64 71 62	33 26 16 80 45	60 11 14 10 95
97 74 24 67 62	42 81 14 57 20	42 53 32 37 32	27 07 36 07 51	24 51 79 89 73
16 76 62 27 66	56 50 26 71 07	32 90 79 78 53	13 55 38 58 59	88 97 54 14 10
12 56 85 99 26	96 96 68 27 31	05 03 72 93 15	57 12 10 14 21	88 26 49 81 76
55 59 56 35 64	38 54 82 46 22	31 62 43 09 90	06 18 44 32 53	23 83 01 30 30
16 22 77 94 39	49 54 43 54 82	17 37 93 23 78	87 35 20 96 43	84 26 34 91 64
84 42 17 53 31	57 24 55 06 88	77 04 74 47 67	21 76 33 50 25	83 92 12 06 76
63 01 63 78 59	16 95 55 67 19	98 10 50 71 75	12 86 73 58 07	44 39 52 38 79
33 21 12 45 29	78 64 56 07 82	52 42 07 44 38	15 51 00 13 42	99 66 02 79 54
57 60 86 32 44	09 47 27 96 54	49 17 46 09 62	90 52 84 77 27	08 02 73 43 28
18 18 07 92 46	44 17 16 58 09	79 83 86 19 62	06 76 50 03 10	55 23 64 05 05
26 62 38 97 75	84 16 07 44 99	83 11 46 32 24	20 14 85 88 45	10 93 72 88 71
23 42 40 64 74	82 97 77 77 81	07 45 32 14 08	32 98 94 07 72	93 85 79 10 75
52 36 28 19 95	50 92 26 11 97	00 56 76 31 38	80 22 02 53 53	86 60 42 04 53
37 85 84 35 12	83 39 50 08 30	42 34 07 96 88	54 42 06 87 98	35 85 29 48 39
70 29 17 12 13	40 33 20 38 26	13 89 51 03 74	17 76 37 13 04	07 74 21 19 30
56 62 18 37 35	96 83 50 87 75	97 12 25 93 47	70 33 24 03 54	97 77 46 44 80
99 59 57 22 77	88 42 95 45 72	16 64 36 16 00	04 43 18 66 79	94 77 24 21 90
16 08 15 04 72	33 27 14 34 09	45 59 34 68 49	12 72 07 34 45	99 27 72 95 14
31 16 93 32 43	50 27 89 87 19	20 15 37 00 49	52 85 66 60 44	38 68 88 11 80
68 34 30 13 70	55 74 30 77 40	44 22 78 84 26	04 33 46 09 52	68 07 97 06 57
74 57 25 65 76	59 29 97 68 60	71 91 38 67 54	13 58 18 24 76	15 54 55 95 52
27 42 37 86 53	48 55 90 65 72	96 57 69 36 10	96 46 92 42 45	97 60 49 04 91
00 39 68 29 61	66 37 32 20 30	77 84 57 03 29	10 45 65 04 26	11 04 96 67 24
29 94 98 94 24	68 49 69 10 82	53 75 91 93 30	34 25 20 57 27	40 48 73 51 92
16 90 82 66 59	83 62 64 11 12	67 19 00 71 74	60 47 21 29 68	02 02 37 03 31
11 27 94 75 06	06 09 19 74 66	02 94 37 34 02	76 70 90 30 86	38 45 94 30 38
35 24 10 16 20	33 32 51 26 38	79 78 45 04 91	16 92 53 56 16	02 75 50 95 98
38 23 16 86 38	42 38 97 01 50	87 75 66 81 41	40 01 74 91 62	48 51 84 08 32
31 96 25 91 47	96 44 33 49 13	34 86 82 53 92	00 52 43 48 85	27 55 26 89 62
66 67 40 67 14	64 05 71 95 86	11 05 65 09 68	76 83 20 37 90	57 16 00 11 66
14 90 84 45 11	75 73 88 05 90	52 27 41 14 86	22 98 12 22 08	07 52 74 95 80
68 05 51 18 00	33 96 02 75 19	07 60 62 93 55	59 33 82 43 90	49 37 38 44 59
20 46 78 73 90	97 51 40 14 02	04 02 33 31 08	39 54 16 49 36	47 95 93 13 30
64 19 58 97 79	15 06 15 93 20	01 90 10 75 06	40 78 78 89 62	02 67 74 17 33
05 26 93 70 60	22 35 85 15 13	92 03 51 59 77	59 56 78 06 83	52 91 05 70 74
07 97 10 88 23	09 98 42 99 64	61 71 62 99 15	06 51 29 16 93	58 05 77 09 51
68 71 86 85 85	54 87 66 47 54	73 32 08 11 12	44 95 92 63 16	29 56 24 29 48
26 99 61 65 53	58 37 78 80 70	43 10 50 67 42	32 17 55 85 74	94 44 67 16 94
14 65 52 68 75	87 59 36 22 41	26 78 63 06 55	13 08 27 01 50	15 29 39 39 43
17 53 77 58 71	71 41 61 50 72	12 41 94 96 26	44 95 27 36 99	02 96 74 30 83
90 26 59 21 19	23 52 23 33 12	96 93 02 18 39	07 02 18 36 07	25 99 32 70 23
41 23 52 55 99	31 04 49 69 96	10 47 48 45 88	13 41 43 89 20	97 17 14 49 17
60 20 50 81 69	31 99 73 68 68	35 81 33 03 76	24 30 12 48 60	18 99 10 72 34
91 25 38 05 90	94 58 28 41 36	45 37 59 03 09	90 35 57 29 12	82 62 54 65 60
34 50 57 74 37	98 80 33 00 91	09 77 93 19 82	74 94 80 04 04	45 07 31 66 49
85 22 04 39 43	73 81 53 94 79	33 62 46 86 28	08 31 54 46 31	53 94 13 38 47
09 79 13 77 48	73 82 97 22 21	05 03 27 24 83	72 89 44 05 60	35 80 39 94 88
88 75 80 18 14	22 95 75 42 49	39 32 82 22 49	02 48 07 70 37	16 04 61 67 87
90 96 23 70 00	39 00 03 06 90	55 85 78 38 36	94 37 30 69 32	90 89 00 76 33

Source: Taken from Table XXXII of Fisher and Yates: *Statistical Tables for Biological, Agricultural and Medical Research* (6th Edition 1974) published by Longman Group UK Ltd. London (previously published by Oliver and Boyd Ltd, Edinburgh) and is reprinted by permission of the authors and publishers.

TABLE 2 Critical Values for the Pearson Correlation Coefficient

	Level of Significance for a One-Tail Test				
	.05	.025	.01	.005	.0005
	Level of Significance for a Two-Tail Test				
df	.10	.05	.02	.01	.001
1	.9877	.9969	.9995	.9999	1.0000
2	.9000	.9500	.9800	.9900	.9990
3	.8054	.8783	.9343	.9587	.9912
4	.7293	.8114	.8822	.9172	.9741
5	.6694	.7545	.8329	.8745	.9507
6	.6215	.7067	.7887	.8343	.9249
7	.5822	.6664	.7498	.7977	.8982
8	.5494	.6319	.7155	.7646	.8721
9	.5214	.6021	.6851	.7348	.8471
10	.4973	.5760	.6581	.7079	.8233
11	.4762	.5529	.6339	.6835	.8010
12	.4575	.5324	.6120	.6614	.7800
13	.4409	.5139	.5923	.6411	.7603
14	.4259	.4973	.5742	.6226	.7420
15	.4124	.4821	.5577	.6055	.7246
16	.4000	.4683	.5425	.5897	.7084
17	.3887	.4555	.5285	.5751	.6932
18	.3783	.4438	.5155	.5614	.6787
19	.3687	.4329	.5034	.5487	.6652
20	.3598	.4227	.4921	.5368	.6524
25	.3223	.3809	.4451	.4869	.5974
30	.2960	.3494	.4093	.4487	.5541
35	.2746	.3246	.3810	.4182	.5189
40	.2573	.3044	.3578	.3932	.4896
45	.2428	.2875	.3384	.3721	.4648
50	.2306	.2732	.3218	.3541	.4433
60	.2108	.2500	.2948	.3248	.4078
70	.1954	.2319	.2737	.3017	.3799
80	.1829	.2172	.2565	.2830	.3568
90	.1726	.2050	.2422	.2673	.3375
100	.1638	.1946	.2301	.2540	.3211

Source: Taken from Table VII of Fisher and Yates: *Statistical Tables for Biological, Agricultural and Medical Research* (6th Edition, 1974) published by Longman Group UK Ltd. London (previously published by Oliver and Boyd Ltd, Edinburgh) and is reprinted by permission of the authors and publishers.

TABLE 3 Critical Values of Chi-Square

df	.99	.98	.95	.90	.80	.70	.50	.30	.20	.10	.05	.02	.01	.001
1	.0002	.0006	.0039	.016	.064	.15	.46	1.07	1.64	2.71	3.84	5.41	6.64	10.83
2	.02	.04	.10	.21	.45	.71	1.39	1.41	3.22	4.60	5.99	7.82	9.21	13.82
3	.12	.18	.35	.58	1.00	1.42	2.37	3.66	4.64	6.25	7.82	9.84	11.34	16.27
4	.30	.43	.71	1.06	1.65	2.20	3.36	4.88	5.99	7.78	9.49	11.67	13.28	18.47
5	.55	.75	1.14	1.61	2.34	3.00	4.35	6.06	7.29	9.24	11.07	13.39	15.09	20.52
6	.87	1.13	1.64	2.20	3.07	3.83	5.35	7.23	8.56	10.64	12.59	15.03	16.81	22.46
7	1.24	1.56	2.17	2.83	3.82	4.67	6.35	8.38	9.80	12.02	14.07	16.62	18.48	24.32
8	1.65	2.03	2.73	3.49	4.59	5.53	7.34	9.52	11.03	13.36	15.51	18.17	20.09	26.12
9	2.09	2.53	3.32	4.17	5.38	6.39	8.34	10.66	12.24	14.68	16.92	19.68	21.67	27.88
10	2.56	3.06	3.94	4.86	6.18	7.27	9.34	11.78	13.44	15.99	18.31	21.16	23.21	29.59
11	3.05	3.61	4.58	5.58	6.99	8.15	10.34	12.90	14.63	17.28	19.68	22.62	24.72	31.26
12	3.57	4.18	5.23	6.30	7.81	9.03	11.34	14.01	15.81	18.55	21.03	24.05	26.22	32.91
13	4.11	4.76	5.89	7.04	8.63	9.93	12.34	15.12	16.98	19.81	22.36	25.47	27.69	34.53
14	4.66	5.37	6.57	7.79	9.47	10.82	13.34	16.22	18.15	21.06	34.68	26.87	29.14	36.12
15	5.23	5.98	7.26	8.55	10.31	11.72	14.34	17.32	19.31	22.31	25.00	28.26	30.58	37.70
16	5.81	6.61	7.96	9.31	11.15	12.62	15.34	18.42	20.46	23.54	26.30	29.63	32.00	39.25
17	6.41	7.26	8.67	10.08	12.00	13.53	16.34	19.51	22.62	24.77	27.59	31.00	33.41	40.79
18	7.02	7.91	9.39	10.86	12.86	14.44	17.34	20.60	22.76	25.99	28.87	32.35	34.80	42.31
19	7.63	8.57	10.12	11.65	13.72	15.35	18.34	21.69	23.90	27.20	30.14	33.69	36.19	43.82
20	8.26	9.24	10.85	12.44	14.58	16.27	19.34	22.78	25.04	28.41	31.41	35.02	37.57	45.32
21	8.90	9.92	11.59	13.24	15.44	17.18	20.34	23.86	26.17	29.62	32.67	36.34	38.93	46.80
22	9.54	10.60	12.34	14.04	16.31	18.10	21.34	24.94	27.30	30.81	33.92	37.66	40.29	48.27
23	10.20	11.29	13.09	14.85	17.19	19.02	22.34	26.02	28.43	32.01	35.17	38.97	41.64	49.73
24	10.86	11.99	13.85	15.66	18.06	19.94	23.34	27.10	29.55	33.20	36.42	40.27	42.98	51.18
25	11.52	12.70	14.61	16.47	18.94	20.87	24.34	28.17	30.68	34.48	37.65	41.57	44.31	52.62
26	12.20	13.41	15.38	17.29	19.82	21.79	25.34	29.25	31.80	35.56	38.88	42.86	45.64	54.05
27	12.88	14.12	16.15	18.11	20.70	22.72	26.34	30.32	32.91	36.74	40.11	44.14	46.96	55.48
28	13.56	14.85	16.93	18.94	21.59	23.65	27.34	31.39	34.03	37.92	41.34	45.42	48.28	56.89
29	14.26	15.57	17.71	19.77	22.48	24.58	28.45	32.46	35.14	39.09	42.56	46.69	49.59	58.30
30	14.95	16.31	18.49	20.60	23.36	25.51	29.34	33.53	36.25	40.26	43.77	47.96	50.89	59.70

Source: Taken from Table IV of Fisher and Yates: *Statistical Tables for Biological, Agricultural and Medical Research* (6th Edition 1974) published by Longman Group UK Ltd. London (previously published by Oliver and Boyd Ltd, Edinburgh) and is reprinted by permission of the authors and publishers.

References

References

American Educational Research Association. (1999). *Standards for educational and psychological tests*. Washington, DC: Author.

American Educational Research Association. (2006). Standards for reporting on empirical social science research in AERA publications. *Educational Researcher, 35*(6), 33–40.

American Psychological Association. (2001). *Publication manual of the American Psychological Association* (5th ed.). Washington, DC: Author.

Anderson, G., Herr, K., & Nihlen, A. (1994). *Studying your own school: An educator's guide to qualitative practitioner research*. Thousand Oaks, CA: Corwin.

Babbie, E. R. (2007). *The practice of social research.* (11th ed.). Belmont, CA: Wadsworth.

Berg, B. L. (2004). *Qualitative research methods for the social sciences* (5th ed.). Thousand Oaks, CA: Sage.

Best, S. J., & Krueger, B. S. (2004). *Internet data collection*. Thousand Oaks, CA: Sage.

Bogdan, R. C., & Biklen, S. K. (2007). *Qualitative research in education: An introduction to theory and methods* (5th ed.). Boston: Allyn & Bacon.

Boruch, R. F., & Cecil, J. S. (1979). *Assuring the confidentiality of social research data*. Philadelphia: University of Pennsylvania Press.

Bryman, A. (2007). Barriers to integrating quantitative and qualitative research. *Journal of Mixed Methods Research, 1*(1), 8–22.

Campbell, D. T., & Stanley, J. C. (1963). Experimental and quasi-experimental designs for research. In N. L. Gage (ed.), *Handbook of research on teaching* (pp. 1–80). Chicago: Rand, McNally.

Charmaz, K. (2000). Grounded theory: Objectivist and constructivist methods. In N. K. Denzin & Y. S. Lincoln (Eds.), *Handbook of qualitative research* (2nd ed., pp. 509–535). Thousand Oaks, CA: Sage.

Chatterji, M. (2007). Grades of evidence: Variability in quality of findings in effectiveness studies of complex field interventions. *American Journal of Evaluation, 28*(3), 239–255.

Chicago manual of style (15th ed.). (2003). Chicago: The University of Chicago Press.

Christians, C. (2000). Ethics and politics in qualitative research. In N. K. Denzin & Y. S. Lincoln (Eds.), *Handbook of qualitative research* (2nd ed., pp. 133–155). Thousand Oaks, CA: Sage.

Cohen, J. (1988). *Statistical power analysis for the behavioral sciences*. Hillsdale, NJ: Erlbaum.

Colton, D., & Covert, R. W. (2007). *Designing and constructing instruments for social research and evaluation*. San Francisco: Jossey-Bass.

Comrey, A. L., Backer, T. E., & Glaser, E. M. (1973). *A sourcebook for mental health measures*. Los Angeles: Human Interaction Research Institute.

Cook, C., Heath, F., & Thompson, R. (2000). A meta-analysis of response rates in web or Internet-based surveys. *Educational and Psychological Measurement, 60*, 821–836.

Cook, T. D., & Campbell, D. T. (1979). *Quasi-experimentations: Design and analysis issues for field settings*. Chicago: Rand McNally.

Corbin, J., & Strauss, A. (2007). *Basics of qualitative research: Techniques and procedures for developing grounded theory* (3rd ed.). Thousand Oaks, CA: Sage.

Creswell, J. W. (2007). *Qualitative inquiry and research design: Choosing among five approaches* (2nd ed.). Thousand Oaks, CA: Sage.

Creswell, J. W. (2008). *Educational research: Planning, conducting, and evaluating quantitative and qualitative research* (2nd ed.). Upper Saddle River, NJ: Merrill/Prentice Hall.

Creswell, J. W., & Plano Clark, V. L. (2007). *Designing and conducting mixed method research*. Thousand Oaks, CA: Sage.

De Leeuw, E., Borgers, N., & Smits, A. (2004). Pretesting questionnaires for children and adolescents. In S. Presser, J. M. Rothgeb, M. P. Couper, J. T. Lessler, E. Martin, J. Martin, & E. Singer (Eds.), *Methods for testing and evaluating survey questionnaires* (pp. 409–430). Hoboken, NJ: Wiley.

Denzin, N. K. (1997). *Interpretative ethnography: Ethnographic practices in the 21st century*. Thousand Oaks, CA: Sage.

Denzin, N. K., & Lincoln, Y. S. (Eds.). (2000). *Handbook of qualitative research* (2nd ed.). Thousand Oaks, CA: Sage.

Dillman, D. (2000). *Mail and Internet surveys: The tailor-designed method* (2nd ed.). New York: Wiley.

Endreny, A. (2006). Children's ideas about animal adaptations: An action research project. *Journal of Elementary Science Education, 18*(1), 33–43.

Erickson, F. (1973). What makes school ethnography "ethnographic"? *Anthropology and Education Quarterly, 9*, 58–69.

Fabiano, E. (1989). *Index to tests used in educational dissertations*. Phoenix, AZ: Oryx Press.

Forsyth, D. R., Story, P. A., Kelley, K. N., & McMillan, J. H. (2008). What causes failure and success? Students' perceptions of their academic outcomes. *Social Psychology of Education.*

Gall, M. D., Gall, J. P., & Borg, W. R. (2007). *Educational research: An introduction* (8th ed.). Upper Saddle River, NJ: Pearson.

Gibbons, J. D. (1993). *Nonparametric statistics: An introduction*. Newbury Park, CA: Sage.

Glanz, J. (2003). *Action research: An educational leader's guide to school improvement* (2nd ed.). Norwood, MA: Christopher-Gordon.

Goldman, B., & Mitchell, D. (2002). *Directory of unpublished experimental mental measures* (Vol. 8). Washington, DC: American Psychological Association.

Goodwin, W. L., & Driscoll, L. A. (1980). *Handbook for measurement and evaluation in early childhood education*. San Francisco: Jossey-Bass.

Gorin, J. S. (2007). Reconsidering issues in validity theory. *Educational Researcher, 36*(8), 456–462.

Green, J. C. (2000). Understanding social programs through evaluation. In N. K. Denzin & Y. S. Lincoln (Eds.), *Handbook of qualitative research* (2nd ed., pp. 981–999). Thousand Oaks, CA: Sage.

Grele, R. J. (1996). Directions for oral history in the United States. In D. K. Dunway & W. K. Baum (Eds.), *Oral history: An interdisciplinary anthology* (pp. 60–75). Walnut Creek, CA: AltaMira.

Guba, E. G., & Lincoln, Y. S. (1989). *Fourth generation evaluation*. Beverly Hills, CA: Sage.

Halperin, S. (1978, March). *Teaching the limitations of the correlation coefficient*. Paper presented at the annual meeting of the American Educational Research Association, Toronto.

Hersen, M., & Bellack, A. (1988). *Dictionary of behavioral assessment techniques*. New York: Pergamon.

Hess, F. M., & Henig, J. R. (2008). "Scientific research" and policymaking: A tool, not a crutch. *Education Week, 27*(22), 26, 36.

Hopkins, K. D., & Gullickson, A. R. (1992). Response rates in survey research: A meta-analysis of the effects of monetary gratuities. *Journal of Experimental Education, 61*, 52–62.

Interviewer's manual (1999). Ann Arbor: Survey Research Center, Institute of Social Research.

Janesick, V. J. (1998). *Journal writing as a qualitative research technique: History, issues, and reflections*. Paper presented at the annual meeting of the American Educational Research Association, San Diego.

Johnson, O. G. (1976). *Tests and measurements in child development: Handbook II*. San Francisco: Jossey-Bass.

Johnson, R. B., & Christensen, L. (2008). *Educational research: Quantitative, qualitative, and mixed approaches* (3rd ed.). Thousand Oaks, CA: Sage.

Johnson, R. B., Onwuegbuzie, A. J., & Turner, L. A. (2007). Toward a definition of mixed methods research. *Journal of Mixed Methods Research, 1*(2), 112–133.

Joint Committee on Standards for Educational Evaluation (1994). *The program evaluation standards* (2nd ed.). Thousand Oaks, CA: Sage.

Keyser, D. J., & Sweetland, R. C. (Eds.). (1984–94). *Test critiques*. (Vols. 1–10). Kansas City, MO: Test Corporation of America.

Koshy, V. (2005). *Action research for improving practice: A practical guide*. Thousand Oaks, CA: Sage.

Lasserre-Cortez, S. (2006). *A mixed methods examination of professional development through whole faculty study groups*. Unpublished doctoral dissertation, Louisiana State University, Baton Rouge.

Lather, P. (1991). *Getting smart: Feminist research and pedagogy with/in the postmodern*. New York: Routledge.

Lincoln, Y. S. (1990). Toward a categorical imperative for qualitative research. In E. W. Eisner & A. Peshkin (Eds.), *Qualitative inquiry in education* (pp. 277–295). New York: Teachers College Press.

Maddox, J. (Ed.). (2007). *Tests: A comprehensive reference for assessments in psychology, education, and business* (10th ed.). Kansas City, MO: Test Corporation of America.

Malone, S. (2003). Ethics at home: Informed consent in your own backyard. *International Journal of Qualitative Studies in Education, 16*(6), 797–816.

Maltby, J., Alan, C. A., & Hill, A. (Eds.). (2000). *Commissioned reviews of 250 psychological tests*. New York: E. Mellen.

Marascuilo, L. A., & McSweeney, M. (1977). *Nonparametric and distribution-free methods for the social sciences*. Monterey, CA: Brooks/Cole.

Marshall, C., & Rossman, G. R. (1999). *Designing qualitative research* (3rd ed.). Newbury Park, CA: Sage.

Mason, J. (1996). *Qualitative researching*. Thousand Oaks, CA: Sage.

Maxwell, J. (1992). Understanding and validity in qualitative research. *Harvard Educational Review, 62*(3), 279–300.

McMillan, J. H. (2008). *Educational research. Fundamentals for the consumer* (5th ed.). New York: Longman.

McMillan, J. H. (2007). Randomized field trials and internal validity: Not so fast my friend. *Practical Assessment, Research and Evaluation, 12*(15). Retrieved October 16, 2008, from http://PAREonline.net/pdf/vizn5.pdf

McMillan, J. H., & Workman, D. (2000). *Teachers' classroom assessment and grading practices: Phase 2*. Richmond, VA: Metropolitan Educational Research Consortium, Virginia Commonwealth University.

Mertens, D. M. (2005). *Research and evaluation in education and psychology: Integrating diversity with quantitative, qualitative, and mixed methods* (2nd ed.). Thousand Oaks, CA: Sage.

Miller, D. C., & Salkind, N. J. (2002). *Handbook of research design and social measurement* (6th ed.). Newbury Park, CA: Sage.

Miller, J., McKenna, M., & McKenna, B. (1998). A comparison of alternatively and traditionally prepared teachers. *Journal of Teacher Education, 49*, 165–176.

Mills, G. E. (2007). *Action research: A guide for the teacher researcher* (3rd ed.). Upper Saddle River, NJ: Merrill/Prentice Hall.

Mitchell, M. L., & Jolley, J. M. (2007). *Research design explained* (6th ed.). Belmont, CA: Wadsworth.

Murphy, L. L., Spies, R. A., & Plake, B. S. (2006). *Tests in print VII*. Lincoln, NE: Buros Institute of Mental Measurements.

National Research Council, Committee on Scientific Principles for Education Research. (2002). *Scientific research in education*. Washington, DC: National Academy Press.

O'Donnell, C. L. (2008). Defining, conceptualizing, and measuring fidelity of implementation and its relationship to outcomes in K-12 curriculum intervention. *Review of Educational Research, 78*(1), 33–84.

Oja, S. N., & Smulyan, L. (1989). *Collaborative action research: A developmental approach*. London: Falmer Press.

Osborn, J. W., & Overbay, A. (2004). The power of outliers (and why researchers should always check for them). *Practical Assessment, Research, and Evaluation, 9*(6). Retrieved June 5, 2004, from http://PAREonline.net/getvn.asp?v=9&n=6

Patton, M. Q. (2001). *Qualitative research and evaluation methods* (3rd ed.). Thousand Oaks, CA: Sage.

Pillow, W. (2003). Confession, catharsis, or cure? Rethinking the uses of reflexivity as methodological power in qualitative research. *International Journal of Qualitative Studies in Education, 16*(2), 175–197.

Popham, W. J. (1981). *Modern educational measurement*. Englewood Cliffs, NJ: Prentice Hall.

Richardson, L. (1998). Writing: A method of inquiry. In N. K. Denzin & Y. S. Lincoln (Eds.), *Collecting and interpreting qualitative research* (pp. 345–372). Thousand Oaks, CA: Sage.

Ritter, L. A., & Sue, V. M. (2007). *Using online surveys in evaluation*. Hoboken, NJ: Wiley Periodicals.

Rosenthal, R., & Jacobson, L. (1968). *Pygmalion in the classroom: Teacher expectation and pupil's intellectual development*. New York: Holt, Rinehart & Winston.

Rowntree, B. S. (1941). *Poverty and progress: A second social survey of York*. London: Longman, Green.

Rudner, L. M., & Peyton, J. (2006). Consider propensity scores to compare treatments. *Practical Assessment, Research, and Evaluation, 11*(9). Retrieved October 12, 2008, from http://PARE-online.net/pdf/v11n9.pdf

Rue, G., Dingley, C., & Bush, H. (2002). Inner strength in women. Metasynthesis of qualitative findings and theory development. *Journal of Theory Construction and Testing, 4*(2), 36–39.

Sagor, R. (2005). *The action research guidebook: A four-step process for educators and school teams*. Thousand Oaks, CA: Corwin Press.

Sarndal, C. E., & Lundström, S. (2005). *Estimation in surveys with nonresponse*. West Sussex, England: Wiley.

Schonlau, M., Fricker, R. D., Jr., & Elliot, M. N. (2002). *Conducting research surveys via e-mail and the web*. Santa Monica, CA: Rand.

Schneider, B., Carnoy, M., Kilpatrick, J., Schmidt, W. H., & Shavelson, R. J. (2007). *Estimating causal effects using experimental and observational designs*. Washington, DC: American Educational Research Association.

Schumacher, S., & Esham, K. (1986). *Evaluation of a collaborative planning and development of school-based preservice and inservice education, Phase IV*. Richmond: Virginia Commonwealth University, School of Education. (ERIC Document Reproduction Services No. ED278659)

Schuman, H., & Presser, S. (1996). *Questions and answers: Experiments in the form, wording and context of survey questions*. Thousand Oaks, CA: Sage.

Schutt, R. K. (2009). *Investigating the social world: The process and practice of research* (6th ed.). Thousand Oaks, CA: Sage.

Shadish, W. R., Cook, T. D., & Campbell, K. R. (2002). *Experimental and quasi-experimental designs for generalized causal inference*. Boston: Houghton Mifflin.

Shavelson, R. J., & Towne, L. (Eds.). (2002). *Scientific research in education*. Washington, DC: National Academy Press.

Shepard, L. A. (1993). Evaluating test validity. *Review of Research in Education, 19*, 405–450.

Shulman, L. S. (2005, June 8). Seek simplicity ... and distrust it. *Education Week, 24*(39), 36, 48.

Siegel, S. (1956). *Nonparametric statistics for the behavioral sciences*. New York: McGraw-Hill.

Smith, L. M. (1990). Ethics in qualitative field research: An individual perspective. In E. W. Eisner & A. Peshkin (Eds.), *Qualitative inquiry in education: The continuing debate* (pp. 258–276). New York: Teachers College Press.

Smith, M. L. (2006). Multiple methodology in education research. In J. L. Green, G. Camilli, & P. B. Elmore (Eds.), *Handbook of complementary methods in education research* (pp. 457–476). Washington, DC: American Educational Research Association, and Mahwah, NJ: Erlbaum.

Smith, M. L., & Shepard, L. A. (1988). Kindergarten readiness and retention: A qualitative study of teachers' beliefs and practices. *American Educational Research Journal, 25*(3), 298–325.

Stake, R. E. (1975). *Program evaluation, particularly responsive evaluation*. Kalamazoo, MI, Evaluation Center, Western Michigan University. (Occasional Paper Series, No. 5.)

Stake, R. E. (1995). *The art of case study research*. Thousand Oaks, CA: Sage.

Stake, R. E. (2000). Case studies. In N. K. Denzin & Y. S. Lincoln (Eds.), *Handbook of qualitative research* (2nd ed., pp. 435–454). Thousand Oaks, CA: Sage.

Stake, R. E. (2008). Qualitative case studies. In N. K. Denzin & Y. S. Lincoln (Eds.), *Strategies of qualitative inquiry* (pp. 119–150). Thousand Oaks, CA: Sage.

Stinger, E. T. (1996). *Action research: A handbook for practitioners*. Thousand Oaks, CA: Sage.

Stright, A. D., & Supplee, L. H. (2002). Children's self-regulatory behaviors during teacher-directed, seat-work, and small-group instructional contexts. *Journal of Educational Research, 95*(4), 235–244.

Stringer, E. (2004). *Action research in education*. Columbus, OH: Pearson Education.

Strike, K. A. (2006). The ethics of educational research. In J. L. Green, G. Camilli, & P. B. Elmore (Eds.), *Handbook of complementary methods in educational research* (pp. 57–73). Mahwah, NJ: Erlbaum.

Stufflebeam, D. L., Foley, W. J., Gepart, W. J., Guba, E. E., Hammond, R. L., Merriman, H. O., & Provus, M. (1971). *Educational evaluation and decision-making*. Itasca, IL: F. E. Peacock.

Stufflebeam, D. L., Madeus, G. F., & Kellaghan, T. (Eds.). (2000). *Evaluation models: Viewpoints on educational and human services evaluation*. (2nd ed.). Boston: Kluwer.

Sykes, G., Schneider, B., & Plank, D. N. (2009). *Handbook of education policy research*. London: Routledge.

Tashakkori, A., & Creswell, J. W. (2007). The new era of mixed methods. *Journal of Mixed Methods Research, 1*(1), 3–7.

Teddlie, C., & Yu, F. (2007). Mixed methods sampling: A typology with examples. *Journal of Mixed Methods Research, 1*(1), 77–100.

Thompson, A. (1998, September). Fifty years on: An international perspective on oral history. *The Journal of American History, 84*, 581–595.

Touliatos, J., Perlmutter, B. F., Straus, M. A., & Holden, G. W. (Eds.). (2000). *Handbook of family measurement techniques*. Newbury Park, CA: Sage.

Tuckman, G. (1998). Historical social science: Methodologies, methods, and meanings. In N. K. Denzin & Y. S. Lincoln (Eds.), *Strategies of qualitative inquiry* (pp. 225–260). Thousand Oaks, CA: Sage.

Wainer, H., & Robinson, D. H. (2003). Shaping up the practice of null hypothesis significance testing. *Educational Researcher, 32*(7), 22–30.

Walker, D. K. (1973). *Socioemotional measures for pre-school and kindergarten children: A handbook*. San Francisco: Jossey-Bass.

Wax, R. H. (1971). *Doing fieldwork: Warnings and advice*. Chicago: University of Chicago Press.

Webb, E. J., Campbell, D. R., Schwartz, R. D., & Sechrest, L. (2000). *Unobtrusive measures* (rev. ed.). Thousand Oaks, CA: Sage.

Weiss, H. B., Mayer, E., Kreider, H., Vaughan, M., Dearing, E., Hencke, R., & Pinto, K. (2003). Making it work: Low-income working mothers' involvement in their children's education. *American Educational Research Journal, 40*(4), 879–901.

540